Law and the family

Law and the family

John Dewar, BCL, MA
Fellow and Tutor in Law, Hertford College, Oxford

with

Stephen Parker, LLB, PHD
Reader in Law, Australian National University

Butterworths
London, Dublin, Edinburgh
1992

United Kingdom	Butterworth & Co (Publishers) Ltd, 88 Kingsway, LONDON WC2B 6AB and 4 Hill Street, EDINBURGH EH2 3JZ
Australia	Butterworths, SYDNEY, MELBOURNE, BRISBANE, ADELAIDE, PERTH, CANBERRA and HOBART
Belgium	Butterworth & Co (Publishers) Ltd, BRUSSELS
Canada	Butterworths Canada Ltd, TORONTO and VANCOUVER
Ireland	Butterworth (Ireland) Ltd, DUBLIN
Malaysia	Malayan Law Journal Sdn Bhd, KUALA LUMPUR
New Zealand	Butterworths of New Zealand Ltd, WELLINGTON and AUCKLAND
Puerto Rico	Equity de Puerto Rico, Inc, HATO REY
Singapore	Butterworths Asia, SINGAPORE
USA	Butterworth Legal Publishers, AUSTIN, Texas; BOSTON, Massachusetts; CLEARWATER, Florida (D & S Publishers); ORFORD, New Hampshire (Equity Publishing); ST PAUL, Minnesota; and SEATTLE, Washington

A CIP Catalogue record for this book is available from the British Library.

First edition 1989

ISBN 0 406 00133 2

Layout by Doublestruck Ltd, London
Printed and bound by MacKays of Chatham Plc, Chatham, Kent.

To lizards everywhere, and to one in particular

Preface

My objectives in preparing this second edition remain as they were
for the first. These were (and are), first, to offer a readable account of
the law which contains enough technical detail to satisfy the needs of
undergraduates; and, second, to describe the main areas of debate
and to indicate where further reading may be found. I have also
continued to try to give space to the different perspectives on the
subject, ranging from those of the critical theorist to the practitioner.
I am told that the first edition found a substantial audience among
non-lawyers, especially social workers, and I have tried to bear the
possible needs of such a readership in mind.

The first edition of this book was rapidly overtaken by events.
Much of this new edition has been rewritten to take account of the
Children Act 1989, and the remainder updated as necessary. I am
very pleased that Dr Stephen Parker, Reader in Law at The
Australian National University in Canberra, was able to assist me in
its preparation. Steve is responsible for new sections on the Child
Support Act 1991 in Chapter 4 and on children's rights in Chapter 3,
and for the revised and expanded section on solicitors in Chapter 1. I
am immensely grateful to him.

I am indebted to a great number of people for their help and
support during the preparation of this second edition. First and
foremost, I must thank Henrietta Barclay, who not only gave love
and support in generous measure, but who also read and commented
on many of the chapters in draft.

I have made many new friends since coming to Oxford. In
particular, I would like to mention Roy Stuart, my colleague at
Hertford, who has helped with this edition more than he realises;
Suzanne Gibson of New College, who has proved to be a challenging
intellectual companion; Adrian Briggs of St Edmund Hall (ditto, but
in a different style); John Eekelaar of Pembroke College and all-
round family law guru; Mavis Maclean of the Centre for Socio-Legal
Studies in Oxford; and Ruth Deech, Principal of St Anne's College,
who started all of this by teaching me the subject in the first place.
Christine Gray, Nicola Lacey, Aiden Robertson and Matthew Weait

joined me in the pub when it mattered most.

I would also like to thank Dick Griffiths, Richard Parry, Fiona Shackleton, Sian Blore, Simon Bruce and John Loram (who together comprise the matrimonial group at Farrer & Co) for giving so generously of their time to help me clarify points of law and practice. Many of their insights have found their way into these pages.

The law stated in this book is updated to 1 January 1992.

John Dewar
Oxford
St Valentine's Day, 1992

Contents

Abbreviations

Commonly used abbreviations of statutes, in alphabetical order:

AA 1976	Adoption Act 1976
CA 1989	Children Act 1989
CSA 1991	Child Support Act 1991
DPMCA 1978	Domestic Proceedings and Magistrates' Courts Act 1978
DVMPA 1976	Domestic Violence and Matrimonial Proceedings Act 1976
FLA 1986	Family Law Act 1986
FLRA 1969	Family Law Reform Act 1969
FLRA 1987	Family Law Reform Act 1987
FPR 1991	Family Proceedings Rules 1991
HFEA 1990	Human Fertilisation and Embryology Act 1990
I(PFD)A 1975	Inheritance (Provision for Family and Dependants) Act 1975
LA 1976	Legitimacy Act 1976
LAA 1988	Legal Aid Act 1988
LASSA 1970	Local Authority Social Services Act 1970
MA 1949	Marriage Act 1949
MCA 1973	Matrimonial Causes Act 1973
MEA 1991	Maintenance Enforcement Act 1991
MFPA 1984	Matrimonial and Family Proceedings Act 1984
MHA 1983	Matrimonial Homes Act 1983
MWPA 1882	Married Women's Property Act 1882
SSA 1986	Social Security Act 1986

Table of statutes

References in this Table to *Statutes* are to Halsbury's Statutes of England (Fourth Edition) showing the volume and page at which the annotated text of the Act may be found.

List of cases

Chapter 1
Law and the family: introduction

What is family law?

Most legal disciplines would claim to possess at least one of two forms of coherence. The first stems from the organising legal concept from which the discipline in question derives its name: 'contract', 'negligence', 'trust'. The second relates to the set of 'real world' problems with which the discipline is concerned: labour relations, housing, land use, commerce, government and administration. At first glance, it would seem that the area of study designated as family law possesses a coherence of the second sort. After all, the term 'family' has in itself no legal significance (although attempts are often made to define the family for legal purposes); and the subject usually comprises a mixed bag of legal rules and concepts, such as those concerned with marriage, divorce, parents and children and property, each possessing a different historical origin and pattern of development. The only justification for studying them together is that they all in some way concern the family, a social phenomenon constituted outside the categories of the law. For this reason, family law has grown over the years to include parts of other legal disciplines of relevance to the family, such as property, criminal and housing law, taxation, social security, evidence and procedure; as well as incorporating legal aspects of phenomena thought to have a 'family' connection, such as domestic violence, child abuse, abortion, marital rape, surrogacy, homelessness and pensions (to name a few).

In spite of this, can it still be said that family law is a coherent area of study? It has already been suggested that it cannot satisfy the first criterion of coherence mentioned above; and if it were to satisfy the second, the subject would be a good deal broader than it is now, probably unmanageably so. For if we were really to take the family as the starting point, and were to consider all areas of law relevant to the family, we would want to include much that is not currently considered part of the subject. For example, we might wish to consider the welfare state, the fiscal system and the labour market in more detail than is customary; and we may also want to consider the areas of education and health services. These are all areas of relevance to families and in which the family is encountered as a necessary relay in the implementation of programmes of social action. But family law has not been interpreted as broadly as this. Instead, it focuses primarily on the more traditional question of status and is thus primarily concerned with the means by which status is conferred, such as marriage, parenthood and cohabitation, and on the means by which status may alter, such as divorce or state action to remove children from parents. More recently, it has become concerned with the problem of individuals abused by members of their own family.

It may be, however, that the two criteria of coherence are in any case inadequate to capture the relation between law and the family. For example, they both presuppose that the family exists *apart from* law. But would it not be more accurate to say, as some feminist writers have, that the family is, at least in part, a legal construct; that law is a significant agent in the reproduction of a particular family form? If so, then it may be difficult to settle as an a priori which areas of law should be studied. Further, is it accurate to see law as a discrete social system with a clearly delineated 'inside' and 'outside'; or is it better viewed as a system which, while sometimes effecting a clearly defined closure from its environment, at other times retains a degree of openness to other systems of regulation, and merges with them through a process of mutual reinforcement? If so, then looking exclusively at law and the legal system (however one decides to choose which bits are relevant), would be to focus too narrowly. Both these points are discussed further below.

We may be forced to conclude that family law is an essentially arbitrary area of study. In writing this book, I cannot claim to have made it any less arbitrary or to have superseded the two versions of coherence outlined above. Instead, I have sought to remain aware of the limits of coherence implicit in the book's subject matter, and to take account of the points made above, in so far as the conventions of the textbook format allow. This opening chapter is important for these purposes. First, we will look at the ways in which family law has been thought about in the past. The purpose is not to dismiss previous ways of thinking, but to use them to enrich our own understanding of the relationship between law and the family. In doing so, we will encounter themes that underlie the rest of the book. Second, we will consider the institutional and professional context in which the substantive law described later is decided and applied. Again, this introduces another important theme of the book, which is that 'the law' in family law is not just about legal doctrine.

Ways of thinking about law and the family

In this section, we shall briefly consider three different and influential ways of thinking about the relationship between law and the family. The purpose is not to discuss issues of 'theory' for their own sake, but to draw attention to the fact that in order to understand social phenomena we must begin by asking questions; and that it is important to have a grasp of different ways in which the questions may be framed.

(a) Functionalism

For present purposes, we may take functionalism to mean that an understanding of an institution can be gained by studying what it does or what it is assumed to do. John Eekelaar has advocated a functionalist approach to the study of law and the family. For Eekelaar, family law may be understood as performing at least three important functions:

(i)   the protective function, according to which the law will protect family members from detriment, whether physical, emotional or economic;

(ii) the adjustive function, according to which the law assists individuals whose family unit has disintegrated to adjust to a new set of circumstances; and

(iii) the supportive function, through which law and social administration seek to promote the success of the family (Eekelaar 1978, pp 44–66; 1984, pp 24–26).[1]

The virtues of this functionalist approach are that it offers both a definition of family law itself, and thus a framework for the exposition of the subject (in which respect the functionalist framework has been highly influential – see, eg, Bromley and Lowe 1987, pp 2–3), as well as a yardstick by which to measure the success or otherwise of family law in achieving its functional objectives.

Nevertheless, functionalist explanations are considered by social scientists to suffer from many shortcomings, many of which apply in

---

1   More recently, Eekelaar has offered a slightly different tripartite classification of law's 'functions': the repressive, the normative and the instrumental (Eekelaar 1987). These, he argues, 'comprise the most significant part' of legal functioning; he also argues that the character of law as it affects family living has shifted from repressive to normative and instrumental law. Although, in his view, the social control of family living through law has not been a success, he does not abandon the notion that law remains a means through which desired social objectives may be achieved.

the present context. For example, it is argued that 'the "functions" are rarely unambiguous or obvious' (Morgan 1975, p 57) and that a statement that a particular institution is 'for' something is neither verifiable nor falsifiable. In the present context, for example, we could ask what is meant by 'protection' and when has it been achieved (Freeman 1985a, pp 155–158)? Further, it is unclear whether it is being claimed that the relationship between institution and function is a necessary one and that only the institution in question is capable of performing it (cf Giddens 1984, pp 293–297). Eekelaar has responded to criticisms of his functionalist position by arguing that 'it is very difficult to avoid references to goals and purposes when accounting for social phenomena' and that law lends itself to a functionalist analysis since the 'purposes of laws are usually either explicit in their terms, or their formulation preceded or accompanied by extensive discussion'. The purposes of law, or at least the 'purposes held . . . by that segment of society in control of its law and policy making institutions', are clear (1984, p 16) and its 'minimal tasks can be agreed' (1978, p 44).

Nevertheless, some further points may be made. The first is that functionalism inevitably limits the range of inquiry, in this case to a study of how far family law achieves the 'obvious', 'agreed' or officially defined goals set for it. It does not explicitly acknowledge that law may advance social objectives other than those which are obvious or intended. We return to this point below. Second, the argument is premised on a 'pathological' view of law, that is, as something that is only called into operation when things go wrong – the 'functions' are a response to a problem. The role of law as a constitutive element of social life, and as sometimes itself constituting 'the problem', is ignored (Freeman 1980a; 1985a, p 158).

Third, Eekelaar's argument is premised on a view of law as a particular kind of social system, that is, as a relatively simple and discrete mechanism whose operations may be specified in advance and scientifically monitored; law, in other words, is the vehicle for the implementation of 'social policy' in family matters. This does not allow for the possibility that law and the legal system are highly complex mechanisms composed of a number of different elements, each operating according to its own functional imperative (Rose 1987, pp 66–67); or that the legal system is concerned not only with the internal coherence and the ordering of its parts, but also with negotiating relationships with its environment. For present purposes, the environment may consist not only of demands made of the system by litigants or by government, but also of other institutions or professional bodies concerned with the same family problems, such as social workers, conciliators and therapists. Here, the legal system has retained a degree of openness and has negotiated relations with these non-legal systems or bodies of knowledge in a way that has extended the reach of both. The legal system, in other words, 'is increasingly incorporated into a continuum of apparatuses (medical, administrative and so on) whose functions are for the most part regulatory' (Foucault 1981, p 144; see also Donzelot 1979; Foucault 1979; Luhmann 1982, Chs 2, 5, 6; 1985, pp 281–288; King 1991). This aspect is lost through an exclusive focus on law as a discrete mechanism. We return to this point at various stages later in the book, especially in the context of divorce (Chs 7–9).

Functionalism as described here is perhaps best understood in the context of the enterprise of socio-legal studies, 'part of [whose] purpose is to relate the aims of social policy as manifested in law or otherwise to social life' (Eekelaar and Maclean 1990, p 630). There is no doubt that the empirical findings of socio-legal researchers, particularly those of Eekelaar and Maclean themselves (1986), have been influential in the development of legal policy with respect to the family. As family law has become increasingly concerned with the consequences (or outcomes) of its rules and procedures, as opposed to the rights of the parties involved (Parker 1991), so empirical findings have exercised a greater influence over its initial formulation, since they purport to tell us what those consequences are or might be. Some (eg, Deech 1990) have questioned the submission of law to empiricism in this way, and we shall see that there are increasing doubts about abandoning traditional legal conceptions of rights or traditional legal methods of dispute settlement (see, eg, Ch 7). In any case, modern family law is neither wholly result-oriented nor wholly rights-based. Parker's assessment of Australian family law in the 1980s may be applied equally to our own: 'a kind of normative anarchy [reigns] . . . with some measures tugging in the direction of rights and others in the direction of utility' (Parker 1991, p 24).

(b) The public/private split

Some writers have argued that an understanding of the relation between law and the family can be gained through the perspective of the distinction between the public and the private (see Olsen 1983; O'Donovan 1985; Freeman 1985a). For present purposes, these terms refer to two distinct social realms constituted within liberal political philosophy, the boundary being drawn according to what is and what is not regulated by the state through law. The public realm, a realm of the state, politics and the market, is associated with an ethos of individualism and is the world of men; the private realm, primarily associated with the family, is associated with an ethos of altruism, and is the world of women. It is the unregulated nature of the private realm, the family, that is seen as the root of inequality between the sexes. Legal policy with respect to the family is imbued with respect for family privacy, and the absence of legal regulation that results permits the exercise of absolute power by men over women and children, and thus reinforces inequalities of power between sexes and generations. And yet, the ideology of privacy and of the unregulated family conceals and mystifies the fact that the realm of the private is in fact heavily influenced by structures external to it, such as the labour market and the welfare state; indeed, the state itself defines the boundaries of the private while claiming that what is private is naturally preconstituted as such and exists outside the scope of legitimate state action.

Two general points may be made here. The first is that we cannot regard the public/private dichotomy as stating a literal truth, since there are many ways in which the family is directly 'regulated' through law (see Eekelaar 1989). Divorce, for example, provides a site for what may be extensive regulation of almost all aspects of a couple's relationship, and the introduction of a statutory child support scheme (in the Child Support Act 1991, discussed in Ch 4) amounts to 'the intrusion of overt public policy considerations into the realm of private ordering' (Parker 1991, pp 30–31). Nevertheless, we can still say that the legal system is highly selective of those matters it will single out for regulation, and adjudication may simply reinforce rather than challenge the values of privacy by means, for example, of decisions with respect to child custody or money. Further, it remains the case that there are many matters with respect to which the ideology of privacy has played a part in justifying legal non-intervention or in rendering less effective those legal provisions that do exist. The ideology of privacy is often invoked, for example, in the context of wife or child abuse (see Chs 6 and 10). Thus, the concept of privacy can be said to be a powerful (but, possibly, inadequately realised) formative element in legal policy with respect to the family.

The second point is perhaps more important. We should note that in drawing the line between the public and the private, the writers referred to above have associated 'regulation' exclusively with law. Something is unregulated, and therefore 'private', if the law has nothing to say on the matter. Yet this would be to ignore the variety of other ways in which social programmes have operated by means of the family to shape and promote desired patterns of living. Birth control, domestic hygiene, child care, reproduction, public health, education and domestic architecture are all matters in which the promotion of particular family patterns is the concern. The fact that few may have relied on law, nor even necessarily on the state, does not mean that the family was not an object (if not the effect) of such regulatory programmes.

The family could be said to have become a means of government: 'the family appeared as a positive solution to the problems of the regulation of morality, health and procreation posed by a liberal definition of the limits of legitimate state action' (Rose 1987, p 70; cf Donzelot 1979). As such, the family falls clearly into neither the public nor the private realm: 'the modern private family remains intensively governed . . . [G]overnment acts not through mechanisms of social control and subordination of the will, but through the promotion of subjectivities, the construction of pleasures and ambitions and the activation of guilt, anxiety and disappointment' (Rose 1989, p 208). Again, the point is that an exclusive focus on law will reveal only a part of the full picture. Nevertheless, as suggested above, the public/private dichotomy may be helpful in analysing specifically legal policy with respect to the family, even though its usefulness may be limited in other respects.

(c) Familialism

More recently, there has emerged a new strand of feminist thinking about law and the family, which we may broadly term 'familialist', which goes beyond the public/private dichotomy in two important ways. First, it recognises that law is not the only means by which the family may be regulated and that the legal system forms merely one element of a broader regulatory framework which includes welfare professionals and government agencies. Second, it rejects the notion of law as a coherent or homogeneous entity that is reduced to the expression of male interests. Instead, it is argued that by taking women rather than law as the starting point, it can be seen that the effect of (but not necessarily the intention behind) law is the promotion of a particular family form. Law, it is argued, reproduces the material and ideological conditions under which patriarchal relations may survive, a process that is particularly visible in the operations and effect of the legal processes of divorce. It is here that women's economic vulnerability and dependence is most evident, and it is here that the law most obviously reproduces those conditions in the post-divorce lives of the parties. Stephen Parker (1990, Ch 6) has developed a similar argument in relation to the growing legal recognition of cohabitation. This he sees as 'a changing strategy of family regulation' in that law now seeks to recognise and regulate 'support/dependency structures of the patriarchal family' whether enshrined in the legal form of marriage or not (see further Ch 2).

A further 'familialist' feature of modern family law is that it has become increasingly child-centred. This has led to women being increasingly subjected to discretionary and welfarist intervention 'for the sake of the children'. The law as it concerns the family is thus of central concern to feminist politics since by contributing to this construction of women in the family sphere, it indirectly assists in the oppression of women in other areas of society – patriarchal relations in the family, as it were, 'spill over' (see Smart 1984, Ch 1; Smart and Brophy 1985; Brophy 1985; Brown 1986, pp 436–437).

This model of understanding law and the family, with its emphasis on effects of rather than intentions behind law, and on the diversity rather than homogeneity of regulatory practices, could hardly be further removed from the 'functionalist' model with which we began, which focused on originating intentions 'behind' the law and tended to regard law as a relatively discrete and unproblematic mechanism. For this reason alone, the 'familialist' model of understanding law and the family seems more fruitful in that it opens up rather than closes down avenues of thought. Nevertheless, the 'familialist' model may not be free of difficulties. For example, it may be said that these writers have placed too much emphasis on the position of women in law, and correspondingly too little emphasis on the needs and rights of children as legal subjects in their own right. Children, after all, are just as vulnerable and deserving of legal protection as are women, if not more so, and there may be many circumstances where the children's interests are not coterminous with those of the mother. Nevertheless, one of the virtues of the 'familialist' position is that it alerts us to the difficulty of arriving at a scientific or neutral view as to where a child's interests lie, and that placing emphasis on the needs of children may turn out to be simply another form of coercion.

Institutions and personnel

It was suggested earlier in this chapter that to regard family law as a homogeneous and undifferentiated system operating according to an identifiable set of 'functions' is to miss much of the complexity of this fascinating subject. Instead, it was suggested that we should recognise that the unity ascribed to 'family law' is an artificial one, and that we should approach the subject as comprising a complex amalgam of interrelating systems and regulatory practices. In this section, it is proposed to examine what some of these are. We begin with a description of the courts administering family law, and then go on to discuss the role of relevant professionals (such as solicitors) and state agencies (such as the social services, police and welfare state).

(a) Courts

In this section, we are concerned with the jurisdiction of courts to make orders in family proceedings. These include: proceedings for divorce, nullity and judicial separation; orders for financial provision; injunctions in cases of domestic violence; orders under the Children Act 1989 in relation to children in public and private proceedings; adoption; and orders in wardship proceedings. We consider first the origin of the jurisdiction of the different courts and will then look at the changes to the court structure introduced by the Children Act 1989. Finally, we shall consider proposals that have been made for a new family court.

(i) Magistrates' court

The magistrates' court occupies the lowest position in the hierarchy of courts, but is the most geographically widespread. It usually consists of three lay magistrates, advised and assisted by a qualified clerk. Although it is primarily concerned with criminal law, it also sits as a 'family proceedings court' to hear matrimonial, domestic or child care matters, such as care proceedings under the Children Act 1989. Magistrates sitting in the family proceedings court are selected from a panel of experienced and specially trained magistrates, known as the family proceedings panel. Under present law,[2] magistrates have the power to make orders in favour of spouses for financial provision and in relation to children as well as domestic violence injunctions, although the magistrates' powers in these respects are more limited than the equivalent powers available in the county or High courts (see Chs 4 and 6). There is no power to issue decrees of divorce, nullity or judicial separation. Magistrates also exercise, concurrently with the higher courts, the power to make orders for adoption (see Ch 11). Under the Children Act 1989, most care proceedings will have to be initiated in the family proceedings court (see below). What is more questionable, however, is the future role of this court in private cases.

The origins of the magistrates' jurisdiction in domestic matters lies in the Matrimonial Causes Act 1878, which enabled magistrates to

2 Primarily, the DPMCA 1978 and the CA 1989.

award a wife, whose husband had been convicted of an aggravated assault on her, a separation order coupled with an order for maintenance. This legislation was born out of a specific concern with wife battering amongst the working classes, and, although the grounds on which orders could be sought were gradually extended between 1886 and 1960, it remained the case that the magistrates provided a 'secondary system designed for what were considered to be the special and cruder requirements of the poor' (Finer and McGregor 1974, para 36); for, until 1967, the only other source of matrimonial relief lay in the more expensive procedures of the High Court. The unfairness of this dual system of matrimonial relief, in which one system catered almost exclusively for the poor, became most obvious following the reform by the Divorce Reform Act 1969 of the substantive law of divorce administered in the county and High courts, which (in theory at least) removed the 'fault' basis for awarding divorce decrees. For, despite this change to the powers of the higher courts, the magistrates continued to dispense their more limited forms of relief on the basis of a long list of 'fault' grounds.[3]

One purpose of the Domestic Proceedings and Magistrates' Courts Act 1978 was to reduce this disparity in the two jurisdictions (see Law Commission 1976) by:

(i) reducing the 'fault' grounds on the basis of which applications were to be made;
(ii) giving magistrates powers to award financial provision similar to, but more limited than, those available in divorce proceedings in the higher courts; and
(iii) giving magistrates power to make protection orders in cases of domestic violence.

In doing so, the Law Commission hoped to transform the role of the family proceedings court into that of a 'casualty clearing station', offering immediate assistance to those marriages in trouble. Those that were in retrievable difficulty could be assisted through the various orders available in the court; those that were not would be passed on to the divorce court for final termination (Law Commission 1973b, para 24). Despite the Law Commission's intentions, however, this is not the function currently performed by the family proceedings court, for a number of reasons.

First, the availability of legal aid for defended divorce and ancillary proceedings, the wider powers available to the divorce court and the tendency of magistrates to make only low orders for maintenance have combined to mean that many couples simply

3   MP(MC)A 1960, s 1(1).

bypass the domestic court by suing straightaway for divorce. This is reflected in the fact that between 1968 and 1978, the family proceedings court experienced a threefold decline in the number of broken marriages resorting to it for matrimonial relief, and that in 1978 the court dealt only with 6% of all broken marriages that resorted to a court (Gibson 1982; see also Smart 1984, pp 194–200). There is no evidence to suggest that the 1978 Act has altered this position. Indeed, the use of the magistrates' jurisdiction in private family cases has continued to decline steadily during the 1980s (see Home Office 1989, Volume 2, Graphic C2).

Second, for those couples who do make use of the family jurisdiction of magistrates there is evidence that in a significant proportion of cases no further action is taken by the parties in relation to their marriage, even though their relationship is at an end (Gibson 1982). The family proceedings court is, in other words, effectively the final point of contact between the legal system and many broken marriages. Even where there are subsequent divorce proceedings, in many cases the magistrates' order continues in force since, for reasons discussed in Chapters 4 and 8, the effect of any increased order made by the divorce court would simply be to benefit the DSS. Third, the availability of the enforcement mechanism in the magistrates' court for divorce court maintenance orders (under the Maintenance Orders Act 1958 – see Ch 9) has meant that the family proceedings court is in practice more concerned with the variation, revocation and enforcement of maintenance orders made in the higher court than with the making of new orders of its own (Gibson 1982, p 138).

Nevertheless, significant use continues to be made of the magistrates' jurisdiction to make orders for maintenance (see Ch 4) and physical protection orders (see Ch 6) even though other courts offer competing jurisdictions for both types of order. It remains to be seen what use is made of the family proceedings court's jurisdiction in private child-related cases. Unlike public cases under the Children Act 1989, which must in most cases be started in the family proceedings court, private cases will be self-allocating. The choice of which court to use for the resolution of domestic disputes will depend on a variety of factors, including: the habits and preferences of individual practitioners, the social class of the parties, the influence of legal aid area committees, and the policies of local government housing departments and local DSS offices, for whom a court order is evidence of entitlement to assistance. All these factors may help to explain why it is that the magistrates' family jurisdiction is more widely used in the northern parts of the country and hardly at all in London and the south-east (Priest and Whybrow 1986).

(ii) County court

The county court, which sits between the family proceedings court
and the High Court, is now the most important of all courts dealing
with family matters. All applications for decrees of divorce,
separation and nullity must be made initially in this court[4] provided
that it has been designated by the Lord Chancellor as a county
'divorce court' (as most have been).[5] Certain county courts have
been specified as care centres and family hearing centres for the
purposes of proceedings under the Children Act 1989 (see below).
The county court also has a limited jurisdiction to deal with certain
matters in wardship proceedings, and may make orders in relation to
adoption and domestic violence.

The preeminence of the county court is a recent development.
Before 1967, sole jurisdiction in all but a small number of
matrimonial causes, except for that vested in the magistrates'
court, was in the High Court. The MCA 1967 transferred
undefended causes to the county court, and the Matrimonial and
Family Proceedings Act 1984 (Part V) continued this process by
transferring more business from the higher to the lower court. In
large part, this was a bureaucratic response to the growing volume of
matrimonial causes, especially divorce petitions, and should be seen
in conjunction with changes in the procedure by which divorces are
granted, especially the 'special procedure' (see Ch 7). The court
structure introduced by the Children Act 1989 further underlines the
central position of the county court, especially in relation to child
care cases (see below).

The distribution of family business between the High and county
courts in private cases is governed by statute and by directions issued
by the President of the Family Division of the High Court.[6] In
general, most cases will be heard in the county court save those that
raise particular difficulties of law or fact, or which contain an
international dimension. Certain matters continue to be reserved for
the exclusive jurisdiction of the High Court (see below). The county
court is staffed by circuit judges and district judges (formerly
registrars), and the distribution of work between them is governed by
rules of court. In general, financial issues are dealt with by the latter
and contested children issues by the former. In child care cases, the
allocation and transfer of business between courts is governed by
rules of court (see below and Ch 10).

---

4   MFPA 1984, s 33(3).
5   MFPA 1984, s 33(1).
6   MFPA, s 37; FLA 1986, ss 2–7; *Practice Direction* [1987] 1 All ER 1087.

(iii) High Court

The Family Division of the High Court, as it is now known,[7] exercises the High Court's jurisdiction in all family proceedings. This jurisdiction derives historically from two main sources. The first is the jurisdiction formerly exercised by the Probate, Divorce and Admiralty Division of the High Court to grant decrees of divorce, nullity and separation, which in turn derived from the jurisdiction of the ecclesiastical courts which was transferred (and extended to include judicial divorce) to the divorce court in 1857, and then transferred to the High Court in 1873. The second is the inherent jurisdiction, originally exercised with respect to children by the Chancery Division of the High Court in wardship. Although originally based exclusively in London, the High Court now operates in London and twenty provincial centres. It is staffed by High Court judges who are family law specialists, and by district judges who are based in the Principal Registry in London.

Although, as we have seen, much of the work in family proceedings has been transferred to the divorce (county) court, there are some areas in which the High Court retains an exclusive jurisdiction. These include: declarations of legitimacy or validity of marriage under s 45 of the Matrimonial Cause Act 1973; financial provision after a foreign divorce; certain child law matters with an international dimension (eg, adoption of children resident abroad) and, perhaps most importantly, applications to make children wards of court.[8] Appeals under the Children Act 1989 lie to the High Court, and certain difficult Children Act cases may be transferred for initial hearing to the High Court (see below and Ch 10).

(iv) The court structure under the Children Act 1989

The Children Act 1989 introduces a new and comprehensive legal framework for resolving legal issues in relation to children. The details of the substantive law introduced by the Act will be discussed at several points throughout this book. A significant feature of the Act is that it ensures that the same law and procedure[9] is now applicable in every court dealing with child law issues under the Act. This rationalisation of the substantive law has in turn permitted a rationalisation of the court structure dealing with cases under the Act. There are three important aspects of this rationalisation. The

7 AJA 1970, s 1.
8 *Practice Direction* [1987] 1 All ER 1087.
9 See the Family Proceedings Rules 1991 and the Family Proceedings Court (Children Act 1989) Rules 1991.

first is that there are now rules governing the choice of court in which proceedings are to be initiated, applicable primarily to public law cases.[10] These rules also make it easier for a particular case to be transferred up or down the hierarchy of courts according to the needs of the case. For example, cases requiring a special degree of expertise may be heard in the High Court; while cases needing to be decided quickly could be transferred down to the family proceedings court. These rules are of primary relevance to public law proceedings and are therefore discussed in Chapter 10. The second is that it is now easier to consolidate different proceedings that may be on foot with respect to the same child, since the relevant legal concepts will be the same. Where consolidated proceedings present particularly difficult issues, it is possible to transfer the case to the most appropriate court.

The third aspect is that all family and child law business is now allocated to specific courts staffed by specially nominated and trained judges. Family cases heard at magistrates' court level will be heard by the family proceedings court (see above). At county court level, there are two specially designated types of court, the 'care centre' and the 'family hearing centre'.[11] Care centres will be staffed by specially designated or nominated circuit and district judges[12] and will have jurisdiction in both public and private law cases. Family hearing centres will be staffed by nominated family judges and district judges and will have jurisdiction in private law cases. There will also continue to be divorce county courts, which will have only the limited jurisdiction accorded to district judges in private cases. Other county courts will have jurisdiction only in relation to injunctions. Cases in the High Court will be heard by judges of the Family Division.

The objective of these elaborate rules is to ensure the development of a specialist group of judges, all of whom will have received special training. The most important of these are the designated family judges who will number about fifty in total and will be based at the care centres. Each care centre will be supported by a Family Court Business Committee (FCBC), chaired by the designated family judge, 'whose function is to examine the process of litigation under the Act and ensure that cases are efficiently and effectively dealt with at local level'.[13] The FCBC has particular responsibility for ensuring:

10 The Children (Allocation of Proceedings) Order 1991.
11 Ibid, Schs 1 and 2.
12 CLSA 1990, s 9; Family Proceedings (Allocation to Judiciary) Directions [1991] Fam Law 487.
13 Lord Chancellor's Department, Children Act Progress Report No 6, May 1991.

(i) that the rules governing the allocation and transfer of business between the family proceedings court and the care centre are working effectively; and

(ii) that the local guardian ad litem panel (see below and Ch 10) and the probation service (see below and Chs 7 and 9) are aware of the needs of the court.

The membership of the FCBC ensures that those responsible for various aspects of family law administration are brought together. Membership includes representatives from court administrators, justices' clerks from the family proceedings panel, the local authority social services and legal departments, the local guardian ad litem panel and the area legal aid board.[14] Each care centre will also have a Family Court Services Committee (FCSC), which 'will be geared towards issues rather than management'.[15] It is designed to provide a forum in which all those involved in family proceedings can meet to discuss the issues of policy arising from the operation of the Act:

> '[t]hese issues might include, for example, assessment techniques and the handling of refusal to consent to treatment or assessment, local services that divert children from court proceedings [and] the availability of expert witnesses.' (Harris and Scanlan 1991, p 184)

Finally, there is a Children Act Advisory Committee, currently chaired by the Honourable Mrs Justice Booth, whose role is to advise the Lord Chancellor on whether the aims of the Act are being achieved.

(v) Towards a family court?

The substantive and procedural changes introduced by the Children Act 1989 go a long way to eliminating the most criticised aspects of the court system in family matters (see Dewar 1989, pp 11–22). In particular, the elimination of the differences in the concepts employed in, and the powers of, the different courts, together with the possibility of consolidating different proceedings in relation to the same child, are in themselves considerable improvements. In addition, the creation of a pool of trained and specialist family judges should be welcomed. Nevertheless, these changes do not go as far as some commentators would like in the direction of creating a separate, specialist family court equipped with its own welfare personnel.

14 Lord Chancellor's Department, Children Act Progress Report No 6, May 1991.
15 Ibid.

Proposals for such a court were made by the Finer Committee in 1974 (pp 170–222), and have since been reiterated, in differing forms, by a number of groups and individuals (see, for example, Graham Hall 1977; Law Society 1979, 1982, 1985; Murch 1980, Part IV; British Association of Social Workers 1984). Most recently, political impetus has been given to the idea of a family court through its espousal by the Butler-Sloss Report on Child Sexual Abuse in Cleveland (1988, p 236), although the report was unspecific about the form such a court should take. However, there is a danger that 'there are as many models of a family court as there are proponents of it' (Hoggett 1986, p 16) and that the shape of the family court as a solution is determined by the particular problem to which it is considered relevant.

For example, the Finer Committee's main purpose in proposing a family court was to eliminate the magisterial jurisdiction in family matters, which it regarded as responsible for what it saw as a class-based dispensation of matrimonial justice (McGregor 1987); similarly, Murch's proposals (1980) stem from a concern to construct a more coherent relationship between courts and welfare agencies in family matters. In neither case was any consideration given to the possible role of a family court in care proceedings involving parents and the state; and it has been suggested that the proposals that have been made for a family court as a way of dealing with care proceedings, which suggest a more interventionist and supervisory role for the court, run counter to the trend exemplified by Finer and Murch towards less reliance on court-based adjudication and greater reliance on conciliation (Hoggett 1986). In other words, the family court 'tends to be perceived as some utopian tribunal capable of dealing with a whole array of family problems as well as meeting some of the deficiencies of the welfare agencies' (Szwed 1984, p 266). This may conceal the fact that the problems to which the family court is advanced as a solution cannot be resolved within the framework of a single family court concept.

The creation of a family court would thus require some careful thought as to both ends and means. In particular, the Lord Chancellor's Department's Review of Family and Domestic Jurisdiction (1986) identified four important questions concerning the family court requiring resolution:

(i) What should be the scope of the proposed court's jurisdiction? In particular, should it include care proceedings and criminal proceedings in relation to juveniles?

(ii) What should be the role within the court of the lay magistracy, if any?

(iii) According to what criteria should the business of the court be distributed between the various available personnel?

(iv) What should be the relationship between the court and the various welfare agencies who currently provide court-related welfare services such as reporting and conciliation? (see para 9.6).

On one point, however, the review was clear: that a family court would remain a judicial institution rather than a therapeutic one (paras 7.3–7.8). In this respect, the review echoed the views of the Finer Committee, who stated as the most important criterion of a family court that it should 'be an impartial judicial institution, regulating the rights of citizens and settling their disputes according to law . . . the individual in the family court must in the last resort remain the subject of rights, not the object of assistance' (paras 4.283 and 4.285).

(b) Solicitors

Solicitors are the most important group of legal professionals in family law. Despite the introduction of simplified divorce procedures in the 1970s and the emergence of alternative forms of dispute resolution (see generally Ch 7), solicitors continue to dominate the scene. In the overwhelming majority of cases, both spouses consult a solicitor at some stage in a divorce (Davis 1988, p 85). Although it was once thought that solicitors were the last resort when things go wrong in a marriage, recent empirical research suggests that solicitors are actually the first resort for many petitioners (Davis and Murch 1988, p 55). In other words, no other agency is contacted beforehand.

In practical terms solicitors are the gatekeepers of the legal system in family law, as in almost all other parts of the law. They are an important source of initial advice and assistance, they are the means of access to legal aid (see below) and they see many people whose problems do not come to court at all. Even after court proceedings are commenced, solicitors retain a central role in determining which of the available procedures should be invoked. They may also influence the atmosphere in which the proceedings and any attendant negotiations are conducted.

Relatively little is known about the kinds of solicitors who practise family law. It is clear that the work is heavily dependent on legal aid and that it is not one of the most lucrative areas of practice. It certainly does not carry the status and prestige of other kinds of better remunerated legal work. Some firms of solicitors do none of it at all and the trend in the 1980s was for large firms to close down their matrimonial departments. In some regions, good specialist practitioners may be hard to find and those there are will almost certainly be heavily overworked.

Recent research has shed some light on the behaviour and beliefs of those solicitors who do practise family law.[16] In the past there was a common view that solicitors, because of their training in adversarial litigation, tended to favour conflict over amicable resolution and accordingly exacerbated problems in some cases. Research findings now suggest a more complex picture. Whilst undoubtedly some solicitors have a *style* which can make things worse rather than better, it now seems that the system as a whole leans heavily towards the settlement of disputes through negotiation towards 'agreed' outcomes. This is so much the case that the contemporary concern is that clients may be sold short and that the values of lawyers, as individuals and as an occupational group, may intrude too prominently.

Carol Smart's study consisted of interviews with 34 solicitors who had substantial matrimonial practices in Sheffield (Smart, 1984). She found that the 'practice of matrimonial law is . . . primarily about negotiation between solicitors according to mutually agreed rules' (p 162), and that these rules consist partly of case law, partly of what solicitors know to be acceptable to local registrars (now called district judges) and magistrates, and partly of what they know on the basis of past dealings to be acceptable to other solicitors.

Smart canvassed solicitors for their views on certain aspects of their work, particularly on maintenance and child custody. On the former, she found that most solicitors saw women's dependence on men, and thus their need for maintenance on divorce, as an individual rather than collective or structural problem. This tended to be associated with sympathy for husbands and with support for the idea of restricting the wife's right to maintenance as a wife (rather than as a mother) by means of the removal of the so-called 'meal-ticket' for life (which, if it ever in fact existed, was removed by the MFPA 1984 – see Ch 8). On the issue of child custody, Smart

---

16 The Newcastle Conciliation Project Unit (1989) looked at solicitors' perceptions of their general role in matrimonial matters. They found that most indicated their role in legal/professional terms, ie taking instructions, advising and doing the best for their client. Some, however, emphasised the social work or counselling aspects of their work and others that their objective was to obtain agreement without going to court. The majority of solicitors claimed that they adopted a 'conciliatory' approach to their work, but their understanding of what this meant related largely to a 'settlement-seeking approach' that did not involve moving very far from the traditional role of a solicitor in adversarial proceedings (Newcastle CPU 1989, paras 9.24–9.37).

found that solicitors tended to favour women, but only because of a largely inaccurate stereotype of women as exclusively concerned with the domestic sphere.

The crucial importance of negotiated settlements in family law, and the solicitor's role in negotiations, is increasingly appreciated by those researching into the everyday operation of family law. As Davis and Murch note (1988, p 85), bipartisan negotiation conducted through or alongside legal advisers is still by far the dominant mode of dispute resolution in family matters. Research in the United States suggests that divorce lawyers actually push disputes towards settlement rather than litigation, one reason being that lawyers are supreme in the world of settlements whereas in the courts they must cede power to the judges (Sarat and Felstiner 1986). In the British context at least, factors other than lawyers' imperialism are clearly also present. A settlement is often objectively in both parties' interests when compared with the financial and personal consequences of contested litigation. At the same time, some of the pressures which *make* it in clients' interests to settle may in part stem from the financial interests of the courts and professional personnel rather than from any immutable external reality (Davis 1988, p 203). The courts wish to restrict demands on judicial time, the Legal Aid Board is reluctant to devote public funds to contested cases when the same amount of money could finance a larger number of negotiated settlements and, by and large, it is in the interests of solicitors to have a high volume of routine work (Davis 1988, 107–108 and Ingleby 1988a, p 48). For a client to swim against the tide of negotiation may involve unacceptable risks and costs. Yet, as Davis says (1988, p 203), ' "[s]ettlements" arrived at in these circumstances may make not the slightest contribution to a resolution of the problem as this is experienced by the parties'.

To summarise the discussion so far, it seems that solicitors have considerable influence over the course of a family law case, they tend to prefer settlement to litigation and the manner in which they settle cases may be influenced partly by their values, ideologies and financial interests. Clearly, other considerations must be taken into account to give a more balanced picture. As we have seen, Smart noted that solicitors' knowledge of case law and of what is acceptable to local magistrates and judges are also factors in whether a case is settled and, if so, on what terms. Nevertheless, enough has been said to suggest that considerably more empirical research is required into the practices and motivations of lawyers before some suspicions about them can be allayed.

Much of the work on family lawyers has concerned the impact of their practices on one or other of the adults. If family law becomes more child-centred, and the overall movement is in this direction (see Ch 3), then increasing attention may need to be paid to the consequences on children of lawyers' advice. This raises some difficult issues of legal ethics. In the normal course of events the solicitor will only be acting for one of the spouses (separate representation of children is discussed in Ch 10). If the solicitor even *sees* the children of the family – and this is unlikely – it will be as part of the adult client's case (Greenslade 1988, p 157; Murch 1980, p 27). The solicitor owes various duties to the client, breach of which can have serious professional repercussions. In particular, the solicitor owes duties of loyalty and confidentiality to the client which require her or him to act only in the client's interests and not to divulge what the client has said without consent (Law Society 1990, Part II).

Suppose, however, that complying with these obligations harms the interests of the children, or at least promotes them less than an alternative course of action would? The most graphic example of this arises in cases of sexual or other physical abuse of children. Take the husband who discloses to his solicitor that he has abused the children but who says that the wife knows nothing about it. He also swears that he has ceased abusing them and that they will be safe if he wins custody of them. Prima facie, the solicitor is obliged to remain silent about the admission. If, however, the husband gains custody of the children following contested litigation and then does abuse them further, the question arises whether the solicitor bears some of the responsibility for the abuse by having remained silent. As will be seen below, on these facts it seems clear that the solicitor bears no *legal* responsibility; but that is simply a consequence of what the law currently says. If one takes the view that the solicitor nevertheless bears *moral* responsibility, then one is faced with the very difficult task of saying how the law should be changed.

The whole question of confidentiality in cases of child abuse and abduction has recently been addressed by the Law Society (Law Society 1991b, p 42). It is difficult to summarise the guidance given because much depends on the particular kind of dilemma facing the solicitor. In general, however, the Law Society concedes that there are some exceptional circumstances where the duty of confidentiality to the client may, in the solicitor's discretion, be broken. To qualify as an exceptional circumstance, the solicitor must believe that on these facts the public interest in protecting children outweighs the public interest in maintaining the duty of confidentiality.

No direct legal authority is adduced for the Law Society's proposition and the position cannot be regarded as free from doubt. As it stands, however, the advice is more significant for asserting that there *can be* justification for breaching confidentiality rather than for its assistance in determining what kind of case qualifies. How does the individual solicitor weigh up the relative merits of two kinds of public interest? Why, in fact, is it expressed like this at all? Admittedly, there are public advantages in the community believing that they can repose trust in their own lawyers, but it seems curious to talk about the *public* interest in protecting children. Closer to the point are the interests of the *children themselves* in not being abused. Put like this, it is difficult to see how a solicitor who, after diligent inquiry, believes there is a real possibility of a child being abducted or seriously assaulted, could ever be justified in remaining silent. Nothing in the Law Society's recent guidance goes so far as to impose a *duty* to disclose.

The situation considered above is a dramatic kind of ethical dilemma. Important as it is, one should not be distracted from the more mundane reality that negotiations routinely take place over the extent of contact, the children's living arrangements or the appropriate level of financial support. The outcome of these negotiations has an important effect on children and yet the children themselves may hardly feature in the process. In so far as this stems from the traditional ethical position in the adversary system that the lawyer's first duty is to her or his client, the time may well have come for a reappraisal of the situation in family matters. In other words, if we are to take seriously the position of children in family law, can we any longer afford to see litigation as disputes between two adults each with their own legal gladiator? To insist on the separate representation of all children in all cases would be extraordinarily expensive and often unnecessary. More desirable, perhaps, is a careful restructuring of the solicitor's role so that no one is in any doubt that the solicitor has broad-ranging responsibilities to children and is not merely the paid mouthpiece of one of the so-called parties.

It is often easier to criticise lawyers than to find ways of praising them. In fact, Murch (1980, Ch 1) found evidence of widespread satisfaction amongst clients with their solicitors (the children were not asked). Most clients found their solicitor approachable and diligent and they relied heavily on her or him for counselling and support, often in preference to relying on those welfare professionals whose training might have better suited them to a counselling role. Murch attributed this to the fact that solicitors are a more socially acceptable source of such support. Most clients saw their solicitor's stance in relation to their case as clearly partisan, that is as a 'fighter' on the client's behalf, and most clients approved of this in their own solicitor, seeing it as an essential part of the role. However, Murch found evidence in some cases that this partisanship created conflict between the parties where none had existed before. More recent research has supported many of these findings, although it should be said that higher levels of discontent have also been found (Davis 1988, p 86). It might be added that clients usually have little or no prior experience of the divorce process. As a result, they may only have limited information on which to judge the quality of the service they have received.

This discussion of solicitors has been designed to remind readers that family law is as much about the beliefs and practices of professional people as it is about rules in statutes or case law. The issues raised here reappear later in the book; in particular in Chapters 7 to 10 where the relative merits of lawyers and welfare professionals are discussed in the context of divorce, financial matters, custody disputes and care proceedings.

(c) **Legal aid**

The Legal Aid Scheme, first introduced in 1950, provides certain qualifying individuals with financial assistance from state funds, which may be recoverable from contributions made by the assisted person, or from any costs or property awarded to the assisted person in court proceedings. The Legal Aid Scheme is of considerable relevance to the subject matter of this book, since many of those who encounter the various aspects of the legal system described here will only be able to afford to do so with the assistance of legal aid. This is particularly true of women, most of whom are likely to be legally aided (Smart 1984, p 164). Further, 'family' matters in general account for a large part of civil legal aid expenditure. For the year 1986/7, for example, matrimonial legal aid accounted for almost a third of the total cost of the Legal Aid Scheme (Law Society 1988, p xiii). Thus, policies pursued by those administering the scheme may have a significant effect on how the available procedures are used. The poor rates of remuneration for legal aid work, and the frequent and lengthy delays in processing legal aid applications, are now such that many practitioners doubt whether they can offer their legally-aided clients a proper service.[17]

The scheme, which is now contained in the Legal Aid Act 1988, is administered by the Legal Aid Board.[18] The Board is a statutory corporate body with responsibility for ensuring that the Legal Aid Scheme is administered in accordance with the terms of the Legal Aid Act 1988. There are 15 area committees and area directors, who

17 See, for example, the editorial by Henry Hodge in the January 1992 issue of *Family Law*.
18 For the background, see Lord Chancellor's Department 1986a, 1987; for discussion, see Zander (1988), Ch 2 and White (1991), pp 321–323.

have responsibility for the day-to-day running of the scheme in their areas, including making decisions about granting, extending or revoking legal aid certificates. The Board has considerable flexibility as to the means by which advice, assistance and representation shall be made available, subject to the ultimate scrutiny of the Lord Chancellor. For example, the Board may enter contracts with any person or body to secure the provision of these services.[19] This would enable the Board to contract with non-lawyers for the provision of certain services, or to enter franchise agreements with firms of solicitors for the provision of certain categories of legally-aided work. Given that matrimonial work accounts for a significant proportion of legal aid expenditure, it seems likely that these new powers will, once exercised, have a significant impact on the availability and nature of matrimonial legal services.

There are at present three different forms of assistance under the scheme:

(i) the 'Green Form' Scheme;
(ii) Assistance by Way of Representation (ABWOR); and
(iii) full civil legal aid.

We will consider each in turn.

(i) Advice and assistance: the 'Green Form' Scheme

Where an individual satisfies the criteria of eligibility (see below), a solicitor may provide oral or written advice on the legal position relating to the client's circumstances and on the appropriate legal action that a person might take, and may provide that person with limited forms of assistance in taking that action.[20] The kind of work covered by this general description would include advice, correspondence, negotiation, drafting and applying for full legal aid or Assistance by Way of Representation (below). There is a limit of £78.50 to the level of refundable costs that may be incurred in this kind of work, although it is possible for a solicitor to apply to the area committee for an extension.[1] Assistance is not available under this scheme for the institution of, or conduct by, the solicitor of court proceedings, for which the other forms of assistance considered below would be necessary. Eligibility for advice and assistance depends on an assessment of the individual's means, which includes both capital and income, and is carried out by the solicitor using the Green Form

19 LAA 1988, s 4.
20 LAA 1988, ss 2 and Pt III; Legal Advice and Assistance Regulations 1989.
1 LAA 1988, s 10(1); LAAR 1989, reg 21.

Key Card. Depending on the assessment of means, advice will either be free, unavailable under the scheme, or available but with a contribution from the individual.[2]

Since the withdrawal in 1977 of full legal aid from undefended divorces[3] (see further Ch 7), advice and assistance under this scheme has assumed a primary role in the majority of divorces. In recognition of this, the limit of costs beyond which an extension must be sought in undefended divorces is set at a higher level of £117.75.[4] Nevertheless, this still means that advice and assistance under the Green Form Scheme may not cover the filing of divorce petitions and acknowledgments of service, although it will include advice on these matters as well as the drafting of the petition itself.

(ii) Assistance by Way of Representation

This is an extension of the Green Form Scheme to include representation in court, introduced by the Legal Aid Act 1979.[5] A solicitor acting for a client under the Green Form Scheme may apply to the area director for authorisation to conduct court proceedings on the client's behalf. In deciding whether to grant authorisation, the director will apply the same criteria as apply to the granting of full legal aid (see below). The director may prescribe a limit to the value of assistance that may be given that is higher than that available under the Green Form Scheme. This scheme applies primarily to proceedings in the magistrates' court (ie, the family proceedings court) with the effect that full legal aid has been almost entirely superseded in that court. As compared with legal aid, Assistance by Way of Representation is quicker to obtain since the assessment of means is carried out by the solicitor rather than by the DSS; however, the criteria of eligibility for full legal aid are slightly more generous.

---

2   LAA 1988, s 9(6) and LAAR 1989, Sch 3. At present, the lower income limit (below which no contribution need be paid) is £70 pw, and the upper limit (above which eligibility ceases) is £135 pw; the limit on disposable capital is £935. It is unlikely in most family cases that the income and capital of spouses and cohabitees will be added together for these purposes, since they are likely to have a 'contrary interest' in the matter (see LAAR 1989, Sch 2). It is for this reason that women are more dependent on legal aid in family cases than men.
3   LAMPR 1977.
4   LAAR 1989.
5   See now LAA 1988, ss 2(3), 8(2) and LAAR 1989.

(iii) Legal aid

Legal aid provides assistance with the costs of court proceedings, including almost all family proceedings except for (i) undefended divorces and (ii) proceedings in the family proceedings court where Assistance by Way of Representation is available. Entitlement to legal aid depends on the grant by an area director of a legal aid certificate. The grant of a certificate will depend on (a) the applicant coming within the financial eligibility rules (a means test), and (b) the decision by the area director to grant the certificate on the merits of each particular case (a merits test). In some circumstances, the cost of the proceedings from the legal aid fund can be recovered. The Children Act 1989 has extended the availability of legal aid in care proceedings and vests in the Lord Chancellor new powers to dispense with means and merits tests in certain cases.[6] There are also provisions which allow for legal aid to be granted without means testing in emergencies, such as applications for injunctions in cases of domestic violence.[7]

Eligibility   An applicant's eligibility for legal aid will be determined by a DSS assessment officer and will depend on the amount of disposable income and capital available to the applicant.[8] An applicant may be entitled to free legal aid, to no legal aid or to legal aid only on condition that the applicant makes a contribution towards the legal costs. The assessment officer will determine the maximum contribution payable, while the actual contribution will be determined by the area director.[9]

Criteria   Provided that the applicant satisfies the financial eligibility rules, he or she will be granted a certificate unless:

(i) the area director takes the view that there are no reasonable grounds for taking, defending or being a party to the proceedings in question;[10]

(ii) it is considered unreasonable that the applicant should receive legal aid, or where Assistance by Way of Representation would be more appropriate;[11] or

6 CA 1989, s 99 and Sch 2, para 45. See, for example, the Legal Aid Act 1988 (Children Act 1989) Ord 1991, which widens the availability of legal aid to the child, its parents and anyone with parental responsibility in care proceedings.
7 CLA(G)R 1989, regs 19, 20. There is some evidence that emergency legal aid can be difficult to obtain, usually because the telephone and fax lines of the area committee are engaged.
8 LAA 1988, s 15; CLAARR 1989.
9 CLA(G)R 1989.
10 LAA 1988, s 15(2).
11 LAA 1988, s 15(3). See also LAA 1988, s 15(3B) (inserted by CA 1989, s 99).

(iii) where only a trivial advantage would be obtained from the proceedings in question, or where they are too simple to require involvement of a solicitor.[12]

This third exclusion, sometimes called the 'paying client test', may be most relevant in matrimonial cases where assistance is being sought for proceedings for maintenance or for variation of an existing maintenance order, in which the evidence may suggest that the chances of a significant amount being ordered or actually paid in the applicant's favour are remote.

Recovery of expenditure   There are three means by which legal aid expenditure may be recouped. First, any costs awarded in favour of the assisted person will be paid into the legal aid fund.[13] Second, the assisted person may be called upon to make a contribution up to the maximum amount specified by the assessment officer.[14] Finally, if there is still a shortfall, the legislation provides for a charge (enforceable by the Legal Aid Board) to be levied on any property 'recovered or preserved' in the proceedings.[15] The effect of this is to transform 'an out and out grant into a loan'.[16] In the matrimonial context, this charge would apply to any transfer of lump sums or of the matrimonial home, provided that the property in question has been in issue in the proceedings. Property will be 'in issue' where it is the subject of a dispute concerning its ownership, transfer or realisation.[17]

The charge is of greater significance in matrimonial than in any other civil proceedings: in 1986/7, just over 8% of the value of legal aid awards were recovered by means of the charge, whereas for other civil proceedings the equivalent figure was just over 2% (Law Society 1988, Appendix 2N). The existence of the charge has clearly affected the exercise by judges of their discretion in disputed cases concerning matrimonial property and finance, and is discussed further in Chapter 8. It should also affect the way solicitors define any disputed issues in legally-aided proceedings, and provides a strong incentive to minimise costs.

---

12 CLA(G)R 1989, reg 29.
13 LAA 1988, s 16; CLA(G)R 1989, reg 29.
14 LAA 1988, s 16(1).
15 LAA 1988, s 16(6).
16 Per Donaldson MR in *Watkinson v Legal Aid Board* [1991] 1 WLR 419 at 421, CA.
17 See *Hanlon v Law Society* [1981] AC 124; *Curling v Law Society* [1985] 1 All ER 705. There is a discretion to postpone the operation of the charge where the assisted person receives either money or land: CLA(G)R 1989, regs 96, 97. The power to postpone the charge over money only arises where the money is to be used for the purpose of the purchase of a home for the assisted person or her dependants.

(d) Welfare professionals

Judges, magistrates and solicitors are not the only professionals who will be encountered in this book. There is also a rather disparate group of professionals who also play a major role. At this stage it is only possible to outline in general terms what role that is; more detailed discussion will follow later at appropriate points. Just as with social welfare provision in general, the provision of welfare services in relation to family matters consists of a 'mixed economy of welfare' in the sense both of function, objective and organisation (see Webb and Wistow 1987, Ch 1). The major components of this 'mixed economy' are:

(i)   local authority social services;
(ii) the Divorce Court Welfare Service;
(iii) conciliation and mediation services;
(iv) guardians ad litem;
(v)   Department of Social Security (DSS); and
(vi) the police.

(i) Local authority social services[18]

The primary function of these bodies for present purposes is to provide for children in need in their geographical area of responsibility; they are also the bodies charged primarily with the task of child protection, with statutory powers to act if necessary. The extent of these powers, together with the administrative framework in which they are exercised, is considered further in Chapter 10. Social services departments may also find themselves involved in 'private' family proceedings where, for example, a child whose place of residence is disputed between his or her parents has been under the previous supervision of a local department, or where the court is considering whether or not to make a care order rather than giving residence to either parent (see further Ch 9). Social services may also find themselves involved in adoption proceedings, where they may be obliged to provide reports to court (see Ch 11).

(ii) Divorce Court Welfare Service

The primary task of the Divorce Court Welfare Officer (DCWO) is to provide reports to the divorce court whenever requested by the court to do so (see Ch 9). The power of the court to request a report

---

18 The legislative framework for local authority social services departments may be found in the Local Authority Social Services Act 1970.

arises in family proceedings under the Children Act 1989,[19] and the task of the Reporting Officer is to provide the court with background information concerning the circumstances of the child and his or her parents (see Ch 9; also March 1980, Part 2; Clulow and Vincent 1987). Reports are usually, but not always, requested in cases where there is a dispute over residence. Thus, DCWOs have also become involved in conciliation, although as we shall see in Chapter 7 the functions of reporting and conciliating must be kept separate.

This service is provided by the Probation Service. The way in which the service is organised will vary geographically. Thus, while some officers are divorce specialists working in a 'divorce unit', others will carry out their divorce work alongside their other responsibilities to the criminal courts (Clulow and Vincent 1987, Ch 3). If the family court were to become a reality, the weight of opinion is against retaining a divorce welfare role for the Probation Service, not least because of the association of the service with criminal work (Finer 1974, paras 4.318–4.322; March 1980, Ch 17).

(iii) Conciliation and mediation services

Recent years have witnessed the growth of conciliation and mediation as a way of encouraging settlement or agreement in divorce and other matrimonial proceedings. Conciliation and mediation are discussed further in Chapter 7, where it will be seen that conciliation has a mixed economy of provision of its own – some services may be provided by the Probation Service as part of the Divorce Court Welfare Service, and some by independent volunteers whose experience may be of probation, social work or marriage guidance.

(iv) Guardians ad litem

The general function of a guardian ad litem, who will often be a trained social worker, is to represent the child's interests to the court. Legislation now provides for the appointment and function of guardians in certain proceedings such as care and adoption proceedings. This is discussed further in Chapters 10 and 11. In other proceedings, such as wardship or private custody disputes, the role of guardian ad litem may be taken by the Official Solicitor (see Turner 1977 and Chapters 9 and 12). The relationship between the guardian and any lawyer representing the same child may sometimes be unclear, in that the latter is obliged to represent his or her client's

19 CA 1989, s 7.

views (as far as possible) rather than the child's best interests (which may not be the same). Where the guardian is a lawyer and is the sole representative for the child, the role of the guardian may be ambiguous. We return to this later.

(v) Department of Social Security (DSS)

The Department of Social Security is responsible for the administration of the system of welfare benefits, including income support, family credit and child benefit, all of which are discussed in Chapter 4. Since, as we shall see in Chapter 8, many ex-spouses and parents are dependent on these welfare benefits as a major component of their household income, the Finer Committee's view that the DSS in effect administers a 'third[20] system of family law' remains as true now as it was in 1974. Of particular relevance is the administration by the Department of the 'liable relative' and 'diversion' procedures, discussed more fully in Chapters 4 and 8, and of the 'cohabitation rule', discussed in Chapter 2. The close relationship between the administrative structure of the welfare benefit system and the practical operation of many aspects of the legal system dealing with family matters will be considered at various points throughout the book.

(vi) Police

For present purposes, the role of the police is threefold. First, to enforce the criminal law in the context of domestic violence or abuse; second, to enforce certain orders of the court restraining the use of violence by one partner against another; and third, to take certain forms of action for the emergency protection of children by means of a place of safety order. Chapter 6 is concerned with the first two of these, Chapter 10 with the last.

Summary

The purpose of this chapter has been to introduce a number of themes which underlie much of the material presented in this book. Three in particular may be identified. The first is that we should

---

20 Third, that is, behind (i) the higher courts (county and High) exercising jurisdiction in matrimonial causes, and (ii) the summary jurisdiction of the magistrates.

question the coherence of family law as a subject and the homo-geneity of the legal system as a set of identifiable institutions and practices. Neither is as straightforward as is sometimes suggested. The second is to caution against looking exclusively at the law. Law does not describe a reality: it does not 'tell the truth'. It is merely one form of regulation amongst others, the balance between which may shift. At present, if one were to look at trends in law as it relates to the resolution of family disputes, one might identify a process of liberalisation or 'dejuridification' in which the constraining character of law is being replaced by the enabling character of other forms of dispute resolution. However, it may be that this obscures the way in which law has merged with other forms of regulation, and that rather than liberalisation there is instead a reassembling of the elements of the regulatory mechanisms in which law as traditionally understood plays a smaller part. Finally, it is important to consider not only the official intentions 'behind' legal provisions, but also their effects and outcome on individuals.

Chapter 2
Marriage and cohabitation

Introduction

Marriage is a social practice which may be endowed with a variety of meanings and functions. It is also the organising concept for the purposes of defining and attaching significance to a certain set of legitimate heterosexual familial relations in English law. However, marriage as a social practice and marriage as a legal concept may, but need not, overlap. Thus, while legal marriage remains a popular state for many people, there is evidence of a significant number of couples who choose to live outside the formal legal framework of marriage but who are nevertheless 'married' in the social sense of maintaining a stable cohabiting and sexual relationship. Thus, the rate of first (legal) marriages has been falling since the early 1970s, with a large proportion of marriages being remarriages for one or both partner, usually following a divorce (Central Statistical Office 1987, Tables 2.12, 2.14; 1991, Tables 2.10, 2.11 and 2.12; OPCS 1991, p 8); and between 1981 and 1988, the proportion of women aged between 16 and 49 who were cohabiting more than doubled (CSO 1991, Ch 2). It has been estimated that in 1986/7, there were about 900,000 cohabiting couples, with over 400,000 dependent children living in such families (Haskey and Kiernan 1989, 1990; see also Foster et al 1990, pp 31–34). Over half of cohabiting couples are single and under thirty (ibid). While this may be explained in part as a growth in pre-marital cohabitation, it is striking how many divorcees, especially divorced men, are cohabiting. Haskey and Kiernan (above) estimate that about a third of divorced men are cohabiting.

However, informal cohabitation is by no means a new phenomenon, but may be viewed as a return to an earlier practice of widespread disregard for formalisation of sexual relationships (Stone 1979; Parker 1990) and as evidence of a growing social acceptance of a practice previously confined to certain social groups (O'Donovan 1984). The growing legal recognition attaching to such 'cohabiting' relationships in modern law, examined later in this chapter, suggests that marriage is losing its central significance as a determinant of the status of the parties. In this way, the legal distinction between formal and informal marriage becomes blurred, as the legal effects of marriage are gradually extended to informal relationships (see Weyrauch 1980). Whether or not this trend is to be welcomed is discussed later. Another important means of determining status in modern law requiring consideration, competing in significance with both formal and informal marriage, is that of parenthood, discussed in the next chapter.

In this chapter, we consider the formalities required for the purposes of marriage, and the legal definition of marriage as expressed in the law of nullity. We then consider the legal effects of marriage, both from the point of view of private and of public law. Finally, we consider the extent to which the law seeks to define and attach consequences to informal cohabitation.

Formalities

(a) Introduction

The insistence on compliance with formality as a precondition of a valid marriage is a comparatively recent phenomenon in English law. The jurisdiction exercised by the Church over matrimonial matters from the twelfth century onwards was relatively lax in this respect, since '[i]n order to reduce the chances of exposure to deadly sin through sexual waywardness, the church maximised the number of ways in which a lawful union could be contracted' (Finer and McGregor 1974, para 3). Thus, there existed not only the possibility of the solemnisation of regular marriages in church, but also that of a clandestine and informal exchange of promises (on marriage practices, see Parker 1990, Ch 2). The common law discriminated between regular and irregular marriages in the only way it knew how, through the law of property (see Bromley and Lowe 1987, pp 34–36). Another distinctive feature of English law until the mid-eighteenth century was the effective absence of a power of parental veto over the marriage; in this respect, English law was apparently unique amongst the nations of Europe (MacFarlane 1986, Ch 4), although parents would have exercised considerable influence over the choices made by their children through their ability to disinherit their offspring (Glendon 1977, pp 34–35).

The absence of necessary formality, combined with the ability to marry without parental consent, was considered to have disastrous consequences in view of the growing importance in the eighteenth century of marriage as a means of managing and advancing the wider family's economic interests (Stone and Stone 1984). This led to the passage in 1753 of Lord Hardwicke's Act, the avowed aim of which was the suppression of clandestine marriage and the adverse proprietorial consequences of such unions (O'Donovan 1985, pp 44–50; Parker 1987, 1990). The effect of this Act was to require rigid compliance with formality in the regularising of marriage, together with an insistence that all marriages be celebrated in a Church of England church or chapel. Further, parental consent was required for the marriage of persons aged under twenty-one. The penalties for breach of these provisions were severe, and included not only the invalidity of the marriage itself, but, in certain cases, the criminal penalties of transportation and death.

The legislation came under attack for two reasons. First, by insisting on celebration according to the rites of the Church of England (excepting Jews and Quakers), the Act displayed little tolerance of religious dissent; and second, the system of parochial registration of marriages was extremely inefficient. For these reasons, certain provisions of the Act were repealed in 1823;[1] and, more importantly, the Marriage Act 1836, together with the Birth and Deaths Registration Act of the same year, introduced a civil procedure for the formalising and recording of marriage. It has been suggested that while the 1753 Act was 'a response to the demands within a particular class to gain greater control over the nuptial behaviour of the young and the deviants within the class . . . [the 1836 Act] was designed to acquire greater bureaucratic control over the poor and moral control over working class behaviour, particularly that of women' (Parker 1990, p 94).

Although the law as to formality has been amended many times,[2] this 'dual' framework of religious and civil formality remains the basic framework of the modern law. It has been said that the purpose of the modern law of marriage formalities ought to be 'to guard against clandestine marriages [and to ensure] that there should be proper opportunity for legal impediments to be declared or discovered, that all marriages should be publicly solemnised and that the marriage should be duly recorded in the official registers' (Law Commission 1973a, Annex, para 4). Whether the present law lives up to this ideal is doubtful; and the Law Commission has recommended certain changes to the law, in particular that there should be uniform civil preliminaries (ibid,

---

1 Marriage Act 1823.
2 Most significantly, by the Marriage Acts of 1898 and 1949.

para 12).[3] The dual nature of the law concerning formality has led to considerable complexity; but 'the apparent complexity of the system masks the fact . . . [that it] . . . exercises little control over the formation of marriage', and 'the English state takes little advantage of the occasion of marriage to promote any particular social policies' (Glendon 1977, p 45).

The following discussion, which offers only an outline of the relevant law, concerns first the required preliminaries to both civil and ecclesiastical marriages, and second the rules concerning solemnisation in each case. Failure to comply with certain of these formalities will render the marriage void.[4] There are also a range of criminal penalties for knowing and wilful infringements of certain requirements.[5]

(b) Preliminaries

(i) Civil

Superintendent registrar's certificate   This is the usual civil procedure. The parties must first give notice in prescribed form to their local superintendent registrar (in whose area they must have been resident for seven days preceding the giving of notice) of their intention to marry.[6] If the parties reside in different areas, notice must be given to the local registrar of each party. Notice must be accompanied by a declaration that there are believed to be no lawful impediments to the marriage and that the requisite consents (as to which, see below) have been obtained or dispensed with.[7] The notice is then displayed for 21 days, at the end of which time the registrar must issue a certificate of marriage[8] which must then be presented to the person solemnising the marriage.[9] During the 21-day period, any person may enter a caveat against the issuing of the certificate, for example on the ground that requisite parental consent has not been given.[10]

3   The Government White Paper *Registration: Proposals for Change* (Cm 939, Ch 3, 1990) decided against introducing uniform civil preliminaries. The General Synod of the Church of England (1988) was opposed to such a change, and the White Paper states that a 'wider consensus is needed before such fundamental changes can be contemplated' (para 3.3).
4   MA 1949, ss 25, 49.
5   MA 1949, ss 75–77.
6   MA 1949, s 27 (as amended); the Government White Paper *Registration: Proposals for Change* (Cm 939, Ch 3, 1990) proposes that notice must be given to the registrar in the district in which the parties are ordinarily resident.
7   MA 1949, s 28.
8   MA 1949, s 31.
9   MA 1949, s 31(4).
10   MA 1949, s 29 (as amended).

In such a case, a certificate may only be issued once court permission for the marriage has been obtained.[11] Determination by a court may also be required where an objection is lodged on the grounds of prohibited degrees. In the event of any other objection being made, the registrar must be satisfied that it ought not to obstruct the issue of a certificate before issuing one.[12]

Superintendent registrar's certificate with licence This procedure is broadly similar to the ordinary certificate without licence, except that:

(i) the notice is not displayed publicly and the certificate must be issued at the end of one week-day unless an impediment has been shown;[13]
(ii) notice need only be given to one registrar, and may be given by either party provided only that one of the parties has been resident in the registrar's district for a period of 15 days preceding the notice and that the other is resident in England and Wales;[14] and,
(iii) it is more expensive.[15]

Although intended as an exceptional procedure, it is in fact used in a substantial minority of cases. It has been pointed out that 'there is far less opportunity of checking the accuracy of the notice and declaration and little time for anyone to raise an objection' (Law Commission 1973a, Annex, para 9). The Government White Paper *Registration: Proposals for Change* proposes the abolition of this procedure.

Registrar General's licence This is a power, conferred in 1971,[16] to authorise the solemnisation of a marriage in a place other than a registered building or registry office (see below).

(ii) Ecclesiastical

Publication of banns This is 'overwhelmingly the most commonly used preliminary' (Law Commission 1973a, Annex, para 12). The banns must be published in the parish church of the parish (or

11 MA 1949, s 30.
12 MA 1949, s 29(2).
13 MA 1949, s 32.
14 MA 1949, s 27(2).
15 Currently £42, as opposed to £15 for an ordinary certificate – MA 1949, s 32(5) and SI 1990/2515, Art 2, Schedule.
16 Marriage (Registrar General's Licence) Act 1970.

parishes) in which the parties are resident on three Sundays preceding the marriage.[17] There is no requirement that the parties provide a declaration, and the ecclesiastical authorities are not obliged to satisfy themselves as to the absence of impediments, or that requisite consents (see below) have been obtained. However, in the latter case a public declaration of dissent by a parent at the time of the publication of the banns will render the publication of the banns ineffective.[18] The parties need give only seven days' notice to the clergyman, together with details of their names, and place and length of residence.[19]

Common licence   This is the ecclesiastical equivalent of the super-intendent registrar's certificate and licence in that it enables the parties to marry in a church while avoiding the publication of banns, and similar requirements as to the provision of declarations concerning the absence of impediments and the obtaining of consents apply. One difference is that the Bishop (who technically grants the licence) need not wait a whole week-day before doing so.[20]

Special licence   The Archbishop of Canterbury may, entirely at his discretion, grant such a licence, the effect of which is to permit solemnisation of marriage according to the rites of the Church of England in a place other than a church or chapel.[1]

(c) Solemnisation

Where preceded by civil preliminaries, a marriage may be solemnised:

(i)   in a registry office;[2]

---

17 MA 1949, ss 6, 7.
18 MA 1949, s 3(3).
19 MA 1949, s 8.
20 MA 1949, ss 15, 16.
1   MA 1949, s 79(6).
2   MA 1949, s 45; the form of words to be used is set out in MA 1949, s 44(3). The Government White Paper *Registration: Proposals for Change* (Cm 939, Ch 3, 1990) proposes to relax the law in this respect in a number of ways: (i) the present requirement that the marriage must take place in the registry office of the district in which at least one of the parties is resident will be removed 'as a helpful move to give the public greater freedom of choice in where they may marry' (para 3.16); (ii) it is proposed that civil ceremonies need not take place in a registry office at all, but in other appropriate buildings; and (iii) alternative, more modern, forms of wording for the ceremony itself will be made available, and it will be open to registrars to agree in advance to additional elements to the ceremony, such as poetry readings (para 3.24).

(ii) in the place of residence of a housebound or detained person;[3]
(iii) in a 'registered building';[4]
(iv) in any place following the issue of a Registrar General's licence (above); or
(v) according to the rites of the Quaker or Jewish communities.[5]

In (i)–(iv), the marriage must take place between 8.00am and 6.00pm in the presence of at least two witnesses[6] and the marriage must be presided over by a registrar or, in the case of marriages solemnised in registered buildings, by an 'authorised person' (who will usually be a minister or senior member of a religious group). Thus English marriage law permits valid marriages to be contracted according to the rites of non-Anglican religions.[7]

Where preceded by ecclesiastical preliminaries, the marriage must be solemnised in one of the churches in which the banns were published[8] or, in the case of a common licence, in the church or chapel specified in the licence.[9] It must be solemnised by a member of the Holy Orders of the Church of England in the presence of at least two witnesses between the hours of 8.00am and 6.00pm.[10] A special licence permits solemnisation in the place specified in the licence at any time. Marriages of housebound or detained persons may also be celebrated according to the rites of the Church of England, but only following the issue of a superintendent registrar's certificate.

(d) Parental consent

We have seen that one of the purposes of Lord Hardwicke's Act of 1753 was to give greater control to parents over the marriage

3 See MA 1949, ss 26(1)(dd), 27A, 78(3), (4), (5) (inserted by MA 1983).
4 See Places of Worship Registration Act 1855 and MA 1949, ss 41–44 (as amended); to qualify, the building must be used for the purposes of 'religious worship', on the meaning of which see *R v Registrar General, ex p Segerdal* [1970] 2 QB 697. It need not be separate, but may 'form part of another building': MA 1949, s 41(7) as amended by the Marriage (Registration of Buildings) Act 1990.
5 See MA 1949, ss 26(1)(c)(d), 47.
6 MA 1949, s 4.
7 See Poulter (1986), pp 33–39; the Government White Paper *Registration: Proposals for Change* (Cm 939, Ch 3, 1990) proposes a simplification of the procedures for recognising registered buildings and authorised persons, the most important implication of which is that a wider range of buildings, or parts of buildings, will be eligible for recognition. This should make it easier for religious minorities to have their places of worship registered where the building in question is not used exclusively for religious worship. The Marriage (Registration of Buildings) Act 1990 (above) goes some way towards achieving this.
8 MA 1949, s 12.
9 MA 1949, s 15.
10 MA 1949, s 4.

decisions of their children. However, the social conditions giving rise to that legislation no longer prevail, although it may be thought that a requirement of parental consent now serves other useful purposes. However, the age beneath which consent is required was lowered in 1969 from 21 to 18,[11] and it is no longer the case that a marriage contracted without parental consent is void;[12] although, as we have seen, it is open to a person whose consent is required to lodge an objection during the course of civil or ecclesiastical preliminaries, the effect of which will be to prevent the marriage going ahead. However, 'the enforcement of the rules relating to consents[13] is notoriously difficult and it is well known that the rules can be easily evaded' (Law Commission 1973a, Annex, para 48).

Defining marriage

(a) Introduction

Marriage in English law consists of a heterosexual and monogamous union to which the parties have freely consented and in which they are able to enjoy at least a minimum of a sexual relationship, between individuals who are not related to each other in a certain number of ways, who are of requisite capacity and who have complied with the necessary formalities. This model of legitimate relations is sanctioned in a number of ways in that non-compliance with any element of this 'definition' of marriage may have a number of possible consequences. Thus, a marriage may be void, that is, will be regarded as never having existed; alternatively, a marriage may be voidable only, that is, valid until terminated by decree at the instance of one of the parties (see further below). Further, certain forms of non-compliance may result in criminal prosecution which may or may not result also in a defect in the validity of the marriage itself. Thus, the sanction for non-compliance with any element of the definition is not necessarily automatic invalidity; and the distinction between valid and invalid has been eroded by the fact that for certain purposes a void or voidable marriage will have similar consequences to a marriage terminated by divorce.

---

11 FLRA 1969, s 2(1)(c).
12 MA 1949, s 48(1).
13 See MA 1949, s 3 (as amended by CA 1989).

This variety in the means by which the required elements of marriage are enforced is matched by a variety in the types of restriction at work in the definition itself. At least four types of restriction may be identified:

(i)   those concerning compliance with formality;
(ii) those concerning capacity to marry ('who may marry?');
(iii) those concerning forbidden types of relation ('who may marry whom?'); and
(iv) those concerned with more substantive issues such as consent and consummation.

The more serious sanctions of total invalidity and criminal penalty are reserved for restrictions falling into categories (i)–(iii), although not all restrictions in these categories are enforced in this way; the sanction of potential invalidity, as expressed in the concept of a voidable marriage, is confined almost entirely (but again, not exclusively) to the final category. Recent years have witnessed a tendency towards the relaxation of the restrictions on the definition of marriage; but this has been associated with a decline in the significance of marriage itself as the central organising framework of familial relations in law (Glendon 1977, Ch 2).

Before examining the elements of marriage in English law, and the legal means by which they are underwritten, it should be noted that these rules have acquired a particular significance for immigrant and ethnic minority communities resident in this country (see Poulter 1986, Chs 2–4; Pearl 1986a, Chs 2–4). The law of marriage in England and Wales still bears the marks of its ecclesiastical, and hence Christian, origins. To what extent, then, does the law of this country accommodate or recognise non-Christian religious beliefs and practices concerning marriage? This may raise questions concerning the validity of marriages solemnised in this country by ethnic and religious minorities according to their own rites and practices; it may also raise questions concerning the recognition by English law of marriages contracted abroad which are valid according to the laws of the country of celebration, but which may contravene the definition of marriage in this country. The latter question raises issues of private international law, a full discussion of which is beyond the scope of this book.[14] Nevertheless, the extent to which English law extends or withholds recognition to or from such practices is an important underlying theme of the following discussion.

---

14 For a fuller account, see Bromley and Lowe (1987), pp 56–64.

(b) Void and voidable marriages

Nullity of marriage is an important means by which the restrictions outlined above are sanctioned. However, the law draws a distinction between void and voidable marriages. This distinction has a significance at a number of different levels. First, the grounds on which a marriage is void[15] are distinct from those on which it is voidable.[16] Second, a void marriage is void from the start, and does not require a decree to bring it to an end; whereas a voidable marriage is a valid marriage up until the date of a decree of nullity.[17] This may be important in determining the legitimacy of any children of the parties,[18] the property or pension rights of the parties and of the children[19] and the capacity of the parties to marry a third party.

Third, there exist certain statutory bars to a decree of nullity of a voidable marriage which do not apply to void marriages. Thus, a court may refuse a decree if the petitioner, with knowledge that it was open to him to have the marriage annulled, so conducted himself in relation to the respondent as to lead the respondent reasonably to believe that he would not seek to do so and that it would be unjust to grant the decree.[20] Time restrictions apply to petitions brought on all but two of the grounds of voidability so that a nullity petition in respect of a voidable marriage must be brought within a certain period of time of the marriage.[1] Fourth, while it is only possible for the parties to petition for a decree in the case of voidable marriages,[2] it seems to be possible for a third party to petition for a decree that the marriage is void (Bromley and Lowe 1987, pp 73–74). Finally, an important similarity between the two should be noted. A petitioner for a decree of nullity on whatever ground may invoke the powers of the court to make orders for income and property and for the custody of any children.[3] In this respect, a nullity decree is the functional equivalent of a divorce.

The case for retaining the concept of voidable marriage is not as strong as that for retaining void marriage. The latter is a means of withholding recognition from relations that do not comply with certain key elements of the legal construction of marriage. Voidable marriage, by contrast, relates to less fundamental elements of

15 MCA 1973, s 11.
16 MCA 1973, s 12.
17 MCA 1973, s 16 (this applies to decrees granted after 31 July 1971).
18 As to which, see Ch 3.
19 See, for example, *Ward v Secretary of State for Social Services* [1990] 1 FLR 119.
20 MCA 1973, s 13(1).
1   MCA 1973, s 13 (2)–(5).
2   Section 13 appears to be based on this assumption.
3   MCA 1973, s 21(1); MCA 1973, s 42(10) (see Chs 8 and 9).

marriage and the decision as to termination is left to the decision of the individual parties. The Law Commission considered the argument that the grounds of voidable marriage should instead be made grounds for divorce, but concluded that the concept of voidable marriage should be retained since it reflected an important religious distinction (articulated in the canon law) between marriages that never existed and marriages that have existed but have been terminated. In particular, it was thought that nullity should be available to those who might have religious or other objections to divorce (Law Commission 1970, paras 21–28).

(c) The required elements of marriage

We turn now to examine the required elements of a valid marriage according to the categories of restriction outlined above.

(i) Formalities

A marriage of persons who 'knowingly and wilfully intermarry' in breach of certain specified formalities, either preliminary to or during the solemnisation of marriage, will be void.[4] The formalities specified include marriage without a certificate, solemnisation in the absence of a registrar or other authorised person (or, in the case of church marriage, in the absence of a clerk in holy orders), or solemnisation in an unauthorised place. All other defects[5] will not invalidate a marriage, including a failure to obtain parental consent for the marriage of a person under the age of 18.[6] Certain procedural defects may be liable to a criminal sanction. Thus, providing false information to the registrar would amount to perjury;[7] and the MA 1949 creates certain offences relating to the 'knowing and wilful' solemnisation of a marriage by a person in breach of certain requirements.[8] For example, solemnisation of a marriage outside the hours of 8.00am and 6.00 pm is an offence carrying a penalty of up to 14 years' imprisonment.[9] However, despite the criminal penalty, there is nothing to suggest that a marriage solemnised in such a way would be anything but valid.

4   MA 1949, ss 25, 49; MCA 1973, s 11(a)(iii).
5   Some defects not affecting validity are listed in MA 1949, ss 24 and 48; other defects are assumed not to affect validity even though no specific mention is made of them in the legislation.
6   MA 1949, s 48(1)(b).
7   Perjury Act 1911, s 3.
8   MA 1949, s 75.
9   MA 1949, s 75(1)(a).

(ii) Who may marry?

Age   A marriage solemnised between two persons, one or both of whom is aged under 16, will be void.[10] This is one of the few matters with respect to which English law is more restrictive than it used to be. Until the Age of Marriage Act 1929, a marriage could be validly contracted by a boy of 14 and a girl of 12; the Act of 1929 raised the age to 16 for both sexes, and rendered such marriages void rather than voidable. The Law Commission has rejected the proposal that under-age marriages should be made voidable once again rather than void on the grounds that there should be as little doubt concerning the status of the marriage as possible, that it should not be up to the parties to decide on the validity of their marriage and that there should be consistency with the age of consent to intercourse for the purposes of the criminal law[11] (Law Commission 1970, paras 16–20). Parental consent is required for persons aged between 16 and 18; but the absence of consent will not, as we have seen, invalidate the marriage.

Under-age marriages contracted abroad by foreign domiciliaries will be recognised as valid in this country provided that the marriage is valid according to the law of the parties' domicile;[12] however, when contracted abroad by a domiciliary of this country, such a marriage will be void even though the under-age party was domiciled in the country of celebration, according to the laws of which the marriage was valid.[13] This may be important where a member of an ethnic minority domiciled in this country returns to his family's country of origin to marry.

Either party already lawfully married: bigamy   A marriage will be void if at the time of the ceremony either party was already lawfully married.[14] This restriction is underlined by the existence of a criminal penalty for bigamy. However, the sanction of invalidity and the criminal penalty may not always overlap. For example, it will be a defence to a criminal charge of bigamy that the party already married reasonably believed that his or her previous marriage had

---

10 MA 1949, s 2; MCA 1973, s 11(a)(ii).
11 See Sexual Offences Act 1956, s 6.
12 If the marriage is valid on this principle, it also seems that no criminal offence of sexual intercourse with a minor (Sexual Offences Act 1956, s 6) is committed: see *Alhaji Mohamed v Knott* [1969] 1 QB 1, [1968] 2 All ER 563. It will not now be possible for a man to bring a female aged under 16 into this country as his wife under the immigration rules – Pearl (1986a), pp 87–88.
13 *Pugh v Pugh* [1951] 2 All ER 680.
14 MCA 1973, s 11(b).

been terminated by death;[15] but the reasonableness of such a belief will not prevent the marriage from being void.[16] Further, a marriage solemnised in England will be void where one of the parties is already party to a polygamous marriage contracted abroad which satisfies the conditions for recognition as valid in English law (see below); however, such a marriage would not involve a criminal offence, since it seems that bigamy is only committed where the first marriage is a monogamous rather than a polygamous one.[17]

Transsexuals   A marriage between parties who are not respectively male and female is void.[18] This clearly applies to homosexual marriages (although there may be a question as to when a 'marriage' has taken place – see below) and thus amounts to an exclusion from marriage of a type of relationship rather than individuals. However, this may amount to a restriction on individuals where the law regards a person as being of one sex while they regard themselves as being of another. In such circumstances, a marriage that to them would appear heterosexual, and thus 'normal', will be regarded in law as homosexual and void. This is presently the case with transsexuals, who exhibit the biological characteristics of one sex but who feel themselves to be members of the 'opposite'[19] sex. In other words, their 'gender identity' does not match their physical characteristics.

English law currently adopts a narrow biological test of sex and gender for the purposes of the law of marriage. If a person possesses the genitals, gonads and chromosomes of one biological sex, that person is immutably a member of that sex for legal purposes despite the fact that they may be living the life of a person of the 'opposite' sex.[1] All evidence of a person's gender identity is ignored. This has been justified on the ground that 'marriage is a relationship which depends on sex and not gender', since only a person who, according to the biological criteria, is female is capable of engaging in 'natural heterosexual intercourse', which was regarded as 'the essential role of a woman in marriage'.[2] A reluctance to recognise sex as more fluid

---

15 Offences Against the Person Act 1861, s 57.
16 Unless a decree of presumption of death and dissolution of marriage has been obtained – see MCA 1973, s 19.
17 *R v Sagoo* [1975] QB 885.
18 MCA 1973, s 11(c).
19 There is no reason why sex and gender should be regarded as falling into one of two exhaustive and mutually exclusive categories – see O'Donovan (1985) Ch 3. There is no biological inevitability about this, since there are well-documented cases of biological hermaphrodites.
1 *Corbett v Corbett* [1971] P 83.
2 Per Ormrod J at pp 107, 105, 106; but see *SY v SY (otherwise W)* [1963] P 37.

for legal purposes may be justified on the basis that the recognition of
a legal change of sex, in the absence of legislation, may create some
technical difficulties (Dewar 1985); but at present English law forces
such individuals into a legal personality manifestly at odds with their
social one.[3] The only recognition accorded to a marriage of a
transsexual consists in the fact that it may be annulled and thus
attracts the ancillary powers to deal with property and finance,
provided (presumably) that a genuine marriage took place (see
below).

Mentally handicapped   Those suffering from a mental handicap may
be incapable of understanding the nature of the marriage contract
and would thus be regarded as incapable of giving consent. This
would render the marriage voidable.[4] A marriage is also voidable if
at the time of the marriage either party, though capable of giving a
valid consent, was suffering from a mental disorder within the
meaning of the Mental Health Act 1983[5] of such a kind or to such an
extent as to be unfit for marriage.[6]

(iii) Who may marry whom?

Homosexuals   We have seen that marriages between persons of the
same sex are void. Whether this means that homosexual marriages
may be annulled and thus attract the court's ancillary powers is
unclear. The Law Commission were originally against including
what is now s 11(c) of the Matrimonial Causes Act 1973 as a ground
of nullity on the ground that it might involve the extension of the
courts' ancillary powers to homosexual unions (1970, para 32). One
view would be that the present ground of nullity is confined to those
cases where there is genuine doubt concerning the sex of one of the
parties and would not include cases where the parties had engaged in
deliberate deception in going through a marriage ceremony.

---

3   A position supported by the European Court of Human Rights – see *Rees v United
     Kingdom* (1986) 9 EHRR 56 (not following *Van Oosterwijck v Belgium* (1980) 3
     EHRR 557, on which see Taitz (1988)) and *Cossey v United Kingdom* [1991] 2 FLR
     492 (no violation of Articles 8 or 12 of the European Convention of Human
     Rights). The ECHR held, amongst other things, that since a refusal to recognise
     legal sex reassignment does not prevent a transsexual from marrying (because
     Caroline Cossey could still have married a woman and Mr Rees could have
     married a man), English law does permit a transsexual to marry in the sense
     guaranteed by the Convention.
4   MCA 1973, s 12(c); see *Re Park's Estate* [1954] P 112.
5   See MHA 1983, s 1(2).
6   See *Bennett v Bennett* [1969] 1 All ER 539.

Prohibited degrees Although it would be true to say that restrictions on certain types of sexual relation are a universal feature of primitive and advanced societies, it should be remembered that 'this must be understood as meaning that some sort of prohibition on mating is universal, not that a particular set of relations is universally tabooed' (Glendon 1977, p 43). Thus, a wide variety of restrictions are possible, ranging from 'elementary' systems in which prohibitions on certain relations are accompanied by a requirement that individuals marry only from within a certain group,[7] to 'complex' systems in which only certain relations are excluded and the choice of partner is left to the individual (Segalen 1986, pp 56–61). In common with other advanced Western legal systems, English law adopts a 'complex' system in which certain core relations of blood (relations of consanguinity) are excluded from marriage, together with certain relations of marriage (affinity). However, outside the core relations of consanguinity, not all Western systems adopt the same set of prohibited relations. Differences emerge especially with respect to prohibitions on relations of affinity (relations through marriage) which are regarded as being within a 'zone of tolerance' (Glendon 1977, p 40).

At present, the restrictions on blood relations in English law are as follows: a man may not marry his mother, daughter, grandmother, granddaughter, sister, aunt or niece; a woman may not marry the equivalent male relations.[8] This is a wider set of restrictions than those found in the criminal law of incest, which prohibit sexual intercourse only with mother, daughter, granddaughter or sister but not with grandmother, aunt or niece (or equivalent male relations in the case of women).[9] The restrictions on relations of affinity, which have been progressively relaxed over the years,[10] are of two types:

(i) those prohibiting a man or woman from marrying the ex-spouses of certain blood relations;[11] and

---

7 These positive rules may require what in other societies would be regarded as 'incestuous' relations – see MacFarlane (1986), p 248.

8 MA 1949, s 1 and Part 1, Sch 1. These prohibited relations include illegitimate and half blood relations, as well as adoptive relations for the purposes of parents and children.

9 Sexual Offences Act 1956, ss 10, 11.

10 Deceased Wife's Sister's Marriage Act 1907; Deceased Brother's Widow's Marriage Act 1921; Marriage (Prohibited Degrees of Relationship) Act 1931; Marriage (Enabling) Act 1960; Marriage (Prohibited Degrees of Relationship) Act 1986.

11 Subject to MA 1949, s 1(2)–(5) (as inserted by the Marriage (Prohibited Degrees of Relationship) Act 1986), a man may not marry the former wife of his father, grandfather or son; equivalent restrictions apply to women – Parts II and III of Sch 1 to MA 1949.

(ii) those prohibiting a person from marrying certain relations through marriage of the opposite sex.[12]

However, these prohibited relations of affinity are now subject to the provisions of s 1 of the Marriage Act 1949 (as amended by the Marriage (Prohibited Degrees of Relationship) Act 1986) which permit such marriages in certain circumstances. Except in the case of a marriage between a man and his former mother-in-law or daughter-in-law, a marriage shall not be void by reason only of affinity if both parties are aged 21 or over and provided that the younger party had not at any time before reaching the age of 18 been a 'child of the family'[13] in relation to the other party.[14] A marriage between a man and his former mother-in-law or daughter-in-law (or a woman and her former father-in-law or son-in-law) is permissible only if the former spouses of both parties are dead.[15] Thus, prohibitions on relations of affinity are of declining significance and are no longer absolutely barred save where they are a potential source of disruption to pre-existing family relations.

These restrictions have been justified in a variety of ways. For example, it is possible that there are genetic dangers involved in permitting procreation between close blood relations, although these dangers are not conclusively proven in relation to all the prohibited degrees of consanguinity, such as relations between uncle/niece or aunt/nephew, and do not exist at all between affines.[16] It has been argued that the present rules prohibit relations that people in general view with 'instinctive revulsion' (Law Commission 1970, para 52); it has also been argued that the rules are designed to prevent the disruption or distortion of family relations, and the reforms of 1986 appear to be premised on this assumption.[17]

Polygamy Another respect in which English marriage law has become more lenient[18] is in relation to the recognition of polygamous

---

12 A man may not marry (subject to MA 1949, s 1(2)–(5)) an ex-wife's mother, daughter or granddaughter, or the ex-wife of a son; equivalent restrictions apply to women – see Parts II and III of Sch 1 to MA 1949.

13 For a definition, see Ch 11.

14 MA 1949, s 1(2), (3).

15 MA 1949, s 1(4), (5).

16 There may be a case for relaxing the restriction on uncle/niece or aunt/nephew marriages so as to enable religious or ethnic minorities to marry in this way where it is permitted as part of their religion (Poulter 1986, p 15). The most common form of kinship marriage found in elementary systems, that between first cousins, would be permitted in English law.

17 For an alternative view on the origin and function of the incest taboo, see Theweleit (1986), pp 363–385.

18 For an example of the earlier approach of English law, according to which such marriages were accorded no recognition, see *Hyde v Hyde* (1866) LR 1 P&D 130.

marriages, that is, marriages in which one of the parties (usually the man) is able to marry a second wife while being already married to a first, or has actually done so. The status of such marriages will be of particular interest to many immigrant communities whose marriages may have been contracted in countries permitting polygamy (Pearl 1986a, Ch 4; Poulter 1986, Ch 3). Greater lenience has recently been manifested by extending the conditions under which such marriages will be recognised as valid, or at least as having some legal consequence, in English law, not only for the purposes of matrimonial relief[19] but also for the purposes of the status of the children,[20] succession,[1] taxation,[2] entitlement to social security and child benefit,[3] and immigration. A polygamous marriage that is not recognised as valid, and is thus void under MCA 1973, s 11(d),[4] will still attract the ancillary powers of the court to award maintenance and to make orders for the custody of any children.[5]

The recognition by English law of a polygamous marriage will turn on three questions. First, does the country in which the marriage was celebrated permit polygamous marriages? Second, does the law of the parties' domicile permit polygamy? Third, is the marriage actually polygamous or actually monogamous? Applying these questions, it seems that a polygamous marriage (whether actually polygamous or not) contracted abroad in a country permitting polygamy will be valid in English law provided that the parties' domiciliary law permits polygamy (Law Commission 1985b, para 2.3).[6] Further, a man (but not a woman) domiciled in England and Wales may validly contract a polygamous marriage abroad provided that it is actually monogamous.[7] The Law Commission has recommended that the sex discrimination implicit in this be

---

19 MCA 1973, s 47; *Chaudhry v Chaudhry* [1976] Fam 148; MHA 1983, s 10(2).
20 Legitimacy Act 1976, s 1.
1   See *Re Sehota* [1978] 1 WLR 1506.
2   *Nabi v Heaton* [1981] 1 WLR 1052; revsd [1983] 1 WLR 626, CA.
3   Social Security and Family Allowances (Polygamous Marriages) Regulations 1975 – see Poulter (1986, pp 54–55); Pearl (1986a, pp 49–50).
4   Which states that a polygamous marriage entered into outside England and Wales will be void if at the time of the marriage either party was domiciled in England and Wales. This section has been held to have extended the recognition of polygamous marriages entered into after 31 July 1971 in English law – see *Hussain* (below).
5   This would not include attempts to contract polygamous marriages in England or Wales since MCA 1973, s 11(d) refers only to polygamous marriages contracted abroad, although such a marriage may be void as bigamous under MCA 1973, s 11(b).
6   But see *Radwan v Radwan (No 2)* [1973] Fam 35.
7   *Hussain v Hussain* [1982] 3 All ER 369; this applies only to marriages entered into after 31 July 1971, ie the date on which what is now MCA 1973, s 11(d) came into force.

removed so that any person domiciled in this country may validly contract a legally polygamous but actually monogamous marriage in a country permitting polygamy (Law Commission 1985b, para 2.17). This will enable members of ethnic minorities domiciled in this country to return to their country of origin for the purposes of marriage.

(iv)   Other defects rendering a marriage voidable

The grounds discussed under this head are all grounds leading to voidable rather than void marriage.[8] The notion of a voidable marriage, that is a marriage which is valid until annulled,[9] arose through the assumption by the common law courts following the reformation of jurisdiction over matrimonial causes, and has had a rather uneven history in the law of nullity. Thus, while incapacity to consummate has been a ground of voidability for some time, the ground of wilful refusal to consummate was introduced as comparatively recently as 1937 by the Matrimonial Causes Act of that year; and lack of consent has only recently been made a ground of voidability, having previously been regarded as rendering a marriage void but ratifiable. The more widespread availability of divorce may have diminished the strength of the case for retaining the notion of voidable marriage; and, as we saw above, the case for its retention is largely based on religious grounds. However, an increasingly important issue is whether the grounds on which a marriage is voidable are available to annul arranged marriages entered into by members of ethnic and religious minorities. Such cases present the difficult issue of how far the courts should respect the minority customs by upholding the marriage as valid, possibly at the expense of the wishes of one or both of the individual parties to it (see Pearl 1986a, Ch 2; Poulter 1986, pp 33–39).

Incapacity and wilful refusal to consummate   These two grounds are set out in s 12(a) and (b) of MCA 1973 respectively. 'Consummation' for these purposes is an act of sexual intercourse following solemnisation of marriage. Male penetration of the female body is the privileged and definitive form of sexual relation for the purposes of defining consummation in this context: the courts have developed a precise calibration of the male performance of the sexual act, a 'penile economy' (Moran 1987). Thus, intercourse must be 'ordinary

8   The nature of this distinction has been discussed above, at pp 40–41.
9   For an illustration of the practical effects of the distinction, see *Ward v Secretary of State for Social Services* [1990] 1 FLR 119.

and complete, and not partial and imperfect';[10] there must be full penetration, which may hinge upon precise measurement,[11] while maintaining an erection; ejaculation is not essential.[12] The procreation of children is neither a necessary nor sufficient condition of consummation. Thus, the use of contraception will not prevent sexual intercourse from counting as consummation;[13] and the birth of children following conception by means other than intercourse will not count as a consummation.[14]

Either spouse may petition for nullity under s 12(a) on the grounds of incapacity to consummate, including the petitioner's own incapacity. There is no requirement in s 12(a) that the incapacity exist at the date of the marriage, although it is likely that a court would insist on this (Cretney and Masson 1990, pp 49–50) in keeping with the canon law doctrine that nullity is only available for defects existing at the time of the marriage.[15] Incapacity may consist of impotence (but not sterility), whether of psychological or physiological cause,[16] or of an 'invincible repugnance'.[17] The incapacity may be general, or relate only to the other party;[18] but it must be incurable, or curable only by resort to hazardous surgery.[19] A mere lack of desire to have sexual intercourse is not enough to establish incapacity. Thus, a female party to an arranged marriage who took a dislike to her partner was held not to be able to petition for a decree of nullity on the basis of her own incapacity.[20]

A petition is also available under s 12(b) on the ground that the respondent has wilfully refused to consummate the marriage. This is of more recent origin than the incapacity ground, as we have seen, and is only available on the grounds of the respondent's refusal. Wilful refusal consists of a 'settled and definite decision come to without just excuse'.[1] A refusal to undergo reasonable curative treatment will be regarded as a wilful refusal;[2] however, a 'loss of ardour' will not.[3] A failure, following a civil marriage, to arrange a

10 Per Dr Lushington in *D-E v A-G* (1845) 1 Rob Eccl 279 at 298.
11 For the purposes of which the court has power to order the physical examination of the parties, usually the woman.
12 *R v R* [1952] 1 All ER 1194; *W (otherwise K) v W* [1967] 1 WLR 1554.
13 *Baxter v Baxter* [1947] 1 All ER 387.
14 *Clarke v Clarke* [1943] 2 All ER 540.
15 Nullity for wilful refusal clearly breaches this principle, however.
16 *G v G* [1924] AC 349.
17 *Singh v Singh* [1971] 2 All ER 828.
18 *C (otherwise H) v C* [1921] P 399.
19 *S v S* [1956] P 1.
20 *Singh* (above).
1 *Horton v Horton* [1947] 2 All ER 871; *Ford v Ford* [1987] Fam Law 232.
2 *S v S (otherwise C)* [1954] 3 All ER 736.
3 *Potter v Potter* (1975) 5 Fam Law 161.

religious ceremony without which the parties cannot according to their religion consummate the marriage, will be regarded as a wilful refusal for these purposes.[4] It has been suggested that by regarding the absence of the religious ceremony as fatal to the marriage in cases such as this, the courts are 'upholding important minority customs in a most sensitive area' (Poulter 1986, p 36).

Invalid consent   Lack of freely given consent to marriage was regarded as invalidating a marriage according to the canon law, and at common law lack of consent rendered a marriage void. However, such marriages were ratifiable and thus effectively equivalent to voidable marriages. This was formalised in 1971 when lack of valid consent was made a ground on which a marriage was voidable.[5] Lack of consent may arise from duress, mistake, unsoundness of mind[6] 'or otherwise'.

No clear test for establishing duress emerges from the case law. On one view, the petitioner must establish that his or her will has been overborne by a genuinely and reasonably held fear caused by an immediate threat to life, limb or liberty for which the petitioner is not responsible.[7] Thus, a marriage will be invalidated where the alternative is imprisonment or death[8] but not where the marriage is an arranged marriage and the petitioner has merely experienced family pressure to go through with it.[9] However, the courts have recently adopted a wider test in the context of an arranged marriage so that duress need not take the form of a physical threat, but need only consist of pressure (including social pressure) such that the reality of consent is destroyed.[10] This development has been welcomed on the ground that 'to uphold forced marriages under the misapprehension that [the courts] are giving effect to the respectable custom of arranged marriages would be a great mistake' (Poulter 1986, pp 31–32).

However, it remains the case that to talk of consent being destroyed is somewhat misleading, since there remains a sense in which a party to such a marriage does intend to marry: the question is rather one of the types of threat or inducement to marriage from which a party is entitled to expect protection. Nevertheless, it has been suggested that '[if] one reviews the actual decisions of the courts

4   *Jodla v Jodla* [1960] 1 All ER 625; *Kaur v Singh* [1972] 1 All ER 292; *Singh v Kaur* (8 March 1979, unreported), CA; *A v J* [1989] 1 FLR 110.
5   Law Commission (1970), paras 11–15; see now MCA 1973, s 12(c).
6   Considered above, at p 44.
7   Per Simon P in *Szechter (otherwise Karsov) v Szechter* [1970] 3 All ER 905 at 915.
8   *Szechter* (above); *Buckland v Buckland* [1967] 2 All ER 300.
9   *Singh v Singh* [1971] 2 All ER 828; *Singh v Kaur* (1981) 11 Fam Law 152.
10   *Hirani v Hirani* (1982) 4 FLR 232; see also *Scott v Sebright* (1886) 12 PD 21.

rather than some of the reasons advanced in reaching some of those decisions, . . . what in effect they have done is to distinguish legitimate threats from illegitimate ones' (Law Commission 1970, para 66).

A mistake will only vitiate consent where the mistake is as to the other party's identity (but not attributes, for example that she is a millionairess or that he is an international footballer);[11] or where the mistake is as to the nature of the marriage ceremony itself, but not as to its effects.[12]

The parties will be taken to have consented to the marriage even where their intention in marrying is limited to, for example, conferring nationality on one of the parties, and where the parties have no intention of living together.[13] However, recent changes to the immigration rules have enabled immigration officers to refuse entry clearance to certain categories of spouse or intended spouse where it is considered that the marriage was entered into, or is being entered into, with the 'primary purpose'[14] of obtaining admission to the United Kingdom (see Pearl 1986a, pp 22–28).

Venereal disease and pregnancy per alium Two further grounds on which a marriage will be voidable are:

(a) that at the time of the marriage the respondent was suffering from venereal disease in a communicable form;[15] and

(b) that at the time of the marriage the respondent was pregnant by some person other than the petitioner.[16]

These grounds were added by the MCA 1937, and were left unchanged when the law was reformed in 1971. It is unclear whether Acquired Immune Deficiency Syndrome (AIDS) would count as a 'communicable venereal disease' for these purposes.

The effects of marriage

It was suggested above that marriage is the organising legal concept for the purposes of defining and attaching significance to a certain set of legitimate heterosexual familial relations. Indeed, the elaborate

---

11 *Wakefield v Mackay* (1807) 1 Hag Con 394.
12 *Mehta v Mehta* [1945] 2 All ER 690; *Kassim v Kassim* [1962] P 224.
13 *Vervaeke v Smith* [1983] 1 AC 145.
14 See *R v Immigration Appeal Tribunal, ex p Kumar* [1987] 1 FLR 444 (discussed by Gordon (1987)) and *R v Immigration Appeal Tribunal, ex p Rajput* [1989] 2 FLR 200.
15 MCA 1973, s 12(e).
16 MCA 1973, s 12(f).

definition of marriage just discussed serves a purpose, and makes sense, only to the extent that marriage makes a difference to the legal rights and remedies of those who marry – to the extent, in other words, that marriage confers a status[17] on married couples. However, it has been noted above that the rules governing entry into marriage have been relaxed in recent years, and that this may be associated with a decline in the significance and exclusiveness of marriage as a status-conferring institution. It has been further suggested that marriage could be dispensed with altogether as the necessary mediating legal concept in ascribing rights and remedies to family members (Clive 1980), and that the objectives implicit in modern family law of economic and physical protection of weaker family members could be more satisfactorily achieved by the development of alternative mediating legal concepts, such as parenthood or the existence of a de facto familial relationship (Hoggett 1980a). However, as we shall see, marriage has a significant effect on the legal position of spouses in many areas that are not part of 'family law' as conventionally defined: the maintenance of marriage as the privileged definition of familial relations may serve a variety of purposes additional to those sought to be attributed to it within 'family law' itself. Thus, it has been said that 'marriage is not . . . *a* legal relationship between two parties; it is many legal relationships between the two parties' (Gibson 1991, p 149).

In this section, we are concerned with the question of how, and the extent to which, marriage continues to affect the rights and remedies of married couples. Much of the law discussed in this section has been influenced by the common law fiction that husband and wife were one person, that person being the husband. The existence of this fiction explains the historical development of the law, much of which has taken the form of 'emancipating' the wife from the various disabilities imposed in the name of marital unity. However, there are still traces of this fiction at work in the modern law.

In the final section of this chapter, we shall consider the question of how far the law has recognised de facto cohabiting relations as giving rise to legal rights and remedies; and in Chapter 3, we shall consider the significance attaching to parenthood. It will be argued that cohabitation, and especially parenthood, are becoming more

---

17 'Status' in this context refers to legal rights and remedies accruing exclusively to a class of individuals defined by reference in this case to the fact of a valid marriage (see Austin 1863, pp 381–400). 'Status' may also be taken to refer to rights and remedies arising otherwise than through the agreement of the individuals concerned – as distinct, that is, from 'contract' (see Maine 1861). The former formulation is preferred for the purposes of the present discussion.

important as the determinants of legal status of family members, outgrowing marriage in importance in this respect.

(a) Property, finance and succession

(i) Private maintenance

The status right attaching to marriage frequently considered the most significant is the right of spouses to claim private maintenance from each other either during the currency of the marriage (see Ch 4) or following a divorce (see Ch 8). This right is not available to those who are merely cohabiting. However, the practical significance of the exclusivity of this right may be overestimated, for two main reasons. First, private inter-spousal maintenance, if claimed and awarded, only rarely forms a significant element of the recipient's overall income. More significant are earnings from employment and welfare benefits provided by the state. This is explored in more detail in Chapter 8. Second, an increasingly important factor influencing the availability of private spousal support is the presence of children in the relationship, regardless of the marital status of the parents. For example, the rights of an unmarried parent to seek maintenance from the other parent on behalf of the child have been greatly improved by the provisions concerning child maintenance contained in the Children Act 1989 (consolidating earlier legislation: see Chs 3 and 4); while the rights of spouses to claim maintenance following divorce are increasingly defined in terms of the needs of any children for which that spouse is caring (see Ch 8). In other words, there is a practical convergence of the position of the married and unmarried in this respect, centred on the presence of children. This convergence will be further emphasised by the implementation of the Child Support Act 1991, under which liability to maintain children will be imposed irrespective of marital status and may in many cases soak up all resources available for redistribution at the end of a relationship. The implications of this 'child-centred' tendency, particularly for women, are considered further in Chapter 8.

(ii) Matrimonial property

As we shall see in Chapter 5, English law has devised no legal regime specifically attaching to matrimonial property. Thus, with some minor exceptions, the general law of property applies unmodified to property acquired and used by married couples; the same rules apply to unmarried couples. It is only on divorce that the legal distinction between married and unmarried becomes significant, since the divorce court has a wide-ranging discretion to allocate property between the partners on divorce under the MCA 1973 (as amended). However, it may be that the 'child-centred' tendency noted above will apply equally to the exercise of these powers by the divorce court, and that in the absence of children a spouse will receive no more on divorce than s/he would have been entitled to according to the ordinary rules of property. Further, as noted above, the practical effect of the Child Support Act 1991 may well be to debar a spouse altogether from receiving maintenance or a property distribution in his or her own right after divorce.

(iii) Inheritance and succession

As we shall see in Chapter 5, English law permits complete freedom of testation. There is no requirement that a testator leave a certain proportion of the estate to immediate members of a marital family. However, this freedom is balanced by a right in certain family members to apply for financial provision out of the estate of the deceased under the Inheritance (Provision for Family and Dependants) Act 1975. This right is not confined to those related to the deceased through blood or marriage, but extends to any person who can show dependence on the deceased (see further below). Where a person dies intestate however, the statutory rules privilege marital relations by according the surviving spouse a priority claim. In the absence of a surviving spouse, priority is given to blood relations. No provision is made for informal non-marital relations, except according to the statutory right to apply for provision out of the estate.

(b) Children

The significance of marriage for the relationship in law between a parent and child has traditionally found expression through the concepts of legitimacy and illegitimacy, according to which the legal rights of both parent (in particular the father) and child hinged upon the marital status of the child's parents. The policy of the Family Law Reform Act 1987 (and now the Children Act 1989) was to remove the legal distinction as far as possible in relation to the child, while resisting the assimilation of the legal position of the father to that of the married father. For some, this has meant that it is questionable whether the 1987 Act has 'abolished' illegitimacy as a status (eg Cretney 1987, pp 242–243). This is discussed further in Chapter 3.

(c) Women's bodies: abortion and rape

(i) Abortion

A woman's right to an abortion does not depend on her marital status, but on satisfying the conditions of the Abortion Act 1967.[18] This requires a medical judgment to the effect that the continuance of the pregnancy would involve a risk to the life, physical or mental health of the pregnant woman greater than if the pregnancy were terminated, or that there is a 'substantial risk' that the child will be born handicapped.[19] Neither a married woman's husband nor an unmarried woman's partner has any right to be consulted or to veto the abortion by means of an injunction.[20] Further, the courts will not assume jurisdiction in wardship proceedings with respect to an unborn child, including where the child is capable of being born alive.[1] However, it is unclear whether the courts will entertain proceedings brought by a next friend (for example the woman's partner) on behalf of a child capable of being born alive to restrain the mother from having an abortion on the grounds that the abortion would constitute an offence under s 1 of the Infant Life (Preservation) Act 1929,[2] even where the conditions of the Abortion Act are otherwise complied with. This point was left open in *C v S*,[3] a case involving an attempt by an unmarried father to restrain the mother from having an abortion, in which the court concerned itself almost exclusively with the question of whether the foetus in that case was 'capable of being born alive'[4] for the purposes of the 1925 Act (see de Cruz 1987a).

(ii) Rape

Sexual relations between married partners are largely regulated in law through the invocation by the parties of the remedies available in matrimonial law rather than through the more coercive intervention of the criminal law. Thus, as we have seen, at least one act of consummation is a precondition of a fully valid marriage in law; and a reluctance, or over-enthusiasm, for sexual relations

18 As amended by Human Fertilisation and Embryology Act 1990, s 37.
19 Abortion Act 1967, s 1.
20 *Paton v British Pregnancy Advisory Service Trustees* [1979] QB 276; *Paton v United Kingdom* (1980) 3 EHRR 408; see also *C v S* [1987] 1 All ER 1230.
1 *Re F (in utero)* (1988) 2 All ER 193.
2 This offence was specifically retained by the s 5 of the 1967 Act.
3 *C v S* [1987] 1 All ER 1230.
4 See also *Rance v Mid Downs Health Authority* [1991] Fam Law 24.

may form the basis for a divorce decree.[5] In such cases, the decision to invoke proceedings for nullity or divorce is a matter for the decision of the parties.

Until recently, the criminal law was significantly less interventionist in the realm of sexual relations between husband and wife than in other categories of sexual relation.[6] Thus, although a husband was liable to a charge of assault on his wife if he used excessive force in his sexual relations with her, or of indecent assault with respect to acts committed preliminary to the act of intercourse (such as fellatio) to which the wife has not consented,[7] he was otherwise not chargeable with the crime of rape.[8] This 'marital rape exemption' derived from the common law view that a wife is taken to consent to all sexual demands made of her by her husband by virtue of the fact of marriage itself.[9] The scope of this exemption had been somewhat narrowed by a series of court decisions which established that a husband may be charged with rape where there is in force a decree nisi of divorce,[10] a decree of judicial separation,[11] a separation agreement,[12] a non-molestation order or a personal protection order,[13] or where he had forced his wife to have intercourse with a third party.[14] Nevertheless, it was argued that the existence of the exemption 'implies . . . that there is a hierarchy of dominance and submission in marriage' (O'Donovan 1985, p 119).

The House of Lords has recently held, however, that the supposed 'marital rape exemption' is no longer part of the common law.[15] Lord Keith held that 'marriage is in modern times regarded as a partnership of equals, and no longer one in which the wife must be the subservient chattel of the husband' and that the proposition that 'by marriage a wife gives her irrevocable consent to sexual intercourse under all circumstances . . . [is] quite unacceptable'.[16]

---

5   Eg *Holborn v Holborn* [1947] 1 All ER 32; *Arthur v Arthur* (1964) 108 Sol Jo 317; *Sheldon v Sheldon* [1966] 2 All ER 257.
6   In one study, it was found that in almost two-fifths of cases, the rape offender was well known to the victim and that current or former husbands or cohabitants accounted for 15% of these offenders who were well known to the victim: see Smith (1989), pp 17–18.
7   *R v Kowalski* [1988] Fam Law 259.
8   *R v Miller* [1954] 2 All ER 529.
9   *R v Clarence* (1888) 22 QBD 23; see Temkin (1987), pp 43–50.
10   *R v O'Brien* [1974] 3 All ER 663.
11   *R v Clarke* [1949] 2 All ER 448.
12   *R v Roberts* [1986] Crim LR 188.
13   *R v Steele* (1976) 65 Cr App Rep 22; but see *R v Sharples* [1990] Crim LR 198.
14   *R v Cogan and Leak* [1976] QB 217.
15   *R v R* [1991] 4 All ER 481; see also *S v HM Advocate* 1989 SLT 469, which removed the exemption from Scots law.
16   [1991] 4 All ER 481 at 484.

Given that, in the view of the House of Lords, the exemption is a matter of common law rather than statute, and that the common law 'is capable of evolving in the light of changing social economic and cultural developments',[17] it was open to the House to declare that it no longer formed part of English law. This view is not uncontroversial, since it has been argued that rape is defined as 'unlawful sexual intercourse'[18] and that the term 'unlawful' can only refer to intercourse outside marriage.[19] On this view, the exemption is preserved by statute and only Parliament can remove it. Thus it may be that legislation will still be necessary.

In its Fifteenth Report on Sexual Offences, the Criminal Law Revision Committee (1984) decided against abolishing the exemption, for a number of reasons. These included the argument that to include marital rape within the definition of rape would diminish the seriousness of the offence of rape as a whole since marital rape does not share the 'peculiarly grave' circumstances usually associated with rape in other circumstances (para 2.64); and because convicted husbands would be dealt with more leniently in sentencing this might lead 'to all rape cases being regarded less seriously' (para 2.65). It was also suggested that police involvement might prevent the parties from becoming reconciled and that investigation of the offence would give rise to difficulty (paras 2.66–2.68). Some of the Committee considered that 'the criminal law should keep out of marital relations between cohabiting partners – especially the marriage bed – except where injury arises' (para 2.69).[20] The Committee unanimously agreed that the exemption should be removed where a married couple had ceased cohabiting, provided that a satisfactory definition of cohabitation could be arrived at (paras 2.81–2.85; for a critical discussion of the Committee's views, see Temkin 1987, pp 54–57; and see Lacey, Wells and Meure (1990), pp 330–335).

In its Draft Criminal Code, the Law Commission (1989c) incorporated the CLRC's proposals. However, the Law Commission has considered the matter again (1990) and has provisionally recommended that the exemption be removed altogether. In the Commission's view, the notion that on marriage a wife is deemed to consent to intercourse is anomalous and inconsistent with modern marriage law, which instead views marriage as a partnership of equals (para 4.4). The growth of 'exceptions' to the immunity has

---

17 [1991] 4 All ER 481 at 483.
18 Sexual Offences (Amendment) Act 1976, s 1(1)(a).
19 See eg the comment by JC Smith in [1991] Crim LR, p 477.
20 For further discussion of the reasons for and against the exemption, see Freeman (1985); Temkin (1987), pp 50–52.

led to a law which is 'uncertain, confusing and anomalous' (para 4.13); and the reasons for having a crime of rape at all, to enable women to decide when they do and do not wish to have intercourse, apply with equal force to non-consensual intercourse within marriage as they apply outside (para 4.19). The physical and emotional consequences of marital rape are every bit as serious, and in some cases may be more so, than rape outside marriage. The Commission rejected the arguments that allowing wives to bring charges of rape against their husbands would threaten the particular marriage or the institution of marriage in general, that existing matrimonial remedies are sufficient, that it would lead to inconsistencies in sentencing, that there would be difficulties of proof or that it would create possibilities of false accusation or blackmail. It has been argued that the Law Commission has now recognised that '[m]any of the so-called "arguments" against the criminalisation of wife rape are mere excuses, masking . . . a reluctance to accept that such behaviour is wicked' (Barton 1991, p 75; see also WAR (1990); for arguments against the proposals, see Williams 1991).

(d) Contract and tort[1]

(i) Contract

At common law, a wife was unable to enter into contracts in her own right (see Morrison 1957). This disability was associated with the fact that a married woman was also unable at common law to own her own property (see further Ch 5). The only contractual capacity conferred on married women by the common law concerned:

(i)   contracts entered into by the wife before marriage, which on marriage became the liability of the husband;[2] and
(ii) contracts entered into by the wife as agent for the husband, an agency which arose in certain defined circumstances. This agency is discussed further in Chapter 4.

The removal of this disability by statute proceeded in tandem with the introduction of separate property for married women,[3] although

1   For a discussion of the significance of marriage for criminal liability, see Mendes da Costa (1957); Bromley and Lowe (1987), pp 136–139.
2   Abolished by Law Reform (Married Women and Tortfeasors) Act 1935, s 3.
3   Eg, by the Married Women's Property Act 1882; since the effect of this Act was to introduce a statutory version of the wife's separate equitable estate, the wife was initially only able to contract if she possessed separate property within the statutory principle; this would not have included, for example, any property subject to a 'restraint on anticipation'. She did not have freedom to contract simply to the extent of the property that she possessed: a subtle and illogical distinction.

full capacity to contract, which also entailed full personal liability on contracts entered into, was not achieved until the passage of the Law Reform (Married Women and Tortfeasors) Act 1935.

Husband and wife may also enter into contracts between themselves,[4] and any agreements entered into on separation will be binding (see Ch 4). However, where they are still cohabiting, it will be a question of whether they possessed the necessary intention to enter into legal relations.[5]

(ii) Tort

At common law, a wife could only sue or be sued in tort if her husband was joined as a party to the action, including where the wife's liability had arisen prior to the marriage (Morrison 1957a). The requirement that the husband be joined as a party in actions in which the wife was plaintiff was removed in 1882,[6] and in which the wife was defendant, in 1935.[7] The common law imposed the further limitation that husband and wife could not sue each other in tort. This rule was gradually eroded,[8] and finally abolished by the Law Reform (Husband and Wife) Act 1962. Further, spouses may be convicted of acting together in conspiracy with each other.[9]

(e) Evidence

At common law, neither spouse was a competent witness for or against the other in either civil or criminal proceedings to which the other spouse was a party. Since 1853, spouses have been both competent and compellable witnesses in civil proceedings;[10] and since 1898, they have been competent (with certain exceptions), but not compellable, witnesses in criminal proceedings.[11] Section 80 of the Police and Criminal Evidence Act 1984 now makes a spouse a compellable witness in criminal proceedings for either defence or prosecution if (and only if) one of the following three conditions is satisfied:

---

4   *Hunt v Hunt* (1908) 25 TLR 132.
5   *Balfour v Balfour* [1919] 2 KB 571.
6   MWPA 1882, ss 13–15.
7   LR(MWT)A 1935, s 3; there had been some doubt as to the effect of the 1882 Act on the husband's liability in this respect, resolved (against him) in *Edwards v Porter* [1925] AC 1.
8   MWPA 1882, s 12 (wife permitted to sue husband in tort for protection of her separate property).
9   *Midland Bank Trust Co Ltd v Green (No 3)* [1981] 3 All ER 744.
10 Evidence Amendment Act 1853, s 1.
11 Criminal Evidence Act 1898.

(i)   the offence charged involves an assault on, or injury or threat of injury to, the spouse of the accused or a person who was at the material time under the age of 16;

(ii) the offence charged is a sexual offence alleged to have been committed in relation to a person aged under 16; or

(iii) the offence charged consists of attempting or conspiring to commit, or aiding and abetting the commission of, either category of offence mentioned in (i) and (ii).

Spouses will, in other words, be compellable in cases of domestic violence and cases of child sexual abuse. The evidential privilege thought to attach at common law to marital communications has been removed by statute.[12]

Cohabitation

(a) Differences from marriage

We have seen that a significant number of adults and children are living in cohabiting relationships outside the formal framework of marriage. We have also seen that marriage confers a particular 'status' on those who choose to formalise their relationship in the prescribed way. This does not mean, however, that cohabitation is completely unregulated by law. Before looking at the legal implications of cohabitation, it will be helpful to summarise the ways in which the legal treatment of cohabitation differs from that of marriage. To some extent, this question may be answered by stating that the status accruing to married couples (outlined above) does not extend to unmarried cohabitees; but the full picture is slightly more complex.[13]

(i) We have seen that the marriage laws place restrictions on who may marry and who may marry whom. There are no restrictions on those who may cohabit, saving those contained in the laws on sexual offences. Thus, cohabitation will be the only option for those who are already married, gay couples, transsexuals or those within the prohibited degrees. However, cohabitation may also be chosen by those who are otherwise free to marry. There may be a number of reasons for making this choice (see Oliver 1982; Scottish Law Commission 1990, para 1.4).

---

12 Civil Evidence Act 1968, s 16(3); Police and Criminal Evidence Act 1984, s 80(9).
13 For a helpful layperson's guide, see Bowler et al (1991).

(ii) Cohabitees are under no obligation to support each other during or at the end of their relationship. However, cohabitees are liable to maintain their children whether under private[14] law or under the Child Support Act 1991 (see Chs 4 and 8). As we shall see, this may be a more significant obligation in practice than the obligation to support a spouse.

(iii) There are special procedures and judicial powers available for resolving disputes between married couples over money and property (discussed in Ch 8). These are not available to cohabitees who must rely on the general law of property (discussed in Ch 5) and on the ordinary procedures for declarations as to their rights of ownership under the relevant rules of court.[15] If there are also proceedings on foot for child maintenance, this may lead to an 'unwieldy fusion' of Queen's Bench and Family Division proceedings, a fact that has prompted recent judicial guidance on the conduct of such proceedings.[16]

(iv) Although married couples are officially encouraged to reach agreement on disputed matters in divorce proceedings (see Ch 7), they are at present unable to make enforceable pre-marriage contracts governing property and finance at the outset of their relationship (see Law Society 1991, pp 22–28). By contrast, it is open to cohabitees to make enforceable cohabitation contracts, or 'living together agreements', dealing with precisely these matters. This is discussed further below. They may also make use of conveyances and declarations of trust to achieve a finality as to their property ownership which is not available to married couples, since a divorce court has complete discretion to review the divorcing couple's needs and resources and distribute property and income accordingly. This has been described as 'a paradox' (see Barton 1990). It has recently been proposed that married couples should be able to make enforceable pre-marriage contracts (Law Society 1991, above, discussed in Ch 8) governing the financial outcome of divorce. If implemented, this would remove the peculiarity of the present law that gives cohabitees freedom of contract concerning financial

14 CA 1989, Sch 1. The orders now available for all children, irrespective of their parents' marital status, include periodical payments, lump sums, and settlements or transfers of property.

15 The Law Commission (1989d) has suggested that 'it might be worth considering' introducing a new procedure enabling cohabitees to seek declarations as to their rights of ownership in the county court, possibly by extending MWPA 1882, s 17 (as to which, see Ch 5) to cohabitees: 'it is difficult to justify imposing a more costly procedure for determining [property disputes] upon those who have not agreed to marry' (para 6.8).

16 Per Waite J in *Hammond v Mitchell* [1991] 1 WLR 1127.

matters but denies it to married couples (who at present are only able to agree terms within the framework of compulsorily invoked legal procedures).

(v) Married parents have automatic 'parental responsibility' for their natural children; only the unmarried mother has automatic responsibility for a child. However, the unmarried father may obtain an equal footing in respect of his children either by court order or by private agreement. This is discussed further in the next chapter.

(vi) There are specific provisions relating to matrimonial property, which offer a spouse certain rights (eg, in relation to occupation of the family home and rights in bankruptcy), which are not available to cohabitees. These are discussed further in Chapter 5. Marriage may also confer entitlements to pension rights or to inheritance that cohabitation does not.

(b) Statutory recognition

There is at present no comprehensive legal framework for cohabitation. The attitude of English law has been to leave the parties to their rights and remedies as individuals rather than as bearers of a special status.[17] In relation to parenthood, we shall see in the next chapter that the increasing tendency is to ignore marital status in constructing legal relationships between parents and children, especially in the matter of financial support. However, there are a number of instances in which rights have been extended by statute to cohabitees for specific purposes. Although these instances may be seen as examples of 'protective' rather than 'adjustive' legislation, they have accumulated as a series of ad hoc initiatives rather than representing a coherent response to the fact of cohabitation. Whether a more coherent framework can, or should, be devised will be discussed further below. In this section, we focus on the definition and effect of the relevant statutory provisions.

(i) Statutory succession to tenancies

Certain members of a statutory or protected tenant's family of, respectively, privately and publicly rented housing are accorded the right in certain circumstances to succeed to the tenancy on the tenant's death (see further Ch 5, at pp 214–216). The members who benefit include co-resident spouses and, in the case of publicly rented

17 For comparative studies, see Muller-Freienfels (1987); Glendon (1989) Ch 6.

property, specified categories of blood relation.[18] They also include cohabitees who, in the case of Rent Act tenancies,[19] can show that they were 'members of the tenant's family' or, in the case of tenancies under the Housing Acts of 1985 (public) and 1988 (private) can show that they were living with the tenant as husband and wife. Litigation has concentrated on the meaning of this phrase in connection with the Rent Act provision;[20] the same meaning presumably applies to the public sector and to tenancies under the Housing Act 1988, although here the statutory definition specifically refers to a person who has lived with the deceased 'as husband and wife'.[1] This clearly excludes homosexual or lesbian relations from the definition in the latter context; although it also seems unlikely that such relations would fall within the more open-ended definition found in the Rent Act.[2]

The case law establishes that, in order to qualify as a member of the tenant's family for these purposes, the test is one of the popular meaning to be attached to the word 'family'.[3] This will include a cohabiting couple who have children;[4] it will also include a cohabiting couple whose relationship exhibits all the characteristics of marriage, defined as permanence and lifelong commitment.[5] Relevant factors in determining whether these features of a relationship exist will include whether the parties hold themselves out as husband and wife, for example by the woman taking the man's name (although this is not essential).[6] If the parties go out of their way to maintain their independence of each other, if their relationship is considered casual or temporary, if one party is much older than the other, or if one has treated the other as a sub-tenant in relation to the premises in question, it is less likely that the definition will be satisfied.[7] The fact that one party has remained married throughout the relationship to a third party is not fatal.[8] Purely platonic relations, however intimate or long-lasting, will not be included in the definition, since 'family' is not as wide as 'household'.[9]

18 Housing Act 1985, s 113(1)(b).
19 The Rent Act regime now applies only to tenancies created before 15 January 1989; tenancies created after that date are subject to the Housing Act 1988 – see Ch 5, pp 214–216.
20 Rent Act 1977, Sch 1, para 3.
1 HA 1985, s 113(1)(a); HA 1988, s 17(4).
2 *Harrogate Borough Council v Simpson* [1986] Fam Law 359.
3 *Dyson Holdings v Fox* [1976] QB 503.
4 *Hawes v Evenden* [1953] 1 WLR 1169.
5 *Dyson Holdings v Fox* (above); *Watson v Lucas* [1980] 1 WLR 1493.
6 *Watson v Lucas* (above); *Helby v Rafferty* [1979] 1 WLR 13.
7 *Helby v Rafferty* (above); *Gasking and Co v Evans* (1981) 131 NLJ 903, CA.
8 *Watson v Lucas* (above).
9 *Ross v Collins* [1964] 1 WLR 425; *Carega Properties SA v Sharratt* [1979] 1 WLR 928; *Sefton Holdings Ltd v Cairns* [1988] Fam Law 164.

(ii) Domestic violence

As we shall see in Chapter 6, the Domestic Violence and Matrimonial Proceedings Act 1976 confers jurisdiction on the county court to make certain orders to restrain the use of violence in the home. This jurisdiction is available where the parties involved are unmarried, provided that they are 'living together as husband and wife'.[10] The factors determining whether a particular relationship falls within this definition will presumably be similar to those outlined above. It has been held that the 1976 Act is not excluded from applying to cohabitees where the applicant has no proprietary interest in the family home (although this may be a relevant factor in deciding what form of order to make);[11] nor is it excluded where the parties are living separately under the same roof, since this would be comparable to a married couple whose relationship was in the process of breaking down.[12] However, the Act may not apply where the parties have not cohabited for some time. Thus, where cohabitation ceased six months prior to the application, it is unlikely that an order will be made under the Act;[13] but jurisdiction exists wherever the evidence of violence relied upon in the application took place before the cessation of cohabitation.[14]

(iii) Income support

As we shall see in Chapter 4, marriage is relevant in many ways in determining entitlement to state welfare and job-related benefits. Cohabitation is treated like marriage for only some of these purposes, the most notorious being its treatment as identical to marriage in determining the needs and resources of the 'assessment group' for the purposes of entitlement to income support where a cohabiting couple are living together as husband and wife.[15] The effect of this is to disable cohabiting couples from claiming income support in their own rights as separate individuals: only one of them may make a claim on behalf of the assessment unit. The justification for this rule is that where two people are living together and sharing resources it would be unfair to treat them as two separate individuals; but the argument against the rule is that it assumes a level of support which

10 DVMPA 1976, s 1(2); see *Harrison v Lewis* [1988] 2 FLR 339.
11 *Davis v Johnson* [1978] 1 All ER 1132.
12 *Adeoso v Adeoso* [1981] 1 All ER 107.
13 *O'Neill v Williams* [1984] FLR 1.
14 *McLean v Nugent* (1980) 1 FLR 26; *O'Neill v Williams* (above). No jurisdiction exists where the conduct complained of took place after the end of cohabitation – see *Harrison v Lewis* (above).
15 Income Support (General) Regulations 1987, regs 2(1), 17.

neither party has a legal right to enforce. This will affect women in particular.

This rule is applied in practice by DSS adjudication officers, who, in deciding whether to regard a couple as cohabiting for these purposes, will consider the factors laid out in official guidance.[16] These include factors such as the presence of and mutual care for children, mutual financial support and sharing of expenses, the existence of sexual relations and a public 'holding out' as husband and wife. The fact that two people are living in the same household does not automatically mean that they are living there as husband and wife. Thus, a housekeeper or someone who is caring for a sick person will not fall within the rule.[17]

(iv)   Inheritance

A cohabitee may be eligible, but is not entitled, to claim a share of a deceased partner's estate if it can be shown that the applicant was, immediately before the death of the deceased, being maintained either wholly or partly by the deceased;[18] and a person is treated as falling into this category if the deceased, otherwise than for full valuable consideration, was making a substantial contribution in money or money's worth towards the reasonable needs of that person.[19] The interpretation of this legislation is considered further in Chapter 5.

(v)   Fatal accidents

A cohabitee will have a claim under the Fatal Accidents Act 1976 where it can be shown that the applicant was:

(i)   living with the deceased in the same household immediately before the date of death;
(ii)   had been so living for two years preceding the death; and
(iii)   was living during the whole of that period as the husband or wife of the deceased.[20]

Again, presumably the phrase 'living as husband and wife' has the same meaning as it does in relation to similar statutory formulations encountered elsewhere.

---

16   Supplementary Benefits Handbook (HMSO, 1982), paras 2.9–2.12; Adjudication Officer's Guide, Part 15 (DSS Leaflets).
17   See, eg, *Crake v Supplementary Benefits Commission* [1982] 1 All ER 498; *Butterworth v Supplementary Benefits Commission* [1982] 1 All ER 498.
18   I(PFD)A 1975, s 1(1)(e).
19   I(PFD)A 1975, s 1 (3).
20   FAA 1976, s 1(3)(b) (as amended).

(c) **Should recognition be extended?**

The growing acceptance of cohabitation outside marriage has raised the question of the extent to which marriage should retain its position as the exclusive means by which legal status is conferred in law on family members. In particular, should the legal framework of marriage be extended to de facto cohabiting relationships? A number of different views are possible. It could be argued that there should be no recognition of cohabitation in order that the privileged status of marriage be retained.[1] The case against legal recognition of cohabitation could also be made on the ground that couples who live outside marriage have deliberately chosen to do so in order to escape the ideological values implicit in legal marriage, and that their autonomy and freedom of choice in this respect should be respected. This is associated with the view that marriage should be 'deregulated' and thus made more like cohabitation, rather than vice versa. In such cases, the preferred means of ordering such relations in law would be through express contracts, and associated mechanisms such as trust, tort and restitution. Thus, it has been argued, 'the settlement of cohabitants' disputes by existing legal principles is fair and workable. The creation of special laws for cohabitants or the extension of marital laws to them retards the emancipation of women, degrades the relationship and is too expensive for society in general and men in particular' (Deech 1980, p 310; see also Weitzman 1981; Shultz 1982; Freeman and Lyon 1983, Ch 7).

A different view is that increased legal recognition of cohabitation is an inevitable consequence of a 'new' family law which is 'less concerned now with legal status than with economic reality' and in which 'marriage is being displaced by "family" and the wife is being displaced by the "mother"' (Parker 1990, p 97). This explains the creation of an informal marriage status in law which has as its primary aim the construction of a set of economic relationships clearly demarcated from, and thereby reducing the burden on, the state. Given the objectives of this 'new' family law, it would be possible to dispense with marriage altogether as a necessary mediating legal concept (see Clive 1980). It will be argued at various points in this book that there is much in modern family law to support this view; and that, in particular, it is parenthood that is becoming an increasingly important determinant of the parties' rights and responsibilities in law.

In its Discussion Paper on Cohabitation, the Scottish Law Commission (1990) considered whether any of the 'private law'

1   See, eg, the comments of Baker P in *Campbell v Campbell* [1977] 1 All ER 1 at 6.

consequences of marriage should be extended to cohabitees. The paper deals with obligations of support, ownership of household goods, savings from housekeeping allowances, intestate succession, occupation of the family home and cohabitation contracts, and arrives at a number of provisional conclusions. The most interesting part of the paper is that dealing with 'the difficult and controversial question' (para 5.1) of claims for financial provision between cohabitants on the termination of the relationship (Part V). The Commission's starting point is that there is a difference between, first, those rights available to married couples deriving 'from the special nature of marriage . . . and the public commitments undertaken on marriage' and, second, 'those related to the simple redress of economic inequities arising out of the factual situation of cohabitation and child-bearing' (para 5.1). It argued that 'the balance between liberty and protection would not be tipped too far in favour of protection if rules of [the second type] were applied to certain cohabitants' (ibid).

Applying this principle to the current Scottish law on the redistribution of property on divorce would mean that only two of the five principles guiding the Scottish courts' exercise of their discretion[2] would apply to cohabitees. These would be:

(i) the principle that fair account should be taken of any economic advantage derived by either party from contributions by the other and of any economic disadvantages suffered by either party in the interests of the other party or the family;[3] and
(ii) the principle that any economic burden of caring, after divorce, for a child of the marriage aged under 16 should be shared fairly between the parties.[4]

In both cases, the Commission felt, the relevant principle is not based on any particular view of marriage but is directed towards ensuring that the economic losses that may be incurred as a necessary result of living together and having children are fairly shared and not allowed to lie where they fall. On the other hand, the Commission did not consider it appropriate to apply to cohabitees the remaining three principles in s 9(1) (ie, those concerned with equal sharing of property and with transitional maintenance to overcome serious hardship flowing from divorce or to assist one party who has been substantially dependent on the other): these principles 'go further than is necessary to redress imbalances arising from the relationship' (para 5.8) and are more concerned to recognise losses flowing from

2 Contained in Family Law (Scotland) Act 1985, s 9(1)(a)–(e).
3 FL(S)A 1985, s 9(1)(b).
4 FL(S)A 1985, s 9(1)(c).

the loss of marital status itself, especially the loss of the right to financial support.

If implemented, the Scottish proposals would not be the first to create a legal regime for cohabitees' property. In Australia, the New South Wales' De Facto Relationships Act 1984 permits a court to award short-term maintenance to a cohabitee if the applicant is unable to support him- or herself adequately as a result either of child care responsibilities or of a reduction in earning capacity which is attributable to the cohabitation; there is also power to make a property adjustment order as seems 'just and equitable' having regard to the parties' financial and non-financial contributions to the couple's property and family. This legislation reflects a division between 'corrective' and 'prospective' factors similar to that envisaged by the Scottish proposals, in that only the former apply to cohabitees while the latter also apply to divorcing spouses (see Finlay and Bailey-Harris 1989, pp 388–394). In Victoria, the Property Law Amendment Act 1987 enables the courts to make property adjustment orders, but not to award maintenance. Similar legislation exists in Canada (see Scottish Law Commission 1990, para 5.2) and Sweden (see Glendon 1989, pp 273–277).

(d) Contract

We have seen that an alternative means of regulating cohabiting relations in law preferred by some writers is that of express contracts, sometimes called 'living together agreements'.[5] Such contracts could incorporate terms dealing with the ownership of property and money, and rights to maintenance on the termination of the relationship (see Barton 1985, Ch 5; Bowler et al 1989, 1991). However, there is only limited scope to contract as far as rights and responsibilities for children are concerned. There are two reasons for this. The first is that a parent with automatic parental responsibility (who, in the case of children whose parents are unmarried, will be the mother[6]) cannot surrender or transfer parental responsibility to another.[7] An unmarried father must either seek a court order giving him parental responsibility or must enter a 'parental responsibility agreement' in a form prescribed by statute[8] (see Ch 3). The second is that any 'maintenance agreement' made between a child's parents in

5 Courts may also imply contracts between cohabitees, eg, in relation to occupation of the home: see *Tanner v Tanner* [1975] 1 WLR 1346; *Horrocks v Forray* [1976] 1 WLR 230; *Chandler v Kerley* [1978] 1 WLR 693.
6 CA 1989, s 2(2).
7 CA 1989, s 2(9).
8 CA 1989, s 4(1).

respect of the child is reviewable by the courts (see Ch 4). This is consistent with the argument made in the next chapter that parenthood is becoming an increasingly important determinant of the rights and responsibilities of family members; this is illustrated here by the fact that matters relating to children have been removed from the contractual competence of parents, a fact which, on one definition, indicates that parenthood is now a matter of status irrespective of marriage.[9]

The enforceability of cohabitation contracts or 'living together agreements' is not beyond doubt.[10] As a matter of contract law, they may be vulnerable to attack on a number of grounds, including illegality, undue influence, an absence of intention to create legal relations, uncertainty and lack of consideration. These problems may be avoided if the parties are independently advised, if the contract is executed as a deed and if the terms deal only with 'hard' issues of money, property and finance and not with the parties' personal or sexual relationship.

The advantages of contracts are that, if enforceable, they confer rights on the parties that they would not otherwise have and may encourage them to clarify their expectations and level of commitment at the outset of the relationship. They also 'increase the variety of options open to people in making their household arrangements' (Kingdom 1988, p 78) and may avoid the considerable expense involved in resolving ownership disputes within the framework of property law (see Barton 1985, Ch 9; Jackson 1990). However, some writers (especially Weyrauch 1980; O'Donovan 1984; 1985, pp 187–194) have questioned the suitability of contracts for this purpose. There are four main reasons for concern. First, it is argued that contract law presupposes a degree of equality of bargaining power between the parties that may not be matched in reality. Second, it is pointed out that, possibly in recognition of this and other similar factors, the courts would be likely to imply contractual terms or to introduce doctrines overriding the parties' expressed intentions that would be as expressive of objectionable views of family living as current marriage laws are said to be. Third, it is argued that private arrangements cannot alter the way in which assumptions concerning women's dependence are expressed in certain areas of public law, such as taxation or in relation to the welfare state (as to which see Ch 4). Finally, it is argued that contracts are ill-adapted to accommodating to changes in the parties' circumstances over long periods of time. In other words, those who favour contract over

9 See Maine (1861) and note 17, p 52, above.
10 See, eg, *Layton v Martin* [1986] FLR 227; for discussion, see Freeman and Lyon (1983), Appendix; Barton (1985), Ch 3; Parker (1987a), pp 144–147.

marriage make two erroneous assumptions: (i) that it is possible to escape state regulation of contracts; and (ii) that the legal framework of marriage is the only way in which objectionable familial values find expression.

Chapter 3
Parents and children

Introduction

(a) From marriage to parenthood?

It was suggested in the previous chapter that we are witnessing a shift in the focus of the legal regulation of family relations. There is now less emphasis on the exclusivity of the legal status of marriage and evidence of a move towards constructing status-like relationships around new organising concepts. The primary aim, it was argued, is to construct a set of legal–economic relations among family members that are clearly demarcated from, and thereby reduce the financial burden on, the state. In this process, the legal concept of marriage is logically, and is *de facto* becoming, redundant. In the preceding chapter we considered the arguments in favour of treating cohabitation as an alternative means of conferring status. In this chapter, we will turn our attention to parenthood. There is growing evidence that, while marriage is an increasingly dissoluble relationship, parenthood is in contrast increasingly regarded as being 'for life'; and that the fact of parenthood is now likely to have a more significant effect than marriage on the rights and responsibilities of family members. Such is the growing 'child-centredness' of the modern law, that one writer has recently tentatively suggested that the legal regulation of relationship breakdown should revolve not around marriage, but around parenthood:

> '[i]f the bonds of parenthood are now assuming the degree of indissolubility once accorded to marriage, any significant readjustment in the relationship between the parents themselves and between parents and children is just as deserving of regulation as the dissolution of marriage itself' (Eekelaar 1991, p 173).

If marriage is to be superseded by parenthood as the central determinant of the legal rights and responsibilities of family members, what then do we mean in a legal sense by 'parent'? Who in law is regarded as a parent, and what is the legal significance of being one? What are the implications of this trend for women, who will increasingly be visible to the law only as mothers rather than as individuals in their own right? Will this trend lead to the legal empowerment of children? These are some of the issues that will be addressed in this chapter and later in this book.

Before doing so, however, we must consider the structure of the Children Act 1989, which is now fundamental to any discussion of the law in this area and which has done much to emphasise the trend noted above.

(b) The Children Act 1989

(i) Background

The Children Act 1989 (together with rules of court[1] and regulations and guidance[2] issued by virtue of it) represents the single most comprehensive legislative reform of child law this century. It deals with both the 'private' and 'public' aspects of child law and provides for the first time a consistent and coordinated set of concepts and procedures for dealing with disputes in relation to children. It clarifies the interrelationship between previously disparate sets of rules concerning, for example, the rights and responsibilities of parents between themselves, third parties and local authorities. It also makes a number of substantive changes of considerable significance, especially to the powers and duties of local authorities in relation to their statutory function of providing for children in need or at risk. Although it does not deal directly with the law of adoption and wardship, it enacts substantive changes that considerably affect those areas of law.

The Act is the outcome of a lengthy process of law reform.[3] It has been officially described as resting 'on the belief that children are

---

1 See particularly the Family Proceedings Courts (Children Act 1989) Rules 1991, the Children (Allocation of Proceedings) Order 1991 and Part IV of the Family Proceedings Rules 1991.
2 The Department of Health has issued several volumes of 'Guidance and Regulations' to accompany the Act dealing with different aspects of the legislation, the status of which is explained in Department of Health (1989a). There is also *An Introduction to the Children Act 1989* (Department of Health 1989) which purports to explain rather than interpret the provisions of the primary legislation.
3 The most important documents are the *Review of Child Care Law* (DHSS 1985), the 1987 White Paper *The Law Relating to Child Care and Family Services* (Cm 62) and the Law Commission's Report No 172, *Guardianship and Custody* (1988), together with the *Report of the Inquiry into Child Abuse in Cleveland* (1988, Cm 412). For a review of the background to the Act, see Parton (1991).

generally best looked after within the family with both parents playing a full part and without resort to legal proceedings' (Department of Health 1991, para 1.5). This official view has been reflected in academic commentary on the Act, in which the new legislation has been seen as evidence that '[t]he law is in retreat from the private realm of family life' (Cretney 1990b) and as effecting a 'privatisation of the public interest in children' (Bainham 1990). While there may be some grounds for this view, it may be argued that the Act represents a more complex process.

In relation to private law, two themes can be seen to predominate: the first is the construction wherever possible of a full set of (heterosexual) legal parental relationships for the child, whether consisting of the child's natural parents or not; and the second is a refocusing of legal resources (in the shape of resources for adjudication) on those parents who cannot agree between themselves. Parents who can agree are allowed to do so free from interference by the courts (Dewar 1991). In the realm of child care (public) law, the Act inaugurates a regime under which the practice of child care by social workers will be increasingly 'legalised', both in the sense of creating a more central role for the courts in decision-making in child care cases, as well as in the sense of permitting a greater standardisation of social work practice through the issuance of guidance and regulations; but at the same time creating a greater dependence than previously of legal decision-makers on social work expertise (see Parton 1991, Ch 7). These arguments will be pursued further in later chapters (especially Chs 9–11).

For the present, we are more concerned with the basic concepts enshrined in the Act and it is to those that we now turn.

(ii) Basic concepts

Paramountcy of the child's welfare In determining any question relating to the child's upbringing or the administration of a child's property, a court is obliged to treat the child's welfare as the 'paramount consideration'.[4] This replaces the very similar provision contained in GMA 1971, s 1, but there are a number of differences. The first is that the child's welfare is the 'paramount' rather than the 'first and paramount' consideration as it was under the 1971 Act. The purpose of the change is to emphasise that the child's welfare is the court's only concern. Although the courts had in any case read the old law in this way,[5] the Law Commission were anxious to avoid

---

4 CA 1989, s 1(1); a 'child' is defined as a person under the age of 18: CA 1989, s 105(1).
5 *J v C* [1970] AC 668; *Re K D (a minor)* [1988] 2 FLR 139.

the possibility of a litigant arguing that other considerations could be balanced against the child's welfare (1988, para 3.14).

A second difference is that, in certain cases,[6] the courts will be obliged, in determining the child's welfare, to apply a statutory checklist of factors.[7] These are:

'(a) the ascertainable wishes and feelings of the child concerned (considered in the light of his age and understanding);

(b) his physical, emotional and educational needs;

(c) the likely effect on him of any change in his circumstances;

(d) his age, sex, background and any characteristics of his which the court considers relevant;

(e) any harm which he has suffered or is at risk of suffering;

(f) how capable each of his parents, and any other person in relation to whom the court considers the question to be relevant, is of meeting his need;

(g) the range of powers available to the court under this Act in the proceedings in question.'

This checklist is based on the recommendations of the Law Commission, which advocated it 'as a means of providing greater consistency and clarity in the law and . . . as a major step towards a more systematic approach to decisions concerning children' (1988, para 3.18). However, the statutory list contains only 'the essentials' and 'must not be applied too rigidly or be so formulated as to prevent the court from taking into account everything which is relevant in the particular case' (paras 3.19–3.20; see Bainham 1990a). The checklist is applicable in any contested application for a 's 8 order' and in care proceedings, and is considered later in those contexts (see Chs 9 and 10).

There is also a new broad power that enables a court, when considering any issue arising under the 1989 Act, to ask a probation officer or local authority to prepare a report to the court. The contents of such reports will be governed by delegated legislation and by the requirements of the court requesting it.[8] Finally, there is a new principle that in every case (and not just those to which the checklist applies) the court must 'have regard to the general principle that any delay in determining the question is likely to prejudice the welfare of the child'.[9] Other sections of the Act and the

6 Those involving disputed applications for 's 8 orders' (see below) and any proceedings for making, varying or discharging care and supervision orders – see CA 1989, s 1(4). The checklist will thus not have to be considered in uncontested s 8 applications, on an application by an unmarried father for a 'parental responsibility order' (see below), or on application for Emergency Protection or Child Assessment Orders (see Ch 10).

7 CA 1989, s 1(3).

8 CA 1989, s 7.

9 CA 1989, s 1(2).

rules of court empower the courts to draw up timetables for the proceedings and to give directions to ensure that the timetable is adhered to.[10] This has been described as according the courts a new 'managerial' role in that the court, rather than the litigants, will set the pace of events (Cretney 1990b, p 71–72). Official guidance is anxious to stress that delay may be justified if it is necessary for a conciliated outcome, on the assumption, it appears, that such outcomes are for the benefit of children (Department of Health 1989, para 3.25).

Non-intervention   The Act introduces a new principle that where a court is considering whether to make an order under the Act in respect of a child, it shall not make the order unless it considers that doing so would be better than making no order at all.[11] This, it has been said, 'creates a presumption against a court order being made: no order may be made unless it can be shown to be beneficial to the child' (Department of Health 1989, para 3.21). This principle is of general application to all orders that might be made under the Act, but it should be noted that it has quite different implications for public as against private orders.

In the private context, the principle is designed to alter the pre-existing practice of regarding an order in relation to children as simply part of the 'package' of orders made, for example, in divorce proceedings. If parents can reach an amicable agreement over arrangements for the children, 'the law should seek to disturb this as little as possible' (Law Commission 1988, para 3.2). Thus, judicial resources are to be concentrated on those parents who are unable to agree. It has been pointed out, however, that 'this scheme, by regarding private agreements as sacrosanct, fails to give adequate recognition to the public interest in children' or, alternatively, that it redefines the public interest 'as best served by facilitating parental agreements' (Bainham 1990, p 210). We have noted above that official guidance on the Act also appears to equate agreed outcomes with the child's best interests. We will return to these issues in Chapter 9 in the context of children in divorce.

It remains to be seen when courts will treat an order as being necessary. Suppose a mother is seeking a formal order in order to assist her in her claim to be rehoused? As we shall see in Chapter 6, many housing authorities have insisted on formal court orders

---

10 CA 1989, s 11(1) and 32(1); Family Proceedings Courts (Children Act 1989) Rules 1991, rr 14(2)(a), 15; Family Proceedings Rules 1991, rr 4.14(2)(a), 4.15. In addition, the court will fix the dates for direction appointments and hearings automatically: Family Proceedings Courts (Children Act 1989) Rules 1991, r 4(2); Family Proceedings Rules 1991, r 4.4(2).
11 CA 1989, s 1(5).

relating to children before treating an applicant for rehousing as being in a 'priority need' category. Would this justify the making of a formal order? We return to this in Chapter 9.

In public proceedings, the principle of non-intervention serves the different function of adding an additional overriding 'threshold criterion' that must be satisfied before an order may be made. It emphasises that merely because the conditions for an order have been made out, a care or supervision order (for example) is not necessarily the best course for the child (DHSS 1985, para 15.22). This will be discussed more fully in Chapter 10.

'Parental responsibility'   The Act introduces the new concept of 'parental responsibility'[12] to describe the collection of rights, duties, powers, responsibilities and authority which the law gives a parent in relation to a child. The Act goes no further in defining this concept, so for a fuller definition we must turn to the general law (see below). The new definition serves a number of purposes:

–   it introduces a single statutory concept to replace the different statutory definitions that appeared in the previous law;[13]
–   it recognises that as a result of case law developments, it is no longer accurate to talk of parental 'rights' since such 'rights' have been held to be merely a necessary concomitant of the parental duties of parents towards their children[14] and are in any case overridden where the child's welfare demands it;[15]
–   it assists in clarifying many aspects that were unclear in the previous law by providing a single concept and clearer rules about the allocation and acquisition of parental rights and duties for children (discussed below). Briefly, married parents and unmarried mothers automatically acquire parental responsibility (and, in the case of married parents, retain it after divorce), while unmarried fathers and certain categories of others may acquire it by court order.[16] Parental responsibility may be shared, and a person with parental responsibility does not lose it merely because someone else has acquired it.[17] The implications of these rules are considered in more detail in Chapters 9, 10 and 11.

12 CA 1989, s 3.
13 Eg, 'parental rights and duties' (Children Act 1975, s 85), the 'powers and duties' of a parent (Child Care Act 1980, s 10(2)).
14 See, for example, *Gillick v West Norfolk and Wisbech Area Health Authority* [1986] AC 112.
15 *Re K D* [1988] 2 FLR 139.
16 In particular, a residence order made in favour of a person who is not a parent or guardian of the child has the effect of conferring parental responsibility on that person: CA 1989, s 12(2).
17 CA 1989, s 2(5), (6).

We will return to this concept at various points in this chapter and later in this book. Two points should be noted at this stage. The first is that the new concept does not do away with the need to identify a child's 'parents', since the Act allocates parental responsibility primarily to them (although the rules differ according to whether the parents are married to each other or not). The Act itself does not assist in identifying who they are but assumes that they are otherwise identifiable, by the means discussed in the next section. However, for non-parents the concept of parental responsibility is the most important means by which they may acquire a legal status in relation to the child.

Another reason for identifying parents separately from parental responsibility is that the latter is only 'concerned with bringing the child up, caring for him and making decisions about him, but does not affect the relationship of parent and child for other purposes' (Department of Health 1991, para 2.2). Thus, the question of liability to maintain a child, or of succession rights, is determined independently of the question of whether the parent in question has parental responsibility for a child.[18] For example, an unmarried father will be liable to maintain his child whether or not he has acquired parental responsibility for it.[19] This may seem odd in view of the fact that maintenance is officially regarded as the most important of all parental responsibilities: too important, it seems, to be incorporated within the concept itself. Further, the Children Act at various points uses the term 'parent' as distinct from 'person with parental responsibility'.[20] The term 'parent' will include both parents of the child whether they are married to each other or not,[1] irrespective of whether both parents have parental responsibility under the Act.[2] Thus, the concept of parental responsibility only partially determines the legal position of parents.

18 CA 1989, s 3(4).
19 Liability to maintain a child is defined by reference to parenthood rather than to parental responsibility: see CA 1989, Sch 1, para 1 and Child Support Act 1991, s 1 (discussed in Ch 4).
20 Compare, for example, CA 1989, s 20(8) (removal of child from local authority accommodation only by a 'person with parental responsibility') and CA 1989, s 34(1) ('parent' allowed reasonable contact with a child in care) or Sch 1, para 1(2)(a) (orders for financial provision of children may be made against 'parents'). By contrast, CA 1989, s 5(3) (which deals with appointment of guardians) talks of 'parents with parental responsibility'. A 'parent' is entitled to apply for a s 8 order without leave: CA 1989, s 10(4)(a).
1 As a result of FLRA 1987, s 1: see below.
2 For example, a 'parent' is entitled to apply for a s 8 order: CA 1989, s 10(4). The parent in question need not have parental responsibility, although in fact most will, the only exception being unmarried fathers: see below.

The second point is that the concept of parental responsibility is itself ambiguous. Eekelaar (1991a) has noted that it is capable of bearing two different meanings: first, that parents are responsible *to* their children;[3] and second, that it is parents rather than the state who should care for children – in other words, that it is parents (rather than anyone else) who are responsible *for* children. The implications of the two are different. Whereas the first suggests a child-centred focus, the latter suggests a concern with the allocation of parenting functions to 'the family' (and not necessarily the 'natural family'). Eekelaar argues that the Act embodies the second rather than first meaning and that this 'sharply reflects an identifiable political position' (p 40; see also Bainham 1990a and Fox Harding 1991).

'Section 8 orders' and 'family proceedings'   The Act creates the framework for a considerable simplification of the private orders that may be made and the means by which they may be sought. It does this in two ways. First, it introduces a new range of private orders ('s 8 orders') that may be made in relation to children. These not only replace the former orders for custody, care and control and access (whose effects were not always clear) with 'residence' and 'contact' orders, but also introduce two new types of very flexible order ('specific issues' and 'prohibited steps' orders) part of whose purpose is to introduce into lower courts the flexibility of the orders available in wardship proceedings (Law Commission 1988, Part IV). The nature and effect of these orders will be considered in more detail in Chapter 9. For present purposes, they can be summarised as follows:

– a residence order is an order settling the arrangements to be made as to the person with whom the child should live;
– a contact order is an order requiring a person with whom a child lives to allow the child to visit or stay with the person named in the order, or for that person and the child otherwise to have contact with each other;
– a specific issue order is an order giving directions for the purpose of determining a specific question which has arisen, or which may arise, in connection with any aspect of parental responsibility for a child;
– a prohibited steps order is an order that no step which could be taken by a parent in meeting his parental responsibility for the

---

3   For a discussion of whether a moral duty exists on parents to care for their children, see Eekelaar (1991b).

child, and which is of a kind specified in the order, shall be taken by any person without the consent of the court.[4]

The Act also clarifies who may apply for such orders, their effects and the interrelationship between such orders and local authority care. It should be noted that, in addition to those who are entitled to apply for s 8 orders, the court has power to grant anyone else leave to apply for one[5] (see below).

Second, the Act makes these orders available in any proceedings designated as 'family proceedings'. This has been widely defined to include virtually any proceedings in which questions relating to children are likely to arise. Thus, it includes wardship proceedings, proceedings under the 1989 Act itself, divorce or nullity proceedings, applications for ouster or non-molestation orders, adoption applications and domestic proceedings in the magistrates' court.[6] At one level, this merely resolves a technical question of jurisdiction. At another, however, it represents a considerable extension of the courts' powers to make orders for children, which is underlined by the fact that the court has power in any 'family proceedings' to make s 8 orders of its own motion,[7] and may grant anyone leave to apply to court for one (see below). This is one reason why it must be questioned whether the Act does indeed represent a withdrawal of legal regulation, or whether, as argued above, it effects instead a refocusing of legal resources, unhindered by jurisdictional limitations, towards those cases where parents are unable to agree.

Who can apply for s 8 orders? The Law Commission's objective in devising rules of eligibility for orders was to replace the old inconsistent scheme of orders with 'a unified scheme which is consistent and clear' (1988, para 4.33) which retains sufficient flexibility 'to enable anyone with a genuine interest in the child's welfare to make applications relating to his upbringing' (ibid, para 4.41). The Act divides applicants for s 8 orders into two categories:

(i) those entitled to apply for all s 8 orders; and
(ii) those entitled to apply only for residence and contact orders.

In addition, anyone not falling into either (i) or (ii), or someone falling into category (ii) who wishes to apply for a specific issue or prohibited steps order, may apply, but only with leave of the court. We will consider each category in turn.

4 CA 1989, s 8(1).
5 CA 1989, s 10(2)(b) and (9).
6 CA 1989, s 8(3), (4).
7 CA 1989, s 10(1)(b).

(i)   Those entitled to apply for all s 8 orders

A parent, guardian or any person in whose favour a residence order has been made with respect to the child is entitled to apply for any s 8 order.[8] 'Parent' includes an unmarried father.

(ii)   Those entitled to apply for residence and contact orders

The Act lists a number of people who may apply without leave for a residence or contact order.[9] They are:

- any party to a marriage, whether or not subsisting, in relation to whom the child is a 'child of the family';
- any person with whom the child has lived for a period of at least three years;[10]
- where a residence order is in force with respect to the child, any person who has the consent of each person in whose favour the order was made;
- where the child is in the care of a local authority, any person who has the consent of that authority;
- in any other case, any person who has the consent of each of those who have parental responsibility for the child (if any).

These provisions would permit, for example, relatives or step-parents to obtain residence or contact orders, provided that one of the conditions is satisfied. If not, then leave of court will have to be sought (see below). If a residence order is made, it automatically confers parental responsibility for the child on the person in whose favour it has been made.[11]

Local authorities are expressly excluded from seeking residence or contact orders,[12] and must rely on their statutory powers contained elsewhere in the Act if there is a need to protect the child. In addition, only residence orders may be made with respect to a child in local authority care[13] and, once made, a residence order discharges a care order.[14] This means that local authorities cannot seek prohibited steps or specific issue orders with respect to children in their care, but would be able to do so with respect to a child not in their care provided it had obtained leave to do so (see below).

8   CA 1989, s 10(4).
9   CA 1989, s 10(5).
10 The period of three years need not be continuous, but must have begun at least five years before the making of the application and must not have ended more than three months before the making of the application: CA 1989, s 10(10).
11 CA 1989, s 12(2).
12 CA 1989, s 9(2).
13 CA 1989, s 9(1).
14 CA 1989, s 91(1).

(iii) Leave of court

Anyone not qualifying under the first two categories may still seek the court's leave to apply for an order. The Law Commission was anxious to preserve the position under the old law which enabled anyone with a genuine interest in a child's welfare to make applications relating to his or her upbringing by means of wardship. The leave requirement was intended as 'a filter to protect the child and his family from unwarranted interference in their comfort and security, while ensuring that the child's interests are properly respected' (1988, para 4.41). Examples of applicants who would need to seek leave would include: a medical practitioner concerned about a parent's decision concerning the medical treatment of the child;[15] a local authority wishing to obtain a specific issue or prohibited steps order with respect to a child not in its care; or a relative who has not had the child living with them for long enough and who does not have the requisite consents.

In deciding whether or not to grant leave, the court must have regard to the following criteria:[16]

- the s 8 order sought;
- the applicant's connection with the child;
- any risk there might be of the proposed application disrupting the child's life to such an extent that he would be harmed by it; and
- where the child is being looked after by a local authority, the authority's plans for the child's future and the wishes of the parents.

A child may also seek leave to apply for a s 8 order in respect of him- or herself, but the court may only grant leave if the court is satisfied that the child has sufficient understanding to make the proposed application.[17]

The Act imposes a restriction on seeking leave in one type of case. A person who is, or has been at any time in the last six months, a local authority foster parent must satisfy one of the following conditions before seeking leave of the court.[18] These are that the foster parent must either (i) have the consent of the local authority who originally placed the child with the foster parents, or (ii) be a relative of the child or (iii) have had the child living with him for at

---

15 Eg, *Re D (a minor) (wardship: sterilisation)* [1976] 1 All ER 326. Wardship will still be available for such cases.
16 CA 1989, s 10(9).
17 CA 1989, s 10(8).
18 CA 1989, s 9(3).

least three years[19] preceding the application. The reason for this added restriction is the need to maintain the confidence of parents in the voluntary care system, even though the Law Commission did not think that this justified a difference of treatment (1988, para 4.43; see Ch 11 for further discussion of the legal position of foster parents).

Who is a parent?

The question 'who is a parent?' may arise in a variety of circumstances. It will assist in determining who is a 'parent', and who has parental responsibility for a child, under the Children Act 1989, and will be important in ascribing liability to support a child (whether under private law or the Child Support Act 1991). It may also arise with respect to issues of inheritance and succession to property, or between individuals and the state over the care, education or medical treatment of the child. Greater difficulties arise in identifying the father than the mother. The mother will be identifiable from the fact of giving birth to the child, including, as we shall see, where the mother is not genetically related to the child following infertility treatment. There is no similarly obvious method of linking fathers to children.

Two features of the legal definition of parenthood should be noted. First, the Children Act 1989 widens the range of people who may be entitled to some legal standing in relation to a child. This has been achieved through an extension of the courts' powers to confer parental responsibility[20] in favour of non-parents (see further Ch 11 and below under the heading of 'Social parenthood'). Thus, although the Act accords parental responsibility initially to the 'natural' parents, it ensures that substitutes may be made available. This is consistent with the argument outlined above, that the Act is concerned to allocate parenting functions as far as possible within 'the family', and not necessarily within the 'natural family'. Second, the legal definition presupposes that two (heterosexual) parents are better than one. Indeed, it might be said that the real focus of the legal definition is on attaching children to fathers (Smart 1987). Yet, the absence of any obvious biological link between a father and a child has meant that fatherhood is inevitably a social construct.

---

19 The period of three years need not be continuous, but must have begun at least five years before the making of the application: CA 1989, s 9(4).
20 By granting a residence order in their favour, which has the effect of conferring parental responsibility on the person in whose favour the order has been made – CA 1989, s 10(5) (eligibility) and CA 1989, s 12(2) (effects of a residence order).

There is no single means by which the legal attachment of fathers to children has been achieved.

Two recent developments have served to complicate matters considerably. The first is the improvement in techniques of blood testing, which now enable biological paternity to be determined more accurately than previously. The second is that advances in techniques of artificial reproduction have for the first time placed in question the nature of the biological link between mother and child. The practice of surrogate motherhood, which involves a woman being fertilised for the sole purpose of bearing the child for someone else, sometimes for payment, has in particular placed in issue the social and legal construction of motherhood (see Morgan 1985; Lewis and Cannell 1986; Zipper and Sevenhuijsen 1987). There is thus a double tendency to attach men to children through a biological link, while dissociating women from children through the 'artificial' manipulation of genetic material.

(a) Marriage: the presumption of legitimacy

At common law, a child born to a married woman is presumed to be the child of the woman's husband.[1] Although described as a presumption of 'legitimacy', it in practice serves as a presumption of paternity in that it identifies a particular man as the father of the child. It is instructive to note that, for legal purposes, it is assumed that the status of a child rests on the proof (or, at least, the absence of disproof) of a link with a particular man. It should also be noted that this presumption is not the only means of attaching a child to a man through marriage by means of the concepts of paternity or legitimacy; a child may also be 'legitimated' by the subsequent marriage of its parents. We shall return to discuss these matters in the context of the significance of marriage in determining parent–child relations in law (below).

This presumption operates even where the child is born very soon after the marriage or following a decree of divorce.[2] It does not operate where the parties are separated by a decree of judicial separation. The strength of the presumption is unclear. According to FLRA 1969, s 26 it may be rebutted 'by evidence which shows that it is more probable than not that that person is illegitimate or legitimate, as the case may be'. On one judicial view, the effect of the presumption is now merely to establish the evidential burden of proof, so that the presumption will only be conclusive in those rare

1 *Banbury Peerage Case* (1811) 1 Sim & St 153.
2 *Knowles v Knowles* [1962] 1 All ER 659; *Re G (a minor)* [1988] 1 FLR 314.

cases where the evidence is so evenly balanced that the court is unable to reach a decision on it.[3] More recently, however, the courts have tended to emphasise that the weight of evidence necessary to rebut the presumption will vary according to the importance of the consequences of a finding of legitimacy or illegitimacy.[4] Thus, the standard of proof required to rebut the presumption is higher than the civil standard of the balance of probabilities, but not as high as the criminal standard of beyond reasonable doubt.[5]

The sort of evidence that would be relevant would be any evidence tending to show that the husband was not, or could not be, the biological father of the child. This would include, but is not confined to, blood test evidence (as to which see below) and evidence of the husband's infertility.[6]

(b) The biological link

In the absence of a marital link between a man and a child (or, more accurately, the child's mother), there exists no presumption as to the paternity of the child. It might be thought that an obvious alternative would be to rely on actual proof of a biological relationship. However, English law does not recognise, and never has recognised, biological paternity as a sufficient condition of entitlement to the legal rights and duties of parenthood (although it is sufficient – and necessary – for the purposes of liability to maintain the child). Proposals made by the Law Commission for the abolition of the status of illegitimacy (1979) would have amounted in effect to the elevation of biological paternity to the status of a sufficient condition of parenthood. According to those proposals, all unmarried biological fathers would automatically have acquired full parental rights over their biological offspring just as married fathers do (Law Commission 1979, Part III). But the proposals drew such wide criticism (eg, Hayes 1980; Deech 1980a; ROW Family Law Sub-Group 1985) that they were modified before being incorporated into the FLRA 1987 (Law Commission 1982, Part IV; now reenacted, with some differences, in the Children Act 1989).

As we shall see below, the effect of the relevant Children Act provision[7] is that, subject to the exception of reproductive technol-

---

3 Per Lord Reid in *S v S, W v Official Solicitor* [1972] AC 24 at 41.
4 *Re J S (a minor)* [1980] 1 All ER 1061; *Serio v Serio* (1983) 4 FLR 756.
5 *W v K (proof of paternity)* [1988] Fam Law 64.
6 *W v K (proof of paternity)* (above).
7 CA 1989, s 4.

ogies (see below), biological paternity is a necessary but not sufficient condition of exercising the legal rights and duties of parenthood: the father must also either obtain the mother's agreement that he should have parental responsibility (in a prescribed form 'parental responsibility agreement') or apply to court for an order giving him parental responsibility in which he must satisfy the requirement that his exercising of parental responsibility is in the interests of the child. However, if the courts take the view that 'children need fathers'[8] in the interests of their 'welfare', then there would appear to be little difference from the proposals as originally envisaged, save the formality of a court application (or a 'parental responsibility agreement') for the conferment of the rights of paternity. This is discussed further below. The Family Law Reform Act 1987 also effected small but significant extensions in the rights of biological fathers, for example to enter their names as father on the register of births without the mother's consent (see below).

(c) Social parenthood

As noted above, the Children Act 1989 has extended the courts' powers to grant parental responsibility[9] for a child to those who can establish neither a marital nor biological link with the child, but who are nevertheless caring for the child. There are, in addition, two examples of legal recognition being accorded to 'social parenting' which may be mentioned here. The first is the legal fiction of adoption (see Ch 11), which creates an entire parent–child relationship between biological and marital strangers. The second is the 'child of the family' formula, which appears in legislation conferring powers on the courts, for example, to make orders for maintenance and property adjustment for children.[10] The effect of the formula is to construct a link between a spouse and any children who are not the biological offspring of that spouse but who have been treated by that spouse in the required way. Once the link is established, parental duties with respect to maintenance arise as if the spouse

---

8 As Baker P did in *S v O (illegitimate child: access)* [1977] 3 FLR 15.
9 By means of a residence order: CA 1989, s 12.
10 MCA 1973, ss 21–25, 41, 52; DPMCA 1978, ss 1–3, 8, 16–18, 88. A person who is a party to a marriage in relation to whom a child is a child of the family is liable (as a 'parent') to maintain the child: CA 1989, Sch 1, paras 4(2) and 16(2). By the same provisions, such a person is entitled to apply for maintenance on the child's behalf and is also entitled to apply for residence or contact orders (CA 1989, s 10(5)): see Ch 11. The definition of 'child of the family', which can be found in CA 1989, s 105(1), is discussed more fully in Ch 11.

were the natural parent of the child, but only in the limited context
of the proceedings to which the definition applies.

(d) **Reproductive technologies and the determination of parenthood**

The growing use of 'artificial' reproductive techniques has posed new
questions of the legal definition of parenthood with respect both to
fatherhood and motherhood. What follows is not an exhaustive
discussion of the legal problems associated with these techniques.
The focus is more directly on the question: how is the legal
parenthood of such children to be determined? The complexities
involved in answering this question arise from the fact that the
traditional legal methods of determining parenthood for legal
purposes (namely marriage, biology and social parenthood) may
be irrelevant or produce inappropriate results. As we shall see, the
current law combines elements of all three methods as well as
introducing new ones. This emphasises how flexible the notion of
parenthood has become as a consequence of the breaking of the
connection, not just between procreation and marriage, but also
between procreation and sexual intercourse.

(i) The 'reprotechnologies'

For present purposes, the technologies with which we are concerned
may be classified as follows:[11]

(1) Artificial insemination by donor (AID)   Except where employed
as part of a surrogacy arrangement, the use of AID (sometimes
known as Therapeutic Donor Insemination, or TDI) is related to the
alleviation of male infertility (see Dewar 1988). The wife or female
partner is inseminated with sperm provided by a third party donor,
so the husband or partner of the woman will not be related
biologically to the child. Usually, the woman and partner will
conceal the nature of conception (Snowden and Mitchell 1981) and
will register the child in the Register of Births as being the natural
child of them both, thus technically committing perjury.[12] However,
the term AID/TDI need not be confined to the use of donated sperm.

11 For more detailed discussion, see Cusine (1990), Dickens (1990), Morgan and Lee
(1991) (especially Ch 5; and see the helpful glossary at pp ix–xiv); Douglas
(1991a), Ch 6.
12 Perjury Act 1911, s 4.

It may include the use of a husband's sperm (sometimes called AIH) or the use of donated eggs for fertilisation in the recipient woman's body (which overlaps with GIFT – see below).

(2) In vitro fertilisation (IVF)   This is the creation of an embryo outside the human body which is then inserted in the womb of the carrying mother (popularly known as 'test-tube babies'). The embryo may be the genetic product of the carrying mother and her husband or partner, or it may involve the use of donated sperm or ova or both. A child born as a result of IVF may thus be genetically related to both, one or neither of its 'parents' (ie, the carrying mother and her partner or husband).

(3) Gamete intrafallopian transfer (GIFT)   This involves the insertion in the womb of egg, sperm, or both, for fertilisation to take place in the womb (in vivo) rather than outside it. The gametes (ie, egg or sperm) may be donated or come from the recipient woman and her partner. Like IVF, the resultant child may be genetically related to one, both or neither of its 'parents'.

(4) Surrogate motherhood[13]   This is not a 'technology' as such, but refers to an arrangement under which the carrying mother agrees to bear a child but to hand it over to someone else (the 'commissioning parents') once born. Surrogacy arrangements may involve any of the techniques described above. Thus, the carrying mother may be inseminated artificially (or 'naturally') with the sperm of the commissioning husband or male partner; or gametes taken either from the commissioning couple or from donors may be used to create an embryo either in vitro or in vivo. The resulting child may thus be genetically related to the commisioning parents, the surrogate mother or a third party donor. It is now an offence for any person to assist for reward in the making of surrogacy arrangements[14] and a surrogacy arrangement is unenforceable by or against any of the persons making it.[15]

(ii) Defining parenthood: Human Fertilisation and Embryology Act 1990

The current law governing the legal parenthood of children born by these means is now (almost) exclusively contained in the Human

13 See Douglas (1991a), Ch 7 for an excellent discussion of the issue.
14 Surrogacy Arrangements Act 1985, ss 1, 2; s 2(2) specifically excludes surrogate mothers and commissioning parents from the scope of the offences created by the Act; for critical comments, see Morgan (1986); Freeman (1986); Harding (1987).
15 Human Fertilisation and Embryology Act 1990, s 36, amending s 1 Surrogacy Arrangements Act 1985.

Fertilisation and Embryology Act 1990.[16] The Act is also concerned
with abortion, embryo research and the regulation of infertility
treatment services which involve the use of donated gametes (see
Morgan and Lee 1991; Douglas 1991; 1991a, Ch 6); but the
discussion below is confined to those aspects that are relevant to the
question of parenthood. The Act creates a licensing framework for
the provision of infertility 'treatment services' by clinics. Treatments
requiring a licence are those involving the use of donated gametes
and thus include AID/TDI and IVF but exclude AIH and GIFT
where the gametes involved come from the man and woman
concerned.[17] The Act does not criminalise 'DIY' treatments (such as
AID, which can be performed without medical assistance), but seeks
to discourage them by treating the donor as the legal father (see
below).

Mother   Where a woman gives birth to a child of which she is the
genetic mother,[18] she will be the legal mother. This is not a
consequence of the Act, but rather of the (often unspoken) legal
presumption that biological motherhood is sufficient for legal
purposes. The Act goes further by providing that a woman who
has carried a child as a result of the placing in her of a donated
embryo or gametes is to be treated as the mother of the child.[19] Thus,
the carrying mother is the legal mother regardless of her genetic
relationship (or lack of it) with the child.

With one exception, this rule will coincide with the parties'
expectations in most cases, and may be justified on the ground that
'since the carrying woman takes the greatest risk in producing the
child, it is right to make her the automatic legal mother' (Douglas
1991a, p 129). The exception is where the carrying mother has
agreed to bear the child for someone else as part of a surrogacy
arrangement. Here, the presumption in favour of the carrying
mother provides a surrogate mother with legal protection from the
commissioning parents if she changes her mind about handing over
the child, and thus acts as a disincentive to surrogacy arrangements.
However, the Act itself introduces a procedure by which the
commissioning parents may by court order become the child's legal
parents, but only with the unconditional agreement of the surrogate
mother (see below).

16 See Warnock (1985), DHSS (1986), (1987). For the argument that the parenthood
    provisions of the Act are consistent with a 'right to reproduce' philosophy, see
    Douglas (1991a), p 129 and Ch 2.
17 HFEA 1990, ss 2(1), 3, 13.
18 Where a person is treated under the Act as a child's parent, they are a parent for all
    legal purposes except in relation to titles of honour: HFEA 1990, s 29.
19 HFEA 1990, s 27(1).

Father   Two policies with respect to fatherhood are identifiable in the Act. The first is to treat as the father any man to whom the woman bearing the child is married or with whom the woman has sought infertility treatment. The second is to discourage infertility treatments being made available to single women (who may seek such treatment, not as a consequence of infertility, but in order to achieve pregnancy without having a sexual relationship with a man). For example, it is a condition of a licence that 'a woman shall not be treated with treatment services unless account has been taken of the welfare of any child who may be born as a result of the treatment (including the need of that child for a father) . . . '.[20] It has been said that this 'is an odd provision. *Ex hypothesi*, the child has a father; the section is not making special provision for parthenogenesis. What the section means to provide for, of course, is that the woman seeking treatment should have a man. That is rather different' (Morgan and Lee 1991, p 155). This is explored further below.

The Act is concerned only to define fatherhood in those cases where the child has been born as a result of gamete donation and where the embryo was not created by the sperm of the man in question. Thus, it would apply where the genetic material came from the mother and a donor or from neither the man nor the mother. The Act draws a distinction between married and unmarried couples. In the case of the former, the presumption of legitimacy is preserved so that a child born to a married woman will be treated as the child of her husband.[1] If the presumption does not apply, the husband is treated as father of the child unless he can prove that he did not consent to the treatment.[2] Thus, even if he can prove that he did not consent, he will still have to rebut the presumption of legitimacy. The rules apply whether or not the treatment was provided in the course of licensed treatment services, so that the husband will be treated as the father in the case of, for example, 'DIY' AID.

In the case of unmarried couples, a man will be treated as the father if (i) the treatment is provided by a licensed provider[3] and

20 HFEA 1990, s 13(5).
1   HFEA 1990, s 28(5).
2   HFEA 1990, s 28(2). These provisions extend FLRA 1987, s 27 (on the background to which, see Law Commission (1982, Part XII) and the Warnock Committee (1985, para 4.17)). There are still uncertainties. For example, the husband of a surrogate mother who has conceived as a result of receiving donated gametes will, unless he is himself the child's genetic father, acquire paternity under these provisions. The presumption of paternity may be easily rebutted, but he may still be the child's father if he did not object to the treatment received by his wife.
3   Thus, in the case of an unmarried woman inseminated by 'DIY' AID her male partner will not be treated as the father; the father will probably be the donor, as we shall see.

(ii) the service was provided for the mother and the man 'together' and (iii) the mother is not married to a third party in whose favour the presumption of legitimacy will operate.[4] This is an exception to the general rule that unmarried fathers do not automatically acquire parental status (see below). If a person is to be treated as father under these rules, then no other person (eg, the donor) is to be treated as the father.[5]

If there is no-one identifiable as the father under these rules, the child may be fatherless since a donor who has given the consents required by the Act to his sperm being used for the purposes of licensed treatments is not to be treated as the father.[6] Thus a child born to a married mother whose husband has not consented to treatment (and who will be able to rebut the presumption of legitimacy), or an unmarried mother who has undergone licensed treatment on her own, will have no legal father. However, in the case of an unmarried woman who undergoes *unlicensed* treatment, the donor may be treated as the father since he is not protected from the legal consequences of his genetic link with the child by the rules concerning statutory consents. In this way, the Act seeks to promote the two-parent heterosexual family unit: it provides a disincentive to using unlicensed treatments (by treating a donor as father) and directs licensed providers to consider the child's need for a (social) father.

Surrogacy   We have seen that the Act establishes the principle that a surrogate mother, as carrying mother, is the mother for legal purposes. However, this provision was thought to pose a potential anomaly in the case of a 'full' surrogacy (ie, where the commissioning parents are also the genetic parents) in that while the commissioning (genetic) father may under the rules discussed above be able to claim paternity,[7] the commissioning genetic mother could not claim maternity (see Morgan and Lee, pp 153–154; Douglas 1991a, pp 157–161).[8] As a result, a provision was included in the Act[9] enabling a married (but not unmarried) couple, one or both of whom is a genetic parent of the child and with whom the child is resident, to apply for an order (a 'parental order') that the child be treated as theirs. Other conditions of a parental order include the free and unconditional agreement of the surrogate mother and the

4   HFEA 1990, s 28(3).
5   HFEA 1990, s 28(4).
6   HFEA 1990, s 28(6) and Sch 3, para 5.
7   For example, where the surrogate mother is single and the genetic father has not given the statutory consents.
8   See, as an example, *Re W (minors)* [1991] 1 FLR 385.
9   HFEA 1990, s 30.

father (if different from the commissioning father) and a requirement that no money has changed hands (although the court may authorise payments and the surrogate is entitled to reasonable expenses). The power to make such an order does not arise where the child was conceived by means of intercourse between the commissioning father and the surrogate mother.[10]

This provision avoids the necessity that would otherwise arise for the commissioning couple to apply to adopt the child.[11] Indeed, the new procedure performs the functional equivalent of an adoption but without the close scrutiny of the applicants encountered in the adoption process.[12] But what is most striking is that the new provision marks a change of legislative attitude towards surrogacy in that it provides a specific procedure for regularising its consequences. To date, legislation on surrogacy has focused on criminal prohibition and legal unenforceability (Morgan and Lee 1991, pp 153–154; Douglas 1991, pp 114–115). This new provision has been criticised for not adopting the Children Act model of permitting anyone (including unmarried commissioning couples) to apply for leave of court to seek parental responsibility for the child by means of a residence order (Montgomery 1991, pp 529–530); but while it does indeed seem odd that only married couples may apply under the new provision, parental responsibility under a residence order would be narrower in scope than an order that the applicants be treated as parents for all purposes (for other criticisms, see Hogg 1991). An application for a parental order constitutes 'family proceedings' for the purposes of the Children Act 1989[13] so that the full range of powers under that Act are available, including the power to make s 8 orders.

Information about origins   The Act permits any person over the age of 18 to apply to the regulatory authority established by the Act for information concerning his or her genetic origins.[14] The regulatory authority is obliged to maintain information concerning the provision of treatment services, the keeping or use of gametes and other information showing that an individual was or may have been

---

10 HFEA 1990, s 30(1)(a).
11 An unmarried commissioning couple will still have to adopt. The fact that money has changed hands under a surrogacy contract will not prevent an adoption taking place – *Adoption Application (adoption: payment)* [1987] 2 All ER 826. For a discussion of the law on adoption following a surrogacy arrangement, see Wright (1986), de Cruz (1988), Douglas (1991a), pp 161–162. Commissioning parents could also seek leave to apply for a s 8 order under the Children Act 1989 (see above).
12 However, HFEA 1990, s 30(9)(a) envisages the possibility that aspects of the adoption regulations could be made applicable to applications under s 30.
13 HFEA 1990, s 30(8)(a).
14 HFEA 1990, s 31.

born as a consequence of treatment services. The information to which an applicant is entitled is of two types. First, an applicant is entitled to know whether s/he has a genetic parent other than those persons defined by the Act as the applicant's parents and, if so, certain (as yet unspecified, but almost certainly non-identifying,[15] information) about that person;[16] and second, whether the applicant is related to any named person that s/he is proposing to marry.

Proof of parenthood

The methods outlined above for linking children to parents, and fathers in particular, may require some form of evidence in their support. Most commonly, this will take the form of blood test evidence as to the biological position concerning parenthood. This kind of evidence will be used most often in disputes between a mother and a man (who may or may not be her husband) who is either claiming or denying paternity and the associated parental responsibility; but it may also be used for the purposes of determining entitlement to rights of citizenship under the nationality and immigration laws. In the latter kind of case, maternity may be in issue as much as paternity. However, there are some purposes for which such evidence will not be necessary and where some other prima facie evidence of paternity will suffice, such as a declaration of parentage or legitimacy[17] or registration of a particular man as father in the register of births (see below).

(a) **Blood tests**

(i)   The nature of blood test evidence

Human blood exhibits certain inheritable characteristics of varying degrees of rarity amongst the population as a whole. The more of these characteristics it is possible to identify, the more likely it is that,

15 Adopted children, by contrast, have a right to their original birth certificate: see Ch 11. For a discussion of the question of disclosure, see O'Donovan (1989) and Morgan and Lee (1991), pp 162–168. For criticism of the 1990 Act's provisions, see Douglas (1991), pp 112–113 and (1991a), pp 132–136.
16 The Act envisages the possibility that this information could extend to the donor's identity, but ensures that no donor's identity will be revealed where at the time of donation it is not open to the authority to provide that information: HFEA 1990, s 31(5).
17 See FLA 1986, s 56 (as amended by FLRA 1987, s 22); note that blood tests may be ordered in proceedings for a declaration under s 56 by virtue of FLRA 1969, s 23(2A) (inserted by FLRA 1987, s 23).

by comparing the characteristics of a child's blood with those of the mother and of a man alleged or claiming to be father, the identity of the biological father will be ascertainable. This is because it will be possible to reveal the presence or absence of common characteristics and so calculate the probability of a given man being the father according to the rarity of the common characteristics identified. Until recently, it was not possible conclusively to identify a man as father; it could only be stated that a certain percentage of the population – say 1% – could be the father (Dodd 1980).

The recent discovery, however, of so-called DNA 'fingerprinting', which uncovers individual strands of DNA which could only have come from two genetic parents, makes it possible for the identity of the parents to be determined positively for the first time (see Bradney 1986; Dodd 1986; Webb 1986; Lygo 1991). Such tests may be conducted on (but are not necessarily confined to) blood samples, and the Home Office has appointed suitably qualified practitioners to the panel of practitioners authorised to conduct blood tests. The greater cost of conducting such tests over normal blood tests has been recognised by an increase in the fees permitted to be charged.[18]

One of the purposes of the FLRA 1987 was to recognise the advances in the techniques of scientific testing (Law Commission 1982, para 10.28). Once implemented, the Act will provide that directions may be made for 'scientific tests' (as opposed to 'blood tests') the purpose of which will be to 'ascertain whether such tests show that a party to the proceedings is or is not the father or mother' of the person whose parentage is in dispute,[19] instead of showing merely that 'a party to the proceedings is or is not thereby excluded from being the father of that person' as at present. The courts will also be empowered to direct the taking of samples of bodily fluids and tissue, such as sperm samples.[20] Until implementation, however, the courts will not be able to order tests to be conducted on anything other than blood and has power to order tests only where paternity, not maternity, is in issue.

(ii) The power to direct blood tests

A court[1] has the discretion in any civil proceedings in which the paternity of a person is in issue to direct the taking of tests or samples,

18 Blood Tests (Evidence of Paternity) (Amendment) Regulations 1989.
19 FLRA 1987, s 23(1) (amending FLRA 1969, s 20(1), (2)).
20 FLRA 1987, s 23(2) (amending FLRA 1969, s 25).
1 High Court (RSC 1965, Ord 112); County Court (CCR 1981, Ord 47, r 5); Magistrates' Court (Blood Tests) Rules 1971. See also, Blood Tests (Evidence of Paternity) Regulations 1971 (as amended by the Blood Tests (Evidence of Paternity) Regulations 1986).

on the application of any party to the proceedings. The court may direct that tests be taken from the child, the mother and from any person claiming or alleged to be the father.[2] The 1987 Act will permit the court to order tests in cases where parentage is in issue (instead of just paternity) and to do so of its own motion;[3] and there will be no restriction on those from whom the court may request samples or tests, provided only that the person sought to be tested is a party to the proceedings, since the purpose of the tests is to show that *a party to the proceedings* is or is not the mother or father.[4]

If the parties consent to providing samples for testing, then there is no need for a direction by the court. It is only where the parties will not agree that a direction may be necessary. However, the courts cannot compel a person aged 16 years and over to give a test or sample. For children under 16, the consent must be given by the person with whom the child is resident.[5] In the event of a person refusing to comply with a direction, the court may 'draw such inferences, if any, from that fact as appear proper in the circumstances'.[6] A failure to comply by a person seeking relief on the basis of the presumption of legitimacy enables the court to dismiss the claim for relief, even though the presumption has not been rebutted.[7]

(iii) When will tests be ordered?

The decision whether to direct that tests should be made is one for the court to determine in its discretion. In *S v S, W v Official Solicitor*,[8] the House of Lords made it clear that the criterion is not the best interests of the child, since it cannot be said whether the determination of paternity by means of testing will or will not be in the child's interests. Thus, tests should usually be ordered, in the interests of ascertaining the truth, unless for some reason it can be shown that tests would clearly be against the child's interests, or where the child is of sufficient understanding to appreciate the purpose and implications of a blood test and its objects.[9] A direction will not be made where the issue of paternity (or, after implementation of the

---

2   FLRA 1969, s 21(1); an applicant for a test may now nominate the tester, subject to the court's approval: FLRA 1969, s 20(1A), (1B) (inserted by CA 1989, s 89).
3   This is primarily to avoid collusion in applications for declarations of parentage (Law Commission 1982, para 10.29).
4   FLRA 1987, s 23(1) (amending FLRA 1969, s 20(1)).
5   FLRA 1969, s 21.
6   FLRA 1969, s 23(1).
7   FLRA 1969, s 23(2).
8   [1972] AC 24.
9   Per Lord Reid in *S v S, W v Official Solicitor* (above) at p 45.

1987 Act, of parenthood) is not directly in issue, or has no significant bearing on any issue in the proceedings.[10]

(iv) The weight attached to blood test evidence

Once the tests have been made, the person conducting them must make a report to the court in which it shall be stated whether the test has excluded a party from paternity or, if not excluded, then the value of the test in determining the likelihood of the party being father.[11] These provisions will be altered by FLRA 1987, s 23 to accord with the changed objectives of the tests (that is, the proof of parenthood rather than paternity – see above). Pending the widespread use of DNA techniques, such a report will either be able definitely to exclude a party from paternity or will be able to offer a measure of the statistical likelihood of a party being the father.

The weight to be attached to this evidence will depend on other evidence available in the case, and on the circumstances in which the issue arises. Thus, a test producing an 85% probability of the mother's husband being father will be treated as conclusive when placed alongside the presumption of legitimacy.[12] A probability of 99.9% derived from a test in the case of an unmarried father would be taken to establish his paternity by way of corroborating the mother's evidence that intercourse took place.[13]

(b) Birth registration

The entry of a man's name as father of a child in the register of births is prima facie evidence of paternity (Law Commission 1982, para 10.59). Where the mother is married, the husband's name will be entered as father by either the husband or the wife, unless the parties are aware that the child is not that of the husband. Where the mother is not married, the father's name may be entered (by the mother only) in three circumstances:

(i) at the joint request of the mother and of the person acknowledging himself to be the father;[14]
(ii) at the request of the mother on production of a statutory declaration made by the person acknowledging himself as father,

---

10 See *Re J S (a minor)* [1980] 1 All ER 1061; *Hodgkiss v Hodgkiss* [1984] FLR 563.
11 FLRA 1969, s 20(2).
12 *Serio v Serio* (1983) 4 FLR 756. Evidence of the man's infertility will also be relevant: see *W v K (proof of paternity)* [1988] Fam Law 64.
13 *Turner v Blunden* [1986] 2 All ER 75.
14 Births and Deaths Registration Act 1953, s 10.

thus dispensing with the need for his attendance at the registration;[15]

(iii) at the request of the mother on production of a court order naming a man as father.[16]

There is also provision for the re-registration of a birth in these three circumstances.[17] The fact that more than half of all non-marital births are registered in the joint names of mother and father (Central Statistical Office 1987, Table 2.20) means that 'the births registration system is . . . an important means of providing evidence of paternity' (Law Commission 1982, para 10.59).

The FLRA 1987 has extended the right of an unmarried father to be entered on the register as father in two ways. First, registration is possible at the request of the man claiming to be father on his producing a statutory declaration both by himself and the mother acknowledging him to be the father; and second, at the request of that man on his production of a court order awarding him any or all parental rights under FLRA 1987, s 4 or GMA 1971, s 9 (or, in cases arising after the implementation of the Children Act 1989, a parental responsibility or residence order: see below), or an order against him requiring him to support the child.[18] In effect, these provisions for the first time enable a man to register himself as father without the mother's consent. There is also provision for the re-registration of a birth in these same circumstances.[19]

These new provisions are based on the proposals of the Law Commission in their 1982 Report on Illegitimacy. The Commission took the view that not permitting registration by the father without the mother's consent was an undesirable form of 'discrimination' against the father (para 10.60). In particular, the Commission gave three reasons for permitting a father to register his name without the consent of the mother. First, registration was seen as a reasonable quid pro quo for accepting the financial obligations of paternity; second, that it was for the benefit of the child to discover his or her biological parentage; and third, that there were benefits to be had from keeping court orders and public records consistent (para 10.61). The Commission took the view that these considerations outweighed the danger that 'if a man adjudged to be father can insist on having his name entered in the births register as a result of maintenance

15 FLRA 1969, s 27.
16 CA 1975, s 93.
17 Births and Deaths Registration Act 1953, s 10A(1). Re-registration will also be possible following a finding of parenthood in proceedings for a declaration of parenthood, legitimacy or legitimation (see below) – FLRA 1987, s 26.
18 FLRA 1987, s 24 (amending Births and Deaths Registration Act 1953, s 10).
19 FLRA 1987, s 25 (amending Births and Deaths Registration Act 1953, s 10A).

proceedings some mothers may be deterred from taking such pro-ceedings' (ibid).

(c) Declarations of parentage and other judicial proceedings

A further means of establishing parentage is to rely on a judicial finding as to parentage. Such findings may arise in two ways. First, the issue may arise in the course of proceedings concerning residence, contact, maintenance or claims to rights of inheritance. In such cases, the court will have to make a finding as to parenthood in order to reach a conclusion on the main issue in the case. Such findings are binding on the parties to the case, and those claiming through them. A finding of paternity in proceedings for child maintenance is prima facie evidence of paternity for all purposes, and will thus require rebuttal in other proceedings[20] (see Law Commission 1982, paras 10.41–10.42). A finding of non-paternity (or of non-parenthood) has no formal effect outside the proceedings in which the issue of paternity or parenthood is raised, although it may be sufficient to lead to the correction of an erroneous entry in the register (ibid, paras 10.44 and 10.67).

A second means of obtaining a judicial determination of parentage is to apply to court specifically for determination of that issue. Following the recommendations of the Law Commission (1982, paras 10.5–10.39; 1984; 1986a, paras 3.14–3.16) the FLA 1986[1] (as prospectively amended by the FLRA 1987[2]) introduced a procedure by which individuals whose status is in issue may apply to court for declarations of their parenthood (and, where necessary, declarations of legitimacy or legitimation). Such a declaration will be binding on the Crown and 'all other persons'[3] and is available to children whose parents are unmarried.

The significance of parenthood

(a) Introduction

It was argued in the introduction to this chapter that parenthood is increasingly becoming the most significant determinant of the rights

---

20 Civil Evidence Act 1968, s 12.
1   Sections 56–60.
2   Section 22.
3   FLA 1986, s 58(1).

and responsibilities of family members, superseding marriage in significance. For example, from the point of view of claims to maintenance for or on behalf of children, the distinction between children whose parents who are and who are not married is now greatly diminished (but by no means abolished) following the enactment of the Family Law Reform Act 1987 (now Sch 1 of the Children Act 1989) and of the Child Support Act 1991 (see Ch 4). Further, in the absence of children, the status of marriage is now no longer a guarantee of maintenance to a spouse in his or her own right following a divorce. In practice, maintenance claims are rarely made or paid in the absence of children; and the MFPA 1984 has formalised a previously informal distinction between divorces involving children and those that do not from the point of view of the distribution of money and property on divorce (see Ch 8). In other words, both as a matter of practice and of formal law, the presence or absence of children in a relationship is increasingly becoming the determinant of the rights and duties of the parties. This is underlined by the Child Support Act 1991, which ignores marital status in defining parental liability to maintain children.

This increasing 'child-centredness' of the law and its procedures also has implications for the content of parenthood itself. The legal position of parents in relation to children (discussed below) has become increasingly mediated through the notion of the child's welfare, both in the context of disputes between parents and between parents and the state. The courts have rejected a 'rights-based' analysis of the legal position of parents. Thus it has been said that '[t]he principle of the law . . . is that parental rights are derived from parental duty and exist only so long as they are needed for the protection of the person and property of the child';[4] and that 'any "right" vested in [the parent] must yield to the dictates of the welfare of the child'.[5] The most striking example of this is the decision by the House of Lords that it is open to doctors to prescribe contraceptives to young women of under 16 without seeking parental permission, where the young woman concerned is of sufficient age and understanding, and where necessary in the interests of her welfare.[6] It was partly (but, as we have seen, only partly) owing to such judicial pronouncements that the Children Act opted for the concept of parental responsibility in preference to the earlier form-ulation of parental 'rights'.

4   Per Lord Scarman in *Gillick v West Norfolk and Wisbech Area Health Authority* [1986] AC 112 at 184.
5   Per Lord Oliver in *Re KD (a minor)* [1988] 2 FLR 139 at 155.
6   *Gillick* (above).

Nevertheless, despite the increasing subjection of a parent's legal position to the test of the child's welfare, there remain good reasons for regarding the rules concerning the allocation and content of parental responsibility as significant. For example, it has been pointed out that 'unless and until a court order is obtained, a person with parental rights [sic] is legally empowered to take action in respect of a child in exercise of those rights' (Law Commission 1982, para 4.19). In other words, a parent has power to act in default of any other person or body intervening in the exercise of the parent's decision.[7] Further, the content and allocation of parental responsibility may be important 'in indicating to third parties what action may or may not be taken in relation to a child without reference to the parents' wishes or resorting to a court' (Law Commission 1985a, para 1.7). Finally, recent case law developments[8] suggest that where a dispute arises between a parent and a third party over physical possession of a child, the parents will be regarded as having a pre-eminent claim to the child which will only be displaced if there is positive evidence demanding displacement of the 'parental right'[9] (see further below).

This part of the chapter begins by discussing how parental responsibility is allocated and then looks in detail at some of the components of the concept. It concludes with a discussion of the idea of children's rights; an idea which has the potential to transform the legal relationship between parents and children as radically as the transformation brought about by the emergence of the welfare principle.

(b) The allocation of parental responsibility

The rules concerning entitlement to exercise parental rights (now responsibility) are the culmination of a gradual extension of formal rights of parenthood by common law and statute (see Bainham 1988, Ch 1; Bevan 1989, pp 6–11). In the case of children whose parents

---

7 See, eg, *Re D (a minor) (wardship: sterilisation)* [1976] 1 All ER 326; *Re B (a minor) (wardship: medical treatment)* [1981] 1 WLR 1421. In both cases, the court, in wardship proceedings, overrode the parents' wishes concerning the withdrawal of life-saving treatment from their seriously ill child. See also *Re C (a minor)* [1989] 2 All ER 782 and *Re J* [1990] 3 All ER 930. The scope for wardship proceedings is reduced where the child is in local authority care: CA 1989, s 100 and below.

8 *Re K* [1990] 2 FLR 64; *Re K* [1991] 1 FLR 57.

9 See, for example, *Re H (a minor)* [1991] 2 FLR 109, in which it was held that the presumption in favour of the natural parents did not exclude other potential carers, such as a grandparent, where it was not in the child's interests to live with the parent.

are married, the common law vested parental rights exclusively and absolutely in the father.[10] Statutory alterations to the common law have progressively extended the rights of a mother;[11] and the formal position now (but only from as recently as 1973) is that the mother and father exercise parental rights equally with each other.[12] The Children Act 1989 also makes it clear that parental responsibility survives the termination of the parents' marriage.[13] However, this extension of the formal rights of the mother has been accompanied by a growing tendency, noted above, to subject parental 'rights' to the test of the child's 'welfare'.[14] Thus the legal position of a mother in relation to her children does not turn on the assertion of formal and unqualified rights, as the father's rights once did at common law, but on prevailing views concerning the mother's role in child-rearing, and on considerations of the individual mother's 'moral' character and fitness for motherhood (Brophy and Smart 1981; see also Ch 9).

With respect to the child whose parents are unmarried, the common law regarded no one as parent until the late nineteenth century, when a series of judicial decisions established that the child's mother was entitled to exercise parental rights.[15] The rights of the father, which are discussed further below, came to hinge on an application to court for custody[16] and now depend either on an application for parental responsibility, on a formal parental responsibility agreement with the mother or on a residence order being made in his favour.[17] His liability to support it was established both through the introduction of affiliation proceedings,[18] and through the imposition by statute of an obligation to recoup the state's expenditure on the child's support (see Ch 4, below).[19]

There are a number of circumstances in which parental responsibility may be acquired by a person other than the parent(s), either concurrently with, or instead of, the parents. Thus, parental responsibility may be held by a guardian (see below),

---

10   *ex p Skinner* (1824) 9 Moore CP 278.
11   Custody of Infants Act 1839; Matrimonial Causes Act 1857, s 35; Custody of Infants Act 1873; Matrimonial Causes Act 1878, s 4; Guardianship of Infants Act 1886; Custody of Children Act 1891; Guardianship of Infants Act 1925.
12   CA 1989, s 2(1).
13   Ibid and CA 1989, s 2(6) and (7).
14   See note 5, p 98, above; and now CA 1989, s 1. See also *Hewer v Bryant* [1970] 1 QB 357; *J v C* [1970] AC 668.
15   *Barnardo v McHugh* [1891] AC 388.
16   Under GMA 1971, s 9(1).
17   CA 1989, s 4; CA 1989, s 12(1).
18   Affiliation Proceedings Act 1957.
19   Poor Law Amendment Act 1868, now SBA 1976, s 17; see Finer and McGregor (1974), pp 115–121; and see the Child Support Act 1991.

or by any person (such as a relative or foster parent) who has a residence order in their favour made in the course of family proceedings.[20] A care order made in favour of a local authority will confer parental responsibility on the authority.[1] Parents whose child is subject to a care order retain parental responsibility, but authorities are empowered to determine the extent to which a parent may meet their responsibility for the child.[2]

(c) Parental responsibility defined

We have seen that the Children Act 1989 altered the legal description of the relationship between parents and children from 'rights' to 'responsibilities'. The Act itself simply defines the term 'parental responsibility' as 'all the rights, duties, powers, responsibilities and authority which by law a parent of a child has in relation to the child and his property'.[3] The Law Commission recognised the practical impossibility of providing a more comprehensive list, not least because the content of such a list 'must change from time to time to meet differing needs and circumstances' (1988, para 2.6). Thus, much depends on the general law.

Before looking in more detail at the legal position of parents and children, two preliminary points should be noted. The first is that the Children Act definition still contains a reference to parental 'rights', suggesting that not all rights-based analysis is obsolete.[4] As we shall see, there remain some areas of parental decision-making which continue to be immune from challenge in the name of the welfare principle. Such areas may arguably continue to be conceptualised in terms of 'rights'. The second is that the older the child, the less likely are the courts to enforce a particular parental right against that child's wishes. It has been said that 'the legal right of a parent to the custody of a child . . . is a dwindling right which the courts will hesitate to enforce against the wishes of the child, the older he is. It starts with a right of control and ends with little more than advice.'[5] This has since been more positively stated: '. . . parental right yields to the child's right to make his own decisions when he reaches a suffUcent understanding and intelligence to be capable of making up

---

20 CA 1989, s 2(5)–(8).
1   CA 1989, s 33(3).
2   CA 1989, s 33(3)(b).
3   CA 1989, s 3(1).
4   For an analysis of the relationship between parents' and children's rights, see Montgomery (1988).
5   Per Lord Denning in *Hewer v Bryant* [1970] 1 QB 357 at 369; see also *Gillick* [1986] AC 112.

his own mind on the matter requiring decision'.[6] Some of the implications of this are explored below.

(i) Parental duties

There is no clear enumeration in English law of parental duties. Parents are clearly under an obligation to maintain their children (although, as we have seen, it is not a precondition of this liability that the parent in question have 'parental responsibility' for the child under the Act[7]), to educate them, and not to harm them in ways prohibited by the criminal law. Further, parents could be said to be under a duty not to abuse or neglect their children in a way that would justify intervention by local authority social services through child care law (see Ch 10). It should be noted that none of these duties is enforceable by the children themselves;[8] they are enforceable only by an adult acting on the child's behalf, or what they perceive to be the child's best interests.

(ii) Physical possession

The claim to physical possession, which includes the power to determine the place and manner of upbringing of the child, may arise in two ways. First, it may arise in the course of proceedings between parents, either where the sole issue is a dispute over the upbringing of the child, or as part of matrimonial proceedings, such as divorce or domestic proceedings in the magistrates' court, in which the court is obliged to consider the position as to the physical residence of children.[9] These proceedings are considered further in Chapter 9. For present purposes, it should be noted that the decision as to the child's residence as between two parents will be determined according to the 'welfare principle';[10] and that the court will also be concerned with issues other than just physical residence, including contact.

Second, a dispute over physical possession may arise as between parents and a third party. In this context, the courts have rejected any 'rights-based' analysis of the parents' position and have

6   Per Lord Scarman in *Gillick* [1986] AC 112 at 186.
7   CA 1989, Sch 1, para 1; Child Support Act 1991, s 1.
8   The Children Act 1989 does, however, permit a child to apply for a s 8 order with the leave of court: see s 10(1)(a)(ii), s 10(8). The 1989 Act also recognises that children of sufficient understanding have a limited degree of decision-making competence: see below.
9   CA 1989, s 8.
10 CA 1989, s 1.

emphasised that any claim to a parental 'right' 'must yield to the dictates of the welfare of the child'.[11] However, this does not mean that parents have no preeminence when asserting a claim to physical possession against a third party. The question to be asked in such cases is not 'which claimant would provide the better home?' but 'are there any compelling factors which require [the court] to override the prima facie right of this child to an upbringing by its [natural parents]?'.[12] Although expressed as a right of the child, this creates a stronger presumption in favour of the parents than a 'pure' welfare test.

Where the third party is a local authority acting under the powers conferred by child care law, the position of parents is considered in detail in Chapter 10. The position of other third parties will depend on the means by which the third party is claiming possession, and on the wishes of the child if it is of sufficient age.[13] A person who has taken a child against the wishes of either the parents or the child may be guilty of the crimes of child abduction, kidnapping or false imprisonment[14] and will have no authority to retain the child. Where the child has been placed with the third party by the parents, for example as part of a private fostering arrangement, the parents will also be entitled to reclaim the child unless the foster parents seek a residence order,[15] in which case the outcome will be determined according to the best interests of the child.[16] If the issue arises in wardship proceedings, we have seen that the claims of the parents will be accorded preeminent, but not overriding, importance.[17] There are provisions enabling the views of the child to be represented in wardship proceedings, but they are rarely used (see Ch 12).

11 *J v C* [1970] AC 668; and per Lord Oliver in *Re KD (a minor)* [1988] 2 FLR 139 at 155; but see *R v United Kingdom* [1988] 2 FLR 445 on Art 8 of the European Convention on Human Rights, which suggests that a parental right to access (now contact) does exist independently of considerations of the child's welfare. In *Re KD*, Lord Oliver sought to reconcile this by arguing that Art 8 is only 'a differing way of giving expression to the single common concept that the natural bond and relationship between parent and child gives rise to universally recognised norms which ought not to be gratuitously interfered with and which, if interfered with at all, ought to be so only if the welfare of the child dictates it' (at p 153).
12 Per Waite J in *Re K* [1990] 2 FLR 64 at 70; see also *Re K* [1991] 1 FLR 57 and *Re H (a minor)* [1991] 2 FLR 109.
13 See *R v D* [1984] AC 778, [1984] 2 All ER 449 (although this will only become a factor once court proceedings are initiated).
14 See, eg, the Child Abduction Act 1984.
15 CA 1989, s 10(5) and 9(3). On the position of foster parents, see Ch 11.
16 CA 1989, s 1(1), (3).
17 Per Waite J in *Re K (a minor)* [1990] 2 FLR 64 at 70; see also *Re K* [1991] 1 FLR 57 and *Re H* [1991] 2 FLR 109.

(iii) Education[18]

Parents are obliged to ensure that their children aged between 5 and 16 receive efficient full-time education suitable to their age, ability and aptitude.[19] This may be fulfilled by education at home or at school, either private or those provided by local education authorities. To this extent, it may be said that parents are able to exercise some degree of choice over how their children are educated, although they are deprived of the 'right *not* to educate their children' (Cretney 1984, p 304). The Education Act 1980 sought to enhance parental choice with respect to local authority-provided schools by introducing the principle that a local authority has a duty to comply with parental preference as to the choice of school.[20] However, this duty is limited where the exercise of parental choice would prejudice the provision of efficient education or the efficient use of local authority resources.[1]

Local authorities are bound to take account of the wishes of the parents in the formulation of education policy, so far as consistent with the provision of efficient education and use of public resources.[2] However, state-maintained schools are also obliged to ensure that pupils should be offered a balanced presentation of opposing views on 'political issues',[3] and that sex education should be given 'in such a manner as to encourage [the] pupils to have due regard to moral considerations and the value of family life',[4] apparently irrespective of parental wishes.

(iv) Consent to medical treatment[5]

A child aged 16 and over may validly consent to surgical, medical or dental treatment.[6] This has two related but separate effects. The first is that the consent will relieve the medical practitioner of any

---

18 See Bevan (1989), pp 461–497.
19 Education Act 1944, s 36; this obligation is enforceable by criminal prosecution of the parents, and care proceedings may be taken with respect to a child who persistently truants from school – see Ch 10.
20 Education Act 1980, s 6.
1   Education Act 1980, s 6(3).
2   Education Act 1944, s 76.
3   Education (No 2) Act 1986, s 45.
4   Education (No 2) Act 1986, s 46.
5   The courts are sometimes called on to sanction medical treatment of those who are unable to consent themselves: see *T v T* [1988] 1 FLR 400 (termination of pregnancy of severely mentally handicapped 19-year-old woman); *Re B (sterilisation)* [1987] 2 All ER 206 (sterilisation of a mentally retarded minor ward of court; on which, see De Cruz (1988) and Montgomery (1989)). See also *Re M* [1988] 2 FLR 497 and *Re P (a minor)* [1989] 1 FLR 182. See Ch 12.
6   FLRA 1969, s 8.

liability for assault, battery or trespass that may have otherwise arisen. The second is that the medical practitioner is not obliged to seek parental consent before providing treatment. In most cases, the issues of liability and consent are the converse of each other since most forms of medical intervention will require at least some physical contact between doctor and patient, leading to the possibility of liability in the absence of a valid consent. However, where the doctor is merely prescribing a course of treatment (such as contraception), the question of parental consent arises independently of liability since it is unclear what liability is being incurred in the absence of a physical examination or operation (see Parkinson 1986).

Where the child is under 16, a doctor will usually require parental consent to medical treatment. The requirement of parental consent will not apply in four instances:

(i)   where the treatment has been ordered by a court;
(ii) where the parents have abandoned the child;
(iii) where there is a life-threatening emergency; and
(iv) where the child is old enough to have sufficient understanding and intelligence to be able to provide a valid consent.[7]

This fourth instance is the most ambiguous of all, and derives from the majority judgments of Lords Fraser and Scarman in the House of Lords in *Gillick v West Norfolk and Wisbech Area Health Authority*.[8]

This case involved an application for a declaration against the respondent Health Authority and the DHSS that a DHSS circular issued to local area health authorities, which permitted doctors to prescribe contraception to young women of under 16 without seeking parental consent, was unlawful on the ground that it amounted to advice to doctors to commit various criminal offences of encouraging unlawful sexual intercourse with a minor. A declaration was also sought against the health authority to the effect that the provision of contraceptive advice and assistance by its employees to a young woman of under 16 would be unlawful without parental consent being sought by virtue of its being an infringement of the plaintiff's parental rights to be consulted. The Court of Appeal granted both declarations. On appeal, the House of Lords, by a majority, overturned both declarations on the ground, first, that the provision of advice and assistance in the circumstances complained of could not amount to a criminal offence; and second, that parental authority was not absolute over children below the age of 16, but dwindled as the child grew older and developed the capacity for independent decision-making.

7   Per Lords Fraser and Scarman in *Gillick* [1986] AC 112.
8   [1986] AC 112, [1985] 3 All ER 402.

There are a number of sources of potential uncertainty in this decision. The first concerns the basis on which parental authority to determine medical treatment has been superseded: is it by decision-making by a doctor in the child's best interests, or decision-making by the child as a mature and autonomous individual? There would appear to be authority for both approaches in the majority opinions. Lord Fraser appeared to adopt the former view in suggesting that the task of the doctor in such cases was to act in accordance with his or her view of the young woman's best interests.[9] Lord Scarman adopted the latter view in suggesting that the sole task for the doctor was to determine whether the patient has a sufficient understanding of the issues involved to give a valid consent.[10] Official guidance issued to health authorities as a result of the *Gillick* decision requires that doctors be satisfied both of the patient's maturity and that contraceptive advice and assistance is necessary in the young woman's interests. The emphasis is on the doctor's individual 'clinical judgment'.[11] However, the Children Act 1989 recognises that in certain circumstances a child 'of sufficient understanding' may exercise an absolute veto over medical treatment.[12]

This difference of emphasis may or may not be important. On the one hand, it may be said that only the latter approach of Lord Scarman achieves any significant extension of the autonomy of the child (Eekelaar 1986) in that it enables the child to insist on treatment (although, as with a fully competent patient, it will be for the doctor to decide whether to accede to the demand); while on the other, it may be said that there is little significant practical difference between asking a doctor to decide whether contraception is in the child's interests, and whether the child is sufficiently mature to make that decision (de Cruz 1987). However, suppose that a child objects to treatment but a doctor wrongly believes that the child is not sufficiently mature to make a decision and obtains parental consent instead? If the emphasis is on the doctor's judgment, then the parent's consent will be enough; but if it is on the actual maturity of the child, parental consent may not suffice (Devereux 1991). The answer to this question may also turn on whether a competent child can veto medical treatment against the wishes of the parent or of anyone else authorised to give it, such as a court in wardship (see below).

A second difficulty stems from what we have already seen may be the peculiar nature of the legal issues arising from the provision of

9   At p 174.
10   At p 189.
11   LAC 86(3), paras 3 and 4 of Appendix.
12   Eg, ss 38(6) (interim care order), 43(8) (child assessment order) and 44(7) (emergency protection order).

contraceptive advice and assistance, and the difficulty of generalising from this case to the legal position as to medical treatment generally. As we saw above, it is unclear what is being consented to in a request for advice and treatment since this may not involve any examination or medical intervention that would otherwise be an assault or trespass without consent. The plaintiff in *Gillick* was simply asserting a 'pure' parental right to be consulted. It is unclear what a doctor's liability would have been if this parental right had been upheld.

A third difficulty concerns the extent to which this decision establishes a right in the child to *refuse* medical treatment against the wishes of the parent. Although it is clear that a refusal of or insistence on a particular course of treatment by parents is challengeable in the courts in wardship proceedings,[13] the *Gillick* case left open the question of whether the child itself can exercise an absolute veto. This question arose in *Re R*,[14] where Lord Donaldson MR suggested (obiter) that a '*Gillick* competent' child has no right to refuse treatment if the parents consent, but that such a child's consent could override a parent's refusal of consent. In addition, a court exercising its wardship jurisdiction could override the refusal of a ward's consent. In other words, a '#Gillick# competent' child has the power to say 'yes', but has no right say 'no' if the parents or the court disagree.

This raises a number of difficult issues, especially in relation to the Children Act 1989. For example, is the parental power of overriding consent in these circumstances included in the concept of 'parental responsibility'? If so, then it may be exercisable by a local authority with a care order even though, as noted above, the Act recognises the child as having a power of veto where there is only an interim care order or an emergency protection or child assessment order.[15] In addition, the effect of a care order is that parental responsibility is shared between the parents and the authority (see Ch 10), but with the authority given the power to decide the extent to which parents may exercise it.[16] Does this mean that the authority can decide whether parents be allowed to override a child's withholding of consent? It could be argued that an authority should in such a case invoke the High Court's inherent jurisdiction in order to decide the question; but if the whole matter is within the scope of 'parental responsibility', then there may be no need to do so.

13 See, eg, *Re D (a minor) (wardship: sterilisation)* [1976] 1 All ER 326; *Re B (a minor) (wardship: medical treatment)* [1981] 1 WLR 1421; *Re C* [1989] 2 All ER 782; *Re J (a minor)* [1990] 3 All ER 930.
14 [1992] Fam 11.
15 For a discussion of this, and of other issues arising from the decision, see Masson (1991).
16 CA 1989, s 33(3)(b).

Finally, what level of understanding must a child have to be '*Gillick* competent'? Lord Scarman thought that, in the case of contraceptive advice, the child should be able to understand not only the advice, but also 'what is involved' including 'moral and family questions'.[17] This has been criticised as setting too high a standard (Montgomery 1988, p 338) and as indicating that 'whether the child has capacity to consent depends less on the child's capacity to understand and more on whether the court thinks the child is making a wise decision' (Devereux 1991, p 292). In *Re R*[18] it was held, in relation to a child suffering a mental disability, that a child whose understanding fluctuated on a week-to-week basis could not be '*Gillick* competent'.[19]

(v) Discipline

Parents have a right to administer reasonable corporal punishment to their children, although the precise measure of permitted parental discipline depends in part on the child's age and emotional maturity, and on the scope permitted within the criminal law and child care law. This right extends to those *in loco parentis* to the child, such as teachers,[20] and arises independently of the parental right (Eekelaar 1973, pp 223–224; Bevan 1989, pp 15–17). Difficult questions could arise in relation to older children since, although as a general principle parental rights diminish as the child grows older, 'it is highly unlikely that . . . the courts would ever allow the parental power wholly to "yield" to the child's right to control his own behaviour' (Bevan 1989, p 17).

(vi) Other rights and responsibilities

Other rights of parents include: the right to determine the religious upbringing of the child;[1] to determine the child's surname; to consent to marriage (see Ch 2) and adoption (see Ch 11); to appoint a guardian for the child (below); to succeed to the child's property

---

17 At p 189.
18 [1992] Fam 11.
19 But see *F v West Berkshire Health Authority* [1989] 2 All ER 545, HL.
20 But see now Education (No 2) Act 1986, s 47(1), which removes the justification for administering corporal punishment in schools 'that it was done in pursuance of a right exercisable by the member of staff by virtue of his position as such', but its administration is not made a matter for criminal proceedings against the member of staff (s 47(4)).
1 See, eg, CA 1989, s 33(6)(a) which requires a local authority to respect parental wishes regarding religious upbringing of children in their care. However, it has been said that the 'parental power to choose the child's religious education . . . does not carry great weight' (Bevan 1989, p 18).

on intestacy, and to administer the child's property (but see Law
Commission 1985a, paras 2.32–2.34).

Children's rights

The concept of parental responsibility in the Children Act 1989
reflects, in part, a change in thinking about the legal relationship
between parents and children that became prominent during the
1970s and 1980s. Instead of conferring rights, parenthood was
increasingly seen as a status which facilitated the protection of
children's interests (see, for example, Dickens, 1981). The idea was
well-captured by the notion of a trust. Parents were trustees and the
object of the trust was the promotion of children's welfare (Dingwall
et al, 1983, p 224). References to parental rights were thought to
send out the wrong signals. We should instead talk about 'parental
powers, authority or responsibility' (Law Commission, 1985a, para
1.11).

Recently, the expression 'children's rights' has increasingly been
used. This has been boosted by the adoption of the United Nations
Convention on the Rights of the child on 20 November 1989. By
18 December 1991 the Convention had been ratified by 107 states,
including, late in the day, the United Kingdom. One can expect that
policy debates concerning parents and children will continue to be
expressed more in terms of the children than the parents. In effect,
there seems to have been a linguistic progression from 'parental
rights' to 'parental responsibility' to 'children's rights'.

There is no doubt that choice of terminology can have symbolic
importance. Merely talking about children's rights, rather than
parental responsibility, might assist in placing the interests of
children more in the forefront of decision-making. More intriguing,
however, is the possibility that 'children's rights' could have a greater
transformative potential and change the distribution of power in
society between adults and children.

A glimpse of the different approaches that can be taken to the idea
of children's rights can be found in the *Gillick* decision discussed
earlier. It was seen that one interpretation of the case could draw on
Lord Fraser's view that a doctor should always keep a young person's
interests in mind so that it may be appropriate to prefer her wishes to
that of a parent. Alternatively, one could draw on Lord Scarman's
view that a child who is competent with regard to the issue in hand
can express a wish that will displace altogether the wishes of a
parent. The former approach can be seen as just a continuation of
the inroads made by the welfare principle into legal disputes
concerning children. If it can be described as a children's rights

approach at all then it certainly signals no revolution in attitudes. It signals only an evolving awareness that, despite the words in statutes, children's interests are, in practice, easily subordinated to the interests of parents and other adults.

What might truly be revolutionary is a policy which has as its working assumption that children are no different from adults, although they do admittedly have special needs. This idea can lead us in quite different directions from the welfare approach to children's rights. Instead of adults acting (or seeming to act) for the welfare of children as they, the adults, perceive that welfare, it is *children* doing the claiming. If adults do not like the result then there are some circumstances when adults will just have to put up with it.

This more radical approach to children's rights might only seem revolutionary because the subject matter is children and we are used to treating them paternalistically (whatever we like to say). In fact, it is arguably merely an extension of orthodox liberal approaches to rights. To the extent that the position of women and ethnic minorities in Western countries has improved during this century, much of it may be due to the values already built into liberal philosophy. After all, if one believes in liberty, equality and individualism then one is on the back foot trying to justify certain kinds of discrimination on the grounds of sex or race. (This is not to deny the importance of struggles by oppressed groups, nor the limited nature of some of the gains made, but merely to point out that liberalism is receptive to claims based on rights.) When looked at in this way, Lord Scarman's apparent approach in *Gillick* – that the law should permit competent minors to decide for themselves – seems unexceptionable. It merely points up the arbitrariness of legal status depending on reaching particular birthdays. No doubt life might be more difficult for parents, schools, doctors, courts and so on as a result, but any transfer of power in society is likely to create difficulties for those who lose it.

The most challenging aspect of the radical approach to children's rights concerns children who on any interpretation of 'competence' are too young to decide for themselves. Are they inevitably to be subjected to a welfare approach, albeit under the banner of children's rights? Eekelaar (1986 and 1991c) and Freeman (1983 and 1991) have suggested ways of maximising children's autonomy and controlling the paternalism which is (allegedly) inherent in welfarism. Freeman, for example, acknowledges that with very young children only adults can make the decisions. In doing so, however, adults should ask themselves: 'what sort of action would we wish, as children, to be shielded against on the assumption that we would want to mature to a rationally autonomous adulthood and be capable of deciding on our own system of ends as free and rational beings?' (Freeman, 1991). To put the matter slightly differently, one can ask whether the child, looking back as an autonomous adult, would appreciate and accept the reasons given for restrictions having been imposed upon her or him.

The sceptic might question whether this is merely a recipe for adults justifying their own actions through the rhetoric of autonomy and rights. Campbell (1991) argues that the whole approach is adult-centred and that it is easy from a position of hindsight 'to welcome sacrifices that were made in the happiness of the child because of the advantages that are now involved. People are inevitably more concerned with their futures than their pasts . . . Moreover, we, as adults, readily forget the miseries of childhood and discount them as childish and unimportant.'

One idea which seeks to prevent substituted judgment from becoming a mere charade is put forward by Eekelaar. He suggests that empirical work be undertaken to find out what children actually want:

> 'No social organisation can hope to be built on the rights of its members unless there are mechanisms whereby those members may express themselves and wherein those expressions are taken seriously. *Hearing what children say* must therefore lie at the root of any elaboration of children's rights. No society will have begun to perceive its children as rightholders until adults' attitudes and social structures are seriously adjusted towards making it possible for children to express views, and towards addressing them with respect.' (Eekelaar, 1991c)

What has been described here as the radical approach to children's rights faces a number of difficulties, apart from the one mentioned of the process becoming subverted by adult-centrism. At a theoretical level, one can question whether 'rights' as a concept is the desirable way to go. Many who do not adopt liberal philosophy as an ideology have argued that a society based on rights may also be an atomised society where connections between people are played down. While being a rightholder might add to the individual's dignity and autonomy, it may be a dignity and autonomy enjoyed within a morally impoverished society. Some recent feminist literature in particular has emphasised the double-edged nature of rights-talk (see, for example, Olsen, 1991).

Another objection is that the whole debate is a distraction from more important matters. While well-fed people in Western countries argue over the possibility of children being rightholders, there are children in all countries of the world who are (preventably) starving, sick and neglected. An injection of adult paternalistic welfarism which actually changes things would not go amiss. (It might also be added that improvements to the living conditions of children in any country in the world tend to be accompanied by improvements to the position of women.)

Finally, there is the practical problem of converting theories about rights into legal remedies. Too often the only people who are well-placed to take action to protect a child's rights are the ones who are currently violating them. To put in place mechanisms whereby children have ready access to help is a challenge to the whole idea that the privacy of the family must be respected (see Ch 1); an idea which, if anything, has been reasserted in some respects by the Children Act 1989. So-called 'pro-family' groups in many states opposed their governments' ratification of the UN Convention on the Rights of the Child precisely because of the supposed threat to family autonomy. One should not underestimate the strength of opposition to the establishment of institutional remedies for children.

We may seem to have wandered a long way from the central issues in a chapter on the law of parents and children. As family law becomes more open-textured, however, so that it is receptive to ideas coming from other systems of thought, it is quite possible that the abstract debates of today become the focus of courtroom and parliamentary battles of tomorrow. It is conceivable, for example, that courts will increasingly give effect to the wishes of children (despite the private reservations of judges) because of a policy of promoting autonomy even where there are thought to be welfare costs to the children. It is conceivable also that the welfare principle which we now find in most legislation concerning children might be cut back or contained so that new, child-centred, tests are implemented. In any event, one must not be captured by the idea that law is only what happens in courts and legislatures. The actions of parents, school teachers, medical professionals and welfare workers are all underpinned by legal powers. Changes to ideas about children may bring changes in the practices of others.

The United Nations Convention on the Rights of the Child could operate as a stimulus to change. It consists of articles dealing with a wide range of issues concerning children. In effect it is a human rights charter for children and deals, inter alia, with discrimination; protection from abuse; health care; nationality; trafficking; freedom of expression, thought, conscience, religion, association and assembly; family life; due process; and education. The Convention is not directly applicable in the domestic law of England and Wales. The enforcement provisions are relatively weak (apparently because that was the best way of inducing states to ratify the Convention) and the main obligation is to report to a UN Committee on the measures the state has adopted to give effect to the rights in the Convention. The reporting requirement will at least force governments to put something in writing which can then be argued over in the public domain.

More importantly, perhaps, one can expect the Convention to be used in argument in the courts. Child law creates a large amount of judicial discretion and the various articles in the Convention could legitimately be brought to a judge's attention when urging her or him to decide a case in a particular way. At the same time, one cannot 'read off' answers from the Convention. International diplomacy required it to be written in very general terms. Significantly one of the controlling articles, Article 3, requires that in all actions concerning children the best interests of the child shall be a primary consideration. This means that the modest, welfare approach to children's rights finds as much sustenance in the Convention as the more challenging, autonomy-based approach.

Perhaps only one thing can be confidently stated. This is that the position of children in society, and particularly the distribution of power between parents and children, will increasingly be debated through the lens of children's, rather than adults', rights.

The significance of marriage

(a) **Introduction**

We saw earlier in this chapter that marriage is an important means of attaching children to fathers, through the presumption of legitimacy (or, more accurately, the presumption of paternity). One implication of this has been that the legal position of the child and its parents has depended on whether it is possible to link a child, via marriage, to a particular man. This has found expression through the concepts of legitimacy and illegitimacy according to which the child whose parents are unmarried has suffered certain legal disadvantages (outlined below). Historically, the distinction of legal treatment between children born in and out of wedlock served an important purpose in ensuring the orderly devolution of inheritable property and titles (Hoggett 1981, p 119; Bevan 1973, p 236), although the disruptive potential of illegitimate offspring would have varied between social classes according to which system of inheritance was adopted (Finer and McGregor 1974, para 59).

Today, the precise legal effects of these concepts are difficult to determine, since they concern not only the position of the child in relation to its parents, but also the position of the parents in relation to the child, to each other and to third parties. The significance of the legal distinction between children whose parents are married and children whose parents are unmarried has also been considerably diminished by recent legislation. These matters are discussed further below. Further, the social significance of these legal categories is difficult to determine. Although there has been a rapid growth in the real and proportionate numbers of non-marital births and conceptions since the mid-1970s (from 9% in 1976 to 19% in 1985: Central Statistical Office 1987, Table 2.20), not all such children will be living in lone parent households, as evidenced by the fact that 65% of non-marital births are registered in the joint names of both parents (ibid). Similarly, not all 'fatherless' children are children whose parents are unmarried: the majority of 'one parent families' arise through divorce or separation rather than single motherhood (Marsden 1969, p 99; OPCS 1987, Table 3.4).

Thus, the absence of a marital link betwen child and father does not necessarily imply de facto fatherlessness, just as the presence of a marital link does not guarantee the presence of a father. As we shall see, the questions of how and to what extent fatherhood of children whose parents are unmarried should be recognised in law has proved to be the most controversial aspect of reform of the law in this area.

(b) Legitimacy and legitimation

At common law, a child was legitimate only if it was born or conceived at a time when the parents were married to each other. This would have included a child conceived before marriage but born during it; and a child conceived during marriage but born after its termination. A child falling outside these categories was regarded as illegitimate, even if the parents subsequently married. Following a series of statutory amendments,[2] the current position is that where the parents of an illegitimate child marry one another, the marriage shall have the effect of legitimating the child from the date of the marriage, provided that the father of the child is domiciled in England and Wales at the time of the marriage.[3] The effect of this statutory legitimation is to confer on the child the same rights, and the same obligations in respect of the maintenance and support of him- or herself or of any other person, as if s/he had been born legitimate; and the provisions of any Act relating to claims for damages, compensation, allowance, benefit or otherwise by or in respect of a legitimate child apply also to legitimated persons.[4]

Where the marriage between the child's parents is void, any child of the marriage born after (but not before) the void marriage[5] shall

---

2 Legitimacy Act 1926; Legitimacy Act 1959.
3 Legitimacy Act 1976, s 2.
4 LA 1976, s 8.
5 *Re Spence* [1990] 1 FLR 286.

be treated as the legitimate child of both parents if at the time of the act of intercourse resulting in the birth,[6] or at the time of the celebration of the marriage if later, both or either of the parties reasonably believed that the marriage was valid;[7] provided that the father of the child was domiciled in England and Wales at the time of the birth.[8] In view of the fact that this provision may cause significant difficulties of proof, it is presumed for the purpose of LA 1976, s 1(1) that one party believed in the validity of the marriage, unless the contrary is shown.[9] Any children born during a voidable marriage which has been annulled will be legitimated, or if legitimated will retain their status, by virtue of the fact that a voidable marriage is a valid marriage up to the date of annulment.[10]

The diminution of the legal distinction between children whose parents are and are not married (see below) has greatly reduced the significance of the rules of legitimacy and legitimation. Their greatest significance is now in relation to questions of inheritance.[11]

(c) The position of children whose parents are unmarried

We have seen that the common law originally regarded the illegitimate child as 'the child of no one'. A series of statutory measures,[12] especially the Family Law Reform Act 1987 and the Children Act 1989 (the latter consolidating and slightly extending some of the provisions of the former), have improved the legal position of the child by recognising legal ties with its mother and father for a variety of purposes. However, there remain three areas of differentiation of treatment between children whose parents are married and children whose parents are unmarried and their parents. These are:

(i)   maintenance of the child (although the differences here are now much reduced: see Ch 4);

6 This includes the time of insemination resulting in the birth – FLRA 1987, s 28(1), amending LA 1976, s 1(1).
7 LA 1976, s 1(1); FLRA 1987, s 28(2) provides (by inserting a new LA 1976, s 1(3)), for the avoidance of doubt, that the belief in the validity of marriage may stem from a mistake of law.
8 LA 1976, s 1(2).
9 FLRA 1987, s 28(2), inserting LA 1976, s 1(4).
10 See MCA 1973, s 16; see also MCA 1973, Sch 1, para 12 (reenacting Law Reform (Miscellaneous Provisions) Act 1949, s 4(1)). This does not apply to marriages annulled before 16 December 1949 (with certain exceptions).
11 See, eg, *Re Spence* [1990] 1 FLR 286 where the issue arose in the context of a dispute over entitlement to suceed to an intestate's estate.
12 Eg, Affiliation Proceedings Act 1957, Family Law Reform Act 1969, Guardianship of Minors Act 1971, Family Law Reform Act 1987.

(ii) the child's rights of succession and citizenship; and
(iii) the legal position of the father.

These are considered below.

One of the most controversial aspects of the debate that preceded the 1987 Act concerned the means by which legal reform of the law relating to illegitimacy should proceed. In its 1979 Working Paper, the Law Commission considered two alternative models for reform (1979, Part III): (a) the abolition of the adverse legal consequences of illegitimacy; and (b) the abolition of the status of illegitimacy and its consequences. The major difference between (a) and (b) was that (b) involved automatically according full parental rights to biological fathers of children whose parents are unmarried unless or until a court ordered their removal. Since the Law Commission assumed that the abolition of the status of illegitimacy necessarily involved the assimilation of the legal position of the unmarried father to his married counterpart, the Commission opted for model (b). This had a certain logic to it since if, as we have seen, the concept of legitimacy hinges on linking a child to a man through marriage, then abolishing the statuses of legitimacy and illegitimacy would involve dispensing with marriage as the necessary precondition of the legal father/child link. However, an equally logical way of proceeding would have been to remove the automatic parental rights of married fathers, an option not considered in the original Working Paper. It was considered briefly in the 1982 Report, but was rejected partly on the ground that the law 'is firmly based on the principle that the family is a unit in which there exists a broad parental[13] authority' (1982, para 4.42).

The proposals met with considerable criticism (Deech 1980a; Hayes 1980; One Parent Families 1980). It was said that the status of the child could be dealt with separately from that of the father, and that the Law Commission's concern was more with the rights of the latter than with the welfare of the former. In particular, the proposals revealed an assumption that 'a child could only have a proper status if it was linked to a man, and that it was not good enough to be the child of a woman' (ROW 1985, pp 194–195). Against the Law Commission's view that the removal of the status in this way was necessary in order to eradicate the stigma and social disadvantage of illegitimacy (1979, para 3.15), it was argued that to the extent that these exist they arise as a consequence of a general moral condemnation of sexual transgression and from the economic difficulties facing all single parent families, rather than being specifically attributable to the absence of an automatic link with a father. It was also argued that it was undesirable to force mothers to

13 Although this should perhaps have read 'paternal authority'.

take proceedings to dispense with the rights of a father, and that this might be a source of additional stress for such women, and may lead to the concealment of the father's identity.

In its final report in 1982, the Commission responded to these criticisms by opting instead for reform model (a). This was the basis for the reforms introduced by the FLRA 1987 (now contained in the Children Act 1989). In doing so, however, the Commission continued to insist that model (a) did not involve the abolition of the status of illegitimacy in the way that model (b) would have done, even though the continuing differences following the implementation of model (a) will concern only the child's parents, and the father in particular. For this reason, the Commission originally recommended that the terms 'marital' and 'non-marital' be used instead of 'legitimate' and 'illegitimate' when referring to such children (1982, para 4.51). However, the Law Commission in its Second Report on Illegitimacy (1986a) decided on a change of policy, according to which references to such children should as far as possible be to the marital status of the parents rather than to the status of the children as such. This accorded with the policy adopted by the Scottish Law Commission (1984a), for whom the terms marital and non-marital were just as discriminatory as the ones they purported to replace (para 9.2). Further, since the continuing legal differentiation will affect only parents, it is logical to distinguish categories of parent rather than of children (Law Commission 1986a, para 2.1).

Thus, FLRA 1987, s 1 provides that in the FLRA 1987 itself, and in any enactments passed and instruments made after the coming into force of s 1, references (however expressed) to any relationship between two persons shall, unless the contrary intention appears, be construed without regard to whether the father and mother of either of them, or the father and mother of any person through whom the relationship is deduced, have or had been married to each other at any time. It is for this reason that wherever the Children Act 1989 refers to a 'parent', that reference will include an unmarried father whether or not he has acquired parental responsibility for a child.

We now turn to a consideration of the areas of differentiation of treatment.

(i) Maintenance

Before the implementation of the FLRA 1987, maintenance for children whose parents are unmarried was only available in the context of affiliation proceedings under the Affiliation Proceedings Act 1957. The FLRA 1987 abolished these proceedings,[14] and

14 Section 17.

replaced them with new proceedings under GMA 1971, s 11B.[15] These provisions have in turn been replaced by those contained in Sch 1 of the Children Act 1989. This is discussed in more detail in Chapter 4. For present purposes, it need only be noted that proceedings under Sch 1 suffer from none of the procedural or substantive limitations that applied to affiliation proceedings, and are available to married and unmarried parents. Further, orders to support children under these provisions may be made against an unmarried father whether or not he has parental responsibility. An unmarried father may also be liable to support his child under s 1 of the Child Support Act 1991 (see also Ch 4).

(ii) Inheritance and citizenship

At common law, an illegitimate child could not inherit on the intestacy of either parent,[16] nor of any relative. Only a limited class of individuals were able to succeed on the illegitimate person's intestacy. Further, a rule of construction applying to wills and other property dispositions presumed that, unless the contrary intention clearly appeared, words denoting a family relationship were presumed to refer only to legitimate relations. This position has been modified by, first, the Legitimacy Act 1926 and, more recently, by the FLRA 1969 so that an illegitimate child has the same rights of inheritance on the intestacy of his or her parents as a legitimate child; and the child's parents may inherit on the intestacy of the child.[17] Further, the rule of construction was reversed so that family relationships are deemed to include illegitimate relations unless the contrary intention appears.[18]

Nevertheless, it remained the case that a child whose parents were unmarried could not partake in the intestacy of remoter relatives, such as grandparents, in the way that a child whose parents were married could; nor could such relatives participate in the intestacy of the child. Following the recommendations of the Law Commission (1982, Part VIII), the FLRA 1987 has now assimilated in all respects the position of the child whose parents are unmarried to that of the child whose parents are married from the point of view of intestacy.[19] Further, the previous inability of children whose parents are unmarried to succeed to entailed interests has also been

---

15 FLRA 1987, s 12.
16 For a more detailed discussion of intestacy, see Ch 5.
17 FLRA 1969, s 14.
18 FLRA 1969, s 15.
19 FLRA 1987, s 18.

removed[20] but the inability of a child to succeed to titles of honour remains.[1]

One respect in which the law will continue to distinguish children whose parents are married from children whose parents are unmarried will be in relation to citizenship. At present, a child whose parents are married may acquire citizenship through its father or mother; a child whose parents are unmarried may acquire it only through its mother.[2] The significance of this is that citizenship, on which hang rights of entry and residence, cannot be acquired by virtue of birth in this country, but only by virtue of the citizenship of the relevant parent. Thus, there will be circumstances in which a child whose parents are unmarried will not be entitled to citizenship where a child whose parents are married would (see Law Commission 1982, Part XI). The Law Commission were of the view that this distinction of treatment should be removed, but since it was 'a United Kingdom matter' did not include any clauses amending the British Nationality Act 1981 in their draft Bill (ibid, para 11.20).

(iii) Parental responsibility

We have seen that parental responsibility with respect to a child whose parents are unmarried vests exclusively in the mother, and that, for reasons discussed above, this remains the case following the FLRA 1987 and the CA 1989.[3] However, the CA 1989 introduces three ways in which an unmarried father may acquire parental responsibility with respect to his child.

Parental responsibility order   A father may apply to court for an order that he shall have parental responsibility for the child.[4] In deciding whether to make an order, the court must, in accordance with CA 1989, s 1, treat the child's welfare as paramount[5] but it is not obliged to apply the s 1(3) checklist.[6] The Law Commission envisaged that this procedure would be used 'where the mother and father were living together and both wanted it, or where the mother had died without appointing the father testamentary guardian . . . , or where

20 FLRA 1987, s 19(2).
1 FLRA 1987, s 19(4).
2 British Nationality Act 1981, ss 1–3.
3 CA 1989, s 2(2).
4 CA 1989, s 4(1)(a).
5 Per Ward J in *D v Hereford and Worcester County Council* [1991] 1 FLR 205.
6 CA 1989, s 1(4).

the parents had separated and he wanted full parental status rather than simply legal custody' (1986, para 3.1). All the reported cases to date (which deal with FLRA 1987, s 4, now replaced by CA 1989, s 4[7]) have fallen into the third category. In such cases, it has been said that the question is whether the father 'has established or is likely to establish such a real family tie with [the child] that he should now be accorded the corresponding legal tie'.[8] Thus, the courts will look to the degree of commitment shown by the father to the child, the degree of attachment which exists between them and the father's reasons for applying for the order.[9] If a local authority is involved, then the authority's long-term plans for the child may also be relevant.[10]

What is so far unclear is how significant the mother's views will be. It has been suggested that 'implacable hostility' by the mother to the father's intervention in the child's life may justify refusing a father's application, but only if it meant that 'no benefit would enure to the child' from granting it;[11] but in another case in which the mother was opposed to the order, it was held that the link established between the father and the child was worth maintaining 'for his sake and for theirs' despite the mother's opposition.[12] Thus, there may be a danger that while the claims of the mother will be mediated through the concept of the child's welfare, those of the father will be treated as claims to abstract rights that are worth maintaining for their own sake.

The effect of an order, if made, is to place the unmarried father in the same legal position as his married counterpart,[13] except that the order may be brought to an end by application to court (see below). Thus, he will share parental responsibility with the mother and will be able to consent, or withhold consent, to adoption,[14] to appoint a guardian for the child[15] and remove the child from local authority accommodation.[16]

However, the significance of a parental responsibility order is limited by two factors. First, as noted above, parental responsibility

---

7   The authority of these cases is diminished by the 1989 Act because, under the Act, an unmarried father will automatically acquire (in his capacity as 'parent') a number of rights which he did not have under the FLRA 1987. This has reduced the number of additional rights conferred by a s 4 order. Nevertheless, the cases remain important as general statements of principle.

8   Per Ward J in *D v Hereford and Worcester County Council* [1991] 1 FLR 205 at 212.

9   *Re H (minors) (No 2)* [1991] 1 FLR 214.

10 Ibid.

11 Per Ward J in *D v Hereford and Worcester County Council* [1991] 1 FLR 205 at 212.

12 Per Mustill LJ in *Re C* (1991) Times, 8 August.

13 Per Mustill LJ in *Re C* (above).

14 Adoption Act 1976, s 72(1) (as amended by CA 1989, Sch 10, para 30(7)).

15 CA 1989, s 5(3).

16 CA 1989, s 20(7), (8).

only partially determines the rights and responsibilities of parents: an unmarried father will be a 'parent' for the purposes of the Children Act 1989 whether he has parental responsibility or not, and is thus, for example, liable to support the child,[17] is entitled to reasonable contact with a child of his that is in local authority care[18] and to be consulted by a local authority who is providing accommodation for his child.[19] Second, a parental responsibility order is not the only means by which he may obtain parental responsibility. He may also seek a residence order, which, if made, will have the same effect, whether or not a parental responsibility order has been made (see below). In other words, a parental responsibility order is neither exhaustive nor exclusive; and questions of residence or contact are treated by the Act as being separate issues from whether a father should have parental responsibility. This emphasises the abstract nature of the parental responsibility order.

The rights conferred by an order (ie, those rights additional to those he already has as a 'parent') are not immediately enforceable. An order merely gives a father locus standi to make applications to court for the same orders for which a married father is entitled to apply.[20] Nor is it a precondition of an order that parental rights be exercisable by the father as a matter of practicality: an order has 'real and tangible value carrying with it rights in waiting which it might be possible to call into play when circumstances changed'.[1]

An order will automatically end on the child attaining majority[2] or by court order. An application to bring a parental responsibility order to an end may only be made by a person with parental responsibility for the child or, with the leave of the court, by the child.[3] Leave to allow a child to bring such an application will only be given if the court is satisfied that the child has 'sufficient understanding' to make such an application.[4]

Parental responsibility agreements The unmarried parents of a child may enter into an agreement (a 'parental responsibility agreement') to confer parental responsibility on the father.[5] This is most likely to be used where the parents are in agreement, although there are no

---

17 CA 1989, Sch 1, para 1(2)(a); see also the Child Support Act 1991.
18 CA 1989, s 34(1).
19 CA 1989, s 22(4).
20 *Re H (minors)* (1989) 2 All ER 353; *D v Hereford and Worcester County Council* [1991] 1 FLR 205; *Re H (minors) (No 2)* [1991] 1 FLR 214.
1   Per Mustill LJ in *Re C* (1991) Times, 8 August.
2   CA 1989, s 91(7), (8).
3   CA 1989, s 4(3).
4   CA 1989, s 4(4).
5   CA 1989, s 4(1)(b).

safeguards in the legislation against mothers being pressurised by fathers into entering into such agreements save that the agreement itself must be in a prescribed form.[6] There is no independent scrutiny by the courts of the agreement or of the circumstances in which it was entered into.[7] The effects of such an agreement are the same as those of a parental responsibility order, and the agreement may be brought to an end in the same way.

A parental responsibility agreement must be made in the prescribed form.[8] Once made, the agreement must be filed at the Principal Registry of the Family Division who will send a copy to each of the father and mother. Once filed, any person may apply to inspect the agreement.[9]

Section 8 orders As a 'parent', an unmarried father is entitled to apply for any s 8 order.[10] In addition, a court may of its own motion make a s 8 order in his favour in any 'family proceedings'.[11] If a residence order is made in favour of an unmarried father, then the court is also obliged to make a parental responsibility order in his favour:[12] thus he need not seek such an order as a precondition of obtaining any s 8 order. In other words, parental responsibility orders or agreements are not the only means by which an unmarried father may obtain parental responsibility.

An unmarried father is also entitled to any other s 8 order, whether or not he has parental responsibility. Thus he may seek contact, specific issue or prohibited steps orders. This raises the possibility of the father being able to question aspects of the mother's upbringing of the child without having to offer himself as a potential caretaker. The Law Commission's argument that unmarried fathers could have achieved this under the old law by means of wardship (1988, para 4.39) is unconvincing.

Guardianship

(a) Introduction

There are a number of ways in which the law provides for parental responsibility to be transferred from the marital or biological parents

6 CA 1989, s 4(2).
7 The statutory form simply advises both parties to seek legal advice before completing the form.
8 The Parental Responsibility Agreement Regulations 1991.
9 Ibid, paras 2 and 3.
10 CA 1989, s 10(4)(a).
11 CA 1989, s 10(1)(b).
12 CA 1989, s 12(1).

to substitute parents. The category of substitute parents recognised in law includes adoptive parents and those non-parents with a residence order in their favour, both of which have already been cited as examples of 'social parenthood' (see further Ch 11). The category of substitute parents also includes those appointed as guardians of children.

Guardianship is unique in this category of substitute parents for a number of reasons. First, guardianship is a 'private' means of arranging for substitute parenting in that, unlike adoption, it need not involve an application to a court, nor involve local authorities. Second, the purpose of guardianship will most often be to provide substitute parents in the event of the death of the marital or biological parent(s); it is not related to the performance by local authorities of their duties under child care law to provide substitutes for inadequate or dangerous parents in the way that adoption and fostering may be (see Chs 10 and 11).[13] Third, guardianship is a means of providing a substitute for a parent, rather than providing a substitute parent (Law Commission 1986, paras 1.12, 3.13); that is, guardianship leaves the child as a member of the same family as before, and a guardian in certain limited circumstances may share parental responsibility with a remaining parent. Finally, proof of social parenthood is not a precondition of appointment as a guardian in the way that it is for adoption or a residence order. For these reasons, guardianship is discussed here rather than in Chapter 11.

The law on guardianship has been considerably simplified by the Children Act 1989, which now provides an exhaustive statutory code for the appointment, removal and status of guardians.[14]

(b) Appointment by parents and guardians

There are two ways in which a guardian may be appointed. First, either parent with parental responsibility,[15] or a guardian, may appoint any person to be guardian of the minor after his or her death.[16] The appointment must be in writing, which must be signed by the person making the appointment, and dated.[17] A person

---

13 Local authorities are also obliged to provide for orphaned children; this duty exists alongside the power of parents or the courts to provide for substitute care for orphans through guardianship.
14 See Law Commission (1988), paras 2.22–2.32.
15 This does not include an unmarried father unless he has obtained parental responsibility.
16 CA 1989, ss 3, 4.
17 CA 1989, s 5. There are detailed provisions concerning revocation of appointments: see CA 1989, s 6(1)–(4) .

appointed as guardian has parental responsibility for the child (but is not, for Children Act purposes, a 'parent').[18]

With one exception, an appointment as guardian takes effect on the death of the last remaining parent with parental responsibility for the child, not on the death of the parent making the appointment.[19] The exception is where there was a residence order in force in favour of the person making the appointment immediately before that person's death, in which case the appointment takes effect on the death of the appointor even though there is another living parent with parental responsibility.[20] The effect of these provisions is to ensure that, unless there has been some dispute in the past requiring a residence order, a surviving parent with parental responsibility will not have to share parental responsibility with a guardian appointed by the dead parent. In those cases where a surviving parent and a guardian do share parental responsibility, any disputes between them may be resolved through s 8 orders.[1] The court also has power to revoke an appointment of a guardian (see below).

(c) **Appointment by the court**

Guardians may also be appointed by the court. The power is exercisable by the court either where an individual has applied to be made a guardian, or of its own motion in 'family proceedings' even though no application has been made for it.[2] In both cases, a court appointment may only be made where there is no parent with parental responsibility for the child or where there was a residence order in favour of a parent or guardian and that person has died while the order was in force.[3] Thus there is no possibility of a court appointing a guardian while a parent with parental responsibility is alive unless there has been some need in the past to make a residence order. In making its decision, the court is bound by the welfare principle, but is not obliged to apply the checklist.

18 CA 1989, s 5(6).
19 CA 1989, ss 5(7), (8).
20 Ibid.
1 An unmarried father without parental responsibility could also use s 8 as a means of bringing disputes to court since he is entitled to apply as a 'parent' for such orders (see above).
2 CA 1989, s 5(1), (2).
3 Ibid.

(d) **Termination of guardianship**

Provided that the person appointed accepts the appointment,[4] guardianship lasts until the child reaches 18 or dies before reaching that age. However, the court also has power to revoke an appointment of a guardian (however appointed) on the application of any person with parental responsibility,[5] the child concerned (with leave of the court), or of its own motion in family proceedings 'if the court considers that it should be brought to an end'.[6] Again, the court is bound by the welfare principle.

---

4 An appointee may disclaim an appointment 'within a reasonable time of the appointment taking effect': CA 1989, s 6(5).
5 Note that this is wider than a 'parent with parental responsibility' and thus includes anyone with a residence order in their favour but excludes an unmarried father who has not acquired parental responsibility.
6 CA 1989, s 6(7).

Chapter 4
Income

Introduction

In this chapter, we are concerned with the law regarding access to, and distribution of, income by and among family members other than in the course of proceedings for divorce, nullity or separation (which are considered separately in Chs 7 and 8). This will involve discussion of a number of different matters, including private maintenance agreements, court proceedings and welfare and job-related benefits provided by the state. However, a number of matters that might be considered relevant to this theme, such as employment and pensions, will not be considered here for the simple reason that such topics fall outside the scope of 'family law' as conventionally defined, and because there is not sufficient space in a book of this size to deal with them adequately. Nevertheless, such matters will be of as great importance in determining the level and distribution of household income to individual family members as any of the matters discussed in this chapter (see Hoggett and Pearl 1991, pp 63–74).

Before looking at the law on this topic, it should be noted that during the currency of a marital or non-marital relationship, the law has relatively little to say on how household income should be distributed between members of the family. With one small exception,[1] all the legal measures discussed in this chapter concerning the reallocation of income arise in the event of the termination of cohabitation; until this occurs, the distribution of family income is regarded as a matter left entirely to the parties themselves. Research is beginning to show, however, that this form of family privacy conceals a great inequity in the distribution of household income, with many women receiving less money to live on from their husbands than they would have received if they had been on welfare benefit (Pahl 1980, 1984, 1989). This suggests that a more

1   DPMCA 1978, s 25(1).

interventionist role for the law is called for, as exemplified by the recent Law Commission's proposals concerning matrimonial property and the legal effects of transfers of money between spouses (see Ch 5; for further discussion of the role of the law in this respect, see Hoggett and Pearl 1991, pp 85–90).

The non-interventionist stance of the law has a long history. The common law imposed a duty on a husband to maintain his wife to an adequate level through the provision of a house and other necessaries, such as food and clothing. This non-reciprocal obligation has to be seen in the context of the contractual and property-owning disabilities to which married women were subjected by the common law, the effects of which were to leave women in a potentially precarious economic position in the event of their husband's failure to support them adequately. Even so, the common law duty was of little practical significance since it was narrowly drawn and difficult to enforce. For example, the wife's right to be supported could be lost on commission by her of a matrimonial offence such as adultery or desertion; and the right to support was enforceable only by means of an implied agency by which the wife could pledge the husband's credit for 'necessaries', an agency which the husband could easily revoke.[2] Further, although the common law recognised a nominal duty on a father to support his legitimate children, it was unenforceable except indirectly through the wife's right to pledge the husband's credit. Of more practical significance was the availability of alimony and maintenance in, respectively, the ecclesiastical courts on judicial separation, and in Parliament in the event of parliamentary divorce, and later under the statutory matrimonial jurisdiction of the civil courts. These remedies were, however, only available once legal procedures for termination of the marital relationship had been initiated, or once marital cohabitation had come to an end; and, as we shall see, the modern statutory remedies largely maintain a stance of non-intervention during the course of a relationship. These statutory remedies form part of the subject of this chapter and the bulk of Chapter 8.

In this chapter, we are concerned with the law as it relates to married couples and to parents' liabilities towards their children. We shall begin by examining the ways in which married couples may themselves provide for the financial consequences of the termination of their relationship.

---

2 The wife's agency of necessity was repealed by MCA 1973, s 41 but apparently resurrected by MCA 1973, Sch 3.

Separation and maintenance agreements

(a) Introduction

A married couple whose relationship has broken down may wish to formalise their financial obligations towards each other by private agreement. They may, for example, have separated amicably and wish to avoid legal proceedings as far as possible; they may simply wish to clarify arrangements quickly and flexibly; or they may have separated without any immediate intention of seeking a divorce. In such cases, it may be appropriate for the parties to enter a separation or a maintenance agreement, which are agreements privately negotiated and enforceable as contracts. A separation agreement will usually provide for the release by each party of the duty to cohabit, but may also provide for income maintenance, property distribution and child custody (Black and Bridge 1989, pp 386–389).[3] A maintenance agreement is similar, but will be concerned only with financial terms. Since a separation agreement would bring a desertion to an end, a maintenance agreement will be appropriate where one party is in desertion and the other intends to rely on that as a ground for an eventual divorce. Both types of agreement, being basically contracts, must comply with the rules for the formation of contracts. Thus, there must be consideration or a deed, and the agreement may be set aside in the event of fraud, mistake, duress or undue influence.

(b) The role of the courts

Although one purpose of such agreements may be to supplant the role of the courts in deciding issues of finance and property, there are two ways in which a role for the courts is retained. Where the agreement in question satisfies the statutory definition of a 'maintenance agreement', then, first, any provision in such an agreement purporting to restrict any right to apply to a court for an order containing financial arrangements shall be void;[4] and, second, there is jurisdiction in the High, county or magistrates' courts to hear applications to alter the agreement itself (see below). For these

---

3   Where a written separation agreement made between two people who are still married contains no provisions concerning financial arrangements, it is nevertheless still open to the court to insert such provisions on the application of one of the parties, provided that there is no other written agreement relating to financial agreements between the parties – see MCA 1973, ss 34(2), 35(2).

4   MCA 1973, s 34(1).

purposes, a 'maintenance agreement' means any agreement in writing made between the parties to a marriage which either:

(i) contains financial arrangements, made during or after the dissolution of the marriage; or

(ii) is a separation agreement containing no financial arrangements, and where there is no other agreement in writing containing financial arrangements between the parties.[5]

In this context, 'financial arrangements' means provisions governing rights and liabilities of the parties to a marriage towards one another and their children when living separately, in respect of the making or securing of payments or the disposition or use of any property.[6]

The powers of the court to alter the terms of such agreements, on the application of either party to the agreement, arise where the court is satisfied either:

(i) that by reason of a change in the circumstances in the light of which the arrangements contained in the agreement were made, or were omitted from the agreement, the agreement should be altered so as to make different, or to contain, financial arrangements; or

(ii) that the agreement does not contain proper financial arrangements for any child of the family.[7]

The court has power to vary or revoke any arrangement contained in the agreement and to insert new provisions in the agreement for the benefit of one of the parties to it, or a child of the family. The powers of the magistrates' court are narrower, and are confined to inserting or altering provisions for the payment of unsecured periodical payments only.[8]

(c) Advantages and disadvantages of private agreements

Although private agreements offer the parties a degree of autonomy in the determination of the consequences of the end of their relationship, they possess some features which may make them less attractive. From the point of view of the party obliged to make payments under the agreement, usually the husband, the fact that the agreement is potentially variable will reduce its attractiveness as against an order of the court. From the point of view of the recipient,

5   MCA 1973, s 34(2).
6   Ibid.
7   MCA 1973, s 35(2)(a). The meaning of 'child of the family' is considered in Ch 11.
8   MCA 1973, s 35(2), (3).

the contractual nature of the agreement means that enforcement of arrears will have to be by court action for breach of contract rather than through the usual enforcement mechanisms available for court orders. These factors may explain why such agreements appear to be rarely used (see Passingham and Harmer 1985, pp 149–150; Reekie and Tuddenham 1988, pp 306–310). Nevertheless, the existence of a privately negotiated agreement may serve the purpose of reducing the level of conflict between the parties, and would either provide a starting point for the divorce court's exercise of its jurisdiction over financial matters on divorce, or form the possible basis of a consent order. (For further discussion of 'private ordering' of financial matters, see Ch 9.)

Failure reasonably to maintain

(a) Introduction

Where the parties have not made an enforceable maintenance agreement and have no immediate intention of petitioning for divorce, there are two alternative statutory provisions enabling one spouse to claim maintenance by court order against the other. One is an application to the magistrates' court under the provisions of the DPMCA 1978, discussed below. The other is an application to a divorce court under MCA 1973, s 27 on the ground that the other party has failed to provide reasonable maintenance for the applicant, or has failed to provide, or to make a proper contribution towards, reasonable maintenance for any 'child of the family'.[9] These grounds are identical to the first two grounds on which proceedings may be brought under the DPMCA 1978.[10] The choice of which procedure to use may be influenced by a number of factors. For example, the powers of the divorce court under s 27 are wider than those of the magistrates' court in that the former can order secured periodical payments and unlimited lump sums, whereas the latter cannot;[11] and the powers of the divorce court under s 27 to make interim orders are wider.[12] However, where a party is legally aided it is unlikely that legal aid will be granted for a s 27 application where the remedies available in the lower court are adequate. This factor

---

9 MCA 1973, s 27(1) (as amended by DPMCA 1978, s 63 and MFPA 1984, s 4). The meaning of 'child of the family' is considered in Ch 11.
10 See DPMCA 1978, s 1(a), (b).
11 Compare MCA 1973, s 27(6) with DPMCA 1978, s 2(1), (3).
12 Compare MCA 1973, s 27(5) with DPMCA 1978, s 19.

may explain why s 27 proceedings are rarely used (Black and Bridge 1989, pp 383–385).

(b) Available orders

On an application under s 27, a court may make one or more of the following orders:

(i) unsecured or secured periodical payments to the applicant;
(ii) a lump sum to the applicant;
(iii) unsecured or secured periodical payments to, or to someone on the behalf of, a child to whom the application relates;
(iv) a lump sum to such a child, or to someone on that child's behalf.[13]

There is no limit on the size of lump sum that may be ordered, but there is no power to order the transfer of property as there is in proceedings ancillary to divorce.[14] The provisions concerning variation, revocation, duration and enforcement of orders for periodical payments are similar to those governing periodical payments ordered by a divorce court in proceedings ancillary to divorce (see Ch 9). One difference is that under s 27 the court has no power to dismiss an application for periodical payments without the consent of the applicant in the way that a divorce court now may by virtue of MCA 1973, s 25A(3). The court has the power also to order interim payments of maintenance where it appears to the court that the applicant or any child of the family to whom the application relates is in immediate need of financial assistance but where it is not yet possible to determine what full order, if any, should be made.[15]

(c) Relevant factors

When considering both (a) whether the applicant has established failure reasonably to maintain either the applicant or a child of the family and (b) what order to make, if any, in favour of the applicant or child, the court must have regard to all the circumstances of the case including those factors listed in MCA 1973, s 25(1)–(4) (see Ch 9), with the necessary modification that the factor in s 25(2)(c) ('the standard of living enjoyed by the family before the breakdown of the marriage') becomes 'the standard of living enjoyed by the

---

13 MCA 1973, s 27(6).
14 MCA 1973, ss 23, 24: see Ch 9 for discussion.
15 MCA 1973, s 27(5).

family before the failure to provide reasonable maintenance'.[16] In practice, it seems,

> '. . . what the court is likely to do when faced with a s 27 application is to decide what order it would have made had it been considering the case under s 23 after a divorce and then to compare what it would have ordered with what the respondent has actually been paying. If his provision does not measure up, the court can be expected to make an order . . . in substantially the same terms as the order it would have made had the application been for ancillary relief.' (Black and Bridge 1989, p 382)

Maintenance in the magistrates' court

(a) Introduction

In the absence of divorce proceedings, and apart from the rarely-used s 27 jurisdiction, the principal judicial means by which financial matters between husband and wife are resolved is by magistrates sitting as a 'family proceedings court' exercising the powers conferred by the Domestic Proceedings and Matrimonial Causes Act (DPMCA) 1978. There is also power to award maintenance for the benefit of children, irrespective of the parents' marital status, under Sch 1 of the Children Act 1989 (see below).

In Chapter 2, we saw how the magistrates' jurisdiction has evolved from its origins as a means of providing working-class wives with a degree of financial and physical protection; and we saw that in proposing the legislation now embodied in the DPMCA 1978, the Law Commission sought to accord to the domestic court the specific function of 'casualty clearing stations' for marriages in trouble (Law Commission 1973b, 1976), that is, a forum in which matrimonial relief was speedily available either as a preliminary to divorce or as a remedy for short-term marital crises. We also saw in Chapter 2, though, that there are a number of reasons why this intention has not been fulfilled, and that the family proceedings court performs only a minor role as a court of first resort for marriages in trouble. Indeed, there has been a steady decline in the use made of the magistrates' matrimonial jurisdiction, including their jurisdiction to order maintenance (Home Office 1989, Vol 2, Graphic C2; Hoggett and Pearl 1991, pp 102–104).

In this section, we are concerned with the power of magistrates to make orders for maintenance between spouses under the DPMCA

16 MCA 1973, s 25(B).

1978.[17] They also have jurisdiction under the Children Act 1989 to make orders in favour, or on behalf of, children, whether the parents are married or not; this is considered below. In each case, the proceedings are 'family proceedings' for the purposes of the Children Act 1989 and Part II of the Magistrates' Court Act 1980. The powers of the magistrates are more limited than those of the divorce court in that there is no power to grant a divorce or to order the transfer of items of property; and there are only limited powers available for the discovery of the parties' means (see Reekie and Tuddenham 1988, pp 294–295). Legal aid is not available for applications to the magistrates' court, but the parties may apply for Assistance by Way of Representation (see Ch 2).

(b) DPMCA 1978

There are three broadly different types of power to order maintenance under this Act:

(i)   contested orders under ss 1 and 2;
(ii) consent orders under s 6; and
(iii) orders following a consensual separation under s 7.

Either party to the marriage may apply to the court for an order under one of these heads. We consider them in turn.

(i) Section 1: grounds for an order

There are four grounds for an order.

That the respondent has failed to provide reasonable maintenance for the applicant[18]   The concept of 'reasonable maintenance' is not defined in the legislation. It has been suggested (Black and Bridge 1989, pp 357–358) that the proper approach is for the court to consider what order it would make in the circumstances, taking into account the factors set out in s 3 (which are almost identical to those set out in MCA 1973, s 25 – see below and Ch 9) and then to compare this notional order with what the respondent is actually providing for the applicant's maintenance, if anything, and, if this is less than what the court would order, to make an order that brings the respondent up to the notional level.

---

17 Their powers to make orders for physical protection and in relation to children are considered in Chs 7 and 10 respectively.
18 DPMCA 1978, s 1(a).

That the respondent has failed to provide, or make a reasonable contribution towards, reasonable maintenance for any child of the family[19]   The phrase 'child of the family' has the same meaning in this context as it has for purposes of the MCA 1973 (see Ch 11 for a discussion of the meaning of this phrase). Presumably, the same approach to the meaning of 'reasonable maintenance' would apply to children as would apply to adults.

That the respondent has behaved in such a way that the applicant cannot reasonably be expected to live with the respondent[20]   The purpose of including this ground was to enable a spouse to leave the other without endangering his or her claim to maintenance (Law Commission 1973b, para 39), although it is not clear why such a case would not be covered by the first two grounds (see Law Commission 1990a, para 4.23). One possibility is that it enables a spouse who is already receiving adequate maintenance to apply to court for an order formalising the position, although this is already to some extent provided for by s 7 (see below). The meaning of 'behaviour' is the same as that attributed to the behaviour ground for divorce[1] (see Ch 8), although presumably adultery could be brought within this ground given that there is no separate adultery ground as there is in divorce. Whether a single act of adultery could be described as 'behaviour' is unclear. The Law Commission has recommended the abolition of this ground since 'all the practical requirements of those who are likely to use this jurisdiction' are covered either by the other grounds or by the powers conferred elsewhere in the 1978 Act (1990a, para 4.27).

That the respondent has deserted the applicant[2]   Desertion has the same meaning for this purpose as it has in the context of divorce (see Ch 8), with the exception that there is no requirement of a minimum period of desertion. The purpose of including desertion as a ground was to enable a spouse to seek an order for maintenance even though s/he was being reasonably maintained (Law Commission 1976, para 2.11), but the Law Commission has now recommended its abolition (1990a, para 4.28).

(ii) Section 2: the available orders

Assuming that one of the grounds in s 1 has been established, it is open to the court to make one of the following orders.

19 DPMCA 1978, s 1(b).
20 DPMCA 1978, s 1(c).
1   *Bergin v Bergin* [1983] 1 All ER 905.
2   DPMCA 1978, s 1(d).

That the respondent shall make to the applicant such periodical payments, and for such term, as may be specified in the order[3]   The court has a discretion as to the period of the order, but it cannot order payments to begin with respect to the period preceding the application, nor beyond the death of either party.[4] In the event of subsequent proceedings for divorce or nullity, the High or county court concerned may direct that the magistrates' order shall cease to have effect from a specified date, and may (or may not) replace it with an order of its own.[5] If the magistrates' order survives the subsequent dissolution or annulment of the marriage, then the order ceases to have effect on the remarriage of the party in whose favour the order was made.[6] The fact that the parties are cohabiting at the date of the order is no bar either to the making or enforcement of an order for periodical payments, provided that the period of cohabitation following the making of the order does not exceed six months; further, the fact that parties resume cohabitation following the making of an order shall not render the order unenforceable, provided again that the period of cohabitation does not exceed six months.[7] As noted above, this is one of the few (albeit limited) examples of legal intervention in the economic affairs of couples who are still cohabiting (see Hoggett and Pearl 1991, pp 87–88). Nevertheless, the dependent spouse may be faced with a difficult choice at the end of the six-month period of whether to stay or leave.

That the respondent shall pay to the applicant such lump sum as may be specified[8]   There is no guidance as to the proper use of this form of order, except that there is no power to award a lump sum greater than £1,000.[9] For reasons discussed below, the guidance offered by the divorce courts in this matter (see Ch 9) is of limited use. It has been decided, however, that it is not a precondition of such an order that the respondent have sufficient capital means to pay a lump sum, since the court has power to order the payment in instalments.[10] Further, it is possible to escape the confines of the £1,000 limit by making separate orders for spouse and children (see below).

That the respondent shall make to the applicant for the benefit of a child of the family to whom the application relates, or to such a child, such periodical

3 DPMCA 1978, s 2(1)(a).
4 DPMCA 1978, s 4(1).
5 DPMCA 1978, s 28(1).
6 DPMCA 1978, s 4(2).
7 DPMCA 1978, s 25(1).
8 DPMCA 1978, s 2(1)(b).
9 DPMCA 1978, s 2(3).
10 MCA 1980, s 75; *Burridge v Burridge* [1982] 3 All ER 80.

payments, and for such term, as may be so specified[11]   Such an order may commence no earlier than the date of application, and, unless specified exceptions apply, shall not extend beyond the child's birthday following the child's attainment of compulsory school age (currently 16).[12]

That the respondent shall pay to the applicant for the benefit of a child of the family to whom the application relates, or to such a child, such lump sum as may be so specified[13]   The £1,000 limit applies here also, although it would be open to a court to make separate lump sum awards to both a spouse in his or her own right together with a further sum either to the spouse on the child's behalf, or directly to the child.

(iii) Relevant factors

In deciding how to make use of its powers to order periodic payments and lump sums in favour of spouses and children of the family, the court is required by DPMCA 1978, s 3 to take into account a list of factors almost identical to those found in MCA 1973, s 25, as amended by the MFPA 1984 (see Ch 9). Included, therefore, is a reference to the parties' conduct;[14] but excluded, for obvious reasons, is the reference to pension and other rights which may be lost through divorce.[15] Also excluded are the provisions in s 25A MCA 1973 which govern the divorce court's powers to impose a 'clean break' on the parties' financial affairs (see Ch 9). The similarity between the two sets of factors suggests that the exercise by the magistrates of their powers will be similar to that of the divorce court, particularly in respect of awards to or for children whose welfare is required to be given 'first consideration' by both courts.[16] However, there are a number of reasons why the practice of the divorce courts may not be a reliable guide in this context.

First, it should be remembered that the powers of the magistrates are not as great as those of the higher courts. Thus, it would be misleading to assume that the approach of the divorce court to the use, for example, of periodic payments can be isolated from that same court's approach to the use of its other wider powers. For example, the making of orders for periodic payments may be linked to the use of property transfers: the exercise of the two may be

11 DPMCA 1978, s 2(1)(c).
12 DPMCA 1978, s 5.
13 DPMCA 1978, s 2(1)(d).
14 *Robinson v Robinson* [1983] 1 All ER 391; see Ch 8 for a full discussion of conduct.
15 MCA 1973, s 25(2)(h) (see Ch 8).
16 DPMCA 1978, s 3(1).

regarded as explicitly interdependent, so that the use of one type of order may reduce or increase the need for another type. Second, the powers of a divorce court are exercisable in a quite different context – the final termination of the parties' legal relationship and associated status – from those of the magistrates, which, at least in theory, fill only a temporary need.

Third, it remains the case that in its limited role as a court of first resort, the family proceedings court continues to deal with predominantly poorer spouses, despite the Law Commission's contrary intention. Magistrates are thus 'dealing routinely with people who are facing considerable financial hardship and who have limited financial resources . . . [and] . . . are constantly required to make decisions concerning the survival of people on or around the poverty line' (Smart 1984, p 193). As we shall see in Chapter 9, one of the most influential factors in determining the divorce court's use of its powers is the means of the parties before it. Thus, many of the rules of thumb developed by the divorce court in relation to wealthier spouses will be of no relevance in the family proceedings court. For this reason, it has been said that '[t]he most important function for magistrates is usually to balance needs and responsibilities against resources'.[17] There will rarely be any need for a more sophisticated consideration of the issue.

(iv) Section 6: consent orders

Either party to the marriage may apply to a court under DPMCA 1978, s 6 for an order formalising an agreement made between the spouses that one spouse (whether the applicant under s 6 or not) shall make financial provision to the other. 'Financial provision' in this context refers to any of the orders that are within the powers of the family proceedings court itself to make under DPMCA 1978, s 2, except that the court may under s 6 sanction an agreement to pay a lump sum greater than £1,000.[18] Before making the order, the court must be satisfied (i) that there is agreement by the paying spouse to making the provision,[19] which may be proved either orally in court or in prescribed documentary form if the paying spouse is not in court,[20] and (ii) that there is no reason to think that it would be contrary to the interests of justice to exercise its powers under s 6.[1]

---

17 Per Dunn LJ in *Vasey v Vasey* [1985] FLR 596 at 603. See also *Day v Day* [1988] 1 FLR 278.
18 DPMCA 1978, s 6(2).
19 DPMCA 1978, s 6(1)(a).
20 DPMCA 1978, s 6(9).
1   DPMCA 1978, s 6(1)(b).

Further, if the proposed provision includes provision for a child of the family, the court must be satisfied (iii) that the provision proposed provides for or makes an adequate contribution towards the financial needs of the child.[2] If either of these last two conditions is not satisfied, it is open to the court to suggest alternative arrangements which do satisfy these conditions. If the parties agree to what the court proposes, the court's proposed terms will be incorporated into the court order.[3]

This power is equivalent to that available in the divorce court to make consent orders (see Ch 9), except that the magistrates' have a much wider discretion to review the terms of the order and to substitute their own terms with the parties' agreement. It has been suggested that one purpose of these provisions may be to prevent spouses colluding to cast the burden of maintenance on to the state by agreeing only minimal provision (Bromley and Lowe 1987, p 612). An order made under this section is, unlike a maintenance agreement (see above), an order of court, and is enforceable and liable to variation as such.

(v)   Section 7: consensual separation and voluntary maintenance

Where the parties have agreed to separate, so that there is no desertion, and where one party has been providing the other (or a child of the family) voluntarily with de facto maintenance, it is open to the recipient to apply to court to formalise the maintenance payments in a court order under DPMCA 1978, s 7. The advantage of this is that it enables a spouse to regularise what may be an erratic and unreliable source of income. This provision differs from s 6 in that the applicant need not prove an agreement to make provision, merely the fact that it has been provided in the past. An applicant must show:

(i)   that the parties have been living apart for a continuous period of more than three months;

(ii) that neither party has deserted the other; and

(iii) that one party has been providing the applicant or a child of the family with periodical payments.

If these conditions are satisfied, the court may order that the respondent make periodic payments to the applicant or to, or for the benefit of, a child of the family. There is no power to order lump sums. A court cannot order a respondent to pay more than either

2   DPMCA 1978, s 6(3).
3   DPMCA 1978, s 5.

(i) the court would have ordered if the application had been made under s 1 or (ii) a sum that in aggregate over a three-month period exceeds the aggregate amount actually paid by the respondent in the three months preceding the application. If the effect of the second of these limitations is that the court cannot order what it considers to be adequate maintenance for either the applicant or a child of the family, it may treat the application as if it had been made under s 2.

It seems that s 7 is designed to fill the gap left by the other provisions of the Act where a spouse has not been deserted and is receiving, but cannot enforce, a reasonable level of maintenance. The section permits an application to court before the paying spouse stops paying. However, an application would be unsuccessful if the applicant could be shown to be in desertion, and will only succeed where the paying spouse has been making 'periodical payments', rather than some other form of provision. In practice, it seems that applications under this section are rare (Reekie and Tuddenham 1988, p 287).

(vii) Additional powers for children

Where an application is made under ss 2, 6 or 7 of the Act and there is a child of the family who is under the age of 18, a court cannot dismiss or make a final order on the application until it has considered whether or not to exercise any of its powers under the Children Act 1989 in respect of the child[4] (see further Ch 9). A power to make financial and property awards in favour of children arises independently under the Children Act 1989, and is considered below.

(viii) Interim orders

On an application under ss 1, 6 and 7 of the Act, the court may make an order for interim maintenance (that is, interim periodic payments) at any time before making a final order on, or dismissing, the application. Interim maintenance may also be awarded where the court refuses to make an order on the ground that the case would be better heard by the High Court, or by the High Court itself on ordering the case to be reheard by magistrates.[5] The period of maintenance of up to three months may be specified by the court; if not, an order will terminate on the magistrates making a

4 DPMCA 1978, s 8.
5 DPMCA 1978, s 19(1).

final order, or at the end of three months following the making of the order, whichever is the earlier.[6] An interim order may be renewed for a subsequent term, subject to the same time limits.[7]

(ix) Variation and revocation

Orders for periodical payments made under ss 1, 6, 7, 11 and 19 of the Act may all be varied, revoked, suspended or revived on the application of either party to the marriage, or, in the case of an order made to or for the benefit of a child of the family, by the child him- or herself if he or she is over 16.[8] Except in relation to applications to vary interim orders or orders made under s 7, it is open to the court on a variation application to make a lump sum order of up to £1,000 even where the person required to pay has already paid a lump sum under a previous order.[9] In exercising its powers of variation, the court shall have regard to all the circumstances of the case, including any change in any of the matters to which the court was required to have regard when making the order to which the application relates. If there is in existence an agreement between the parties in relation to the application, the court shall give effect to it so far as it considers it just to do so.[10]

The relationship between magistrates' orders and later proceedings in the divorce court has already been discussed.

(c) Enforcement of magistrates' orders

Non-compliance with orders for financial provision is an increasingly well-documented phenomenon. Gibson (1981) found that 'only a small minority of husbands regularly pay the court order', and in his survey of maintenance orders in West London Magistrates' Court he classified the majority of husbands as either 'poor' or 'bad' payers of maintenance (ibid, p 141). In a more recent survey of divorce court orders registered for enforcement in the magistrates' court under the Maintenance Orders Act 1958 (see below and Ch 9), Edwards and Halpern (1988a) found that over half of the orders for periodic payments were in arrears, some for many years. The authors attributed this in part to a view taken by husbands that maintenance

6 DPMCA 1978, s 19(5).
7 DPMCA 1978, s 19(6).
8 DPMCA 1978, s 20(1)–(6), (12). The enforcement powers available to Magistrates' courts under Magistrates' Courts Act 1980, s 59 (see below) are available on variation applications: DPMCA 1978, s 20ZA (inserted by Maintenance Enforcement Act 1991, s 5).
9 DPMCA 1978, s 20(1), (7).
10 DPMCA 1978, s 20(11).

is linked to access to children; and also a reluctance on the part of wives to take enforcement proceedings. This reluctance was attributed to a number of factors: a fear of antagonising the husband, a lack of confidence in magistrates actually enforcing the order rather than remitting the arrears (see below), and a lack of incentive where maintenance payments would simply reduce the level of income support payable by the DSS (see further below)(ibid, pp 118–119: see also Westcott 1987, Table 2). The research conducted by the DSS as part of the background to the government's proposals on child support revealed that one-third of all maintenance orders in magistrates' court cases were in arrears for a median period of 15 weeks (Lord Chancellor's Department 1990a, Vol 2, paras 5.1.3 and 5.1.5).

It was evidence of this sort that prompted the government to seek ways of improving the system of enforcing and collecting maintenance payments. In the longer term, this policy will lead to the creation of a child support agency with responsibility for implementing the Child Support Act 1991 (see below). In the meantime, the government has introduced measures, contained in the Maintenance Enforcement Act 1991, to improve the effectiveness of court orders for maintenance (see Wikeley 1991). The provisions of the 1991 Act extend to magistrates', county and High courts. The powers of the magistrates' to enforce maintenance orders[11] are largely contained in the Magistrates' Courts Act 1980, as amended by the 1991 Act. A magistrates' court is now required, when making an order for periodical payments, to direct that the money be paid

(i)   direct to the recipient,
(ii) to the court clerk,
(iii) by standing order from a bank account, or
(iv) by means of an attachment of earnings order.[12]

These powers also apply to an order of the divorce court that has been registered for enforcement in the magistrates' court under the Maintenance Orders Act 1958 (see Ch 9), since the effect of

11 These powers are exercisable where a magistrates' court orders 'money to be paid periodically by one person . . . to another' (MEA 1991, s 2, substituting a new Magistrates' Courts Act 1959, s 59). This includes a lump sum payable by instalments (MCA 1980, s 59(12), as amended). The precise powers available depend on whether or not the order in question is a 'maintenance order' (see below) and, if so, whether it is a 'qualifying maintenance order' (defined as a maintenance order made at a time when the debtor was ordinarily resident in England and Wales). Orders for the payment of money made by a Magistrates' Court under the DPMCA 1978 and CA 1989, Sch 1 are 'maintenance orders' for these purposes: DPMCA 1978, s 32(1); CA 1989, Sch 1, para 12(3).

12 MCA 1980, s 59(1), (3) (as substituted by MEA 1991, s 2). The full range of powers is only available in respect of 'qualifying maintenance orders': see above.

registration is to give the court of registration the same power over the order for the purposes of enforcement and variation as if it were an order of that court.[13]

Most orders of the magistrates' court (and registered orders) will specify that payment should be made to the clerk of the court,[14] who then remits the payments to the recipient or, if the 'diversion procedure' (see below) is in operation, to the DSS. As noted above, the Maintenance Enforcement Act 1991 now in addition permits a court at the time of making the order to make an attachment of earnings order or to direct that the payments be made by standing order (on both of which, see below). The 1991 Act also streamlines enforcement procedures for maintenance arrears. Thus, as soon as payments under a maintenance order are in arrears, so that a need for enforcement arises, the recipient may request the clerk to initiate enforcement proceedings.[15] In addition, the recipient may give the clerk a written authority to proceed to enforce the arrears as soon as they arise.[16] This means that the clerk may take enforcement action without waiting for a request from the recipient to do so. Before the 1991 Act, such action could only be taken once arrears had accumulated to a certain amount and only then at the request of the recipient.

Once enforcement proceedings in respect of arrears have been initiated, it is then up to the magistrates to decide how to exercise their discretion to remit the whole or part of the arrears.[17] In doing so, magistrates should not enforce arrears payable more than one year before the date of the application.[18] If it is decided to enforce payment of all or part of the arrears, one of the following methods may be used.

(i) Distress

This is an order of court enabling the police to seize goods of the liable spouse in order that they may be sold and the proceeds used to discharge the arrears.[19] This means of enforcement is rarely used.

13 Maintenance Orders Act 1958, s 3(1).
14 Magistrates' Courts Act 1980, s 59(3)(b) (as amended by the MEA 1991). This method of payment was used in 73% of magistrates' court orders: Lord Chancellor (1990), Vol 2, para 5.2.2. There is also power (used in 22% of cases: ibid) to direct that the payments be made direct to the recipient (MCA 1980, s 59(3)(a)).
15 MCA 1980, s 59A(1) (as inserted by MEA 1991, s 3).
16 MCA 1980, s 59A(2), (3) (as inserted by MEA 1991, s 3).
17 MCA 1980, s 95(1) as substituted by MEA 1991, Sch 2, para 8. Magistrates may order that the arrears be paid by instalments and when doing so must direct that the instalments be paid (i) direct to the recipient, (ii) to the court clerk, (iii) by standing order, or (iv) by means of an attachment of earnings order: MCA 1980, s 95(2) (as inserted by MEA 1991, Sch 2, para 8).
18 *Dickens v Pattison* [1985] FLR 610.
19 MCA 1980, s 76(1).

(ii)   Committal to prison

Before committing a defaulter to prison, the court must be satisfied, after an inquiry in the presence of the defaulter, that:

(i)   the default was owing to his wilful refusal or culpable neglect; and

(ii)   that an attachment of earnings order, if available (see below), or payment by standing order, are not more appropriate in the circumstances.[20]

The period of imprisonment that may be ordered depends on the amount of arrears, subject to a maximum of six weeks.[1] Imprisonment does not discharge the arrears, but arrears will not usually be regarded as accumulating during the period of imprisonment.[2] It is open to a court to suspend a committal on condition that payments are made regularly and the arrears discharged.[3] An obvious problem with this method of enforcement is that it disables the defaulter from retaining the means of discharging the arrears and may in the long run simply aggravate the position; nevertheless, the power to suspend may prove an effective one in some cases.[4]

(iii)   Attachment of earnings[5]

Where a liable spouse is in paid employment, the most effective method of enforcing financial provision will be an attachment of earnings order under the Attachment of Earnings Act 1971. This is a court order directed to the liable spouse's employer to deduct a certain amount from the spouse's earnings and to remit the amount to the court.[6] In making the order, the court must specify how much is to be deducted (the 'normal deduction rate') and an amount beneath which the liable spouse's earnings must not fall by virtue of the deductions in the event of the actual level of earnings fluctuating (the 'protected earnings rate').[7]

---

20 MCA 1980, s 93 (as amended by MEA 1991, Sch 2, para 7).
1   Ibid.
2   Ibid, and s 94.
3   MOA 1958, s 18(1).
4   According to the 'lifecycle' survey conducted by the DSS as part of the background to the government's proposals on child support, only 2% of enforcement actions resulted in immediate imprisonment and 8% in a suspended prison sentence (Lord Chancellor's Department 1990a, Vol 2, para 5.6.3).
5   Attachment of earnings orders may also be made in the county and High courts, where the applicable rules are the same: Attachment of Earnings Act 1971, s 1.
6   AOEA 1971, s 6 and Pt 1 of Sch 3.
7   AOEA 1971, s 6(5).

Before the Maintenance Enforcement Act 1991, an attachment of earnings order could only be made at the time of the maintenance order itself if the maintenance debtor agreed; and could only be made subsequently if non-payment was attributable to the maintenance debtor's wilful refusal or culpable neglect.[8] Nevertheless, an attachment of earnings order was the most common outcome of enforcement proceedings, being used in 22% of cases (Lord Chancellor's Department 1990a, Vol 2, para 5.6.3). The 1991 Act removes these restrictions on the making of such orders[9] and empowers a magistrates' court to make such an order when making or enforcing an order for periodical payments[10] without the maintenance debtor's consent or proof of actual or likely default. If an order is not made at the time of the maintenance order, it may be subsequently applied for either by the person to whom payments are due under the order for maintenance (which, in the magistrates' court, will usually be the clerk) or by the liable spouse himself.[11] The order will lapse if the spouse ceases to be in the employment of the employer to whom the order is directed.[12]

The effectiveness of such orders will obviously depend on the husband being in paid employment, as opposed to being self-employed or unemployed. Orders are easily avoided by the husband giving up the employment to which the order relates. The 1991 Act does not address these problems. In their study of divorce court orders registered for enforcement in the magistrates' court, Edwards and Halpern (1988a) found that out of 346 orders, only 77 had attachment orders (p 118; see also Westcott 1987, Table 1, in which an even lower percentage of orders with attachment is found).

(iv) Payment by standing order

The MEA 1991 introduces a new power to order that payments under a maintenance order be made by standing order from a bank account or by some similar means.[13] The court also has the power to order that the maintenance debtor open a bank account so that standing order payments may be made from it, but only when satisfied that the debtor has failed without reasonable excuse to open such an account.[14] This power arises both on the initial making of a

8   AOEA 1971, s 3(2), (5).
9   MEA 1991, Sch 3.
10 MCA 1980, s 59(3) (as substituted by MEA 1991, s 2) and MCA 1980, s 76(4) (inserted by MEA 1991, s 7).
11 AOEA 1971, s 3(1).
12 AOEA 1971, s 9(4).
13 MCA 1980, s 59(3)(c), (6) (as substituted by MEA 1991, s 2).
14 MCA 1980, s 59(4) (as substituted by MEA 1991, s 2).

maintenance order and in proceedings for its enforcement.[15] It has been suggested that this new power will be of limited value but may 'have some use where the father is self-employed (and so beyond the reach of an attachment of earnings order) and arrears are due to oversight rather than a concerted effort to avoid payment' (Wikeley 1991, pp 353–354).

(v) Other penalties for non-compliance

Where a maintenance creditor is required to pay money due under a maintenance order to the clerk of the court or by standing order (or its equivalent) and subsequently fails to 'comply with the order . . . as [it] . . . relates to the manner of payment concerned', the maintenance creditor may complain to a justice.[16] The potential penalty for such failure is a fine of up to £1,000.[17] Again, the value of this new provision has been doubted:

> '. . . it seems unlikely that many creditors will avail themselves of this new procedure, given that their priority will be . . . securing the payment of arrears through ordinary enforcement proceedings.' (Wikeley 1991, p 355)

Maintenance for children

(a) Introduction

As things stand at the time of writing, maintenance for children is likely to be paid (if it is paid at all) as a result either of a private agreement between the parents or a court order. In addition, as will be seen later in this chapter, a liable relative of a child might be making payments to the Department of Social Security as reimbursement of the income support that the Department is paying in respect of the child. Leaving aside the liable relative procedure, however, any court order creating the liability to pay maintenance may have been made in divorce proceedings or in other proceedings taken, most probably, after the parents of the child separated. The whole question of maintenance after divorce is dealt with in Chapter 8. For the moment we are mainly concerned with occasions short of divorce when a maintenance liability towards

---

15 MCA 1980, s 76(4) (inserted by MEA 1991, s 7).
16 MCA 1980, s 59B (inserted by MEA 1991, s 3).
17 MCA 1980, s 59B(3), (4).

children arises. The most common of these is where the parents
(married or unmarried) have separated, but all of the discussion
below is equally applicable to parents who have never lived together.
We look first at private maintenance agreements for the support of
children. We then look at court proceedings other than divorce.
Finally, we consider the Child Support Act 1991. The Act is not yet
in force and many of the important details have been left to
regulations which are still to be brought in. The discussion of the Act
is necessarily general for this reason.

(b) Maintenance agreements

We saw earlier that maintenance agreements are contracts like any
other, and enforceable as such. It would thus be open to parents to
agree terms concerning the maintenance of their children. Where the
parents are married, such an agreement, even if concerned only with
child maintenance, would probably fall within the scope of MCA
1973, s 35 and would thus be liable to variation or revocation on
application to a court (see above). Where the parents are unmarried,
Schedule 1 of the Children Act 1989 provides an equivalent to MCA
1973, s 35. This applies to any written 'maintenance agreement'
made between the parents of a child (whether married or not) which
contains provision for making or securing payments, or the
disposition or use of any property, for the maintenance or education
of the child. This will enable a court to vary or revoke any terms
contained in the agreement on the same grounds as the existing
MCA 1973, s 35.[18] Although not expressly confined to unmarried
parents, the significance of the new Sch 1 will be largely felt in that
context since married parents may already invoke MCA 1973, s 35.

(c) Court proceedings: Children Act 1989, Sch 1

Before the implementation of the Family Law Reform Act 1987,
maintenance for children of unmarried parents could be obtained
only in affiliation proceedings in the magistrates' court. Affiliation
proceedings were beset by procedural and jurisdictional limitations
(on which, see McGregor et al 1971, Ch 11). As part of its policy of
reducing the legal disadvantages attaching to illegitimacy (see Ch 3),
the Law Commission proposed that affiliation proceedings be
abolished and replaced by a new and wider set of powers to order

18 CA 1989, Sch 1, para 10. The power of the magistrates' court is limited: see CA
1989, Sch 1, para 10(6).

maintenance and property awards in favour, or on behalf of, children. These proposals were contained in the FLRA 1987, and have since been consolidated in the Children Act 1989, Sch 1. Although available in respect of all children, the fact that the powers of the divorce and magistrates' courts to make orders in favour of 'children of the family' in matrimonial proceedings have been retained (see above and Ch 8) means that these powers will have the greatest significance for children of unmarried parents. In particular, it is now possible for an unmarried parent to obtain lump sums and property transfers on behalf of a child. This was not possible in affiliation proceedings.

We shall now consider the powers of the court. Proceedings under Sch 1 of the 1989 Act, which may be initiated in the magistrates', county or High courts, are 'family proceedings' for Children Act purposes.

(i) Who may apply?

An application may be made by a parent or guardian of a child,[19] or by any person in whose favour a residence order has been made.[20] For these purposes, a 'parent' includes any unmarried parent (whether he has parental responsibility or not)[1] and any party to a marriage in relation to whom the child concerned is a child of the family, which may include a step-parent.[2] A person who has reached the age of 18 may also apply for periodical payments or a lump sum against her or his parents, but only if

(a) the applicant's parents are not living together at the time of the application;
(b) there was no periodical payments order in force with respect to the applicant immediately before she reached the age of 16; and
(c) that the applicant is (or would be if an order were made) undergoing education or training, or there are otherwise special circumstances justifying making an order.[3]

A court may also make an order of its own motion when making, varying or discharging a residence order.[4] Conversely, a court may

---

19 A 'child' generally means a person under the age of 18 (CA 1989, s 105); but there is a power in certain circumstances to make orders in favour of a person aged over 18 (see CA 1989, Sch 1, paras 2 and 6), in which case that person is a 'child' for these purposes: CA 1989, Sch 1, para 16(1).
20 CA 1989, Sch 1, para 1(1).
1 FLRA 1987, s 1(1). See Ch 3 for a discussion of how parenthood is proved.
2 CA 1989, Sch 1, para 16(2).
3 CA 1989, Sch 1, para 2.
4 CA 1989, Sch 1, para 1(6).

make any s 8 order (see Chs 3 and 9) in the course of proceedings under Sch 1, since they are 'family proceedings'. If this power is widely used, it could deter unmarried mothers from seeking orders against fathers for fear that the father will in turn be granted contact by the court acting of its own motion.

(ii) Who is liable?

An order may be made against either or both of the child's 'parents'. Again, this includes an unmarried father (with or without parental responsibility) and anyone linked to the child under the 'child of the family' formula, which may include a step-parent (see above). As we shall see below, the criteria governing the making of orders against step-parents are slightly different from those governing orders made against biological parents. An order cannot be made against a guardian.

(iii) What orders may be made?

The orders available depend on the court to which application is made. A county or High court may make one or more of the following orders:[5]

-   an order for periodical payments (secured or unsecured), payable either to the applicant for the benefit of the child, or to the child direct;[6]
-   an order requiring payment of a lump sum, either to the applicant for the child's benefit, or direct to the child;[7]
-   an order requiring a settlement to be made for the child's benefit of specified property to which either parent is entitled either in possession or reversion;
-   an order requiring either or both parent(s) to transfer specified property to which they are entitled in possession or reversion either to the applicant for the child's benefit or to the child.

A magistrates' court may make orders only for unsecured periodical payments and for lump sums of up to £1,000.[8] There are thus

5   CA 1989, Sch 1, para 1(1), (2).
6   On the duration and variation of orders for periodical payments, see paras 3, 6, 7. There is also a power to make interim orders for periodical payments: CA 1989, Sch 1, para 9.
7   A lump sum may be made for the purpose, among others, of meeting liabilities or expenses connected with the birth or maintenance of the child that have been reasonably incurred before the making of the order: CA 1989, Sch 1, para 5(1).
8   CA 1989, Sch 1, para 5(2).

extremely wide powers available to the higher courts, equivalent to those available to the divorce court (see Ch 8). The only difference from the divorce court's jurisdiction is that applications may only be made for the benefit of the child, not the parent or carer.

(iv) The relevant criteria

In deciding whether, and if so how, to exercise its powers, the court is obliged to have regard to the following circumstances:[9]

(a) the income, earning capacity, property and other financial resources that the applicant, each parent[10] or any other person in whose favour the court proposes to make an order has or is likely to have in the near future;
(b the financial needs, obligations and responsibilities which the applicant, each parent or any other person in whose favour the court proposes to make an order has or is likely to have in the foreseeable future;
(c) the financial needs of the child;
(d) the income, earning capacity, property and other financial resources of the child; and
(e) any physical or mental disability of the child; and
(f) the manner in which the child is being educated or trained.

Thus, although an order, if made, is expressed as being for the child's benefit, the legislation recognises the importance of taking account of the carer's financial position as well as of the needs and resources of the child. Again, there is a striking similarity between these criteria and those governing the making of orders between married couples in the divorce and family proceedings court (see above and Ch 8).

A further similarity between the jurisdictions is that when making an order under Sch 1 against someone who is not the child's natural parent but who is caught by the 'child of the family' formula, the court must have regard to:

– whether that person assumed responsibility for the child's maintenance and, if so, on what basis and for how long;
– whether he or she did so in full knowledge of the facts of parenthood; and
– the liability of any other person, such as a natural parent, to maintain the child.[11]

9 CA 1989, Sch 1, para 4(1).
10 This includes those caught by the 'child of the family' formula, except where a person aged 18 or over is applying in his or her own right under para 2 (above), in which case it includes only the applicant's natural parents: para 4(4).
11 CA 1989, Sch 1, para 4(2). See also DPMCA 1978, s 3(4) and MCA 1973, s 25(4).

(v)   The end of marriage?

Although it remains to be seen how these powers will be used, they have the potential further to undermine the centrality of marriage in family law: for if a parent is able to use these provisions to obtain substantial transfers of income, capital and property, then the courts exercising this jurisdiction will be performing a role equivalent to that of the divorce court. The only difference will be that the parent applying has no entitlement in her or his own right; but, as we shall see in Ch 8, there are grounds for arguing that a wife's entitlement to share in family assets on divorce has in any case come to be increasingly centred on the presence of children. The trend towards treating parenthood rather than marriage as the primary focus of financial obligations of family members is further underlined by the government's scheme for the assessment and enforcement of child support, embodied in the Child Support Act 1991, to which we now turn. As we shall see, the support obligations created by that Act are unaffected by the marital status of a child's parents.

(d)   The Child Support Act 1991

The Child Support Act (CSA) 1991 received the Royal Assent on 25 July 1991 and is to be brought into force by regulations.[12] The main features of the Act were foreshadowed in a White Paper, *Children Come First* (Lord Chancellor's Department, 1990a). Reform of child maintenance laws has taken place in a number of common law countries. Most of the American states passed child support legislation in the 1970s and 1980s. Australia, whose child support scheme was looked at carefully by the British government when it was considering what to do, enacted the Child Support (Registration and Collection) Act 1988 and the Child Support (Assessment) Act 1989. New Zealand passed similar legislation in 1991.

Although there was certainly an element of one country learning from the experience of others in these developments, there was also an element of independent discovery in each jurisdiction that no-fault divorce laws, coupled with judicial discretion[13] to set levels of maintenance, may have failed the very people they were supposed to protect. Empirical research in Australia during the 1980s produced a chronicle of low incidence of court orders, low levels of maintenance

---

12 For discussion, see: Edwards and Halpern (1990b); Eekelaar (1991, Ch 5; 1991d; 1991e); Holmes (1991); Hayes (1991); Smith (1991); Bird (1991).
13 One should add here the discretion of parties to agree privately on levels of maintenance. For a discussion of the problematic aspects of settlements see 'Solicitors' in Ch 1 and 'Children's Rights' in Ch 3.

and low compliance rates. This was remarkably similar to research in England and Wales (see Parker 1991 and 1991a). The result was that sole parents and their children were shown to be some of the poorest people in the community and that social security was increasingly their primary means of support. A reviewer of both the English and Australian schemes need not be particularly cynical to conclude that social security saving was a greater spur to government action than the relief of poverty. The English legislation in particular will do little to benefit sole parents on income support (ie over 70% of sole parents) because every extra pound of child support being paid simply reduces income support by one pound.

Research commissioned for the English White Paper showed that only 30% of lone mothers and 3% of lone fathers in 1989 received regular child maintenance and that the average weekly maintenance was only £16. Maintenance formed less than 10% of lone parents' total net income compared with 45% for income support and 22% for net earnings (Lord Chancellor's Department, 1990, Vol 2, paras 1.4.4 and 5). It was also clear that, from the point of view of government expenditure, the position had worsened during the course of the decade. The proportion of lone parents claiming income support who also received some maintenance fell from 50% to 23% (Family Policy Studies Centre, 1991, p 3). In other words, income support was becoming an increasingly significant contributor to total income.

No doubt a variety of factors contributed to this situation. Going to court can be costly, slow and troublesome. Compliance with orders is notoriously low and enforcement difficult. The custodial parent, typically the mother, may want nothing further to do with a father who has disappeared from the lives of her children. She may fear that maintenance action will revive or exacerbate the difficulties or violence of the past relationship. Policy-makers, realising this, were increasingly attracted to the idea of bypassing the judicial system altogether in favour of administrative assessment of maintenance according to a formula. In this way, individual parents or the Legal Aid Fund would not have to bear the cost of litigation, there would be greater predictability over the amounts to be paid, enforcement could be taken out of the hands of the custodial parent and opting out could be curtailed where she was in receipt of income-tested benefits.

Another factor in the seeming decline in child maintenance needs to be mentioned. To some people, it was a positive factor which has been put in jeopardy by the CSA 1991. In the late 1970s a trend emerged in divorce cases towards a 'clean break'. The idea was to minimise continuing financial contact between former spouses in favour of a once and for all distribution of capital (see Ch 8).

Admittedly the clean break idea was never officially intended for situations where there were dependent children. Nevertheless, a custodial parent who settled for a higher percentage of the capital, and perhaps took all of the family home as a result, was in a more secure position than one who lost the home and who had to rely on an uncertain source of income in the other parent. Not surprisingly, solicitors acting for mothers often pressed for such a settlement and the courts commonly went along with it. The state might pay more in the way of income support because of this arrangement but it did not have to pick up the consequences of homelessness. As will be seen below, the future of the clean break is uncertain if, as is expected, regulations will preclude court orders which have as their consequence increased reliance on means-tested benefits. In addition, existing clean break settlements might be disrupted unless regulations make them secure. Nothing in the Act prevents a custodial parent now from applying for an assessment of child support even though she had agreed to forgo child maintenance in return for a capital sum.

The CSA 1991 will apply to all children, regardless of the marital status of their parents. Because the Act itself provides none of the amounts necessary to make use of the formulae in it, the following discussion gives only an outline of the method by which maintenance is to be calculated in future.

(i) *The duty to maintain and the basic principles*

For the purposes of the CSA 1991, each parent of a 'qualifying child' is responsible for maintaining her or him.[14] To reach the key concept of a 'qualifying child' one needs to make a daisy chain of other concepts, beginning with the meaning of 'child' in the Act.

In simplified form, a person is a child if he or she is an unmarried person under the age of 16 or under the age of 19 and receiving full-time, non-advanced education.[15] A child is a qualifying child if one or both parents are 'absent'.[16] An absent parent is one who is not living in the same household as the child, provided that the child has her or his home with a person who is 'a person with care'.[17] A person with care is a person with whom the child has her or his home, provided that the person usually provides day-to-day care for the child (whether exclusively or in conjunction with any other person),

14 CSA 1991, s 1(1).
15 Ibid, s 55(1) and (2).
16 Ibid, s 3(1).
17 Ibid, s 3(2).

and who does not fall within a prescribed category of person.[18] The Secretary of State cannot prescribe, inter alia, parents or guardians for these purposes.[19] Tying this all together, the normal situation when a child will be a qualifying child is where the child's parents have separated and the child is living only with one of them. It is irrelevant that the parent with care has repartnered.

An absent parent is taken to have met his responsibility to maintain the child by making such periodical payments of maintenance of such amount, and at such intervals, as are determined under the Act.[20] In particular, where a maintenance assessment is in force under the Act, then the absent parent must comply with it.[1] Payments required under a maintenance assessment are referred to as 'child support maintenance'.[2]

Leaving aside cases where a parent with care is receiving income support, family credit or other prescribed benefit (discussed below), either the absent parent or the person with care of the child may apply for a maintenance assessment.[3] Where the assessment is made, the Secretary of State may, if either party applies, arrange for the collection of the maintenance and enforcement of the obligation if there is default.[4] Potentially this is of considerable value to a custodial parent not on income support because she does not have to collect or enforce the payment of the maintenance and the money will actually benefit her rather than the state. It should be noted, however, that the Secretary of State is only *empowered* to collect and enforce the obligation. He or she is not *required* to do so. It is appropriate here to mention a general obligation in the Act imposed upon the Secretary of State and all child support officers (as they are to be called). Under s 2, in considering the exercise of any discretionary power conferred by the Act, they shall have regard to the welfare of any child likely to be affected by their decision. This statutory duty may be of some assistance in applying pressure on a reluctant official. Having said that, the welfare test here is of a limited nature. The requirement is only to 'have regard' to the child's welfare. If the Secretary of State does decide to collect and enforce the child support, a charge can be made for the service.[5]

18 CSA 1991, s 3(3).
19 Ibid, s 3(4)(a) and (b). Nor can the Secretary of State prescribe as a category persons in whose favour residence orders under s 8 of the Children Act 1989 are made (see Ch 3) or, in Scotland, persons having the right to custody of a child; s 3(4)(c) and (d).
20 Ibid, s 1(2).
1 Ibid, s 1(3).
2 Ibid, s 3(6).
3 Ibid, s 4(1).
4 Ibid, s 4(2).
5 Ibid, s 47.

Provision is made in the Act for cases where more than one person has care of a qualifying child.[6] The basic idea is that a person with parental responsibility is to apply. In the common case of a custodial mother who has repartnered, she will make the application because her new partner will not normally share parental responsibility for her child.

If a parent with care is receiving income support, family credit or other prescribed benefit, she can be *required* to authorise the Secretary of State to recover child support maintenance from the absent parent.[7] She cannot, however, be required to do so if the Secretary of State considers that there are reasonable grounds for believing that the parent or any child living with her would be at risk of suffering harm or undue distress.[8] This is likely to be a highly contentious aspect of the administration of the Act. The means test on income support means that many custodial mothers will not be better off if the father makes child support payments. It would be quite understandable if they wished to avoid opening up old wounds by authorising the Secretary of State to recover child support maintenance from him. One should note in this connection that the test is not whether, objectively, there *are* reasonable grounds for believing that the parent or child would be at risk of suffering harm or undue distress. It is whether the *Secretary of State* considers there are such grounds. This will make it much harder to review her or his decisions.

A parent with care who is in receipt of income support, family credit or other prescribed benefit must give the Secretary of State such information as the Secretary of State considers necessary to enable the absent parent to be traced and to enable child support maintenance to be assessed and recovered.[9] The obligation does not apply in prescribed circumstances (as yet unprescribed) or where the Secretary of State, in prescribed circumstances (also as yet unprescribed), waives it.[10] Failure without good cause to comply with an obligation under this section can lead to a 'reduced benefit direction' under s 46(5); meaning a direction that benefit can be reduced by such an amount, and for such a period, as is specified in the direction. The maximum amount and period are to be prescribed in regulations. This provision gave rise to considerable controversy when the Child Support Bill was being debated because it enables a woman who refuses to name the father of her child to be penalised through a reduction in her benefit.

6   CSA 1991, s 5.
7   Ibid, s 6(1).
8   Ibid, s 6(2).
9   Ibid, s 6(9).
10 Ibid, s 6(10).

Before giving a reduced benefit direction the child support officer must consider whether, having regard to any reasons given by the parent, there are reasonable grounds for believing that, if she were to be required to comply with the requirement there would be a risk of her or any children living with her suffering harm or undue distress as a result of complying.[11] If the child support officer considers that there are such reasonable grounds then he or she is to take no further action.

(ii) The place of the courts after the Child Support Act 1991

Section 8 of the CSA 1991 is the crucial section dealing with the future place of the courts in child maintenance. In any case where a child support officer has jurisdiction to make a maintenance assessment, no court is to exercise any power which it would otherwise have to make, vary or revive any maintenance order in relation to the child and absent parent concerned.[12] In other words, the courts' powers have not actually been abolished. They simply cannot be used where the CSA 1991 is applicable. Because it is anticipated that the Act will be brought into force in stages, the courts' powers will be available to those groups who still fall outside it. Even after the Act is fully in force, section 8 preserves the courts' powers in the following five circumstances.

Consent orders The Lord Chancellor may prescribe circumstances allowing a court to exercise its maintenance powers where there is already a written agreement for periodical payments for the child and the order the court makes is, in all material respects, in the same terms as the agreement.[13] The idea behind this exception is that consent orders can still be made. It is highly likely, however, that regulations will not allow such orders where they could lead to an increase in social security payments. If, therefore, the custodial parent is claiming income support, the court will presumably not be allowed to give effect to an agreement which could lead to her claiming more income support than she would be able to claim if there were an administrative assessment in force under the Act. This may well rule out some clean break arrangements which in the past enabled women to take a larger share in, or remain in occupation of, the matrimonial home in return for notionally reduced periodical payments in respect of the children. The exception does not apply at

---

11 CSA 1991, s 46(3). The limited welfare test in s 2, mentioned above, presumably also applies to this decision.
12 Ibid, s 8(3).
13 Ibid, s 8(5).

all where the agreement makes provision for the maintenance of children other than by periodical payments. The courts will not be allowed to convert these maintenance agreements into consent orders at all (at least in so far as children are concerned).

Even where the consent order does have effect because of the regulations, it will presumably not be secure. Section 9 of the Act preserves generally people's ability to make their own maintenance agreements but the existence of an agreement does not prevent either party from applying for a maintenance assessment. Any provision in the agreement purporting to restrict the right to apply for an assessment is void.[14]

The 'alternative formula'   It will be seen below that the normal formula for calculating child support does not apply in certain cases of high income. Here an alternative formula applies which operates to put a ceiling on the child support to be paid.[15] The courts will retain power to require payment of maintenance *in addition* to the maintenance assessed under the alternative formula.[16]

Educational expenses   The court can exercise its powers to order the payment of maintenance to meet expenses incurred in connection with the instruction of a child at an educational establishment or while the child is undergoing training for a trade, profession or vocation.[17]

Expenses of disability   The court can exercise its maintenance powers if the order is made solely for the purposes of meeting expenses attributable to a child's disability.[18] A child is treated as disabled if he or she is blind, deaf or dumb or is substantially and permanently handicapped by illness, injury, mental disorder or congenital deformity or such other disability as is prescribed.[19]

Order against parent with care   Since the changes made to the taxation of maintenance payments by the Finance Act 1988, the possible income tax advantages of an order against a custodial parent are much reduced. There may, however, be some residual and marginal advantages in particular cases.

In addition to these five cases where the courts will retain original jurisdiction to make maintenance orders, there is a curious provision

14 CSA 1991, s 9(3) and (4).
15 Ibid, Sch 1, para 4(3).
16 Ibid, s 8(6).
17 Ibid, s 8(7).
18 Ibid, s 8(8).
19 Ibid, s 8(9).

which seems to apply only to *existing* orders and agreements. Under s 10, the Secretary of State may prescribe conditions under which certain orders and agreements will cease to have effect or will have modified effect. Until the regulations have been made it is impossible to know what is contemplated but presumably the policy of saving social security expenditure will be a controlling factor.

We have been looking so far at circumstances where court orders can have effect despite the enactment of the CSA 1991. It should be remembered that the Act only applies to certain classes of people and there will be cases falling outside the Act altogether. Thus the courts will continue to make orders in respect of step-children[20] and children over the age of 18 who, for example, are undergoing higher education.[1]

(iii) Maintenance assessments under the statutory formula

The amount of child support to be fixed by an assessment is determined under Sch 1, Part 1 of the Act.[2] Provision is also made for interim maintenance assessments.[3] Although the values to be fed into the formula are not yet known, the government's prediction was that, in 1989 figures, the formula outlined in the White Paper would produce an average child maintenance assessment of about £40 per week, compared with an average assessment in the court-based system of £25 per week (Lord Chancellor's Department, 1990a, para 3.37).

The starting point in operating the formula is to work out the particular 'maintenance requirement' for the child or children in question. This represents the minimum amount assumed to be necessary for their maintenance.[4] It is arrived at by aggregating prescribed amounts, including amounts per child and in respect of the person with care, and then deducting the basic rate of child benefit.[5] The prescribed amounts will be the same as the income support allowances which would be paid for the children and person with care if they were entitled to income support. By pegging the formula to income support amounts, it is automatically updated with social security changes (which have, of course, been approved by Parliament).

Once the maintenance requirement for the children has been determined one has to work out how much should be contributed by

---

20 Section 23 of the Matrimonial Causes Act 1973 (see Ch 8) or Sch 1, para 4(2) of the Children Act 1989 (see p 149, above).
1 MCA 1973, s 29(3) and CA 1989, Sch 1, para 2.
2 CSA 1991, s 11(2).
3 Ibid, s 12.
4 Ibid, Sch 1, para 1.
5 Ibid, Sch 1, para 1(2)–(5).

the parents towards meeting it. Both parents, where they have sufficient income, are expected to contribute to the maintenance requirement from their 'assessable income'. This is net income (calculated in accordance with regulations) less exempt income (also calculated in accordance with regulations).[6] The exempt income is expected to be the amount necessary to cover daily expenses (based on income support amounts), reasonable housing costs and the costs of any of the parent's other children who are living with the parent. (The children of a new partner by someone else do not give rise to any increase in exempt income.)

It is assumed that in the vast majority of cases the parent with care will have no assessable income because her income will not be above her exempt level. This is because relatively few custodial parents have income that is higher than the income support allowances, although there will be many who, because they have repartnered, are not actually receiving income support. We begin by assuming that only the absent parent's income is to be fed into the formula.

Once one has the absent parent's assessable income (ie net income minus exempt income), a proportion is applied to it under what is called 'the general rule'.[7] The proportion is expected to be one-half. If, as is expected to be the case with 75% of parents, one-half of their assessable income is *less* than the maintenance requirement for the children, then the absent parent simply pays half of his assessable income as child support maintenance.[8]

The operation of the formula is best illustrated by a simple example, taken from the White Paper itself.

Marie and David have separated. They have two children: Sarah (5) and Mark (3). Sarah and Mark live with Marie.

The maintenance bill for Sarah and Mark will be:

	£ per week
Child allowances	24.70 *(allowance for a child aged under 11 is 12.35 on 1990–1991 figures)*
Family premium	7.35
Lone parent premium	4.19
Parent as carer	36.70 *(adult personal allowance)*
Total	72.85
Less child benefit	14.50 *(7.25 x 2)*
Total maintenance bill	**58.35 per week** *(rounded to 58)*

6   CSA 1991, Sch 1, para 5(1) and (2).
7   Ibid, Sch 1, para 2(1).
8   Ibid, Sch 1, para 2(2).

David is living alone in rented accommodation for which he pays a reasonable rent.

His exempt income will be:

	£ per week
Personal allowance	36.70 *(for single persons)*
Housing cost	31.00[9]
Total exempt income	**67.70** *(rounded to 68)*

David has a net income of £160 per week. Marie is not working and has no income to be taken into account.

David's assessable income is:

	£ per week
Net income	160 *(after tax and national insurance)*
Less exempt income	68 *(see above)*
Total assessable income	**92 per week**

David pays 50% of his assessable income in maintenance. This is £46 (28.8%) of his total net income. He keeps £114 (71.2%).

Where one-half of the absent parent's assessable income *exceeds* the maintenance requirement for the children then a more complex calculation is undertaken.[10] Maintenance does continue beyond the maintenance requirement because the maintenance requirement is only the *minimum* amount considered necessary for the children. In essence, one calculates the amount of income needed to meet the maintenance requirement (ie that amount of assessable income which, when halved, is equal to the maintenance requirement). The balance of the assessable income then has a lower rate applied to it; expected to be between 15% and 25%. This means that the children continue to receive maintenance from the absent father over and above their minimum requirement but they take fewer pence in the pound.

The formula has what might be called lower and upper limits. At the lower end, a liable parent is always to be left with a protected level of income so that he can meet inescapable financial obligations.[11] In this circumstance only, it is expected that his obligations to his current partner or step-children may be taken into

---

9 Said to be 'typical and for illustration'. This raises the concern that what is allowed for housing costs under the scheme will not reflect actual housing costs.

10 CSA 1991, Sch 1, paras 3 and 4.

11 Ibid, Sch 1, para 6.

account. The protected level of income will be set by reference to income support levels, including their housing costs, and an additional £5 per week margin. The effect is that he stops paying his assessed amount at the point when his weekly income would be taken below his protected level of earnings.

The upper limit on maintenance liability operates by virtue of an 'alternative formula' to be applied in working out the absent parent's liability where the children's maintenance requirement is exceeded.[12] It is to operate by putting a ceiling on the income that can be fed into the formula so that no maintenance will be deducted from income above the ceiling.[13]

Finally, the Act allows the Secretary of State to prescribe a minimum amount of maintenance to be paid, whatever the product of the formula. The White Paper mooted the possibility of £3 per week. This minimum cannot apply, however, in a case where s 43 operates or in other cases as may be prescribed. Section 43 deals with the case where an absent parent is receiving income support or other prescribed benefit. Ordinarily, such a parent is taken to have no assessable income.[14] Section 43, however, enables regulations to be made with a view to securing that payments of a prescribed amount (as yet unprescribed) are made in place of child support maintenance and that arrears of child support maintenance are recovered. It is expected that rules will provide that 5% of income support should be deducted and paid as maintenance. The White Paper justified this by saying that the personal responsibility to maintain children is too important a principle to be ignored just because a fit and able parent is on income support. He should be expected to contribute a 'nominal' 5% of his income support (Lord Chancellor's Department, 1990a, para 3.30). When one is living on the poverty line, the loss of 5% of one's income is hardly nominal and the real policy underlying this provision is probably more to do with discipline and punishment than the satisfaction of obligations.

In the small number of cases where the custodial parent *does* have income in excess of her exempt income level, she will be expected notionally to contribute towards the children's maintenance requirement (although no assessment is actually made against her).[15] One simply takes 50% of her assessable income and adds it to the absent parent's contribution (ie 50% of his assessable income). If the combined total still falls short of the children's maintenance

12 CSA 1991, Sch 1, para 4(3).
13 This is one of the occasions when a court is still permitted, by s 8(6), to make an order for maintenance. See above.
14 Ibid, Sch 1, para 5(4).
15 Of course, simply by caring for the children she will already be making a major contribution, in cash and in kind, to the maintenance of the children.

requirement then nothing further is done. If the total exceeds the children's maintenance requirement then provision is made for the parents to continue contributing, pro rata, at the reduced rate of 15–25% (depending on which figure the government ultimately chooses).

(iv) Termination of child support

A maintenance assessment under the Act terminates in a number of circumstances. In particular, it ceases to have effect on the death of the absent parent or the person with care; when there is no longer a qualifying child (for example because of reaching the age of 16); or when the absent parent and the person with care have lived together for a continuous period exceeding six months.[16]

(v) Disputes about parentage

The word 'parent' is not defined very helpfully in the CSA 1991. It means any person who is in law the mother or father of the child.[17] Section 26, however, deals specifically with disputes about parentage. Where there is a dispute, a child support officer must not make a child support assessment unless the case falls within one of those set out in s 26(2). In England and Wales, a person is a parent under that subsection if he or she:

– has adopted the child;
– is treated as such by s 30 of the Human Fertilisation and Embryology Act 1990 (see Ch 3 above);
– is declared as such by a declaration under section 56 of the Family Law Act 1986 (see Ch 3 above);
– is declared as such by a declaration under CSA 1991, s 27;[18] or
– is a man who has been found or adjudged to be the father in court proceedings and that finding or adjudication still subsists.

Somewhat curiously, the presumption of legitimacy (unlike in Australia and unlike the comparable presumption in Scottish law) does not apply here.[19] It follows that the husband of a woman who conceives a child during the marriage cannot be assumed by a child support officer to be the father. This makes it possible for a husband

---

16 See generally CSA 1991, Sch 1, para 16.
17 Ibid, s 54.
18 This section permits a child support officer to apply to the court for a declaration that the alleged parent is one of the child's parents.
19 The presumption of legitimacy is discussed in Ch 3.

to deny paternity, even though he knows full well that he is the father of the child, as a way of stalling the application for child support and forcing an application to the court. The husband might ultimately be penalised in costs but it seems odd that he should even be given the opportunity of strategic advantage.

(vi) Administrative machinery

The government proposes a complex administrative machine to implement the CSA 1991. A Child Support Agency has been established within the Department of Social Security and its staff is expected to grow to about 4,700. The Act provides for the appointment of child support officers[20] to make maintenance assessments and of inspectors to collect information.[1] Assessments will be reviewed periodically[2] or where circumstances change[3] or where the parents believe that the assessment was made in ignorance of a material fact, was based on a mistake as to a material fact or was wrong in law.[4] An appeal system is created so that appeals from reviews and refusals to review go to a child support appeal tribunal.[5] Further appeal is to a Child Support Commissioner on a question of law.[6] Appeal onwards is to a court, with the leave of the Commissioner or the court.

The collection and enforcement of maintenance assessments is primarily in the hands of child support officers. (For those custodial parents fortunate enough not to lose income support or family credit by the same amount as they receive child support, this is one of the significant advantages of the new legislation over the old system because a government department can shoulder the responsibility of tracing the absent parent and extracting money from him.) The Secretary of State may make a deduction from earnings order so that the employer of a liable parent must make payments direct to the Child Support Agency.[7] Alternatively, regulations may provide for other methods of payment so that maintenance can, for example, be paid direct to the custodial parent, by standing order or otherwise.

Where a liable parent is in default the Secretary of State may apply to a magistrates' court for a liability order so that the appropriate amount may be raised by distress and sale of goods.[8] It seems that,

20 CSA 1991, s 13.
1   Ibid, s 15.
2   Ibid, s 16.
3   Ibid, s 17.
4   Ibid, s 18(6).
5   Ibid, s 20.
6   Ibid, s 24.
7   Ibid, s 31.
8   Ibid, ss 33 and 35.

subject to regulations not yet made, the magistrate must make the liability order if satisfied that there has been default.[9] Alternatively, a county court can recover the debt by means of a garnishee or charging order.[10] If all else fails, the Secretary of State may apply to a magistrates' court for a warrant committing the absent parent to prison. This can only be granted if, inter alia, the court is of the opinion that there has been wilful refusal or culpable neglect on the part of the absent parent.[11]

To the disappointment of some people, the enforcement and collection system differs from that operating in Australia. There, the Child Support Agency is established within the Australian Taxation Office rather than the Department of Social Security. The formula is based upon taxable income from previous years (all of which information is already in the possession of taxation officials) and the child support is *routinely* collected by direct deduction from earnings. Indeed, it is relatively difficult to arrange for any alternative method of payment. Although one can say this of all legislation, it is especially true of the CSA 1991 that only time will tell whether it achieves the practical benefits for custodial parents and financial benefits for the Exchequer that the government claimed when the Bill was being debated.

Welfare benefits

(a) Introduction

The importance of welfare benefits provided by the state to an understanding of the economic position of families cannot be overestimated. This is particularly so in relation to those families who are separated or divorced. There is a close link between marriage breakdown and single parenthood, in that most single parents (most of whom are women) are either divorced or separated (Haskey 1986, Fig 1); there is also, in turn, a close link between single parenthood and poverty, in the sense that a single parent family is more likely than a dual parent family to be reliant on the 'safety net' provisions of the welfare state (DHSS 1986a; Lord Chancellor's Department 1990a, Vol 2). Indeed, as we have seen, it was largely because the state shoulders much of the economic cost of

9 CSA 1991, s 33(3).
10 Ibid, s 36. In practice this will mean that the debt may be recovered from an absent parent's bank account or by an order for the sale of his home.
11 Ibid, s 40.

single parenthood that the government took steps to improve recovery of maintenance from absent parents. It has been said that the welfare state provides a 'third system of family law', operating alongside those of the divorce and magistrates' courts, a significant proportion of whose clients are single women with children (see Ch 9 for further discussion). The implementation of the Child Support Act will formalise the relationship between the different systems by excluding the courts' jurisdiction over income maintenance in most cases (see above).

Until the CSA 1991 is implemented, the nature of the interrelation between this third system and the other two is determined by a number of factors. For example, the most significant benefit, income support, is means-tested in such a way that the receipt by a claimant of private maintenance through court proceedings may serve only to reduce the claimant's level of entitlement to the state benefit. This offers the claimant little incentive to pursue a private claim, which may simply replace a steady source of income (income support) with an erratic one (maintenance); but it offers a considerable incentive to the state to encourage use of private claims as a way of reducing the call on its resources. This goes some way to explaining the existence of the 'liable relative' and 'diversion' procedures (see below), and lies at the heart of the CSA 1991. Another question that arises is the extent to which the courts, operating within one of the first two 'systems' of family law, should take into account the availability of state support when fixing the level of maintenance in the event of a private claim being brought. This is discussed further in Chapter 9.

What follows is an outline of those types of benefit that are most important in the context of family breakdown. It will be seen that, without exception, the benefits discussed here fall into only one of the two main categories of state benefit, namely, non-contributory benefits. There is no discussion of the other type of benefit, contributory benefits, even though many of these (such as pensions, widow's benefits and maternity benefits) may be relevant to a full understanding of family economics. The reason for this is that the system of contributory benefits, as introduced by the National Assistance Act 1948 following the scheme of the Beveridge Report on *Social Insurance and Allied Services* (1942), is not at all geared to the needs of single parents following a marital breakdown. Instead, it is premised on the assumption that married women will derive benefits from the scheme, not as contributors in their own right, but as dependants of their husbands: their entitlement derives from their spouse's contribution (see Land 1976, 1983; Wilson 1977, Ch 7). Such a scheme is ill-adapted to providing for women with dependent children who may have lost entitlement to their husband's benefits, but who have made no significant contributions in their own right. Beveridge's original scheme included a proposal to provide 'innocent' separated wives with a temporary separation benefit along the lines of the widow's benefit, but it was never implemented (Finer and McGregor 1974, paras 89–111).

The law in this area was changed by the Social Security Act 1986 (as subsequently amended[12]), which came into force in April 1988. The following discussion is based on that legislation.

(b) Income support

This is the most important state benefit of all for present purposes since it provides a 'safety net' guarantee of a minimum level of income. Although originally it was thought that the need for this benefit would gradually disappear through rising employment and the spread of the state insurance scheme, it has in fact retained a preeminence, especially for single parents. Income support (previously known as supplementary benefit) works on the basis of making up the difference between an individual's income and other resources (as defined) and his or her needs (as defined). What follows is only an outline, with particular emphasis on the place of parents and children in the statutory scheme.

(i) Eligibility

Any person aged over 18 who is not engaged in remunerative work, and whose partner (married or unmarried) is not so engaged, and whose income does not exceed their needs ('the applicable amount') is eligible to claim income support.[13] In most cases, entitlement depends on the claimant being available for work[14] but this does not apply to a lone parent (which includes separated parents[15]) solely responsible for the care of dependent children.[16]

(ii) Who can claim for whom?

In the case of married couples, or of unmarried couples who are living together as husband and wife (see Ch 3), the income and applicable amounts of the couple are aggregated, together with those

---

12 Social Security Acts 1988, 1989.
13 Social Security Act 1986, s 20(3).
14 Income Support (General) Regulations 1987, regs 7–11 (as amended by the Income Support (General) Amendment No 2 Regulations 1989.
15 IS(G)R 1987, r 2(1), 16.
16 IS(G)R 1987, reg 8 and Sch 1.

of any dependent children[17] resident in the same household.[18] Only one adult, which may be either the man or the woman, may claim on behalf of the family unit.[19] It is only once the partners separate and are no longer members of the same 'household' that they will be treated as individuals for claiming purposes, although the partner with children will continue to claim on the children's behalf as well. Lone parents also claim on their own and their children's behalf.

(iii)   Calculating the amount

Since the level of income support is defined as the amount by which a claimant's income falls short of his or her needs, the actual amount payable will depend on a calculation of the two elements of needs ('the applicable amount') and resources.

Needs – the 'applicable amount'   An individual's needs and those for whom an individual is claiming are defined in the legislation according to an annually revised scale of personal allowances and additional 'premiums'. These amounts are deemed adequate to cover all items of normal expenditure, with the exception of certain housing costs which are covered separately by housing benefit. At present, the rates are as follows:[20]

(1) Single claimant aged –
    (a) under 18   £23.65
    (b) 18–25   £31.15
    (c) over 25   £39.65
(2) Lone parent aged –
    (a) under 18   £23.65
    (b) over 18   £39.65
(3) Couple –
    (a) both under 18   £47.30
    (b) one over 18   £62.25
(4) Children –
    (a) under 11   £13.35
    (b) 11–16   £19.75
    (c) 16–18   £23.65
    (d) over 18   £31.15

17 Defined in IS(G)R 1987, regs 15 and 16.
18 SSA 1986, s 20(11), (12)(k). The term 'household' is not defined.
19 IS(G)R 1987, reg 17; Social Security (Claims and Payments) Regulations 1987, reg 4(3) .
20 IS(G)R 1987, Sch 2; Social Security Benefit Uprating Regulations 1991.

In addition, there are available:

(i) the family premium, available to a claimant who is a member of a family which includes at least one child or young person, worth £7.95; and

(ii) the lone parent premium, available to lone parents, worth £4.45.

The family and lone parent premiums may be claimed together. In the case, therefore, of a single parent aged 20 with two children aged under 11, the 'applicable amount' will be £78.75, consisting of:

(a) a personal allowance of £39.65;
(b) two allowances of £13.35 in respect of the children;
(c) the family premium of £7.95; and
(d) the lone parent premium of £4.45.

Limited assistance is also available under the income support scheme for certain housing costs, mainly assistance with repayments of mortgage interest. The proportion of such repayments that are met under the scheme varies according to the age of the claimant and the period of time for which the claimant has been receiving income support.[1]

Resources The 'applicable amount' defines the minimum level of income to which an individual is considered entitled. The extent to which this may be claimed from the state depends on the other resources an individual (or couple) has available to them. It is only if these other resources fall short of the 'applicable amount' that an entitlement to income support arises.[2] For these purposes, 'resources' fall into three main categories:

(a) Income in the form of net earnings from employment or self-employment, both of the claimant, the claimant's partner or the children of the claimant.[3] Certain amounts of earnings are 'disregarded' in the calculation of resources. At present, this stands at £5 of the claimant's and claimant's partner's earnings. If the lone parent premium is or would be included in the calculation of the claimant's 'applicable amount', the disregard rises to £15.[4] In its White Paper on child support, the government rejected the possibility of increasing these disregards as a means of encouraging lone parents back into the job market (Lord Chancellor's Department 1990a, Ch 6).

1 See IS(G)R 1987, Sch 3.
2 SSA 1986, ss 20(3)(b), 21.
3 IS(G)R 1987, Chs II–IV.
4 IS(G)R 1987, Sch 8.

(b) Income from other sources is included.[5] For present purposes, it is important to note that this includes other social security benefits such as child benefit and one parent benefit. It also includes maintenance payments (either periodic or by lump sum) made by a spouse or ex-spouse, whether voluntarily or by court order, and whether to the spouse or ex-spouse in his or her own right or for the benefit of children.[6] There is no 'disregard' applicable to maintenance payments, which explains why many women who are dependent on income support will be in no better position if they claim maintenance, since anything they receive simply diminishes their entitlement to income support. This will also be the case under the CSA 1991.

Again, the government has rejected the possibility of introducing disregards for maintenance payments in calculating entitlement to income support. The White Paper argued that 'if maintenance were to be received in addition to income support payments then the custodial parent would have to earn a higher salary to be as well off in work. So it would act as a disincentive to going to work and further frustrate the ambitions which parents have for themselves' (1990a, para 6.6). Instead, the government proposes to introduce more generous disregards for maintenance payments in respect of those benefits payable to those already in work: family credit, housing benefit and community charge benefit. The policy is clearly to offer incentives to caring parents to enter the job market, rather than to assist those on income support.

(c) Capital is regarded as a resource, and if a claimant or a claimant's partner possesses capital (as defined) worth more than £8,000, all entitlement to income support is lost.

Further, capital over a certain amount is treated as producing a notional income for the claimant's benefit, whether or not that income actually accrues. A claimant's primary dwelling house is not treated as a capital asset for these purposes.[7]

(iv) The liable relative[8]

The Social Security Act 1986 imposes a duty of support on certain categories of relative of income support claimants, the effect of which is to enable the DSS to recover money paid out by way of income

---

5   IS(G)R 1987, Ch V.
6   IS(G)R 1987, Ch VII.
7   IS(G)R 1987, Ch VI.
8   See Webb (1988).

support or from the social fund (see below) from those liable.[9] For present purposes, the two most important categories of liable relative are:[10]

(i)   spouses (but not ex-spouses), who are liable to maintain each other; and
(ii) parents (married, divorced or unmarried) who are liable to maintain their children.

As a result of changes introduced by the Social Security Act 1990,[11] the DSS may also take proceedings to recover any amount they have paid to a custodial parent in her own right where the DSS has been paying income support to the custodial parent for both her own and the children's maintenance. This amounts to the creation of a support obligation between unmarried parents *to each other*, but only where the custodial parent is on income support and caring for the natural child(ren) of the liable parent. The obligation of the liable relative is enforceable by the DSS in civil and, in extreme cases, criminal proceedings.[12]

If, at the time of an application for income support, it appears to the DSS, from information which the claimant is obliged to supply,[13] that there is a liable relative who is failing to support the claimant, the DSS will contact the liable relative and will, if no maintenance proceedings are being brought by the claimant, assess an amount for the liable relative to pay to the claimant according to the 'liable relative formula' and bring proceedings for that amount. This formula, which is entirely non-statutory and was publicly revealed for the first time by the Finer Committee Report (1974, paras 4.188– 4.190), assesses as payable a sum that will leave the liable relative with an amount equal to the current applicable amounts for himself and any new members of his household together with the equivalent of current housing benefit levels, plus an additional allowance of either £5 or a quarter of his net earnings. This leaves the liable relative in a more favourable position than the courts would if awarding maintenance in private proceedings (see Ch 9).

If, according to this formula, the liable relative is unable to relieve the DSS entirely of the obligation to provide income support, the DSS may invoke the 'diversion procedure' under which the liable relative makes payments to the DSS who in turn pay the claimant

---

9   SSA 1986, ss 24, 24A, 33(7); Income Support (Liable Relatives) Regulations 1990.
10 SSA 1986, s 26(3).
11 SSA 1990, s 8, inserting a new SSA 1986, s 24A.
12 SSA 1986, ss 24(1), 26(1).
13 SS(C and P)R 1987, reg 7(1) .

her income support in full.[14] This procedure is also useful where the liable relative's payments are erratic. It is also open to the claimant to pursue her own remedies under the matrimonial legislation; but, for reasons already discussed, she may have little incentive, and DSS local offices should not bring pressure to bear on claimants to do so. Nevertheless, there is evidence that some local offices do precisely that (Priest and Whybrow 1986, para 2.7).

The SSA 1990 also empowers the DSS to revive claims against liable relatives, to enforce periodical payments orders on behalf of an income support recipient and to transfer orders against liable relatives to the income support recipient.[15] Concern has been expressed that the power to revive claims against a liable relative for the personal allowance element paid to a custodial parent for her own benefit could threaten the security of 'clean break' arrangements sanctioned in the divorce court (Wood 1991). For example, a liable relative who has agreed in divorce proceedings to give up his share in the matrimonial home in return for a reduction of periodical payments may find himself being pursued by the DSS for contributions to the cost of the custodial parent's income support.[16] As we shall see in Chapter 8, the same point could be made of the CSA 1991.

One of the more worrying changes introduced by the 1986 Act is the inclusion of payments from the social fund (see below) within the liable relative procedure. Lone parents who have financial needs not covered by the basic level of income support may be discouraged from applying to the social fund for additional help for fear of antagonising a spouse or ex-spouse by increasing their level of enforceable obligation to the DSS.

(v) Passported benefits

Those entitled to income support are automatically entitled to certain other benefits, such as free prescriptions, free dental treatment, milk tokens and free vitamins (for certain groups) and free school meals. These are also available to those in receipt of certain other benefits.

14 Income Support Manual (HMSO, 1988), paras 1015–1019.
15 SSA 1986, s 24A (inserted by SSA 1990, s 8).
16 SSA 1986, s 24A(7) (inserted by SSA 1990).

(c) The social fund

The social fund provisions of the Social Security Act 1986[17] replace the previous system of single payments and urgent needs payments with a new system of grants and loans. The purpose of such a scheme is to recognise that the basic rates of benefit may be insufficient to cover all needs, and that assistance may be needed with certain items such as furniture, bedding or clothing. However, the new social fund differs from the previous system in four major respects. First, each local 'Social Fund Officer', whose job it is to decide whether to grant applications for payment, has to work within a cash-limited budget and cannot make payments that exceed the cash limit.[18] Second, the decision of the Social Fund Officer is entirely discretionary, and is to be made according to the statutory criteria, directions issued by the Secretary of State and the guidance contained in the Social Fund Manual.[19] Third, the majority of payments will be in the form of recoverable loans rather than outright payments, although the precise conditions of any payment are at the Social Fund Officer's discretion. The loans will be recoverable from the claimant through the deduction of benefit, from the claimant's partner and from any liable relative.[20] Finally, there is no provision for an independent appeal against the decision of an officer; instead, there is a system of internal appeal.[1]

Although the purpose of the new scheme is to target money at those most in need of it, many claimants will be discouraged from applying for assistance by the fact that they may be required to repay money received by them and, for reasons already discussed, by the fact that it may be recoverable from a liable relative. It is also the case that assistance may be unavailable because of lack of money at the disposal of the local officer.

(d) Family credit

Family credit, which replaces and modifies family income supplement, is a benefit available to families on low incomes in full-time remunerative employment, defined as remunerative work of 24 hours a week or more. It is thus claimed instead of income support. To

17 Sections 32–35 (as amended by the SSA 1988, 1990).
18 SSA 1986, s 32(8), (9).
19 SSA 1986, s 33(9), (10).
20 SSA 1986, s 33.
1 SSA 1986, s 34.

qualify, a family (which includes married and unmarried couples and single parents[2]) must include at least one child or young person for which the claimant or the claimant's partner is responsible.[3]

Like income support, family credit is a means-tested benefit, and there are rules governing the calculation of income (which includes maintenance payments) and capital resources. The resources of couples, whether married or unmarried, are aggregated, and only one of the partners, usually the woman, may claim.[4] The amount of family credit payable depends on whether the family's income does or does not exceed the 'threshold amount' (currently £62.25 per week). If it does not, then family credit is payable at the full rate, currently £38.30 for an adult and a sum of between £9.70 to £27.95 per child depending on the child's age. If it does exceed the 'threshold amount', the amount of family credit is calculated as the full rate minus 70% of any income in excess of the threshold amount.[5] These rates are set at a level which ensures that those in full-time remunerative employment and dependent on family credit are better off than those who depend on income support. The government proposes to introduce disregards of maintenance payments in calculating entitlement to family credit and to reduce the number of hours of work required before eligibility accrues from 24 to 16 hours a week (Lord Chancellor's Department 1990a, Ch 6).

(e) **Child benefit and one parent benefit**

Child benefit is a universal, non-means-tested, non-contributory benefit payable to anyone with responsibility for a child.[6] It is not taxable, but is counted as income for income support purposes. It is payable by monthly cashable orders, hence directly to mothers or carers. One parent benefit is an additional benefit payable to single parents in respect of the first child of the family only. At present, child benefit is £7.25 pw for each child (together with an additional £1 for the eldest or only child) and one parent benefit is £5.60 pw.

(f) **Conclusion**

One of the purposes of the framework introduced by the 1986 Act was to target benefits more directly at families on low incomes with children and to bring the structure of benefits more into line with the

2 SSA 1986, s 20(11).
3 SSA 1986, s 20(5).
4 Family Credit (General) Regulations 1987.
5 FC(G)R 1987, regs 46–48, Sch 4.
6 Child Benefit Act 1975; Child Benefit (General) Regulations 1976.

structure of tax allowances for families. However, the current framework retains many of the features of the old. For example, the liable relative procedure is not only retained but is extended to cover social fund payments and (in certain circumstances) unmarried couples. Nor is there any special recognition of the needs of single parents beyond the provision of slightly higher rated benefits for lone parents; the Finer (1974) proposal that single parents be paid a substantial allowance (a 'guaranteed maintenance allowance') combined with a total disregard for maintenance payments and a substantial disregard for earnings is no nearer to being a reality. It seems unlikely that the significance of the Social Security system as the 'third system' of family law is to be much reduced.

Chapter 5

Property

Introduction

The previous chapter concerned the entitlement of family members to a share in the household income. By contrast, this chapter is concerned with the rules governing the ownership of property – that is, things that can be bought, sold and given away according to recognised legal principles – by spouses and their non-marital equivalents.

Two preliminary points may be made. The first is that what lawyers count as 'property' is much narrower than one might expect. In particular, it does not include many things that in a modern economy constitute access to resources necessary for the support of the means of life, such as pensions, welfare benefits and other job-related benefits (MacPherson 1978; Glendon 1981). Second, the most significant item of property (in the lawyer's sense) for most families will be the owner-occupied family home. This is a direct result of shifting patterns of land tenure, towards owner occupation, since the last war (see Ball 1983, Chs 1 and 2). For this reason, land law has increasingly become the necessary framework within which the claims of family members to land (in the shape of the family home) have been balanced against the assumed requirements of conveyancers and those for whom land is a commercial asset; and yet this framework is premised on the quite different pattern of family land tenure of the early twentieth century (Murphy and Clark 1984, Ch 1; Murphy and Roberts 1987, Ch 8). This has inevitably led to a good deal of complexity as the courts have sought to accommodate these different needs.

Despite the fact that divorce courts now have an extensive jurisdiction to override the strict rules of ownership on divorce (considered in Ch 8, below), there are many reasons why the rules discussed in this chapter continue to be of importance.[1]

---

1 See also the comments of the Law Commission (1988c) at para 1.4.

(a) A starting point in divorce

Although the divorce court has extensive power to override legal titles to property, the court can only consider the use of its powers once it knows what the parties' respective financial positions are. In most cases, this may simply involve a comparison of the parties' incomes; but it may also involve ascertaining what property each party owns.[2]

(b) Unmarried couples

The power to allocate matrimonial property on divorce does not extend to unmarried couples. For that reason, the property-owning consequences of a non-marital relationship have to be resolved within the terms of the principles outlined in this chapter, excepting those statutory amendments to the law of property which apply only to husband and wife.

(c) Third parties

Whether the parties are married or not, an issue may arise concerning the priority of interest as between one or both parties and a third party in relation to an item of property. The best example of this would be a dispute between a party and a mortgagee with respect to the matrimonial home.[3] The outcome of this dispute would at present turn on the principles discussed here.

(d) Death or bankruptcy of one of the parties

Although the proprietorial consequences of both these events are now to a large extent regulated by statute, the strict question of how much the dead or bankrupt party owned in his or her own right will provide the starting point for the application of these statutory rules.

(e) Power and control

Quite apart from these technical considerations, the formal legal position as to the ownership of family property will be of considerable symbolic and practical significance when disputes arise between parties over how the property is to be dealt with. The relevant legal rules are important statements of principle within which couples may

2 See, eg, *Harwood v Harwood* [1991] 2 FLR 274.
3 Eg, *Williams and Glyn's Bank v Boland* [1981] AC 487; [1980] 2 All ER 408.

arrange their affairs. They also effect a distribution of the powers of management over matrimonial property. For example, the fact that a spouse has rights in the family enforceable against a mortgagee[4] will give him or her a de facto right to be consulted in advance of any mortgage transaction.

A distinctive feature of English law on this matter is that, unlike many other jurisdictions,[5] there is no special regime of rules for determining issues of ownership for these purposes. Instead, there is a complex amalgam of different rules of common law and equity, together with various piecemeal statutory reforms. This makes it difficult to state the law either briefly or simply.

Background to the present law[6]

Like continental civilian systems, the common law imposed on married couples a special legal regime governing the ownership of matrimonial property. But whereas the civil law established a 'community of property' between the spouses, the common law, with some exceptions, effectively subordinated all the wife's property and earnings to the husband's ownership and control. Thus, a wife's chattels vested absolutely in the husband, including those acquired by her own earnings; the earnings themselves also belonged to the husband. The wife's freeholds became subject to the husband's control on marriage, and he was entitled to leasehold income and to the leaseholds themselves if the wife predeceased him.

From the seventeenth century onwards, the Chancery courts alleviated the hardship of the common law rules through the device of the wife's separate equitable estate by which property was settled

---

4   See *Boland*, above.
5   For a comparative study of matrimonial property regimes, see Rheinstein and Glendon (1980) and Freedman et al (1988); and for a comparison of the relevant laws of France, Germany, the United States and England, see Glendon (1989), pp 110–140. Glendon concludes that, despite a degree of convergence between the different regimes, there remain three areas of divergence: (i) the scope of the limits imposed on spouses' freedom to deal with property during marriage; (ii) the degree of certainty as to how property will be distributed on divorce; and (iii) the extent to which spouses may contract out of the relevant regime (see pp 134–135). The Law Commission concluded from its review of comparative community of property regimes that 'experience shows that a community system which does not permit independent management during marriage is unacceptable, hence the move in countries which have community of property towards more independent management and more deferred community'(1988c, para 3.6). For further discussion of community of property regimes, see the final section of this chapter.
6   For a brief historical survey, see Pahl (1989) Ch 2.

to the wife's 'sole and separate use', and thereby escaped the common law regime. However, this device was as much to preserve the property for the benefit of the wife's family as for the benefit of the wife herself. It was in any case only readily available to wealthier families and was of no relevance to those women for whom the important issue was income maintenance and the right to control their own wages (Minor 1979). Reform of the common law position became an important focus of nineteenth-century liberal and feminist politics (Holcombe 1977, 1983).

After two false starts in 1857 and 1870, the common law system was finally abrogated in 1882 by the Married Women's Property Act. This, in effect, extended the principle of the equitable separate estate to all married women without the need for trustees, with the effect that all wives were capable of acquiring and owning their own property free from the legal interference of their husbands. However, it should be remembered that the Act did little more than establish a very formal legal equality between husband and wife. It left untouched the rules governing the acquisition of property so that where couples organise themselves according to the traditional sexual division of labour – that is, where the wife stays at home while the husband goes out to work (Edgell 1980) – these rules tend in practice to favour property acquisition by men.

This principle of separation of property, which accords ownership to the person providing the purchase money, is thus considered to operate unfairly in the context of a typical domestic economy (O'Donovan 1985, pp 112–118). It is also out of step with partners' own views that marriage is a partnership involving a sharing of jointly-acquired and jointly-used property (Todd and Jones 1972, pp 38–40; Manners and Rauta 1981, pp 12–17). Further, by comparison with community of property regimes, it is uncertain in its effects, especially where the parties have not formalised their property relationship in ways recognised by the law, since the law as to precisely what counts as provision of the purchase price for these purposes is unclear. This uncertainty is further compounded by the piecemeal nature of statutory reforms to the law of matrimonial property, especially the family home.

Section 17 of the Act of 1882 empowered the courts to hear and resolve disputes as to the possession and ownership of matrimonial property, and to make such order as they 'thought fit'. Until 1970, with some relatively minor exceptions,[7] this section was the primary means by which the matrimonial property was divided up on divorce. Increasingly, as a consequence of the growth from the 1930s onwards of owner-occupation, the courts came to deal with disputes

7 MCA 1963, s 5(1); MCA 1965, ss 17(1), (2).

concerning the family home under s 17, within the framework of the separate property principle (see Deech 1984). The importance of s 17 is now much diminished, following the introduction in 1970 of discretionary powers on divorce (now MCA 1973; see below, Ch 8); but the principles evolved in those cases[8] are of significance in that they form the basis on which disputes over property are resolved in those cases where strict questions of ownership are still relevant, whether between married or de facto couples, and whether under s 17 or not.

Personal property

As far as family members are concerned, the most important items of personal property will most likely be money and other financial assets, such as stocks and shares, and consumer goods such as cars, furniture and household appliances. Disputes over the ownership of such items are only likely to occur where they are of considerable value.

The basic rules applicable to such items are easy to state. Where money has been earned as income, it will belong to the earner. Property belonging to spouses at the time of marriage (or to de facto partners at the commencement of their relationship) remains the property of the owning partner; and property received by the spouses as gifts belong to them as the donor intended. Other items belong to the person providing the purchase money for them.[9] These rules favour property acquisition by the spouse with a substantial or steady income (often the husband) and it is difficult for spouses to bring about joint ownership of personal property within these rules even where that is what they intend, or would intend if they thought about it (Law Commission 1988c, paras 2.1–2.4). However, these rules are subject to modification in certain circumstances.

(a) **Pooled income**

Where both parties pool their income, from whatever source and in whatever proportion, that fund shall belong to the parties in equal shares as joint tenants.[10] The best example of this would be where the parties operate a joint bank account. However, the contents of a joint

---

8   Especially *Pettitt v Pettitt* [1970] AC 777; *Gissing v Gissing* [1971] AC 886.
9   *Re Vinogradoff* [1935] WN 68; *Heseltine v Heseltine* [1971] 1 All ER 952.
10   *Jones v Maynard* [1951] Ch 572; [1951] 1 All ER 802.

bank account will not automatically be subject to joint ownership where the money is provided exclusively by one spouse unless the parties clearly intended this to occur.[11] However, if the husband is the sole provider, the presumption of advancement (discussed below) may operate in the wife's favour. Ownership of any property bought with money drawn from the joint fund will also depend on evidence of the parties' intentions.[12] It may also depend on the nature of the property bought so that, for example, it might be reasonable to assume that items such as clothing would be owned by the partner for whose use they were bought.

(b) Gifts between partners

Gifts between partners take effect subject to the normal rules concerning the transfer of legal title to chattels. However, the question of beneficial entitlement is determined by certain equitable presumptions. The first of these, the presumption of resulting trust, assumes that wherever A makes a voluntary transfer to B (that is, without receiving consideration), the beneficial entitlement to the property remains with, or 'results to', A under an imputed trust.[13] This may be rebutted by evidence that a gift was in fact intended. It may also be rebutted by the second presumption, that of 'advancement', which assumes as between certain groups of people the necessary intention to make a gift. In particular, it makes this assumption with respect to transfers from husbands to wives, but not vice versa, from parents to children and from a person to a child to whom he stands *in loco parentis*.[14] It may also be rebutted (see Maitland 1936, pp 77–80).

The presumption of advancement is rooted in the notion that husbands and parents are under an 'equitable obligation' to provide for their wives and children respectively. The one-sidedness of the presumption as between husbands and wives may be thought to be undermined by the fact that spouses are now equally liable by statute to maintain each other.[15] The current status of these presumptions is

---

11 See *Heseltine*, above.
12 Compare *Jones v Maynard* [1951] Ch 572, [1951] 1 All ER 802 with *Re Bishop* [1965] Ch 450, [1965] 1 All ER 249.
13 *Fowkes v Pascoe* (1875) 19 Ch App 343
14 See *Bennet v Bennet* (1879) 10 Ch D 474; *Shepherd v Cartwright* [1955] AC 431; *Silver v Silver* [1958] 1 All ER 523; *Sekhon v Alissa* [1989] 2 FLR 94 (presumption of resulting trust not rebutted by evidence of gift or loan in a transaction between mother and daughter, and satisfied by the granting to the mother of a lease of a defined part of the premises).
15 See DPMCA 1978, s 1; MCA 1973, s 21.

unclear following the House of Lords' decision in *Pettitt*. While the majority view appeared to be that the presumption of advancement is now of much reduced force as between husband and wife, the actual range of views ran from Lord Diplock who considered it virtually obsolete,[16] to Lord Upjohn, who considered the presumption to offer a common-sense method of resolving disputes.[17]

The absence of further litigation to resolve this point reflects the fact that most disputes over property concern the family home, or arise between de facto partners. The presumption of advancement is unhelpful in resolving disputes of the former kind, owing to the instalment nature of modern house purchase by mortgage (Murphy and Clark 1984, pp 34–35); and it has no application to the latter. The resulting trust, however, is of central significance in both instances.

(c) Housekeeping allowances and other transfers of money between partners

For those wives who do not have an income of their own, it may be that the only money they receive, apart from child benefit (see Ch 4), is in the form of an allowance from their spouse for household expenses (see Pahl 1980; 1984; 1989 for discussion of the different forms such arrangements might take[18]). At common law, such money was regarded as belonging to the husband, including any money saved from the allowance and anything purchased with those savings.[19] The Married Women's Property Act 1964 altered this rule

16 At p 824; see also *Calverly v Green* (1985) 85 ALJR 111, per Murphy J.

17 At p 815.

18 Pahl (1989, Ch 5) identifies four systems of money management: (i) the wife management/whole wage system, in which one partner (usually the wife) is responsible for managing all household finances; (ii) the allowance system, in which the husband makes a regular allowance to the wife for specified items of expenditure (to which she will add child benefit and her own earnings, if any), retaining the rest for himself; (iii) the pooling/shared management system, which involves the operation of a joint account or 'pool' into which both parties pay earnings and from which both draw money; and (iv) the independent management system under which each partner has an income and retains control over it while undertaking separate responsibility for specific items of expenditure. Pahl found (iii) to be the most prevalent and (iv) the least. The factors determining which system is adopted are complex (see Pahl (1989) Ch 6) although she observes that 'when money is short, so that managing is a demanding chore rather than a source of power or pleasure, then typically women manage and control finances' (ibid, pp 120–121).

Under the present law, the implications of each scheme for the legal ownership of property will be different: as we have seen, operating joint bank accounts or providing housekeeping allowances may well have a legal significance, whereas the 'whole wage' system will not. The effect of the independent management system will be entirely arbitrary, depending on who pays for what.

19 *Blackwell v Blackwell* [1943] 2 All ER 579; *Hoddinott v Hoddinott* [1949] 2 KB 406.

by providing that any money 'derived from' an allowance made by the husband to the wife 'for the expenses of the home or for similar purposes', or any property acquired out of such money, was to be regarded as belonging to the parties in equal shares.[20] The Act does not apply to cohabitees, for whom the ownership of such money will depend on any evidence of their intentions, such as may be derived from their use of joint bank accounts.[1]

Many criticisms may be levelled at the Act (Law Commission 1985, paras 4.4–4.13). It is explicitly discriminatory in that it only applies to allowances made by husbands to wives and not vice versa. It is unclear when an allowance has been made for 'expenses of the matrimonial home'. For example, does it cover money given by a husband to the wife to pay the mortgage? It is also unclear what the phrase 'derived from' means – does it refer to the allowance itself, or only to money saved from the allowance? And what is included in the term 'property acquired' out of such money? Further, the precise impact of the Act is likely to depend on the financial arrangements adopted by individual couples.

(d) **Reform**

The Law Commission has proposed to reform the law relating to (i) household goods, (ii) the presumption of advancement and (iii) the 1964 Act by the introduction of two new principles (1989c, para 4.1):

(a) where money is spent to buy property, or property or money is transferred by one spouse to the other, for their joint use or benefit the property acquired or money transferred should be jointly owned; and

(b) where money or property is transferred by one spouse to the other for any other purpose, it should be owned by that other.

These general rules would give way to a contrary intention on the part of the paying or transferring spouse, provided that the other spouse is aware of that intention at the time of the purchase or transfer of the property. Principle (a) would not apply to land and insurance policies (although principle (b) would, since the Commission's intention is to deal comprehensively with the presumption of advancement); but, unlike the equivalent Scottish provisions,[2] would include motor vehicles and securities. The proposals would not apply to property owned by the parties before marriage, to gifts received by either party during the marriage or to purchases or

---

20 MWPA 1964, s 1.
1 *Paul v Constance* [1977] 1 All ER 195.
2 Family Law (Scotland) Act 1985, s 25.

transfers made wholly or mainly for the purposes of a business. The proposals 'are designed for the property bought or transferred for the purposes of the couple's domestic life together' (para 4.11).

These proposals, if implemented, would considerably simplify the current law and make it less arbitrary. Ownership would no longer depend on the provision of purchase money, but on the purpose for which the property is bought. It would remove the discrimination implicit in the 1964 Act and the current rules concerning advancement (by, in effect, applying the presumption uniformly to all inter-spousal gifts).

However, the scheme has a number of limitations. First, it is possible to foresee evidential problems arising in relation to the question of the purpose for which something is bought and the issue of whether a spouse intended to exclude common ownership. For example, a spouse may purchase some shares as an investment without considering whether they are for the couple's 'joint use or benefit' – they are simply an investment. Indeed, it is possible that transactions in shares will take place without the other spouse's knowledge or consent. Does the scheme apply in such cases? If so, what is the effect of transactions to which the other spouse has not consented? Does title pass to the purchaser or not? Second, given that the scheme would apply only to personal property and not to land, the practical impact of the scheme will vary according to the nature of the property owned by any particular couple. Thus, a couple whose major asset is their home will be less affected by the scheme than by a couple whose major assets are, for example, cars and investments. Finally, it should be noted that the scheme would not apply on either divorce or death, although the Law Commission expressed the hope that 'knowing who owns what . . . is more likely to lead to an early settlement without the need to go to court' (para 4.19). However, the scheme would presumably apply on the bankruptcy of one of the spouses, so that the property available for distribution to creditors would be reduced to the extent that the scheme would give the non-bankrupt spouse property rights s/he would not otherwise have.

The family home

Since we are in this chapter concerned primarily with questions of ownership,[3] our discussion under this heading is concerned almost entirely with the owner-occupied family home. To the extent that

---

3 We are thus not concerned here directly with devices for protecting occupation, such as contractual licences.

the statutory protection accorded to tenants of rented property confers rights that begin to resemble proprietary rights – in particular, the rules concerning succession to the tenancy on the death of the tenant – they will also be considered later in this chapter. However, when we come to consider the question of regulating the occupation of the family home, both later in this chapter and in the next, the relevance of the form of legal tenure of the family home begins to disappear.

Another distinction of varying significance is that between married and de facto couples. While much of the law discussed under this heading applies equally to both – in line with the fact that English law recognises no concept of matrimonial property – there are some instances where the legal status of the parties is relevant. The most obvious example is the Matrimonial Homes Act 1983 (below).

Most family homes are likely to be owner-occupied, as a consequence of the rapid growth of this form of tenure over the last fifty years. Since very few people are wealthy enough to buy their homes outright, most will have been bought with the aid of a mortgage. For those families, the house is likely to be the single most important economic asset, although this will to some extent depend on the amount of the mortgage that remains to be paid off, and on the rate of house price inflation since the mortgage was executed (Todd and Jones 1972, pp 20–21). The dominance of owner-occupation has meant that disputes over the ownership of the family home (other than those arising under MCA 1973 in divorce proceedings) have to be resolved within the framework of land law principles derived from statute and the general law, especially of trusts. As we have seen, this framework was devised to meet the needs of a society that had quite different landholding practices.

This has had two consequences. First, the attempt to accommodate the resolution of family disputes within the land law framework has significantly disturbed the conceptual orderliness of the land law itself. This is not our concern here. Second, the assumed need to maintain the transferability of land has restricted the range of interests of family members that have been legally recognised in the family home, especially those of women, and has been advanced as an argument for further restricting such rights as have been recognised (see especially Law Commission 1982b; and further below).

(a) **Attributing ownership**

(i) Formalities

A distinctive feature of the law relating to land is its insistence on compliance with formality in the creation and conveyance of interests in land. It is a statutory requirement that a conveyance of a legal title to land be by deed, and that the creation or disposal of an equitable interest in land should also be formally evidenced in writing.[4] This means that the ownership of the family home may be made the subject of express arrangements by the parties in the shape of a deed, conveyance or declaration of trust. Provided that the requisite formalities are complied with, the ownership of the property in question, both at law and in equity, will be determined by any such document, and will have nothing to do with the question of who provided the purchase price for the house. Thus, a conveyance of the family home into the joint names of the parties, together with a declaration that the parties hold the property as joint tenants in equity, will (subject to the possibility of rectification or rescission for fraud or mistake) constitute the parties as equal beneficial owners of the property,[5] even though one party has provided no money towards its purchase. Similarly, a declaration that the parties hold as tenants in common in specified shares will also be conclusive.[6] Whether or not this happens depends in large part on conveyancing practice. Such evidence as there is suggests that, at least where married couples are concerned, it is the rule rather than the exception (Todd and Jones 1972, pp 10–12).[7]

(ii) Implied trusts

However, there will be some cases where the formal documents merely record that one of the parties is the legal owner, or that the parties are joint legal owners, but make no declaration as to the beneficial interests of the parties.[8] In such cases the question may arise as to what ownership interest, if any, the non-owning partner has acquired in the house. Since there is no formal record of the non-owner being granted an interest, resort must be had to the sole exception to the statutory rules concerning formalities – that is, that the formal requirements do not apply to 'resulting, implied, or constructive trusts'.[9] All claims to a share in the property in these circumstances

---

4 LPA 1925, ss 52, 53(1).
5 *Wilson v Wilson* [1963] 1 WLR 601; *Goodman v Gallant* [1986] Fam 106; a formal declaration may not always be necessary – see *Re Gorman* [1990] 1 WLR 616.
6 Per Lord Diplock in *Gissing v Gissing* [1971] AC 886 at 905.
7 The 1984 General Household Survey found that 72% of married couples said they were joint owners of their home.
8 See *Hine v Hine* [1962] 1 WLR 1124.
9 LPA 1925, s 53(2).

are to be treated as claims to the existence of one of these 'imputed' trusts in the claimant's favour.[10]

On what basis do these trusts operate? We have already seen that the resulting trust recognises a share only where a financial contribution to the property in dispute has been made by the claimant. In the context of the family home, this basic rule raises two questions. First, how can this rule be applied to the purchase of a house on a mortgage, where payments are made by instalments over a period of time? What, in such circumstances, is to count as a contribution to the purchase? Second, given that this basic rule will tend to favour the partner with the larger income, since that partner will be best able to make the kind of contribution required,[11] is there any way of ameliorating the harshness of the rule when applied to couples operating according to the traditional division of labour? To put it another way, is it possible to recognise non-financial contributions to the household, such as housework or child care, as qualifying for a share? The answer to this second question depends in part on the importance of the policy of formality in land transactions, since the wider the range of qualifying contributions, the less accurate the formal legal documents will be.

The law on this subject is still in the process of development (see Hayton 1990). For present purposes, the relevant principles may be discussed under two heads:

(i) cases turning on the finding of an imputed common intention between the parties that they shall share the equitable ownership; and

(ii) cases where there is evidence of an express but informal promise made by one party to the other that the other shall have a share in the property (see Chesterman and Moffat 1988, Chs 12, 13).

Although at one stage it might have been correct to refer to (i) as cases of resulting trust and to (ii) as cases of constructive trust, the current judicial tendency is to refer to both as examples of constructive trust.[12]

---

10 Per Lord Upjohn in *Pettitt v Pettitt* [1970] AC 777 at 813–814; per Slade LJ in *Goodman v Gallant* [1986] Fam 106 at 239.

11 The decision made by couples as to who should pay the mortgage may be entirely arbitrary and will depend on how the couple choose to organise their finances – see Pahl (1989), pp 145–146 and the discussion above, p 180, note 18. Nevertheless, the evidence supports the suggestion that where the parties' income is higher (so that they are more likely to be buying than renting) mortgage repayments are more likely to be made by the husband than the wife.

12 Eg, Lord Bridge in *Lloyd's Bank plc v Rosset* [1991] 1 AC 107 (although it may be that Lord Bridge assumed that there was no question of a resulting trust in the traditional sense arising on the facts of *Rosset*); for an attempt to clarify the terminological confusion, see Sparkes (1991), pp 41–46.

Imputed common intention: 'financial contributions'   In the absence of an express agreement or promise concerning ownership, the courts will impute an intention to the parties to share the equitable ownership where it is reasonable to do so.[13] However, the courts appear to regard only financial contributions to acquisition of the property in question as sufficient grounds for imputing this intention. It will not be sufficient to show that, for example, 'a house is to be renovated as a "joint venture" [or] that the house is to be shared by parents and children'.[14] One consequence of this narrow approach to the question of imputing intention to the parties may be that in future the courts will be more inclined to find evidence of an express, but informal, agreement between the parties so as to bring into play the broader principles discussed under the next heading.

The types of contribution recognised by the courts as justifying the inference of a common intention may be summarised as follows:

(i)   the payment of a deposit on a house, or any other direct financial contribution to its purchase;[15]
(ii)   the payment of mortgage instalments;[16]
(iii)   the contribution of money to general household expenses which thereby enables the other partner to make the mortgage payments.

It is unclear whether, in order to qualify for (iii), such contributions must be part of an arrangement between the partners, or whether the fact of having made a contribution to household expenses is itself sufficient. If the latter, it is also unclear whether the claimant needs to show that the partner paying the mortgage could only have done so with the claimant's financial help.[17] In *Burns v Burns*,[18] the Court of Appeal were prepared to recognise only contributions to house-hold expenses that were 'substantial' on the ground that 'one way or another' such contributions would enable the other party to pay the mortgage. However, following the House of Lords' decision in *Lloyd's Bank v Rosset*,[19] it may even be doubted whether contributions to

13 Per Lords Reid and Diplock in *Pettitt v Pettitt* [1970] AC 777; and see *Sekhon v Alissa* [1989] 2 FLR 94.
14 Per Lord Bridge in *Lloyd's Bank v Rosset* [1991] 1 AC 107 at 130.
15 *Pettitt* (above); *Gissing v Gissing* [1971] AC 886; *Burns v Burns* [1984] Ch 317, [1984] 1 All ER 244; the realisation of a discount available to a tenant of rented property counts as a contribution to the purchase price for these purposes – see *Marsh v Von Sternberg* [1986] 1 FLR 526.
16 Ibid; undertaking a mortgage liability may be treated as the equivalent of a cash contribution to acquisition – see *Bernard v Josephs* [1982] Ch 391; *Marsh v Von Sternberg* [1986] 1 FLR 526.
17 See especially *Burns* (above), per Fox LJ; compare *Hazell v Hazell* [1972] 1 WLR 301.
18 Above.
19 [1991] 1 AC 107 (see Gardner 1991).

household expenses will qualify the contributor for a share, since Lord Bridge took the view that it was 'extremely doubtful' whether anything less than direct contributions to the purchase price, whether initially or by mortgage instalments, will justify the necessary inference of a common intention.[20] Given that, as we have seen, couples' decisions as to who should pay the mortgage will be dictated by a range of factors, this seems an unnecessarily inflexible and arbitrary rule to adopt.

This focus on financial contributions to acquisition has meant that, in the absence of any express promise or agreement relating to beneficial ownership, the following types of contribution will not be sufficient to impute the necessary common intention to the parties:

- caring for children and running the household[1]
- 'do-it-yourself' improvements to, or redecorations of, the family home[2]
- buying clothes, furnishings or consumer durables for the family[3]
- supervision of building works[4]
- assisting with business entertaining[5]
- 'topping up' the housekeeping.[6]

As noted above, the courts' attachment to purely financial contributions will severely disadvantage those partners (usually women) who give up, or who never undertake, regular full-time employment in order to discharge domestic and child care responsibilities.

Promises, promises: constructive trusts and estoppels The restrictive approach of the courts to the question of what counts as a financial contribution has led litigants to draw on an alternative body of doctrine, which falls loosely under the heading of constructive trust and estoppel.[7] This enables the courts to take a slightly broader

---

20 [1991] 1 AC 107 at 133.
1 *Burns v Burns* [1984] Ch 317, [1984] 1 All ER 244.
2 *Pettitt v Pettitt* [1970] AC 777; *Gissing v Gissing* [1971] AC 886; *Thomas v Fuller-Brown* [1988] 1 FLR 237.
3 *Burns* (above).
4 *Lloyd's Bank v Rosset* [1991] 1 AC 107; *Windeler v Whitehall* [1990] 2 FLR 505.
5 *Windeler v Whitehall* (above).
6 *Burns* (above).
7 On the question of whether there is, or should be, a conceptual distinction between constructive trusts and estoppels, see Hayton (1990), Warburton (1991) and the comments of Nourse LJ in *Stokes v Anderson* [1991] 1 FLR 391, who spoke of 'the burgeoning question of the relationship between . . . constructive trust and proprietary estoppel'; and for an illustration of the different operation of the two, compare *Grant v Edwards* [1986] Ch 638 with *Coombes v Smith* [1986] 1 WLR 808. A useful statement of the modern law of proprietary estoppel may be found in *Taylors Fashions Ltd v Liverpool Victoria Trustees* [1982] QB 133n.

range of contributions into account where the legal owner has expressly promised the claimant a share in the house, and the claimant has relied on that promise.[8] The existence of an express, albeit informal, promise or representation by the defendant is sufficient to establish the common intention necessary to found a claim to an implied trust. There must be evidence of 'express discussions between the partners, however imperfectly remembered' evidencing the necessary intention to share the equity.[9] The claimant must also be able to prove that he or she has acted to his or her detriment in reliance on that promise[10] and the acts of reliance must be 'linked' in some way to the original promise.[11]

The precise nature of this 'link', and the means by which it might be proved, are still unclear. In *Grant v Edwards*,[12] Nourse LJ required evidence of 'conduct on which the woman could not reasonably have been expected to embark unless she was to have an interest in the house'; whereas Browne-Wilkinson V-C was prepared to assume that once there was evidence of a common intention based on a promise or representation, 'any act done by her to her detriment relating to the joint lives of the parties is . . . sufficient detriment to qualify'[13] and the burden is on the defendant to disprove the 'link' between the two.[14] Mustill LJ took the view that the conduct must be 'referable' to the bargain or promise between, or intentions of, the parties and that this would depend on the nature of the conduct on the one hand and of the bargain, promise or intention on the other.[15]

Does this 'alternative' approach offer a means of escaping the attachment to purely financial contributions as the exclusive basis for attributing shares in the equity? Examples to date of successful claims under this head suggest a slightly, but not significantly, broader approach. For example, in *Eves*[16] a female partner successfully claimed a quarter share in the home on the basis of work she had done to the house and garden; and in *Grant v Edwards* itself the woman was awarded a half share on the basis of substantial

8   *Cooke v Head* [1972] 2 All ER 38, [1972] 1 WLR 518; *Eves v Eves* [1975] 3 All ER 768; *Grant v Edwards* [1986] Ch 638, [1986] 2 All ER 426; *Midland Bank plc v Dobson* [1986] 1 FLR 171; *Lloyd's Bank v Rosset* [1990] 2 WLR 867.
9   Per Lord Bridge in *Lloyd's Bank v Rosset* [1991] 1 AC 107 at 132; the promise need not relate to sharing the equity, but may concern rights of occupation, in which case the terminology of estoppel will be used – see *Coombes v Smith* [1986] 1 WLR 808.
10 *Grant v Edwards* (above); *Lloyd's Bank v Rosset* (above).
11 *Midland Bank plc v Dobson and Dobson* [1986] 1 FLR 171.
12 Above.
13 At p 130.
14 On the burden of proof, see *Greasley v Cooke* [1980] 3 All ER 710; *Coombes v Smith* (above).
15 At p 125.
16 Above.

contributions to household expenses.[17] In *Lloyd's Bank v Rosset*,[18] Lord Bridge took the view that even if the wife had been able to prove the necessary express agreement, her activities in supervising building work and redecorating the house would not have been sufficient acts of reliance to qualify her for a share. In *Coombes v Smith*,[19] it was held (albeit obiter) that a woman who had left her husband, become pregnant by the defendant and looked after the house and child had not acted sufficiently to her detriment to entitle her to any equitable relief. Thus, it may be that successful claims will still have to be based on contributions in money or money's worth.

It remains to be seen whether any further development takes place. In *Grant v Edwards*,[20] Browne-Wilkinson V-C expressed a willingness to consider 'any act done . . . to [the claimant's] detriment relating to the joint lives of the parties' which 'need not be inherently referable to the house' as evidence of reliance on a pre-existing understanding that the claimant was to acquire a share. This suggests a broader approach to the question of qualifying contribution.

It may be that the real significance of the growing use of estoppel and constructive trusts is that it permits the court a greater flexibility in determining the claimant's remedy rather than in significantly broadening the range of qualifying contributions (Moffat and Chesterman 1988, Ch 13). This flexibility exists both as to the proportionate share to be awarded to the claimant, which need not be governed by a precise calculation of the amount contributed,[1] and as to the means by which the plaintiff's rights are protected. The latter need not always involve awarding an equitable share by means of a trust since the courts regard their task as doing the minimum necessary to 'satisfy the equity' created by the estoppel. This may include some degree of occupational protection by means of a protected licence.[2] These devices will be of most use in cases

---

17 See also *Risch v McFee* [1991] 1 FLR 105, where a loan which the lender had not asked to be repaid was regarded as a sufficient act of reliance entitling the lender to have the amount of the loan taken into account when calculating her share of the equity; and *Hammond v Mitchell* [1991] 1 WLR 1127, in which a female cohabitee who had acted as 'mother/helper/unpaid assistant and at times financial supporter to the family prosperity' was found to have acted sufficiently to her detriment to justify awarding her a half share.

18 Above.

19 [1986] 1 WLR 808.

20 Above.

1 *Cooke v Head* [1972] 2 All ER 38; *Grant v Edwards* [1986] Ch 638, [1986] 2 All ER 426; in *Stokes v Anderson* [1991] 1 FLR 391, Nourse LJ said that in cases of constructive trust 'there is no practicable alternative to the determination of a fair share' (at p 400).

2 *Greasley v Cooke* [1980] 3 All ER 710; *Re Sharpe* [1980] 1 All ER 198; *Coombes v Smith* [1986] 1 WLR 808.

involving de facto couples for whom the statutory means of protecting occupation are not available.

The most striking example of remedial flexibility is *Pascoe v Turner*[3] where a woman, who had been told by her partner that the house was hers, had spent money on furniture, redecorations and improvements. The Court of Appeal considered that transferring the legal title to her was the 'minimum necessary to do equity' in view of her age, resources and her need for freedom of interference by the male ex-partner.[4] It has been suggested that 'the Court of Appeal was acting like a judge of the family division dividing the family's assets after divorce' (Sufrin 1979, p 577).

(iii) MPPA 1970, s 37

If a husband or wife makes a substantial contribution in money or money's worth to improvements to real or personal matrimonial property, the contributing spouse will receive a share, or increased share, in the improved property, subject to any agreement to the contrary.[5]

(b) Third parties

(i) General principles

Where both partners are on the legal title to the land, then any dealing with the land requires the knowledge and consent of both.[6]

---

3   *Pascoe v Turner* [1979] 2 All ER 945.
4   See *Burrows and Burrows v Sharpe* [1991] Fam Law 67 where the Court of Appeal held that, although the equity will often be satisfied by granting the claimant the interest s/he was intended to have, this will not be the case where that would be produce a result that would be practically unworkable.
5   MPPA 1970, s 37; see *Re Nicholson* [1974] 2 All ER 386.
6   This may not provide a spouse with absolute protection where s/he is not fully aware of the nature or consequences of a particular transaction, eg an 'all-moneys' mortgage. Litigants have resorted increasingly to doctrines of misrepresentation, undue influence, inequality of bargaining power and duties of disclosure to avoid the full consequences of such transactions. These attempts have not been sympathetically viewed by the courts – see *National Westminster Bank plc v Morgan* [1985] AC 686; *Lloyd's Bank plc v Egremont* [1990] 2 FLR 351; but see *Kingsnorth Trust Ltd v Bell* [1986] 1 WLR 119; *Barclays Bank plc v Kennedy and Kennedy* [1989] 1 FLR 356. However, lenders are still well advised to ensure (i) that mortgage documents are executed in the presence of a solicitor, and (ii) that the signatory is told that it is desirable to obtain independent advice. There is, however, no obligation to ensure that such advice is either actually received nor, if received, that it is actually independent (see *Coldunell Ltd v Gallon* [1986] QB 1184; *Kingsnorth Trust Ltd v Bell* (above)).

Where one of the partners is not on the legal title, this may render that partner vulnerable to the legal owner dealing with the legal title to the land without their knowledge. The question may arise as to the protection available for that partner's interest in the land. This interest is not merely in the money value the land represents, but also in the continuing right to occupy the land.[7] The question of the right to occupy as against the other partner is considered later in this, and in the next, chapter. Where the issue is between the partner and a third party, for example a buyer or mortgagee of the land, the outcome depends in large part on the general principles of land law. Where the parties are married, it may also depend on the Matrimonial Homes Act 1983, discussed below.

Where land is co-owned in equity, either expressly or by virtue of the operation of imputed trusts, the statutory mechanism of the trust for sale comes into operation[8] (for further discussion, see Murphy and Clark 1983, Ch 6). For our purposes, this mechanism is significant in two respects. First, in dealing with the land the legal owner is obliged to consult the equitable co-owner.[9] This obligation may be enforceable by injunction in advance of the dealing taking place.[10] Second, the legal owner may only offer third parties a title to the land free of the co-owner's beneficial interest if certain statutory formalities are complied with. The most significant of these is that the sale be effected by two, rather than just one, legal owners.[11] While this provision would have been an unproblematic one in the context of the practice of land transfer in the early part of this century, it has come to form a crucial element in the protection of co-owners' interests in the family home. For where a family home is in the single name of one of the partners, it is unlikely that they will go to the trouble of appointing a second legal owner solely for the purposes of effecting a sale or mortgage.

In this event, the statutory guarantee of a title free of equitable interests is not triggered, and the courts (especially the House of Lords in *Williams and Glyn's Bank v Boland*[12]) have held that where the purchaser or mortgagee has actual or constructive notice[13] of the co-owner's equitable interest (or the equivalent in registered land[14]), the co-owner's interest is binding on them.[15] In practice, this means

---

7   *Bull v Bull* [1955] 1 QB 234.
8   LPA 1925, ss 34–36; *Bull v Bull* (above).
9   LPA 1925, s 26(3).
10 *Waller v Waller* [1967] 1 All ER 305.
11 LPA 1925, ss 2(2), 27(2).
12 [1981] AC 487, [1980] 2 All ER 408.
13 LPA 1925, ss 198, 199.
14 LRA 1925, s 70(1)(g).
15 *Williams and Glyn's Bank Ltd v Boland* [1981] AC 487, [1980] 2 All ER 408; *Kingsnorth Trust Ltd v Tizard* [1986] 2 All ER 54.

that the co-owner is entitled to remain in occupation as against the third party. The effect of this is to prevent the lender from enforcing its security by a sale of the property. The requirement of notice, or 'actual occupation' of the land for registered land, has been defined in such a way that it is easily satisfied by a spouse or partner resident in the family home at the time of the transaction in question.[16]

In recent years, however, the courts have been beating a retreat from protecting occupying equitable co-owners. This retreat has taken three forms. First, where the mortagage is executed by two legal owners, it was held in *City of London Building Society v Flegg*[17] that the overreaching provisions of the Law of Property Act 1925 confer on the mortagagee a guarantee of priority, even where there are other equitable co-owners in occupation at the date of the mortgage.

Second, where the mortgage is executed at the same time as completion of the initial purchase, actual occupation will rarely be established for the purposes of LRA 1925, s 70(1)(g) since the relevant date for deciding this issue is the date of the execution of the mortgage.

This was part of the decision in *Abbey National Building Society v Cann*.[18] The effect of this will be that where a house has been purchased initially with the aid of a mortgage, it will be very difficult to establish 'actual occupation' at the relevant date since occupation will usually only be established at the same time as, rather than before, the execution of the mortgage. It was further held in *Cann* that where a mortgage is contemporaneous with the conveyance (as will often be the case with domestic purchases) there is no 'point in time' at which the legal owner takes the title unencumbered by the lender's charge. As a result, any claim to an equitable interest will be demoted in priority to the lender's charge. In other words, an equitable owner's interest cannot 'bite' on the legal owner's interest in priority to that of the mortgagee.[19]

Finally, the Court of Appeal has been dealing with this question in a less technical manner by developing the concept of a special type of limited equitable interest in residential property. This originated in *Bristol and West Building Society v Henning*.[20] Here, it was held that where the equitable interest arises informally on the basis of the

16 See *William and Glyn's Bank Ltd v Boland* [1981] AC 487, [1980] 2 All ER 408 and *Kingsnorth Trust v Tizard* [1986] 2 All ER 54; and *Lloyd's Bank v Rosset* [1989] Ch 350, CA.
17 [1988] AC 54.
18 [1991] 1 AC 56.
19 Ibid.
20 [1985] 1 WLR 778. See also *Equity and Law Home Loans v Prestidge* [1992] 1 WLR 137.

parties' imputed intentions, it was a necessary part of that intention that the equitable owner had authorised the execution of the mortgage and that the interest was thus not intended to take priority to that of the lender's charge. Although not extensively reasoned, it seems that the principle to be applied is that an equitable owner cannot claim priority over a mortgagee's interest where (i) s/he knew of the mortgage, and (ii) where s/he has benefited from the mortgage by living in the property purchased with its assistance, and (iii) where the equitable interest itself has arisen informally under an implied trust. This view of the matter was confirmed, albeit briefly, by the House of Lords in *Abbey National Building Society v Cann* and in the later Court of Appeal decision of *Equity and Law Home Loans v Prestidge*.[1] The scope of this principle is unclear. For example, when will an occupier be taken to have benefited from a mortgage? Must actual knowledge of a mortgage be proved, or is it sufficient that the occupier in question must have known that the property could only have been bought with one? What is clear, though, is that the concept of the 'limited equitable interest' offers a means of resolving disputes between lenders and occupiers by reference to broad principles of fairness and without needing to use the technical language of the 1925 Law of Property legislation.

The net effect of this judicial retreat from *Boland* is that the protection offered to occupiers by that decision appears now to be confined to cases involving second rather than first mortgages; and even second mortgages may be vulnerable to the concept of the limited equitable interest.

(ii) Reform

Statutory co-ownership   These decisions, especially that in *Williams and Glyn's Bank v Boland*, were thought to create considerable problems for conveyancers and to threaten the certainty of transactions in land (Law Commission 1982b, paras 33–35). In particular, it seems that the decision was thought to pose a particular threat to the institutional suppliers of mortgage finance, since the successful assertion of a right to occupy the matrimonial home undermined the home as security for a loan in the event of foreclosure. In practice this problem may be dealt with by the use of deeds of consent, by which all occupiers of a mortgaged family home sign away any claim to occupy that might affect the lender's title (Murphy and Clark 1983,

1   [1992] 1 WLR 137.

pp 167–170); and the decision in *Abbey National Building Society v Cann* now seems to offer mortgagees sufficient protection where the mortgage in question is a first mortgage of residential property (see above). However, the Law Commission responded to the *Boland* decision by proposing the introduction of the scheme of statutory co-ownership set out in an earlier Law Commission Report on matrimonial property (Law Commission 1978).

The Law Commission's scheme, which would only apply to the homes of married couples, would involve statutory co-ownership of the equitable, but not the legal, title to the property. This equitable co-ownership would carry with it the right both to occupy the home, to have a half-share in the financial value of the home and to have a right of veto on all dealings with the property. However, these rights would only be effective against a third party purchaser or mortgagee of the land if the spouse had registered a new class of statutory land charge (or registered land equivalent) prior to the transaction. Certain items of property could be excluded from the scheme by written declaration, such as property owned before marriage; and a donor of property to one of the spouses could also exclude the property comprised in the gift from the scheme.

The family home's pre-eminence as an item of family property has two consequences in this context. First, the Law Commission's apparent reluctance to introduce a community of property regime on continental lines (discussed further below), under which all matrimonial property would be subjected to automatic joint ownership,[2] derives in part from the view that it is a sufficient answer to the question of matrimonial property to frame rules for the matrimonial home alone (Law Commission 1971, para 0.25).[3] However, it has been argued that there may be couples for whom the home is relatively insignificant. For such spouses, co-ownership of the home alone seems neither relevant nor fair (Scottish Law Commission 1984, para 3).

Second, the proposals exhibit considerable deference to the needs of conveyancers. In effect, they offer the non-owning spouse greater nominal rights in the family home while reducing their enforceability against third parties by insisting on the registration of a statutory charge, as opposed to the operation of the doctrine of notice, as at present (Deech 1980; Murphy and Rawlings 1980; Murphy 1983).

2   See note 5, p 176, above and Cretney (1984a), Ch 24; Scottish Law Commission (1983), Part III; Hoggett and Pearl (1987), pp 145–153; Masson (1988); Freedman et al (1988); see further the final section of this chapter.

3   See also note 5, p 176, above.

The dominance of the concern with conveyancing is underlined by the fact that the presumption of joint ownership is not carried forward into divorce, and the proposals will have no relevance on the death of one of the spouses.

Other criticisms have been made of these proposals. It has been argued that the problem at which the proposals are directed, that is spouses who are not already joint legal owners of their home, is a comparatively small one (Zuckerman 1978). It has also been argued that the scheme is too complex, especially as regards the number of permitted exceptions (Deech 1980).

The Law Commission's most recent proposals on Matrimonial Property (discussed above at pp 181–182), which adopt a different approach, specifically exclude land, despite a recognition that this would 'create a new and potentially serious anomaly, in that where one spouse pays for the matrimonial home and the other buys the furniture, the furniture will become jointly-owned but the house will not' (1989c, para 4.4). It was thought that including land in the proposals would be 'controversial and attract inappropriate opposition' to the rest of their proposed reforms (ibid, para 4.3) even though extending the proposals to include land would, the Commission thought, 'be a simple matter if this were thought desirable' (para 4.5). In the Commission's view, the fact that most matrimonial homes are purchased in joint names, as well as the protection offered to non-owners by the decision in *Boland*, makes such an extension less pressing in any case (para 4.3). However, we have seen that the scope of the protection offered by *Boland* is now much diminished. Proposals for a more radical approach to reform of matrimonial property are discussed in the final section of this chapter.

Reform of the land law framework　　The Law Commission's proposals for a new-style Trust of Land (1989 and 1989a) will, if implemented, have considerable significance in this context. Two particular features of those proposals are relevant here. The first is the proposed widening of the courts' jurisdiction to resolve disputes under LPA 1925, s 30 (see further below). This will enable beneficiaries of the new trust to refer disputes over occupation or disposition of the land to the courts and will give them 'greater scope to challenge the decisions of the trustees and generally influence the management of the trust land' (Law Commission 1989, para 13.6). This will give to the existing duty on trustees to consult beneficiaries a force that it currently lacks. However, this will still require a beneficiary to take the matter to court before a disputed disposition (eg, a second mortgage) takes effect.

The second, and in this context more important, feature of the proposals is the suggestion that where a beneficiary is occupying trust property, and has a right to do so by virtue of his or her equitable interest, that beneficiary's interest should not be overreached unless he or she consents (see Law Commission 1989a). This would amount, in effect, to a statutory codification of the decision in *Boland* and reversal of *Flegg*[4] (see above) and would give qualifying beneficiaries an effective veto over dealings with the land. Even this, though, could be outflanked by the concept of the limited equitable interest: such an interest would automatically lose priority to a lender's charge without having to be overreached at all.

Although not framed with the family home primarily in mind, these proposals offer more effective protection to those family members who are not on the legal title than those devised earlier by the Commission specifically for family property. However, it should be noted that these proposals will only assist those who have an equitable interest in land – the proposals do not themselves extend the range of people qualifying for such interests beyond those who already qualify under the rules discussed above. The earlier proposals for statutory co-ownership would at least have conferred a statutory interest in the matrimonial home where none would otherwise arise. It seems that it is possible to have either a wider distribution of interests in the family home or a more effective means of protecting them against third parties – but not both.

(iii) Matrimonial Homes Act 1983

Further protection against third parties is available to spouses (but not to de facto partners) under the MHA 1983. As we have seen, occupational protection of the owner-occupied family home against third parties under the general land law depends on legal ownership, or on the protection accorded to equitable interests by the doctrine of notice or overriding interests (above). However, this leaves several gaps. The spouse who has no legal or equitable interest in the house is completely unprotected against third parties, and possesses no 'equity' enforceable against third parties to remain in the house by virtue only of her status as wife.[5] Also, the protection available to equitable interests in the matrimonial home is not absolute. They

---

4 But not of *Abbey National Building Society v Cann* [1991] 1 AC 56 since the proposals only apply to beneficiaries in actual occupation who have a right enforceable against the person conveying the legal estate (1989a, para 4.11). The basis of the *Cann* decision was that, in the case of a first mortgage, neither of these conditions is likely to be satisfied.

5 *National Provincial Bank v Ainsworth* [1965] AC 1175.

may be overreached on a sale by two trustees, and there must be circumstances, such as the fact of occupation, which trigger the relevant doctrines of notice. The MHA 1983, originally the MHA 1967, confers certain statutory rights on the non-owning spouse to fill these gaps.

Where only one spouse is legal owner (or is otherwise the only spouse entitled to occupy), the Act confers on the other spouse statutory 'rights of occupation' in the matrimonial home which comprise (i) the right not to be evicted from the house if in occupation, and (ii) the right to enter and occupy if not in occupation.[6] The other spouse is not regarded as having a right to occupy merely by virtue of possessing an equitable interest in the house.[7] One implication of conferring rights of this sort is that they may be enforced not just against third parties, but against the other spouse; and the MHA 1983 does provide for this. Here, the relevance of the form of legal tenure of the family home disappears, since this aspect of the Act applies both where the home is owner-occupied or rented. This is more appropriately considered in the next chapter in relation to other procedures for regulating occupation of the family home. We are here primarily concerned with third-party interests in relation to the owner-occupied family home.

As far as third parties are concerned, these statutory rights of occupation take effect as if they are an equitable charge on the owning spouse's estate or interest, created either at the date of the marriage, or at the date on which the owning spouse acquired the estate or interest in the matrimonial home, whichever is the later.[8] Where the owning spouse's estate is a legal estate in land, this statutory charge will only bind third parties where the non-owning spouse has protected it by registering a notice (in the case of registered land) or a Class F land charge (in the case of unregistered land).[9] Once registered, the statutory interest takes effect in the same way as any other registered equitable interest, particularly in terms of priority to other interests in the home. Thus, a spouse's statutory charge will not have priority over a mortgage that has already been executed at the time of registration; but it will have priority over any subsequent interest, and entitles the spouse registering the charge to continue or enter into occupation as against the later interest holder. The statutory rights are void against any purchaser (including a mortgagee[10]) of an estate or interest in the land for value if not

6   MHA 1983, s 1(1); but see also s 9 which extends the Act in limited respects to
    couples who are joint legal owners – see Ch 6.
7   MHA 1983, s 1(11).
8   MHA 1983, s 2(1).
9   MHA 1983, s 2(8), (9), (11); LCA 1972, s 2(7).
10 LPA 1925, s 205.

registered in the appropriate way.[11] The statutory rights will cease to
bind third parties once the marriage comes to an end either through
death or divorce, even where they have been registered and as a
consequence have taken priority over the third party's interest.[12]
The spouse's rights survive the bankruptcy of the owning spouse (see
below).

The insistence on registration as a precondition to enforceability
against third parties may be criticised. It could be argued that many
non-owning spouses will be unaware of the requirement until it is too
late. It has also been suggested that registration is 'a hostile step
which [the wife] may be unwilling to take' (Law Commission 1982b,
para 75). This is reflected in the comparatively few registrations
made under the Act. In 1977–1978, for example, there were 17,000
registered charges under the Act (Law Commission 1982b, para 78).
This raises once again the question of how far family members should
be expected to formalise their affairs in the interests of achieving
certainty in land transactions. Much will depend on conveyancing
practice; but there is no reason why a solicitor acting for the owning
spouse in the purchase of a house should consider registering a
charge on behalf of the client's spouse unless the client specifically
requests it, which seems unlikely (Murphy 1979).

On the other hand, however, it has also been argued that the
statutory reliance on registration is *too* effective a means of protecting
the statutory rights. For example, the registration of a charge
technically entitles a spouse to occupy the property against a third-
party purchaser where the charge is registered after the exchange of
contracts but before registration of the purchaser's estate contract; in
such circumstances, the vendor will be in breach of contract for
vacant possession, unless the spouse can be persuaded to vacate the
charge.[13] Used in this way, the Act offers the non-owning spouse an
effective veto over all dealings with the property. However, in such a
case it may be open to a court to take the view that this is not a
proper use of the statutory rights, and the charge may be set aside.[14]
Further, there seems to be no reason why the owning spouse should
not be able to apply to have the other spouse's rights under the Act
terminated under the procedure laid down by the Act itself.[15]
Alternatively, the court could dismiss the other spouse's claim to
enforce the statutory rights by taking the purchaser's circumstances
into account.[16]

11 LCA 1972, s 4(8).
12 MHA 1967, s 2(4).
13 *Wroth v Tyler* [1974] Ch 30, per Megarry J.
14 *Barnett v Hassett* [1982] 1 All ER 80.
15 MHA 1983, s 1(2)(a).
16 *Kaur v Gill* [1988] 2 All ER 288 (see Sparkes 1989).

The statutory rights also include the right to take over repayment of the mortgage (or rent) from the spouse who is mortgagee or tenant. Payments are deemed by statute to be made by the mortgagee or tenant spouse.[17] Thus a deserted non-owning spouse may take over such payments without risking forfeiture of the property. The Act also confers on such a spouse the right to be notified of any foreclosure proceedings by a mortgagee, but only where the spouse has registered the statutory charge by the time of the proceedings.[18] This spouse may then apply to be made a party to the proceedings, in which he or she will be able to make a case against foreclosure if there is a prospect of paying off the arrears and the current instalments.[19]

(c) **Valuation**

There may be some circumstances where it will be important to determine the precise value of the parties' shares in the property. In the case of spouses, this may be because of the bankruptcy of one of the parties. For de facto partners, the question may arise at the termination of their relationship. Indeed, as we saw in Chapter 2, there are no special procedures for resolving property disputes between cohabitees, which have to be resolved within the principles stated here.

There are two separate issues. First, in what proportions do the parties own the property? Second, when are those proportions to be valued?

(i) *Apportioning the equity*

If there is a formal document setting out the parties' shares, then that will determine the issue. Where the share to be valued has arisen by virtue of an 'imputed common intention' trust, the starting point will be the relative sizes of the two parties' contributions either to the deposit or to subsequent mortgage repayments.[20] This raises potentially extremely complex issues (Murphy and Clark 1983, pp 47–59). For example, where there is an endowment as opposed to repayment mortgage, or where the parties have not consistently paid the same outgoings, or where the claim is based on contributions to

17 MHA 1983, s 1(5).
18 MHA 1983, s 8(3).
19 MHA 1983, s 8(2); AJA 1970, s 36(1); AJA 1973, s 8(1) .
20 See, eg, *Marsh v Von Sternberg* [1986] 1 FLR 526.

household expenses rather than direct acquisition costs, it may be difficult to determine in what shares the parties have made contributions. Other difficulties include the value to be attributed to mortgage repayments as against money deposits and the attribution of shares as between two people both of whom have been making mortgage repayments or who have jointly undertaken responsibility for the mortgage but have made repayments in unequal amounts (see Sparkes 1991[1]). Nevertheless, the courts have shown themselves willing to take a flexible approach to the question of valuation,[2] and the guiding principle remains the respective size of the parties' contributions (however defined).

Where the share arises by virtue of constructive trust or estoppel, the contribution may be less easily valued and is more likely to be governed by the content of the express but informal understanding on the basis of which the trust arises. It has already been suggested that in such cases the courts may exercise a wide discretion in fixing the size of the share.[3]

(ii)　Occupation rent

Difficulties may also arise where one party leaves and the other stays and continues to pay the mortgage. One solution is to treat those mortgage repayments by the resident partner as in part enhancing the non-resident partner's share of the equity. This offers a means of recognising the benefit to the resident partner of occupying the house.[4] This may be formalised further in the form of an 'occupation rent' payable by the resident partner to the other.[5] A rental element may be allowed for in calculating the price at which one party may be directed to buy out the other. In *Bernard v Josephs*,[6] the 'buy out'

1　Sparkes (1991) identifies two problems: (i) where one party contributes in cash and the other by mortgage, how far should account be taken of mortgage repayments that have actually been made, and are the parties' proportionate shares to be in the gross or net sale proceeds?; and (ii) where more than one person has contributed to mortgage repayments, what relationship should there be between the amount repaid and the proportionate share accruing to each contributor? What allowance, if any, should be made for the fact that some mortgages involve repayment of interest only, while others involve repayment of interest in the early stages and repayment of capital in later stages?

2　*Bernard v Josephs* [1982] Ch 391, [1982] 3 All ER 162; *Walker v Hall* [1984] FLR 126.

3　See, eg, *Cooke v Head* [1972] 2 All ER 38; *Stokes v Anderson* [1991] 1 FLR 391.

4　*Leake v Bruzzi* [1974] 2 All ER 1196.

5　*Dennis v McDonald* [1982] 1 All ER 590; the imposition of a rental liability between tenants in common was once thought to be confined to exceptional cases; it now seems that one will be imposed whenever it is fair to do so: see *Chhokar v Chhokar* [1984] FLR 313.

6　Above.

price was arrived at by deducting from the occupier's half-share in the equity one-half of the amount paid by the non-resident party in mortgage repayments, the other half representing a form of occupation rent. In that case, the mortgage repayments were taken to be a guide to a fair rent; but where there is no mortgage, or where only a very small amount to be repaid, some other basis will have to be used. In *Dennis v McDonald*,[7] the Court of Appeal took the Rent Act concept of a 'fair rent' as its starting point. Whether this will continue to be used following the replacement of 'fair rents' by 'market rents' (by the Housing Act 1988) remains to be seen.

(iii) Date of valuation

In times of high house price inflation (or deflation), this may be an issue of considerable significance. There seem to be three alternative dates on which the courts will determine the value of a share:

(a) the date of the parties' separation (if any),[8]
(b) the date of the hearing,[9] and
(c) the date of the sale of the property.[10]

Although this variation in approach seems hard to justify, relevant factors may be whether the house is still being used as a home, in which case (c) may be applicable, and whether one party is planning to buy the other out, in which case (b) may apply. However, current judicial policy is to value the parties' shares at, or as close as possible to, the effective date of realisation and to disclaim any discretion as to which date to apply.[11] It was once thought that the parties' marital status was relevant and that (a) applied to de facto partners only;[12] this has now been disapproved.[13]

(d) Realisation

There may come a time when one of the parties wishes to convert their equitable share in the house into money by sale. If both parties agree, there is no problem. If they disagree, then resort may be had to the courts who, by virtue of LPA 1925, s 30, may order the sale of

---

7 [1982] 1 All ER 590.
8 *Hall v Hall* (1981) 3 FLR 379.
9 *Bernard v Josephs* [1982] Ch 391, [1982] 3 All ER 162.
10 *Gordon v Douce* [1983] 2 All ER 228.
11 *Turton v Turton* [1988] Ch 542; *Passee v Passee* [1988] 1 FLR 263.
12 *Hall* (above).
13 *Turton v Turton* (above).

the property in question. In practice, s 30 will only be necessary where the partner opposing the sale is a sole or joint legal owner of the property, since equitable owners cannot veto dealings with the property except to the limited extent allowed by LPA 1925, s 26 (above). If the parties are married and getting divorced, then the question of sale may be more effectively dealt with under MCA 1973.[14] Thus this section will now be more concerned with de facto partners (and other unmarried co-owners),[15] and the solutions devised by the courts bear a remarkable resemblance to those deployed by the divorce court with respect to the matrimonial home under MCA 1973 (Thompson 1984).

As we have seen, it is the technical framework of land law created by the Law of Property Act 1925 that is the primary means of resolving questions about co-owned land. Co-owned equitable interests give rise to a trust for sale which, as its name implies, imposes, often unrealistically, a primary duty to sell the land coupled with a 'power' (or discretion) to postpone sale. Technically, this means that if the legal owner(s) (the trustee(s) for sale) cannot agree over whether or not the land should be sold, the legislation supplies a statutory presumption in favour of sale.[16] The courts have displaced this presumption in favour of the view that if the primary purpose for which the property was bought is still subsisting, a sale will be refused.[17] Thus, if the house was bought as a family home, and if the parties have separated, a sale may be ordered.[18] However, if there are children of the relationship living in the house, and they are of an age at which it would be undesirable to order a sale, the sale may be refused.[19] This involves 'a departure from traditional property principles in so far as it takes account of the needs of the children, who will normally not be beneficiaries of the trust' (Murphy and Clark 1983, p 65). Thus, the needs of children may not always be conclusive,[20] for example where the dispute over sale is with a trustee in bankruptcy of one of the parties.[1]

14 *Williams v Williams* [1976] Ch 278.
15 Section 30 offers the only procedure for resolving disputes between unmarried couples over the exercise of their respective rights of occupation, since the MHA 1983 (discussed in this chapter and in Ch 6) only applies to spouses; nor, as we saw in Ch 2, is there any special procedure for resolving disputes over ownership. However, cohabitees may apply under the DVMPA 1976 (discussed in Ch 6) for non-molestation and ouster orders: 'In these circumstances it is not surprising that the courts have on occasions used the 1976 Act in order to resolve matters' (Law Commission 1989d, para 3.35).
16 See LPA 1925, s 35(1); *Re Mayo* [1943] Ch 302.
17 *Jones v Challenger* [1961] 1 QB 176; *Bedson v Bedson* [1965] 2 QB 666.
18 *Jones v Challenger* (above); *Jackson v Jackson* [1971] 1 WLR 1539.
19 *Re Evers' Trust* [1980] 3 All ER 399.
20 *Burke v Burke* [1974] 1 WLR 1063; cf *Richards v Richards* [1984] 1 AC 174.
1 *Re Holliday* [1980] 3 All ER 385; see further below.

The courts may use their power to grant or refuse sale to extract undertakings from the party resisting sale. In *Re Evers*,[2] a sale of the property was refused, but on condition that the resident partner paid the mortgage and other household outgoings; and in *Bernard v Josephs*,[3] the court ordered a sale, but postponed the date of sale to enable the resident party to consider whether to buy the other party's share at a price fixed by the court.[4] The court may also use its power to impose conditions on a refusal of sale to order one party to pay an occupation rent to the other (see above).[5]

The Law Commission has identified a number of shortcomings in the present s 30 jurisdiction (Law Commission 1989, paras 3.19–3.21 and 12.1–12.13). The first is that it is unclear who can apply to court under the section. On its face, the section appears only to confer jurisdiction to hear an application where it is one of the trustees who is refusing to effect a sale.[6] Those entitled to apply presumably include other legal or equitable owners of the land. However, the section does not enable, for example, a beneficiary of the trust for sale (let alone a mere occupier of the land in question) to apply to court to prevent a sale on which the trustee(s) is/are agreed. Second, the powers of the court to make orders are unclear, although we have seen that they have taken an expansive view of their jurisdiction in relation, for example, to occupation rents. Finally, the criteria to be applied in applying the section are unclear, especially in relation to the weight to be given to the needs of children (above). In particular, the Commission considered that the statutory imposition of a primary duty to sell has restricted the development of the courts' jurisdiction.

The Commission propose as part of their new Trust of Land to broaden the courts' jurisdiction to resolve disputes over co-owned land. In particular, the duty to sell will be removed, the courts' powers to make orders widened (and will include the power to regulate the beneficiaries' rights to occupy the land) and eligibility to apply to court will be extended to anyone seeking to force *or prevent* a sale. In addition, criteria for the exercise of the jurisdiction will be set out in statute and the interests of any children will be included in the list of relevant factors. If implemented, these proposals would represent an explicit acknowledgment that in dealing with disputes

---

2   *Re Evers' Trust* [1980] 3 All ER 399.
3   [1982] Ch 391, [1982] 3 All ER 162.
4   In *Cousins v Dzosens* (1981) Times, 12 December, sale was postponed until the resident party could find alternative accommodation.
5   See *Dennis v McDonald* [1982] 1 All ER 590.
6   It has been suggested that a beneficiary in occupation has the right to veto a sale and that a trustee can only dispense with the beneficiary's consent under s 30 – per Lord Denning LJ in *Bull v Bull* [1955] 1 QB 234.

over property rights and their realisation, the courts have been, and are inevitably, involved in an 'adjustive' exercise not dissimilar to that undertaken under the divorce law (see Ch 8). However, these proposals are not confined to 'family' cases, but would extend to all instances of co-owned land; and they do nothing to confer property rights where none would otherwise exist.

(e) Rented property

The discussion so far has centred on the owner-occupied family home. A very substantial minority of family homes, however, will be rented, either from private landlords, public housing authorities or other bodies such as Housing Associations. If certain conditions are satisfied, tenants receive statutory protection from eviction and harassment, and are entitled to controlled rents.[7] These provisions attach to the tenant rather than to the property, that person becoming the protected or statutory tenant. The details of these provisions are not discussed here (see Bromley and Lowe 1987, pp 564–578).

However, there are certain provisions relating to rented property that specifically affect family members. For example, the MHA 1983 provides that the spouse who is not the tenant of the property may nevertheless make payments of rent as if they were the tenant, provided that they are entitled to the statutory 'rights of occupation' under the Act (see above). The provisions governing the regulation of occupation of the family home (see Ch 6) also apply to rented property. The MHA 1983 empowers the divorce court to transfer tenancies between spouses in divorce proceedings (see Ch 8). There are also provisions governing the transmission of statutory protection on the death of the protected or statutory tenant to the tenant's spouse or to certain other members of the family. These provisions are also discussed below and in Chapter 2.

(f) Homeless families

Not all families have permanent accommodation. This state of affairs may arise from a variety of circumstances. For example, immigrant families newly arrived in this country, single mothers, or women with children who have left a violent spouse, may find themselves in this position. Provided that certain statutory preconditions are satisfied, the relevant local housing authority will be under a statutory

---

7 Rent Act 1977 and Housing Act 1988; Housing Act 1985.

obligation to find accommodation for such people.[8] These provisions
are considered more carefully in the next chapter. Local authorities
may also be under an obligation towards such families by virtue of
the statutory obligation resting on them to prevent the reception of
children into care (see Ch 10, below).

Death

It is an easily forgotten fact that more marriages are terminated by
the death of one of the parties than by divorce. For this reason, the
rules governing the transmission of property on death are of
considerable importance. The starting point for considering the
effects of death will be the size of the deceased's estate, determined
according to the rules set out above. The next step will be to ask
whether the dead partner has made a will in compliance with the
requisite statutory formalities.[9] If they have, the terms of the will
govern the destination of the property. English law imposes no limits
on the testator's freedom of disposition, thus permitting the
possibility that the family of the deceased may receive nothing
under the terms of the will. However, certain groups of family
members and dependants are given a statutory right to apply to
court for provision out of the testator's estate under the Inheritance
(Provision for Family and Dependants) Act 1975 (below).

This system of freedom of testation coupled with a right to apply
for provision contrasts with the approach adopted in other
jurisdictions, such as Scotland, where the immediate family are
given 'prior rights' to a certain fixed portion of the testator's estate
irrespective of the terms of the will. The Law Commission has
rejected the introduction of a similar system into English law, on the
grounds that a fixed share is too rigid a means of ensuring that family
members are provided for on death, either in conjunction with or as
replacement for a system of family provision (Law Commission 1971,
1973). Nevertheless, there appears to be wide support for a system of
fixed shares (Todd and Jones 1972, pp 45–51; Manners and Rauta
1981, pp 18–21).

Only a minority of partners make a will (Todd and Jones 1972,
pp 32–37; Manners and Rauta 1981, Tables 4.1, 4.2). A public
opinion survey commissioned by the Law Commission found that, on
average, only one in three people make a will, although the rate
varies according to age and social class (Law Commission 1989b,

8   Housing Act 1985, ss 58–65.
9   Wills Act 1837.

Annex C). Thus, the most significant body of rules are those governing the transmission of property in such circumstances, the rules of intestate succession. These provide a 'safety net for those who have, or think they have, little to leave, or who have not thought about it, or who die prematurely' (ibid, para 5).

(a) Intestacy

The rules of intestate succession have been said to constitute an 'Everyman's will', and to furnish 'the most dramatic illustration of the legal movement of the institution of marriage into the foreground relative to other family relationships' (Glendon 1981, p 21; see also Glendon 1989, pp 238–251). In other words, the rules governing intestate succession have increasingly come to favour the spouse of the deceased as against the blood relations of the deceased. In English law, the decisive shift in this direction came with the passing of the Administration of Estates Act 1925, the basic framework of which still applies, as subsequently amended.[10] These rules take effect subject to the right of family members and dependants to apply for provision out of the deceased's estate (below).

(i) Where there is a surviving spouse

If there is a surviving spouse, all personal chattels pass to the survivor.[11] The destination of the rest of the estate depends on what other relatives of the deceased there are surviving. If there are marital or non-marital[12] children or grandchildren of the deceased, then the spouse takes £75,000[13] from the estate (which will include the matrimonial home up to that value) together with a life interest in half the remainder. The other half is held on statutory trusts[14] for the issue absolutely. If there are no such issue, but if there are surviving blood relations of the deceased (that is, parent, sibling and their issue) then the spouse takes £125,000[15] from the estate, together with an absolute interest in half the remainder, the other half being held on trust absolutely for the blood relations. If there are

10 Intestates' Estates Act 1952; Family Provision Act 1966; Family Law Reform Act 1969; Administration of Justice Act 1977, s 28(1); Family Provision (Intestate Succession) Order 1981; Intestate Estates (Interest and Capitalisation) Order 1977 (amended 1983).
11 AEA 1925, s 33(1).
12 FLRA 1969, s 14; FLRA 1987, s 18.
13 Family Provision (Intestate Succession) Order 1987.
14 AEA 1925, s 47.
15 See note 13, above.

no issue or blood relatives, the entire estate passes to the surviving spouse.[16]

(ii) If no surviving spouse

If there is no surviving spouse, then the estate is held absolutely for the children and grandchildren of the deceased. If there are no issue, then there is a statutory order of priority for the distribution of the estate absolutely amongst the blood relations of the deceased. In descending order of priority: parent(s); brothers and sisters of the whole blood and their issue; brothers and sisters of the half-blood and their issue; surviving grandparents; uncles and aunts of the whole blood; uncles and aunts of the half-blood. If there is no issue and no qualifying blood relative, then the estate goes to the Crown as *bona vacantia*.[17]

(iii) Some problems[18]

The practical effect of these rules will obviously depend on the value of the property comprised in the estate, especially the family home. In the context of modern house prices, especially in the south of England, it is by no means guaranteed that the statutory legacy is sufficient to vest the matrimonial home entirely in the surviving spouse where there are competing offspring or relatives. The effect of the existing rules on the survivor's rights to the home will depend on the possibly arbitrary question of how the house was owned[19] which, in turn, will affect the entitlement of issue or relatives. Although there are statutory protections available to support the survivor's continued occupation, which enable the survivor to require that the home be appropriated in satisfaction of any absolute interest s/he may have in the deceased's estate, it remains the case that if the value of the house exceeds the value of the survivor's half-interest, the survivor must pay the balance to the trustees of the estate.[20] There are also certain restrictions on the trustees selling the house within twelve months of the death.[1] The Law Commission has also pointed out that 'the whole concept of a fixed sum is called in question by the

---

16 AEA 1925, s 46.
17 AEA 1925, s 46.
18 See also Law Commission (1988b), Part III, (1989b) paras 17–23.
19 For example, the problem does not arise where the surviving spouse is a joint tenant of the matrimonial home since s/he will receive the entire interest automatically under the rules of survivorship.
20 Intestates' Estates Act 1952, Sch 2.
1 Ibid, paras 3, 4.

development of types of property which do not form part of a deceased's estate and thus pass to his survivors irrespective of the provisions of a will or the law of intestacy', such as pensions and life insurance (Law Commission 1989b, para 2).

Despite the fact that most people do not make wills, there is widespread ignorance of the rules of intestate succession (Todd and Jones 1972, pp 36–37). Further, there is some evidence to suggest that the current rules do not coincide with what most people regard as a fair distribution of an intestate's property, especially in so far as they exclude the parents-in-law from the statutory list of relatives eligible to participate in intestacy (ibid, pp 52–57). Finally, it should be noted that these rules have no application to de facto partners, for whom the sole means of redress is an application for provision out of the deceased's estate under I(PFD)A 1975, s 1(e) (below).

(iv) Reform

The Law Commission has proposed that the law of intestacy be reformed according to two guiding principles:

(i)   that the rules should be certain, clear and simple to understand and operate; and
(ii) that the surviving spouse should be adequately provided for (1989b, paras 25–26; see also Kerridge 1990; Buck 1990).

The Commission thus made the strikingly simple recommendation that on intestacy the surviving spouse (if any) should receive the whole estate (para 33). Neither of the other two options, namely increasing the surviving spouse's statutory legacy or giving the home automatically to the survivor (with an increased statutory legacy), was thought suitable as a means of achieving the twin aims the Commission set itself. Where there is no surviving spouse, the current law would continue to apply. The Commission also made other technical amendments to simplify the law.

The introduction of such a simple rule further emphasises the trend noted above of placing greater emphasis on the marital relationship in the distribution of property on death. It would have two foreseeable consequences. The first is that greater use is likely to be made of the provisions of the I(PFD)A 1975 (see below), especially perhaps by children of former marriages[2] for whom the proposed rule may

2 See *Re Leach* [1986] Ch 226, [1985] 2 All ER 754 and *Re Callaghan* [1985] FLR 116. Such a claim could be made either on the death of the deceased (who would be the child's parent) or on the death of the surviving spouse (who would be the child's step-parent), although in the latter case there may be difficulties in establishing eligibility for a claim under the 1975 Act – see below, especially in relation to eligibility as a 'child of the family'.

operate especially unfairly, although this will only be worthwhile where the deceased leaves a sizeable estate. The Commission decided against making special provision for children of former marriages (1989b, paras 41–46; for a critical discussion of which, see Kerridge 1990). The second is that there will be a greater incentive to make a will where the proposed rule would not accord with the deceased's wishes. This would be underlined by the potentially disastrous tax consequences of the proposed rule for sizeable estates.

(b) Inheritance (Provision for Family and Dependants) Act 1975

Instead of opting for a system by which a deceased's family took certain fixed shares of the estate, English law has preferred to retain full freedom of testation. The only limit to which this is subject is the statutory right of certain members of the deceased's family and certain dependants to apply for maintenance out of the estate. This legislation, originally passed in 1938, was considerably extended by the I(PFD)A 1975 following the recommendations of the Law Commission (Law Commission 1974).

With one exception, entitlement to provision under the Act is based on proof of need for it. The exception is where the applicant is the spouse, in which case the claim is for a fair share of the estate regardless of need. This is based on the analogy with divorce, where the spouse's claim is not based exclusively on proof of need. It was considered anomalous that a divorced spouse should be in a better position than a widowed one (Law Commission 1974, para 41). Whether this argument remains valid following the MFPA 1984, which appears to have diminished the spouse's right to a fair share in divorce, is perhaps questionable (see Ch 8, below). There may be some support for the view that a widowed spouse should be more favourably treated than a divorced one.

The framework of the Act is quite straightforward. If certain groups of applicants can show that, either on a testate or intestate succession, they have not received 'reasonable financial provision' from the estate, a court may make a range of orders in their favour for provision out of the estate.

(i) Applicants[3]

(1) The spouse of the deceased   This includes any person who entered a void marriage with the deceased in good faith, and where that marriage has not been annulled.[4]

---

3   I(PFD)A 1975, s 1(1).
4   I(PFD)A 1975, s 25(4).

(2) A former spouse of the deceased who has not remarried ('an unremarried spouse')[5]   The view has been expressed that where such a spouse has had the benefit of a financial settlement on divorce, it will only be in exceptional cases that a claim will succeed.[6]

(3) A child of the deceased   This includes a non-marital child[7] but not a child of the deceased who has been adopted by others.[8]

(4) Any person treated by the deceased as a 'child of the family' in relation to a marriage to which the deceased was at any time a party   This is a phrase found elsewhere in statutes governing the court's powers to make orders for the residence and maintenance of children (see Ch 11). However, the scope of the formula is broader in this context, since the treatment of a child as a 'child of the family' need only be 'in relation to' the marriage and not necessarily during it. So, for example, a relationship between a step-mother and daughter came within the formula even though it only developed after the step-mother had been widowed on the death of the daughter's father.[9] Further, the applicant may be a 'child of the family' even if an adult.[10]

(5) Any person who immediately before the death[11] *of the deceased was being maintained either wholly or partly by the deceased*   This definition is satisfied if the deceased, otherwise than for full valuable consideration, was making a substantial contribution in money or money's worth towards the reasonable needs of that person.[12] This section, introduced by the 1975 Act for the first time, permits de facto partners, and any other dependants who can satisfy the relevant conditions, to apply for maintenance.
  The key questions here are:

(i) what is a 'substantial contribution' towards the applicant's maintenance? and
(ii) when has the deceased received 'full valuable consideration' for that contribution?

5 I(PFD)A 1975, s 25(1).
6 See *Re Fullard* [1981] 2 All ER 796; but see also *Re Farrow* [1987] 1 FLR 205; I(PFD)A 1975, s 15(1).
7 Ibid; *Re Debenham* [1986] 1 FLR 404.
8 *Re Collins* [1990] Fam 56.
9 *Re Leach* [1986] Ch 226, [1985] 2 All ER 754.
10 *Re Callaghan* [1985] Fam 1.
11 There must be some settled basis or arrangement existing at the time of death – *Re Beaumont* [1980] 1 All ER 266.
12 I(PFD)A 1975, s 1(1)(e), 1(3).

Until recently, judicial interpretation of this section had been perverse. The approach of the courts[13] had been to answer the first question by taking 'substantial' to mean that the deceased has provided more for the applicant than vice versa, and the second by taking a broad view of consideration so that, for example, it included companionship. The two questions were regarded as simply the converse of each other. The overall task of the court, then, was to weigh the contributions of the deceased against the contributions (broadly defined) of the applicant and only to uphold a claim where the former outweighed the latter.

This presented three problems (Dewar 1982). The first was that it committed the court to weighing two probably incommensurable forms of contribution against each other – for example, the provision of accommodation against the provision of friendship. The second was that a claim was less likely to succeed where the applicant has done a lot for the applicant – say, working unpaid as a housekeeper – than where s/he has done very little. Third, the outcome of this weighing up process bore very little relationship to the purpose of the Act, said to be 'to remedy wherever possible, the injustice of one who has been put by a deceased person in a position of dependency on him'.[14] On this approach, a person who provided the deceased with companionship or housekeeping in return for accommodation, and who could not rely on a similar arrangement being available elsewhere, was regarded as outside the scope of the Act, even though they may in a very real sense have been dependent on the deceased.

However, the Court of Appeal decision of *Bishop v Plumley*[15] suggests that the courts will in future avoid 'fine balancing computations involving the value of normal exchanges of support in the domestic sense'.[16] Thus, the provision of 'extra devoted care and attention' will not disqualify an applicant, provided that the applicant can show that the deceased made the necessary 'substantial contribution' to his or her reasonable needs. The provision of a secure home for the applicant will usually suffice for this purpose. However, the decision casts no light on what in future *will* be regarded as 'valuable consideration' flowing from the applicant so as to disqualify the claim.

The Law Commission's response to the law before *Bishop v Plumley* was to recommend that cohabitants should form a new and separate category of claimant under the 1975 Act. The Commission proposed

13 *Re Wilkinson* [1978] 1 All ER 221; *Re Beaumont* [1980] 1 All ER 266; *Jelley v Iliffe* [1981] 2 All ER 29.
14 Per Stephenson LJ, [1981] 2 All ER 29 at 36.
15 [1991] 1 All ER 236.
16 Per Butler-Sloss LJ.

that those cohabitants who are entitled to bring actions under the Fatal Accidents Act 1976 should automatically be entitled to claim under the 1975 Act without the need to prove dependence on the deceased (see Law Commission 1989b, paras 58–61). Given that *Bishop v Plumley* does not remove all uncertainty from the present law, there may still be good reasons for this reform.

(ii) Reasonable financial provision

The grounds for an application are that the disposition of the deceased's estate effected by the will or the rules of intestacy, or a combination of both, is not such as to make reasonable financial provision for the applicant.[17] 'Reasonable financial provision' is defined as such financial provision as it would be reasonable in all the circumstances of the case for the applicant to receive for his maintenance.[18] The question of the reasonableness of the provision made is an objective one for the court to decide on the date of the hearing.[19] The term 'maintenance' refers to a level of support that is suitable to the circumstances of the applicant.[20] It thus refers to a level higher than that needed merely to survive, but does not extend to the provision of luxuries.[1] The fact that a claimant is in receipt of income support will not be a disqualifying factor.[2]

The relevant factors, both to a finding that reasonable provision has not been made and to the order eventually made (if any), are listed in the Act.[3] These include the financial needs and resources (together with any physical or mental disability) of the applicant, those of any other applicant under s 2 and those of any beneficiary of the estate of the deceased; any obligation or responsibility which the deceased had towards any applicant or beneficiary; the size and nature of the net estate; and any other matter which the court may consider relevant, including the conduct of the applicant or any other person. In this way, the legislation ensures that the task of the court is to consider claims not just in relation to the circumstances of the individual applicant, but bearing in mind the circumstances of all those with possible claims on the estate of the deceased. This underlines the fact that, except in the case of claims by a spouse, the objective is not to apportion the estate according to a notion of fair

17 I(PFD)A 1975, s 1(1).
18 I(PFD)A 1975, s 1(2)(b).
19 I(PFD)A 1975, s 3(5).
20 *Re Coventry* [1980] Ch 461, [1979] 3 All ER 815.
1   *Re Dennis* [1981] 2 All ER 140; *Re Clarke* [1991] Fam Law 364.
2   *Re Collins* [1990] Fam 56.
3   I(PFD)A 1975, s 3(1)(a)–(g).

shares, but according to the greatest satisfaction of the needs of those eligible.

Where the applicant is a spouse of the deceased (but not a former unremarried spouse), there is a different definition of reasonable financial provision, which is such financial provision as it would be reasonable in all the circumstances of the case for the spouse to receive, whether or not that provision is required for the spouse's maintenance.[4] Further, the court must have regard to the provision which the applicant might have reasonably expected to receive had the marriage been terminated by divorce rather than death.[5] The weight of this factor has presumably been altered by the reforms implemented by the MFPA 1984 (see Ch 8). The preferred treatment of the spouse derives, as we have seen, from the analogy with the position of a spouse in divorce.

Where the applicant is either a spouse or a former unremarried spouse, the court must consider two factors in addition to those outlined above.[6] First, the age of the applicant and the duration of the marriage; and second, the contribution made by the applicant to the welfare of the family of the deceased, including looking after the home and caring for the family.

Where the applicant is a child or child of the family, the court must also consider the manner in which the applicant is being or might be trained.[7] Where the applicant is a child of the family, the court must consider whether or to what extent the deceased had assumed responsibility for the maintenance of the applicant, whether in doing so s/he was aware the child was not that of the deceased, and the liability of any other person to maintain the applicant.

Where the application is based on s 1(1)(e), the court must also consider the extent to which and on what basis the deceased assumed responsibility for the maintenance of the applicant and to the length of time over which that responsibility had been discharged. The fact that the deceased has maintained the applicant is sufficient indication of an assumption of responsibility to do so.[8]

(iii) Available orders

The court has available to it a remarkably wide range of orders once an applicant has proved a case. The factors relevant to the question

4 I(PFD)A 1975, s 1(2)(a); see *Re Rowlands* [1984] FLR 813.
5 *Re Besterman* [1984] 2 All ER 656, [1984] Ch 458; this was described as 'a curious exercise' by Anthony Lincoln J in *Re Rowlands* (above) at p 819.
6 I(PFD)A 1975, s 3(2)(a), (b).
7 I(PFD)A 1975, s 3(3).
8 *Jelley v Iliffe* [1981] 2 All ER 29.

of whether reasonable financial provision has been made are also relevant to the making of an order, if any.[9] The court's powers include:[10] the payment of periodical payments or lump sums; the transfer to the applicant of specified property comprised in the estate, or settlement of specified property for the applicant's benefit; the acquisition out of the estate of specified property for the applicant; and the variation of certain settlements in the applicant's favour.[11] The court may attach to its order such consequential and supplemental provisions as it thinks necessary to ensure that the order achieves its purpose or operates fairly as between two beneficiaries.[12] There are also certain provisions preventing the deceased from placing property beyond the operation of the Act[13] (see Bromley 1987, pp 748–756).

(c) Transmission of statutory tenancies on death

Where one member of the family is a statutory or protected tenant of rented property under the Rent Act 1977[14] or Housing Act 1985, the tenancy, together with the statutory protection, may pass according to statutory rules to members of the tenant's family. The rules for public and private sector tenancies differ, and the rules for private sector tenancies differ slightly according to when the tenancy was created.

(i) Private sector

Tenancies created before 15 January 1989   Any surviving spouse of the tenant who was resident in the house at the time of the tenant's death will succeed to the tenancy.[15] If there is no spouse in residence, then the tenancy will pass to any member of the tenant's family who was living with the tenant at the tenant's death, and for the six months preceding death.[16] This formula will include any close relatives of the dead tenant who satisfy the residence condition. It may also include

---

9   I(PFD)A 1975, s 3(1).
10   I(PFD)A 1975, s 2.
11   See, for example, *Stead v Stead* [1985] FLR 16 where the court made orders for periodical payments and a lump sum together with a variation of the terms of the will concerned with sale of the former matrimonial home and investment of proceeds.
12   I(PFD)A 1975, s 2(4).
13   I(PFD)A 1975, s 11.
14   Or, for tenancies created after 15 January 1989, under the Housing Act 1988.
15   RA 1977, Sch 1, para 2; see Ch 2 for a discussion of the relevant case law.
16   Ibid, para 3.

cohabitees. However, mere cohabitation in the same household is not enough. The courts have insisted upon some evidence of the parties maintaining the 'outward appearance' of marriage.[17] Thus, the relationship must be more than merely casual or platonic,[18] and the parties must not go out of their way to avoid pretending to be married, for example, by maintaining their own names.[19] The tenancy may pass twice in this way.[20]

Tenancies created after 15 January 1989   A tenancy created after 15 January 1989 is subject to the new 'assured tenancy' provisions of the Housing Act 1988. An assured tenancy enjoys less statutory protection than Rent Act tenancies. Any surviving spouse of the original tenant who was, immediately before the tenant's death, occupying the house as his or her principal home will succeed to the tenancy.[1] The term 'spouse' includes 'a person who was living with the tenant as his or her wife or husband'.[2] This is narrower than the equivalent Rent Act provision in that it excludes relatives, but is unlikely to affect the types of cohabiting relationship which have already been held by the courts to be included in, or excluded from, the Rent Act 1977.[3] Unlike the Rent Act 1977, the Housing Act 1988 only permits the tenancy to pass once in this way.[4]

(ii) Public sector

The rules governing succession to public sector tenancies are slightly different.[5] As with the Housing Act 1988, succession on death is only permitted once. To qualify to succeed, a person must be either:

(i)   the tenant's spouse, or
(ii) a member of the tenant's family who has lived with the tenant for the twelve months preceding death.

In both cases, the claimant must have been occupying the house at the tenant's death as their main residence.[6] The phrase 'member of the tenant's family' is defined as including certain relatives and any

---

17 *Watson v Lucas* [1980] 3 All ER 647, per Stephenson LJ.
18 *Dyson Holdings Ltd v Fox* [1976] QB 503; *Carega Properties SA v Sharratt* [1979] 2 All ER 1084.
19 *Helby v Rafferty* [1978] 3 All ER 1016.
20 RA 1977, Sch 1, paras 2, 3, 6, 7.
1   HA 1988, s 17(1).
2   HA 1988, s 17(4).
3   See Ch 2 for a discussion of the relevant case law.
4   HA 1988, s 17(1)(c).
5   HA 1985, ss 87, 88.
6   HA 1985, s 87.

person who has lived with the deceased tenant as husband and wife.[7]
Presumably the question of whether cohabitees satisfy this condition
will be decided on the same basis as other similar statutory formulae
(see Ch 2, above). If more than one person qualifies, there is a
statutory preference for the tenant's spouse to succeed; if there is no
spouse, then those qualified must settle the matter between them, or
allow the landlord to decide.[8]

Bankruptcy

A person is bankrupt when his or her liabilities exceed the assets
available to meet them, and the creditors choose to invoke the
bankruptcy procedure by presenting a petition to a court under the
Insolvency Act 1986. If found to be bankrupt, the bankrupt's
property will vest in a trustee in bankruptcy, who is obliged to realise
the bankrupt's assets and distribute them to the creditors in a
statutory order of preference. The impact of bankruptcy on the
property of other family members will depend on how much of the
family property was owned by the bankrupt, according to the
principles already discussed. The trustee in bankruptcy is not
entitled to take property belonging to other family members.
However, certain transactions entered into by the bankrupt,
possibly with other family members, may be voidable at the
instance of the trustee in bankruptcy; and there are now certain
provisions in the Insolvency Act 1986 governing the realisation by
the trustee of the value of any family home in which the bankrupt
might have a share.

(a) **Voidable transactions**

The title of members of the bankrupt's family to property may be
avoided by the trustee in two cases. If within the five years preceding
the presentation of the petition of bankruptcy the bankrupt entered
into any 'transaction at an undervalue', the trustee may apply to the
court for an order restoring the position to what it would have been
had the transaction not been entered into.[9] On such an application,
the court may make such an order 'as it thinks fit'.[10] The term
'transaction at an undervalue' includes not only a gift, but also any
transaction in which the bankrupt has received less consideration

7   HA 1985, s 113.
8   HA 1985, s 89.
9   IA 1986, ss 339, 341.
10 IA 1986, s 339(2).

than s/he has given and any transaction entered into in consideration of marriage.[11] The term of five years is reduced to two if the bankrupt can prove that at the time of the transaction s/he was otherwise able to meet liabilities as they arose.[12]

The significance of this for present purposes is that an equitable share in the family home accruing to the bankrupt's spouse or partner by virtue of the doctrine of estoppel or constructive trust may be open to challenge by the trustee, since the share may be larger than that which would arise according to a strict calculation of financial contributions. This might come within the term 'transaction at an undervalue', and be liable to be set aside.[13] The term may also include an express but voluntary declaration of trust of the family home (or other property) by the bankrupt in favour of the spouse or partner, where the beneficiary's share is unsupported by direct financial contributions to the acquisition of that property.[14]

The trustee, together with certain other groups of creditors, may also apply to have certain other 'transactions at an undervalue' set aside if it can be proved that the transaction was entered into in order to put assets beyond the reach of the creditors, or otherwise to prejudice the interests of creditors.[15] The court may make such order as it thinks fit to restore the position to what it would have been if the transaction had never been made, or to protect the interests of persons prejudiced or capable of being prejudiced by it.[16] Thus, gifts or transfers of property unsupported by consideration between family members, if made in order to preserve the property transferred from the bankrupt, are voidable.

(b) Bankruptcy and the family home

If the bankrupt is the owner of a legal or equitable interest in the family home, then the trustee will be obliged to realise the value of this share by seeking the sale of the property. If the bankrupt were not sole legal and equitable owner of the house, this would formerly have been achieved by an application for sale under LPA 1925, s 30, under which the courts were inclined to order a sale in favour of the trustee, usually within a short period of the application.[17]

11 IA 1986, s 339(3).
12 IA 1986, s 341.
13 *Re Densham* [1975] 3 All ER 726.
14 A compromise of a spouse's claim for a property adjustment order under MCA 1973, s 24 may constitute valuable consideration for these purposes – see *Re Abbott* [1982] 3 All ER 181.
15 IA 1986, ss 423, 424; see *Freeman v Pope* (1870) 5 Ch App 538; *Re Wise* (1886) 17 QBD 290, CA; *Lloyd's Bank v Marcan* [1973] 3 All ER 754.
16 IA 1986, s 423(2), (5).
17 *Re Bailey* [1977] 2 All ER 26; *Re Lowrie* [1981] 3 All ER 353.

The only reported decision in which a sale was deferred for a substantial period is *Re Holliday*[18] where a husband filed his own bankruptcy petition, apparently as a means of defeating the wife's claim in proceedings ancillary to the parties' divorce. This, coupled with the fact that the debts were comparatively small, that the creditors were not pressing for bankruptcy and that an immediate sale would cause great hardship to the wife and considerable disruption to the children's education, led the court to refuse an immediate sale. The general rule, however, is that a sale will generally be ordered unless there are 'exceptional circumstances'.[19] The mere fact that an immediate sale will cause hardship to the bankrupt's family is not an 'exceptional circumstance' for these purposes: '. . . they are the melancholy consequences of debt and improvidence with which every civilised society has been familiar'.[20] It is unclear when 'exceptional circumstances' will exist. The Court of Appeal's decision in *Re Citro*[1] is remarkably unhelpful in this respect, save to assert that 'exceptional circumstances must be identified if and when they arise'.[2] The only clearly established example is where postponement of a sale will not cause hardship to the creditors, as in *Re Holliday*;[3] whether that case could be construed more widely may be a matter of debate.[4]

The Cork Committee on Insolvency[5] recommended that the courts should be empowered to give greater weight to the circumstances of the bankrupt's family (see para 1129) and that the family home of the bankrupt should receive greater protection from the creditors. As a result, two provisions were enacted in what is now the Insolvency Act 1986, although it should be noted that the 1986 Act only partially implements the Cork Committee's proposals (see Miller 1986, at pp 395–396; Gray 1987, pp 879–883).

Where either (i) the bankrupt is joint legal co-owner[6] of the matrimonial home with a spouse (not a de facto partner) or (ii) the

18   [1981] Ch 405, [1980] 3 All ER 385; see also *Re Gorman* [1990] 1 WLR 616 where a sale was delayed for six months to enable the wife to pursue a negligence claim against solicitors which might have provided a sufficient sum to buy out the trustee's half-share.

19   *Re Citro* [1991] Ch 142.

20   Per Nourse LJ in *Re Citro* (above) at p 157.

1   Above.

2   Per Nourse LJ, ibid.

3   Above.

4   See, for example, the dissenting judgment of Sir George Waller in *Re Citro* (above).

5   Cmnd 8558 (1982).

6   The legislation does not apply where the bankrupt is not on the legal title and has an equitable interest only. The Law Commission has proposed that the law be extended to cover such cases. The Commission has also proposed that s 336 should not be confined to cases where the property concerned is a dwelling house, but that the criteria in s 336(4) (see below) should only apply to cases involving a matrimonial home (Law Commission 1989, paras 12.11–12.12).

statutory 'rights of occupation' under the MHA 1983 apply to the bankrupt's spouse,[7] any application for an order for sale under LPA 1925, s 30 or for an order under MHA 1983, s 1 to restrict or terminate the statutory rights of occupation must be made to the court having jurisdiction in the bankruptcy.[8] In deciding what order to make, the court may make such order as it considers just and reasonable having regard to the interests of the creditors, the conduct of the spouse in contributing to the bankruptcy, the needs and resources of the spouse, the needs of the children and all other circumstances except those relating to the needs of the bankrupt.[9]

By contrast, IA 1986, s 337 applies wherever there are children under 18 who had their home with the bankrupt at the time of the bankruptcy, irrespective of the bankrupt's marital status. In such cases, the bankrupt will be deemed to have the statutory rights of occupation under the MHA 1983 against the trustee in bankruptcy, which may be dispensed with by the court having jurisdiction in the bankruptcy.[10] The court may make such order as it thinks just and reasonable having regard to the same list of factors as set out above.[11]

Under either section, if the application comes before the court over a year after the initial vesting of the bankrupt's property in the trustee, then the court is obliged to assume that the interests of the creditors outweigh all other considerations, unless there are exceptional circumstances.[12] It has already been seen that the courts have given a restricted meaning to the words 'exceptional circumstances', and it is likely that the same meaning will continue to apply. Thus, 'the bankrupt's home will rarely be immune from sale for more than a limited adjustment period of one year following his bankruptcy' (Gray 1987, p 881).

Where the bankrupt is unmarried, and s 337 does not apply, applications will still have to be made under LPA 1925, s 30 and will continue to be governed by the existing case law. However, in *Re Citro*, Nourse LJ considered that it was undesirable that different tests should apply to different classes of case and had 'no doubt that [s 336(5)][13] was intended to apply the same test as that which has

---

7   It is specifically provided that the statutory rights continue to be effective against the trustee – IA 1986, s 336(2).

8   IA 1986, s 336(2), (3).

9   IA 1986, s 336(4); see Miller 1986, pp 397–401, for a discussion of these criteria.

10 IA 1986, s 337 (1), (2), (3).

11 IA 1986, s 337(5).

12 IA 1986, s 337(6); it is unclear whether a court order deferring sale made *within* a year may be challenged by the trustee after a year has elapsed – see Wheeler (1989) for discussion of this, and other aspects, of the legislation.

13 And, presumably, s 337(5).

been evolved in the previous bankruptcy decisions'.[14] Thus, the only real changes effected by the Insolvency Act provisions, where they apply, are (i) to alter the forum in which the issue is heard, and (ii) to give the court power to make a wider range of orders.

It will not alter the criteria by which the courts decide priorities between creditors and family members, except possibly providing a year's grace.[15] It is doubtful whether this will realise the Cork Committee's intention of conferring greater protection on members of the bankrupt's family:

> 'If the Insolvency Act 1986 intended to promote the idea that the family home should as far as possible be inviolable from the claims of creditors . . . it is a failure.' (Wheeler 1989, p 106)

An integrated approach to reform? Community of property

In 1988, the Institute of Fiscal Studies published a report advocating the introduction of a new regime of family property law, to be called a regime of 'mixed community of gains' (Freedman et al 1988). The report identified a number of shortcomings of the existing law. The first was that the present law is ill-adapted to a society in which women are increasingly equal economic partners and in which divorce is a common, rather than exceptional, phenomenon. Another was that, although there have been, as we have seen, a number of statutory and case-law developments, these have been piecemeal and directed at specific issues rather than resting on an integrated view of family property. Thus, related areas (such as property law, family law, pensions and social security law, bankruptcy, succession and intestacy law) have been treated as discrete and separate from each other. In particular, as we have noted, there has been a tendency to separate the position during marriage (which has been viewed as raising largely technical conveyancing issues) from the position on death, divorce or bankruptcy, where (as we shall see in Ch 8) heavy reliance is placed on the exercise of judicial discretion within a framework of statutory guidelines. The proposed 'mixed community of gains' would not only bring together previously disparate types of property

---

14 Per Nourse LJ in *Re Citro* [1991] Ch 142.
15 In *Lloyd's Bank v Egremont* [1990] 2 FLR 351, Booth LJ considered s 336 to provide a wife 'with no defence whatever' against a trustee in bankruptcy after the expiration of the one-year period (at p 360).

into one regime, it would also seek to apply consistent principles both during the marriage and on its termination.

The main features of such a regime would be as follows.

(a) All financial gains and liabilities incurred during marriage would be shared equally on termination of the marriage by death or divorce, or on bankruptcy. In this respect, the proposed system is similar to (but, for reasons given below, not identical to) systems of deferred community of property under which property and liabilities are shared at the termination of the relationship. The report discusses how different assets, such as 'unspent' earnings, pension rights, earning capacity, insurance policies, damages for personal injury and 'windfalls' (such as pools winnings) would be dealt with.

(b) Any property acquired by either spouse before the marriage would be excluded from the regime, as would gifts and inheritances received by either party during the marriage. This would require a valuation of all excluded property at the date of the marriage. The proposed system is thus a 'community of gains' rather than a 'community of acquests', since not all property would be subject to the scheme.

(c) Certain assets, such as the home and (importantly) pensions, would be co-owned during the marriage and equal division of these assets on divorce would be the starting point, subject to the joint liability to provide for any children of the marriage. Further, pooled income, and property acquired with it, would also be jointly owned. For this reason, the proposed system is distinct from a deferred community of gains since it would affect ownership during the marriage.

(d) Parties would be able to contract out of the regime.

The scheme would also have implications for the tax and social security systems (see ibid, Chs 5 and 7) and for the law of bankruptcy (Ch 4).

The introduction of such a system has not been generally supported (see Scottish Law Commission 1984; Law Commission 1988c, paras 3.3–3.6; Law Society 1991, paras 2.3–2.13). There have been two main reasons for this. The first is that such a system would lead to legal complexity. There would be difficulties in defining precisely what property should be subject to such a scheme, and allowing contracting out would create two different categories of property to which different rules would apply, posing problems for third-party purchasers of family property. The second is that such a system would be too rigid. If the presumption of equal sharing were to be applied on divorce, it might lead to unsatisfactory results which could only be avoided by retaining a discretion to redistribute property in other ways; yet retaining such a discretion would remove the principal benefits of consistency and certainty created by such a regime. Experience from those jurisdictions which have introduced a community regime have shown that many couples choose to opt out and that there is a legislative tendency to move towards greater independent management of community property during marriage.[16] Further, it is thought to be simpler to allow spouses to opt for equal ownership within a separate property system (whether by means of joint conveyances, declarations of trust or enforceable premarriage contracts) than to impose a regime of community property which allows for contracting out and departure from the principle of equal ownership in certain circumstances.

Thus, it is considered simpler and more effective to retain the principle of separate property while legislating for specific matters, such as distribution on death or divorce, rights in bankruptcy or ownership during marriage. However, the simplicity and fairness of the current law, whether or not reformed along the lines proposed by the Law Commission, may, as we have seen, be questioned.

16 See note note 5, p 176, above.

Chapter 6

Violence, breakdown and regulating occupation of the family home

Introduction

(a) Remedies in law and the family

So far in this book, we have been primarily concerned with the way in which the law structures the economic, sexual and parental relationships within marital and non-marital families. This has been conducted largely without reference to what happens when things 'go wrong'. In this chapter, we begin consideration of those remedies and procedures to which spouses or cohabitees might turn at the first signs of disharmony. This is the more traditional perspective of family law, which views law as performing adjustive or protective 'functions' in the event of family breakdown (see Parker 1985, pp 97–98; see also Ch 1, above). Nevertheless, although it is attractive to see the operation of the law in this area from this 'functional' perspective, we should recall the arguments made in Chapter 1 that the relationship between law and the family may be a good deal more complex than a functionalist perspective would suggest.

There are two primary reasons why, in this context, this is so. The first is that the existence of these remedies does not necessarily mean that they are *effective*, nor that they operate smoothly according to the functional imperative assigned to them. Indeed, we shall see at many points in this chapter that there are reasons why the remedies discussed here may be ineffective in practice. The second is that a 'functionalist' perspective cannot account for the ways in which the law itself contributes to the incidence of domestic violence through its construction of women as powerless and dependent:

> 'Violence by husbands against wives should not be seen as a breakdown in the social order so much as an affirmation of a particular kind of social order, namely a patriarchal one . . . The legal system plays a significant part in producing this for it operates in such a way as to impose particular structural forms on social relationships both within and without the family.' (Freeman 1980a, p 216)

Edwards (1989) has developed this further by arguing that the law reinforces, in a variety of ways, the perception that 'violence against wives or female partners is in certain ways distinct from violence towards non-family members in the street' (p 49). For example, the availability of civil remedies (discussed below), which must be initiated by the victim, serves to reinforce the police attitude that the criminal law has a lesser role to play in such cases; and this may be reinforced by the attitudes of those responsible for the prosecution of criminal offences towards the strength of evidence required for, and likelihood of, a successful prosecution for crimes of domestic violence. However, whether the automatic criminalisation of all 'domestic' violence would offer better protection to those who suffer it is perhaps open to debate (see below).

The primary focus of this chapter is on the legal remedies available to protect partners from violence and to regulate occupation of the family home. However, the remedies discussed here are not exhaustive, since questions of income support, housing and child custody (which may, but need not be, resolved in the context of divorce proceedings – see Chs 4, 7–9) will also be of relevance to a partner seeking effective protection from violence; and these 'private' remedies have to be considered alongside other sources of assistance available from public agencies, such as the police, housing authorities, social and medical services. The discussion in this chapter of such 'public' sources of assistance is confined to the first two of these, partly because only they raise distinctively legal issues, but also because the most pressing needs of 'battered' partners are for protection from further violence and alternative accommodation (Binney et al 1981, Ch 2). Other, and in practice just as important, sources of assistance are the women's refuges provided by charitable groups such as Women's Aid Federation and Gingerbread.

(b) Domestic violence: definition and responses

Despite a large body of literature seeking to determine the causes and incidence of 'marital' or 'domestic' violence (see Martin 1978; Dobash and Dobash 1980; Borkowski et al 1983; Pahl 1985, Ch 3; Smith 1989, Chs 1, 3) there is no agreed definition of the phenomenon itself (although there is agreement that there are many more 'battered women' than 'battered men'). Even amongst those professionals to whom the victims of such violence might turn, such as solicitors, social workers, health visitors and doctors, one group of researchers found no consistent view as to what constituted 'marital violence' (Borkowski et al 1983, Ch 4). For present purposes, this is not a serious difficulty, since a more significant question is whether the circumstances of a particular case will be regarded as constituting the victim as an object of possible assistance. For example, is it a crime, and if so, will the police define it as part of their work of law enforcement? Are the circumstances such as to justify the issue of an injunction by the courts, or to require a housing authority to offer assistance with respect to accommodation? As we shall see, the different agencies involved operate according to different criteria in answering these questions.

This underlines the frequently-made criticism that the various forms of assistance available to battered women are characterised by 'complexity and lack of integration' (Parker 1985, p 98; see also Binney et al 1981, p 22). This may stem in part from the varied nature of the needs of such women; but it may also stem from the fact that domestic violence is a low priority of government (Select Committee on Violence in Marriage 1975, paras 5, 13); which in turn may be associated with a view that domestic violence is a private matter, and that the measures necessary to offer battered women adequate protection would constitute an invasion of privacy (O'Donovan 1985, pp 122–125). As we shall see, this is particularly characteristic of the police view. However, as one writer has asked: 'Whose privacy? Whose liberty?' (Faragher 1985, p 124).

The police and the criminal law

(a) Introduction

If we take 'domestic violence' to refer to 'serious or repeated injury' administered by one co-resident partner to another (Select Committee 1975, para 6), then it is a crime. The criminal law provides a range of alternative relevant offences, including assault, aggravated assault, assault causing actual bodily harm, assault causing grievous bodily harm, wounding, manslaughter and murder.[1] One consequence of this is that the police have a duty to investigate and assist the victim. However, this does not mean that a failure to obtain an eventual conviction is an indication that the initial police action was not justified (Select Committee 1975, para 44), although, as we shall see, supposed difficulties in obtaining convictions in such cases may in practice affect police attitudes to 'domestic' cases (see, eg, Dow 1976).

---

1 Offences Against the Person Act 1861, ss 18, 20, 42, 43, 47 (as amended); see Edwards (1989), pp 73–80, and the discussion of rape in Ch 2.

(b) The police

There is a considerable body of evidence to suggest that the police are not an effective source of assistance for battered women (Binney et al 1981, Ch 2; Pahl 1982; Faragher 1985; McGann 1985, pp 88–94; Edwards 1989, pp 172–175).[2] Many women do not request police assistance at all, preferring to turn first to relatives, friends or other formal agencies (Smith 1989, pp 39–40, Ch 9). Edwards (1989, Ch 4) found that the police tend to regard domestic violence as a private matter and that many police officers feel unable from a practical point of view to be able to offer much assistance to the victim. Such work is regarded as 'boring' and outside the proper scope of police work. They appear to regard domestic violence as a 'crime' in only the most serious cases, and to 'evaluate the need for their intervention by the degree to which the woman appears prepared to embark on legal action' (Faragher 1985, p 117; Edwards 1989, pp 102–110). Edwards found that 'the police initiated independent action only when the violence inflicted was unusually severe . . . or where the aggressor had threatened the police and behaved belligerently' (1989, p 102).

To some extent, the police response is geared to the circumstances of the couple involved. Thus, the police are less likely to intervene if the violence occurs between a married couple who are living together than if it occurs between an unmarried couple who are living apart; further, the police were more likely to provide assistance if the woman concerned had an injunction (see below) in her favour, or if she had recently returned home from a refuge (Pahl 1985).

The police justification for this attitude is that their task is primarily to maintain the 'unity of the spouses' (see the evidence of the Association of Chief Police Officers and the Metropolitan Police to the Select Committee on Violence in Marriage 1975, Vol II) and that there are often difficulties in persuading the woman to pursue a complaint to a conclusion (Dow 1976; for discussion of the supposed 'unreliability' of women complainants in domestic cases, see Faragher 1985, pp 117–118; Sanders 1988, pp 360–365; Edwards 1989, pp 104–105; Smith 1989, pp 56–58).

There is, however, evidence that the Home Office and the police are beginning to take domestic violence more seriously. The Metropolitan Police issued a force order in 1987 encouraging officers to treat domestic violence as criminal and to use powers of

---

2   Many aspects of police procedure in cases of domestic violence have been criticised, eg record-keeping, response times to calls for assistance, the adoption of non-arrest policies and the lack of any systems for referrals to other agencies (summarised by Smith (1989), pp 39–53).

arrest more frequently; it also recommended that closer cooperation be developed between the police and other agencies able to offer support to the victims of violence. This has led a number of stations in London to set up special units with particular responsibility for responding to domestic violence cases (see Edwards 1989, pp 197–207; Smith 1989, pp 61–62). More recently, the Home Office has issued a circular which suggests that 'what victims want is enforcement of the law' and that 'the arrest and detention of an alleged assailant should therefore always be considered, even though the final judgment may be that this is inappropriate in the particular case'.[3]

(c) Criminal prosecution

Although the police response is linked to the question of whether an eventual prosecution will result, these issues are now technically severable since the transfer in late 1986 of the task of prosecution to the Crown Prosecution Service. It remains to be seen whether this has any impact on the role of the police, or on the number of prosecutions arising out of incidents of domestic violence (see Sanders 1988, p 377; Edwards 1989, pp 218–226; Smith 1989, Ch 8).

A prosecution is usually a necessary precondition of the woman being eligible for compensation under the Criminal Injuries Compensation Scheme (Freeman 1986a; Bromley 1987, pp 154–155). In the event of a prosecution, it is now the case that a wife may now be made a compellable witness against her husband in criminal proceedings[4] (see further, Ch 2 above). If there is no prosecution by the Crown, the woman may initiate a private prosecution by laying a complaint before the magistrates' court, but legal aid is not available and the court is unlikely to do more than fine the guilty spouse. This is also true of Crown prosecutions (Binney et al 1981, p 15), although the Court of Appeal has recently indicated a tougher sentencing policy for domestic crimes of violence.[5]

This raises the question of whether criminal proceedings are an appropriate means of dealing with marital violence. It has been argued that in many cases, the criminal law is a blunt instrument and its use may simply be counter-productive to the woman involved since the unlikelihood of imprisonment offers her no protection from recriminations by the man (Maidment 1980). However, it may also be argued that only the criminal law can offer a clear condemnation

3 Home Office Circular 60/1990.
4 Police and Criminal Evidence Act 1984, s 80.
5 *R v Cutts* (1987) Fam Law 311, CA.

of the conduct and a statement of the offender's personal responsibility, together with the best hope of immediate and effective protection (Maidment, op cit; Parnas 1978). Edwards has argued that:

'. . . in the short term the criminalisation of violence and a new police response may lead to more violence against women by men who are charged with assault and released on bail, returning to abuse the woman. In the long term criminalisation will serve to convey a powerful message, creating a public attitude of intolerance of and repugnance towards violence against women.' (1989, p 187)

(d) Children

Apart from the offences mentioned above, there are also specific offences relating to the physical and sexual abuse of children.[6] Similar points concerning the appropriateness of the criminal law as a means of dealing with such offences may be made as those made above with respect to marital violence between spouses. However, the issue is inevitably affected by the fact that there exists a range of non-criminal powers vested in local authorities to intervene to safeguard the well-being of children, which are discussed in Chapter 10.

Civil injunctions

(a) Introduction

There are a number of statutory provisions enabling a spouse or cohabiting partner to apply for injunctive relief from domestic violence. These take two forms:

(i) injunctions preventing a spouse or partner from molesting the applicant (a 'non-molestation order'); and

(ii) an order preventing a spouse or partner from entering the family home (an 'ouster order').

These are the only legal provisions devised specifically to deal with the problem of domestic violence. Unlike the criminal sanction, proceedings for injunctive relief are initiated exclusively by the individual seeking protection. There is no public agency, like the police, whose task it is to seek this form of protection on the applicant's behalf. Nevertheless, there is some overlap with the criminal law in that failure to observe the terms of an injunction may be

6 Eg, CYPA 1933, s 1.

punishable ultimately by imprisonment; further, it is now possible for a court to attach a power of arrest to an injunction (see below).

The law on this matter is complicated by the coexistence of four different statutes relating to the courts' jurisdiction in such matters. The powers of the High and county courts are wider than those of the magistrates' courts; and while the powers of the higher courts are concerned with both protection from violence and with regulating occupation of the family home, those of the magistrates are confined to protection from violence. In addition, the remedies in the higher courts are available to cohabitees, while the magistrates' powers are exercisable only with respect to married couples. It has been said that

'. . . the remedies have . . . been developed to meet a variety of needs. Some were specifically devised to deal with the problem of domestic violence, and other forms of molestation, where protection of the person is the predominant purpose. Others were originally devised to secure the right to occupy the family home in the short or longer term, but have since developed to include a power to oust one party in the interests of the other.' (Law Commission 1989d, para 1.7)

Matters have been further confused by the House of Lords decision in *Richards v Richards*[7] (discussed below).

Many advantages are claimed on behalf of the injunction as a means of dealing with a violent spouse, in particular that it is a speedy and effective procedure. It is certainly true that injunctions may be obtained very quickly by means of an *ex parte* procedure,[8] but an official preference has been expressed for a proper hearing of the issue[9] which will inevitably cause some delay (see Barron 1990, pp 65–70, 73–75). Whether the injunction is effective is a matter that will be considered below in relation to the question of the enforcement of injunctions. However, it may be said that the law in this area has become needlessly complex, a fact which must inevitably diminish its effectiveness in practice, as the opportunities for legal challenge to the granting of injunctions proliferate. It is arguable that the legal remedies are neither clear (nor always fully understood by legal advisers), speedily available, nor affordable by clients (whose eligibility for legal aid may not always be clear-cut).[10]

7 [1984] AC 174.
8 CCR 1981 Ord 13, r 6.
9 *Practice Note* [1978] 2 All ER 919, which requires an applicant to show 'a real immediate danger of serious injury or irreparable damage' before the making or granting of an ex parte order (and see *Ansah v Ansah* [1977] 2 All ER 638 and *G v G* [1990] 1 FLR 395). This requirement has been criticised by the Law Commission (1989d), para 5.3.
10 On the difficulties encountered by women in obtaining legal aid, and in some cases obtaining it quickly in cases of emergency, see Barron (1990), pp 34–36.

Further, official judicial policy with respect to the legislation appears to have undergone a series of metamorphoses. In early decisions under the legislation, such as *Davis v Johnson*[11] and *Spindlow v Spindlow*,[12] it was clear that the judges regarded the legislation as primarily concerned with protection from violence, threatened violence or intolerable living conditions, and with the question of how best to house the parties, and the children in particular, in the short term.[13] The courts were willing to exclude one partner from the family home on the basis that the other found continued cohabitation impossible and needed somewhere for the children. However, in the more recent decision of *Richards v Richards*,[14] the courts appear (as we shall see) to have become more concerned with the 'justice' of the matter as between the adult parties and to have demoted the housing needs of children in significance, and in doing so have considerably added to the complexity of the existing law (see Edwards and Halpern 1988).

The following discussion is arranged according to the different statutes conferring jurisdiction. It will be seen that, with one minor exception, the courts' powers hinge around the existence of (i) a marriage; (ii) marriage-like cohabitation; or (iii) children. This means that the powers of the court are not exhaustive since they will not apply to homosexual couples, or to couples who are unmarried but who do not satisfy the statutory definition of cohabitation (eg, because they have separated). Their application to divorced spouses is unclear. We shall see, in addition, that when it comes to ouster orders, the courts are influenced by the formal question of ownership of the family home. It is also unclear when an injunction will be available against a third party who is neither a husband, cohabitee or father.[15]

(b) Injunctions ancillary to other proceedings

The High Court has a general power to grant an injunction 'in all cases in which it appears just and convenient to do so', on 'such terms and conditions as the court thinks just'.[16] Similar powers are

11 [1979] AC 264.
12 [1979] 1 All ER 169.
13 See, eg, Lord Scarman in *Davis v Johnson*, at pp 348–349; Ormrod LJ in *Spindlow v Spindlow* [1979] 1 All ER 169 at 173.
14 [1984] AC 174.
15 See, eg, *Chaudhry v Chaudhry* [1987] 1 FLR 347; *Patel v Patel* [1988] Fam Law 213; for a discussion of the gaps in the present law, see Law Commission (1989d), Part IV.
16 Supreme Court Act 1981, s 37(1), (2).

conferred on the County Court.[17] This power includes the power to order the types of injunction under discussion here. However, there are two significant limitations on this power.

(i) The need for ancillary proceedings

First, such an injunction may only be sought where there are substantive proceedings either in progress (or about to be initiated[18]) to which the injunction sought is ancillary, or which is within the scope of the remedy sought within the main proceedings. For present purposes, this requirement will be satisfied if there are matrimonial proceedings (except those initiated under s 27 of the MCA 1973[19]), proceedings under the Children Act 1989 with respect to the residence of a child,[20] wardship proceedings[1] or proceedings in tort for damages for assault. The last of these forms the exceptional case referred to above. The jurisdiction survives the dissolution of a marriage where such an order is necessary for the protection of the children.[2] It may also be available to an ex-spouse in his or her own right following dissolution, although it is unclear on what basis the jurisdiction will be exercised.[3]

(ii) Ouster orders not available?

The second limitation on the power of the court stems from the decision in *Richards v Richards*,[4] in which it was held that a court acting under this head of jurisdiction has no power to make an ouster order on the application of a party to a marriage. Instead, ouster orders may only be made by virtue of MHA 1983, s 1 or, under certain circumstances, under the DVMPA 1976 (both below). Such applications would have to be made separately from those made under the present head of jurisdiction. Nevertheless, the decision in *Richards* may not have completely eliminated the availability of ouster orders under this head since the MHA 1983 has no application to divorced or unmarried couples.

---

17 County Courts Act 1984, s 38(1) as amended by Courts and Legal Services Act 1990, s 3.
18 *McGibbon v McGibbon* [1972] 3 All ER 836; *Beard v Beard* [1981] 1 All ER 783, CA.
19 *Des Salles d'Epinoix v Des Salles d'Epinoix* [1967] 2 All ER 539.
20 By analogy with *Re W (a minor)* [1981] 3 All ER 401, CA; but a court cannot always make an ouster order in the course of such proceedings: see *Ainsbury v Millington* [1986] 1 All ER 73, *M v M* [1988] 1 FLR 225.
1 *T v T* [1987] 1 FLR 181.
2 *Beasley v Beasley* [1969] 1 WLR 226; *Stewart v Stewart* [1973] 1 All ER 31.
3 *Webb v Webb* [1986] 1 FLR 541; *Lucas v Lucas* [1991] FCR 901, CA.
4 [1984] AC 174.

For example, the House of Lords expressly preserved the power of the court to make ouster orders under this head following the dissolution of marriage where necessary to safeguard the welfare of children.[5] It is also clear that the court has power to make such an order where there are proceedings concerning children (see above), although (confusingly) it has also been decided that in such cases the ouster order must not only be necessary to safeguard the welfare of the child but must also be founded on a legal right of the plaintiff, such as a property right in the home forming the subject of the application.[6] The effect of this will be that the court may have no jurisdiction at all to make an ouster order if the parties are divorced (so that the MHA 1983 does not apply), if they are not living together (so that the DVMPA 1976 does not apply) and if the applicant has no proprietary right in the family home from which s/he is seeking to exclude the other party.

If the court does assume jurisdiction to make an order, it is now clear that the welfare of the child is not a paramount consideration,[7] even though the child's welfare is paramount in determining the substantive issue of residence or upbringing. In practice, it seems that any attempt to separate the issue of residence from that of ouster is likely to be artificial.[8]

(iii) Criteria for making orders

With respect to non-molestation orders (whether sought under this or any other head), the applicant must prove both that there has been molestation in the past, and that an injunction is necessary to protect the applicant and any child of the applicant.[9] Molestation includes, but is not confined to, physical violence. It would also include, for example, verbal harassment or pestering.[10] However, research suggests that it is rare for a court to make such an order in the absence of evidence of violence: molestation on its own will not usually suffice (Edwards and Halpern 1991, p 103). A usual form of order would restrain the respondent from 'assaulting, molesting or otherwise interfering with the petitioner' and/or named children

---

5 See *Stewart* [1973] 1 All ER 31; *Wilde v Wilde* [1988] 2 FLR 83; but see *Ainsbury v Millington* [1986] 1 All ER 73 and *M v M* [1988] 1 FLR 225.
6 *Ainsbury v Millington* (above); *M v M* (above).
7 Per Lord Hailsham in *Richards* [1984] AC 174; *Ainsbury* (above).
8 See, eg, *Re T (a minor), T v T* [1987] 1 FLR 181.
9 *Spindlow v Spindlow* [1979] 1 All ER 169.
10 *Vaughan v Vaughan* [1973] 1 WLR 1159; *Horner v Horner* [1982] Fam 90; 'harassment includes within it an element of intent to cause distress or harm': per Donaldson MR in *Johnson v Walton* [1990] 1 FLR 350 at 350.

(Black and Bridge 1989, p 240). The lack of a statutory definition of molestation has been criticised (Law Commission 1989d, para 3.28).

Given the limited availability of ouster orders under this head of jurisdiction, the criteria for granting them are considered further below. The enforcement of both non-molestation and ouster orders is also considered below.

(c) DVMPA 1976

The Select Committee on Violence in Marriage identified three major shortcomings in the powers of the court under the previous head. The first was the requirement that injunctions were only available once other proceedings were under way (para 47). As Susan Maidment has pointed out, 'because a woman wants her husband to stop beating her does not mean that she wants a divorce' (Maidment 1977, p 419). The second was that the procedures for enforcing injunctions through the law of contempt (see below) were inadequate (para 45). The third was that unmarried partners had limited protection (para 52). The DVMPA 1976 provided a right to apply (in both the county[11] and High[12] courts) for non-molestation and ouster orders as ends in themselves, independently of any other proceedings.[13] It also provided for the attachment of a power of arrest to an injunction in certain circumstances.[14] The right to apply was extended to cohabitees.

(i) Who may apply?[15]

Applications may be made by a party to a marriage for orders restraining the other party to the marriage.[16] This means that the Act is not available for the protection of divorced spouses. By s 1(2), the right to apply extends to 'a man and a woman who are living with each other as husband and wife in the same household'. The meaning of this phrase has already been discussed in Chapter 2. One

---

11 DVMPA 1976, s 1(1).
12 RSC Ord 90, r 30.
13 DVMPA 1976, s 1(1).
14 DVMPA 1976, s 2(1).
15 Applications under the 1976 Act grew steadily during the 1980s, while applications under the 1983 Act and under the DPMCA 1978 declined over the same period: see Edwards and Halpern (1991), p 101.
16 DVMPA 1976, s 1(1); the court will not have jurisdiction to make an order under the Act if the applicant intends to continue to cohabit with the respondent – see *F v F* [1989] 2 FLR 451.

difficulty that may arise in this context is where cohabitation has ceased prior to the application as a consequence of the violence itself. It has been decided that the court's jurisdiction exists where the violence relied upon in the application took place while the parties were cohabiting,[17] but not where cohabitation ceased before the conduct complained of occurred.[18] In the former case, a long delay between termination of the cohabitation and the application will reduce the applicant's chances of receiving protection under the Act.[19]

(ii) Orders available

There are four different provisions that may be inserted in the injunction ordered by the court.

Section 1(1)(a) – a provision restraining the other party to the marriage from molesting the applicant   The basis on which such orders are made has already been discussed above.

Section 1(1)(b) – a provision restraining the other party from molesting a child living with the applicant   The terms 'child' and 'living with' are not defined, but they appear to bear wider meanings than the phrase 'child of the family'. There seems no obvious reason, however, why the policy of the Act should have been that the protection of children should hinge upon co-residence with the applicant. It should be noted that the Act confers no rights on the children themselves to apply for an injunction on their own behalf. Orders cannot be sought for the protection of any child living with the respondent (ie, the person against whom the order is sought).

Children may also be protected by means of ouster orders: but, as we shall see, the decision in *Richards* has demoted the welfare of children in significance as a factor governing the exercise of the jurisdiction to make such orders; and where there is no jurisdiction to make such an order under the MHA 1983 or the DVMPA 1976 (eg, because the parties are divorced or have ceased to cohabit), we have already seen that the courts have taken a restrictive view of their power to grant such an order as an exercise of their inherent jurisdiction.[20]

17 *McLean v Nugent* (1980) 1 FLR 26.
18 *Harrison and Another v Lewis* [1988] 2 FLR 339.
19 *O'Neill v Williams* [1984] FLR 1; on the legal difficulties facing unmarried partners who fall outside the scope of the statute, see Law Commission (1989d), paras 4.7–4.11. The problems are compounded by the absence of any specific statutory procedure for resolving cohabitees' disputes over ownership or occupation of the family home – see Ch 2.
20 See *Ainsbury v Millington* [1986] 1 All ER 73; *M v M* [1988] 1 FLR 225.

The Children Act 1989 is relevant here in two respects. First, proceedings under the DVMPA 1976 and the MHA 1983 are 'family proceedings' for the purposes of that Act. Thus, a court has power in the course of those proceedings to make 's 8 orders' in respect of children (see Chs 3 and 9). Second, a 'prohibited steps order', which may be made in *any* 'family proceedings', could conceivably be framed in such a way as to amount in effect to an ouster order. Whether the courts will use such orders in this way remains to be seen.

Section 1(1)(c) – a provision excluding the other party from the matrimonial home or a part of the matrimonial home or from a specified area in which the matrimonial home is included   The decision in *Richards*, that applications for ouster orders by spouses may only be made under the MHA 1983, affects this subsection. For this reason, the basis on which ouster orders are made is considered further below in relation to that Act. However, the judges in *Richards* cannot have intended to render this provision entirely redundant given that, as we have already noted, the MHA 1983 is not itself exhaustive. For example, it does not apply where the parties are not married or already divorced. Further, as we saw in the previous chapter, the MHA 1983 only applies where one spouse has a legal right to the matrimonial home while the other does not. Thus, where neither party has a legal right to the home, the Act has no application. Where both parties have such a legal right, the Act nevertheless remains available as a consequence of an amendment to the original Act by the DVMPA 1976 itself.[1] Without this amendment, it would be very hard to sustain the House of Lords' claim in *Richards* that the 1967 (now 1983) Act offered an exhaustive code for the resolution of disputes over occupation since, but for the 1976 amendment, the Act would have been inapplicable to all cases where the matrimonial home was jointly owned.

Quite apart from this, the decision in *Richards* makes little sense in this context given that the powers of the court under s 1(1)(c) of the DVMPA 1976 are wider than those available under the MHA 1983, in that the former permits the court to exclude the respondent from the area of the home, as opposed to just the home itself. Further, it is unclear whether the court may attach a power of arrest to an ouster order under the MHA 1983 in the way that it may under the DVMPA 1976 (see below). If either of these provisions is sought as part of the order, it may be that an application under the 1976 Act will have to be made simultaneously with that under the 1983 Act. This is merely one further respect in which the decision in *Richards*

1   DVMPA 1976, s 4, now MHA 1983, s 9.

has contributed unnecessarily to the complexity of the law on this matter.

Where, for the reasons just discussed, applications have to be made under the 1976 Act for ouster orders, it appears that the criteria to be applied are those contained in the 1983 Act.[2] These criteria are discussed below. About one-third of all orders made under the 1976 Act are ouster orders, although there is a geographical variation in the propensity to grant such orders (Edwards 1989, p 63).

Section 1(1)(d) – a provision requiring the other party to permit the applicant to enter and remain in the matrimonial home or a part of the matrimonial home   This is only likely to be effective if coupled with one of the other provisions mentioned above; but it seems likely that this section has been entirely superseded by the MHA 1983 following *Richards*.

(d) MHA 1983

In the context of domestic violence, this legislation has assumed an increased importance following the case of *Richards*, in which the House of Lords decided that applications for ouster orders by one spouse against another could only be made under s 1(2) of the MHA 1983. However, as we have seen earlier in this chapter, the MHA 1983 is not exhaustive in this respect in that it has no application to divorced[3] or cohabiting couples, nor to couples neither of whom has any right or interest in the matrimonial home. This is because the Act applies only to *spouses* where one of them has a legal right to occupy the home and the other does not.[4] The Act confers on the non-owning spouse the statutory 'rights of occupation', which consist of the right not to be evicted and the right to be permitted to enter into occupation.[5] In the previous chapter, we saw how the Act operates to protect these rights against third parties; we are here concerned with those provisions in the Act that enable the courts to determine how those rights shall be exercised between spouses. In this aspect of its operation (and only in this aspect), the MHA 1983 now applies also to couples who are joint owners of their home.[6]

Statistical evidence suggests that applications under the 1983 Act decreased steadily during the 1980s, while there was a corresponding increase in applications under the 1976 Act (Edwards and Halpern 1991, p 101).

2   Per Lord Brandon in *Richards* [1984] AC 174; see also *Lee v Lee* [1984] FLR 243.
3   Subject to MHA 1983, s 2(4).
4   MHA 1983, s 1(1).
5   MHA 1983, s 1(1)(a), (b).
6   MHA 1983, s 9.

(i) The powers of the court

Provided that the conditions for the operation of the Act are satisfied, either spouse may apply to the court for an order

(i) declaring, enforcing, restricting or terminating the statutory rights of occupation of a spouse;
(ii) prohibiting, suspending or restricting the exercise by either spouse of a right to occupy that has arisen by operation of law independently of the Act; or
(iii) requiring either spouse to permit the exercise by the other of that right.[7]

The difference in terminology between (i) and (ii), and in particular the difference between 'terminating' (which applies to the statutory rights) and 'prohibiting' (which applies to legal rights of occupation), is unlikely to be of practical significance given that both terms include ouster from occupation. The difference appears to lie in the fact that the latter leaves intact the underlying property right while removing the right to its enjoyment.

The court is not empowered to make a non-molestation order under these provisions, which will require a separate application under the DVMPA 1976; nor is it empowered to restrain the respondent from entering the geographical area of the matrimonial home, as it is under the DVMPA 1976. However, the court may make orders for periodical payments, and may impose on either spouse obligations as to the repair and maintenance of the house or the discharge of any obligations with respect to it.[8] The court may also order that certain parts of the house be excepted from a spouse's right of occupation.[9] There are thus discrepancies between the powers conferred under the two statutes.

(ii) Criteria governing ouster orders

Prior to the decision in *Richards*, the case law concerning the circumstances in which an ouster order will be granted exhibited two differing tendencies. One line of cases[10] tended to emphasise the question of whether it was unreasonable to expect the spouses to continue cohabitation having regard to their personalities and conduct; while another[11] approached the issue from the point of view

7 MHA 1983, s 1(2)(a)–(c).
8 MHA 1983, s 1(3)(b), (c).
9 MHA 1983, s 1(3)(c).
10 Eg, *Myers v Myers* [1982] 1 All ER 776.
11 Eg, *Samson v Samson* [1982] 1 All ER 780.

of the housing needs of the children, irrespective of the justifiability or otherwise of the wish of the applicant to exclude the other. The House of Lords in *Richards* held that the correct criteria to apply were those contained in s 1(3) of the MHA 1983, namely:

(a) the conduct of the spouses;
(b) their needs and financial resources;
(c) the needs of any of the children; and
(d) all the circumstances of the case.

These are considered in more detail below. By virtue of *Richards*, the criteria in s 1(3) apply also to applications brought under the DVMPA 1976 for ouster orders, for example by cohabitees.[12]

One feature of this list is that it refers to both the criteria considered important in the pre-*Richards* case law – that is, the parties' conduct and the needs of children – without indicating which is the more important. This has meant that in subsequent case law it is still possible to encounter differing emphasis on conduct as against the needs of children,[13] and vice versa,[14] and it may be questioned whether *Richards* has done much to resolve the difference. The question seems to be whether an applicant for an ouster order must prove some conduct on the part of the other spouse which justifies their exclusion, or whether the court may take the applicant's refusal to live with the other spouse at face value and consider the question from the point of view of how the children are to be best housed. A reading of the decision in *Richards* suggests that the House of Lords had a strong preference for the former approach, since the applicant in *Richards* itself was denied an ouster order on the grounds that her allegations against her husband were 'rubbishy' and 'flimsy', despite the fact that she was living with the children in very unsuitable conditions.

It may be that the decision in *Richards* was born out of a recognition of the fact that ouster orders may significantly alter the terms on which the parties are able to negotiate once they embark on the divorce process. For this reason, the 'drastic' nature of an ouster order is increasingly emphasised by the courts,[15] as is the fact that the remedy is for short-term protection rather than a final solution (see further below on the duration of orders). Nevertheless, the corollary

12 *Lee v Lee* [1984] FLR 243.
13 Eg, *Summers v Summers* [1986] 1 FLR 343.
14 Eg, *Lee v Lee* (above).
15 *Burke v Burke* [1987] Fam Law 201; *Summers v Summers* (1986) 1 FLR 343; as a result, courts should not grant ouster orders on the basis of affidavit evidence alone – see *Tuck v Nicholls* [1989] 1 FLR 283; *Whitlock v Whitlock* [1989] 1 FLR 208; *G v G* [1990] 1 FLR 395; *Shipp v Shipp* [1988] 1 FLR 345.

of this appears to be that women, such as the applicants in *Summers*[16] and *Wiseman v Simpson*,[17] whose relationship has broken down but who cannot prove any serious allegations against their partner, and who have children to care for, will be forced to live with their partner in the family home or move elsewhere. It has been said that the effect of the *Richards* decision has been to make 'the interests of adults paramount over those of the children' (Law Commission 1989d, para 6.31; see also Edwards and Halpern 1988, who suggest that *Richards* had an immediate effect of reducing the level of applications for ouster orders and made them more difficult to obtain).

We turn now to a consideration of the individual criteria in s 1(3). It should be borne in mind that – at least in theory – no factor is dominant, and the weight to be accorded to each depends on the facts of each individual case.[18]

The conduct of the parties   It is not clear what forms of 'conduct' are to be considered relevant. From the point of view of the applicant, the Court of Appeal has recently come close to suggesting that some form of serious molestation or violence on the part of the respondent is a precondition of an order.[19] The courts are reluctant to oust a spouse against whom no allegations of misconduct can be proved, even though there may be evidence suggesting that the children would be affected by continued cohabitation.[20] This appears to accord to 'conduct' the overriding role that the House of Lords said it should not have. After *Richards*, it also seems open to the court to take account of the applicant's bad conduct, as well as the respondent's good conduct.[1] Quite why this wide-ranging review of the parties' conduct prior to divorce is considered appropriate when it is, strictly speaking, excluded from divorce itself, is unclear. It has been pointed out that the court may now be 'obliged to hold a full-scale trial of the parties' relative matrimonial blameworthiness in order to resolve the short-term question of how the parties should be accommodated pending their divorce' (Law Commission 1989d, para 3.11).[2]

16 [1986] 1 FLR 343.
17 [1988] Fam Law 162.
18 Per Lord Brandon in *Richards* [1984] AC 174.
19 See *Summers* [1986] 1 FLR 343 and *Wiseman v Simpson* [1988] Fam Law 162.
20 See, eg, *Blackstock v Blackstock* [1991] 2 FLR 308, in which the Court of Appeal upheld a judge's refusal to oust a husband against whom no misconduct could be proved, even though the children were living in unsatisfactory accommodation.
1 Per Lord Brandon at p 830.
2 The consequences of this are well illustrated in *Shipp v Shipp* [1988] 1 FLR 345, [1988] Fam Law 168 where the court insisted on a full oral hearing of hotly contested cross-allegations of violence before deciding whether to grant an interim ouster order; and see the dissenting judgment of Lord Scarman in *Richards*. On the problems flowing from 'pre-divorce litigation involving issues of conduct', see Law Commission (1989d) para 3.22.

The parties' needs and resources   An obvious concern will be the ability of the parties to obtain housing elsewhere in the event of an ouster order being made or refused. It has been held that the prospect of the parties being rehoused by a local authority is a relevant factor to the court's decision so that an application by a wife will be refused if the housing authority has a statutory obligation to rehouse her but not her husband.[3] Where the parties are joint tenants of public housing under the Housing Act 1985, it has been held that an ouster order ought to be regarded as a drastic remedy since it will deprive the ousted party of the 'secure and valuable rights' accorded to council tenants under that legislation.[4]

There is a complication arising out of the fact that the 'courts are in effect being used [by housing authorities] to provide a lever which enables the authority to take certain decisions which it is reluctant to take without a court order' (Pearl 1986, p 21). For example, authorities may insist on an unsuccessful ouster application being made before it will consider an application for rehousing. This arises partly as a result of the greater security of tenure available to council tenants under Part IV of the Housing Act 1985 which has restricted local authority discretion to reallocate tenancies, and partly as a consequence of shortages in the public housing stock itself.

The courts have been reluctant to 'play the authorities' game' in this sense;[5] and in any case, it is questionable whether, by approaching the question on the basis of the law as it stands after *Richards*, the courts are the most appropriate forum for making 'welfare' decisions of this sort. One effect of this has been that neither the housing authorities nor the courts are obliged to consider the matter from the point of view of the needs and welfare of the parties (see generally Pearl 1986). There is also a risk that 'battered women will be shuttled between courts and housing departments' (Bryan 1984, p 206) as the latter insist that the former make a decision to oust, while the former refuses to be used to make what it regards as a decision for the latter:

> 'If the authorities concerned continue to insist upon exclusion orders as a prerequisite to housing, they will risk trapping battered women in a "Catch 22" position, unable to secure rehousing without an order, and unable to obtain an order because of the housing duties owed to them.' (Thornton 1989, p 73)

The needs of any children   The House of Lords in *Richards* made it clear that the needs of children were not to be regarded as a

---

3 *Wooton v Wooton* [1984] FLR 871; *Thurley v Smith* [1984] FLR 875.
4 *Wiseman v Simpson* [1988] Fam Law 162.
5 *Warwick v Warwick* (1982) 12 Fam Law 60.

paramount factor, as they had been in some of the earlier case law, but merely as one of the factors to be considered in relation to all the others. This would still permit a court to make an order where the children would be at risk of violence or abuse if the order were not made; but in the absence of this element, it seems unlikely that a court would make an order simply on the basis that the custodial parent no longer wished to continue cohabitation. In *Lee v Lee*,[6] however, the Court of Appeal accorded considerable weight to 'the needs of children to re-establish a family unit in the family home'. *Lee* may be an unusual case in that the child in question was in care, and the only way in which the local authority social services would have countenanced a return of the child to the mother was in the event of the mother's accommodation being improved. It may be that the decision was motivated by a desire to avoid continued reliance on local authority care. A more representative case may be *Blackstock v Blackstock*[7] in which the Court of Appeal refused to grant an ouster order even though there was clear evidence that the children were living in unsatisfactory accommodation.

The relevance of the Children Act 1989 to cases of violence and molestation has been considered above.

All the circumstances of the case   It is unclear what this might include. It is not open to the court to make orders for the purposes of 'allowing the dust to settle'.[8]

The Law Commission (1989d) has criticised the current position with respect to the criteria governing ouster orders. First, the application of the MHA 1983 criteria to all cases fails to distinguish between the different circumstances in which an ouster order may be sought. For example, there is a difference between an applicant who is seeking immediate protection from violence and one who is seeking a longer-term adjustment of joint rights in the family home (para 3.19). Second, the criteria, which were originally contained in the 1967 Act, were drafted before much of the current law of divorce was enacted and before the awakening of public concern in the problem of domestic violence or the increased legal recognition of cohabitation. Thus, the criteria fail to acknowledge that 'personal protection for the victims should be given priority over hardship to the respondent' (para 3.21). Third, there is a risk that the welfare of children will not be given the weight it requires, and that this runs counter to modern policy in law and the family (para 3.23). Finally, the 1983 Act provides no clear guidance as to how the criteria should

6   [1984] FLR 243.
7   [1991] 2 FLR 308.
8   *Summers* [1986] 1 FLR 343.

be applied to unmarried couples. This is simply because the criteria were intended only to be applied to spouses.

The Law Commission's preference is for a 'balance of hardship' test (para 6.33). Under this test, the courts would 'consider with care the accommodation available to both spouses, and the hardship to which each will be exposed if an order is granted or refused, and then consider whether it is really sensible to expect [the applicant] and child to endure the pressures which the continued presence of the other spouse will place on them'.[9] The long-term effects on the children of conflict between parents would be a major consideration. This test would not remove all consideration of the parties' conduct, since there would still have to be evidence that continued cohabitation is not a reasonable thing to expect; but it would restore the emphasis placed by pre-*Richards* decisions on assessing the impact of continued cohabitation of the parents on the children.

(iii) Duration of ouster orders

As we have seen, the courts have been concerned to emphasise the 'drastic' and remedial nature of an ouster order. This is reflected in the judicial policy,[10] consolidated in a Practice Note,[11] of placing time limits of up to three months on the period of ouster orders made under the DVMPA 1976. Presumably this policy applies equally to orders made under the MHA 1983.[12] This stems partly from a reluctance to allow an ouster order to effect a once-and-for-all de facto determination of the parties' living arrangements,[13] and partly to constrain the potential of such orders to deprive property owners of the right to occupy their property.[14] However, there may be some cases where an indefinite order may be appropriate, for example where there have been regular breaches of an ouster order in the past.[15] The Law Commission would prefer to see 'more comprehensive and flexible guidelines, which distinguish the circumstances in which time-limited and indefinite orders are appropriate' (1989d, para 3.37).

---

9   Per Cumming-Bruce LJ in *Bassett v Bassett* [1975] Fam 76.
10   *Hopper v Hopper* [1979] 1 All ER 181; the practice of delaying implementation of ouster orders pending the outcome of ancillary proceedings in divorce, in which a final solution to the issue of ownership and occupation would be imposed, has been discouraged: see *Dunsire v Dunsire* [1991] Fam Law 266.
11   [1978] 2 All ER 1056.
12   MHA 1983, s 1(4) permits time limits on orders under the Act.
13   *Hopper v Hopper* (above).
14   *Davis v Johnson* [1978] 1 All ER 1132; *Freeman v Collins* (1983) 4 FLR 649, CA.
15   *Spencer v Camacho* (1983) 4 FLR 662.

(e) Enforcement

Assuming that an injunction has been ordered under the rules discussed above,[16] by what means is it to be enforced? This is as important as the granting of the original injunction, since without effective enforcement an injunction may be worth little. Ultimately, 'enforcement' in this context refers to some form of criminal sanction, usually a fine or imprisonment. In this sense, there is evidence that there is little effective enforcement of injunctions in practice, and that breaches of injunction are sanctioned by a criminal penalty in only a minority of cases (Binney et al 1981, pp 17–18). However, Pahl found in her study that the existence of an injunction 'served to label the women as people whose complaints to the police ought to be taken seriously; and [it] gave an effective remedy to the police if violence recurred' (1985, p 89).

As we have seen, an injunction is an order of a civil court. Until 1976, the only means of enforcement was by way of committal for contempt of court. This remains an important means of enforcement. The DVMPA 1976 also provided that a court may attach a power of arrest to certain orders. Both of these are discussed here.

(i) Committal for contempt

Application may be made in both the county[17] and High[18] courts to commit a person for contempt of court for breach of the terms of an injunction issued by the court or of an undertaking[19] given to the court. In committal proceedings, the court may impose the sanctions of immediate or suspended terms of imprisonment, or may impose a fine.[20] The use of imprisonment is generally considered appropriate

16 In 1987 (1989), there were 11,081 (14,239) non-molestation orders granted and 4,903 (6,180) 'other' orders, which presumably included ouster orders; of these, 4,623 (5,870) had powers of arrest attached. There were 817 (727) arrests made by virtue of these powers of arrest and 274 (193) persons were committed to prison: see Lord Chancellor's Department (1988), Table 5.17 and (1990), Table 5.13.
17 CCR 1981 Ord 29, r 1.
18 RSC Ord 29, 52.
19 *Hussain v Hussain* [1986] 1 All ER 961; but note that a power of arrest cannot be attached to an undertaking and, once accepted, an undertaking cannot be replaced by an injunction – *Carpenter v Carpenter* [1988] 1 FLR 121. There is evidence to suggest that judges and legal advisers will often encourage applicants to agree to accept an undertaking from the respondent; and yet an undertaking provides lesser legal protection and is often disregarded by the police – see Barron (1990), pp 56–58. However, Butler-Sloss LJ has recently emphasised that 'an undertaking has all the force of an injunction' – see *Roberts v Roberts* [1990] 2 FLR 111 at 113.
20 *Banton v Banton* [1990] 2 FLR 465.

in only the most serious cases where the respondent has persistently breached the injunction.[1] The courts have refused to lay down any guidelines as to the matter of sentencing,[2] but it has recently been said that breaches of an injunction are in a 'wholly special category' from a sentencing point of view and will be treated more severely than criminal offences committed against a person who is not under the injunctive protection of the courts.[3] If the court decides to commit the respondent for contempt, the warrant is enforced by the officers of the court (ie, the bailiff) rather than by the police. If a power of arrest (see below) has been attached to the injunction, then the court may suggest that the power of arrest be activated, especially if the committal proceedings have been held up for technical reasons.[4]

One difficulty associated with contempt proceedings has been the tendency for there to be serious defects in the committal procedure, either in the service of documents, the court procedure or the order of the court itself. While this may sometimes be attributable to unforeseen circumstances, such as the detention of the respondent by the police on unrelated matters which prevents him from attending the committal hearing,[5] a more common cause appears to be a lack of diligence on the part of professional advisers. While there is little excuse for this, the difficulty has been compounded by the reluctance of the courts to take up a consistent stand on when defects will or will not invalidate the procedure[6] (see Prime 1987; and see Barron 1990, pp 63–65).

(ii) Power of arrest

The procedure for committal discussed above can be lengthy and offers no immediate protection. Section 2 of the DVMPA 1976 now provides that a power of arrest may be attached to an injunction whether issued under s 1 of that Act or otherwise,[7] provided that

---

1   *Ansah v Ansah* [1977] 2 All ER 638; *Wright v Jess* [1987] 1 WLR 1076; *Smith v Smith* [1988] 1 FLR 179; *Mesham v Clarke* [1989] 1 FLR 370; *Brewer v Brewer* [1989] 2 FLR 251; *Wilsher v Wilsher* [1989] 2 FLR 187; *Goff v Goff* [1989] 1 FLR 436; but compare *George v George* [1986] 2 FLR 347. Only a very small number of injunctions are enforced by committal proceedings, and there are regional variations in the annual number of committals – see Edwards (1989), p 67.
2   *Re H* [1986] 1 FLR 558.
3   Per Donaldson MR in *Miller v Juby* [1991] Fam Law 97.
4   *Newman v Benesch* [1987] Fam Law 128.
5   Eg, *Aslam v Singh* [1987] 1 FLR 122.
6   Compare *Linnett v Coles* [1986] 3 All ER 652 with *Linkletter v Linkletter* [1988] Fam Law 93; and see *Clarke v Clarke* [1990] 2 FLR 115.
7   *Lewis v Lewis* [1978] 1 All ER 729.

certain conditions, discussed below, are satisfied. It is unclear whether the power is exercisable with respect to ouster orders made under the MHA 1983.

The advantage of a power of arrest is that it enables a police constable who has a reasonable suspicion that a person has breached the terms of an injunction[8] to arrest and detain that person for up to 24 hours. At the end of that period, the person must be brought before a judge.[9] Provided that the applicant is able sufficiently to prove the breach of injunction, the judge may then decide whether to commit him for contempt in the same way as in ordinary committal proceedings (above). There is provision in the rules of court for court staff to notify the police of all injunctions currently in force.[10] The significance of the power of arrest is that by making a breach of injunction itself a ground for arrest it permits a holder of an injunction to call on police assistance at an earlier stage, rather than having to wait for the commission of a criminal offence. It also offers speedier protection than the civil committal process.

A power of arrest may be attached to an injunction, granted on the application of a party to the marriage against the other party, provided that it contains any of the following provisions:

(a) a provision restraining the other party from using violence against the applicant; or
(b) restraining the other party from using violence against a child living with the applicant; or
(c) excluding the other party from the matrimonial home or from the area of the home.[11]

In addition, the judge must be satisfied that the other party has in the past caused actual bodily harm to the applicant or to the child concerned and considers that he is likely to do so again.[12] The term 'party to the marriage' includes a man and woman living together as

---

8 Proceedings for committal for contempt in respect of acts of violence falling outside the scope of an injunction cannot be dealt with under the expedited procedure contained in CCR Ord 47, r 8(7). Thus, a husband who damaged the car of a friend of a woman who had been granted a non-molestation order to which a power of arrest had been attached was entitled to be served with notice of the committal proceedings, since the acts complained of did not amount to a breach of the order – see *Bowen v Bowen* [1990] 2 FLR 93.
9 DVMPA 1976, s 2(3), (4); *President's Direction* [1991] 1 FLR 304; *Roberts v Roberts* [1991] 1 FLR 294.
10 RSC Ord 90, r 30; CCR Ord 47, r 8.
11 DVMPA 1976, s 2(1).
12 DVMPA 1976, s 2(1); 'actual bodily harm' includes an injury to state of mind, but there must be evidence of 'real psychological damage . . . a real change in the psychological condition of the person assaulted': per Glidewell LJ in *Kendrick v Kendrick* [1990] 2 FLR 107.

husband and wife.[13] It should be noted that it is only to injunctions restraining the respondent from violence, as opposed merely to molestation, that the power of arrest may be attached. The exception to this is ouster orders, to which s 2 permits the attachment of the power of arrest; but it has already been suggested that the fact that such orders may now only be made under the MHA 1983 (subject to the exceptions discussed above) may mean that this possibility no longer exists.

The courts do not regard the addition of a power of arrest as a routine measure, but as something to be resorted to only when the respondent has persistently disobeyed the terms of the injunction.[14] Indeed, there is considerable evidence that courts prefer wherever possible to dispose of cases by extracting an undertaking from the respondent; and we have seen that powers of arrest cannot be attached to undertakings. Statistical evidence suggests that powers of arrest are attached to orders in only a minority of cases, usually only in cases of extreme violence, although practice varies geographically (Smith 1989, pp 34–35; Edwards 1989, Ch 2; Edwards and Halpern 1991, pp 107–108). This reluctance to attach powers of arrest has been criticised on the ground that 'to give an abuser a warning without imposing any penalty at all should that warning be flaunted is to give no warning at all' and that an injunction without a power of arrest 'is not worth the paper it's written on' (Edwards 1989, p 61; Edwards found this view shared by the police, who are responsible for activating powers of arrest – ibid, p 107).

A Practice Note suggests that a time limit of three months should usually be placed on the power of arrest, unless the judge is satisfied that a longer period is necessary.[15] This is justified on the ground that it eases the burden on the police and enables them to concentrate on cases where action may be required. Even where a power of arrest is attached, the police still appear reluctant to arrest for a breach of the injunction, especially where they suspected the woman concerned of having invited the man back into the home (Edwards 1989, p 107).

(f) The magistrates' court: DPMCA 1978

One of the original purposes of the magistrates' jurisdiction in matrimonial causes was to offer spouses protection from violence (see Ch 1, above). This jurisdiction is now contained in DPMCA 1978,

13 DVMPA 1976, s 2(2).
14 *Lewis* [1978] 1 All ER 729.
15 [1981] 1 All ER 224.

ss 16–18, and exists concurrently with the jurisdiction of the county and High courts already discussed. However, the magistrates' jurisdiction is narrower in two respects. First, the orders are only available to married couples and not to cohabitees, and apply only to 'children of the family'; and second, the criteria for the making of orders are more minutely specified in the legislation and are more restrictive than in the other courts. This means that an applicant may be successful in obtaining an order in the county court where they would not have been successful before the magistrates.[16]

However, where an applicant seems likely to be able to satisfy the more restrictive requirements of the DPMCA 1978, an application to the magistrates has the advantage of being cheaper, more convenient and sometimes quicker; and legally-aided clients may not have any choice since legal aid for county court proceedings may be refused (Black and Bridge 1989, p 250). However, this has not prevented a steady decline in the use made of the magistrates' jurisdiction in this area (Law Commission 1989d, n 72; Edwards and Halpern 1991, pp 100–101). Indeed, there has been a decline generally during the 1980s in the use made of the magistrates' family jurisdiction (see Home Office 1989, Vol 2, Graphic C2). Barron (1990) found that solicitors gave a number of reasons for preferring to use the county court, including a preference for affidavit over oral evidence; knowing and trusting the judges; and the fact that Magistrates tended to require greater evidence of violence and higher standards of proof (pp 100–103).

(i) The orders available

Magistrates may make two different types of order on the application of either party to the marriage:[17]

(i) an order that the respondent shall not use or threaten to use violence against the person of the applicant or of a child of the family[18] ('a personal protection order'[19]);[20]

(ii) an order requiring the respondent to leave the matrimonial home, or prohibiting the respondent from entering the matrimonial home ('an exclusion order'[1]). Where an exclusion

---

16 See, eg, *O'Brien v O'Brien* [1985] FLR 801.
17 DPMCA 1978, s 16(1).
18 See DPMCA 1978, s 88(1).
19 DPMCA 1978, s 16(2)(a), (b).
20 The court may include a provision that the respondent shall not incite or assist any third party to use or threaten to use violence against the applicant or a child of the family. DPMCA 1978, s 16(10).
1 DPMCA 1978, s 16(3)(i), (ii).

order is made, the court may also order the respondent to permit the applicant to enter and remain in the matrimonial home.[2]

The legislation provides for expedited applications for both types of order in emergencies.[3] Before making a personal protection order, the court must be satisfied that the respondent has used or has threatened to use violence (not defined) against the person of the applicant or a child of the family and that it is necessary for the protection of the applicant or child of the family that an order should be made.[4] It should be noted that this order hinges around the notion of violence as opposed to the broader concept of 'molestation', which applies in the higher courts. Thus, there must be evidence of previous actual or threatened violence to the respondent or a child of the family, and the order itself only restrains the respondent from acts of violence rather than molestation. Further, the requirement that the order be 'necessary' for the applicant's or child's protection is a more restrictive test than in the higher courts. It is for the court to judge necessity for the order rather than the applicant.[5] An applicant seeking protection from non-violent molestation must apply under the DVMPA 1976.

Before making an exclusion order, the court must be satisfied that one of the following conditions exists:

(i)   that the respondent has used violence against the person of the applicant or a child of the family;

(ii) that the respondent has threatened to use violence against the person of the applicant or child of the family and has actually used violence against some third party; or

(iii) that the respondent has broken the terms of a personal protection order by threatening to use violence against the applicant or child of the family.

In every case, the court must be further satisfied that the applicant or a child of the family is in danger of being physically injured by the respondent, or would be if the respondent were allowed into the matrimonial home.[6] The threat of danger need not be immediate, but it must be considered reasonably to exist.[7] Again, the powers of the court hinge around the concept of actual violence; threatened violence only counts where it is coupled with actual violence to a

---

2   DPMCA 1978, s 16(4).
3   DPMCA 1978, s 16(5)–(8).
4   DPMCA 1978, s 16(2).
5   *McCartney v McCartney* [1981] 1 All ER 597.
6   DPMCA 1978, s 16(3).
7   *McCartney* (above).

third party or where a personal protection order is already in existence.

Both types of order may be made subject to specified conditions or exceptions, and there is no limit in the legislation as to what form these may take. It is thus difficult to say whether the powers of magistrates in relation to, say, imposing conditions on exclusion orders, are wider or narrower than those available under the MHA 1983 or DVMPA 1976 (Law Commission 1989d, para 3.4). Similarly, the court may specify the duration of both personal protection and exclusion orders.[8] Presumably the same policy with respect to duration would apply in magistrates' courts as prevail in the higher courts (see above).

(ii) Enforcement

The court may attach a power of arrest to an order made under s 16 restraining the respondent from using violence against the person of the applicant or a child of the family, or from entering the matrimonial home. The court must be satisfied that the respondent has physically injured the applicant and is likely to do so again.[9] The power of arrest works in the same way as those attached to orders made in the higher court.[10] It should be noted that there is clearly jurisdiction to attach the power of arrest to an exclusion order. The courts have stressed that powers of arrest should not be routinely attached to orders, and that magistrates should give their reasons for doing so.[11]

If no power of arrest has been attached, it is open to the applicant to apply to the court for the issue of a warrant of arrest for breach of any order made under s 16.[12] Such a warrant is executed by the police. The magistrates have power to remand any person brought before them by virtue of such a warrant,[13] and it may fine or imprison the respondent.[14]

8 DPMCA 1978, s 16(9).
9 DPMCA 1978, s 18(1); Edwards (1989, p 69) has criticised this statutory criterion for attaching a power of arrest: 'No one can crystal-ball gaze and predict whether a man will reoffend.'
10 See also Magistrates' Courts (Matrimonial Proceedings) Rules 1980, r 19.
11 *Widdowson v Widdowson* (1982) 4 FLR 121.
12 DPMCA 1978, s 18(4).
13 DPMCA 1978 s 18(5).
14 Magistrates' Court Act 1980, s 63.

(g) **Reform**

The Law Commission (1989d) has suggested two alternative approaches to reform. The first would be to 'retain the basic structure of the present law but seek to remove as many inconsistencies, gaps and deficiencies as possible'; while the second would be to 'restructure the law so as to provide a single, consistent set of remedies' (para 6.1).

Under the first approach, the Commission recommended a number of reforms aimed at eliminating many of the problems identified above. These would include

- bringing divorced spouses and separated cohabitees within the courts' jurisdiction (paras 6.2-9);[15]
- extending the power to make orders to protect children who are at risk of abuse (para 6.13);
- extending the powers of magistrates to make orders on grounds of molestation (as well as violence) prohibiting a wider range of harassing behaviour (paras 6.16, 6.34–6.35) and to enable them to regulate spouses' rights of occupation and to enforce a spouse's right to re-enter the matrimonial home (paras 6.21, para 6.35);
- to harmonise the courts' powers with respect to making orders excluding the respondent from the area of the home or from part of the home (para 6.17);
- to introduce new statutory guidelines concerning the grounds on which orders may be made; in the case of ouster orders, this would mean replacing the MHA 1983 criteria with a 'balance of hardship' test[16] (paras 6.26–6.33).

The Commission's preferred approach, however, is to introduce a unified structure under which all courts would have the same powers to make non-molestation, ouster and reentry orders as well as orders regulating occupation of the family home, coupled with a power to make a range of ancillary orders. Magistrates' powers may be limited in some specified respects. Orders would be available either in the course of 'family proceedings' (as defined in the Children Act 1989) or in their own right. They would be available to spouses,

---

15   Edwards and Halpern (1991) would suggest going even further and would extend protection to those who have never lived together, eg girlfriends, and that the orders should be available to 'a broader spectrum of family relationships (including relationships between homosexuals and lesbians)' (pp 102–103).

16   As set out by Cumming-Bruce LJ in *Bassett v Bassett* [1975] Fam 76; for a criticism of this test, see Edwards and Halpern (1991) at p 105.

cohabitants and former spouses or cohabitants, although entitlement to ouster orders would be restricted in the case of cohabitees and former spouses to those with a legal, beneficial or statutory right to occupy the property in question; such applicants would only be eligible if they applied within a short period of the divorce or of the cohabitation ceasing and even then would only be entitled to short-term orders. The criteria for making orders would be set out in legislation along the lines of the 'balance of hardship' test suggested above, as would the criteria for attaching powers of arrest (paras 6.46–6.68).

Hayes (1990) has argued that the Commission's proposals gloss over two key distinctions in this area. The first is that between those cases of violence or threatened violence, on the one hand, and, on the other, cases where a relationship is in the process of breaking down and where the parties are seeking a short-term resolution of the question of which party should continue to occupy the family home pending the final resolution of all financial and property issues. The former class of case requires a stronger and more urgent response than the latter; while the latter raises the question of the interrelationship between orders regulating occupation of the family home in the short term and other procedures, such as divorce, which are designed to provide longer-term solutions. At present, as we have seen, the legislation covers both types of case without distinguishing between them; and the relationship with divorce remedies and procedure is unclear. The Commission's proposals would do little to alter this. The second is the distinction between married and unmarried couples. In the former case, 'the occupation rights of spouses must have a coherent link with the present and contemplated future structure of divorce law' (Hayes 1990, p 223).

There may therefore be a case for creating separate powers and procedures to provide short-term assistance to divorcing spouses, where no violence is involved, possibly as an extension of the powers of the divorce court. As we shall see in the next chapter, the current law of divorce is structured in such a way that the wide powers of the court to resolve questions over property and money only arise once a decree of divorce has been granted – ie, at the end of the procedure. The Law Commission's proposals for reform of the law of divorce, discussed in the next chapter, would make these powers available earlier in the process: but these powers would still only become available once the divorce procedure had been initiated. Perhaps we need to think more radically still, and to sever altogether the link between divorce proceedings and the power to make interim or final orders regarding children, property, money and occupation of the home: 'issues which arise as a result of . . . a relationship breakdown need to be heard together, rather than as at present, separately, under different statutes and procedures and in different courts' (Edwards and Halpern (1991), p 107).[17]

Alternative accommodation

One of the most pressing needs of women who leave their violent spouses is for substitute accommodation. Temporary provision is made by women's refuges (on which, see Smith 1989, pp 76–79); but most women who enter such refuges have need of a permanent substitute. Only a minority return to their spouse or partner (Binney et al 1981, Table 25, p 78). To this end, the vast majority of women approach local authority housing departments for rehousing according to the latter's statutory duties to provide for the homeless. These duties are set out in Part III of the Housing Act 1985. According to this legislation, a local authority is only obliged to provide permanent accommodation if the applicant can prove that

(i)   s/he is 'homeless' within the statutory definition;
(ii) the applicant is in a category of 'priority need' as defined by the Act; and
(iii) s/he is not 'intentionally homeless'.

Each of these requirements will be examined in turn from the point of view of the 'battered woman'.

(a) Homelessness

The Act defines homelessness as the absence of a legal right to occupy accommodation which it would be reasonable for the applicant to continue to occupy.[18] Under normal circumstances, this would exclude separated spouses since the MHA 1983 confers on non-owning spouses the right to occupy the matrimonial home, assuming that it is fit for habitation. However, the definition of homelessness includes individuals who have a legal right to occupy accommodation, but who cannot secure entry to it, and cases where it is probable that occupation of it will lead to violence from some other person

---

17 See, for example, the response of the Family and Civil Committees of the Council of HM Circuit Judges to the Law Commission's proposals ([1990] Fam Law 225), where similar possibilities are canvassed.
18 HA 1985, s 58, as amended by Housing and Planning Act 1986, s 14 (inserting s 58(2A), discussed below in note 19).

residing in it or to threats of violence from some other person residing in it who is likely to carry out those threats.[19] If these conditions are satisfied, the fact that a woman has temporary accommodation in a refuge does not lift her out of the category of 'homeless'.[20]

Many women experience difficulty in persuading housing authorities to treat them as homeless (Binney et al 1981, pp 78–85; Smith 1989, pp 35–36; Thornton 1989). There is evidence that some authorities require a court order relating to child custody or maintenance, or an application for a non-molestation or ouster order, as evidence of 'genuine' homelessness (see Priest and Whybrow 1986, pp 14–15; Thornton 1989, pp 70–73). There is also some evidence of judicial support for this practice, either as a precondition of a finding of homelessness or of unintentional homelessness.[1] This seems to fly in the face of the Code of Guidance issued to accompany the Act which encourages housing authorities to treat battered women as homeless without the need for a court order;[2] and we have already seen that the courts are reluctant to allow the housing authorities to shift their decisions on to the courts.[3] However, it has been argued that the Code 'begs too many questions' and that it is hardly surprising that hard-pressed housing authorities should require a court order before allocating accommodation out of a diminishing stock of public housing (Pearl 1986, p 30). In other words, the requirement of court proceedings becomes 'an important control device' (Bryan 1984, p 199); but, as Thornton has pointed out, 'the grant or refusal of an order under the domestic violence legislation, decided upon entirely different criteria from those applying under the Housing Act, is also peculiarly inappropriate as evidence of the risk of battering' (1989, p 71).

---

19 HA 1985, s 58(3); Thornton (1989) found, on the basis of a postal questionnaire, that some authorities would not treat as homeless within s 58(3) a woman who could not occupy a home from which her partner had been excluded for fear of attacks on it by the excluded partner (but on this, see *R v Broxbourne Borough Council, ex p Willmoth* (1989) 22 HLR 118 in which it was held that the possibility of threats from a person not living in the accommodation was relevant to whether it was accommodation that the applicant could reasonably be expected to occupy under s 58(2A); see also *R v Kensington and Chelsea Royal London Borough Council, ex p Hammell* [1989] 2 FLR 223); Thornton also points out that where there is no violence, but merely a failed relationship, the rights of a woman seeking rehousing as 'homeless' will turn entirely on whether she has any rights to occupy the home in question (pp 74–75).

20 *R v Ealing London Borough Council, ex p Sidhu* (1982) 3 FLR 438.

1 Eg, *R v Eastleigh, ex p Evans* (1986) 17 HLR 515; *R v Wandsworth London Borough Council, ex p Nimako-Boateng* [1984] FLR 192; but see also *ex p Sidhu* (above).

2 Paragraph 2.16.

3 See *Warwick v Warwick* (1992) 12 Fam Law 60.

(b) **Priority need**

A housing authority is only obliged to guarantee provision of permanent accommodation to those falling into the statutory 'priority need' category. In this context, the most significant categories of 'priority need' are where the homeless person has dependent children who either reside or might reasonably be expected to reside with her,[4] where the homeless person is pregnant, or is 'vulnerable' for any other special reason.[5] This final category may be wide enough to include childless women who have been battered, but such an interpretation is not guaranteed by the statute. Although the Code of Guidance urges authorities to treat such women as in the category of priority need, many authorities do not do so (Thornton 1989, pp 76–78). If a homeless person is not in any category of priority need, the authorities' obligation is simply to offer advice and appropriate assistance.[6]

Since in this context the definition of 'priority need' hinges on the presence of children normally resident with the homeless applicant, some authorities have insisted upon a full custody order relating to the children in favour of the applicant. In *R v Ealing London Borough Council, ex p Sidhu*[7] it was held that there is no justification for this practice, but, again, not all authorities appear to have followed this and continue to insist on a court order (Thornton 1989, p 79).

(c) **Intentional homelessness**

Another category of homeless applicants excepted from the obligation to rehouse are those who are within the statutory definition of 'intentionally homeless'. A person is intentionally homeless if s/he deliberately does or fails to do anything in consequence of which he ceases to occupy accommodation which is available for his or her occupation and which it would have been

---

4   The child need not be residing exclusively with the applicant. Thus, a parent with whom the child lives for half of the week may fall into the category of priority need – see *R v London Borough of Lambeth, ex p Vagliviello* [1991] Fam Law 142, 22 HLR 392, CA; but a parent with an order for reasonable access to a child will not qualify: see *R v Port Talbot Borough Council, ex p McCarthy* (1991) 23 HLR 207, in which Butler-Sloss LJ said that cases in which children might reside with both parents for the purposes of defining 'priority need', following separation or divorce, would be exceptional.

5   HA 1985, s 59; 'vulnerable' refers to vulnerability in the housing market – see *R v Bath City Council, ex p Sangermano* (1984) 17 HLR 94.

6   HA 1985, s 65.

7   (1982) 3 FLR 438.

reasonable for him to continue to occupy.[8] In this context, must the battered woman seek a non-molestation order or ouster order before she will qualify as unintentionally homeless? Despite the Code of Guidance which suggests that battered women should be regarded as unintentionally homeless, we have seen that many authorities do in practice require such a course of action, and that there is a measure of judicial support for this (see above). Thornton (1989) found that a number of authorities will threaten a woman with a finding of intentional homelessness if she does not exhaust her legal remedies (pp 80–81).

8 HA 1985, s 60.

Chapter 7
Divorce and conciliation

Introduction

(a) Divorce and marital breakdown

Divorce is the formal legal termination of the status of marriage. It is the concluding point of a process that might have begun with the invocation of the remedies outlined in the preceding chapter and Chapter 4. For this reason, the annual number of divorces (or the divorce 'rate') is not necessarily an accurate reflection of the rate of marital breakdown, but is in part related to a variety of factors peculiar to the legal system and its procedures (Eekelaar 1984, pp 11–15). For example, the rapid rise in the divorce rate since the 1930s (ibid, Figure 2) may be attributable, in part, to the widening of the grounds for divorce in 1937[1] and in 1969,[2] to the introduction of legal aid in 1949,[3] to procedural changes introduced during the 1970s (see below) and to the reduction of the length of the time bar to divorce from three years to one year.[4] Further, there are some couples who, as we saw in Chapter 4, may not get as far as formally terminating their relationship in the divorce court, and may be content with the orders that have been made in the family proceedings court. If neither party wishes to remarry, and if they do not wish to invoke the wider redistributive powers of the divorce court with respect to property, there may be no obvious reason to seek a divorce.

However, there is evidence that although legal and procedural reforms do have some impact on the divorce rate, there has been an underlying and steady increase in the 'real' rate of post-war divorce (Burgoyne et al 1987, pp 20–22), the explanation for which is debated (Dominian 1982; Burgoyne et al 1987, Chs 1 and 3; Law

1 MCA 1937.
2 DRA 1969.
3 LAA 1949.
4 MFPA 1984, s 1.

Commission 1988a, 2.14–2.22; Richards 1991). In 1987, there were 182,934 petitions for divorce. This compares with a figure of 115,048 for 1973 (Lord Chancellor's Department 1988, Table 5.18). The proportion of marriages that these figures represent will depend on the size of the married population at any one time. It has been estimated that about one in three marriages will end in divorce within twenty years of the marriage (Haskey 1989). However, since 1978 the number of petitions filed each year has remained relatively stable, as has the median length of marriages ending in divorce (Elliott 1991, pp 91–94).

The proportion of petitions filed by wives has grown to about 71% of all petitions. There is a marked difference in the grounds used by husbands as opposed to wives, with husbands preferring to rely on adultery and wives preferring the behaviour ground (Elliott 1991, p 93; Law Commission 1990a, Appendix C, Table 1). The rate of divorce varies between social groups, being more prevalent among the unskilled and the unemployed (Haskey 1984). There is also a relationship between social class and the grounds relied on in the divorce petition: adultery is favoured by social classes I and II, while behaviour is preferred in classes III to V (Law Commission 1990a, Appendix C, Table 2).

(b) Background to the present law

The control exercised by the Church over matrimonial matters through the canon law from the twelfth century onwards had the consequence that divorce in its modern sense was unavailable. Marriage was regarded as an indissoluble union, although there was an 'elaborate theory of nullity' combined with a power to order the equivalent of the modern judicial separation (Finer and McGregor 1974, paras 4, 5). From the late sixteenth century, it became possible for those wealthy enough to afford it to petition Parliament by a Private Act of Parliament for the dissolution of the petitioner's marriage (see Anderson 1984). The grounds recognised by Parliament were adultery and, in the rare case of the petition being presented by a wife, of the husband's adultery which had been aggravated in some way. This differentiation of treatment was apparently justified on the ground that wives stood to lose less than the husband by way of interference with property and inheritance through adultery and the production of illegitimate offspring.

The introduction of judicial divorce in 1857 by the Matrimonial Causes Act of that year 'was in fact little more than a codification of the practice developed in relation to private divorce Acts and its transfer from parliamentary private bill committees to a court of law'

(Burgoyne et al 1987, p 46). In particular, the Act specified adultery as the sole ground for divorce and retained the distinction between husbands and wives as petitioners, the latter having to prove that the adultery was aggravated by incest, cruelty, desertion, sodomy or bestiality.[5] It also sought to codify the Parliamentary practice of refusing dissolution if there was evidence of collusion, condonation or of the petitioner's own adultery, through the formulation of absolute and discretionary bars to divorce.[6] Although the discriminatory basis of the law was removed in 1923,[7] and the grounds extended in 1937 to include desertion, cruelty and incurable insanity,[8] the 'offence' basis of the law of divorce (that is, the general principle that divorce is only available to a petitioner able to prove that the other party has committed one of a number of specified matrimonial offences) remained intact until the Divorce Reform Act of 1969.

The 'offence' basis of the divorce law came under increasing criticism. First, the fact that many cases were not contested rendered the judicial function in the divorce process unclear, and the statutory grounds an almost empty formality. Ingenious means were devised for manufacturing the evidence necessary for the satisfaction of the grounds and for avoiding the statutory bars to divorce (Burgoyne et al 1987, pp 48–54). Second, where the case was contested, the nature of the grounds rendered the proceedings lengthy and acrimonious, and the allocation of 'fault' by judicial process was increasingly seen as an unreal characterisation of the true causes of divorce. When the Archbishop of Canterbury's Group, appointed to consider the grounds of divorce, reported in 1966, it described the offence-based divorce law as 'quite simply, inept': it failed either to uphold the sanctity of marriage or to offer a humane system for its termination (SPCK 1966, para 45).

The Archbishop's group wished to see the replacement of a fault-based system with a sole ground, which would be that the parties' marriage had 'irretrievably broken down' (ibid, para 55). This would have involved an extensive judicial inquiry into the state of the parties' marriage. This proposal was regarded as an unworkable one by the Law Commission, to whom the matter was speedily referred, owing to the time and resources that would be necessary for such an inquiry in every case (Law Commission 1966, para 120). Instead, the Law Commission recommended the adoption of a 'dual system', that is, a system that would retain the existing offence grounds in a reformulated form, while introducing alongside them

5   MCA 1857, s 27.
6   MCA 1857, ss 30, 31.
7   MCA 1923.
8   MCA 1937, ss 2, 3.

the 'no-fault' ground of separation for a certain period of time. The law now provides that the sole ground for divorce is 'irretrievable breakdown', but this may only be evidenced by proof of one of five facts.[9] These 'facts' consist of three offence grounds of adultery, cruelty and desertion and two separation grounds, one of two years' separation with the respondent's consent, and five years' separation. Unlike the offence grounds, the separation grounds are coupled with certain financial safeguards.[10]

This substantive reform to the law still left open the question of the judicial role in divorce proceedings, especially where they were not contested. There was evidence that court hearings in such cases were perfunctory, and served no obvious function (Elston et al 1975). Partly in recognition of this, but also (and more importantly) out of a desire to reduce the growing burden on the civil legal aid budget of matrimonial costs (Gibson 1980), in 1973 there was introduced a streamlined procedure for certain cases which reduced the judicial function to an absolute minimum. This 'special procedure' (discussed below) was eventually extended to all undefended petitions. Since about 99% of petitions are undefended (Law Commission 1990a, para 2.2), the 'special' procedure thus became the rule rather than the exception. This procedural change probably did more to alter the nature of the divorce process than any substantive change introduced by the 1969 Act: divorce, it has been said, has become an administrative process (Freeman 1976a).

(c) Divorce: from juridical to administrative regulation

Divorce refers not only to the formal legal termination of the relationship of marriage, but also to the process by which all aspects of the parties' relationship, such as money, property and children, are 'adjusted'. The overwhelming concern in modern divorce is with these matters, rather than with the formal legal issue of the fulfilment of the statutory grounds of divorce:

> '. . . the work of the court in its matrimonial jurisdiction is primarily concerned with . . . how best to secure the welfare of the children and how best to achieve an equitable adjustment of the available income and capital.' (Booth 1985, para 2.7)

This has been underlined by the recent procedural changes, especially the introduction of the 'special procedure' for undefended divorces, the net effect of which has been to turn the divorce itself

---

9 MCA 1973, s 1(1).
10 MCA 1973, ss 5, 10.

into an administrative rather than judicial process (Freeman 1976a). It has been argued that the modern law of divorce in effect offers divorce 'on demand' (ibid). This may be regarded as a de facto liberalisation of the divorce law. Alternatively, it may be regarded as simply a shift in the focus of the regulation of divorce from judicial process towards a looser alliance of judges, welfare officers, social workers, conciliators and mediators, all of whom may become involved with the matters regarded as ancillary to the divorce itself (cf Donzelot 1979, pp 90–92; Smart 1984, p 55). Whether the net effect of modern divorce in practice, when considered in the broader sense of including all the matters negotiated with it, is that of a progressive liberalisation as claimed, is a question underlying this and the following two chapters (see also Weitzman 1985). The Law Commission's proposals for reform of the law and procedure of divorce, considered next, could be seen as an attempt to improve the administrative management of the divorce process in its widest sense.

(d) Legal and procedural reform

(i) Criticisms of the present law

In its 1966 Discussion Paper 'The Field of Choice', the Law Commission set out what it considered to be the objectives of a good divorce law. These were:

(i) that it buttress rather than undermine the stability of marriage; and

(ii) that it enable the empty legal shell of a marriage to be destroyed with the maximum fairness and the minimum bitterness, distress and humiliation (Law Commission 1966, para 15).

In its review of the current law, the Law Commission (1988a, 1990a) argued that it serves to promote neither objective. As to the first, the Commission argued that the law places obstacles in the way of reconciliation by requiring allegations of past misconduct to be made which 'may destroy any lingering chance of saving the marriage'; and that by focusing attention on the grounds for divorce, rather than on the practical realities that flow from it (such as arrangements for the children, the house and money) which do 'not have to be contemplated in any detail until the decree nisi is obtained', the current law loses an opportunity to encourage the parties to 'think again' (1988a, paras 3.6–3.11; 1990a, para 2.17). As to the second, it argued that the retention of fault grounds prevents both the speedy termination of dead marriages and may aggravate rather than reduce bitterness and humiliation (1988a, paras 3.22–3.27; 1990a, para 2.16; see also Booth 1985, para 2.10). This may be detrimental to the children, since it may prevent both parents retaining good relationships with them.

Several other criticisms may be made of the present system. First, the fault grounds in MCA 1973, s 1 are used in just under 70% of all petitions (Law Commission 1990a, Appendix C, Table 1). To the extent that the Law Commission's original intention was to reduce the reliance on the fault grounds, the 1969 Act has thus been only a partial success. Second, the current statute is 'capricious in operation' because it 'seeks to single out forms of conduct which justify one spouse treating the marriage as ended. Hence, it represents an evaluation . . . as to the limits of toleration within the marital partnership', an evaluation that may vary from case to case (Eekelaar 1984, p 43). Even so, the ground relied on may have no connection with the real reason for the breakdown of the marriage: 'the sex, class and other differences in the use of facts[11] make it quite clear that these are chosen for a variety of reasons which need have nothing to do with the reality of the case' (Law Commission 1990a, para 2.9).

The law is thus doubly dishonest: it sets up 'irretrievable breakdown' as the sole ground for divorce, but then insists on 'proof' of that breakdown, in practice provided most often by evidence of 'fault'; it then permits, indeed encourages, that fault to be attributed in an arbitrary way. Further, it may be entirely arbitrary whether one party has grounds for divorcing the other on the basis of fault. This could be used to distort the parties' bargaining positions and could operate unfairly to those who are unable to make use of separation grounds, owing to their inability to move away from the family home or to oust the other spouse from it (Law Commission 1990a, paras 2.8–2.19; for a critical view of the Commission's reasoning, see Mears 1991).

Despite these criticisms, cogent enough in themselves, it is arguable that the greatest failing of the present law, in the Commission's view, is that 'the law does nothing to give the parties an opportunity to come to terms with what is happening in their lives, to reflect in as calm and as sensible a way as possible upon the future, and to renegotiate their relationships' (Law Commission 1990a, para 2.21). This foreshadows the key elements of the Commission's proposals for change: a shift of emphasis towards conciliation (albeit voluntary) and away from court-based procedures unless absolutely necessary;

11 The use of the grounds was found to vary according to the sex of the petitioner, the social class of the parties and the presence of children: see Law Commission (1990a), Appendix C, Tables 2–4.

and an attempt to force the parties to come to terms with the practical consequences of their actions sooner rather than later.

(ii) The preferred option: divorce by 'process over time'

Having considered a number of alternatives,[12] the Commission's preferred model for reform was 'divorce over time'. Under this model, considered in more detail below, divorce would be obtained by one or both parties filing a statement that one or both of the parties believes that the marital relationship has broken down. After 11 months have elapsed, either party could apply for a divorce order, which would be granted a month later. The 12-month period would be used to resolve any differences between the parties over property, finance and children. In the intervening period, the courts would have the power to deal with all practical matters including regulating occupation of the matrimonial home and protection from violence. This would sever the link that exists at present between, on the one hand, the availability of the powers to make final orders and, on the other, a decree nisi of divorce. The Commission's reasons for preferring this option were that the lapse of a period of time provides

> '. . . solid evidence of a permanent breakdown in the marital relationship, . . . restrains hasty or rash applications and ensures that the couple have given some consideration to what the future will hold before finally committing themselves to a divorce. It [also] provides an opportunity to reflect upon the children's best interests and to explore the possibility of reconciliation.' (1990a, para 3.26)

(iii) Key aspects of the proposals

The Commission's proposals are detailed and come with a draft Bill attached. They cover all aspects of the divorce process, including procedure[13] and the impact of the proposals on other matrimonial

12 Including: (i) a return to exclusively fault-based grounds; (ii) judicial inquest into the issue of irretrievable breakdown; (iii) immediate unilateral demand; (iv) mutual consent; (v) retention of the current dual system; and (vi) a sole separation ground. The last of these, probably the most serious alternative, was rejected because it would be unfair to those who could not move out of the home and who could not oust the other spouse, and would create problems in defining when parties who were still under the same roof would be 'separated': Law Commission (1990a), Part III, especially paras 3.20–3.25.

13 Many of the procedural reforms were foreshadowed in the report of the Booth Committee (1985), whose proposals are summarised in Dewar (1989), pp 175–177. See also Eekelaar (1986b).

remedies. For present purposes, two aspects of the proposals deserve particular consideration.

The first is that the 12-month period will be more than just a period for 'consideration and reflection'. The parties will be required to use the period to agree on all ancillary matters. Several features of the proposals seek to ensure this. The first is that a divorce petition will have to be accompanied by much more information than is currently required. At present, a divorce petition must be accompanied only by a 'Statement of Arrangements' for the children (if there are any): disclosure of information relating to property and financial matters only comes at a later stage (see Ch 8), not least because the courts' power to make final property and financial orders only arise at the date of the decree nisi (very nearly at the end of the process). This means that the decree of divorce is often merely a prelude to years of negotiation over money and property.

Following the Booth Committee (1985, paras 4.31 and 4.39) the Commission proposes that *all* information relevant to ancillary matters will have to be lodged with the application (preferably jointly) and the courts will have the power to make final orders in these matters at any time during the 12-month period, including of its own motion (paras 5.21–5.24 and 5.53–5.55). The explicit purpose of this is to force the parties to face the harsh realities of their position sooner rather than later:

'. . . [t]he preparation and completion of such forms should encourage couples to start thinking seriously about the future and emphasise exactly what will be involved if the separation or divorce is to proceed' (para 5.22).

In addition, the availability of the divorce order may be conditional on satisfactory arrangements being made, since the courts will have the power to extend the 12-month period if they consider that 'such financial arrangements . . . as the court would consider proper . . . have not been made [and] it appears impractical to make them' before the expiration of the 12-month period (para 5.58).

To emphasise the business-like nature of this 12-month period, there will be a 'preliminary assessment' of each case conducted by the court after three months of the 12-month period in which the court will be required to review the progress made by the parties towards agreement, to make final orders that have been agreed, to consider the position of the children, to identify outstanding areas of dispute and to give directions for the conduct of proceedings relating to disputed matters (paras 5.50–5.52). Thus, the period of consideration and reflection is in fact a period in which the parties, under the watchful managerial eye of the court, come to terms with their circumstances and each other. The 'preliminary assessment' is roughly equivalent to the Booth Committee's proposal for an 'initial hearing' (Booth 1985, paras 3.5–3.9, 4.53–4.90), except that it is to take place later in the process: '[t]his is in order to avoid rushing the parties into precipitate decision-making or inducing the feeling that a separation or divorce is inevitable in every case' (para 5.50).

The second important aspect of the proposals is the emphasis they place on encouraging the parties, whenever possible, to resolve their differences through mediation or conciliation (discussed more fully below). The Commission rejected the suggestion that conciliation or mediation (which they regard as interchangeable terms) should be made compulsory, preferring instead to rely on 'encouragement'. One reason for this, in the Commission's view, is the evidence (discussed below) that the most successful form of conciliation is that which is voluntary and clearly demarcated from the court. In addition, the Commission was anxious to retain a role for traditional adjudication in some cases:

'Where time permits, alternative methods can be explored so as to enable the parties to try and reach their own agreements away from the pressures of the court door. Where, however, an immediate decision is needed in the interests of either party or of their children, the courts should be prepared to give it.' (para 5.34)

A number of specific proposals seek to provide this encouragement towards conciliation and mediation. First, on the making of the divorce application both parties will be supplied with an information pack containing (among other things) an explanation of the nature and purpose of conciliation and details of conciliation services available locally. Second, solicitors acting for either party will be obliged to certify whether they have informed their clients of these matters. The hope and expectation is that this will encourage legal advisers to refer their clients to conciliation services where appropriate. Finally, the courts will be obliged at the preliminary assessment to consider how best to 'encourage' the parties to resolve their differences through conciliation and will have the power at any stage in the proceedings both to direct that the parties meet a specified conciliator to 'discuss the nature and potential benefits' of conciliation and to adjourn hearings of disputed issues to allow conciliation to take place (paras 5.29–5.39).

(iv) Easier, harder, or just different?

It would be tempting, but inaccurate, to characterise these proposals as making divorce 'easier'. Although the need to allege and prove fault will be removed, and although the periods of separation will be reduced to a period in which no separation need be shown, there are a number of ways in which the proposed scheme would make divorce harder. It would, for example, lengthen the divorce process for most people: the median length for adultery and behaviour petitions from start to finish is currently only six months (Law Commission 1990a, Appendix C, Table 5). It would also force the parties to address the practical consequences of a divorce much sooner. In any case, the interest of these proposals lies not in whether they would make divorce easier or harder, but in the changes they imply in the role of the legal system in divorce cases.

The scheme marks the final withdrawal of any normative or evaluative content from the divorce law. Instead, the focus is on two managerial goals. The first is the effective management of the divorce process through the creation of a more active role for the relevant formal institutions of the legal system. This is evidenced, for example, by the proposals for fixed hearing and directions appointments and the discretion to extend the period if suitable financial or child care arrangements have not been made. The second is a refocusing of judicial and court resources on those cases where they are most needed. Those considered suitable for conciliation or mediation will be 'encouraged' in that direction, leaving the courts free to concentrate on those cases requiring quick and decisive court action: extra-legal conciliation is being co-opted as a further element in the strategy of diverting litigants away from the courts (cf Davis 1988, p 114). At the heart of the proposals, however, lies a lack of any clear articulation of the proper boundary between the different forms of dispute resolution.

There is a third, but not expressly articulated, goal: that by forcing divorcing couples to think sooner rather than later about the practical consequences of what they are doing, they will be discouraged from divorcing at all. As Eekelaar has suggested, 'instead of attempting to influence behaviour by incorporating moral precepts into its substantive provisions (as under the fault-based system), the goal is now to influence it through procedures' (1991, p 143).

Procedure

(a) Undefended divorces

The overwhelming majority of divorce petitions are not defended by the respondent. In such cases, the procedure, very briefly, is as follows. The petitioner files a petition,[14] the contents of which are prescribed by rules of court.[15] The petition must be accompanied by a statement of the arrangements proposed for any children of the family[16] (see further, Ch 9, below). The petition is then served on the respondent by the court. The respondent acknowledges service in prescribed form, following which the petitioner files an affidavit in support of the allegations in the petition.[17]

The district judge[18] then examines the documents and considers the evidence, and if satisfied that the contents of the petition have been sufficiently proved, makes a certificate to that effect.[19] This is known as the 'special procedure', although in practice it is the ordinary procedure.[20] Once the district judge certifies the case as proved, the decree nisi is pronounced by a judge in open court at a later date.[1] The parties' attendance is not required, although the petitioner may be required to attend a judicial appointment for the purposes of considering the arrangements for the children, the date of which will be arranged by the district judge[2] (see Ch 9). The petitioner then applies for the decree absolute, which finally terminates the marriage.[3]

As we have seen, one purpose of this procedure was to save money. The simplified procedure meant not only that there would be savings in judicial time, through the transfer of the bulk of the work to district judges, but also that savings in legal aid could be made. Thus, the extension of the procedure to all divorces in 1977 was accompanied by the withdrawal of legal aid from undefended petitions for divorce.[4] Advice and assistance is still available under the Green Form Scheme (see Ch 1, above), and full legal aid continues to be available for defended causes, for ancillary matters and for disputed residence cases.[5] Under the Green Form Scheme, the solicitor may do almost all the work preparatory to the examination of the documents by the district judge, and may advise as to the obtaining of the decree absolute. However, the scheme does not cover the judicial appointment to consider the arrangements for the

---

14 Family Proceedings Rules 1991, r 2.2(1).
15 Family Proceedings Rules 1991, r 2.2(1) and Appendix 2.
16 Family Proceedings Rules 1991, r 2.2(2) and Form M4.
17 Family Proceedings Rules 1991, r 2.24(3).
18 Previously known as a registrar. In this chapter, the new term will be used except where referring to research or procedures that pre-date the change of name.
19 Family Proceedings Rules 1991, r 2.36(1).
20 Per Ormrod LJ in *Day v Day* [1979] 2 All ER 187.
1   Family Proceedings Rules 1991, r 2.36(2).
2   Family Proceedings Rules 1991, r 2.39(3).
3   Family Proceedings Rules 1991, r 2.49.
4   Legal Aid (Matrimonial Proceedings) Regulations 1977.
5   Legal Aid (Matrimonial Proceedings) Regulations 1977, paras 2, 3.

children, at which the petitioner will be unrepresented unless there is likely to be a dispute over residence, or the solicitor is willing to attend unpaid. Where the solicitor is advising a petitioner, the normal expenditure limit is increased.[6]

The removal of legal aid from undefended divorces has not greatly diminished the involvement of solicitors in undefended divorce proceedings (Davis et al 1982). However, it seems that some solicitors find it necessary to do work not covered by the Green Form Scheme, and some clients are confused about the availability of assistance and the distinction between the Green Form Scheme and the full Legal Aid Scheme (ibid). Nevertheless, '[t]here is as yet no evidence that the removal of legal aid from undefended petitions has brought hardship or undue inconvenience to petitioners' (Gibson 1980, p 624).

(b) Defended divorces

A respondent to a petition may wish to defend it for a variety of reasons. S/he may not wish to be divorced, may wish to dispute the allegations made in the petition or may wish to cross-petition for divorce by alleging that the petitioner has given grounds for doing so. Nevertheless, divorce petitions are very rarely defended, although Davis and Murch suggest there are many undefended cases in which 'opposition to the award of a decree (or to the contents of the divorce petition) still strongly persists. It is just that this resistance is dealt with at some preliminary stage' (1988, p 101).

The rules governing the drafting and service of petitions are the same as undefended cases. A respondent wishing to defend must indicate an intention to do so in the acknowledgment of service and then file an answer to the petition.[7] The petitioner may, in certain circumstances, file a further reply, for example to defend a cross-petition.[8] The rules of court provide mechanisms for the exchange of pleadings and discovery of documentary evidence.[9] Once the exchange of pleadings is complete, the district judge fixes the date, time and place of the hearing.[10] The hearing takes place before a High Court judge, and the normal rules of evidence, especially as to hearsay and documentary evidence, apply. The evidence of witnesses is prima facie to be given orally in court, but this is expressed to be subject to the Civil Evidence Act 1968.[11]

6 See Ch 1.
7 Family Proceedings Rules 1991, r 12.
8 Family Proceedings Rules 1991, r 2.13.
9 Family Proceedings Rules 1991, r 2.20.
10 Family Proceedings Rules 1991, r 2.24.
11 Family Proceedings Rules 1991, r 2.28(1).

Substantive law

(a) Jurisdiction

The courts of England and Wales have jurisdiction to hear a petition for divorce if either of the parties to the marriage is domiciled in England and Wales when the proceedings are begun, or was habitually resident in England and Wales throughout the period of one year ending with that date.[12] There are provisions permitting or requiring the staying of proceedings when proceedings have been begun in another jurisdiction in relation to the same marriage.[13] 'Domicile' includes both domicile of origin and domicile of choice.

(b) One-year bar

There is an absolute bar on the presentation of a petition for divorce within one year of the celebration of the marriage.[14] There is no exception to this bar. This rule was introduced by MFPA 1984, s 1. Previously, the bar lasted for three years but was subject to exceptions where the petitioner suffered 'exceptional hardship' or where the respondent was 'exceptionally depraved'. The present rule was proposed by the Law Commission (1982c), who considered that the old exceptions were unsatisfactory but regarded the maintenance of a time bar as important in order to avoid the devaluation of marriage as an institution and to prevent 'the apparent scandal of divorce petitions being presented immediately after the marriage' (para 2.33).

Under the Law Commission's proposed new scheme, parties will in effect be prevented from obtaining a divorce until they have been married for two years: the one-year bar would thus be retained, and the period for consideration and reflection would be added to it. However, there would be nothing to prevent a couple from making a statement of marital breakdown during the first year of marriage, or from applying for a separation order at the end of the period for consideration (see below). The courts would simply have no power to issue a divorce order until two years since the date of the marriage had elapsed (Law Commission 1990a, paras 5.82–5.84).

(c) The five 'facts' evidencing irretrievable breakdown

A petition for divorce may be presented by either party to the marriage on the ground that the marriage has broken down

---

12 Domicile and Matrimonial Proceedings Act 1973, s 5(2).
13 DMPA 1973, s 6(3), Sch 1, paras 7, 8, 9.
14 MCA 1973, s 3.

irretrievably.[15] However, the court shall not hold the marriage to have broken down irretrievably unless the petitioner satisfies the court of one of the five 'facts' set out in MCA 1973, s 1(2). The court is under a duty to inquire, so far as it reasonably can, into the facts alleged by either party,[16] although as we have seen the court's ability to do this will be very limited in undefended cases: '. . . the registrar's scrutiny may well be effective in picking up technical errors in procedure or presentation but is unlikely to reveal defects of substance, particularly in behaviour cases' (Law Commission 1990a, para 2.2). If one of the facts is proved, then the court shall grant a decree unless it is satisfied that the marriage has not broken down irretrievably.[17] In other words, proof of one of the facts is a necessary but not a sufficient condition of a decree.[18] The irretrievable breakdown need not be consequent on the particular fact relied on.[19] The five 'facts' are as follows:

Section 1(2)(a) – that the respondent has committed adultery and the petitioner finds it intolerable to live with the respondent

'Adultery' for this purpose is defined as voluntary heterosexual sexual intercourse between two people who are not married to each other, but at least one of whom is married to a third party.[20] 'Sexual intercourse' is defined as the penetration by the male of the female genitalia.[1] The requirement of voluntariness excludes the victim of rape from the definition of adulterer; the requirement of heterosexuality excludes homosexual intercourse, although the respondent's homosexuality may be sufficient for a petition based on s 1(2)(b) (see below). A petitioner will be prevented from relying on this ground where s/he has lived with the respondent for more than six months following the disclosure to the petitioner of the adultery relied on in the petition;[2] but any such period of cohabitation of less than six months will be disregarded in determining whether or not the petitioner finds it intolerable to live with the respondent.[3]

The petition must provide brief particulars of the evidence supporting the allegation of adultery. Consistent with the proposals of

15 MCA 1973, s 1(1).
16 MCA 1973, s 1(3).
17 MCA 1973, s 1(4).
18 *Pheasant v Pheasant* [1972] 1 All ER 587; *Richards v Richards* [1972] 3 All ER 695.
19 *Buffery v Buffery* [1988] FCR 465.
20 *Clarkson v Clarkson* (1930) 46 TLR 623.
1 *Dennis v Dennis* [1955] 2 All ER 51.
2 MCA 1973, s 2(1).
3 MCA 1973, s 2(2).

the Booth Committee (1985, para 4.14), the name of the party with whom the adultery was committed need no longer be given.[4] If a name is given, that person is then made co-respondent. In the event of further evidence being necessary, for example in a defended petition or where the district judge requests more information under the special procedure, there are a number of ways in which this may be provided. For example, direct evidence from an inquiry agent, a written admission by the respondent, the identity of a child's father or a finding of adultery in other proceedings may be sufficient to prove adultery. The standard of proof is high, but falls short of the criminal standard.[5] However, it will only be in very rare cases that evidence such as this will be needed. For the most part, thinly substantiated allegations will suffice in undefended cases.

For a time, it was unclear whether the requirement in s 1(2)(a) that the petitioner find it intolerable to live with the respondent was to be proved by evidence other than adultery, or whether the 'intolerability' had to be consequent on the fact of adultery itself. In *Cleary*,[6] the Court of Appeal held that the former was the correct interpretation, although doubts have been expressed as to whether this is the correct approach,[7] especially in view of the wording of MCA 1973, s 2(2) which presupposes that intolerability is linked to the adultery. In practice, however, it will be sufficient for the petitioner simply to assert the fact of intolerability in the petition without attributing it to a specific cause.

Adultery is the second most widely used ground (Law Commission 1990a, Appendix C, Table 1). This may be owing in part to the fact that minimal supporting evidence will be required in most cases. This has been emphasised by the removal of the requirement that a co-respondent be named in the petition.

Section 1(2)(b) – that the respondent has behaved in such a way that the petitioner cannot reasonably be expected to live with the respondent

The requirement is not that the respondent has behaved unreasonably, but that the petitioner cannot reasonably be expected to continue cohabitation. This imports both a subjective and an objective element. Thus, the court is not only concerned with the conduct of the respondent, but also with the effect of that conduct on the petitioner.[8] Nevertheless, the court must also view all the facts from

4   Family Proceedings Rules 1991, r 2.7(1).
5   *Serio v Serio* (1983) 4 FLR 756.
6   [1974] 1 All ER 498.
7   *Carr v Carr* [1974] 1 All ER 1193.
8   *Balraj v Balraj* (1980) 11 Fam Law 110; *Ash v Ash* [1972] 1 All ER 582.

the point of view of the 'right-thinking person' and ask whether, taking into account all the circumstances, together with the character and personalities of the parties, the petitioner can be reasonably expected to live with the respondent.[9]

Thus defined, the category includes a wide range of behaviour, from outright physical violence,[10] alcoholism,[11] and deliberate persecution,[12] to a series of acts which, though trivial in themselves, together constituted 'a constant atmosphere of criticism, disapproval and boorish behaviour'.[13] However, mere lack of affection,[14] moodiness,[15] refusal of sexual contact[16] and desertion (and conduct immediately preceding desertion[17]) have not been regarded as sufficient.

Nevertheless, although a state of affairs or state of mind has not been regarded as 'behaviour',[18] it has been held that 'behaviour' may consist of both positive acts and omissions, although spouses may reasonably be expected to tolerate the latter to a greater degree than the former.[19] Further, 'behaviour' need not consist of conduct over which the respondent has control. Thus, it is possible for a petitioner to obtain a divorce from a respondent who has become so ill as to require full-time medical care, although it may be that the nature of the illness must also be to cause behaviour that cannot be tolerated, rather than simply to leave the respondent in a vegetable-like state.[20]

Where the petitioner continues to live with the respondent following the last incident relied upon in the petition, that period of cohabitation shall be ignored for the purposes of determining the reasonableness of continued cohabitation unless it comes to more than six months;[1] but even then, a long period of cohabitation will not prevent a decree being made where the petitioner had no alternative but to remain with the respondent.[2] In other cases, however, the fact of continued cohabitation will clearly be relevant

---

9 *Livingstone-Stallard v Livingstone-Stallard* [1974] 2 All ER 766; *O'Neill v O'Neill* [1975] 3 All ER 289.
10 *Bergin v Bergin* [1983] 1 All ER 905.
11 *Ash v Ash* [1972] 1 All ER 582.
12 *Stevens v Stevens* [1979] 1 WLR 885.
13 *Livingstone-Stallard v Livingstone-Stallard* (above).
14 *Pheasant v Pheasant* [1972] 1 All ER 587.
15 *Richards v Richards* [1972] 3 All ER 695.
16 *Dowden v Dowden* (1977) 8 Fam Law 106.
17 *Stringfellow v Stringfellow* [1976] 2 All ER 539.
18 *Katz v Katz* [1972] 3 All ER 219
19 *Thurlow v Thurlow* [1975] 2 All ER 979.
20 *Thurlow* (above).
1 MCA 1973, s 2(3).
2 *Bradley v Bradley* [1973] 3 All ER 750.

to the question of whether the petitioner can reasonably be expected to continue it.

In the petition, brief particulars of the behaviour to be relied upon should be pleaded but not the evidence by which they are to be proved.[3] As a rule of thumb, it has been suggested that the petition should allege about six incidents, including 'the first, the worst and the last' (Black and Bridge 1989, p 80). This recital of allegations is not calculated to encourage amicable divorce, as evidenced by the fact that respondents to petitions based on this ground are more likely to indicate an initial intention to defend than any other ground (Eekelaar 1984, pp 46–47). This is the most widely used ground of all (Law Commission 1990a, Appendix C, Table 1).

Section 1(2)(c) – that the respondent has deserted the petitioner for a period of two years immediately preceding the presentation of the petition

This is the least used ground of all, accounting for only 0.8% of petitions (Law Commission 1990a, Appendix C, Table 1). This is not surprising given that a spouse in desertion for two years will be likely to consent to a petition based on two years' separation under s 1(2)(d), below. This would avoid the necessity of satisfying the rather technical and convoluted legal definition of desertion, much of which derives from pre-1969 case law. It will only be necessary to rely on this ground where the deserting spouse will not consent to a decree based on separation and has given no other ground for divorce, and where the petitioner does not wish to wait for the expiration of the five-year period for the purposes of s 1(2)(e). The following is therefore only a very brief account of the law on this subject.

(i) Separation   A prerequisite of desertion is that there has been a complete withdrawal by one of the parties from cohabitation. The most obvious example of this is where one spouse simply leaves the matrimonial home; but there may be a desertion even though the parties continue to live under the same roof, provided that the parties lead completely separate lives.[4] It has been said that 'desertion is not the withdrawal from a place, but from a state of things'.[5] Thus, desertion may occur where the separation was initially involuntary[6] (eg, work abroad or imprisonment) or

3   Family Proceedings Rules 1991, Appendix 2.
4   *Naylor v Naylor* [1961] 2 All ER 129.
5   *Pulford v Pulford* [1923] P 18.
6   *Beeken v Beeken* [1948] P 302.

consensual, provided that the deserter forms the necessary intention to withdraw (see below). Although the period of separation must be continuous, it is provided that the continuity shall not be broken by any period of cohabitation coming to a total of not more than six months, although any such period shall not count towards the period of separation.[7]

(ii) Intention to desert   A deserting spouse must be shown to have intended to withdraw permanently from cohabitation. This will usually be inferred from the fact of departure. If the initial separation was either by mutual consent (see below) or involuntary (ie, foreign employment or imprisonment) and a spouse forms an intention to desert during such a period, it must be communicated to the other spouse before desertion will be regarded as having occurred.[8] If the deserting spouse suffers from a mental illness, the question is whether that spouse was capable of forming the necessary intention to desert.[9]

(iii) Deserted spouse does not consent   The deserted spouse must not be a willing party to the departure of the deserting spouse, although consent will not be implied from relief at the departure.[10] Consent may take the form of an express separation agreement, or may be implied from conduct, for example where one spouse actively assists the other with preparations for departure.[11] Consent may pre- or post-date departure, in the latter case bringing a desertion to an end.[12] Prior consent may be for a determined period, in which case desertion will begin at the end of the period;[13] or it may be for an indefinite period, and may be withdrawn by means of a genuine offer to resume cohabitation. If the offer is rejected without consideration, desertion begins from that point.[14]

(iv) No good cause for desertion   There will be no desertion if the departed spouse can prove that there existed good cause for the departure. There may be justifying circumstances related to illness and (again) imprisonment or foreign employment.[15] Alternatively, there may have been behaviour on the part of the petitioner justifying the departure. The courts have recognised this in cases

---

7 MCA 1973, s 2(5).
8 *Nutley v Nutley* [1970] 1 All ER 410.
9 See also MCA 1973, s 2(4).
10 *Harriman v Harriman* [1909] P 123.
11 *Spence v Spence* [1939] 1 All ER 52.
12 *Pizey v Pizey* [1961] P 101.
13 *Shaw v Shaw* [1939] P 269.
14 *Gallagher v Gallagher* [1965] 2 All ER 967.
15 See *Tickle v Tickle* [1968] 2 All ER 154.

where the conduct complained of has been 'grave and weighty'.[16] It has been argued that the meaning of this phrase must be closely linked to the definition of 'unreasonable behaviour' in s 1(2)(b) (above),[17] since it would be odd if a spouse could be regarded as justified in leaving the other while not having any ground for divorce in his or her own right; or conversely as being in desertion while having grounds for a decree under s 1(2)(b) (Bromley and Lowe 1987, pp 194–195).

(v)   Termination of desertion   Desertion will come to an end if any of the elements so far discussed cease to exist. Thus, if cohabitation is resumed, or an intention to cohabit is manifest,[18] or if the deserted spouse consents to or condones the desertion, or provides the deserter with good cause, then the desertion will be regarded as at an end. Desertion may also be terminated by a decree of judicial separation, since such a decree relieves the parties of the obligation to cohabit; but if the decree has been granted on the basis of two years' desertion, it may be transformed into a decree of divorce at a later stage.[19]

(vi)   Constructive desertion   Instead of deserting, a spouse may choose instead to behave in such a way as to force the other to leave. This is known as constructive desertion, and also constitutes grounds for divorce under s 1(2)(c). It has been argued that the conduct necessary to amount to constructive desertion is the same as that which would justify a divorce under the 'behaviour' head of s 1(2)(b) (Bromley and Lowe 1987, p 196). This would render constructive desertion redundant. However, there may be cases where a spouse has been forcibly evicted, or told to leave, in a way that might not come under the 'behaviour' ground.[20]

Section 1(2)(d) – that the parties to the marriage have lived apart for a continuous period of at least two years immediately preceding the presentation of the petition . . . and the respondent consents to a decree being granted

This is a 'pure' breakdown ground in the sense that it does not require proof of a matrimonial offence. It is relied upon in about 23% of cases (Law Commission 1990a, Appendix C, Table 1). There are two requirements: (i) that the parties 'lived apart' for the

16 Per Lord Penzance in *Yeatman v Yeatman* (1868) LR 1 P&D 489 at 494.
17 *Pheasant v Pheasant* [1972] 1 All ER 587.
18 Subject to MCA 1973, s 2(5) (see above).
19 See MCA 1973, s 4(1)–(3).
20 *Morgan v Morgan* (1973) 117 Sol Jo 223.

required period, and (ii) that the petitioner has consented to being divorced. The two-year period of separation must be 'continuous', but the continuity will not be broken by any period or periods of cohabitation the total of which does not exceed six months.[1]

One of the virtues of a separation ground is assumed to be the fact that separation offers objective and easily verifiable proof of breakdown (see Eekelaar 1984, pp 48–51). However, taken literally, a straightforward requirement of physical separation may cause hardship in two types of case. First, it may not always be easy for a spouse to leave the other, possibly because of lack of resources or because of the needs of any children of the family. This will be a factor particularly affecting women. Second, the parties may be separated involuntarily, with initially no thought of divorce. In these circumstances, it may be considered unfair to permit such a period of separation to count towards the two-year total. The legislation offers little assistance, save that it provides that spouses will not be 'living apart' if they are living 'in the same household'.[2] The term 'household' is not defined.

The courts have responded to these two difficulties, but not in an entirely satisfactory way. On the first point, it has been held that spouses may not be 'in the same household' even though they are in the same house.[3] However, the requirements that must be satisfied before parties living under the same roof will be regarded as 'living apart' have been stringently defined by reference to the standard required for similar purposes under the law of desertion.[4] Thus, there must be no aspect of their domestic lives which is shared. If, for example, the wife cooks and washes for the husband, they will not be living apart.[5] If, however, the wife has left to live with a third party and subsequently takes the husband in as lodger, and cares for him during an illness, the parties will be regarded as living apart even though living under the same roof.[6]

With respect to the second issue, the courts have held that physical separation must be accompanied by an intention to treat the marriage as at an end in order to count as 'living apart'.[7] However, *unlike* the law of desertion, the courts have held that the parties will be 'living apart' even where one spouse forms a unilateral view that the marriage has ended and has not communicated that view to the

1 MCA 1973, s 2(5).
2 MCA 1973, s 2(6).
3 *Fuller (otherwise Penfold) v Fuller* [1973] 2 All ER 650, CA.
4 See eg *Naylor v Naylor* [1961] 2 All ER 129.
5 *Mouncer v Mouncer* [1972] 1 All ER 289.
6 *Fuller* (above).
7 *Santos v Santos* [1972] 2 All ER 246.

other spouse.[8] To have insisted upon communication would have seemed fairer to the other spouse, and would have avoided the task of inquiring into the petitioner's state of mind; a task which is in any case impossible to perform in undefended cases. Thus the present interpretation of 'living apart' appears neither to maintain the objective simplicity of the ground, since the court will be potentially engaged in a detailed consideration of the parties' domestic arrangements, or of a spouse's state of mind, nor to offer a resolution of the unfairness implicit in such a ground.

The respondent's consent must be freely and clearly given. The rules of court provide that an acknowledgment of service containing a statement that the respondent assents to the petition, which has been signed by the respondent and his or her legal representative (if any), will suffice.[9] The respondent may withdraw consent at any time prior to the granting of a decree nisi.[10] There is a limited power to rescind the decree nisi once granted if the respondent can prove that he or she was misled by the petitioner, either intentionally or unintentionally, about any matter which the respondent took into account in deciding to give his consent.[11] There are certain limited provisions protecting the financial position of the respondent to a petition based on this ground (see below).

Section 1(2)(e) – that the parties to the marriage have lived apart for a continuous period of at least five years immediately preceding the presentation of the petition

The terms 'continuous' and 'living apart' carry the same meaning as they do for the previous ground. There is no requirement that the respondent consent to the petition; thus, respondents may be divorced against their will. However, there are financial safeguards additional to those available to respondents to petitions based on the previous ground (see below). This is the least used ground, accounting for only 7–8% of petitions annually (Law Commission 1990a, Appendix C, Table 1). It has been argued that the availability of two different periods of separation, one requiring consent and the other not, 'implicitly perpetuates the offence system', since 'the longer period can only be justified as a penalty against a spouse who wishes to divorce an unwilling partner and cannot establish an "offence" against him or her' (Eekelaar 1984, p 49).

8   *Santos v Santos* [1972] 2 All ER 246.
9   Family Proceedings Rules 1991, r 2.10(1).
10 Family Proceedings Rules 1991, r 2.10(2).
11 MCA 1973, s 10(1).

(d) Financial protection of respondents to petitions based on separation 'facts'

Another way in which the present law implicitly perpetuates the fault basis of divorce is by offering respondents to petitions based on two and five years' separation certain financial safeguards which are not available to respondents to petitions based on the first three 'fault' grounds. We are encouraged to assume that the latter, being at fault, are not considered deserving of such protection. The protections are of two types, the first applying to both separation 'facts', the second only to five years' separation.

(i) Two and five years' separation: s 10(2) MCA 1973

Once a decree nisi has been granted with respect to a petition based on two or five years' separation, the respondent may apply to the court to prevent the decree being made absolute, unless the court is satisfied that *either* the petitioner should not be required to make any financial provision for the petitioner, *or* that the financial provision made for the respondent is reasonable and fair or the best that can be made in the circumstances.[12] In considering any such application, the court is directed to have regard to a list of factors very similar to that contained in MCA 1973, s 25[13] which governs the exercise by the courts of their powers to make orders for ancillary relief (discussed in detail in Ch 8).

In practice, an application under s 10 will be made at the same time as an application for ancillary relief, and it seems that s 10 adds nothing of substance to the applicant's rights to receive maintenance or property transfers to those that already exist.[14] The sole purpose of a s 10 application is to delay the granting of the decree absolute until the terms of a financial settlement have been agreed and implemented. In cases to which s 10 does not apply, by contrast, a decree absolute may be granted even though there is an unresolved dispute between the parties over money and property. Thus, where the petitioner is anxious to remarry, a s 10 application may provide the respondent with a powerful bargaining counter. However, there are signs that the courts may be concerned to discourage the use of s 10 applications.[15] Further, the court has power to refuse the application if it considers it desirable that the decree be made

---

12 MCA 1973, s 10(2), (3).
13 MCA 1973, s 10(3).
14 *Lombardi v Lombardi* [1973] 3 All ER 625.
15 Eg, *Robertson v Robertson* (1982) 4 FLR 387.

absolute without delay, provided that the petitioner has made an undertaking to the court (of which the court approves) as to the provision s/he will make for the respondent.[16]

(ii) Five years' separation: MCA 1973, s 5

MCA 1973, s 5 permits a respondent to a petition based on s 1(2)(e) to oppose the grant of a decree of divorce on the ground that the dissolution of the marriage will result in 'grave financial or other hardship' to him or her, and that it would be wrong in all the circumstances to dissolve the marriage. This differs from s 10 in two main ways. First, it relates to non-financial as well as financial hardship; second, it permits the court to refuse a decree altogether, rather than merely to postpone a decree absolute. The Law Commission have proposed that this bar be retained in the context of a reformed divorce law, even though the bar is rarely invoked: 'it provides an important protection for a small group of people who may still face serious hardship which the law is unable to redress at present in other ways', especially those for whom divorce would mean the loss of pension rights (Law Commission 1990a, para 5.75).

An applicant under this section must prove:

(i)   that there is grave hardship, financial or otherwise;
(ii) that the hardship is a consequence of the legal dissolution of marriage, rather than of the mere fact of breakdown;[17] and
(iii) that it would be wrong to dissolve the marriage.

Grave financial hardship flowing from dissolution   The most obvious example of financial loss flowing from the legal dissolution of marriage will be the loss by a spouse of the status of dependant for the purposes of state or private pension rights. The statute specifically identifies 'the loss of the chance of acquiring any benefit which the respondent might acquire if the marriage were dissolved'.[18] However, this might also include rights of inheritance under an existing testamentary settlement, although a decree has never been reported as withheld for this reason.

The loss of pension rights will only be considered to cause 'grave hardship' where there is a real likelihood of the rights accruing to the applicant, and where the income from the pension will not be made up from other sources, such as supplementary benefit.[19] The more valuable the rights are, especially when they arise under private or

16 MCA 1973, s 10(4).
17 *Talbot v Talbot* (1971) 115 Sol Jo 870.
18 MCA 1973, s 5(3).
19 *Reiterbund v Reiterbund* [1974] 2 All ER 455, [1975] 1 All ER 280, CA.

occupational schemes, the more likely it is that their loss will be considered a source of grave hardship.[20] If grave financial hardship is established, the court has no power to order the petitioner to compensate the respondent, but the prospect of the decree being withheld may be a sufficient inducement on the petitioner to make an improved offer of a financial settlement.[1] Where the petitioner does not have sufficient resources to make good the loss of income, the marriage remains in existence.[2] The difficulties involved in protecting spouses against the loss of pension rights on divorce is considered further in Chapter 8.

Other hardship flowing from dissolution   Although there is no definition of what might count as other hardship, all reported cases have (unsuccessfully) sought to rely on the social stigma attaching to divorce in religious communities or foreign countries of which the respondent is a member or inhabitant. While the courts take note of the strength of the respondent's feelings or views, the matter falls ultimately to be determined according to an objective (and possibly ethnocentric) standard of reasonableness.[3]

Wrong to dissolve the marriage   In deciding whether it would be wrong to dissolve the marriage, the court is directed to consider the conduct of the parties together with the interests of the parties and of any children or other persons concerned.[4] The courts will also take account of the length of the marriage, the age of the parties[5] and, perhaps most importantly, of the need not to allow s 5 to override the statutory policy of dissolving marriages that have clearly broken down.[6] It is open to a court to dissolve a marriage even though grave hardship has been established.

Reconciliation and conciliation

(a) Reconciliation

A longstanding official policy with respect to divorce procedures has been the encouragement of attempts at reconciliation between the

20 *Le Marchant v Le Marchant* [1977] 3 All ER 610, CA.
1 *Le Marchant* (above).
2 See eg *Julian v Julian* (1972) 116 Sol Jo 763; *Johnson v Johnson* (1981) 12 Fam Law 116.
3 *Rukat v Rukat* [1975] 1 All ER 343, CA; *Balraj v Balraj* (1980) 11 Fam Law 110.
4 MCA 1973, s 5(2)(b).
5 *Mathias v Mathias* [1972] 3 All ER 1, CA.
6 Per Finer J in *Reiterbund v Reiterbund* [1974] 2 All ER 455, [1975] 1 All ER 280, CA.

parties (see Finer 1974, paras 4.290–4.298). Reconciliation has been defined as 'the provision of support and counselling which has the aim of bringing estranged spouses back together again' (Burgoyne et al 1987, p 172). This policy is reflected in the provisions, already encountered in this chapter, according to which periods of separation or desertion are not broken by aggregated periods of cohabitation of less than six months;[7] and also by the requirement in MCA 1973, s 6(1) that the petitioner's solicitor certify in prescribed form[8] whether he has discussed the possibility of reconciliation with the petitioner.

Further, the court has power to adjourn divorce proceedings at any time if it appears that there is a reasonable prospect of the parties becoming reconciled, for such a period as it thinks fit to enable attempts to be made to effect such a reconciliation.[9] However, it seems unlikely that either of these provisions is particularly effective, since they only apply once one of the parties has filed for divorce, by which time reconciliation seems a remote prospect. Further, s 6(1) does not require a solicitor to do anything: it requires only that s/he certify whether or not reconciliation has been discussed. Despite this, it has been suggested that the possibilities of reconciliation, even at the stage at which solicitors become involved, may be greater than is sometimes supposed (Davis and Murch 1988, Ch 4); but for most petitioners, the decision to seek a divorce is usually only taken after considerable thought (ibid, Ch 3).

(b) Conciliation

Growing emphasis is now being placed on the different concept of 'conciliation'.[10] This may be explained by a variety of factors. One set of explanations points to concern about the social and economic consequences of divorce both for the individuals involved and for society at large; growing dissatisfaction with the adversarial nature of divorce and the conflict thought to be engendered by it; and concern about the effects of divorce on children (see, eg, Parkinson 1986, pp 1–9; see also pp 67–72). Other writers have tended to place more emphasis on the advantages of conciliation for the individual parties, arguing that it permits them greater control over the resolution of their differences (eg Davis 1983a, p 6; Roberts 1983). Eekelaar has argued that a shift away from legal procedures and

7   MCA 1973, s 2(5).
8   Family Proceedings Rules 1991, r 2.6(3) and Form M3.
9   MCA 1973, s 6(2).
10 For a description of the development of conciliation, see Eekelaar and Dingwall (1988a); Newcastle Conciliation Project Unit (1989), pp 10–16.

personnel is essential if the 'adjustive' function of the law is to be perfected, since the 'adjustive function, properly applied, demands that the institutional arrangements direct the parties' attention towards the future and maximise their opportunities to realign their lives towards new family arrangements which cause the minimum friction to all concerned' (1984, p 54).

Whatever the explanation, there is increasing support for the idea of conciliation, including at the official level (eg, Booth 1985; Law Commission 1990a); although official interest may, in part, be attributable to the possibility thought to be offered by conciliation of cutting the costs associated with adversarial court proceedings (Eekelaar and Dingwall 1988, pp 19–20). However, 'conciliation' remains a vague concept. A useful starting point for discussion, therefore, is to attempt a definition of the term itself.

(i)   What is conciliation?

The Finer Committee (1974) offered the first official articulation of conciliation as something distinct from reconciliation. They defined it as 'assisting the parties to deal with the consequences of the established breakdown of their marriage, whether resulting in a divorce or separation, by reaching agreements or giving consents or reducing the area of conflict upon custody, support, access to and education of the children, financial provision, the disposition of the matrimonial home, lawyers' fees, and every other matter arising from the breakdown which calls for a decision on future arrangements' (para 4.288). The Interdepartmental Committee on Conciliation ('The Robinson Committee', 1983) adopted this definition and added that '[i]n more general terms, . . . conciliation means some kind of structured scheme or facility for promoting a settlement between parties' (para 1.2).

More recently still, the Booth Committee on Matrimonial Procedure (1985), while also adopting the Finer definition, added the further gloss that 'the essence of conciliation [is] that responsibility remains at all times with the parties themselves to identify and seek agreement on the issues arising from the breakdown of their relationship' (para 3.10). Another writer defines conciliation as 'a structured process in which both parties to a dispute meet voluntarily with one or more impartial third parties (conciliators) who help them to explore possibilities of reaching agreement, without having the power to impose a settlement on them or the responsibility to advise either party individually' (Parkinson 1986, p 52).

While this last definition is more precise as to the institutional embodiment of the general idea of conciliation – that is, as involving some independent third party intervention (see Roberts 1983) – it still leaves many practical aspects of the concept somewhat vague. For example, uncertainty surrounds the role of the conciliator(s). It has been pointed out that the term 'conciliator' may refer both to someone who merely attempts to promote communication between the parties, as well as to someone who actively seeks to shape the outcome of the process (Roberts 1983, p 549). The nature of conciliation will differ according to which posture is adopted, as will the extent to which the objective of according the parties greater control over their affairs is achieved.

The ambiguities of conciliation are further underlined by the evidence obtained by the Newcastle Conciliation Project Unit[11] of the views of relevant professional bodies as to the objectives of conciliation. While some saw it as confined to being part of the process of settling disputes over practical problems without having to go to court, others saw it as an opportunity for providing counselling and therapy; and while some saw it as a means of parents retaining relationships with their children, others saw it as a means of giving the children themselves a voice in the proceedings (Newcastle CPU 1989, paras 5.1–5.12). Views also differed over the scope of conciliation, its relationship with formal legal processes (and in particular whether it should be compulsory) and over the involvement of lawyers (ibid, Ch 5). However, there appeared to be more consensus as to the aims of conciliation among judges, registrars, probation officers and those involved in independent schemes. The most important of these were 'saving court time' and 'shortening proceedings' (Table 8.9). Those more closely involved with the legal process (such as judges and registrars) considered 'clarifying the issues' to be more important than those less closely connected (such as probation officers); similarly, the latter group considered 'counselling and dealing with personal feelings' to be more important than the former group (ibid).

The proper place of conciliation within legal procedures is unclear. For example, should legal officials act as conciliators (bearing in mind that they may have the power to impose solutions), and should lawyers be present at conciliation attempts (Roberts 1983,

---

11 The Newcastle Conciliation Project Unit (CPU) was established by the Lord Chancellor's Department, on the recommendation of the Robinson Committee (see below), with the purpose of researching the cost and effectiveness of all conciliation schemes in operation in England and Wales and of submitting a report to the Lord Chancellor to enable him to decide whether, and if so how, a national family conciliation service might be established. The report was published in March 1989. See Roberts (1990) and Eekelaar (1991), Ch 7 for discussion. For a discussion of the CPU's research design in relation to the issue of costs analysis, see Ogus, Jones-Lee, Cole and McCarthy (1990).

pp 551–557)? Further, it is unclear what is meant by 'impartial' as it applies to a conciliator (Davis 1983b). Is it consistent, for example, with a conciliator actively taking sides in the course of the conciliation process? If not, then there is a danger that conciliation will merely reinforce inequalities of power.

The fact that there is no coherent set of answers to these questions reflects the comparative novelty of conciliation as a practice, together with the ad hoc and somewhat uncoordinated nature of conciliation services as they exist in this country at present, combined with the differing objectives sought to be realised through it. It has been said that conciliation 'takes on the role of a code word which says everything and therefore does not need to say anything' (Bottomley 1985, p 165). Nevertheless, one consistent theme that does emerge from discussions of conciliation is that its primary justification and focus is the 'welfare' of children involved in divorce (Bottomley, op cit; Newcastle CPU 1989, para 5.6). This is reflected in the National Family Conciliation Council's Code of Practice, which states that the longer-term aim of conciliation is to help 'both parents (a) maintain their relationships with their children, and (b) achieve a co-operative plan for their children's welfare' (Parkinson 1986, Appendix A, para 1). It has been suggested, however, that it is difficult to reconcile this aim with the supposedly neutral stance of a conciliator since it implies a preferred outcome of the conciliation process (Newcastle CPU 1989, para 5.7).

(ii) Conciliation in practice

One of the tasks of the Interdepartmental Committee on Conciliation (1983, hereafter the 'Robinson Committee') was to review and report on existing arrangements for conciliation. The Committee estimated that at that time there were over fifty conciliation services in operation (para 3.8), a number which has since grown. The Robinson Committee classified the services into four types (paras 3.10–3.16). This classification remains a useful starting point, although, as we shall see, a more complex typology has since been devised.

1 Independent voluntary schemes   Characteristically, these are run by voluntary committees and staffed by voluntary or partly-paid workers; they 'run with the support of the local courts without being formally connected with them' (Parkinson 1987, pp 112–113; see also CPU 1989, paras 8.18–8.38). This means that such schemes are sometimes referred to as providing 'out-of-court' conciliation in order to distinguish them from 'in-court' schemes (below). The best known and longest established of these is the Bristol Courts Family Welfare Service (as to which, see Parkinson 1986, pp 74–79), but there are now about fifty such services nationwide (Pearce 1990). Such schemes vary in a variety of ways, for example, with respect to the types of work undertaken (Robinson 1983, Appendix 3), methods of working, sources of funding, systems of referral and the qualifications and background of staff (Parkinson 1987; Newcastle CPU 1989, para 2.36–2.38). Greater uniformity of practice may arise from the promulgation in 1985 by the National Family Conciliation Council[12] (to which independent services will be affiliated) of a Code of Practice for Family Conciliation Services (Parkinson 1986, App A).

Many advantages are claimed for such schemes. It is argued, for example, that they are available to couples at an earlier stage than the in-court schemes, that they are quickly and easily accessible (Parkinson 1987, pp 119–120) and that the effectiveness of conciliation is increased when undertaken independently of the judicial process (Davis and Bader 1985). However, such schemes have difficulty in attracting funding, despite the fact that legal aid may be available under the Green Form Scheme to cover some of the costs. More importantly, such schemes are not widely used (see Kleanthous and Kane 1987, p 175). This may be accounted for by a lack of awareness of their availability or their value by the public, solicitors and the courts,[13] or, alternatively, by the fact that there is no significant demand for such services (see Robinson 1983, paras 4.2– 4.4). The overwhelming tendency of conciliation to concentrate on disputes involving children means that it is only where there is a real difference between the parties on this issue that conciliation will have a role.

2 Out-of-court services based on the probation service   As we shall see, the probation service undertakes a role in in-court schemes in its capacity as the Divorce Court Welfare Service (see also Ch 9). However, in some areas probation workers with experience in family cases have set up independent out-of-court services. Such services 'accept referrals in a similar manner to other out-of-court services . . . , but may also seek to conciliate where there is a welfare report' (Robinson 1983, para 3.13). The latter may be more likely in areas where there is an out-of-court service already established; here the

---

12 On the history of the NFCC, see Pearce (1990). A precondition of affiliation to the NFCC is a background of training in marriage guidance or social work.

13 Independent schemes rely either on being approached directly by members of the public, or on referrals from solicitors or from the courts: see Fraser (1990); CPU (1989), para 8.30. A *Practice Direction* ([1986] 2 FLR 171) encourages judges to consider conciliation before ordering a Welfare Report, 'where local conciliation facilities exist'.

probation service may set up specialist 'Divorce Units' to provide continuity in its provision of assistance to the courts (see further Ch 9), and to offer support to the other out-of-court service (Clulow and Vincent 1987, pp 57–65). As we shall see, the question of whether a Divorce Court Welfare Officer should combine the functions of reporter and conciliator has proved controversial.

3 In-court mediation   Where such a scheme has been established at local level, the 'usual procedure is that, once an issue has been filed in court, an appointment is fixed before the registrar at an early date, at which the parties and their legal advisers, if any, and the Divorce Court Welfare Officer attend . . . If the issue has not been previously resolved by the parties (as often happens) the registrar seeks to establish the area of disagreement, following which the parties, their advisers and the Divorce Court Welfare Officer confer in a separate room and attempt to resolve the dispute . . . If they succeed an order is made. If they fail, the registrar gives directions for the trial of the dispute' (Robinson 1983, para 3.14; see also Eekelaar 1991, p 156). The CPU found, however, that an equally common procedure was for the court to make a specific conciliation appointment with a welfare officer (1989, Table 8.1).

Within this general framework, there are considerable local variations with respect (for example) to the respective roles allotted to registrars, solicitors and welfare officers, the procedure at appointments and their duration, the initiation of the procedure, the selection of cases for conciliation, the matters considered at such appointments and whether both or only one party was present (Davis and Bader 1985; Kleanthous and Kane 1987, p 177; CPU 1989, paras 8.5–8.17, 9.6–9.9). The best known of these schemes are those initiated by the Bristol County Court (see Parmiter 1981; Parkinson 1986, pp 72–74) and the Principal Divorce Registry in London.[14] A recent survey of 85% of local courts found that such schemes were in operation in 65% of courts,[15] all of which had been established since 1978, and that some of the remainder had plans to set up a scheme in the near future (Kleanthous and Kane 1987, p 177). Eekelaar found that 76% of registrars in his study ran a scheme for children issues, but that only 18% coupled this with a pre-trial review of property and financial matters (1991, pp 155–159). However, there are suggestions in recent case law of growing judicial support for pre-trial reviews and in-court mediation in financial and property disputes;[16] and there is evidence of a growing

14 *Practice Direction* [1982] 3 All ER 988; *Practice Direction* [1984] 3 All ER 800.
15 The CPU found schemes established in 82 of 176 divorce county courts (para 8.5).
16 Per Booth J in *Evans v Evans* [1990] 2 All ER 147.

use of in-house conciliation for this purpose (Davis 1991, 1991a; Rose and Gerlis 1991).

Several concerns have been voiced about the use of such schemes. In their research into the 'consumer's' view of in-court conciliation, Davis and Bader (1985) found that many couples experience an almost complete loss of control over the course of negotiations, as the various professionals involved (that is, lawyers and welfare officers) come to dominate the proceedings. A particular concern was the way in which the close relationship between such forms of conciliation and the personnel of the court, such as the registrar and welfare officer, tended to blur the distinction between conciliation and adjudication. This tendency was emphasised by the common reliance on solicitors to conduct negotiations (see also Parkinson 1986, pp 96–101). Davis and Bader point to the dangers that in-court conciliation may simply boil down to 'endless delay', 'crude arm twisting' and 'a search for a compromise' (p 84). Davis concludes from his experience of researching the area that 'decision-making on court premises can never have a genuinely mediatory character, if by that is meant a form of negotiation which continues to reflect the *disputants'* view of the quarrel, rather than that of professional third parties' (1988, p 109). It has also been suggested that in-court schemes are considered useful as means of 'clearing Registrar's desks' rather than as offering the litigants any significant advantages (Newcastle CPU 1989, para 5.18).

Another concern was the way in which welfare officers have attempted to combine conciliation with their function as reporting officers to the court (see Ch 9, below). Reporting and conciliation, it has been argued, are two entirely separate functions (Davis 1982). This has caused considerable debate (eg, Pugsley and Wilkinson 1984; James 1988); and it is now provided that welfare officers who act as conciliators under in-court schemes should not report in the same case.[17] However, many welfare officers who are asked to report to the court may also see it as part of their function to attempt to promote agreement (see further, Ch 9 below).

4 Magistrates' courts   The magistrates' court has jurisdiction to hear applications for various forms of matrimonial relief (see Chs 1 and 4). Some courts operate a court-based conciliation service in conjunction with the Divorce Court Welfare Service, whose duties include the preparation of welfare reports for magistrates in the same way as for the divorce court (see Ch 9). There is evidence of greater use

---

17 *Practice Direction* [1986] 2 FLR 171.

being made by magistrates of the facilities offered by the welfare service to effect conciliation (Robinson 1983, para 3.15–3.16; Guymer and Bywaters 1984).

An alternative classification: judicial or probation control　The Newcastle CPU adopted a slightly different classification for the purposes of their research. Instead of treating the independent/court-based classification as primary, they preferred instead to classify schemes according to the degree of control exerted over them by the judiciary or the probation service (in its role as the Divorce Court Welfare Service: see Ch 9). They thus arrived at the following classification.

(a) *Court-based schemes*
  (i) where a judge or registrar was present with the court welfare service at the beginning of the conciliation appointment ('Category A'); and
  (ii) where conciliation was predominantly controlled by the court welfare service ('Category B').

A further classification was according to whether legal advisers were or were not present at the conciliation appointment.

(b) *Independent schemes*
  (i) where there was some form of 'probation control', through the provision of premises, funding, conciliators, administration or supervision ('Category C'). This category was further sub-divided according to the strength of probation control; and
  (ii) where there was no probation control, except possibly in the form of representation on the management committee ('Category D'). This category was also further sub-divided according to whether judges and registrars were or were not represented on the management committee (CPU 1989, paras 7.8–7.14).

The complexity of this classification reflects the variety of means by which conciliation services are provided. The conclusions of the CPU Report are considered below.

(iii) Criticisms

Despite the widespread support for conciliation, there has also been a less widespread expression of concern at its implications. As we have seen, the main advantages claimed for conciliation are that it offers the parties greater control over the proceedings, and that it encourages agreement by shifting the focus away from adversarial court-based proceedings. Against this, it has been argued that conciliation necessarily implies a degree of loss of control by the parties, since by definition they have been unable to resolve the dispute on their own (Roberts 1983, p 541). This in turn may lead to a situation in which the conciliator actively encourages a certain form of settlement, rather than allowing the parties to define the terms of their own agreement (see Bottomley 1984, p 298; Dingwall 1988). For this reason, one commentator has pointed to the dangers of 'dragooning the parties into a settlement'(Davis 1983b, p 135).

This is in turn associated with the view that, rather than offering an alternative to adjudicatory proceedings and thus a form of deregulation, conciliation offers an extension of regulation (see Bottomley 1984, 1985). This arises from the fact that, first, conciliation as practised is not confined only to those cases that would have gone on to be disputed in a full hearing, but is applied in any case manifesting a dispute at an early stage, even though that dispute might have been settled by other means, probably through solicitors, if conciliation had not been available. Second, as we have seen in relation to in-court schemes, the fear has been expressed that conciliation has not in practice dissociated itself from the adjudicatory function of the court and its personnel; rather, it has become 'effectively assimilated into the standard practice of the courtroom' (Davis 1987, p 306). In other words, the rhetoric of 'private control' and 'informal decision-making' conceals the reality of a dramatic extension of the coercive regulation of the divorce process.

This is argued to have particularly adverse consequences for women, since the focus of much conciliation is, as we have seen, the needs of children (Bottomley, op cit). The professional ideology of those most closely associated with mediation, that is Divorce Court Welfare Officers, is focused on 'child saving' (see Davis 1983a, p 10). Thus, in the process of conciliation, women may be pressurised to make concessions in the interests of securing agreement 'for the sake of the children', even though their view of the needs of their children may be quite different; and this may in turn weaken the bargaining power of women in relation to property and finance. Nevertheless, it should be remembered that conciliation is characterised by a wide diversity of practice, not all of which will present the dangers outlined here. What remains in question, though, is the extent to which conciliation actually achieves the objectives that have been set for it, rather than simply becoming an administratively convenient method of processing disputes.

(iv) The future of conciliation

Conciliation and mediation seem set to play a central role in the divorce process, especially if the Law Commission's proposed new divorce law were to be introduced. At the very least, the Commission's proposals presuppose that conciliation will be available locally, although the Commission expresses no clear preference for in-court or independent conciliation. There nevertheless remains a fundamental uncertainty about the relationship that would exist under the new scheme between formal adjudication in court and the non-legal alternatives. We saw that the Law Commission did not wish to make conciliation compulsory, preferring to rely on 'encouragement'; but it remains unclear how this would work in practice. Will the choice between the two lie with the parties, or will the parties fail to see the distinction between encouragement and compulsion? Would registrars and judges respect an individual's refusal to go to conciliation, or would such a refusal be penalised? It has been suggested that 'the aggrandising tendency of the conciliation "movement", coupled with the rationing, deflecting strategies employed by courts, could lead to adjudication becoming so much a last resort that it is stigmatised as the refuge of the obsessive and the intransigent' (Davis 1988, p 114; see also Eekelaar 1991, pp 165–171 for a discussion of the role of judicial supervision of mediated agreements).

As to the organisation of conciliation and mediation services themselves, the findings and conclusions of the Newcastle Conciliation Project Unit are unlikely to prove decisive. On the question of cost, the Unit found that conciliation 'involves a significant net addition to the overall resource cost of settling disputes' (para 20.5). They estimated this additional cost at about £150 per case in the case of court-based conciliation and £250 in the case of independent conciliation.[18] On the question of effectiveness, which was measured both in terms of 'dispute resolution' and 'therapeutic' criteria, it was found that court-based services with heavy judicial control (Category A, above) were less effective than the others and that independent schemes with little probation control (Category D) were marginally the most successful. However, they were unable to draw any clear conclusions as to the effectiveness of conciliation as compared with conventional adjudication, although the Unit acknowledged that conciliation could have benefits that cannot be measured through conventional research methods (para 20.11):

---

18 For a critical discussion of these costings, see Eekelaar 1991, pp 160–161; but Eekelaar accepts that 'there is no evidence that conciliation saves overall costs'.

'Our research suggests that conciliation (except that of Category A) is at least as effective as other, more traditional, procedures in generating satisfactory settlements and on several measures of effectiveness often achieves much more than that.' (Para 20.11)

On the issue of a possible national conciliation service, the Unit's view was that, if such a service were to be introduced, it should be firmly based on the principle of voluntary participation and that 'its distinguishing feature should be to enable couples to retain control of the decision-making process consequent on separation and divorce, encouraging them to reach their own agreements' (para 20.19). Conciliation would be seen as a genuine alternative to litigation, and not an adjunct to it. This would free conciliators from the tension 'between the belief that parents know best what is appropriate for their children and should therefore retain responsibility for decision-making, and the consensus among professionals that, for example, the access of the non-custodial parent is a "good thing" and to be encouraged (or insisted on)' (para 20.32). Conciliation would not be regarded as better or worse, simply different; and the parties would have the right to choose their forum, aware of the different underlying values of each.

A national conciliation service would also permit a standardisation in welfare approaches and processes, and the development of a standard and unambiguous terminology. Any national service should not be based on any of the existing models (Categories A–D, above) but be 'one part of a network of local services, independent of the courts and the probation service'. Any such service would not be confined to providing conciliation, but could cater for a 'range of relationship difficulties' by means of advice, counselling and 'divorce experience courses' (para 20.33; for a critical view of the proposals, see Roberts 1990).

Judicial separation

(a) Introduction

It was suggested in Chapter 6 that one possible remedy for domestic violence was to petition for divorce. Not only would this trigger the ancillary powers of the divorce court over matters such as custody of children, maintenance and occupation of the family home; it would also enable the court immediately to issue injunctions to prevent molestation or to oust one partner from the family home (subject to the limitations and criteria discussed in Ch 6). However, there may be many reasons why the initiation of divorce proceedings is not possible or appropriate.

For example, an insufficient time may have elapsed since the marriage so that a petition for divorce is time-barred. This is likely to be less significant a constraint now that the time bar on divorce has been reduced from three years to one (see above). Alternatively, the spouse concerned may not want a divorce, possibly for religious reasons; or may wish to preserve pension rights, which would be lost on divorce; or a 'blameless' spouse may have no desire to concede to the other's wish for a divorce, so enabling that other to remarry. Quite legitimately, such a spouse may regard the refusal of consent to a divorce as a significant bargaining counter in ancillary matters. In such circumstances, the appropriate procedure is to petition for judicial separation, a petition for which may be presented at any time after a marriage. From the point of view of invoking the ancillary powers of the divorce court over children and property, and the powers of the court to issue injunctions, judicial separation is the functional equivalent of a divorce. The only difference is that neither party may remarry. In other words, a decree of judicial separation creates a 'legal limbo between being married and divorced' (Maidment 1982, p 75).

(b) Grounds for judicial separation

The DRA 1969 (now MCA 1973) assimilated the grounds for judicial separation with those of divorce.[19] These grounds are discussed above. The only difference is that the court is not required to be satisfied, as it is in divorce proceedings, that the marriage has broken down irretrievably.[20] Further, ss 5 and 10 of the MCA 1973, (which provide financial safeguards for certain classes of respondents to divorce petitions – see above) do not apply to petitions for judicial separation. The granting of a petition on a particular ground serves as sufficient proof of that ground for subsequent divorce proceedings, provided that irretrievable breakdown can be proven and also that the parties have not resumed cohabitation since the decree of judicial separation. A large number of petitions for judicial separation are eventually followed by a petition for divorce, or are converted into a petition for divorce as part of a property and financial settlement (Maidment 1982, pp 21–25; Garlick 1983, pp 722–723).

---

19 MCA 1973, s 17(1); MCA 1973, ss 1(2), 2.
20 MCA 1973, s 17(2).

(c) **Effects of a decree**

The granting of a decree of judicial separation relieves the petitioner of the obligation to cohabit with the respondent. This would bring any desertion to an end (see above). From the point of view of the rules of intestacy, a judicial separation is deemed to have the same effect as death.[1] Most significantly, however, the effect of a decree will be to invoke the ancillary powers of the court with respect to property, finance and children.

(d) **The use of judicial separation**

The use of judicial separation grew rapidly, both in absolute numbers and as a proportion of the matrimonial causes, during the latter half of the 1970s. In 1970, there were 231 petitions for judicial separation which formed 0.32% of all petitions for matrimonial decrees; in 1980, the equivalent figures were 5,423 (3.06%) (Maidment 1982, Appendix, Table 1). Since, as we have seen, judicial separation serves as the functional equivalent of divorce in all but the provision of a licence to remarry, the best explantion may lie in the fact that it was used as a means of escaping the bar on petitions for divorce within the first three years of marriage (ibid, pp 34–45; Garlick 1983, pp 723–725). This is underlined by the fact that the number of petitions has declined since 1984, when the length of the bar was reduced from three years to one. In 1987, there were 3,199 petitions (Lord Chancellor's Department 1988, Table 5.18). The restrictions placed by the House of Lords in *Richards* (above) on the power of the courts to make ouster orders ancillary to matrimonial proceedings will also diminish the attractiveness of the procedure as a means of obtaining injunctive relief.

Nevertheless, there will remain some cases in which, for reasons outlined above, a spouse will find judicial separation a preferable course of action. This is underlined by the fact that practitioners may prefer their clients to use this procedure as a means of obtaining financial remedies where the alternative is to go to the family proceedings court or to petition under MCA 1973, s 27 (see Ch 4, above). This is partly because practitioners appear to prefer the county court to the magistrates' court as a general practice (Maidment 1982, pp 60–63; Garlick 1983, pp 727–731); but also because the powers of the court with respect to property, finance and custody are much more extensive in judicial separation proceedings than in either of the alternatives. Nevertheless, it seems unlikely that

1   MCA 1973, s 18(2).

judicial separation will be more than rarely used for this purpose (Maidment 1982, pp 74–75; see also the figures given above).

Perhaps the most controversial aspect of judicial separation is that it permits a spouse to 'have their cake and eat it' (Black 1989, p 133), in the sense that it allows a spouse to obtain the benefits of divorce in the shape of the court's ancillary powers while refusing the other spouse permission to remarry. On this basis, it has been suggested that judicial separation in its present form be abolished (see Maidment 1982, pp 69–79 for discussion). However, this seems to assume that divorce is a process in which one spouse (usually the man) buys from his wife the right to remarry according to terms set out and enforced by the courts. There is otherwise no reason to assume that the two issues should be linked. Further, it also seems to assume that it is wrong for spouses (often referred to as 'spiteful wives') to refuse consent to a divorce as a way of increasing their bargaining power with respect to ancillary matters, often pejoratively referred to as employing 'tactics'.

The Law Commission has recommended that judicial separation be retained (and renamed a 'separation order'), primarily for those who cannot divorce (because they have not been married for long enough) or those who have religious or other objections to divorce (1990a, paras 4.2–4.19). They thus propose that, like divorce, judicial separation be available after the expiration of a year following the initiation of a period of consideration and reflection. The difference from divorce would be that the period could be initiated within the first year of marriage, so that separation would retain the advantage of being available earlier. A separation order under the proposed scheme would thus not be available until at least a year after the marriage, so in this sense it would become harder to obtain than at present.

Chapter 8
Money and property in divorce

Introduction

(a) Background to the present law

In this chapter, we are concerned with the powers of the divorce court to make orders concerning the allocation of income and property amongst family members on divorce, powers which, as we have already seen, historically formed one of the three 'systems' of family law. Although the wider availability of legal aid has reduced the social exclusivity of the remedies considered in this chapter, it should still be remembered that for many ex-spouses the economic consequences of divorce are to be reckoned in terms of entitlement to welfare benefit rather than the transfer of income or property ordered by the divorce court (see Ch 4). It has been said that 'private or family law does little to solve these economic difficulties, partly because it can only allocate resources: it cannot create them' (Maclean 1991, p 33). For this reason, we are not concerned in this chapter with the divorce court's powers in isolation: an important task will be to examine the interrelation between orders made by the divorce court and the system of welfare benefit entitlement, an interrelation that will be formalised by the implementation of the Child Support Act (see Ch 4 and below).

(i) Before 1970

The present legal framework governing the distribution of property and income on divorce is to be found in the Matrimonial Property and Proceedings Act 1970 (now MCA 1973), and is thus of comparatively recent origin. Prior to this, the question of property entitlement on divorce was determined according to the ordinary principles of property law, with only limited powers available to the courts to vary the strict operation of these principles.[1] The courts also

---

1 MCA 1965, s 5(1); MCA 1965, s 17(1), (2).

had the power to order a husband to maintain his ex-wife out of his income, according to a set of guidelines developed by the courts, derived from previous parliamentary practice (see Finer and McGregor 1974; Eekelaar and Maclean 1986, Ch 1).

Following the introduction of judicial divorce, the continuing post-divorce support obligation was overtly dominated by moral considerations and was not regarded as 'simply a projection into post-divorce life of the obligations of marriage' (Eekelaar and Maclean 1988, p 141). For those who could afford to take advantage of divorce, the concern was not so much to protect women and children from economic hardship (as it was with the public law obligations of support enforced through the Poor Law) as to uphold conventional morality (ibid). In making orders for income maintenance, the courts were 'concerned to protect the public purse, shield women from "temptation" and, most of all, deter against irresponsible rejection of marriage vows' (ibid, p 35). For example, the liability of husbands to maintain their ex-wives could be diminished if the wife had committed adultery or was otherwise guilty of a matrimonial offence. However, the changes implemented in 1970 as part of the more general reform of the divorce law (as to which, see Ch 7) altered this legal construction of the economic consequences of divorce.

(ii) MPPA 1970

The MPPA equalised the liabilities of husband and wife to provide for each other on divorce, and removed many of the technical distinctions of the old law which had rendered the financial remedies available dependent on the type of proceeding invoked. The courts were also given more extensive readjustive powers over the parties' property and income, and the exercise of these powers was made subject to a statutory list of criteria which marginalised any moral considerations and focused attention primarily on questions of need (Gray 1977, pp 313–315).[2] The overriding objective, taken without debate from earlier case law (Law Commission 1969), was to place the parties in the position in which they would have been had the marriage not broken down (subsequently christened the 'principle of minimal loss', Eekelaar 1978, Ch 9). It has been argued that the effect of this new statutory regime was to alter 'the legal axes of regulation of the family' in such a way as to reveal 'the marriage contract to be an economic or financial one rather than a contract based on sexual fidelity and moral obligation' (Smart 1984a, pp 99–100).

2 See now MCA 1973, s 25.

By the end of the 1970s, however, there was growing demand for the reform of the law. The statutory guidelines, and in particular the overriding principle of minimal loss, had become a 'crumbling edifice' (Eekelaar 1979, p 262), owing to the fact that in most cases it was impossible to fulfil. Instead, the courts had developed their own priorities; and while there was a measure of agreement among appeal judges as to what these should be, research showed that there was less consistency amongst county court registrars (now district judges), who were responsible for deciding the majority of cases (Barrington Baker et al 1977). Further, the justifiability of a continuing support obligation after divorce was widely questioned, most effectively by pressure groups acting on behalf of ex-husbands and second wives. The Law Commission considered the matter in a discussion paper (1980), in which a range of alternative models for reform were discussed (Part IV; see also Eekelaar and Maclean 1986, Ch 3). A year later, the Commission produced a final report (1981).

The report's approach was to avoid a wholesale reconsideration of the basis of the law, but instead to suggest certain 'changes of emphasis' within the statutory framework laid down in 1970. This contrasted markedly with the approach adopted by the Scottish Law Commission in their proposals published at the same time, which involved introducing a principle of equal division of property on divorce together with restrictions on the use of income maintenance after three years of the divorce (Scottish Law Commission 1981; Dewar 1984).[3] The changes of emphasis suggested by the English Commission were:

(i)   to give greater priority to the needs of children;
(ii) to place greater emphasis on the need for the parties to become self-sufficient following divorce; and
(iii) to promote the use of the so-called 'clean break' in financial matters, which results in a once-and-for-all financial settlement involving no continuing economic links between the parties.

There was also found to be widespread support for the abandonment of the principle of minimal loss. To a very large extent, these changes merely reflected the priorities in fact pursued by the judges during the 1970s (Eekelaar 1982; Dewar 1986).

(iii) MFPA 1984

These proposals were embodied in the MFPA 1984, which effected certain amendments to the MCA 1973, the details of which are con-

---

3   See now Family Law (Scotland) Act 1985, s 9 (on which see Thomson 1987, Ch 7).

sidered below. The Act has been widely criticised. It has been argued that the objectives of the Act are contradictory (Symes 1985; Dewar 1986; Douglas 1990). For example, according priority to the needs of children may be inconsistent with the priority to be accorded to self-sufficiency and the clean break, since it may not be in the best interests of the children for the wife to go out to work or to be dependent on welfare benefit. The primary objective of the Act is clearly to restrict the use of income maintenance following divorce; but it should be remembered that the guidelines apply equally to property awards (see Eekelaar 1982; Dewar 1986). Much is left by the legislation to judicial interpretation, and we shall see later in this chapter how the higher courts have interpreted and applied the legislation.

It has also been argued that the 1984 Act was founded on the myth of the existence of a large group of ex-wives living parasitically on the earnings of their ex-husbands (for which, as we shall see, there was very little evidence at the time of the passage of the Act); and that it was unfair to legislate to reduce ex-wives' rights to maintenance, however nominal, without at the same time increasing the public support available to women through the benefit system (O'Donovan 1982) possibly along the lines of the 'guaranteed maintenance allowance' recommended by the Finer Committee (1974). Divorce, it has been argued, exposes the economic dependency in marriage; but the 1984 Act, by confining reform exclusively to the private law of maintenance, characterises the 'problem' of dependency as soluble in terms of private initiative rather than public action (Smart 1984b; Symes 1985). However, it has been argued that in the political climate prevailing at the time it would have been naive to expect any proposals for increased state support for women to be seriously considered by government (Cretney 1986b).

Empirical evidence (Edwards and Halpern 1987, 1990, 1990a; Edwards, Gould and Halpern 1990; Eekelaar 1991, pp 68–70) suggests that, since the Act came into force, there has been a decline in the use of periodic payments to ex-spouses and only a small corresponding increase in the use of lump sum or property awards. There is some evidence to suggest that the Act has increased the number of orders for financial provision in favour of children, although this does not necessarily mean that the Act has had the effect of increasing the amounts paid in child support: it may simply mean that any income available is ordered to be paid for children rather than the ex-spouse.

(iv) A need for further reform?

A number of criticisms have been levelled at the current law. One is that 'it is almost impossible to say what [individuals'] precise rights and liabilities are' and that it should be possible, in the interests of saving time, costs and emotional distress, 'to introduce more precision into the determination of financial provision in divorce than exists at present' (Green 1987, pp 1–2[4]). A second is that, given that most divorcing couples have no 'tangible assets to divide on divorce . . . elaborate rules about property settlements are usually irrelevant' (Jackson and Maclean 1990, p 1). In other words, the rules have been devised for one social class but are actually applied, for the most part, to another. As a consequence, many important intangible assets that are available on divorce, such as future earning capacity and pensions, are ignored. On this view, what is required is a rethinking of spousal maintenance as the assertion of a property right to a share in an ex-spouse's earnings, derived from a spouse's contribution to the other's earning capacity, rather than as 'women demanding money from their husbands [because] they are either too weak to support themselves or are alimony drones wreaking financial revenge on their spouses' (ibid, p 7; see also Maclean and Johnston 1990). In addition, some form of 'pension-splitting' should be introduced to empower courts to share the value of pension rights attributable to the period of the marriage.

On the question of greater certainty, we have seen in Chapter 4 and above that this is one of the objectives of the Child Support Act 1991. Whether a similar degree of certainty should be introduced into the allocation of property on divorce between spouses by the introduction, for example, of a presumption of equal sharing (as in Scotland) has, as we saw in Chapter 5, so far been resisted in this country; and evidence from other jurisdictions concerning the economic effects of such a presumption is not encouraging (see Weitzman 1986, 1988; but see further below). The question of pension rights is considered later in this chapter. As far as spousal maintenance is concerned, there has so far been little evidence of an official willingness to reconceptualise its purpose along the lines suggested above. Indeed, since the introduction of the MFPA 1984,

---

4   Green proposes clearer (and firmer) rules governing the allocation of capital and property and the assessment of spousal maintenance; Eekelaar (1991), who is also critical of the law's failure 'to set out any clear model upon which courts can base their approach to the exercise of their powers' (p 76), canvasses an 'individualistic' model for the exercise of such powers, which would provide 'remedies to restore the individual's investment in a joint enterprise and to compensate each individual for damage caused by the failure of the enterprise' (p 88). This would involve two elements: (i) restitution to each of the parties of an amount drawn from the common assets equivalent to the parties' respective contributions (broadly defined) to the marriage; and (ii) compensation, usually to the wife, for loss of earning capacity arising from the marriage and from child care. Such a model would be similar to that now enshrined in Scottish law (note 3, above; for a discussion of which see Dewar 1984).

it has been statutory policy to discourage the use of spousal maintenance, although, as we shall see, the courts have sought to restrict the impact of this legislation.

(b) The economic consequences of divorce

The reform debate that preceded the 1984 Act took place against a background of almost total ignorance of the short- and long-term economic consequences of divorce for the parties. Much valuable work has since been completed on this matter, both in England and Wales (Davies et al 1983; Eekelaar and Maclean 1986; Gregory and Foster 1990), in Australia (McDonald 1985) and in the United States (Weitzman 1985, Chs 9 and 10 and 1988; Wishik 1986; Garrison 1990). Only the details of the English findings are discussed here; but the patterns appear to be similar in the other two jurisdictions. All the studies suggest that, whatever the jurisdiction, divorce has especially adverse economic consequences for women with children (for a review of the evidence, see Maclean 1991, Ch 1).

This raises the question of the extent to which divorce laws (and the associated rules concerning property distribution and maintenance) can affect the economic consequences of divorce. For example, in the case of the United States, Weitzman (1986 and 1988) attributes the hardships faced by women and children to the introduction there of 'enlightened' no-fault divorce laws, coupled with the introduction of principles of equal sharing of property on divorce (see also Glendon 1987). However, the strength of this causal link between the nature of divorce and property distribution law on the one hand, and the economic consequences of divorce on the other, may be doubted in view of the fact that in England and Wales, where divorce law continues to be partly fault-based and where there is no automatic presumption of equal sharing, similar findings of economic hardship have been made (see below).[5] The economic impact of the introduction into Scots law of a presumption of equal sharing of matrimonial property on divorce has yet to be explored.[6]

The most important factor affecting the ex-wife's economic position following divorce, measured in terms of household income, is the presence or absence of children (Eekelaar and Maclean 1986, p 69; Gregory and Foster 1990, Table 4.3). For the majority of single

---

5 For American evidence contradicting the hypothesis that no-fault divorce and equal division of property have in themselves caused a worsening in the economic position for ex-wives and children, see Garrison (1990) and Sugarman (1990).
6 See Family Law (Scotland) Act 1985, s 9; but see Wasoff, Dobash and Harcus (1990) for a study of the impact of the Scottish law on solicitors' practice.

parents, most of whom are women, welfare benefits are their main source of income (Eekelaar and Maclean, Table 5.2; Gregory and Foster 1990, Table 4.8). Another important factor is the remarriage of the parties, which improves the economic position of both divorced men and women (ibid). Single-parent families were found to be two-and-a-half times more likely than reconstituted families to have a household income below a notional family average (Eekelaar and Maclean 1986, p 72). Eekelaar and Maclean also found that the presence of children closely determined whether or not income maintenance was sought following the termination of marriage, usually by the wife. In no case where there were no children was a transfer of money between ex-spouses found to be taking place (Eekelaar and Maclean, p 91; but see Gregory and Foster 1990, who found payments being made in 7% of such cases: Table 8.1).

Where there were dependent children, a transfer was found to be taking place in 68% of cases (ibid; Gregory and Foster 1990, Table 8.11 suggests a similar pattern). Although the actual amounts transferred were found to be small, they represented a significant contribution to the household income of the recipient. For half of the recipients, maintenance payments accounted for between a tenth and a third of household income (Table 6.2). Paradoxically, however, it was found that these payments only rarely achieved an increase in the overall level of household income, since the payments merely diminished the wife's entitlement to supplementary benefit (now income support). Thus, maintenance payments only increased household income where the wife was in full-time employment and not dependent on benefit (Table 6.2; pp 94–95). This may explain why a higher proportion of women not receiving maintenance have been found to be on income support than of those women who are:

'. . . not receiving maintenance may make it more difficult for a woman to survive on a low-paid or part-time job, and therefore [the woman] is more likely to prefer to live on welfare income.' (Maclean 1991, p 91)

This raises the question of the interrelationship of maintenance payments and welfare benefits. We have seen in our discussion of income support (Ch 4, above) that it is based on a calculation of needs and resources. Any maintenance payments in fact received from the ex-husband are regarded for these purposes as 'a resource' and thus diminish the ex-wife's level of benefit. In some cases, particularly where the level of maintenance ordered is below the level of benefit and where payment of maintenance is irregular, it may be more convenient for the wife to use the 'diversion procedure' (see below) whereby the maintenance order is registered with the local magistrates' court. This entitles the justices' clerk to enforce the order and to divert any payment received from the husband to the

DSS, who in turn pay the wife the appropriate level of benefit without having to reassess the wife's level of resources every time the husband fails to pay.[7] If the husband fails to make the payments with respect to the children (or, following the Social Security Act 1990, an ex-wife or partner) then the DSS may alternatively enforce payment under the 'liable relative' procedure, discussed in Chapter 4.

The net effect of the 'diversion procedure' is that so long as the ex-wife's resources remain below the level at which entitlement to benefit ceases, any payments made by the husband for the wife's benefit have no effect on the overall level of household income. This may explain why income transfers have been found to be taking place where the wife is working and not in receipt of supplementary benefit, since the ex-husband feels that his payments are making a genuine contribution rather than diminishing the burden on the public purse (Davies et al 1983, Table 3). This is precisely the opposite of the relationship between self-sufficiency through employment and income maintenance to that envisaged by the 1984 Act.

Further, the ability of ex-wives to obtain an adequate level of income through employment is related to a variety of factors both affecting women workers in general (such as skill-downgrading following a return to work after long periods of child care; Eekelaar and Maclean 1986, pp 89–90) and arising from differences of social class (Davies et al 1983, Table 6). There is evidence to suggest that single parents are less likely than married women as a whole to be in employment, but, if in employment, are more likely than married women to be in full-time rather than part-time work (Maclean 1991, p 39). However, a single parent's ability to work is clearly affected by the age of the children: the younger the children, the less likely it is that the mother will be working (Gregory and Foster 1990, Ch 3). Those adverse factors in the employment market facing women in general are especially severe for single parents since theirs is a sole rather than additional income (Eekelaar and Maclean 1986, pp 89–90; see generally, Maclean 1991, Ch 5).

Thus there appears to be little relationship between the payment of maintenance and the ability of women to become self-sufficient. Indeed, the present system ensures that the payment of maintenance is only significant where the ex-wife is already in reasonably well-paid employment. This suggests that there is a 'distinction between middle- and upper-income groups for whom the debate about maintenance for ex-wives may still have relevance, and the remainder of the population who are likely to be caught in the poverty trap' (Davies et al 1983, p 224).

7 Supplementary Benefits Handbook (HMSO, 1982), para 13; see *Peacock v Peacock* [1984] 1 All ER 1069.

(c) **Summary**

The empirical evidence suggests that the economic position of women following divorce depends partly on their social class, partly on their continuing status as mothers, and partly on their ability to find a new partner. This de facto position has effectively been consolidated in law by the MFPA 1984, which, by emphasising the needs of children, has done much to reduce the significance of the distinction between spouse maintenance and child maintenance. The latter is now accorded priority, although the care-giving wife may benefit from it during the period of child care. In this way, the debate over the ex-wife's right to income support after marriage in her own right (classically stated by Deech 1977 and O'Donovan 1978) has received legislative resolution in a way that weighs against any such continuing obligation.

For this reason, it could be argued that the 1984 Act represents a further shift in the axes of the legal regulation of marriage and divorce, from a financial and economic relationship to a relationship centred on the presence and needs of children. Even where there are children, however, we have seen that in many cases child support payments received from a former spouse are only rarely a significant component of a single mother's income package and are overshadowed by state benefits and, to a lesser extent, earnings from employment.

Several problems remain, however. First, although it is clear that income maintenance is not to be used to relieve women of more general economic inequalities, it is unclear how far the law now permits recognition of special needs of individual wives *as wives* (rather than as mothers) to form the basis of a claim to continuing support. The attempt of the Scottish Law Commission (1981) to formulate the necessary distinction ran into conceptual difficulty (Dewar 1984), but nevertheless resulted in legislation. Second, as already pointed out, the principles governing property (as opposed to income) division are unclear. English law has no presumption of equal sharing, unlike that found in Scots law[8] and other jurisdictions (Gray 1977, Ch 2; Glendon 1981, Ch 2). Finally, the 1984 Act focused attention on what had previously been a marginal issue: the appropriate principles of child support (see Eekelaar and Maclean 1986, Ch 7).

Procedure

An application for 'ancillary relief', which includes all the orders discussed in this chapter,[9] is made by the petitioner in the divorce

8   FL(S)A 1985, s 9(1)(a).
9   Except an order for sale under MCA 1973, s 24A.

petition or by the respondent in an answer to the petition claiming relief.[10] In either case, the application must be followed by the filing of a prescribed form of notice.[11] Application is made to the court seized of the divorce petition, that is, to the county court where the main petition is undefended, and to the High Court where defended. In the former case, there is no time limit on the application, which may be made at any time following the decree of divorce provided that the court is prepared to grant leave,[12] and provided also that the applicant has not since remarried.[13]

The application must be accompanied by an affidavit setting out the applicant's financial position.[14] This will usually include details of the applicant's income, assets and outgoings (see Barnard 1983, p 157; Passingham and Harmer 1985, pp 506–514). If the applicant has applied for a transfer of property, certain details concerning the property in question must also be included in the affidavit.[15] The other spouse must then file a similar affidavit in answer.[16] Either party may then request further information from the other by letter or questionnaire, or in the event of non-compliance, by court direction for discovery of documents[17] or by means of a 'production appointment'.[18] The relevant documents will be any item that provides information as to the parties' financial position. This may include: bank accounts, building society and other savings accounts, wage slips, tax returns, business accounts (if relevant), credit card accounts, and details of pension entitlement, insurance policies and share holdings (Barnard 1983, pp 193–196; Black and Bridge 1989, pp 162–163). The courts also have the power to prevent or set aside dispositions made or about to be made with the intention of defeating claims to financial relief.[19]

Although the fact-finding powers of the court appear considerable, it would be a mistake to overestimate their efficacy. There seems to

---

10 Family Proceedings Rules 1991, r 2.53.
11 FPR 1991, Appendix 1, Form M13.
12 FPR 1991, rr 10.9, 2.53(2).
13 MCA 1973, s 28(3).
14 FPR 1991, r 2.58(2).
15 FPR 1991, r 2.59(1).
16 FPR 1991, r 2.58(3).
17 FPR 1991, r 2.59; RSC Ord 24; CCR Ord 14; see *B v B* [1990] 2 FLR 180.
18 This new procedure enables a court to order that any person attend before the court and produce any document specified in the order: FPR 1991, r 2.62(7). This does not permit a court to require disclosure of documents from a person who is otherwise not under an obligation to produce them: it is merely a speedier means of getting documents before the court.
19 MCA 1973, s 37; there is also power to issue injunctions to preserve assets (such as Anton Piller and Mareva injunctions): see Cretney (1991), pp 172–173; Edwards and Halpern (1991a).

be a variation in practice as to the use made of them, with some district judges arranging a preliminary directions hearing, while others may leave it to the parties to apply for directions as they deem necessary (Black and Bridge 1989, pp 163–164). More importantly, the information in affidavits has not always been found to be reliable, and failure to supply affidavits is widespread (Barrington Baker et al 1977, paras 4.8–4.15). Difficulties are greater where the husband's whereabouts are not known.

The available orders

(a) Maintenance pending suit and interim orders

The court may order such payments for the applicant's maintenance 'as it thinks fit' for the period between the presentation of the petition and the decree absolute of divorce.[20] There is no guidance in the legislation as to what level of order to make or as to what factors are relevant. The purpose of the order is simply to ensure adequate provision for the applicant until the court is in a position to make a full order,[1] that is, at any time from the granting of a decree nisi of divorce onward.[2] Since the order is for a temporary period only, and is not made with the assistance of full information as to the parties' resources nor as part of a wider financial settlement, the level of order is likely to be less than that awarded as a full order. Maintenance pending suit is not available for children, since full orders for maintenance may be made in their favour from the presentation of the petition.[3]

An application for maintenance pending suit entails the disclosure of affidavit evidence of resources, as outlined above. Thus, one purpose of an application (apart from obtaining payment of money) is to force an early disclosure of means (Barnard 1983, pp 188–189). Once there is a decree nisi of divorce, it is possible for the applicant to obtain interim maintenance, which the district judge may order as he 'thinks just'.[4] Since, unlike maintenance pending suit, interim maintenance is available beyond the decree absolute, the applicant is thereby enabled to pursue further inquiries as to the other partner's means.

---

20 MCA 1973, s 22.
1   See *Peacock v Peacock* [1984] 1 All ER 1069; *Re T v T* [1990] FCR 169.
2   MCA 1973, s 23(1).
3   MCA 1973, s 23(2).
4   FPR 1991, r 2.64(2).

(b) Income maintenance

(i) Who may apply?

Once a decree nisi has been granted, the court may make an order against either party to the marriage in favour of the other party to take effect at the date of the decree absolute.[5] Orders may be made in favour of any 'child of the family' (as to the meaning of which, see Ch 11 below) under the age of 18 from the date of the presentation of the petition,[6] although it may be more appropriate to rely initially on interim maintenance and to await seeking a full order until there is full financial disclosure. This avoids the necessity of varying a full order. Orders may be made in favour of children of the family aged over 18 where the recipient is undergoing full-time education or training, or where there are 'special circumstances'.[7] An example of the latter might be where the child is handicapped.

Usually, the spouse with custody of the child(ren) will apply for maintenance on their behalf, and the court may order payment to be made to that person.[8] However, the statute does permit payment directly to the child.

(ii) Types of order

There are two types of income maintenance order: for secured or unsecured periodical payments, for such term as may be specified in the order.[9] These are the most common form of order made in ancillary proceedings (Barrington Baker et al 1977, para 3.3). An order to make secured payments is, in effect, an order to set aside a certain amount of property, the income from which is paid to the recipient. The advantage of this is that, provided the liable spouse complies with the order, the payments are guaranteed and there is no problem of continuing enforcement. The disadvantage is that any shortfall in the income produced by the property is borne by the recipient, although the order may be varied (see below). Alternatively, non-income-producing assets may be set aside and charged with any arrears if they accrue.

There is no guidance in the Act as to when secured payments are appropriate. Obviously, the liable spouse must have sufficient revenue-producing assets for the purposes of security which can be

5   MCA 1973, s 23(1).
6   MCA 1973, ss 23(1), (2), 29(1), (3).
7   MCA 1973, s 29(3).
8   MCA 1973, s 23(1)(d) (f).
9   MCA 1973, s 23(1)(a), (b), (d), (e).

set aside for the duration of the order without causing undue hardship. It may be appropriate where there is reason to believe that the liable spouse may seek to avoid an unsecured order. The property charged reverts to the liable spouse at the end of the period of the order.

(iii) Duration

An unsecured order in favour of a spouse cannot last beyond the death of either party or the remarriage of the recipient spouse. A secured order similarly terminates on remarriage, but not on the death of the liable spouse.[10] Secured or unsecured payments in favour of children of the family should initially only be made up to the age at which the child may leave school, and in any case not beyond 18 (subject to the exceptions discussed above).[11]

Within these limits, the court may order payments over a specified period.[12] In the past it seems that the courts have not done this except in certain defined cases (Barrington Baker et al 1977, para 3.4), but have left it to the parties to seek variation or discharge as appropriate. However, certain provisions enacted as part of the MFPA 1984 may ensure that greater use is made of time limits. Apart from the general provision encouraging the 'clean break'[13] (see below), the courts are directed to consider, when making an order for secured or unsecured periodical payments, whether to require those payments to be made or secured only for such period as would in the opinion of the court be sufficient to enable the recipient to adjust without undue hardship to the termination of financial dependence on the other party.[14] A similar principle applies on an application for variation or discharge of an order for periodical payments.[15] The courts appear willing to interpret 'self-sufficiency' as being a level of income relative to the standard of living enjoyed during the marriage, rather than as a basic minimum required for survival.[16] A court may direct that the recipient shall not be entitled to apply for an extension of the period of the order.[17]

---

10 MCA 1973, s 28(1).
11 MCA 1973, s 29(2).
12 MCA 1973, s 23(1)(a), (b), (d), (e).
13 MCA 1973, s 25A(1).
14 MCA 1973, s 25A(2). See the discussion of the 'clean break' below, pp 325–329.
15 MCA 1973, s 37(1) (see below).
16 *M v M (financial provision)* [1987] 2 FLR 1.
17 MCA 1973, s 28(1A); the power will not be used where there is 'real uncertainty' over the future: see *Waterman v Waterman* [1989] 1 FLR 380.

It should be noted that these time limit provisions do not apply to orders to or for the benefit of children; and that the presence of children may influence any awards made for the benefit of the recipient spouse in his or her own right (see below).

(iv) Enforcement

There is evidence of widespread non-compliance with orders for maintenance, especially when ordered in favour of the wife alone (Gibson 1982; Eekelaar and Maclean 1986, Ch 4; see also Weitzman 1985, Chs 5 and 9; Edwards and Halpern 1988a; Lord Chancellor's Department 1990a, Vol 2). There are a variety of methods of enforcing a divorce court order for maintenance. These are either aimed at the liable spouse's income or at his property. The former category includes: judgment summons, which requires the liable spouse to attend before a judge who may make such order as he thinks fit; an order under the Attachment of Earnings Act 1971[18] ordering the liable spouse's employer to deduct a certain amount from the salary paid to the liable spouse and to forward it to the court (see Ch 4); and a power to order payment by standing order and to require the payer to open a bank account for that purpose.[19] The latter category includes: a garnishee order, which orders any third party debtor of the liable spouse (such as a bank) to pay the debt to the applicant to the extent necessary to discharge the arrears; a charging order, which charges certain property belonging to the debtor, the charge being enforceable if necessary by an application for sale of the charged property; and a warrant of execution, entitling the creditor to seize property of the liable spouse and sell it to satisfy the debt.

It is also possible for a maintenance order to be registered in the magistrates' court, in which case the order is enforceable (subject to the discretion to remit arrears) as if it were an order of that court (see Ch 4). The money is paid to the court rather than the recipient;[20] the court then forwards the money to the recipient or, if the 'diversion procedure'(see above) is in operation, to the DSS. The advantage of this is that a record of payments may be kept, and any enforcement proceeding may be taken by the clerk to the court on the recipient's behalf (see Westcott 1987). There is evidence that a large proportion

---

18 The powers of the High and county courts in this respect are wider following the Maintenance Enforcement Act 1991: see Ch 4 for a discussion of the powers of the magistrates' court, which are substantially similar.
19 Maintenance Enforcement Act 1991, s 1, on which see Ch 4.
20 Maintenance Orders Act 1958.

of divorce court orders are registered in this way (Barrington Baker et al 1977, Table 23) because there is no effective equivalent enforcement procedure available in the divorce court, although there is also evidence of a decline in the use of this procedure (Edwards, Gould and Halpern 1990, p 32). This has meant that the family proceedings court has become closely involved with enforcement of orders made in the divorce court (Gibson 1982; and Chs 1 and 4, above). Registration also transfers responsibility for applications for variation of registered orders to the magistrates' court, and there is evidence that magistrates are inclined more to vary orders downwards rather than up (Edwards and Halpern 1988a, pp 119–120).

(c) Lump sums

The court may order that one party to the marriage transfer a lump sum of money to the other spouse both for that spouse's benefit and for the benefit of any child of the family.[1] Application must be made before the applicant remarries and, where the order is in favour of a child, before the child reaches 16.[2] Once a lump sum has been transferred, it does not present the problems of enforcement encountered in relation to orders for periodic maintenance.[3] If it is necessary to enforce payment of the money, the same provisions as those already discussed apply.

Lump sums are rarely used (Barrington Baker et al 1977, paras 3.7–3.10; Eekelaar 1991, p 70). A necessary precondition of such an order would appear to be that the parties are relatively wealthy,[4] in which case it might be used to compensate for a property transfer, for example of the matrimonial home (ibid).[5] Lump sums will very rarely be ordered purely for investment purposes (and will probably be confined to 'big money cases'); but if they are, 'the recipient of the lump sum is expected to expend it, or so much of it as is intended to meet future income needs, by drawing both upon its capital as well as relying upon the income it can produce'.[6] A starting point for

---

1   MCA 1973, s 23(1)(c), (f).
2   MCA 1973, ss 28(3), 29.
3   Unless the lump sum ordered takes the form of a charge for a specified amount (or, preferably, for a specified percentage of the proceeds) on the matrimonial home, in which case delaying tactics by the other spouse in effecting the sale may give rise to problems – see, eg, *Hope-Smith v Hope-Smith* [1989] 2 FLR 56.
4   *Potter v Potter* [1982] 3 All ER 321.
5   *Smith v Smith* [1970] 1 All ER 244; *Backhouse v Backhouse* [1978] 1 All ER 1158.
6   Per Ward J in *B v B* [1990] 1 FLR 20 at 24; but a recipient of a lump sum is not obliged to deal with the money in any particular fashion – per Butler-Sloss LJ in *Gojkovic v Gojkovic* [1990] 1 FLR 140 at 145.

calculating a lump sum for these purposes is the so-called 'Duxbury' calculation, which produces a figure 'which, if invested on the assumptions as to life expectancy, rates of inflation, return on investments, growth of capital, incidence of income tax, will produce enough to meet the recipient's needs for her life'.[7] Accountants have devised computer programmes for precisely this purpose (see Lawrence 1990). However, the calculation is only directed to ascertaining the size of lump sum needed to meet proper future living expenses; it does not take account of special needs, such as the need for housing, nor does it reflect all the factors which the courts are directed to take into account (such as contributing to building up a family business[8]), which may affect the overall amount of provision awarded.[9] Thus, the calculation is 'a means to an end, not an end in itself'.[10]

A lump sum may also be used as a means of reducing or avoiding reliance on periodic maintenance,[11] especially after the MFPA 1984. In such a case, the amount awarded by way of lump sum is not to be diminished on the ground that the recipient is likely to remarry, even though periodic payments, if ordered, would have ceased on remarriage.[12]

(d) Property transfers

The court has the power to order the transfer of specified property by one spouse to the other. This power is exercisable in favour of the other party to the marriage, and of any child of the family under the age of 18 (subject to the exceptions outlined above).[13] Any order so made takes effect once the decree of divorce has been made absolute.[14]

The property that may be made subject to such an order is only briefly defined in the legislation as property to which the liable spouse is entitled, either in possession or reversion.[15] It is thus a question of ascertaining what that spouse is entitled to at the date of the order. As far as a reversionary interest is concerned, it is a question of construing the terms of the instrument under which the

7 *Gojkovic v Gojkovic* [1990] 1 FLR 140.
8 Ibid.
9 *B v B* [1990] 2 FLR 180.
10 Ibid.
11 *S v S* [1987] 2 All ER 312.
12 *Duxbury v Duxbury* [1987] 1 FLR 7.
13 MCA 1973, s 24(1)(a).
14 MCA 1973, s 24(3).
15 MCA 1973, s 24(1)(a).

interest arises. However, this formal definition of property may be extended in practice by two provisions in MCA 1973, s 25(2), which direct the court to take account, first, of all the parties' financial resources, including those that they are likely to have in the foreseeable future,[16] and second the value to each of the parties of any benefit (such as rights to a pension) which the parties stand to lose by reason of the divorce.[17]

These provisions are discussed in detail below. Their significance for present purposes is that although the courts cannot deal directly with property rights that have not yet materialised, such as pension rights, it is open to the courts to use their powers to make transfers or lump sum payments of 'property' as conventionally defined in recognition of the fact that other rights will come into existence at some time in the future, or that one spouse will lose entitlement to those future rights. For example, a court may order the transfer of property to a wife in recognition of the fact that she will lose pension entitlements as a result of the divorce.[18] While this does not mean that the courts can reallocate the pension rights themselves, it does mean that a compensating transfer of existing property can be made.

The technical implementation of property transfers may take a variety of forms, including settlement of 'property' as defined.[19] This is a question that is most closely connected with transfers of the matrimonial home and is considered below in that context.

(e) Variation of settlements

The courts may also vary, reduce or extinguish the terms of any ante- or post-nuptial settlement in favour of the parties to the marriage and any children of the family.[20] This power dates back to the introduction of judicial divorce itself, and until 1970 was virtually the only redistributive power available to the divorce court. For this reason, the term 'settlement' has been widely defined by the courts so that, for example, it includes even a conveyance of a house into the joint names of husband and wife.[1] The only restriction is that the 'settlement' must be for the benefit of the spouses as spouses, or for their children.

---

16 MCA 1973, s 25(2)(a).
17 MCA 1973, s 25(2)(h).
18 Eg *Milne v Milne* (1981) 2 FLR 286.
19 MCA 1973, s 24(1)(b).
20 MCA 1973, s 24(1)(c)(d); see *E v E* [1990] 2 FLR 233.
1 *Brown v Brown* [1959] 2 All ER 266.

(f) Order of sale

Section 24 of the MCA 1973 confers only powers of transfer, resettlement and variation. It does not include a power to order a sale of any property, even though there may be many circumstances where a sale would be appropriate to realise matrimonial assets as a precondition to their redistribution. For this reason, a new s 24A was inserted in 1981[2] which empowers a court when making an order for secured periodical payments, a lump sum or property transfer to order the sale of property. The section also confers very wide powers to specify the terms on which the sale is to take place and the way in which the proceeds are to be distributed.[3] This is considered further in relation to the matrimonial home, below.

(g) Transfer of tenancies

The MHA 1983 conferred a power on the courts to transfer certain protected tenancies on the granting of a decree of divorce.[4] The court may also make orders concerning responsibility for the payment of outgoings on the property.[5]

The statutory guidelines

These extensive readjustive powers are exercisable according to a statutory list of criteria, contained in MCA 1973, s 25 and s 25A. It was on these criteria that the debate preceding the MFPA 1984 focused. It will be remembered that one consequence of that Act was to remove the overriding 'principle of minimal loss' without introducing a replacement. The following discussion is based on reported case law, which consists mainly of cases appealed to the High Court or Court of Appeal.

There are two important limitations on the value of reported case law. The first is that it is unclear how far these principles are in fact

---

2 Matrimonial Homes and Property Act 1981, ss 7, 8; for a discussion of the background and effect of this provision, see *R v Rushmoor Borough Council, ex p Barrett* [1988] 2 FLR 252.
3 MCA 1973, s 24A(1), (2), (4); but it does not permit a court to make an order for vacant possession against a spouse with an equitable interest in the property in question – see *Crosthwaite v Crosthwaite* [1989] 2 FLR 86.
4 MHA 1983, s 7, Sch 1.
5 Sch 1, para 5.

applied by district judges (previously divorce court registrars), who deal with the majority of cases of financial provision. The existence of wide regional variations in awards (Edwards and Halpern 1990, pp 78–81) suggests that the influence of the case law is limited, since the variation is attributed to 'the exercise of discretion by registrars' who 'clearly have views about the policies which underpin the operation of the law in this field' (ibid, p 87). Other research has found that 'when asked to articulate a general goal towards which they are working, the registrars are unable to produce a cohesive model. This is not surprising because the law has provided none' (Eekelaar 1991, p 62). The second is that only a minority of divorces involve an application for financial provision (see below). Thus, post-divorce economic arrangements may either take place without the direct intervention of the courts, or simply do not exist. The significance of the Child Support Act in this context is that, at least where children are involved, the economic consequences of divorce or relationship breakdown will in future be subjected, in some cases compulsorily, to legal/bureaucratic regulation outside the courts.

(a) The welfare of children

(i) An overriding concern?

We have seen that, as a purely empirical matter, 'post-divorce support is essentially child support' (Eekelaar and Maclean 1988, p 147); yet, from a legal point of view, it is often characterised merely as an adjunct of adult support (ibid, p 148). Although the 1984 Act directed the court, in exercising its powers, to have regard to all the circumstances and to give 'first consideration' to the welfare of any 'child of the family' who is under 18,[6] it failed to specify any clear criteria by which the courts are to measure levels of child support. Even though MCA 1973, s 25(3) requires the court to have regard to a variety of factors (such as the financial needs of the child, the child's financial resources, any physical or mental disability of the child, the manner of his education or training, together with the financial needs and resources of the child's parents) it remains the case that court decisions as to the level of child support awards remain arbitrary and their basis undisclosed (Sax et al 1987). In practice it seems that the size and form of awards for children are heavily influenced by considerations of taxation and

---

6   MCA 1973, s 25(1); 'first' is not the same as 'paramount', so the presence of children will not exclude a 'clean break': see *Suter v Suter and Jones* [1987] 2 All ER 336.

welfare entitlement (Eekelaar and Maclean 1986, Ch 2). Indeed, there is much evidence to suggest that awards of child maintenance vary widely both in terms of their size and the proportion they represent of the payer's income (Lord Chancellor's Department 1990a, Vol 2, Ch 4; Eekelaar 1991, pp 94–96).

Very little guidance has emerged from the reported cases. In the leading case of *Wachtel*,[7] for example, the wife was awarded a sum calculated according to the 'one-third rule' (see below); the court then awarded an 'additional sum' for the child without specifying the basis of the calculation. Beyond this, the case law establishes very few guidelines, except that the level of child maintenance is not to be affected by the custodial parent's misconduct[8] (although any reduction in the parent's award will of course affect the household income as a whole), and that it is irrelevant to the level of award that the children are being supported by welfare benefit.[9] Where the child is not the natural child of the liable spouse, but comes within the child of the family formula, the statute directs the court to have regard to whether or to what extent the spouse assumed responsibility for the child's maintenance, to whether or not the spouse knew that the child was not his or her own, and to the liability of any other person to maintain the child.[10]

The welfare of children will be relevant to the way in which the court exercises its powers in favour of the adult parties to the marriage. It has been stated that the primary concern of the courts as far as the children are concerned is that they receive 'shelter, food and education according to the means of the parents'.[11] Thus, it is rare for courts to award property transfers or lump sums directly to children.[12] It has also been decided that the welfare of children is not such an overriding factor as to exclude the possibility of a 'clean break' (as to which, see below).[13] 'First' importance is not the same as 'paramount'.

Although the MCA 1973 technically retains the distinction between spouse and child maintenance, the 1984 amendments have probably served to erode it, since continuing support of a spouse following divorce will become increasingly dependent on his or her status as caretaker of children (see Edwards, Gould and Halpern 1990). This would be welcomed by those who regard the distinction between spouse and child maintenance as artificial, on the basis that

---

7 [1973] 1 All ER 829.
8 Eg *West v West* [1977] 2 All ER 705, CA.
9 *Tovey v Tovey* (1978) 8 Fam Law 80.
10 MCA 1973, s 25(4).
11 *Harnett v Harnett* [1973] 2 All ER 593.
12 *McKay v Chapman* [1978] 2 All ER 548; *Lord Lilford v Glynn* [1979] 1 All ER 441.
13 *Suter v Suter and Jones* [1987] 2 All ER 336.

the economic position of the child and custodial parent are in any case inextricably linked (Cretney 1984, p 813; Eekelaar and Maclean 1986, p 107); but it would tend to support the view that the 1984 Act has considerably diminished the spouse's claim to continuing maintenance following divorce in her own right. Whether this is the case or not will turn on the interpretation given to 'first consideration'. Does it mean, for example, that the child's needs take priority over an ex-spouse's claim, even where the child's needs may soak up all the available resources? And what standard of living is the paying spouse to be left with once the child's needs have been satisfied? The current law (including the MFPA 1984 itself) offers remarkably little guidance; although the answers will become clearer once the Child Support Act 1991 has been implemented.

(ii)   The impact of the Child Support Act 1991

We saw in Chapter 4 that the Child Support Act will introduce a new system for the assessment and enforcement of child maintenance. Once implemented, this scheme will have a significant impact on the material discussed in this chapter, although much will depend on detailed regulations that have yet to be made public. Two points may be made at this stage. The first is that, by giving priority to child support, the scheme will in many cases soak up most of the resources available to the parties; 'the practical effect is likely to be to propel child support issues into the forefront of matters to be dealt with in agreed settlements or if there is any dispute' (Eekelaar 1991, p 120). The second is that by removing the issue of child maintenance from the jurisdiction of the courts (with some limited exceptions), the scheme may well make negotiated agreements less likely. At present, a husband may be willing to concede transfers of property (such as the matrimonial home) in return for a reduced support obligation. By making that obligation non-negotiable, there is at least the possibility that such agreements will become harder to negotiate: 'it will be in the father's interest to cling to his capital' (Eekelaar 1991d, p 16).

(b)   Other relevant factors

As far as claims between spouses are concerned, the court must have regard to 'all the circumstances' and 'in particular' to those listed in MCA 1973, s 25(2)(a)–(h). There are also certain additional factors introduced by MFPA 1984, and now contained in MCA 1973, s 25A. Consideration of all these factors is subject to the needs of children;

but we have seen that the extent to which the welfare of children is an overriding factor is unclear.

(i) Section 25(2)(a) – '. . . the income, earning capacity, property and other financial resources which each of the parties has or is likely to have in the foreseeable future, including in the case of earning capacity any increase in that capacity which it would in the opinion of the court be reasonable to expect a party to the marriage to take steps to acquire'

Income The parties' income should have been disclosed in the exchange of affidavits and documents before the hearing. The best proof of income is a salary or wage slip, and these are produced in most (but not all) cases. However, these do not include evidence of earnings from overtime and bonuses (Barrington Baker et al 1977, paras 4.14–4.15; Table 11). Where the spouses' financial affairs are more complex, the courts look as far as possible to the realities of the position.[14] Although case law has established that the court should work with a gross (ie, before tax) rather than net figure of earnings,[15] practice varies as to the extent to which outgoings and expenses (such as travel to work) are deducted before arriving at a level of income regarded as being available for distribution (ibid, para 2.10; Table 3). The courts in any case regard their task as being to arrive at appropriate figures once the effects of taxation on the overall package have been taken into account.[16] Benefits in kind, such as company cars, are also taken into account.[17]

The receipt of state benefits, such as supplementary benefit, housing benefit and family income supplement, may also be regarded as income and therefore as relevant to the award. This is discussed further below in relation to the economic outcome of divorce for low-income families.

Earning capacity The courts must also have regard to what the parties are capable of earning, and since the MFPA 1984, to any increase in capacity that it would be reasonable to expect a party to acquire. It is unclear to what extent the new provision adds anything, since the courts were in any case prior to 1984 willing to

---

14 Eg *Brett v Brett* [1969] 1 All ER 1007.
15 *Rodewald v Rodewald* [1977] 2 WLR 191; following the changes to the taxation of maintenance payments introduced in the 1988 Finance Act, maintenance is calculated on the net rather than gross incomes of the parties: see Green (1988), p 13. This will make the 'net effects' calculation easier to apply.
16 *S v S* [1977] Fam 127; *Stockford v Stockford* (1981) 3 FLR 58.
17 *Sibley v Sibley* (1979) 2 FLR 121.

have regard to the possibility of a spouse earning more[18] (Barrington Baker et al 1977, paras 2.16–2.18). There is similarly some confusion over whether the new provision applies to the earning capacity of the claimant (so as to reduce the award) or of the liable spouse (so as to increase it) (Dewar 1986, p 104). The provision has been applied in a case where the wife was in part-time employment, and the fact that she would be able to increase the number of hours she worked was taken into account.[19]

The question of how far a spouse should be expected to enter employment and become self-sufficient is related to the use by the courts of their powers to impose a clean break (discussed below) and the welfare of the children. Thus, Eekelaar found that registrars took the view that:

> '. . . a former spouse would be considered to be under a duty to support the other where the interests of their common children inhibited the care-giving parent from seeking employment . . . [They] were not anxious to force such a parent into employment. In the absence of this inhibiting factor, the emphasis switched towards encouraging employment, and, where this could be easily achieved, continuing support was likely to be very restricted.' (1991, p 68)

Earning capacity is not regarded as an item of intangible property to be split between the parties, as some have suggested it should be (eg, Jackson and Maclean 1990: see above). Rather, it is relevant only to deciding what the applicant's needs are and what the liable spouse can reasonably afford to pay.

Property and other resources   The court will have regard both to property to which the parties are presently entitled, and to assets or resources which are likely to become available to them in the near future, such as gratuities,[20] insurance policies, pension rights and distributions from discretionary trusts;[1] and the likelihood of a party coming into an inheritance may also be considered in certain limited circumstances.[2] The courts will also take account of any damages for personal injuries received by one of the parties,[3] of the value of any share in another house which either party has acquired since the

18 Eg *McEwan v McEwan* [1972] 2 All ER 708; *Ward v Ward and Greene* [1980] 1 All ER 176n.
19 *Leadbeater v Leadbeater* [1985] FLR 789; see also *Mitchell v Mitchell* [1984] FLR 387.
20 *Happe v Happe* [1990] 2 FLR 212.
1   Although a beneficiary of a discretionary trust has no enforceable right to receive money from the trustees, the court will look to 'the reality of the situation' but without placing improper pressure on the trustees to exercise their discretion in a particular way – see *Browne v Browne* [1989] 1 FLR 291; *J v J (C intervening)* [1989] 1 FLR 453.
2   *Michael v Michael* [1986] 2 FLR 389.
3   *Daubney v Daubney* [1976] 2 All ER 453.

breakdown of the marriage[4] and of any property actually inherited after divorce.[5]

Although the enjoyment of rent-free accommodation is not to be regarded as a resource,[6] the fact that a party is securely housed is a significant factor when considering the needs of the parties under the next heading.[7] The court may also have regard to the fact that a liable spouse has a new partner who is also earning or is providing the spouse with housing, but only as part of the 'overall picture'.[8] Third parties can be ordered to attend and give evidence at the hearing of a claim for ancillary relief,[9] but cannot be compelled to supply an affidavit of means.[10]

It is possible that although a spouse is very wealthy on paper, he or she may not easily have access to certain assets. An example would be where the spouse is self-employed. In such cases, the needs of the business may set a limit to the value of assets available for distribution.[11] It is highly unlikely that the business will be sold (since it is the only source of the husband's income), and the courts have warned parties against becoming involved in 'titanic struggles' to produce evidence as to what the business is worth.[12] The courts have emphasised that consideration of the husband's resources in such cases is of a general rather than detailed nature and that the wife's reasonable requirements will be balanced against the husband's ability to pay.[13]

(ii) Section 25(2)(b) – '. . . *the financial needs, obligations and responsibilities which each of the parties to the marriage has or is likely to have in the foreseeable future'*

Needs   In most cases, the primary need of the parties will be housing. This is considered below. Beyond this, the concept of need is interpreted in a 'relative' rather than an 'absolute' sense, so that, for example, the needs of wealthy spouses will be regarded as being

---

4   *W v W (financial provision: lump sum)* [1975] 3 All ER 970; *Ibbetson v Ibbetson* [1984] FLR 545.

5   *Lombardi v Lombardi* [1973] 3 All ER 625; *Pearce v Pearce* (1979) 1 FLR 261; *Schuller v Schuller* [1990] 2 FLR 193.

6   *Wills v Wills* [1984] FLR 672.

7   *Browne v Pritchard* [1975] 3 All ER 721; *Martin v Martin* [1977] 3 All ER 762.

8   *Wilkinson v Wilkinson* (1979) 10 Fam Law 48; *Macey v Macey* (1981) 3 FLR 7.

9   FPR 1991, r 2.62(4).

10   *Wynne v Wynne and Jeffers* [1980] 3 All ER 659; *Re T v T* [1990] FCR 169.

11   *Smith v Smith* (1982) 4 FLR 154, CA; *Potter v Potter* [1982] 3 All ER 321.

12   *B v B* [1989] 1 FLR 119. On the valuation of shares in a family business for divorce purposes, see *Holt v Holt* [1990] BCC 682.

13   *Potter* (above); *P v P* [1989] 2 FLR 241; see Cretney (1991).

greater than the equivalent for poorer ones. In *Preston v Preston*,[14] for example, Ormrod LJ interpreted 'needs' as meaning 'reasonable requirements', and refused an appeal by a wealthy husband against a lump sum to the wife of £600,000. However, Ormrod LJ made it clear that the meaning attributed to 'needs' was coloured by the overriding, and now defunct, 'principle of minimal loss'. Nevertheless, the decision in *Preston* was referred to with approval in the post-1984 case of *Duxbury v Duxbury*.[15] In such cases, the line between need and entitlement as providing the basis of an award is somewhat blurred. For the less well-off, the concept of 'need', apart from housing, will include what is considered reasonable to cover necessary outgoings, such as food and travel expenses for work. Thus where a husband takes on an unreasonably large mortgage following separation, he cannot use that to argue for reduced payments to the wife.[16]

The interpretation of need may be affected by the remarriage of the claimant. The fact that a spouse has acquired a legal right to be supported by someone else has been regarded as increasing the level of their resources, and so to reduce their needs.[17] This principle has been extended to a claimant spouse who was likely to remarry,[18] and to one who was cohabiting[19] and has been taken to reduce the claimant's need both for periodic payments and for lump sums or property transfers. This may seem at odds with the fact that lump sums and property transfers, once made, cannot be varied on the remarriage of the recipient, and are generally not regarded as capitalised periodic payments.[20] If anything, this serves to underline the confused rationale of the law.

Obligations and responsibilities   This may include both legally imposed and voluntarily assumed obligations of support. Although the courts have regarded the primary responsibility of a husband to be to

14 [1982] 1 All ER 41.
15 [1987] 1 FLR 7.
16 Eg *Cowie v Cowie* (1983) 13 Fam Law 250, CA.
17 *H v H (financial provision: remarriage)* [1975] 1 All ER 367.
18 *Tinsdale v Tinsdale* (1983) 4 FLR 641.
19 *MH v MH* (1981) 3 FLR 429; but see *Atkinson v Atkinson* [1988] 2 FLR 353, where the court refused to equate cohabitation with remarriage: a cohabiting ex-spouse will not automatically lose maintenance by virtue of the cohabitation itself, although a decision not to remarry so as to preserve the right to maintenance may be relevant as 'conduct' under s 25(g) (see below) or, on an application to vary or discharge an order for periodical payments, as a relevant change in circumstances under MCA 1973, s 31(7) (see below); see also *Hepburn v Hepburn* [1989] 1 FLR 373, where Butler-Sloss LJ said that 'it is not the job of the court to put pressure on parties to regularise their irregular unions' (p 378) (see Hodson 1990).
20 See *Duxbury* (above).

maintain his first family,[1] they have increasingly recognised the claims of a second family on the husband's income.[2] Thus, just as a second partner's income is taken into account as part of the 'overall picture' (see above), so the fact of a second partner's dependence is also taken into consideration.[3] The courts are willing to recognise the fact that there is 'life after divorce': in *Delaney*,[4] Ward J said that a husband is 'entitled to order his life in such a way as will hold in reasonable balance the responsibilities to his existing family which he carries into his new life, as well as his proper aspirations for that new future', provided that he does not behave in 'an extravagant fashion' in undertaking new liabilities.[5]

(iii) Section 25(2)(c) – '. . . the standard of living enjoyed by the family before the breakdown of the marriage'

This paragraph has survived the 1984 reforms in an unaltered form, but its status as a factor must now be unclear following the removal of the overriding principle of minimal loss. In *Gojkovic*,[6] Butler-Sloss LJ suggested that the repeal of the principle of minimal loss did not prevent the court, where finances permit, from keeping the parties' post-divorce standards of living in proportion to each other[7]. Under the old law it was clear that this factor will not depress the level of an award where the wife has accepted a lower standard of living in the interests of the husband's business.[8]

(iv) Section 25(2)(d) – '. . . the age of each party to the marriage and the duration of the marriage'

Age The age of the parties may be relevant to their earning capacity and prospects, and thus to the question of their needs. For example, while a young wife might be expected to retrain and

1   *Tovey v Tovey* (1978) 8 Fam Law 80; *Cowie v Cowie* (1983) 13 Fam Law 250.
2   *Barnes v Barnes* [1972] 3 All ER 872; *Winter v Winter* (1972) 140 JP Jo 597; *Blower v Blower* [1986] 1 FLR 292.
3   *Macey v Macey* (1981) 3 FLR 7.
4   [1990] 2 FLR 457.
5   Ibid, at p 461.
6   [1990] 1 FLR 140.
7   The family's standard of living may also be relevant to the weight to be attached to the children's welfare; thus, an ex-wife of a very wealthy husband with custody of children may get more than she would have done in her own right since it may not be in the children's interests for the mother to be living in 'straitened circumstances': per Ewbank J in *E v E* [1990] 2 FLR 233.
8   *Preston v Preston* [1982] 1 All ER 41.

enhance her earning capacity,[9] an older one might not. Further, the position of an older wife with respect to pension rights may also have to be considered.[10]

Duration of the marriage   Where the marriage has been short,[11] this will usually result in a reduced or nominal award,[12] especially where the parties are young. Where the claimant is not responsible for the brevity of the marriage, the level of the award may be more than nominal by virtue of a consideration of the conduct of the parties (see below) or of 'all the circumstances' under the opening words of s 25(2).[13] Where the parties are older, the effect of even a short marriage on their financial position may be extremely adverse, for example from the point of view of housing or pension rights. In such cases, the courts look to the 'overall effect' of the marriage, and seek to relieve its most serious consequences.[14] Although technically a period of premarital cohabitation does not count towards the duration of the marriage,[15] it may be taken into account either by means of a consideration of contributions made to the family (below) or as one of 'all the circumstances'.[16] Presumably, the needs of any children are not related to the length of the marriage.

(iv)   Section 25(2)(e) – '. . . any physical or mental disability of either party to the marriage'

(v)   Section 25(2)(f) – '. . . the contributions which each of the parties has made or is likely to make in the foreseeable future to the welfare of the family including any contribution by looking after the home or caring for the family'

This provision offers explicit recognition of domestic labour and child care provided by a spouse. However, it may also serve to reduce an award where the court takes the view that the wife has not performed these duties adequately.[17] This paragraph may also include unpaid work in a family business (which may operate to

9   *Khan v Khan* [1980] 1 All ER 497.
10   *S v S* [1977] 1 All ER 56.
11   For the meaning of 'short' in this context, see *Gengler v Gengler* [1976] 2 All ER 81; *M v M* (1976) 6 Fam Law 243, CA.
12   Eg *Graves v Graves* (1974) 4 Fam Law 124; *Leadbeater v Leadbeater* [1985] FLR 789.
13   *W-S v W-S* (1974) 5 Fam Law 20; *Soni v Soni* [1984] FLR 294.
14   *S v S* [1977] 1 All ER 56.
15   *Campbell v Campbell* [1977] 1 All ER 1.
16   *Kokosinki v Kokosinki* [1980] 1 All ER 1106; *Foley v Foley* [1981] 2 All ER 857.
17   *West v West* [1977] 2 All ER 705, CA.

increase substantially the level of award[18]), or the provision of finance to the other spouse for business purposes.[19]

(vi) Section 25(2)(g) – '. . . the conduct of each of the parties if that conduct is such that it would in the opinion of the court be inequitable to disregard it'

The removal of the principle of minimal loss from s 25 necessitated the redrafting of the reference to conduct, since they previously appeared together in the same sentence. It was unclear whether this reformulation was intended to widen the relevance of conduct as a factor to be considered, or simply to codify the previous law.[20] If the latter, it is a matter of some speculation what the previous law was on this matter.

Two different approaches emerge from the case law. Under the first, conduct will only be considered relevant if it is 'obvious and gross'.[1] This formulation was clearly aimed at ensuring that considerations of fault are not reintroduced in a no-fault system of divorce at the ancillary stage.[2] This formula has been found to apply to cases in which, for example, a spouse had physically attacked another,[3] where one spouse was persistently harassing the other,[4] where one spouse had refused to set up a household with the other from the date of the marriage,[5] and where a husband had committed adultery with his daughter-in-law.[6] On this view, conduct will only rarely be a decisive factor, and it has been emphasised that in most cases a comparison of the parties' conduct will usually reveal an equality of 'guilt'.[7]

The second, and more recent, approach involves asking whether it would be 'inequitable' to disregard a particular pattern of behaviour, and to find conduct to be a relevant factor where one party was substantially more responsible for the marriage breakdown than the other[8] or where 'the imbalance of conduct one way or the

---

18 See eg *Gojkovic v Gojkovic* [1990] 1 FLR 140 (see Cretney 1990).
19 *Kokosinki* [1980] 1 All ER 1106; *Preston* [1982] 1 All ER 41.
20 For the former view, see *Kyte v Kyte* [1988] 1 FLR 469, per Purchas LJ.
1 Per Denning MR in *Wachtel v Wachtel* [1973] 1 All ER 829.
2 Ibid.
3 *Jones v Jones* [1975] 2 All ER 12; see also *Evans v Evans* [1989] 1 FLR 351 (ex-wife convicted of inciting others to murder her husband).
4 *J (HD) v J (AM)* [1980] 1 All ER 156.
5 *West v West* [1977] 2 All ER 705.
6 *Dixon v Dixon* (1975) 5 Fam Law 58, CA.
7 *Vasey v Vasey* [1985] FLR 596; but see *Kyte* (above).
8 *Robinson v Robinson* [1983] 1 All ER 391; *Bailey v Tolliday* (1982) 4 FLR 542; *Ibbetson v Ibbetson* [1984] FLR 545; *B v B* [1988] 2 FLR 490 (wife penalised for obstructing discovery). Note that para (g), along with the rest of s 25, will also be relevant on

other would make it inequitable to ignore the comparative conduct of the parties'.[9] On this basis, conduct after the parties' divorce will be relevant, for example where one spouse has made much greater efforts than the other to improve his or her financial position since the end of the marriage.[10]

Once established, conduct may either decrease or increase an award; in the latter cases of 'good conduct', there will usually be an overlap with paragraph (e) (above).[11] It is also clear that the court may compare the conduct of the parties and allow one to cancel the other out.[12] Given the expense involved in the proving and hearing of allegations of fault, it may be better for all concerned simply to agree to leave fault out as an issue in the proceedings,[13] although some clients (especially those with the money to fight) may be reluctant to do this.

(vii) Section 25(2)(h) – '. . . the value to each of the parties to the marriage of any benefit (for example, a pension) which, by reason of the dissolution or annulment of the marriage, that party will lose the chance of acquiring'

This paragraph includes future pension rights, the surrender value of any insurance policy,[14] the value of a retirement lump sum[15] and any money obtained from the sale of a family business.[16] Although the court may not be able to deal with these rights directly (see below), the present or future value of these rights may be taken into account by the court in deciding what order to make out of property as conventionally defined. Thus, a court may order a husband to transfer money or property to his wife in recognition of the fact that the wife will lose entitlement to a widow's pension as a consequence of the divorce.

The court may also make an order requiring a lump sum to be transferred on the occurrence of a specified future event, such as the

---

an application for variation or discharge of an order (discussed below). It has been held that a wife's cohabitation with another partner may be relevant to the question of 'conduct' on such an application, but only if there is evidence that the claimant has deliberately chosen not to remarry in order to preserve the right to maintenance, or of 'financial irresponsibility or sexual or other misconduct': per Waterhouse J in *Atkinson v Atkinson* [1988] 2 FLR 353 (followed in *Hepburn v Hepburn* [1989] 1 FLR 373: see Hodson 1990).

9   *Kyte v Kyte* [1988] 1 FLR 469, per Purchas LJ at p 478; *K v K* [1990] 2 FLR 225.
10 *K v K* (above).
11 Eg *Kokosinski* [1980] 1 All ER 1106.
12 *Harnett v Harnett* [1974] 1 All ER 764; *Leadbeater* [1985] FLR 789.
13 Per Ackner LJ in *Duxbury* [1987] 1 FLR 7.
14 *Bennett v Bennett* (1978) 9 Fam Law 19, CA.
15 *Richardson v Richardson* (1978) 9 Fam Law 86, CA.
16 *Trippas v Trippas* [1973] 2 All ER 1.

husband's retirement.[17] This avoids the difficulty that, at the time of the divorce, the extent or value of a spouse's accrued pension entitlements may be unclear. The court may order the transfer of a specified amount, or of a specified proportion of the pension lump sum when it is eventually received. However, in the particular case of service pensions, an order requiring the transfer of a part of a pension or its monetary equivalent may constitute a contravention of other statutory provisions.[18] Pension rights of ex-wives may be preserved in cases of petitions for divorce based on five year's separation, by means of the refusal of a decree (see Ch 7) and by applications by unremarried divorced spouses for financial provision out of a deceased's estate.

It is doubtful whether these provisions adequately compensate a wife for the loss of pension rights (see Morgan 1984; Masson 1986, 1988). The courts' powers are limited by a number of factors: there is no power to order a husband to take out insurance for the wife, to assign pension benefits (which may in any case be prohibited by the terms of the pension scheme itself), or to continue paying pension or insurance premiums; there are difficulties in valuing pensions; and there are rarely sufficient assets which can be transferred to the wife to compensate for the loss of entitlement (see Law Society 1991, pp 17–18).

Pensions are increasingly recognised as significant items of 'new' property (eg, Glendon 1981) and the value of pension rights significantly affects the overall distribution of wealth. Women are disadvantaged in relation to this form of property, since pension entitlement depends on a steady record of contributions from earnings either to the state or to a private pension scheme. Women who have given up work to care for children may not have made sufficient contributions to qualify; and divorced women with children have a more limited earning capacity and will thus be unable to build up significant pension contributions in their own right (see generally Joshi and Davies 1991). Thus, for many women, entitlement to pension rights will be in the capacity of dependant on a husband; and divorce will remove even this form of entitlement. The problem is especially acute for older wives. It has been estimated that the proportion of divorced women aged over 60 will increase from 3% in 1985 to 13% by 2025 (ibid, Ch 2). As we have seen, the courts have no power to deal with the pension rights themselves, but are merely obliged to take their present or future existence into

---

17 *Priest v Priest* (1978) 1 FLR 189; *Milne v Milne* (1981) 2 FLR 286.
18 Eg Air Force Act 1955, s 203: see *Ranson v Ranson* [1988] 18 Fam Law 128; but once such benefits have been received, they become available for distribution: see *Happe v Happe* [1990] 2 FLR 212.

account, and the various ways in which they may do this, outlined above, may not always adequately reflect the value of the loss of entitlement suffered by the wife.

Although the Law Commission has recognised the importance of dealing with pensions in divorce (1981, paras 31–33) and despite a consultation paper from the Lord Chancellor's department (1985), no action has yet been taken to improve the position;[19] but, despite recent official silence on the matter, a number of proposals have recently been canvassed that would enable courts to divide pension rights on divorce (eg, Law Society 1991, pp 17–21). This would involve changes to both family and pensions law, since the courts would have to be empowered to direct pension fund trustees, or the state (depending on the type of pension involved), to pay accrued benefits to someone other than the contributor or his/her legal dependants: 'the court would need to obtain a transfer value for each pension, to be able to direct the fund trustees to pay this to another scheme and . . . to require the new scheme to accept the transfer' (Masson 1988, p 688). This is sometimes called 'pension-splitting', or apportionment of pension rights (Joshi and Davies 1991, Ch 1).

There are two ways in which the split could be calculated (ibid). The first would be to split pension rights accruing to both parties during the marriage. Since these are likely to be unequal, this will involve transferring future pension entitlement from one spouse to another (which the recipient could pay into her own scheme, or use to start one). The split would be calculated at the time of divorce, although the precise value of the transferred rights would, in the case of some types of pension, inevitably depend on a forecast of future events, such as actual earnings to retirement. The second would be to split benefits after the end of the working lives of both parties at the time of the later retirement of the two parties. The gap in pension entitlements would then be split, the split being weighted to take account of the length of the marriage and any associated child care responsibilities (which might persist after the termination of the marriage).

The advantage of the second approach over the first would be that it would allow recognition of any increase or decrease of earning capacity attributable to the marriage; the disadvantage is that it would postpone the calculation of the division of rights until long after the divorce. The disadvantage of both would be that '[i]f the

19 For discussion, see Eekelaar and Maclean (1986) pp 149–152; Masson (1986, 1988); Gray (1977) pp 155–167; Jackson and Maclean (1990). Scottish law now explicitly includes accrued rights under life insurance policies and occupational pension schemes referable to the period of the marriage as matrimonial property to which the principle of fair sharing applies – see FL(S)A 1985, s 10.

marriage was short the wife's share would probably be too insignificant to justify the prolonged contact and the administrative machinery necessary to enforce the pension splitting . . . if the marriage was a long one, the wife's share may be such that the husband would be deprived of a substantial part of his pension' (Jackson and Maclean 1990, p 8). This has led to proposals for an alternative 'yearly accrual scheme', under which parties would accrue rights under their spouse's scheme according to the number of years of marriage (eg, Goodhart 1988; for a contrary view, see Masson 1988 who would prefer pension splitting to 'preserving for the wife a pension in her former husband's scheme': p 688).

(c) The clean break

(i) The legislative background

We have seen that one of the objectives of the 1984 Act was to reduce the use of periodic maintenance following divorce. The Act sought to achieve this in a variety of ways. First, it encouraged courts to impose time limits on orders for periodic payments, either when initially made (see above) or on an application for variation or discharge (see below). The Act also permits a court to prevent a spouse from applying for an extension of a fixed-term order for periodical payments.[20] Second, it enabled a court to dismiss an application for periodic payments against the wishes of the applicant and to direct that the applicant shall not be entitled to make any further application in relation to that marriage.[1] Differences of judicial opinion had emerged under the previous law as to whether this was technically possible.[2] Finally, the Act sought to introduce the principle that 'the financial obligations of each party towards the other will be terminated as soon after the grant of the decree as the court considers just and reasonable'.[3] Although this provision is new to the statute books, it may be seen as a codification of a policy of the 'clean break' that had been developing in the case law from the late 1970s onwards.[4]

---

20 MCA 1973, s 28(1A): see *Waterman v Waterman* [1989] 1 FLR 380.
1 MCA 1973, s 25A(3): see *Thompson v Thompson* [1988] 2 FLR 170.
2 *Minton v Minton* [1979] 1 All ER 79; *Dunford v Dunford* [1980] 1 WLR 5; *Dipper v Dipper* [1981] Fam 31.
3 MCA 1973, s 25A(1).
4 *Minton* (above).

(ii) Mechanics of the clean break

The legislation leaves open the question of how the clean break is to be implemented (see Cretney 1990). Possible alternatives include:

- dismissing all claims for periodic maintenance, possibly coupled with a transfer outright to the claimant of all interest in the matrimonial home (and possibly subject to a charge or postponed order for sale – see below);
- making an order for periodical payments for a specified term, with or without a direction preventing the applicant seeking an extension of the term;
- making a nominal periodical payments order, which will permit an application to vary upwards at a later date;
- making a substantial periodical payments order, thus leaving it to the parties to apply at a later date for a variation (see below), at which point the court may impose any of the above solutions.

It has been suggested that 'it would be helpful to have some judicial guidance about the consequences of these various options' (Cretney 1990, p 91).

(iii) Applying the clean break

It is unclear when a 'clean break' will be considered 'just and reasonable'.[5] Under pre-1984 law, there was widespread, though not unanimous, agreement that it would not be appropriate where there are small children of the family.[6] However, it may be that pre-1984 decisions are unhelpful since they were made on the assumption that a clean break could not be imposed on the parties. Decisions made since the Act suggest that the courts will not consider the presence of children to exclude the clean break, on the basis that the welfare of the children is only a 'first' and not a 'paramount' consideration.[7] If the children's welfare was paramount, then one might expect the clean break to be excluded by small children, since it might be against their interests to require the mother to work full-time (see Law Commission 1981, para 24).

Other cases where it has been argued that a clean break would be appropriate are:[8]

5   See, eg, the judicial disagreement in *Whiting v Whiting* [1988] 2 FLR 189, a case arising under MCA 1973, s 37(1).
6   See Lords Scarman and Fraser in *Minton v Minton* [1979] 1 All ER 79 and Ormrod LJ in *Carpenter v Carpenter* (1976) 6 Fam Law 110, *Carter v Carter* [1980] 1 WLR 390 and *Moore v Moore* (1980) 11 Fam Law 109, CA.
7   *Coley v Coley* [1986] 1 FLR 537; *Suter v Suter* [1987] 2 FLR 232.
8   See generally Douglas (1981); Cretney (1990); Wright (1991). For evidence of registrars' views on their use of clean break powers, see Eekelaar (1991), pp 63–68.

- where the parties have only small incomes and some degree of reliance on welfare benefit is inevitable;[9]
- where the parties have significant means and it is possible to meet the claimant's future needs by means of a lump sum arrived at according to the 'Duxbury calculation' (see above);[10]
- where the marriage has been short[11] (although we have already seen that awards of maintenance are rare in such cases);
- where the husband may prove unreliable in making the payments;
- where, owing to a serious physical handicap, periodical payments could do little to enhance the quality of life of the recipient;[12] and
- where there has been considerable bitterness between the parties.[13]

It may be said that the courts have blunted the impact of the 'clean break' principle. For example, it has been held that the duty imposed on a court to consider whether to impose a fixed term on an order for periodical payments[14] does not amount to a presumption in favour of imposing such a limit. It is merely one factor among all the others to be considered and does not limit the discretion of the court.[15] The clean break is not a 'principle' requiring the court to strive for it regardless of all other considerations: the court is required merely to consider whether it would be appropriate.[16]

The courts have placed particular emphasis on the fact that the powers to impose time limits are only exercisable where a time-limited order would enable a party to adjust 'without undue hardship' to the termination of payments.[17] Thus, a clean break is not inevitable where an ex-wife is in her mid-40s, whose career opportunities have been restricted by child care responsibilities, and who is looking for, but having difficulty in obtaining, a job.[18] A clean

---

9 In *Ashley v Blackman* [1988] 2 FLR 278, Waite J held that the 'clean break' could, in appropriate cases, override the policy (discussed below) of preventing a husband from leaving his ex-wife to claim state benefits: 'No humane society could tolerate – even in the interests of saving its public purse – the prospect of a divorced couple of acutely limited means remaining manacled to each other indefinitely . . .' (at p 284).
10 *B v B* [1990] 2 FLR 180.
11 *Hedges v Hedges* [1991] 1 FLR 196.
12 *Seaton v Seaton* [1986] 2 FLR 398,
13 *C v C* [1989] 1 FLR 11.
14 MCA 1973, s 25A(2).
15 *Barrett v Barrett* [1988] 2 FLR 516; *Fisher v Fisher* [1989] 1 FLR 423.
16 *Clutton v Clutton* [1991] 1 FLR 242, per Lloyd J at p 245.
17 MCA 1973, s 25A(2) (on an original application) and s 31(7) (on a variation application).
18 *M v M* [1987] 2 FLR 1; *Barrett* (above).

break will be more likely in such a case where the wife has access to substantial capital, since it will be easier to find that she will be able to adjust to the termination of dependency on the husband without undue hardship.[19]

Nor does the clean break exclude altogether the possibility of a nominal order being made, or a substantial order being reduced to a nominal order on a variation application, as a 'long-stop' enabling the claimant to reapply for variation upwards at a later date.[20] Further, it has been held that the power to prevent a spouse applying for an extension of an order for periodical payments[1] should not be used where there is 'a real uncertainty' about the wife's future, especially where she is caring for a young child (even though a separate order has been made for the child).[2]

Two points should be made here. The first is that orders in favour of children (as opposed to orders for parties to the marriage) are not affected by the clean break principle. Second, the court may compensate for refusing to order periodic payments by ordering lump sums or property transfers, though this obviously depends on there being assets available to do this. Certain forms of property transfer, such as a transfer of the matrimonial home subject to a charge in favour of the transferor, may be regarded as a continuing 'financial obligation' and thus discouraged in pursuit of the clean break. However, in *Clutton*, Lloyd LJ expressed doubt as to whether such an order would offend against the principle of the clean break and was clearly of the opinion that a 'Martin order' (that is, an order granting the non-resident party a charge over the matrimonial home to be realised on sale on the death, remarriage or cohabitation of the resident party) offended against the clean break in only the most extended sense of the term.[3]

An outright transfer of the house combined with no order for periodic payments may be a convenient means of effecting a clean break.[4] There is evidence to suggest that this is precisely the impact of the Act in practice in the middle wealth range of cases where the transfer of the matrimonial home to the custodial parent leaves the transferor with virtually no capital so that a reduction or elimination of periodic payments is more likely (Edwards and Halpern 1987,

---

19   See *C v C* [1989] 1 FLR 11.
20   *Suter v Suter* [1987] 2 FLR 232; *Whiting v Whiting* [1988] 2 All ER 275; *Hepburn v Hepburn* [1989] 1 FLR 373.
1   MCA 1973, s 28(1A).
2   *Waterman v Waterman* [1989] 1 FLR 380.
3   1 FLR 242 at 245–246.
4   Although this solution has the disadvantage that any property transferred may be subject to the statutory charge for recovery of legal aid expenditure: see below, and *Hanlon v Hanlon* [1978] 2 All ER 889; *Mortimer v Mortimer-Griffin* [1986] 2 FLR 315.

1990, 1990a; Edwards, Gould and Halpern 1990; see also Eekelaar 1991, pp 69–70); but the same research suggests that, despite judicial willingness in reported case law to limit the impact of the 'clean break', its introduction has led to a significant reduction in the use of periodic maintenance (with only a small increase in the use of lump sum or property orders), leading to a general decline (except in 'big money' cases) in the amounts received by ex-wives.

However, it should be noted that these figures are based on those cases in which an application for financial provision has been made. What is striking about the statistical evidence is the number of divorces in which no such application is made. Edwards and Halpern (1990) found that only 30–40% of divorce petitions filed led to such an application and suggest, on the basis of this, that 'the existing legislation may be both unworkable and (or) unwelcoming. Unworkable because there may be no money, no need or a reluctance to pay. Unwelcoming because courts may be too remote and inaccessible, and the law and the judicial process too complex and time consuming' (ibid, pp 77–78).

The guidelines applied

In this section, we consider how the courts have approached their task in resolving disputes over money and property. First, we shall consider how the courts deal with the question of housing the parties. Second, we consider the different approaches adopted according to the wealth of the divorcing parties. It is now well established that this is a factor of major importance in the practical exercise of the court's powers.[5] This in turn raises the question of the extent to which the statutory guidelines discussed above have a bearing on court decisions. It has, for example, been argued that '(t)here will be many who doubt whether it can be realistically claimed that English statute law now embodies any clear principle at all' and that we are left with 'a heavy reliance on accumulated case law and . . . the exercise of a wide judicial discretion' (Cretney 1984, p 850; see also Deech 1982; Dewar 1986).

(a) The matrimonial home

In exercising their powers on divorce, the courts regard one of their most important tasks as being to ensure that both parties to the

5 Per Ormrod LJ in *Preston* [1982] 1 All ER 41.

marriage and any children of the family are rehoused adequately.[6] This raises more complex issues where the matrimonial home is owner-occupied than where it is publicly or privately rented, since the ability of the parties to rehouse themselves will in such cases depend on their overall economic position, rather than simply on their level of income (Eekelaar and Maclean 1986, p 73). The courts are faced with the problem of how best to divide up the owner-occupied matrimonial home in both its aspects as a home and as probably the parties' most significant economic asset. For this reason, the primary focus of this section is on the owner-occupied home.

However, it should be remembered that the courts have the power to transfer publicly or privately rented tenancies from one party to another on divorce, and there are a number of associated ancillary powers governing orders regarding the payment of outgoings (see above). Where the tenancy is public, the courts may regard the issue as best left to the local authority to sort out as a matter of its own policy,[7] unless the authority is unwilling or legally unable to do what the court regards as most appropriate (see Pearl 1986, pp 21–23).[8]

We have already seen that the courts have a wide range of powers to transfer, resettle or order the sale of matrimonial property. In relation to the owner-occupied matrimonial home, these powers are exercised in the light of information as to the housing needs of the parties and any children, their existing accommodation arrangements and the value of the home and of any other assets available to the parties. The objective is to ensure that, whether there are children of the family or not,[9] the parties are adequately rehoused; but if there are children, there is evidence of a strong preference for trying to keep the children in the home (Eekelaar 1991, p 71).

The courts may employ one of the following devices:

(i) The 'Mesher order'

This form of order, which derives its name from the case in which it was made,[10] requires that the home be held on trust for sale in equal shares, with sale postponed until the children of the family reach a certain age (say, 17), during which time the custodial parent would be able to live in the house while paying all the outgoings (including

6   *Browne v Pritchard* [1975] 3 All ER 721; *Martin v Martin* [1977] 3 All ER 762.
7   *Warwick v Warwick* [1982] 12 Fam Law 60.
8   *Hutchings v Hutchings* (1975) 237 Estates Gazette 571, CA.
9   *Martin v Martin* (above).
10 [1980] 1 All ER 126n (originally 1973).

rates and mortgage interest repayments). Any repayments of mortgage capital may be ordered to accrue equally to both parties' share in the equity. The purpose of this order is to preserve the home for the child of the family during minority, while enabling the non-custodial spouse to realise his share of the equity at a later date.

However, this form of compromise between retention and sale of the family home will only be appropriate under certain circumstances, for example where both parties have remarried, so that at the eventual date of sale the resident spouse will not be without resources to find alternative accommodation. Thus, if there is real doubt about a wife's ability to rehouse herself on the charge taking effect, the order should not be made.[11] Unless such conditions exist, a Mesher order will not be a satisfactory way of resolving the case since it will leave the resident spouse homeless at some future date.[12] The order has been criticised as 'likely to produce harsh and unsatisfactory results' and should 'no longer [be] regarded as the "bible"'.[13]

Nevertheless, such an order may be appropriate where, but for the presence of children, the court would have regarded an immediate sale as appropriate, such as where the non-resident spouse has no secure accommodation[14] or the marriage has been short,[15] or where there are sufficient resources to rehouse both parties but where the interests of the children require that they stay in the home.[16] The deferred housing needs of the resident spouse may be met by increasing her proportionate share under the trust for sale.[17] A Mesher order may also be made contingent on the happening of other events, such as the death, cohabitation or remarriage of the resident spouse (sometimes called a 'Martin order').[18] This variant of the order has been said not to suffer from the disadvantages of a Mesher order,[19] presumably because, at the time the charge takes effect, the needs of the resident partner will either be non-existent or may be met in other ways.

11 Per Lloyd LJ in *Clutton v Clutton* [1991] 1 FLR 242 at 248.
12 *Hanlon v Hanlon* [1978] 2 All ER 889; *Carson v Carson* [1983] 1 All ER 478.
13 Per Parker LJ in *Mortimer v Mortimer-Griffin* [1986] 2 FLR 315 at 319. Despite disapproval from the higher courts, Eekelaar (1991) found some registrars who regarded them favourably: pp 71–72.
14 *Cawkwell v Cawkwell* (1978) 9 Fam Law 25, CA.
15 *Drinkwater v Drinkwater* [1984] FLR 627.
16 Per Lloyd LJ in *Clutton* (above) at p 248.
17 *Scott v Scott* [1978] 3 All ER 65.
18 *Martin v Martin* [1977] 3 All ER 762; *Tinsdale v Tinsdale* (1983) 4 FLR 641.
19 Per Lloyd LJ in *Clutton* (above) at p 248.

(ii) Outright transfer

The drawbacks of the Mesher order may be avoided by transferring the entire interest in the home to the custodial spouse. This may be accompanied by a reduction or refusal of periodic payments to the resident spouse,[20] the payment by the resident spouse of an immediate lump sum (possibly raised by mortgage on the property itself)[1] or the execution of a charge of a fixed or proportionate amount of the value of the house enforceable on the death or remarriage of the resident spouse, on the children reaching a certain age or on the sale of the property[2] (for discussion of the interrelationship between this form of order and welfare benefits, see Cretney (1990a)).

The order adopted will depend on a consideration of all the circumstances, the overriding purpose being to ensure as far as possible that both parties and any children are adequately housed. An outright transfer, whether or not accompanied by a compensating order for the transferor, has the advantage of crystallising the parties' interests in the home at an early stage and may thus be preferable from the point of view of the 'clean break'.[3] It may also be appropriate where the sale of the house and division of proceeds at some point in the future will yield an insufficient amount to rehouse the resident spouse,[4] or where the non-resident spouse is adequately provided for elsewhere.[5] A charge will be preferable to an immediate lump sum where the latter would in effect force an immediate sale of the property.[6] This may be a particularly important consideration where there are children who need a home.

Although a charge may appear in substance to be the same as a Mesher order, it has been argued that it has the advantage of enabling the non-resident spouse to be released from liability for the mortgage on the property so as to raise a mortgage on another property, and of demoting the non-resident spouse from co-owner to chargee, which may be important where relations between the parties are tense (Hayes and Battersby 1986). Against this, however, it has been argued that the Mesher order has the advantage of

---

20 *Hanlon v Hanlon* [1978] 2 All ER 889.
1   *White v White* (1972) 116 Sol Jo 219, CA; *Backhouse v Backhouse* [1978] 1 All ER 1158; *Scipio v Scipio* (1983) 4 FLR 654.
2   *Hector v Hector* [1973] 3 All ER 1070; *Blezard v Blezard & Mul* (1978) 9 Fam Law 249, CA; *Dunford v Dunford* [1980] 1 All ER 122; *Simmons v Simmons* [1984] 1 All ER 83.
3   *Scipio* (above).
4   *Hanlon* (above).
5   *White* (above); *Backhouse* (above).
6   *Blezard* (above).

greater flexibility if, for example, the resident spouse wishes to move house (Hayes and Battersby 1985).

Another important consideration in relation to these different forms of order will be the differential effect of the Law Society's statutory charge for the recovery of costs incurred by way of legal aid.[7] The charge may be attached to any property 'recovered or preserved' in legally-aided proceedings. This will include any outright transfer of the matrimonial home or order for a lump sum made in ancillary proceedings, as well as any case in which the assisted party has successfully claimed realisation of his or her share in the property.[8] Where the charge attaches to property, there is jurisdiction in the court to postpone the operation of the charge; but where it attaches to a lump sum or to the proceeds of sale of property, no such jurisdiction exists[9] unless the proceeds of sale are to be used for the purchase of a home for the legally-aided party or her dependants.[10] In practice, the operation and effect of the charge may closely affect the court's exercise of its powers.[11]

(iii) Other orders

The court may allow a spouse to occupy the home until for a defined period, for example, the spouse's lifetime, and order the non-resident spouse to pay all outgoings;[12] the court may also order that the resident spouse pay the other an occupation rent, either immediately or from a certain specified date, for example, the date of the final mortgage instalment.[13] The court also has power to order a sale by virtue of MCA 1973, s 24A (see above).

(b) Low income divorces: private maintenance and income support

The relationship between private maintenance and public income support is of considerable importance in many cases. Divorce is most likely to occur amongst low income groups (Haskey 1984), and, as

---

7 Legal Aid Act 1988, s 16(6). See Ch 1.
8 *Hanlon v Law Society* [1981] AC 124; *Curling v Law Society* [1985] 1 All ER 705.
9 *Simmons v Simmons* [1984] 1 All ER 83; *R v Law Society, ex p Sexton* [1984] 1 All ER 92; *Simpson v Law Society* [1988] Fam Law 19.
10 Civil Legal Aid (General) Regulations 1989, reg 96; see *Scallon v Scallon* [1990] 1 FLR 194.
11 *Simmons* (above).
12 *Tinsdale v Tinsdale* (1983) 4 FLR 641.
13 *Harvey v Harvey* [1982] 1 All ER 693; *Brown v Brown* (1981) 3 FLR 161.

we saw above, there is evidence that income support is a significant source of household income for many single parents following a divorce. Given that most families reliant on income support are unlikely to have significant assets or property, the only question will be the extent to which the fact of reliance on income support is to affect the level of periodic payments (if any) ordered by the court (see Hayes 1978/9; Cretney (1990a)).

In principle, the courts will ignore the fact that an applicant is in receipt of income support when assessing the applicant's resources. This is because a husband cannot shift his responsibility to the state by arguing that his ex-wife is adequately provided for through income support.[14] This is the case, even though the applicant is unlikely to receive any benefit from the payments[15] (either for herself or her children[16]) unless, for reasons already discussed above (pp 299–301), she is in employment. However, where the husband himself is on a low income or in receipt of income support, the fact that any payments will not raise the recipient's level of household income may be relevant in assessing the level of payments.[17] In addition, if, after taking account of new commitments reasonably undertaken by the payer, there are insufficient resources properly to maintain the claimant and children without making a 'financially crippling' order, then 'the court may have regard to the fact that in proper cases social security benefits are available to the wife and children'.[18]

It has been held that the principle of the 'clean break' may be applied in such circumstances.[19] However, the willingness of husbands to consent to a clean break (especially one involving a transfer to the wife of all his interest in the family home in return for a dismissal of all claims for maintenance) is likely to be lessened by the fact that the husband remains a 'liable relative' under social security legislation (discussed in Ch 4). He will thus continue to be liable to contribute to the maintenance of his children and their mother if they are in receipt of income support, despite the terms of any order made in the divorce court.[20] In other words, a husband will not be released from all obligations to support his ex-spouse and

---

14 *Ashley v Ashley* [1965] 3 All ER 554; *Tovey v Tovey* (1978) 8 Fam Law 80.
15 *Peacock v Peacock* [1984] 1 All ER 1069; *Berry v Berry* [1986] 2 All ER 948.
16 *Supplementary Benefits Commission v Jull* [1980] 3 All ER 65.
17 *Stockford v Stockford* (1981) 3 FLR 58; *Chase v Chase* (1982) 13 Fam Law 21.
18 Per Ward J in *Delaney v Delaney* [1990] 2 FLR 457 at 462.
19 *Ashley v Blackman* [1988] 2 FLR 278.
20 Social Security Act 1986, s 24(1), s 24A (the latter provision having been introduced by Social Security Act 1990, s 8). For further discussion, see Ch 4. For an argument that a clean break order could be relied on to escape liability under the new s 24A (to contribute to the support of an ex-wife with whom children under 16 are living), see Mears (1991).

children no matter how generous the terms of a clean break package. We have seen that similar criticisms may be made of the scheme to be inaugurated by the Child Support Act 1991.

Where the husband is employed, the courts will not usually make an order against him that reduces his level of income below that which he would receive for himself and for any newly-acquired dependants by way of income support.[1] The courts have refused to adopt the more generous 'liable relative formula' employed by the DSS in liable relatives proceedings (see Ch 4) as the basis for calculating the level of income to be left to the husband after payment of maintenance.[2] This level of subsistence is only a rough starting point, however, and an application will not automatically be dismissed if it would result in the husband falling below this notional level.[3] If the husband is himself receiving income support, then the courts will usually make only a nominal order for maintenance, which may be varied upwards at a later date if his circumstances improve.[4]

(c) Medium wealth divorces: one-third or net effects?

A starting point often adopted by the courts in assessing awards has been the so-called 'one-third rule', according to which the applicant would be awarded one-third of the joint gross income (subject to certain deductions) of the parties together with one-third of the joint matrimonial assets. In later cases, it became clear that the courts regarded this as a useful guideline only where the parties were neither very wealthy nor very poor[5] (see also Barrington Baker et al 1977, paras 3.25–3.26). In the former case, one-third might yield too high a figure, and may force a husband to sell assets that would impair a family business;[6] in the latter case, other considerations prevail (see above). Thus, the rule would be useful in those cases where the parties had a comfortable income, but where the only significant asset was the family home.[7] Although the rule had been justified (at least in part) by reference to the 'principle of minimal loss',[8] it seems that it has survived the 1984 Act and is still regarded as useful in appropriate cases.[9]

1   *Chase v Chase* (1982) 13 Fam Law 21; *Berry v Berry* [1986] 2 All ER 948; *Fletcher v Fletcher* [1985] 2 All ER 260.
2   *Shallow v Shallow* [1978] 2 All ER 483; but see *Allen v Allen* [1986] 2 FLR 265.
3   *Tovey v Tovey* (1978) 8 Fam Law 80; *Freeman v Swatridge* [1984] FLR 762.
4   *Chase, Berry* and *Fletcher* (all above).
5   *Slater v Slater* (1982) 3 FLR 364.
6   *Preston v Preston* [1982] 1 All ER 41.
7   Per Ormrod LJ in *O'D v O'D* [1975] 2 All ER 993, CA.
8   Per Denning MR in *Wachtel v Wachtel* [1973] 1 All ER 829, CA.
9   *Bullock v Bullock* [1986] 1 FLR 372.

Even in such cases, however, the rule is still only regarded as a starting point, and it may be that the facts of any particular case will justify a departure from it. The courts will be as concerned to determine the 'net effect' of any order they make once all liabilities to tax and other reasonable outgoings have been taken into account, to compare the income position of both the parties under a proposed order, and to balance the applicant's reasonable needs against the respondent's ability to pay[10] (see Greenslade 1988, Appendix 2, for a 'net effects' calculator). There are two further limitations on the rule. The first is that the needs of any children will now take precedence over any precise mathematical starting point for the division of income and assets, although the one-third rule may remain appropriate for childless divorces. The second is that the rule may have no application to the distribution of capital, especially where the capital is substantial or tied up in a business.[11] However, in *Bullock v Bullock*[12] it was held that the rule applied to a capital award in a case of substantial assets.

The precise status of the rule is thus unclear from the case law. In practice, it seems that it is regarded by district judges as a useful starting point only in the middle wealth range of cases which will usually be departed from according to the facts of the case (Barrington Baker et al 1977, paras 3.22–3.29) and it may be that the 'net effects' approach is more widely used (Cretney 1987, p 128 and Appendix). The primary usefulness of the rule has been in providing practitioners with an indication of the likely level of awards. The present uncertainty surrounding the status of the rule diminishes its usefulness in this respect.

(d) Wealthy divorces

Where there are large assets available, we have already seen that the one-third starting point will produce figures regarded as too high. In such cases, the courts will have resort to the criteria in s 25(2), and in particular to the parties' needs, their previous standard of living, any contributions made by the applicant to, for example, a family business, and the husband's liquidity.[13] In *Dew v Dew*,[14] the

---

10 *Slater v Slater* (1982) 3 FLR 364; *Stockford v Stockford* (1981) 3 FLR 58; *Titheradge v Titheradge* (1982) 4 FLR 552; *Allen v Allen* [1986] 2 FLR 265.
11 *Potter v Potter* [1982] 3 All ER 321.
12 [1986] 1 FLR 372; but see also *Dew v Dew* (1986) Fam Law 335.
13 *S v S* (1980) Times, 10 May; *Preston v Preston* [1982] 1 All ER 41; *Leadbeater v Leadbeater* [1985] FLR 789.
14 (1986) Fam Law 335.

husband's assets, which consisted mainly of shares in a company in which both he and the wife had previously worked, were valued at about £1m. Anthony Lincoln J held that while one-third would give the wife too much (about £300,000), she was entitled to more than a figure suggested by her reasonable requirements in order to recognise her contributions to the business. He thus awarded her a lump sum of £135,000, an amount which the husband would be able to realise without seriously overstretching his resources.

As we have seen, the 'needs' of wealthy spouses are interpreted in a 'relative' sense (above, pp 317–318). Thus, in *Duxbury v Duxbury*,[15] where a husband's assets were valued at between £2.6m and £2.75m, the Court of Appeal upheld an award of a lump sum (based on what is now known as the '*Duxbury* calculation', discussed above) of £600,000 to the wife, together with the matrimonial home and its contents valued at £150,000. The lump sum was intended to provide the wife with an annual income of £28,000 for the rest of her life. The figure of £28,000 was taken (allowing for inflation) from the case of *Preston v Preston*, where the Court of Appeal upheld a similar award as being the right figure to produce the luxurious standard of living considered to be appropriate. In *B v B*,[16] a husband worth between £2m and £2.5m was ordered to pay the wife a lump sum of £570,000: £270,000 for the purchase of a house and £300,000 which, on the basis of the '*Duxbury* calculation', would provide the wife with an income of £15,000 pa.

Private ordering

The discussion so far has been premised on the assumption that the parties are in dispute over property and financial matters; yet many divorcing couples will reach an agreement at some stage as to the financial terms of the divorce. There may be in existence a maintenance agreement (see Ch 4, above), possibly dating back to the date of the parties' separation. Alternatively, the parties may at some stage in the course of an application for ancillary relief agree terms, possibly with the assistance of conciliation. The agreed terms may then be submitted to the court, which will make an order in the terms agreed between the parties. Such an order is termed a 'consent order', and is discussed below.

15 [1987] 1 FLR 7.
16 [1990] 2 FLR 180.

As we have seen, it is currently official policy to encourage private agreement between the parties on all aspects of the divorce process.[17] This is particularly so with respect to financial matters, where 'there is the potential for proliferation of affidavits and documents, for accusation and counter-accusation, for protracted and unnecessary delay and for the expenditure of costs which can far exceed what is reasonable having regard to the nature of the claim' (Booth 1985, para 4.146). This policy would be thwarted if the courts were too ready to overturn agreements privately arrived at. However, private agreements present dangers of their own which also need to be guarded against. For example, agreements may be reached on the basis of inadequate financial or other information or with inadequate professional advice. Further, where financial arrangements are negotiated together with arrangements for the children (as is often the case), a spouse may feel pressurised to concede financial claims in order to avoid disputes relating to the children. In such cases, the formal protections offered in contested hearings may be extremely valuable (see Bottomley 1985).

The difficulty, then, is in determining the balance to be struck between conceding an area of private decision-making to the parties in the 'shadow' of the law as described above, and retaining a supervisory jurisdiction in the courts to guard against the dangers outlined (see Eekelaar 1991, pp 145–146 for discussion).

(a) Maintenance agreements

We saw in Chapter 4 that there are two reasons why such agreements may not be conclusive of all financial matters. First, provided that the agreement comes within the statutory definition of 'maintenance agreement',[18] it is specifically provided by statute that any provision restricting a party's right to apply to court for an order containing financial arrangements shall be void.[19] Second, it is open to either party to apply to court (including a magistrates' court) for a

---

17 For a discussion of the 'unintended limits' placed on private ordering by the legal process (particularly in relation to the rules governing the operation of the legal aid scheme and access to public sector housing, which either penalise or discourage privately negotiated settlements), see Ingleby (1988). In so far as the courts have control over the negotiation process, they have sought to encourage private ordering through the making of offers in settlement, especially through so-called 'Calderbank letters' (see, eg, *Evans v Evans* [1990] 1 FLR 319). Failing to make or accept offers may be penalised by an award of costs against the party refusing to settle (see *Gojkovic v Gojkovic (No 2)* [1991] 2 FLR 233 for a helpful discussion; and Bennett (1990)).

18 MCA 1973, s 34(2).

19 MCA 1973, s 34(1).

variation of the order on the grounds set out in MCA 1973, s 35 (see Ch 4, above).

Nevertheless, the existence of a maintenance agreement may be regarded as relevant by the courts in hearing later claims for financial relief in divorce proceedings. In *Edgar v Edgar*,[20] for example, the wife of a wealthy man who had accepted the husband's offer of a lump sum and periodical payments under a deed of separation in spite of professional advice that she could obtain better by going to court, was held to be bound by the terms of the agreement and therefore her later claim for ancillary relief in divorce proceedings was dismissed. It should be remembered that this is a separate issue from that of whether the jurisdiction to vary the maintenance agreement itself has arisen under s 35. Further, the court may ignore the agreement in ancillary proceedings if to hold the spouse to it would cause unfairness or hardship.

(b) Consent orders[1]

(i) Procedure

If the parties have agreed terms, then the court may make a consent order in those terms on the basis only of 'prescribed information' supplied with the application, unless it has reason to think that there are other circumstances into which it ought to inquire.[2] The 'prescribed information' should include information relating to: the duration of the marriage, the age of the parties and of any minor child of the family; a summary estimate of the value of the parties' capital and net income; the arrangements for the children of the family; the actual or intended remarriage or cohabitation of either of the parties; and 'any other especially significant matters'.[3] Where the consent order contains a clean break as far as periodical payments are concerned, the court must be satisfied that it is appropriate that the parties be financially independent, and that the claimant consents to the dismissal.[4]

Since a consent order is an order of court, no order may contain an arrangement which it is beyond the technical power of the court to order.[5] However, it is open to a court to approve a consent order

---

20 [1980] 3 All ER 887.
1 See Eekelaar (1991), pp 145–154 for evidence as to the use of consent orders in practice, focusing in particular on the supervisory role of the court.
2 MCA 1973, s 33A(1).
3 FPR 1991, r 2.61(1).
4 *Practice Direction* [1961] 2 All ER 256.
5 MCA 1973, s 33A(3).

containing a declaration that neither party shall make any further claim for financial provision, even though there is no specific statutory authority for this;[6] and the scope of a consent order may be extended beyond the powers of the court by incorporating in it undertakings made by one or both spouses.[7]

(ii) Variation and appeals

Another consequence of the fact that a consent order is an order of court is that it may be varied in the same way as an order made in contested proceedings (see below). Thus, since lump sums and property transfers are not generally variable, the same applies to any such provision in a consent order. A provision contained in a consent order to the effect that a spouse will not seek an increase in the amount awarded will not be binding.[8] However, if the agreement has either a time limit on the period of maintenance, or if it is a 'clean break' order, then any direction that the claimant shall not be able to apply for any further periodical payments order[9] or for an extension of the defined term,[10] will presumably be as effective as if the order had been made in a contested hearing.

Similar rules as to appeals apply, and leave to appeal out of time against a consent order will only be given where there has been fraud or unconscionable conduct. A mere change in circumstances since the making of the order will not suffice.[11] If there is an appeal within the required period, then the courts may substitute an order that fairly takes account of any change. The courts have emphasised the importance of careful drafting of consent orders.[12]

(iii) Setting consent orders aside

In common with all orders for ancillary relief, consent orders may be set aside if there has not been full and frank disclosure of all relevant facts.[13] In *Livesey v Jenkins*,[14] for example, a consent order was set aside on the ground that the wife had failed to reveal that she was

---

6   *H v H* [1988] 2 FLR 114.
7   Per Lord Brandon in *Livesy v Jenkins* [1985] AC 424.
8   *Jessel v Jessel* [1979] 3 All ER 645.
9   MCA 1973, s 25A(3) (above).
10 MCA 1973, s 28(1A) (above).
11 *Barder v Barder* [1986] 2 All ER 918.
12 *Sandford v Sandford* [1986] 1 FLR 412; *Dinch v Dinch* [1987] 2 FLR 162.
13 For a detailed consideration of the relevant procedure, see Ward J's judgment in *B-T v B-T* [1990] 2 FLR 1 (see Scott and White 1990).
14 [1985] AC 424.

engaged to be remarried. Although, as we have seen, there is extensive provision in the rules of court for extracting all relevant information from parties, this is no guarantee of full disclosure. However, the non-disclosure must be 'material'.[15] Consent orders may also be set aside on the grounds of mistake, fraud or misrepresentation.[16]

(c) **Pre-marriage contracts?**

An alternative to all the above would be for the parties to agree *before* marriage on the property and financial consequences of death or divorce (Law Society 1991, pp 22–28). Such a contract could cover the ownership of income and assets acquired before, in contemplation of or during the marriage, the barring of any statutory claims, eg to maintenance, as well as the treatment of gifts and inheritances, ownership of personal items (eg jewellery) and liability for debts and taxes. The enforceability of pre-marriage contracts of this sort is unclear in English law, and may be open to attack on grounds of public policy, lack of consideration and intention to create legal relations, and as an attempt to oust the jurisdiction of the courts.

The Law Society (above) has recommended that such contracts should be enforceable, subject to certain safeguards (including receiving independent legal advice and obligations of disclosure of assets). One difficult problem would be the relationship between a pre-marriage contract and the powers of the divorce court. The Law Society canvas three possibilities: that a contract would not oust the courts' jurisdiction, but would be taken into account as one of the factors under s 25; that the courts' jurisdiction would be completely ousted; or that the contracting parties could choose between these two alternatives.

The disadvantage of the first is that it would destroy much of the purpose of (and the source of much of the current interest in) the pre-marriage contract, which, as the Law Society acknowledges, is to enable 'the very rich' or 'those who have already experienced the trauma of divorce to protect themselves in the future' (ibid, para 3.46). The disadvantage of the second would be that it would provide no protection for a party for whom the contract operates unfairly either through making a bad bargain or as a result of changed circumstances. The Society suggest that this could be dealt with by defining certain circumstances that would invalidate the contract (such as fraud or lack of disclosure) or certain events that

15 *Barber v Barber* [1987] Fam Law 125.
16 *Payne v Payne* [1968] 1 All ER 1113.

would trigger a revocation or review of the terms, such as the birth of a child or permanent disablement.

Enforceable pre-marriage contracts would represent a different type of private ordering from those discussed above in that any such agreement would be reached before marriage rather than at its end, and would have the deliberate objective of escaping the 'shadow' of the law in which other forms of private ordering take place. They may be seen as the functional equivalent of an old-style wife's separate equitable estate, in that they seek to preserve family wealth from the legal effects of marriage. The differences would be that they would be entered into by the couple themselves, rather than by their families; and would take effect by contract, rather than through the law of property.

Variation and revocation of orders

(a) Powers of the court

Under MCA 1973, s 31 a court may vary or discharge the financial provision orders listed in s 31(2). These include any periodical payments order (secured or unsecured), an order for the payment of a lump sum by instalments and an order for sale under MCA 1973, s 24A(1). There is no power to vary or revoke property transfers or lump sums (with one exception[17]). On the making of an application, the court has no power to order property transfers or lump sums in place of the order sought to be varied. However, in *S v S*,[18] the court held that it was possible to accede to a proposal put forward by the paying spouse that an order for periodic payments be 'varied' to a lump sum, as a means of capitalising the periodic payments. The court justified this on the basis of s 31(7) which requires the court to consider whether it would be appropriate to limit the period over which payments be made. The courts do not have the power to order a lump sum against the wishes of the payer,[19] and in any case will only do so where the lump sum offered is sufficiently large.

---

17 Section 31(2)(e) – an order for settlement of property or variation of settlement made on a decree of judicial separation.

18 [1986] 3 All ER 566, [1987] 1 FLR 71; *Boylan v Boylan* [1988] Fam Law 62.

19 *Peacock v Peacock* [1991] 1 FLR 324, in which Thorpe J criticised the lack of such a power: 'Cases in which spouses move to the goal of clean break by two stages are commonplace. In such cases, it is surely unfortunate if the court does not have the jurisdiction to set and enforce the fair level of capital commutation' (at p 330).

On an application for variation, the district judge may order that the parties file affidavits of means. The order may be varied from the date of the original order.[20] The court may also order that any variation or discharge take place on the expiry of a specified period.[1]

(b) Relevant considerations

In determining applications for variation or revocation, s 31(7) requires that the court have regard to all the circumstances of the case, first consideration being given to the welfare of any minor child of the family, together with any change in any of the matters to which the court was required to have regard when making the order to which the application relates. Thus, the court 'must apply s 25 and review the whole situation afresh'.[2] In the case of periodic payments (secured or unsecured) the court must also have regard to whether or not it is a suitable case for a 'clean break' in the shape of a time limit 'for such further period as will in the opinion of the court be sufficient to enable [the recipient] to adjust without undue hardship to the termination of those payments'.[3]

In practice, most variation applications will be where there has been a significant change in the parties' financial circumstances, either for the better or worse.[4] Where it is sought to vary a consent order, an important consideration may be that the courts will be reluctant to vary them too freely for fear of discouraging their use in the first place.

(c) Clean break and time limits

The power to vary orders has now to be considered alongside the power of the court in the original proceedings to exclude the possibility of future variation applications. As we have seen, the court

---

20 *Morley-Clarke v Jones (Inspector of Taxes)* [1985] 1 All ER 31.
1 MCA 1973, s 31(10).
2 Per Wood J in *MH v MH* (1981) 3 FLR 429.
3 MCA 1973, s 31(7)(a); but see *Whiting v Whiting* [1988] 2 All ER 275, in which an application to delete a nominal order in favour of an ex-wife earning more than the liable ex-husband was refused. Balcombe LJ dissented, saying that 'to make mutual orders for periodical payments in nominal amounts just in case something should happen to either party . . . is to negate entirely the principle of the "clean break" (at pp 199–200); see also *Ashley v Blackman* (above).
4 See *Atkinson v Atkinson* [1988] 2 FLR 353 and *Hepburn v Hepburn* [1989] 1 FLR 373, where an ex-wife's cohabitation was considered a relevant 'change of circumstance'; but 'it is not the job of the court to put pressure on parties to regularise their irregular unions' (per Butler-Sloss LJ in *Hepburn* (above), at p 378).

may dismiss a claim for periodical payments and order that no further application shall be made by the spouse in relation to that marriage.[5] It may also make a time-limited order, accompanied by a direction that the recipient shall not be entitled to apply for an extension of the term.[6]

5   MCA 1973, s 25A(3).
6   MCA 1973, s 28(1A).

Chapter 9
Children and divorce

Introduction

Divorce is estimated to affect approximately 150, 000 children aged under 16 each year (Law Commission 1986, para 4.1; Hoggett and Pearl 1991, p 501).[1] In this chapter, we are concerned with the law and procedures governing the making and approving of arrangements for how children will live following a divorce. Much of this is now governed by the Children Act 1989 and by new procedural rules.[2]

An important theme of this chapter is that the relevant legal rules, and especially the relevant procedures, display two apparently contradictory tendencies of intervention and abstention. On the one hand, we shall see that a petitioner for divorce is obliged to submit a detailed 'statement of arrangements' which outlines how the parties propose to organise their children's future living arrangements. In some cases, the court has extensive powers to order reports and enquiries and to specify arrangements in detail through court orders. In extreme cases, the court has the power to postpone the granting of the divorce decree itself if it is not satisfied with the arrangements proposed.

On the other hand, though, we should not overestimate the significance of the courts' role in these matters. The vast majority of divorces affecting children involve no dispute over living arrangements that the courts are called upon to arbitrate. Research conducted under the pre-1989 law revealed that only about 6% of custody cases were disputed, in the sense of going to a hearing (Eekelaar and Clive 1977; Maidment 1984, Ch 3). In uncontested

---

1 For evidence of the effects of divorce on children, see Wallerstein and Kelly (1980); Maidment (1984), pp 161–176; Block, Block and Gierde (1986); Maclean and Wadsworth (1988); Schaffer (1990), pp 155–167; Wallerstein and Blakeslee (1989); Elliott, Ochiltree, Richards, Sinclair and Tasker (1990); Elliott and Richards (1991, 1991a); Clulow (1991).
2 Family Proceedings Rules 1991, Part IV; Family Proceedings Courts (Children Act 1989) Rules 1991.

cases, the court's role in scrutinising the parties' proposed arrangements for the children has been formally curtailed by the Children Act 1989 (see below). Even under the old law, under which the court was formally required to approve the parties' proposed arrangements in every case, the court's role was described as 'symbolic and incidental' (Law Commission 1986, para 4.10) and approval of the parties' proposed arrangements was granted in the overwhelming majority of cases. Most of these proposed arrangements involved the children living with the mother (Eekelaar and Clive 1977; Dodds 1983).

It is important to remember that the courts are in any case limited in the extent to which they can protect the interests of the children that come before them. In uncontested cases, it would be difficult to challenge the arrangements the parties propose since the court itself has extremely limited powers or resources to suggest or enforce alternatives. As we shall see, a court may order a local authority investigation, or make a 'family assistance order', but this inevitably depends on the availability of the appropriate resources. It may commit care to a third party (such as a relative), but this seems to be a rare occurrence (Priest and Whybrow 1986, paras 7.2–7.5). Similarly, in contested cases a court will usually be faced with a choice between the two parents. The courts are also limited in the extent to which they are able to supervise the post-divorce relationship between parents and children, especially in relation to the question of contact.

Nevertheless, although the dominant logic at work is one of abstention, we should not underestimate the powers of the court to scrutinise and supervise the lives of the divorcing couples that come before them in the minority of cases where the courts and legal procedures operate according to an interventionist logic (see, for example, Rights of Women 1986). Further, the axis around which the logic operates – the distinction between disputed and undisputed cases – may not always be clear-cut. A case will be classified as undisputed if it does not go to a hearing of the disputed issue; but this does not mean that the parties have always been in agreement, since the need for a hearing may have been avoided by means of conciliation; and, as we saw in Chapter 7, conciliation may operate as just as effective a form of regulation as a judicial hearing. Indeed, it has been suggested that conciliation is in part a response to the perceived limits of the courts' capacities to promote the welfare of children (Bottomley 1985).

The law and procedures which form the subject of this chapter provide a good illustration of the argument advanced in Chapter 1, that, rather than effecting a 'liberalisation', the relaxation of the divorce laws has permitted a proliferation of opportunities for the investigation and supervision of children in their families. Ostensibly concerned exclusively with the child's welfare, these processes are as much concerned with the child's family and its parents; the child becomes the instrument for the dissemination of proper familial practices (Thery 1986, p 345; Commaille 1982, Ch 5). However, while some families are singled out for detailed scrutiny by means of welfare reports and conciliation, the rest are allowed to determine the child's future by agreement between themselves, which is later ratified by the courts. It is this phenomenon that has been termed the 'double logic' of abstention and intervention (Thery 1986, pp 351–354).

Procedure

(a) In every case: statement of arrangements

(i) Background

Under the old law, a court could only grant a decree of divorce if it declared itself satisfied that the arrangements that the parties were proposing to make for their children after the divorce were 'satisfactory' or 'the best that could be devised in the circumstances'.[3] The basis on which it made this declaration was the statement of arrangements for the children that a petitioner for divorce was obliged to file with the divorce petition. The requirement applied in every case, irrespective of whether the divorce itself was contested. Coupled with this was a requirement in every case that the petitioner attend a hearing with a judge in chambers to consider the arrangements (a 'children's appointment'). The aim of these requirements was the entirely laudable one of ensuring that the interests of the children were scrutinised by the court in those cases where the parents themselves were not in dispute over the children (Morton 1956, paras 371–372). However, research evidence showed that they were largely ineffective.[4]

(ii) The 1989 Act

As a result, the 1989 Act (implementing the proposals of the Law Commission (1988, paras 3.5–3.11)) gives the court the more modest role of considering whether, in the light of the arrangements

3 MCA 1973, s 41. For the history behind this provision, see Hall (1990).
4 Summarised in Dewar (1989), pp 243–244.

proposed for any children of the family,[5] it should exercise any of its powers under the 1989 Act[6] (which would include making a s 8 order of its own motion,[7] making a 'family assistance order'[8] (see below) or directing a local authority to investigate a child's circumstances[9]). Thus, the court is no longer obliged to declare itself satisfied with the arrangements, and there is no requirement of a children's appointment, unless the court considers that it is a case in which it should exercise its powers.[10]

The power to withhold a decree of divorce remains, but is exercisable only where the court considers that the case may be one in which it should exercise its powers and where the court needs to consider the matter further before doing so.[11] In addition, the court must also be satisfied that there are 'exceptional circumstances' which make it desirable in the interests of the child to withhold the decree.[12] The Law Commission's intention was to ensure that children did not become 'pawns in their parents' own battles' (1988, para 3.8) while enabling the court to use the sanction of withholding a decree 'where the parties are refusing to consider how best to meet their parental responsibilities in the changed circumstances' (ibid, para 3.9).

The requirement that a petitioner for divorce files a statement of arrangements for the children with the divorce petition is retained.[13] Following the proposals of the Booth Committee (1985, paras 2.23–2.27, 4.33–4.37 and Ch 7) the new rules of court permit a petitioner and respondent to submit an agreed statement;[14] and the statement of arrangements form itself has been considerably expanded, now running to eight sides.[15] The purpose of the enlarged statement of arrangements is to 'remind parents of their responsibilities towards their children' and to place the court 'in a better position to identify those children whose welfare requires further action' (Law Commission 1988, para 3.10).

5 'Child of the family' is defined in CA 1989, s 105(1), and discussed below in Ch 11.
   A 'child' (and hence a 'child of the family') is defined as someone aged under 18, but s 41 applies only to 'children of the family' who are under 16 (MCA 1973, s 41(3)(a)) and to any child of the family aged over 16 in relation to whom the court directs that the section shall apply (MCA 1973, s 41(3)(b)).
6 CA 1989, Sch 12, para 31.
7 CA 1989, s 10(1)(b).
8 CA 1989, s 16.
9 CA 1989, s 37 (see further, Ch 10).
10 In which case, a judge may request further evidence, direct that a welfare report be prepared and require the parties to attend an appointment: FPR 1991, r 2.39(3).
11 MCA 1973, s 41(2) (as amended).
12 MCA 1973, s 41(2)(c) (as amended).
13 FPR 1991, r 2.2(2).
14 Ibid.
15 Form M4; the old form, which consisted of a series of headings rather than (as the new one does) of a detailed questionnaire, can be found in Barnard (1983), p 267.

A respondent may file a written statement of his or her views on the proposed arrangements for the children.[16] If these differ from those proposed by the petitioner, then there will either be an application by one of the parties for a s 8 order (see below), or the court may treat it as a case in which it should exercise its powers, which it may do, for example, by making a s 8 order of its own motion. The parties may also be directed towards conciliation (Law Commission 1988, para 3.10)

(iii) 'De-legalisation'?

It has been said that the new s 41 'marks a radical and restrictive view of the right of the state to interfere in private arrangements' and that, when taken with the presumption of no order (discussed below), is evidence that the law 'is in retreat in relation to intervention in family life' (Cretney 1990b, pp 60 and 58). It has also been said that the new s 41 'is likely to curtail severely the extent of court involvement in divorce cases' and that 'an area which hitherto was thought appropriate for legal regulation will in future be substantially de-regulated' (Bainham 1990, pp 209–210). This may be termed the 'de-legalisation hypothesis'.

Two points may be made about this hypothesis. The first is that it equates legal regulation exclusively with a court making an order. In that sense, the hypothesis is likely to prove valid, not least because of the presumption of no order: parents will be encouraged to resolve any disagreement by other means, with the court acting as a long-stop. But if we take 'regulation' to include not just court orders, but also the legal framework within which private agreements are to be negotiated (often within conciliation), we shall see that the 1989 Act creates a very clear framework for describing parental responsibility following a divorce: a framework in which both parents, irrespective of the practical arrangements made for the children, retain and share responsibility (see below). This at least clarifies the old law; at most, it changes it by creating what would once have been thought of as a presumption in favour of 'joint custody' (see Roche 1991, at pp 345–346, for a similar argument). If, therefore, we take 'regulation' in this broader sense of the law casting a shadow in which parties negotiate, then the 1989 Act is very much concerned to regulate the consequences of divorce for parents and children.[17] This is discussed further below.

16 FPR 1991, r 2.38(1).
17 The 'deregulation of divorce does not mean "minimal intervention" by the judiciary, but the displacement of this intervention and the transformation of procedures' (Thery 1989, p 94).

Second, it may be argued that the Act is primarily concerned with 'making more effective use of resources' and ensuring that 'these will be directed at the cases where they are needed most' (Law Commission 1988, para 3.10). As noted above, there was evidence that the old s 41 procedure was largely ineffective, and the 1989 Act provisions amount to little more than a recognition of this fact, coupled with a more precise targeting of judicial resources. Thus, the new provisions may be seen, not as straightforward de-legalisation, but as a refocusing of judicial resources towards those cases where the parties cannot agree, or where there is evidence that the children may be suffering harm at the hands of parents who appear to be in full agreement with each other. In addition, as we have already seen, in those cases in which the court is involved, it now performs a more managerial and directive role than previously; and we shall see later that when the court makes an order, it has greater powers to specify in detail the content and conditions of an order.

Instead of the 'de-legalisation hypothesis', we may thus argue that the 1989 Act conforms to a 'double logic of abstentionism and interventionism' which 'polarises . . . two categories of divorcing spouses: those for whom the law rubber stamps their autonomous decisions; and those upon whom control and regulation are to be imposed' (Thery 1989, p 94).

(b) Where a s 8 order is sought

(i) Introduction

Under the old law, only a small minority of divorces involved a dispute over the custody of children (Eekelaar and Clive 1977, paras 6.1–6.8; Maidment 1984, Ch 3), but this did not prevent the courts from making a formal order as to custody in over 90% of cases (Priest and Whybrow 1986, para 8.2). The Law Commission attributed this to the fact that orders 'may [have been] seen by solicitors as "part of the package" for their matrimonial clients and by courts as part of their task of approving the arrangements made in divorce cases' (1988, para 3.2). The Commission wished to see a 'more flexible approach' under which it would not be assumed that an order is inevitable, but would only be made where it is necessary to promote the child's welfare (ibid, para 3.3). This is reflected in the 1989 Act by the 'presumption of no order' under which the court is directed not to make an order 'unless it considers that doing so would be better for the child than making no order at all'.[18]

18 CA 1989, s 1(5).

It is unclear from the legislation itself when an order will be considered necessary according to this criterion (see below), but it seems likely that the most important reason for making an order will be where the parents are unable to agree about residence or contact arrangements, or any other significant matter relating to the child's upbringing.[19] Historically, as we have seen, this has proved to be the case in only a small number of divorces: but it should be remembered that the 1989 Act makes a wider range of orders available in all 'family proceedings' (which includes divorce proceedings) coupled with a more extensive range of powers vested in the court when making such orders (see below). It would be unfortunate if the 1989 Act had the effect of increasing the level of litigated disputes between divorcing parents.

(b) Procedure

The procedure governing orders relating to children in divorce proceedings are the same as those governing all applications for s 8 orders. The new rules of court[20] make a number of significant procedural changes, which have the effect of giving the court a much greater degree of control over the conduct and timing of a case.

An application for a s 8 order in divorce proceedings must be made to the court dealing with the divorce petition.[1] The application must be made on the appropriate form[2] which must be filed with the court and served on the respondent.[3] The rules expressly prevent an applicant from submitting any documentary evidence other than that required in the prescribed form, without the leave of court.[4] The respondent must file an answer to the application in the prescribed form.[5] If the respondent wishes to challenge the application, s/he

---

19 A significant factor in the making of applications for s 8 orders will be the courts' attitudes to questions of costs. Traditionally, orders for costs have rarely been made in proceedings relating to children (see Butler-Sloss LJ in *Gojkovic (No 2)* [1991] 2 FLR 233 at p 236); but it may be that courts will in future penalise what they see as unneccessary s 8 applications by awarding costs against the applicant. It is virtually certain that the courts will use the costs weapon to penalise any party who fails to comply with a court direction relating to the conduct of a s 8 application.
20 Part IV Family Proceedings Rules 1991; Family Proceedings Courts (Children Act 1989) Rules 1991.
1 FPR 1991, r 2.40(1).
2 Form CHA 10 (which runs to seven sides).
3 The respondent will be any person with parental responsibility for the child: FPR 1991, Appendix 3. There is a power to join others as a party: FPR 1991, r 4.7.
4 FPR 1991, r 4.17(4).
5 Form CHA 10A.

must indicate his or her intention to do so on the answer form. Meanwhile, the court will automatically fix a date for a directions appointment or a hearing,[6] which all parties are obliged to attend.[7] The court has a wide power to give, vary or revoke directions either of its own motion or on the application of a party. Directions may relate to the timetable of the proceedings, the attendance of the child, the service of documents or submission of evidence, or the preparation of a welfare report (as to which, see below).[8]

The net effect of these rules is to give the court a much greater role in the management and conduct of a case. In part, this flows from the general principle that the courts must have 'regard to the general principle that any delay in determining the question is likely to prejudice the welfare of the child'.[9] The rules are aimed at ensuring that cases do not drift and that the courts are not inundated with irrelevant evidence. However, it remains to be seen whether the courts will be able to discharge this new managerial role effectively (see Cretney 1990b). In particular, it is possible to envisage problems with the new procedure for the automatic fixing of dates for hearings or directions appointments.

Regulating post-divorce relationships

Under the old law, the legal position of parents following divorce was thought to hinge very largely on the type of court order made in relation to custody. As we have seen, formal court orders were made in the majority of cases. The 1989 Act, by contrast, seeks to limit the making of an order to cases where an order is necessary to promote the welfare of the child. This means that court orders will in future have less significance in determining the legal position of divorced parents. Before discussing the available orders, therefore, we need to consider the primary means by which the 1989 Act describes the post-divorce position of parents: the concept of parental responsibility.[10]

---

6   FPR 1991, r 4.4(2)(a).
7   FPR 1991, r 4.16.
8   FPR 1991, r 4.14(2). As noted above, failure to comply with directions will be penalised through an award of costs.
9   CA 1989, s 1(2).
10 See Ch 3 for a discussion of the content of, and limits to, this concept.

(a) Parental responsibility

(i) Introduction

The old law as to orders for custody and their effects was confusing and uncertain (see Law Commission 1998, paras 4.2–4.4). In particular, the differences between orders for 'sole custody' (which were the most common form of order) and orders for 'joint custody' were unclear, especially in relation to the legal position of the non-custodial parent (see Dewar 1989, pp 254–255). The Law Commission, heavily influenced by 'the clear evidence that the children who fare best after their parents separate are those who are able to maintain a good relationship with them both',[11] proposed that there should be enshrined in law the principle that both parents should retain equal parental responsibility for their children after divorce, irrespective of any order that the court may make. The Commission's aim was that of 'encouraging both parents to feel concerned and responsible for the welfare of their children' and of '"lowering the stakes" in cases of parental separation and divorce' (1988, paras 2.10–2.11). The Commission recognised that the law may not be able to achieve effective co-parenting in every case, but that 'at least it should not stand in their way' (1988, para 4.5).

(ii) The 1989 Act

The 1989 Act gives effect to these proposals. Thus, parents who are married to each other automatically acquire parental responsibility for their child and retain it following divorce. The Act states that any person with parental responsibility may act independently of the other in meeting that responsibility unless to do so would be incompatible with the terms of a court order made with respect to the child.[12] Thus parental responsibility following divorce is retained by, and shared between, both parents (and anyone else who has acquired it) independently of any order that may be made about the child's residence or upbringing; and either parent may act independently of the other in fulfilling their responsibility to the child, provided always that it does not conflict with a court order.

The Law Commission offered the following example of how this would work in practice:

> 'If . . . the child has to live with one parent and go to a school near its home, it would be incompatible with [an order relating to the child's residence] for the other parent to arrange for him to have his hair done

---

11 See Wallerstein and Kelly (1980); Maidment (1984), Ch 6.
12 CA 1989, s 2(1), (7), (8).

in a way which will exclude him from the school. It would not, however, be incompatible for that parent to take him to a particular sporting occasion over the weekend, no matter how much the parent with whom the child lived disapproved.' (1988, para 2.11)

In addition, a

'. . . parent who does not have the child living with him should still be treated as a parent. He should be treated as such by schools and others so that he can be given information and an opportunity to take part in the child's education.' (ibid, para 4.6)

(iii) Criticisms

A number of criticisms have been made of the way in which the 1989 Act has sought to create a legal framework of co-parenting. It has been said that the Act provides for 'joint *independent* rather than *co-operative* parenting' (Bainham 1990, p 212). For example, there is no obligation on either parent, even during a marriage,[13] to consult the other about any particular matter. Instead, a parent who objects to a decision taken by the other will have to go to court to seek an order (see below). This is 'difficult to square with the stated aims and purposes of the reforms' which is underlined by the fact that '[t]here is no provision in the Act positively encouraging co-parenting' (ibid). Thus, 'the law sets standards [of co-parenting] unless a parent disagrees with these standards' (Brophy 1989, p 232). It has also been argued that the presumption of co-parenting enshrined in the law is unrealistic:

'[I]t assumes and thereby attempts to impose a particular model of parenting on divorcing parents whose marriages, for the most part, lack both the formal structures and mutuality necessary to achieve this ideal. Thus a legal presumption based on the notion of co-parenting may simply be a presumption to continue substantial inequalities of power and responsibilities.' (ibid, p 233; see also Eekelaar 1991, pp 134–138; Roche 1991)

One incidental effect of the new law could be to weaken the bargaining capacity of women in relation to money and property. The issues of custody and finance 'are often negotiated together and involve implicit or explicit trade-offs' (Weitzman 1985, p 310; see also Eekelaar and Clive 1977, para 6.6). Under the old law, a wife agreeing to joint, as opposed to sole, custody was perceived, rightly or wrongly, as having made a 'concession'. The new Act, by creating

---

13 In contrast to the old law, which appeared to provide both parents with a veto over decisons taken by the other: CA 1975, s 85(3). The significance of this provision was, however, unclear.

a presumption of parental equality, introduces a presumption of joint custody in all but name, thereby removing a potential bargaining counter.[14] Indeed, it is possible that by providing greater opportunities for legal challenge to the decisions of the parent with whom the child is living (usually the mother), especially through 'specific issue' and 'prohibited steps' orders (below), the new law may serve to subject the caring parent to greater judicial scrutiny and control. To the absent parent, parental responsibility may easily be seen more as a right to 'have a say' and raises the prospect of power *without* responsibility. This is associated with another criticism, indicated above and pursued below, that the new Act creates the opportunity for greater (rather than less) 'legalisation' of disputes over children in the minority of cases in which the parents cannot agree (see also King 1991).

It remains to be seen whether the new law has the effect of encouraging either more flexible residence arrangements (so that, for example, a child might spend substantial time with both parents) or greater contact between the child and the parent with whom it is not living. There was evidence under the old law that the majority of children following divorce lived with their mothers (Priest and Whybrow 1986, Part IV and Tables 6 and 8) and that contact between the child and the absent parent diminished rapidly (Eekelaar and Clive 1977, Table 15). This was not necessarily evidence, as some suggested, of the law 'favouring' mothers, but was 'more a general affirmation of the current sexual division of labour' (Brophy 1985, p 100).

(b) The available orders: s 8 orders

The Law Commission's intention in introducing the new scheme of court orders was to get away from the 'proprietorial connotations of "custody"' (1988, para 4.10) and from the idea that court orders are concerned with the allocation of rights rather than with 'ensuring that each parent properly meets his responsibilities while the child is with him' (ibid, para 4.8). The new orders are confined to dealing with the practical questions of where the child[15] is to live and how much he is to see of the other parent (ibid). The scheme was also intended to deal with cases in which there 'is concern that one parent will cause difficulties for the other in the way he exercises his responsibilities' (ibid, para 4.9).

14 For a summary of the debate surrounding joint custody, see Dewar (1989), pp 255–258; and see Smart (1989).
15 The court's jurisdiction extends to 'any child' in relation to whom a question has arisen in any family proceedings as to that child's welfare: CA 1989, s 10(1).

Before looking at the new orders, a number of points should be made. The first is that, as we have seen, the significance of an order is now diminished in view of the continuing retention by both parents of parental responsibility (see above) and by the presumption of no order (see below). Where an order is made, however, the court has considerable power to specify conditions, and the exercise of parental responsibility is subject to the terms of any order made. Also, the new 'menu' of orders introduced by the 1989 Act ('s 8 orders') include two types of order (specific issue and prohibited steps orders) which explicitly permit a court to regulate aspects of post-divorce parenting, potentially in great detail, and to resolve disputes between parents (and others).

There is thus considerable scope for the 'legalisation' of parental disputes over children according to the dual logic of intervention and abstention noted above: parents who agree will be allowed to do so free from court interference, while those who cannot agree will be able to invoke a number of wide-ranging judicial powers. The 1989 Act thus privileges the agreement/disagreement distinction as the primary axis around which judicial intervention revolves: this, it has been said, is hard to reconcile with the paramountcy of the child's welfare (see Bainham 1990a).

Finally, it should be noted that s 8 orders are available in any family proceedings, not just divorce proceedings. However, they are discussed in this context because it is likely that it is in divorce proceedings that they will be most widely used and it was for this purpose that they were primarily devised.

Residence orders

A residence order is an order 'settling the arrangements to be made as to the person with whom a child is to live'.[16] Thus, the order is simply concerned with the question of residence and, as we have seen, does not affect the ability of the other parent to meet his responsibility for the child so far as is consistent with the order.[17] The Law Commission was anxious to ensure that this new form of order should be capable of accommodating a much wider set of living arrangements than was possible under the old law (1988, para 4.12). Thus, the Act envisages the possibility of a residence order being made in favour of two or more persons who do not themselves all live together and that, if made, such an order may (but need not) specify the periods during which the child is to live in each household.[18]

---

16 CA 1989, s 8(1).
17 It may be unclear what actions would amount to conduct inconsistent with a residence order.
18 CA 1989, s 11(4). Such orders were disapproved of under the old law: see *Riley v Riley* [1986] 2 FLR 429.

Such an order would be appropriate, for example, where the child is to spend term-time with one parent and holidays with another (ibid), and would be preferable to making a residence order to one and a contact order to the other since it would be 'a far more realistic description of the responsibilities involved' (ibid).

Where a residence order has been made with respect to a child as a result of which the child lives with one of two parents, both of whom have parental responsibility for the child, the order shall cease to have effect if the parents live together for a continuous period of six months.[19] This is because 'it is unrealistic to keep in being an order . . . when both are living together' (Law Commission 1988, para 4.13). The Act also clarifies the effect of residence orders in two important respects. Where a residence order is in force, no person may either change the child's surname or remove the child from the United Kingdom without either the written consent of every person with parental responsibility or the leave of court.[20] This does not prevent the child's removal from the United Kingdom for a period of less than one month by the person in whose favour the residence order is made.[1] Residence orders may be enforced in the magistrates' courts.[2] If a residence order is made in favour of a person who does not otherwise have parental responsibility for the child, that person will acquire parental responsibility by virtue of the order itself.[3]

As with all s 8 orders, the court has extensive powers to make directions as to how the order is to be implemented and to impose conditions on individuals.[4] These powers are discussed below. At this stage, it need only be noted that these powers include making a residence order for a fixed period.[5] Anyone entitled to apply for a s 8 order is also entitled to apply for its variation or discharge, since the Act defines a s 8 order as including an order varying or discharging a s 8 order.[6]

Contact orders

A contact order is an order requiring a person with whom a child lives to allow the child to visit or stay with the person named in the

---

19 CA 1989, s 11(5). This would apply to an order made in respect of a child whose parents are unmarried, where the father has acquired parental responsibility.
20 CA 1989, s 13(1).
1 CA 1989, s 13(2). When making a residence order the court may grant the necessary leave to remove the child either generally or for specified purposes: CA 1989, s 13(3).
2 CA 1989, s 14.
3 CA 1989, s 12(2).
4 CA 1989, s 11(7).
5 CA 1989, s 11(7)(c).
6 CA 1989, s 8(2).

order, or for that person and the child otherwise to have contact with each other.[7] This replaces the old order for access, but differs from it in that it does 'not provide for the "non-custodial" parent to have access to the child [but] for the child to visit and in many cases stay with the parent' (Law Commission 1988, para 4.17). A contact, as opposed to a residence, order would be appropriate 'where the child is to spend much more time with one parent than the other' (ibid). It is envisaged that in most cases a contact order will be for 'reasonable contact', which would include allowing the child to stay with the person in the order. During periods of this form of contact, the parent in question may exercise all parental responsibility consistently with any court order. It is open to the court to impose conditions on contact[8] (for example, that the child is not to be taken to certain sporting events); and if reasonable contact is not practicable or desirable, then the court may order other forms of contact, such as letters or telephone calls (ibid). As with a residence order, a contact order will come to an end if the parents cohabit for more than six months,[9] and anyone entitled to apply for a s 8 order may also apply for its discharge or variation.[10]

In the light of evidence that children derive long-term benefit from continued contact with both parents following a divorce (Maidment 1984, Ch 10; Clulow and Vincent 1987, pp 18–23), there is considerable concern at the fact that contact between the child and the non-custodial parent tends to diminish rapidly (eg, Eekelaar and Clive 1977, Table 15; Richards 1982, 1986). Contact reveals the limits of the court's power to supervise the post-divorce arrangements of divorced families (Maidment 1984, Ch 10). There is little that can be done to force contact to take place. The non-custodial parent cannot be obliged to visit the child; and if the custodial parent is opposed to contact taking place, it is highly likely that the 'cure' (that is, a change of residence or a committal for contempt of court) will 'be worse than the disease' (Law Commission 1986, para 2.57).[11] Nevertheless, where specific conditions have been attached to the exercise of contact by the non-custodial parent, it may be argued that the sanction of the removal of contact is extremely effective – perhaps, in some cases, too effective (ROW Lesbian Custody Group

---

7 CA 1989, s 8(1).
8 CA 1989, s 11(7).
9 CA 1989, s 11(6). The 'living together' rule in s 11(6) applies to 'parents', whereas the equivalent rule in s 11(5) for residence orders refers to parents with parental responsibility.
10 The Act defines a s 8 order as including an application for the variation or discharge of one of the orders contained in s 8(1): CA 1989, s 8(2).
11 See *Churchard v Churchard* [1984] FLR 635, CA; *Thomason v Thomason* [1985] FLR 214; *I v D (access order: enforcement)* [1988] Fam Law 338.

1986, p 154). In this respect, contact conforms to the 'dual logic' of abstention and intervention noted earlier.

Specific issue orders

A specific issue order is an order giving directions for the purpose of determining a specific question which has arisen, or which may arise, in connection with any aspect of parental responsibility for a child.[12] In other words, it is a means of resolving disputes over particular matters that relate to a child's upbringing. It was possible under the old law to invoke legal proceedings for this purpose, both under an obscure statutory provision[13] and under the wardship jurisdiction (see Ch 12); but the former was very rarely used, and the latter an extremely expensive means of conducting a private parental dispute. Thus, the introduction of this new form of order may open the way to increased litigation over specific disputes (eg, as to education or medical treatment) that may arise; and in making its order, the court has extensive powers, discussed below, to make conditions or give directions. This opens the way for potentially extensive judicial scrutiny of the arrangements to be made between parents who cannot agree.

A specific issue order may be made in conjunction with a residence order. The courts are not permitted to make a specific issue order with a view to achieving a result which could be achieved by making a residence or contact order.[14] Finally, it should be noted that a specific issue order may only decide a question that has arisen in connection with any aspect of parental responsibility; it cannot be made in respect of a matter that has nothing to do with parental responsibility.

Prohibited steps orders

A prohibited steps order is an order that no step which could be taken by a parent in meeting his parental responsibility for the child,

---

12 CA 1989, s 8(1).
13 GA 1973, s 1(3).
14 CA 1989, s 9(5)(a). A court is similarly prevented from making a specific issue order in any way that is denied to the High Court in the exercise of its inherent jurisdiction: CA 1989, s 9(5)(b) (see below). The significance of this is that, although a local authority may apply for a specific issue order in respect of a child not in its care (CA 1989, s 9(2)), it cannot by means of such an order obtain any parental responsibility for the child that does not derive from the statutory code. It does mean, however, that an authority may bring an issue to the court for the court to decide.

and which is of a kind specified in the order, shall be taken by any person without the consent of the court.[15] An example would be that the child could only be removed from the jurisdiction with the court's approval.[16] Like the specific issue order, this new order is designed to introduce the flexibility of the wardship jurisdiction into the lower courts, and in particular the rule applicable in wardship that no 'important steps' are to be taken with respect to the child without court consent (modified in this context so that the 'steps' requiring consent are specified in advance); but, again like the specific issue order, it raises the possibility of increased litigation.

Although a prohibited steps order may be made against anyone, the 'step' in question must be one which could be taken by a parent in meeting his parental responsibility. Thus, it would not apply to any step that had nothing to do with parental responsibility, such as publicity relating to the child (White, Carr and Lowe 1990, para 3.19). As with a specific issue order, a court cannot make an order with a view to achieving a result which could be achieved by making a residence or contact order.[17]

Additional powers when making s 8 orders

When making a s 8 order, a court has power to give directions as to how it is to be carried into effect, to impose conditions and to 'make such incidental, supplemental or consequential provisions as the court thinks fit'.[18] Conditions may be imposed on the person in whose favour the order is made, on a parent of the child concerned, on anyone with parental responsibility or on anyone with whom the child is living. In addition, the court may make an order for a specified period or may direct that any provisions it contains shall have effect for a specified period. The intention behind these provisions was to preserve the flexible order-making powers that the divorce courts had interpreted s 42 of the MCA 1973 as giving them (Law Commission 1988, para 4.21). Nevertheless, it could be argued that the courts now have much greater powers when making orders than previously, or at least powers that are more clearly conferred. This is consistent with the 'dual logic' of abstention and intervention noted above in that, although fewer orders will be made, the court now has extremely wide powers to specify, potentially in great detail,

15 CA 1989, s 8(1).
16 If a residence order has also been made, the restrictions on removal from the jurisdiction of the child to whom the order relates will apply: see CA 1989, s 13(1).
17 CA 1989, s 9(5)(a). A court is similarly prevented from making a prohibited steps order in any way that is denied to the High Court in the exercise of its inherent jurisdiction: CA 1989, s 9(5)(b) (see below).
18 CA 1989, s 11(7).

the terms of an order in those cases where it is considered appropriate to make one.

One area of potential uncertainty is the relationship between residence and contact orders on the one hand and specific issue and prohibited steps orders on the other. A court is prevented from making the latter kind of order with a view to achieving a result which could be achieved by making the former.[19] The scope of this prohibition is unclear, since it will often be possible to resolve a specific issue or prohibit a particular step by means of a condition, direction or provision in a contact or residence order (see, for example, the Law Commission (1988), para 4.23, who suggest that disputes over schooling can be dealt with by means of a condition in a residence order). Another potential difficulty concerns the relationship between s 8 orders and other court orders, such as non-molestation and ouster orders (see Ch 6). Although it is theoretically possible for s 8 orders to be made that have the same effect as, for example, an ouster order, there are differences in the means, and effectiveness, of the enforcement of s 8 orders.

Duration of s 8 orders

A court cannot make a s 8 order which is to have effect for a period which will end after the child has reached the age of 16, unless it is satisfied that the circumstances of the case are 'exceptional'.[20] Similarly, a court cannot make a s 8 order with respect to a child who has already reached the age of 16 unless it is satisfied that the circumstances of the case are exceptional.[1]

Family assistance order

If a court has power to make a s 8 order,[2] it may also make a 'family assistance order' whether a s 8 order is made or not.[3] This is a new form of order, introduced on the recommendation of the Law Commission, and is in effect a limited form of supervision order.[4] It replaces the power that existed under the previous law to make supervision orders in private proceedings.[5] Its purpose is to 'formalise

19 CA 1989, s 9(5).
20 CA 1989, s 9(6).
1   CA 1989, s 9(7).
2   Ie, in 'family proceedings', which would include care proceedings.
3   CA 1989, s 16(1). An order may only be made by a court of its own motion, and cannot be applied for.
4   Supervision orders are discussed in more detail in Ch 10.
5   Eg, MCA 1973, s 44(1).

the involvement of a welfare officer for a short period in helping the family to overcome the problems and conflicts associated with their separation or divorce' (Law Commission (1988), para 5.19). An order may be made only where the court is satisfied that the circumstances of the case are exceptional and that the consent of every person named in the order, except for the child, has been obtained.[6] Orders will therefore not be available routinely and cannot be made against the wishes of those involved. Although the checklist does not apply to the making of such orders, there is nothing to prevent a court from seeking the child's views. Official guidance stresses the importance of the court making 'it plain at the outset why family assistance is needed and what is hoped to be achieved by it' (DoH 1991, para 2.52).

The Law Commission was particularly concerned at evidence suggesting that there was confusion as to the purpose of the old form of supervision order made in private proceedings, and of an overlap of function in discharging the duties imposed by such orders between the divorce court welfare service (based on the probation service) and local authorities with responsibility for child protection. The Commission thought that

'. . . a clearer distinction between the two types of supervision would be helpful in clarifying the expectations of all concerned [especially local authorities and the probation service], in developing and targeting specialist skills within the two agencies, and in ensuring that families who would benefit from some help during the crisis of separation and divorce are not faced with the prospect of "permanent, long-term intervention in family life on grounds of divorce".'[7] (1988, para 5.13; see also Priest and Whybrow 1986, paras 7.12–7.26; Maidment (1984), pp 86–87; Dewar (1989), pp 261–262)

Thus, although the order may impose a requirement on those named in it to maintain contact with the welfare officer, a family assistance order does not impose the wider-ranging conditions encountered in a supervision order.

A family assistance order is an order requiring either a probation officer or a local authority officer to be made available to 'advise, assist and (where appropriate) befriend' any person named in the order.[8] A parent, guardian, any person with whom the child is living or in whose favour a contact order is in force, or the child, may be named in the order.[9] A person named in the order (or any specified person named in the order) may be directed to take specified steps to

---

6   CA 1989, s 16(4).
7   The quote is from Maidment (1984), p 87.
8   CA 1989, s 16(1).
9   CA 1989, s 16(2).

keep the officer concerned informed of the addresses of all those named in the order and to ensure that the officer is able to visit the child concerned.[10] An order may last for up to six months.[11] Where a s 8 order is in force with respect to the child, the officer concerned may refer to the court the question whether the s 8 order should be varied or discharged.[12]

(c) Power to direct a local authority investigation

The divorce court's power to commit a child to local authority care[13] has been removed. Instead, where it appears to the court (in any 'family proceedings' that it 'may be appropriate' for a care or supervision order to be made with respect to the child, it may direct a local authority to undertake an investigation of the child's circumstances.[14] The removal of the power to commit a child to care in divorce proceedings is consistent with the policy of requiring local authorities to establish that the conditions in s 31 of the CA 1989 are met before obtaining a care order. Thus, a local authority which, having undertaken an investigation, decides that a compulsory order is required must make a separate application for a care or supervision order under s 31. However, if a court orders an investigation and is satisfied that there are reasonable gounds for believing that the conditions contained in s 31 are satisfied, it may make an interim care or supervision order.[15]

If the local authority directed to conduct the investigation decides against making an application for a care order, it must inform the court of the reasons for its decision and of any assistance which it is providing, or is intending to provide, for the child and its family, and of any other action they propose to take.[16]

The criteria for making orders

In this section, we are concerned with the criteria governing whether, and how, the courts will exercise their order-making powers. This is admittedly speculative, since much will turn on judicial interpretation of the new legislation. The same criteria will apply wherever s 8 orders are applied for in family proceedings. They

10 CA 1989, s 16(4).
11 CA 1989, s 16(5).
12 CA 1989, s 16(6).
13 MCA 1973, s 43(1). On the use of this power, see Priest and Whybrow (1986), para 7.8.
14 CA 1989, s 37(1).
15 CA 1989, s 38(1), (2).
16 CA 1989, s 37(3).

would therefore apply equally, for example, to disputes between unmarried parents (ss Ch 3). They also apply to the making of care and supervision orders in care proceedings (see Chs 3 and 10).

(i) Presumption of no order

We have already encountered the principle introduced by the 1989 Act[17] that a court shall only make an order if doing so would be better for the child than making no order at all (the 'presumption of no order'). It was suggested above that, far from being evidence of a 'delegalisation' of the divorce process, the new presumption instead amounts to a refocusing of judicial resources towards those parents who cannot agree. This is because it is most likely to be in cases of parental disagreement that the presumption will be rebutted and an order made. This was the intention of the Law Commission, who wished to ensure that parents could, if they wished, 'make responsible arrangements for themselves without the need for a court order' (1988, para 3.2). According to Official Guidance, 'if orders are restricted to where they address a demonstrable need this should reduce conflict and promote parental agreement and cooperation' (Department of Health (1989), para 1.17).

However, it may be that parental disagreement will not be the sole criterion determining whether an order is made. If parents disagree, it may be hard to see how an order can be avoided; but there may be cases in which, although the parents agree, an order may still be appropriate. The Law Commission recognised that 'in many, possibly most, uncontested cases an order is needed in the children's own interests, so as to confirm and give stability to existing arrangements, to clarify the respective roles of the parents, to reassure the parent with whom the children will be living, and even to reassure the public authorities responsible for housing and income support that such arrangements have in fact been made' (1988, para 3.2). So, for example, a court may be justified in making an order if there is a danger of the child being abducted or for the purpose of assisting a parent to obtain rehousing from a local authority. Thus, the order/no order distinction may not precisely mirror that of parental agreement/disagreement. This is an area that can only be clarified by the courts.

(ii) The checklist

An important innovation introduced by the 1989 Act is the statutory checklist of factors to be considered in making decisions concerning the upbringing of a child.[18] The checklist is based on the

17 CA 1989, s 1(5).
18 CA 1989, s 1(1), (3).

recommendation of the Law Commission (1988, paras 3.17–3.21) who saw it as a means of 'providing greater consistency and clarity in the law' and as a 'major step towards a more systematic approach to decisions concerning children' (ibid, para 3.18). In addition, the Commission considered that such a checklist would have the advantages of ensuring that the same basic factors were used to implement the welfare criterion by the wide range of professionals involved in child cases and would help parents and children understand how decisions were made (ibid). It was also thought that a checklist would assist solicitors 'in focusing their clients' minds on the real issues and therefore in promoting settlements' and would reduce the length of contested hearings by encouraging the parties to identify and prepare relevant evidence at the outset (ibid).

However, it was also considered necessary to restrict the application of the checklist to contested cases in order to prevent the courts intervening unnecessarily in uncontested cases in the course of considering the arrangements proposed for the children (para 3.19). The 1989 Act therefore provides that the checklist applies only where an application to make, vary or discharge a s 8 order is opposed.[19] The Commission also stressed that any checklist would not be exhaustive but would be confined to the 'major points', leaving it to the courts to take other factors into account that may be relevant in a particular case. In addition, it should be remembered that the checklist is confined to decision-making about practical arrangements such as residence and contact. These issues must now be seen in the wider context of the framework, also introduced by the 1989 Act, of continued sharing of parental responsibility following divorce. As we have seen, the practical significance of this is that the legal position of the parents no longer turns on the type of court order made and is thus removed from the area of decision-making governed by the welfare criteria.

Although it remains to be seen how the checklist will affect decision-making both in and out of court, a number of points may be made. Although there is no attempt made in the checklist to prescribe particular outcomes, there is no indication in the checklist itself as to the relative importance of the factors it contains. This means that the 'rules of thumb' developed under the old law (for example, that small children are better off with their mothers[20] or

---

19 CA 1989, s 1(4)(a). It also applies to the decision whether to make care or supervision orders, but not to whether to make Emergency Protection or Child Assessment Orders: see Ch 10.
20 Eg, per Cumming-Bruce LJ in *Re W (a minor)* (1982) 4 FLR 492; per Ormrod LJ in *Plant v Plant* [1982] 4 FLR 305 at 310; *Bowley v Bowley* [1984] FLR 791; per Bingham LJ in *A v A (custody: appeal)* [1988] Fam Law 57, CA; *Dicocco v Milne* (1983) 4 FLR 247. For empirical evidence of judicial decision-making under the old law, see Eekelaar & Clive (1977); Maidment (1984); Priest & Whybrow (1986).

that heterosexual parents are more suitable than lesbian or homosexual ones[1]) could persist under the checklist, but now with statutory sanction. It would be open to a judge to argue, for example,
that either of the two examples given above would still be justifiable
by reference to the child's age, the child's needs and the parents'
respective capacities to meet those needs (see below).

For this reason it has been suggested that, although a failure to
consider the checklist in full may leave a decision open to challenge
on appeal, 'if a judge goes through the checklist, it might now
become even more difficult to overturn even an apparently
idiosyncratic decision' (Eekelaar 1991, p 127). It has also been
suggested that some items in the checklist may conflict with others,
and that in any case 'the individual items on the list do not speak for
themselves. It will still fall to individual judges, magistrates, court
welfare officers and social workers to "interpret" the meaning and
scope of the checklist items – professional and social judgment will
still be central' (Roche 1991, p 349). In other words, the checklist
will not eliminate subjective value judgments about parenting and
child care arrangements, but may serve to immunise them from
challenge on appeal.[2] It has been argued, however, that adjudication
in child custody disputes is inevitably indeterminate given that it is
person-oriented rather than act-oriented and that it concerns
predictions of the future rather than determinations of past facts
and events (Mnookin 1975).

On the positive side, the checklist, by including a specific reference
to the wishes and feelings of the child, may help to increase the
significance attached to the child's own views (see below). It could
also be argued (as indeed it was by the Law Commission) that the
checklist may assist parents to resolve differences without resorting to
contested proceedings. It will provide part of the backdrop to the
bargaining, negotiation and advice-giving that goes on in solicitors'
offices and barristers' chambers in cases that may never assume the
character of a formal dispute over residence. In such cases, the
assumptions underlying the law relating to child disputes 'influence
the bargaining power of each party in the negotiations' (Weitzman
1985, p 217) not just with respect to residence itself but also with
respect to financial matters which may be intimately linked to custody arrangements. In practice, 'the two issues are often negotiated
together and involve implicit or explicit trade-offs' (Weitzman 1985,

1   *C v C* [1991] 1 FLR 223; but see *B v B* [1991] 1 FLR 402 and *C v C (No 2)* [1992] 1
     FCR 206 (see Tasker and Golombok 1991).
2   The House of Lords has held that the principle to be adopted by appellate courts in
     hearing custody appeals should be to overturn a judge's decision only when the
     judge in question has 'exceeded the generous ambit within which a reasonable
     disagreement is possible': per Lord Fraser in *G v G* [1985] 1 WLR 647 at 652.

p 310; see also Eekelaar and Maclean 1986); and 'the threat of a custody suit might be used in negotiations over property or support awards' (ibid, p 224). If this is so, then it may be helpful for the parties to know what assumptions underlie the law. As Eekelaar has argued, 'that legal ideology plays some role in the development of social behaviour can hardly be disputed. It is important that the grounds for decisions should be clearly articulated so that they can be openly scrutinised and, if necessary, adjusted by statutory enactment' (Eekelaar 1991, p 134). Finally, the checklist may help eliminate the apparent discrepancies between the criteria prescribed in reported case law and those applied by judges at first instance (Maidment 1984, Ch 3).

We will now consider the contents of the checklist. Before doing so, it should be noted that many, if not all, of the listed factors have been considered to be important ones in previous case law.

(a) 'The ascertainable wishes and feelings of the child concerned (considered in the light of his age and understanding)' The inclusion of this as the first item of the checklist may be attributable in part to the *Gillick* decision, discussed in Chapter 3. There is also some evidence that the courts were willing to take the child's wishes into account under the old law.[3] However, there is no suggestion that the child's wishes should be conclusive: they are merely one factor to be weighed against all the others. The weight to be attached to the child's wishes and feelings will depend on the age and maturity of the child,[4] and on the nature of the issue to be resolved. Thus, the implacable opposition of a 12-year-old child to contact with the absent parent may be conclusive;[5] as may the wishes of a 14-year-old child concerning schooling.[6] It has been said, however, that it is important to avoid facing the child with a choice between the parents.[7] According to official Guidance, the Act's objective is 'to strike a balance between the need to recognise the child as an independent person and to ensure that his views are fully taken into account, and the risk of casting on him the burden of resolving problems caused by his parents or requiring him to choose between them' (DoH 1989, para 1.25).

A more practical issue is the means by which the child's views are to be ascertained and represented to the court. The report of the Divorce Court Welfare Officer, if there is one, will contain some information about the child's wishes. This is considered further

3 Eg, *M v M* [1988] FCR 39; *Re P (minors)* [1991] 1 FLR 280, CA.
4 See *Peters v Peters* (1974) 4 Fam Law 165, CA.
5 *M v M* (above).
6 *Re P* (above).
7 *Adams v Adams* [1984] FLR 768.

below. In addition, a judge may choose to interview the child[8] but this is entirely a matter for the judge's discretion. One effect of the checklist may be to increase the use of judicial interviews. Children may be brought to in-house conciliation appointments, although it has been argued that this both threatens the conciliation process and places an intolerable burden on the child (Davis and Bader 1985, p 46).

There are provisions allowing for the representation of children in private family proceedings. The court has power to direct that the child be made a party to the proceedings,[9] and if in any case it appears to the court that the child ought to be separately represented, it may appoint the Official Solicitor or some other proper person to be the child's guardian ad litem with authority to take part in the proceedings on the child's behalf.[10] A child may also apply for a s 8 order,[11] but only with the leave of court (see above). If leave is granted, the child will automatically be a party.

It has been official policy to discourage the use of the power to make children parties,[12] and children are rarely separately represented. Even where they are represented, there may be some confusion as to the precise role of the representative (Maidment 1984, pp 82–84). For example, are they to represent the child's views, or to advocate the course considered to be in the child's best interests? In care proceedings, where the provisions regarding the representation of children are more detailed, these different functions are explicitly divided between the child's lawyer on the one hand, and the social worker acting as guardian ad litem on the other (see below, Ch 10). The confusion may be compounded in private cases by the fact that there may already be a welfare officer involved in the case either as a reporter to the court, or as in-court conciliator, who may have been informally pursuing the role of child's representative (Eekelaar 1982; see also Law Commission (1988), paras 6.22–6.29).

(b) 'His physical, educational and emotional needs'   It is difficult to generalise about what children need: 'children's individuality must be taken into account' (Schaffer 1990, p 222). It should also be remembered that the court is usually making a choice between two parents, not looking for the 'best' solution. In effect, the courts are considering the 'least detrimental alternative' (Goldstein, Freud and Solnit 1973.

8   *Elder v Elder* [1986] 1 FLR 610, CA.
9   Family Proceedings Rules 1991, r 4(7)(5)(a); Family Proceedings Courts (Children Act 1989) Rules 1991, r 7(5)(a).
10 Family Proceedings Rules 1991, r 9.5.
11 CA 1989, s 10(8).
12 *Practice Direction* [1982] 1 All ER 319.

A child's physical needs may include proper housing, food and clothing. Whether these can be guaranteed will turn in part on the economic resources available to the parties. The question of who the child is to live with will often be inextricably bound up with that of who is to occupy the matrimonial home. In such cases, the courts have stressed the importance of dealing with all the matters together, rather than making an order to one parent conditional on that parent remaining in the home.[13] A child's educational needs may be affected by the process of separation and divorce itself (Elliott and Richards 1991 and 1991a). In some cases, the question of how to meet a child's educational needs will be directly related to the issue of with whom the child is to live.

A child's emotional needs are perhaps the least determinate factor of all. Bowlby's theory of 'maternal deprivation', which stressed the 'absolute need of infants and toddlers for the continuous care of their mothers' (Bowlby 1965, p 18), has exercised a considerable influence over the minds of the judges;[14] although Maidment suggests that 'current judicial thinking displays a tension between the earlier maternal preference and a less a priori, more open-minded approach of whatever is in the best interests of the child' (1984, p 177). Recent decisions of the Court of Appeal have continued to display this tension. For example, it has been said that although there is no presumption that young children should be with their mothers, it is nevertheless the case that it is 'natural for young children to be with mothers but, where it is in dispute, it is a consideration but not a presumption'.[15] Other considerations, such as the continuity of the mother–child relationship, are equally important.[16]

However, it has also been said that it 'is not a principle but a matter of observation of human nature in the case of upbringing of children of tender years, that given the normal commitment of a father to support the family, the mother, for practical and emotional reasons, is usually the right person to bring up her children'.[17] This has been reinforced by a reluctance by the Court of Appeal to permit fathers either to share care of children with other members of their own family, or to give up employment in order to care for the

---

13 *Re B (a minor)* [1991] 2 FLR 405, CA.
14 See, eg, *Re W (a minor)* (1982) 4 FLR 492. For empirical evidence, which does not provide strong support for the existence of a 'maternal preference', see Eekelaar and Clive 1977, Ch 6 and Maidment 1984, Ch 3; but see Priest and Whybrow 1986, paras 4.20–4.27.
15 Per Butler-Sloss LJ in *Re S* [1991] 2 FLR 388, CA.
16 See, eg, *Re A (a minor)* [1991] 2 FLR 394.
17 Per Sir Roualeyn Cumming-Bruce in *Re H (a minor)* [1990] 1 FLR 51, CA.
18 *Plant,* above; *Dicocco v Milne* (above).

children themselves.[18] Such statements are, however, also explicable, not as an expression of a maternal 'preference', but as 'a general affirmation of the current sexual division of labour' (Brophy 1985, p 100) in which women are primarily responsible for child care during marriage and after. This is reflected in the fact that in uncontested cases, as we have seen, the vast majority of couples decide to leave the children with the mother.

More recently, writers have emphasised the importance of a child feeling 'wanted' by a parent, who need not be the child's 'natural' parent, and of continuity in that relationship (Goldstein et al 1973). These factors will also be relevant to other items in the checklist.

(c) 'The likely effect on him of any change in his circumstances'   There is much evidence to support the view that children require consistency in their relationships and surroundings. This is especially important when parents separate, because it can 'bring about a whole network of changes: loss of contact with a parent, move to a new neighbourhood, a change of school, the need to make new friends, a different life-style because of reduced circumstances, and so on . . . [C]oming together, they may add up to more than a child can cope with' (Schaffer 1990, p 227). Some change is inevitable, but the courts have been consistently reluctant to disturb established arrangements where they have been working well over a period of time.[19] This is reflected in those studies of adjudication in custody disputes which establish the preservation of the status quo as the most significant factor (Eekelaar and Clive 1977, Ch 6; Maidment 1984, Ch 3). As a consideration, it operates equally in favour of fathers and mothers.[20]

(d) 'His age, sex, background and any other characteristics of his which the court considers relevant'   The age and gender of a child may, as we have seen, be directly relevant to the issue of residence. A child's 'background' or 'characteristics' may be a more relevant consideration when the proceedings involve someone other than the child's parents.

(e) 'Any harm which he has suffered or is at risk of suffering'   'Harm' in this context has the same meaning as it does in care proceedings, that is, 'ill-treatment or the impairment of health or development'.[1]

---

19 Eg, *D v M (minor: custody appeal)* [1982] 3 All ER 897; *Dicocco v Milne* [1983] 4 FLR 247; *Pountney v Morris* [1984] FLR 381; *Re H* [1990] 1 FLR 51; *Re A (a minor)* [1991] 2 FLR 394. See also Maidment (1984), Ch 6.
20 *B v B (custody of child)* [1985] FLR 166, CA.
1   CA 1989, ss 105(1) and 31(9). See Ch 10 for further discussion.

(f) '*How capable each of his parents, and any other person in relation to whom the court considers the question to be relevant, is of meeting his needs*' A number of factors may be relevant under this head. It is important to note that the emphasis is on parental capability and not parental behaviour or blameworthiness. It used to be thought that the child's welfare in custody cases was significantly influenced by the question of parental responsibility for the breakdown of the marriage. Thus, adulterous wives were thought to be 'bad' mothers[2] and so were to be deprived of custody (now residence). More recently, it has been stressed that parental responsibility for the marital breakdown is irrelevant to the determination of residence, and that parental behaviour is only relevant where it has a direct bearing on the child's welfare,[3] for example where the parent has a criminal record of violence, or a record of habitual drinking.[4] The checklist confirms this view by excluding any reference to parental behaviour. Nevertheless, parental sexuality continues to be subjected to scrutiny where either parent is homosexual. For example, it has been held that it does not promote a child's welfare to be brought up in a lesbian household, on the basis that it would cause the child social embarrassment in the community[5] (see ROW 1986).

Frequently, the courts find themselves forced to make a choice between two parents as between whom the factors discussed so far are evenly balanced. In such cases the courts will compare the standard of care on offer from both parents. Relevant factors may include material circumstances, geographical location and the character of any new partners there may be, and the child's relationship with them.[6] A father's case is usually strengthened by the presence of a female partner or second wife who is capable of being a good mother[7] and by an ability to rearrange work commitments around child care responsibilities.[8] Another factor relevant to parental capability may be the religious or other convictions of a parent. There may be extreme cases where the beliefs held by a parent are considered so damaging to a child that the matter is decisive as to the child's welfare. The best recent

2   *Re L (infants)* [1962] 1 WLR 886, CA.
3   *Re K (minors) (wardship: care and control)* [1977] 1 All ER 647, CA; *Re H (a minor)* [1991] Fam Law 422, CA.
4   *Re R (minors) (custody)* [1986] 1 FLR 6.
5   See *S v S (custody of children)* [1978] 1 FLR 143 and *C v C* [1991] 1 FLR 223; but see *B v B* [1991] 1 FLR 402 and *C v C (custody of child) (No 2)* [1992] 1 FCR 206 which suggest a more open-minded approach.
6   Eg, *Re C (a minor) (custody of child)* [1980] 2 FLR 163, CA; *Re W (a minor) (custody)* [1982] 4 FLR 492.
7   *Pountney v Morris*, above.
8   *B v B* [1985] FLR 462.

example concerned a parent who belonged to the Church of Scientology.[9] Otherwise, religious belief will only be relevant if the parents choose to make it the basis of the dispute, or where there is a dispute between the parents and a third party.[10]

(g) 'The range of powers available to the court under this Act in the proceedings in question' This item was not contained in the Law Commission's original proposal. It is primarily relevant in care and related proceedings where its purpose is to remind the court that a compulsory order should only be used as a last resort and where there is no case for the court using its power to make a s 8 order instead of a care order. However, it may be relevant in private proceedings:

'. . . the court may make any other private order if it thinks it is best for the child or may trigger a local authority investigation [see above] to see whether the authority should apply for one of the orders available to protect the child.' (DoH 1989, para 1.22)

(iii) Acquiring additional information

There are two ways in which a court may increase the information available to it on which to base a decision in a disputed case.

(a) Welfare reports A court considering any question with respect to a child in any family proceedings is empowered to seek a welfare report from a Divorce Court Welfare Officer or from a local authority[11] at any time during proceedings affecting the welfare of a child.[12] This includes, but is not confined to,[13] proceedings for s 8 orders. Under the old law such reports were available in 53% of contested divorce cases as compared with 8.2% of uncontested cases (Eekelaar and Clive 1977, para 4.6). The Act gives no guidance on when a report should be ordered. The Law Commission exhorted courts to be 'moderate' in their use of this power and that they

---

9   *Re B and G* [1985] FLR 134.
10   *J v C* [1970] AC 668.
11   The power to seek a report from a local authority is new. Previously, only the Probation Service (ie, Divorce Court Welfare Officers) could be called on to report.
12   CA 1989, s 7(1). The Children Act rationalises and simplifies the powers of the court in this respect: see Law Commission (1988), paras 6.14–6.21. For example, there was no power under the old law to order a report in proceedings brought by an unmarried father for a parental rights order. This limitation has now been removed.
13   A report may be ordered in care proceedings, but the presumption in favour of appointing a guardian ad litem may reduce the need to do so.

should be 'targeted on those cases in which it will be most valuable' (1988, para 6.15). An important factor in ordering a report will be the delay (sometimes as long as six months) involved in preparing the report since the courts are enjoined to have regard to the general principle that any delay in determining the question is likely to prejudice the welfare of the child.[14]

The task of the welfare officer is to report, orally or in writing,[15] to the court on such matters relating to the welfare of the child as the relevant regulations and the court direct.[16] However, Divorce Court Welfare Officers have in the past seen their function as extending to assisting the parties to reach agreements on disputed matters through conciliation and also to making recommendations to court as to a course of action (Wilkinson 1981; James and Wilson 1984; Clulow and Vincent 1987; James 1988; Newcastle CPU 1989, paras 8.46–8.60). It has been said that 'for most CWOs the goal is agreement (or what may appear to be agreement) and the avoidance of that nasty monster, "the trial"' (Kingsley 1990, p 187). There is some evidence of their success in encouraging settlement of disputes (Eekelaar 1982), and that their efforts in this respect are appreciated by the divorcing couple. Where welfare officers are *formally* entrusted with the task of conciliation under in-court conciliation schemes (see above, Ch 7) it is specifically directed that the roles of reporter and conciliator should be strictly separated[17] (Latham 1986). The informal combination of the two functions during the compilation of welfare reports should perhaps be open to doubt (Booth 1985, paras 4.61–4.63), and it has recently been directed that welfare officers should not attempt conciliation in the course of the compilation of reports, but may encourage parties to settle their differences if the likelihood of a settlement arises.[18]

In compiling reports, officers may have access to the documentation in the divorce file; they should also interview the parents, any new partners, and most but not all will interview the child (James and Wilson 1984). They may also seek information from schools, doctors, health visitors, the police and any other agency that may have relevant information concerning the child (Wilkinson 1981, pp 93–121; Hoggett and Pearl 1991, pp 552–554; Newcastle CPU 1989, para 8.51–8.52). There is evidence, however, that welfare officers show little consistency in defining their objectives when making a report (Kingsley 1990, p 184; Foden and Wells 1990). Since welfare

14 CA 1989, s 1(2). See *Re C* (1980) 2 FLR 163.
15 CA 1989, s 7(3).
16 CA 1989, s 7(1), (2).
17 *Practice Direction* [1982] 3 All ER 988; *Re H (conciliation: welfare reports)* [1986] 1 FLR 476.
18 *Practice Direction* [1986] 2 FLR 171; see *Clarkson v Winkley* [1987] 1 FLR 33.

officers are not, strictly speaking, witnesses in court, but rather its independent officers, they may include hearsay evidence in their reports,[19] but should make it clear when they are doing so,[20] and are not subject to cross-examination other than with the consent of the judge.[1] The report is confidential, but may be inspected by the parties and their advisers.[2] The report will usually contain a recommendation to the court which is not binding but which is often followed. A court must give reasons for dissenting from a welfare officer's recommendation.[3] This may give the welfare officer a considerable degree of power in the eyes of the parties.

It has been argued that the availability of these reports and the recommendations they contain throws into relief the uncertainty underlying the court's role in these cases, for if a court departs from a recommendation it is unclear on what basis it does so; yet if it follows the recommendation, then it may merely be 'rubber-stamping' the views of an expert. Further doubt is cast by the suggestion that in making recommendations, welfare officers are guided by what they think the court will do anyway (James and Wilson 1984). One writer has concluded from his research into the work of welfare officers that 'too often, the CWO appeared to act in tandem with, or as a mouthpiece for, the judge' (Kingsley 1990, p 188). This suggests that the ordering of a welfare report amounts to little more than the mutual reinforcement of professional decisions, or what Michael King has termed 'symbiotic legitimation' (King 1981, pp 122–126). In King's view, the Children Act will serve only to confirm this feature of adjudication procedures in child cases:

> '. . . by holding up the legal system as the primary institution for the construction of any dispute concerning children, [it] has effectively forced the purveyors of child-welfare knowledge to display their wares before the distorting mirrors of the law' (King 1991, pp 319–320).

In view of both this, and the fact that welfare reports may cause considerable delay to the final decision as to custody, it may be argued that the resources devoted to compiling these reports would be better spent on providing practical assistance to the parties. However, it has also been argued that the welfare officer is usually the only professional involved in divorce proceedings capable of independently representing the interests of the child (Eekelaar 1982; James and Wilson 1984).

---

19 CA 1989, s 7(4).
20 *Thompson v Thompson* [1986] 1 FLR 212n, CA.
1 *Cadman v Cadman* (1981) 3 FLR 275, CA.
2 *Practice Direction* [1984] 1 All ER 827.
3 *Re T (a minor)* (1977) 1 FLR 59; *Stephenson v Stephenson* [1985] FLR 1140; *W v W* [1988] 2 FLR 505; *Re B (minors: access)* (1991) Times, 15 July.

(ii) Expert witnesses

The courts have tended to discourage the use of 'independent' expert witnesses by the parties unless there is a real reason to think the child is disturbed in some way, and only then with the leave of the court.[4] It has been directed that leave should only be granted where there is a specific problem requiring the assistance of an expert and where the child is separately represented or in the care or supervision of a local authority and the representative or local authority supports the application.[5]

---

4 Per Ormrod LJ in *W v W and Hampshire County Council* (1979) 2 FLR 68, CA; see also Family Proceedings Rules 1991, r 4.18(1); Family Proceedings Courts (Children Act 1989) Rules 1991, r 18(1). For guidance on how experts should present their reports, see *Re R (a minor)* [1991] 1 FLR 291.
5 *Practice Direction* [1985] 3 All ER 576.

Chapter 10

The state as parent

Introduction

In this chapter we are concerned with the powers of local authorities[1] to act for the welfare and protection of children in their areas of geographical responsibility. These include, but are not confined to, duties to children in need and the power to assume parental responsibility with respect to a child in certain defined circumstances. Local authorities' powers and duties in this context are now contained in the Children Act 1989, which has made extensive and significant changes to the law and seeks to promote new policies and practices in child care work. The background to the 1989 Act is discussed further below.

However, a proper understanding of this area of state activity in relation to the family cannot be gained from a discussion of the statutory provisions alone. Equally important are the developments in child care policy since 1945, and the organisational framework within which these powers are exercised.

Child care law and policy from 1945

(i) Pre-1989

It has been said that '[t]he development of the child care policies in Britain since the war is characterised by a series of parliamentary acts which resulted from an expressed dissatisfaction or concern with

---

1 The organisation of local authority social services is currently governed by the Local Authority Social Services Act 1970, which, following the recommendations of the Seebohm Committee Report of 1968, created social services departments (SSDs) in each authority answerable to a Social Services Committee of the authority (see Webb and Wistow 1987, Ch 1; see also Dingwall and Eekelaar 1982, Ch 2). Certain powers are also exercisable by the National Society for the Prevention of Cruelty to Children (NSPCC) and by the police.

existing services' (Sinclair 1984, p 1). Most often, this 'dissatisfaction or concern' is expressed by means of an inquiry and report into a particular case. The best known of these is the inquiry into the death of Maria Colwell (DHSS, 1974), which, as we shall see, has proved highly influential on child care policy. More recent examples include the inquiries into the deaths of Tyra Henry and Kimberly Carlile and the Report of the Inquiry into Child Abuse in Cleveland (Secretary of State for Social Services, 1988).

The Children Act of 1948 was in part a response to the reports of the Monckton Inquiry (1945) into the death of Denis O'Neill and the Curtis Committee on the Care of Children (1946) in which criticisms were made of the level of service provided, the lack of professional expertise, the standards of institutional care, and of the lack of an organisation with primary responsibility for child care. This led to the creation by the 1948 Act of local authority children's departments which were to be the primary providers of a state child care service, staffed by trained professionals. The practice of the children's departments was founded on a belief in the effectiveness of fostering as a means of providing substitute care, and much time was devoted to fostering placements (Packman 1981, Ch 2) in preference to institutional care. During the 1950s, increased attention was paid to the question of preventing the need for substitute care from arising through the provision of support to natural parents, a policy which found expression in the Children and Young Persons Act 1963. As we shall see, modern child care law continues to place great emphasis on these themes of 'prevention' and 'family support'.

Throughout the 1960s, the primary focus was on delinquent children, and the Children and Young Persons Act 1969 was an attempt to decriminalise juvenile delinquency by providing a uniform procedure – care proceedings – both for children who were abused or neglected and for children who had committed crime. However, the Conservative government which took office in 1970 decided not to implement all of the provisions of the 1969 Act, with the result that juvenile delinquents continued to be dealt with by criminal prosecution, and the 1969 Act's procedures became exclusively associated with cases of abuse or neglect. Nevertheless, many aspects of the 1969 Act were influenced by the criminal model of proceedings, with several adverse effects.

Child care policy throughout the 1970s was shaped by three factors. The first was the death in 1973 of Maria Colwell and the consequent inquiry, in which the emphasis placed by social work practice on retaining links between a child and its natural family came to be questioned. Maria Colwell had died after being abused by her step-father following the decision by social services to return her to her natural mother from foster parents with whom Maria had

had her home for six years. The second was the publication of research by Rowe and Lambert (1973) of evidence that there were many children in care with no serious prospect of being reunited with their natural families and whose future was unplanned; as a consequence, such children were 'drifting' in care. The third was the publication of Goldstein, Freud and Solnit's book *Beyond the Best Interests of the Child* (1973) in which the authors argued that psychological links between a child and parent were more important than ties of blood, and that children benefited from stable and continuous relationships with parents, whether 'natural' or not (see Sinclair, Ch 1).

The combined effect of these factors was that greater emphasis came to be placed on 'planning for permanence', according to which children in care would either be 'rehabilitated' with their parents as soon as practicable, or, if that proved impossible, a permanent alternative in the form of either fostering or adoption would be pursued. It was these considerations that, together with the recommendations of the Houghton Committee on Adoption (see Ch 11), lay behind the provisions of the Children Act 1975. The overall purpose of the Act was to strengthen the hand of local authorities, foster parents and prospective adopters, and to weaken the legal position of the child's natural parents. The Act also improved provision for the separate legal representation of children. Several administrative changes were also introduced during the 1970s as a response to the Colwell case. Foremost among these were the introduction of the register of 'non-accidental injuries', of case conferences and area review committees (ARCs) (see DHSS 1974a, 1976), all of which are discussed below.

(ii) The Children Act 1989

(a) The background

The 1980s witnessed increasing pressure for reform of child care law. Concern was expressed that the legal framework in some respects conferred insufficiently wide powers on local authorities, especially in relation to the definition of the grounds on which compulsory powers could be assumed; and in others conferred powers that were too wide, particularly in the form of the 'parental rights resolution' and 'place of safety' procedures. By the mid-1980s, it could be said that 'social work practice with children and families [had] become far more authoritative and decisive and [had] increasingly come to intervene in ways which [could] be experienced by families as threats or punishments' (Parton 1985, p 127). Research evidence (summarised in DHSS 1985a) revealed that although there was evidence of an increased use of compulsory powers, their use was often counter-productive in that it damaged relations between parents, their children and social work departments without any corresponding benefits accruing to the child in terms of planning or security. In addition, there was strong evidence that parents were denied assistance to avoid the need to invoke compulsory measures; and that once such measures had been employed, parents were almost entirely excluded from future planning for the child. There was also a widespread loss of faith in the rehabilitative possibilities of child care practice (Parton 1990).

In 1984, the Social Services Select Committee issued a report that was highly critical of child care law, and recommended that the DHSS set up a working party to consider reform. The working party reported in 1985 (DHSS 1985) and the government accepted most of the proposals it contained (White Paper 1987). The Report of the Inquiry into Child Abuse in Cleveland (Secretary of State for Social Services 1988)[2] was also influential, especially in relation to local authorities' emergency powers and the mechanisms for cooperation between the different agencies involved in child care work, such as the police and medical services. It has been said that 'the events in Cleveland were significant precisely because they flagged the . . . oppressive potential of child protection' which provided a stimulus for arguments for 'privacy, autonomy, justice and control of executive or professional power'; and that 'subsequent policy and legislation (of which the Children Act 1989 is a key example) have had to reflect [this]' (Harris 1990, p 337). In this respect, Cleveland differed from earlier child care inquiries,[3] which, as we saw above, were more concerned with a failure to act than with over-intervention.

(b) The main changes

We have already discussed the broad framework of the 1989 Act's scheme for child law in general (see Ch 3), and we have seen in particular that the Act creates common concepts and terminology which apply to both the public and private aspects of child law. However, the Act makes many important changes to child care law itself (discussed in more detail below) which may be summarised as follows:

2   On Cleveland and its significance, see Campbell (1988); Parton and Martin (1989); Harris (1990); Parton (1991), Ch 4.
3   Such as those into the deaths of Maria Colwell (1974), Jasmine Beckford (1985), Tyra Henry (1987) and Kimberly Carlile (1987).

- it reformulates the duties owed by local authorities to children in their area;
- it removes the power to assume parental rights over children who have been placed in voluntary local authority care (a concept which has itself been abandoned) and seeks to promote the concept of 'partnership' between parents and local authorities who are looking after their children;
- it reformulates the grounds for compulsory orders and almost completely eliminates wardship as a route to such orders;
- it seeks to discourage the use of compulsory orders except as a last resort;
- it introduces new forms of emergency order and clarifies the effect of all compulsory orders;
- it effects significant changes to court procedure in child care cases, in particular by extending provisions requiring representation of the child and by requiring greater pre-hearing disclosure of evidence;
- it requires local authorities to establish a complaints procedure in relation to the discharge of some of its powers; and
- it extends jurisdiction to hear care cases, under certain conditions, to the county and High courts.

(c) Analysis

We saw in Chapter 3 that there are good reasons for doubting the claim (frequently made in academic commentary) that the 1989 Act effects a straightforward withdrawal of the state from family life. It may be argued that the Act represents a more complex and subtle process. Indeed, it has been suggested that the 1989 Act embodies as many as four distinct and potentially competing views of the proper relationship between parents, children and the state (Fox Harding 1991). For present purposes, however, it may be said that the 1989 Act, rather than effecting a 'privatisation' of the family, instead represents a refocusing of state resources in the sense that, although compulsory intervention is subjected more closely to court scrutiny, there are (as we shall see) wider powers to act once the statutory conditions for intervention are made out.

It has also been argued that the Act is concerned to 'legalise' child care-related social work. This involves the transfer of ultimate decision-making authority to the court[4] and according priority to the rule of law, 'if necessary at the expense of other considerations,

4   Eekelaar and Dingwall (1990, pp 43–47) distinguish three possible models for understanding the court's role under the new legislation: (i) decision-taker (under which the court decides on the basis of information presented to it); (ii) referee (under which the professionals take the decision while the court ensures merely

including that which may be deemed (by the professionals concerned) to be optimally therapeutic or "in the best interests of the child"' (Parton and Martin 1989, p 23). It also involves the creation of a framework within which social work practice may be rendered more consistent and accountable (Parton 1991, Ch 7).

One suggested cause for this increased emphasis on legalism is 'the serious political and public scepticism and uncertainty about the child care system. Faith in procedure provides a substitute for conviction as to the substantive "solution" to the problem' (Parton and Martin 1989, p 37).[5] Another possible explanation is that greater emphasis on legal procedures also serves to confer legitimacy on the exercise of state powers (ibid). This is particularly important in view of the fact that, as we shall see, there are many respects in which the 1989 Act extends the powers of the state to act in certain cases (Fox Harding 1991, pp 189–192; and see below).

Despite the centrality of the courts, however, the decisions required to be made there are by no means wholly legal. For example, the paramountcy of the child's welfare and the concept of 'significant harm' (see below) are not susceptible of legal definition, but depend crucially on professional or expert advice, foremost among which will be the advice of social workers (whether as local authority employees or independent guardians ad litem):

> 'Thus, while the reconstituted system of child care is . . . subject to an increased emphasis on legalism and accountability to the court, . . . the forms of knowledge and types of expertise which are . . . crucial in helping to make decisions are crucially dependent on social work.'
> (Parton 1991, p 213)

Law and social work are thus constituted as mutually interdependent. The infiltration of each by the other will inevitably affect the character of both.

As an example of the way in which the new regime seeks to promote consistency in child care practice, the introduction of the Act has been seized as an opportunity to introduce not only several

---

that there are proper grounds for the decision); and (iii) broker (under which the court conciliates between parents and professionals to arrive at a mutually acceptable result). They suggest that (i) is the appropriate role where the question is whether the child should enter local authority care, but that (ii) is more appropriate once the child is in care.

5 Another view is that greater reliance on court procedures is one form of response to a perceived crisis in the capacity of the political processes of the (welfare) state to affect social behaviour: see Offe (1984). According to Offe, other forms of response include greater reliance on community institutions (such as schools or the family) to communicate norms concerning social behaviour: hence the political emphasis on 'parental responsibility' and on the family as the natural setting for child-rearing; and greater reliance on 'impartial regimes of truth', such as courts.

volumes of guidance on the detailed provisions of the legislation, but also 'shared principles' governing social work with children and families. These are aimed particularly at social work professionals in an attempt to standardise social work practice. Although specific aspects of child care work are already covered by delegated legislation, by statutory guidance or by Codes of Practice, it has been said that there is still 'some room for manoeuvre' which may lead to 'inconsistency which is rightly perceived as both unjust and incompetent' (DoH 1989, p 4). Thus, the Department of Health has issued a document (1989) which lays down 42 'principles of good child care practice' (1989, Ch 2) and which states that it 'is the responsibility of managers to be fully conversant with these principles and to base their policy and agency guidelines on them' (p 6), even though they do not formally have the status of law.

The organisational framework of child care

Although 'in the area of child protection, social workers control virtually all the key resources – money, substitute care placements, domiciliary support workers and access to the courts if legal sanctions are necessary' (Dingwall and Eekelaar 1982, p 21), it is nevertheless the case that social workers are not best placed to detect abuse or neglect in the first place, and they must rely on a variety of other agencies for this purpose. These will include: health workers, such as health visitors, district and school nurses, general practitioners, hospital doctors and nurses, as well as school teachers, the police and the probation service (Dingwall and Eekelaar 1982, Chs 1 and 2; DHSS 1982a, Section 1; Dingwall et al 1983, pp 12–20, Ch 2; Eekelaar and Dingwall 1990, Ch 4). The coordination of these different agencies is managed by means of three organisational principles, introduced through government guidelines following the Colwell inquiry (DHSS 1974a, 1976; see Parton 1985, Ch 5) and further reviewed in the light of the Cleveland Report (Home Office 1991). These are Area Child Protection Committees, the child protection register and child protection conference.

Area Child Protection Committee

This is a body comprising senior representatives of all the relevant agencies concerned with child care. Its usual function is to develop coordinated child care policies and guidelines, and to oversee the operation of the local 'at risk' or child protection register (see below).

It is a 'joint forum for developing, monitoring and reviewing child protection policies' (Home Office 1991, para 1.9). Many aspects of these arrangements for cooperation were criticised in the Cleveland Inquiry, and further guidance on the organisation, accountability and management of ACPCs has recently been issued (Home Office 1991, Part 2). This is a document aimed at those working in the social services, the police, the health and education services, the probation service, day care services, the armed services, the NSPCC and other voluntary organisations, family court committees as well as guardians ad litem and reporting officers.

Child protection register

This is a consolidated list of children who are formally considered by a relevant agency to be suffering or likely to suffer significant harm (Dingwall and Eekelaar 1982, p 24; Eekelaar and Dingwall 1990, pp 61–63). Once a child is registered, it will usually become the subject of an inter-agency plan to prevent the predicted abuse or neglect. For this reason, entry of a child's name on to the register is an important step. Criteria for registration are laid down by official guidance (Home Office 1991, paras 6.39–6.48) and registration in an individual case will usually require the sanction of a case conference (below). The purpose of the register is 'to provide a record of all children in the area for whom there are unresolved child protection issues and who are currently the subject of an inter-agency protection plan and to ensure that the plans are formally reviewed every six months' (Home Office 1991, para 6.37). The recent official Guidance stresses the importance of involving parents fully in the decision-making process (ibid, paras 6.11–6.23). This is underlined by the fact that a decision to enter a child's name on the register is judicially reviewable (see below).

Child protection conference

A child protection conference 'brings together the family and the professionals concerned with child protection and provides them with the opportunity to exchange information and plan together' (Home Office 1991, para 6.1). The most important role of a CPC is to decide whether to place, or continue to keep, a child on the child protection register and to agree a plan for the child and monitor its implementation. The role of a child protection conference will usually be advisory, since the decision whether to devote resources or to invoke legal procedures in a particular case will remain the responsibility of the individual agency. Official Guidance provides detailed information about the function and organisation of the CPC (Home Office 1991, Part 6).

As noted above, the fact that the powers to invoke the legal procedures discussed in this chapter are vested almost exclusively in local authorities will mean that the social services will have a pre-eminent role in the formulation and implementation of child care policy. This is emphasised by the fact that the various relevant authorities are now obliged to respond to requests for assistance from a local authority which is conducting an inquiry into the case of a particular child (see below).

Family support services and prevention

(i) Introduction

The 1989 Act contains for the first time a comprehensive code concerning the duties of local authorities to children in their area, and specifies the powers by which these duties may be fulfilled. Leaving aside the powers of authorities to seek care, supervision and emergency or child assessment orders (discussed below), these duties fall into two categories: 'family support' (to help parents bring up their children) and 'preventive' (to prevent the admission of children to care or the need for court proceedings) (see DHSS 1985, para 5.7). Although there were similar provisions in place before the 1989 Act, the 'family support' duties and powers were 'scattered about in a number of pieces of legislation' (ibid, para 5.10);[6] and the 'preventive' obligation (contained in Child Care Act 1980, s 1) was defined exclusively by reference to the need to avoid care and thus laid 'insufficient stress on the value of positive family support, and [gave] an impression of care as a last resort' (ibid). In addition there was uncertainty as to the precise meaning of the obligation contained in CCA 1980, s 1[7] and inconsistency in its implementation in local authority practice.[8]

6   Eg, Nurseries and Child-Minders Regulation Act 1948, National Health Service Act 1977, National Assistance Act 1948, Chronically Sick and Disabled Persons Act 1970.
7   See, eg, *A-G (on the relation of Tilley) v Wandsworth London Borough Council* [1981] 1 All ER 1162.
8   See Heywood and Allen (1971); Murray (1980); Freeman (1980), (1983b, pp 150–155); Packman (1981). The arguments are summarised in Dewar (1989, pp 269–272).

The expressed purpose of the 1989 Act is to state the relevant provisions 'clearly in general terms of making services available at an appropriate level to the needs of the area rather than in terms of duties owed to individual children or families, in order to leave local authorities a wide flexibility to decide what is appropriate in particular cases while providing for a reasonable overall level of provision' (DHSS 1985, para 5.8). Although the emphasis is on local authority discretion, however, official guidance accompanying the Act also stresses that '[t]he Act's emphasis on family support and partnership with parents requires local authorities to adopt a new approach to child care services. To give family support a high priority in resource allocation may require new thinking across departments on matters such as devolving budget management and accountability' (DoH 1991a, para 1.10). If realised, this will mark a reversal of pre-1989 practice in which 'preventive' and 'family support' work received low budgetary priority (Parton 1985, pp 190–193).

The obligations imposed by the Act relate to local authority (and other) services as a whole, not just to social services departments. Thus, they will be relevant to housing and education authorities, as well as health authorities. Indeed, the Act imposes duties on these authorities to cooperate with social services,[9] and requires local authorities to coordinate the provision of services with voluntary organisations.[10] Official Guidance stresses the need for a 'corporate policy and clear departmental procedures in respect of interdepartmental collaboration [to] ensure good cooperation at all levels' (DoH 1991a, para 1.13). This suggests that an important subsidiary purpose of the new regime is to create consistency in practice between different local authorities, something which, as noted above, was lacking under the old law.

(ii) Duties to all children

The duties of local authorities are primarily towards those children within their area who are 'in need' (see below). However, some of the specific duties and powers of local authorities contained in Part 1 of Schedule 2 of the Act (considered below) are equally relevant to all children, whether 'in need' or not. The Act states that the Schedule 2 duties and powers are for the purpose 'principally' (and hence not

---

9 CA 1989, s 27. An authority whose help is requested is obliged to comply with the request, but only 'if it is compatible with their own . . . duties and obligations and does not unduly prejudice the discharge of any of their functions': CA 1989, s 27(2).

10 CA 1989, s 17(5).

exclusively) of facilitating the discharge of their general duty to children in need.[11] Thus, local authorities are obliged in respect of all children:

(i) to take reasonable steps to prevent children within their area suffering ill-treatment or neglect;[12]

(ii) to take reasonable steps to reduce the need to bring proceedings for care or supervision orders, criminal proceedings, any family proceedings which might lead to children being placed in their care and proceedings under the inherent jurisdiction of the High Court;[13]

(iii) to 'encourage' children in their area not to commit criminal offences;[14]

(iv) to avoid the need for the use of secure accommodation;[15] and

(v) to provide such 'family centres'[16] as they consider appropriate.[17]

The ways in which these duties may be discharged are considered further below.

(iii) Children 'in need'

The primary obligation of local authorities is to children in their area who are 'in need'. A child is 'in need' for these purposes if it satisfies one of the following criteria:[18]

– the child is unlikely to achieve or maintain, or have the opportunity of achieving or maintaining, a reasonable standard of health or development without the provision for him of services by a local authority under the Act;

– the child's health or development[19] is likely to be significantly impaired, or further impaired, without the provision for him of such services; or

– the child is disabled.[20]

---

11 CA 1989, s 17(2).
12 CA 1989, Sch 2, para 4.
13 CA 1989, Sch 2, para 7 (a).
14 CA 1989, Sch 2, para 7(b).
15 CA 1989, Sch 2, para 7(c).
16 A 'family centre' is defined as a centre providing various activities, advice, guidance or counselling and accommodation: CA 1989, para 9(2). On the different types of family centre, see DoH (1991a), paras 3.18–3.24.
17 CA 1989, Sch 2, para 9.
18 CA 1989, s 17(10).
19 'Health' and 'development' have the same meaning as in the conditions for care and supervision orders: CA 1989, s 31(9), (10) (see below).
20 A 'disabled' child is one who is blind, deaf, dumb, suffers from a mental disorder or is substantially or permanently handicapped: CA 1989, s 17(11).

It should be noted that this definition is considerably wider than just those children who are at risk of significant harm. Thus, the child's needs include 'physical, emotional and educational needs according to his age, sex, race, religion, culture and language and the capacity of the current carer to meet those needs' (DoH 1991a, para 2.4). The definition is 'deliberately wide to reinforce the emphasis on preventive support and services to families' (ibid).

(iv) Duties and powers with respect to children 'in need'

In addition to the duties owed to all children, described above, the 1989 Act imposes two general duties on local authorities towards children 'in need', to be discharged by providing 'a range and level of services appropriate to those children's needs'. The first is to safeguard and promote the welfare of such children; the second, to promote the upbringing of such children by their families so far as is consistent with their welfare.[1] For these purposes, 'family' is not confined to the natural or biological family, but includes anyone who has parental responsibility for the child and any other person with whom the child has been living (whether that person has parental responsibility or not).[2] The services need not be aimed exclusively at the child, but may be provided to the child's family, or any member of the child's family, if provided with a view to safeguarding or promoting the child's welfare;[3] and the services may include giving assistance in kind or, in exceptional circumstances, cash.[4]

The Act provides for the discharge of this general duty to children in need through a combination of specific duties and powers. Thus, an authority is obliged:

- to take 'reasonable steps' to identify the extent to which there are children in need in their area;[5]
- to publicise the availability of services;[6]
- to maintain a register of disabled children in their area[7] and to provide services for disabled children so as to minimise the effect

---

1 CA 1989, s 17(1).
2 CA 1989, s 17(10).
3 CA 1989, s 17(3).
4 CA 1989, s 17(6). Assistance may be provided on condition that it, or its value, is repaid, depending on the means of the child and its parents: CA 1989, s 17(7)–(9).
5 CA 1989, Sch 2, para 1. This is not an obligation to identify particular children in need, but authorities have, in certain cases, a power to assess a particular child's needs for the purposes of the Act: CA 1989, Sch 2, para 3.
6 CA 1989, Sch 2, para 1(2).
7 CA 1989, Sch 2, para 2.

on them of their disabilities and to give them the opportunity to lead lives which are as normal as possible;[8]

— to make 'such provision as . . . is appropriate' for certain services to be made available to children while they are living with their families, such as advice, guidance and counselling, organised activities, home helps, assistance with the expenses of travelling to take advantage of any service, and assistance to enable the child and its family to have a holiday;[9]

— to take 'such steps as are reasonably practicable' to enable a child who is separated from its family, but is not being looked after by the authority, to live with its family or to promote contact between the child and its family, if it is necessary to do so to safeguard or promote the child's welfare.[10]

In addition to the duty, already noted, to provide 'family centres', authorities are also obliged to provide day care for young children in need who are not attending school, 'as is appropriate'.[11] Finally, authorities are obliged to 'provide accommodation' for certain categories of children in need. This is discussed in more detail below.

It should be noted that many of these duties are qualified by reference to concepts of 'reasonableness' or 'appropriateness'. As a result, local authorities are relatively free to decide on the level of provision of certain services, and on whether to provide others at all. This will have to be done in the light of an authority's assessment of the level and type of need in their area, the resources available locally from within the voluntary sector and, probably most importantly, the size of the relevant budgets. One consequence of this is that it will only be in rare circumstances that an individual will be able to challenge a particular authority's policy as to the discharge of its duties through judicial review (see below). Indeed, it was one of the intentions behind the legislation that the duties should be framed as being owed to children in general, rather than to particular children, precisely so as to avoid the possibility of legal challenge from individuals: 'It is for local authorities to decide on their priorities within the resources available to them' (DHSS 1985, para 5.8). There is, however, an obligation to establish a procedure

8   CA 1989, Sch 2, para 6.
9   CA 1989, Sch 2, para 8.
10 CA 1989, Sch 2, para 10.
11 In making day care arrangements, authorities must have regard to the different racial groups to which children in need belong (CA 1989, Sch 2, para 11). Authorities are obliged to conduct regular reviews of day care provision (CA 1989, s 19) and have regulatory functions in relation to child-minders and those providing day care (CA 1989, Part X).

for hearing complaints[12] (see further below), the effectiveness and impact of which remains to be seen.

Another consequence of the qualified nature of the duties is that, apart from the services that authorities are obliged to provide, there may be a number of ways of discharging the duty to children in need. Official Guidance lists a number of services which authorities may provide in meeting their duties. These include: day nurseries, playgroups, child-minding, out-of-school clubs and holiday schemes, supervised activities, befriending services, parent/toddler groups, toy libraries, drop-in centres and playbuses (DoH 1991, paras 3.3–3.17). Official Guidance emphasises that '[i]t is important to recognise the benefits of developing packages of services appropriate to the assessed needs of individual children and their families, rather than directing them to existing services which may not be appropriate' (DoH 1991a, para 2.11).

In this respect the Children Act 1989 must be thought of as a considerable advance, in that it 'gives a positive emphasis to identifying and providing for the child's needs rather than focusing on parental shortcomings in a negative manner' (DoH 1991a, para 2.15). However, as we have seen, the duties are for the most part qualified, and will be shaped in practice by the available resources: 'State support for the family . . . is in the end best measured not by rhetoric and not by a tidy statute book but by the level of financial commitment a government is prepared to make' (Bainham 1990b, p 234). Further, if the aims of the Act in this respect are to be achieved, there will be a need for 'a change of attitude on the part of some practitioners and a change of organisational culture on the part of some agencies' (Parton 1991, p 209).

(v) Duties to investigate

In addition to the duties outlined above, a local authority is also obliged, in certain circumstances, to make such enquiries as it considers necessary to enable it to decide whether to take any action to safeguard or promote the welfare of a particular child.[13] The duty arises where a local authority is informed that a child who lives or is found in their area is the subject of an emergency protection order (see below), is in police protection (also below) or where the authority has reasonable cause to suspect that such a child is suffering, or is likely to suffer significant harm (see also below). A similar provision was contained in CYPA 1969, s 2(1), but the new

12 CA 1989, s 26(3).
13 CA 1989, s 47(1).

provision is slightly wider in that the duty arises even though an authority does not have reason to believe that there are grounds for bringing care proceedings in relation to the child.

The Act also specifies the purposes of an investigation more clearly as being to establish whether the authority should make an application to court or exercise any of its other powers under the Act.[14] This suggests that (for example) an application for a care or supervision order is not an inevitable consequence of an investigation; the authority may decide instead to offer assistance under the powers discussed above (although if for any reason, such as lack of resources, an authority has no relevant support to offer, it may have no alternative but to seek an order). There is no obligation, as there was under the old law,[15] to initiate care proceedings if the necessary grounds are found to exist (see below). It has been said that it 'is surprising that the imposition of... duties to enquire do not lead to a clear and unambiguous duty to take action' (Eekelaar 1990, p 487). If the authority decides not to apply for a care, supervision, emergency protection (EPO) or child assessment order (CAO), it must consider whether the case should be reviewed at a later date and, if so, set a date for the review.[16] If, on the other hand, an authority does plan to seek one of these orders, an investigation will usually be an essential preliminary step to court proceedings (DoH 1991, para 4.73).

A local authority is entitled to assistance from other authorities (such as a health or education authority) in the conduct of an investigation.[17] An authority is obliged to obtain access to the child (unless satisfied that they already have enough information), and if this is unreasonably refused by a parent, the authority will be able (and is obliged) to seek an EPO or CAO (see below).[18]

Accommodating children

(i) Introduction

There may be many families who are unable, through no fault of their own, to provide proper care for their children, either

---

14 CA 1989, s 47(3)(a). There are similar purposes where the child is the subject of an EPO or is in police protection: CA 1989, s 47(3)(b), (c).

15 CYPA 1969, s 2(2).

16 CA 1989, s 47(7).

17 CA 1989, s 47(9)–(11).

18 CA 1989, s 47(4), (6).

temporarily or over a long period. This could be attributable to a number of reasons, the most common being debt, homelessness, the collapse of personal relationships or illness (One Parent Families 1982, pp 8–9). Under the old law, local authorities were empowered to assist families in such cases by providing 'voluntary care' (that is, care provided by a local authority on a voluntary basis as opposed to care provided under a court order). This was, however, one of the most criticised aspects of the old law: the legal position of children in voluntary care, and that of the parents, was unclear; and, despite its name, voluntary care often led to the assumption by local authorities of parental rights over the child by means of the infamous 'parental rights resolution' procedure, which offered very little procedural protection to the parents (see Dewar 1989, pp 273–276, 279–288).

The Review of Child Care Law proposed a new model of 'respite care' and 'shared care' with a view to giving voluntary care a more positive image and to encouraging and emphasising parental responsibility and involvement in the child's care (DHSS 1985, Chs 6 and 7). Although the government did not accept the 'respite' and 'shared' care distinction,[19] the Act in its final form reflects the other policies espoused by the review. Thus, the term 'voluntary care' is replaced by 'provision of accommodation' and becomes one of the ways in which local authorities may discharge their duties to children in need, and the parental rights resolution procedure is abolished. As we shall see, parental involvement is emphasised by the fact that parents may remove the child at any time and are entitled to be consulted about plans for the child. This is further underlined by the fact that authorities are obliged to agree a plan for the child with the parents:[20] 'The Act assumes a high degree of co-operation between parents and local authorities in negotiating and agreeing what form of accommodation can be offered and the use to be made of it' (DoH 1991, para 2.25).

(ii) **Duty to provide accommodation**

The duty to provide accommodation is owed to 'children in need' (see above) who appear to the authority to require it as a result of:

19 Cm 62, para 26.
20 A local authority is obliged to agree proposed arrangements for the child 'so far as reasonably practicable' with (i) a person with parental responsibility, or (ii) if there is no such person, with the person who is caring for the child. Such arrangements should be recorded in writing: Arrangements for Placement of Children (General) Regulations 1991, r 3. The matters to be included in agreed arrangements are set out in Sch 4 to the Regulations.

(i)   there being no person who has parental responsibility for him;[1]
(ii) the child is lost or has been abandoned;[2] or
(iii) the person who has been caring for the child is prevented (whether or not permanently and for whatever reason) from providing him with suitable accommodation.[3]

These grounds are similar to those relating to voluntary care under CCA 1980, s 2 (which they replace) except that it is now clear that (iii) applies where the problem arises from the special needs of the child as well as from the disability of the parents. In every case, an authority is obliged, before providing accommodation, to ascertain the child's wishes regarding the provision of accommodation, so far as is reasonably practicable and consistent with the child's welfare, and to give 'due consideration' to any ascertained wishes of the child having regard to his age or understanding.[4]

No duty to provide accommodation arises in respect of a child who is not 'in need', but an authority has a power to provide accommodation for any child if they consider that to do so would safeguard or promote the child's welfare.[5] The use of this power must be seen against the background of the general duty to prevent ill-treatment or neglect and to reduce the need to bring court proceedings (see above).

Where the duty to provide accommodation arises, it is likely that in many cases, given the definition of a child who is 'in need', there will also be sufficient grounds for proceedings for a care or supervision order (see below). Although authorities are under a general duty to avoid the need for court proceedings, and are exhorted in official Guidance to explore voluntary arrangements before initiating such proceedings (see, eg, DoH 1991, para 3.10), there is nothing in the Act to *require* an authority to resolve the problem by providing accommodation on a voluntary basis. The strengthened position of parents whose children are being provided with accommodation (discussed below) may have the effect of dissuading authorities from considering this course. As Eekelaar has pointed out, '. . . the dim-

---

1   This refers to the absence of a legal rather than 'social' parent. However, if the child is in fact being looked after by a person who does not have parental responsibility for the child, that person may obtain it by seeking a residence order.
2   Neither of these terms is defined, but 'abandon' has been judicially defined as 'leaving a child to its fate': see *Watson v Nikolaisen* [1955] 2 QB 286 and *Wheatley v Waltham Forest London Borough Council* [1980] AC 311.
3   CA 1989, s 20(1). The duty arises in certain other circumstances. For example, they must accommodate any child in need aged 16 or over whose welfare they consider is likely to be seriously prejudiced if they do not provide accommodation: CA 1989, s 20(3). See also CA 1989, s 21.
4   CA 1989, s 20(6).
5   CA 1989, s 20(4).

inution of an authority's capability to exercise what may be termed a 'middle-range' degree of control could, in certain circumstances, push it unnecessarily towards using the more powerful interventive measures' (1991a, p 48; see also Bainham 1990b, pp 233–234).

(iii) Legal effects of the provision of accommodation

A local authority which is accommodating a child does not acquire parental responsibility for it: it remains vested in the person(s) who had it before the child was accommodated. Further, any person who has parental responsibility for an accommodated child may remove the child at any time;[6] and an authority is prevented from providing accommodation where a person with parental responsibility, who is willing and able to provide (or arrange) for the child's accommodation, objects.[7] These rules do not apply where anyone who has a residence order in respect of the child,[8] or has been granted care of the child in wardship, agrees to the child being accommodated;[9] nor where a child aged 16 or over agrees to being accommodated.[10]

The purpose of these provisions, which mark a significant change from the previous law, is to emphasise the voluntary nature of accommodation. However, as noted above, their effect may be to encourage authorities to consider more drastic steps. As we have seen, authorities are obliged to enter into written agreements with parents of the child who is being accommodated, and this agreement should cover the likely duration of the placement in accommodation and arrangements for terminating the placement;[11] but even if parents have agreed to a certain duration of the placement, and to giving notice of their intention to remove the child, it is unlikely that they will be prevented by the fact of the agreement from taking the child whenever they wish. One option open to authorities would be to seek a prohibited steps or specific issue order,[12] but this may not be entirely satisfactory from the authorities' point of view; and these orders cannot be used to achieve the same ends as residence or contact orders (see Ch 9).

Another consequence of the written agreement should be noted. A parent who places a child in accommodation is, technically,

6 CA 1989, s 20(8).
7 CA 1989, s 20(7).
8 So that, for example, if there has been a dispute between the parents necessitating a residence order, the non-custodial parent cannot remove the child.
9 CA 1989, s 20(9).
10 CA 1989, s 20(11).
11 Arrangements for Placement of Children (General) Regulations 1991, Sch 4.
12 CA 1989, s 9(2) prohibits local authorities from seeking residence or contact orders.

arranging for some or all of his or her parental responsibility to be met by one or more persons acting on his or her behalf.[13] It is envisaged (DoH 1991b, para 2.62) that the written agreements will cover a number of matters encompassed within the concept of parental responsibility,[14] such as decisions about the child's health care, education and the parent's day-to-day role in relation to the child. In this way, an authority's powers will derive from the agreement, and it is likely that practice will differ between, and even within, authorities. It has been said that this may 'perpetuate a degree of uncertainty about the precise allocation of responsibility between the parents and the authority which it was one of the aims of the legislation to remove' (Bainham 1990b, p 233).

The powers of local authorities to provide for children they are accommodating, and the position of parents, is considered further below in the context of local authorities' powers and duties to children 'looked after' by them, which includes children in care under a care order, as well as children being voluntarily accommodated. The contents of written agreements will also be considered further in that context.

Emergencies

We have seen that local authorities are under a duty to reduce the need to bring proceedings for care or supervision orders;[15] but that they are also under a duty to investigate the circumstances of a particular child if they have reasonable cause to suspect that a child who lives in their area is suffering or is likely to suffer significant harm.[16] If, as a result of these enquiries, the local authority conclude that they should take action to safeguard or promote the child's welfare, they may (but are not obliged to[17]) seek a care or supervision order (see below); but the circumstances may demand swifter action to protect the child, in which case resort may be had to the emergency protection order (EPO), which replaces what under the old law was termed the 'place of safety order' (POSO).

13 CA 1989, s 2(9).
14 See Arrangements for Placement of Children (General) Regulations 1991, Sch 4, para 4, which refers to 'what delegation there has been [to the authority] of parental responsibility for the child's day to day care' as a matter that should be covered in written agreements.
15 CA 1989, Sch 2, para 7.
16 CA 1989, s 47(1).
17 CA 1989, s 47(8) states that authorities are only obliged to take action 'so far as it is ... reasonably practicable for them to do so'. This is discussed further below, in the context of initiation of care proceedings.

The POSO had been criticised for a number of reasons. The old procedure was drawn in very wide terms and, although designed for emergencies, could easily be used as a means of initiating care proceedings in circumstances where the immediate removal of the child from the family was not strictly necessary. Some magistrates expressed concern that the procedure was used by local authorities as a short cut to care in circumstances where there was no immediate justification for emergency treatment (DHSS 1985, Annex C) and there was some evidence to suggest that this concern was well founded (Packman et al 1986, pp 52–54). The Inquiry into Child Abuse in Cleveland (1988) found that different agencies were unclear as to its legal effects, especially on the issue of access (ibid, Chs 10 and 16 and p 246). In addition, a POSO authorised removal of the child for up to 28 days, while providing parents with virtually no means of legal challenge.

The new order seeks to meet these criticisms; but, as we shall see, there are some respects in which the new order is wider than the old POSO. In this respect, the EPO exemplifies the point made above, that the 1989 Act does not mark a withdrawal of the state, so much as a redirection of state authority. This is evident in official Guidance: the order 'is limited to what is necessary to protect the child [and] remains an extremely serious step . . . [but] nevertheless decisive action to protect the child is essential once it appears that the circumstances fall within [the statutory grounds for an order]' (DoH 1991, para 4.30).

(i) Who may apply?

'Any person' may apply for an EPO.[18] However, it is likely that in most cases the applicant will be a local authority or an 'authorised person' (ie, the NSPCC). In such cases, as we shall see, the grounds for an order are wider than in the case of a non-local authority or NSPCC applicant.

(ii) The grounds for an order

A court may only make an order if it is satisfied that there is reasonable cause to believe that the child is likely to suffer significant harm if he is not either removed to accommodation provided by or on behalf of the applicant or if he does not remain in the place in which he is then being accommodated.[19] These grounds are stricter than those under the POSO in that:

18 CA 1989, s 44(1).
19 CA 1989, s 44(1)(a).

(i)   the likely harm must be 'significant' (the meaning of which is considered below);
(ii) the applicant must specifically demonstrate a need to remove or keep the child from its family; and
(iii) it is the court, rather than the applicant, who must be convinced that the grounds are made out.[20]

The purpose of the new grounds is to avoid the EPO being used as 'a matter of course where care proceedings are a likely option' (DHSS 1985, para 13.8). Instead, there must be a need, proved to the court, to remove the child immediately.

However, there are a number of respects in which the new grounds are significantly wider than under the POSO. First, the harm need not be current: it need only be 'likely'. Under the old grounds, it was unclear whether future harm was sufficient. This was especially problematic where the child was, for example, in hospital. The new grounds refer exclusively to future harm, and specifically envisage cases where the child is away from its family but likely to be harmed if returned. Second, the grounds are significantly wider where the applicant (as will usually be the case) is a local authority or an 'authorised person'. Here, it will be sufficient if the applicant can show:

(i)   that it is making enquiries with respect to the child's welfare; and
(ii) those enquiries are being frustrated through an unreasonable denial of access to the child.

In such cases, a local authority need only show that it (rather than the court) has reasonable cause to believe that access to the child is required as a matter of urgency. An authorised person must show in addition that he or she has reasonable cause to suspect that the child is suffering or is likely to suffer significant harm.[1] The Act does not specify when refusal of access will be 'unreasonable'.

The purpose of these provisions concerning refusal of access was to meet concern that a duty to investigate is meaningless unless those making enquiries can gain access to the child concerned. They were originally included in the Children Bill to satisfy those who wished to introduce a new power enabling local authorities to seek access to the

20 The s 1(3) checklist does not apply to the issue of whether an Emergency Protection or Child Assessment Order should be made, but the 'principle of no delay' does apply.
1 See CA 1989, s 44(1)(b), (c). A local authority that has been refused access to the child or denied information concerning its whereabouts in the course of making investigations is specifically enjoined to seek a compulsory order 'unless they are satisfied that his welfare can be satisfactorily safeguarded without their doing so': CA 1989, s 47(6).

child specifically for investigative purposes (see Parton 1991, pp 176–190). As we shall see, the original Bill was eventually amended to include a new child assessment order (CAO: see below), which is designed for a similar purpose; but although this new power was finally enacted, it was not thought necessary to delete these added grounds from the EPO.

This raises the question of how in practice the EPO and CAO will be used in relation to each other. According to official Guidance, an EPO should only be used in cases of emergency (DoH 1991, para 4.38); but the drafting of the legislation fails to reflect this, in that it may well prove easier to obtain an EPO on grounds of refusal of reasonable access than to obtain a CAO, which requires proof that (among other things) the applicant has reasonable cause to suspect current or likely 'significant harm' (see further below). This is unfortunate, given that the EPO represents, as we shall see, a more intrusive form of order. Much will depend on the meaning accorded by the courts to 'unreasonable refusal' of access and on the effect in practice of the 'presumption of no order'. For example, will the courts insist that an order will only be made where the parents' co-operation cannot under any circumstances be obtained and where a CAO would not be more appropriate?

(iii) Effect of an order

The effect of an EPO is different in a number of respects from its predecessor. First, there is a shorter maximum time limit of eight days[2] (as opposed to 28 days under the POSO). Where an EPO has been made in favour of a local authority or an authorised person, it is possible to apply for a single extension of up to seven days.[3] Second, the legal effects of an order are clarified (and in some respects extended). Thus, in addition to conferring parental responsibility on the applicant for the duration of the order (which will be shared with anyone else who already has it),[4] an order operates as a direction to anyone who is in a position to do so to comply with a request to produce the child and authorises the child's removal to, or retention in, alternative accommodation.[5]

This is reinforced by further powers to obtain information about the child and to authorise entry and search of premises. Thus a court may include in an EPO a direction requiring any person to disclose

---

2 CA 1989, s 45(1).
3 CA 1989, s 45(3)–(6). An EPO may only be extended if the court has reason to believe that the child is likely to suffer significant harm if it is not extended: CA 1989, s 45(5).
4 CA 1989, s 44(4)(c) and s 2(6).
5 CA 1989, s 44(4).

any information s/he may have about the child's whereabouts, failure to comply with which will amount to a contempt of court.[6] Further, a court may authorise the applicant to enter and search premises for the child, and for any other child who may be on the premises and in respect of whom an EPO ought to be made.[7] Any person who intentionally obstructs the exercise of the power of entry and search is guilty of a criminal offence;[8] and the court may issue a warrant authorising a constable to assist the applicant, using reasonable force if necessary.[9] A court may also direct that, in executing the warrant, the constable may be accompanied by certain medical personnel.[10] Taken together, these powers amount to a formidable range of interventionist measures which go beyond those available under the POSO. In particular, an applicant may now require information concerning the child to be given, may search premises without the compulsory involvement of the police and may search for more than one child.

If an order is made, the applicant may only exercise parental responsibility in order to safeguard the child's welfare and may only take such action in meeting his or her parental responsibility as is reasonably required to safeguard or promote the child's welfare.[11] This means that if an applicant, on gaining access to the child, discovers that it is not likely to suffer significant harm (eg, because the abuser has left the home[12]), the applicant may not remove the child. However, if circumstances change during the currency of the order, the applicant may remove the child. If the child is removed (or is already accommodated away from its home), the applicant is obliged to return, or permit the removal of, the child once it appears to the applicant that it is safe to return the child, or to allow the child to be removed.[13]

---

6   CA 1989, s 48(1). No person may refuse to give information on the grounds of self-incrimination, but any statement or admission made in compliance will not be admissible in evidence against that person in proceedings for any offence other than perjury: CA 1989, s 48(2).

7   CA 1989, s 48(3), (4). An order made in relation to another child on the premises shall have effect as an EPO if the child is found on the premises and if the *applicant* is satisfied that the conditions for an EPO exist with respect to that child.

8   CA 1989, s 48(7).

9   CA 1989, s 48(9).

10 CA 1989, s 48(11).

11 CA 1989, s 44(5).

12 The abuser may be forced to leave by means of the procedures considered in Ch 6, but these may only be initiated by a spouse or cohabitee. In addition, local authorities are empowered to provide assistance to the abuser in such cases, either in cash or by helping to obtain alternative accommodation, but only if the abuser 'proposes to move from the accommodation': CA 1989, Sch 2, para 5.

13 CA 1989, s 44(11), (12).

The 1989 Act clarifies the position concerning medical or psychiatric examinations, which was unclear under the POSO. Thus, a court may give directions (either at the time of the application or at any time during the currency of the order) concerning the medical or psychiatric examination or assessment of the child, including a direction that no such examination shall take place, or shall take place only with the leave of the court.[14] It is anticipated that a direction that such an examination should take place will only be made where the applicant and the parents cannot agree on whether there should be an examination or on who should conduct it (DoH 1991, para 4.63). However, it is difficult to envisage how such agreement is to be reached in urgent cases, and there is a high likelihood that applicants will seek directions as a matter of course, often before the parents are aware that an application is being made. A child of sufficient understanding to make an informed decision may refuse to submit to the examination or assessment.[15]

The 1989 Act also clarifies the position of parents, which under the POSO was either unclear or considered unfair. Thus, parents (and certain others) are entitled to reasonable contact with the child during the order, although the court may impose conditions on such contact and may prohibit it altogether (see further, the discussion of contact below).[16] As with directions concerning medical examination, directions concerning contact may be made either at the time of making the order, or at any time during its currency.[17] Thus, applicants for an EPO should, but need not, give thought to issues of contact and medical assessment at the time of the application. However, it is likely that 'the court will leave contact to the discretion of the authority or order that reasonable contact be negotiated between the parties unless the issue is disputed, in which case specific directions can be sought' (DoH 1991, para 4.62).

Finally, the 1989 Act permits a parent (and the child) to apply to discharge the order, but only after a period of 72 hours beginning with the making of the order, and only if the person seeking the discharge did not receive notice of, and was not present at, the original hearing of the application.[18] This is some improvement on the POSO, under which parents had only very limited means of challenging an order. However, it remains to be seen whether courts will be inclined to discharge orders, especially where the applicant has not completed its assessment of the child (see DoH 1991, para

14 CA 1989, s 44(6)(b), (8), (9).
15 CA 1989, s 44(7).
16 CA 1989, s 44(6)(a), (13).
17 CA 1989, s 44(9).
18 CA 1989, s 45(8), (9).
19 CA 1989, s 45(10).

4.69). As under the POSO, there is no right of appeal against the making of the order or against any directions it contains.[19]

It remains to be seen whether these provisions will in practice improve the position of parents; or whether the courts will instead exercise the considerable discretion vested in them to favour the applicant's point of view. If they do the latter, there may be little incentive for local authorities to resolve matters by agreement wherever possible, as they are exhorted to do in official guidance.

(iv) Procedure

An application for an EPO is subject to the same procedural requirements as apply to other applications made under the 1989 Act. Thus, an applicant must file and serve in advance of the hearing (i) written statements[20] summarising oral evidence on which it is intended to rely and (ii) copies of any documents, including experts' reports, which will form part of the applicant's case.[1] However, the urgent nature of such applications means that these strict procedures may be departed from. Thus, it is possible for the applicant to seek leave of the court, either orally or without giving notice to the other parties (or both), to depart from these requirements.[2] It remains to be seen how rigorously the courts will wish to test the evidence offered in support of applications.

Further, it is possible to apply for an EPO ex parte,[3] which means that an order may be made without giving notice of the application to those who would otherwise normally be entitled to it, and in the absence of those normally entitled to attend the hearing.[4] Indeed, the rules envisage that an application may be made by telephone,[5] without the need to file the application in the appropriate form, provided only that the formal documents are filed within 24 hours of the application. Where an order has been made ex parte, the applicant must serve a copy of the application on all respondents within 48 hours of the making of the order.[6] However, the court has

20 Such a statement need not be a sworn affidavit but must be (i) dated, (ii) signed by the person making it and (iii) contain a declaration that its maker believes it to be true and understands that it may be placed before the court: FPR 1991, r 4.17(1)(a); FPC(CA 1989)R 1991, r 17(1)(a).
1 FPR 1991, r 4.17(1); FPC(CA 1989)R 1991, r 17(1).
2 FPR 1991, r 4.14(3), (4); FPC(CA 1989)R 1991, r 14(3), (4).
3 FPR 1991, r 4.4(4); FPC(CA 1989)R 1991, r 4(4).
4 Those entitled to notice of an application and to be respondents to an application are set out in FPR 1991, Appendix 3 and FPC(CA 1989)R 1991, Sch 2 discussed below.
5 FPR 1991, r 4.4(4); FPC (CA 1989)R 1991, r 4(4). Applications may be made to a single justice: CA 1989, s 93(2)(i).
6 Ibid.

a discretion to refuse to make an order ex parte and to insist on a full hearing.[7] As we have seen, the Act permits respondents to an ex parte application to apply for a discharge of the order after 72 hours. The rules concerning the appointment of a guardian ad litem and a child's solicitor (discussed below) apply to applications for EPOs and CAOs.[8]

The 1989 Act relaxes the rules of evidence for the purposes of applications for EPOs. Thus, a court hearing such an application is given a broad power to take account of any statement made in any report to the court that has been prepared in the course of, or in connection with, the hearing, and may take account of any other evidence given during the hearing that, in the court's view, is relevant to the application.[9] This enables the court to take into account evidence that would otherwise be excluded as hearsay (see further below).

Finally, it should be noted that applications for EPOs do not count as 'family proceedings', so that it is not open to the court to make an order other than the one applied for. A local authority applicant who is unsuccessful will need to consider whether to seek an interim care order, and will need to initiate fresh proceedings for that purpose.

(v) Police powers

As under the old law, the police have certain powers to remove children in emergencies, although their practical significance may be reduced now that social workers may obtain authority to enter and search premises and may enlist police assistance in doing so (see above). Official guidance emphasises the importance of ensuring that 'effective inter-agency working is achieved' between local authorities and the police (DoH 1991, para 4.77).

A constable may take a child 'into police protection'[10] where s/he has reasonable cause to believe that a child would otherwise be likely to suffer significant harm. The constable may either remove the child to suitable accommodation or prevent the child's removal from hospital, or other place in which he is then being accommodated.[11] Parental responsibility for a child taken in this way is not transferred to the police, but the 'designated officer' (that is, the police officer designated for the area concerned as responsible for children taken in this way) must do what is reasonable in all the circumstances to

---

7 FPR 1991, r 4.4(5); FPC (CA 1989)R 1991, r 4(5).
8 CA 1989, s 41(6)(g).
9 CA 1989, s 45(7).
10 CA 1989, s 46(2).
11 CA 1989, s 46(1).

promote the child's welfare.[12] A child may only be kept in police protection for up to 72 hours;[13] but the constable taking the child must ensure that the case is enquired into by the designated officer.[14] The constable must also inform the relevant local authority, the child (if capable of understanding) and the parents of the steps that have been, and are proposed to be, taken for the child.[15]

Once the designated officer has completed the inquiry, that officer must release the child unless s/he considers that there is still reasonable cause for believing that the child would suffer significant harm if released.[16] The designated officer may also apply on behalf of the local authority for an EPO, whether the local authority knows of, or agrees to, the application or not.[17] The designated officer must also permit the parents (and certain others) to have such contact with the child as, in the designated officer's opinion, is reasonable and in the child's best interests.[18] Whether an EPO is sought or not, the local authority comes under an obligation to make enquiries:[19] 'In practice this means that the police and local authority will need to be in close liaison as soon as possible after the child has been taken into police protection' (DoH 1991, para 4.74).

Child Assessment Orders

The Child Assessment Order (CAO) is an entirely new form of order. It enables a local authority or an authorised person to gain access to the child for the purposes of assessment in circumstances which are not emergencies, but 'where the harm to the child is long-term and cumulative rather than sudden and severe' (DoH 1991, para 4.8). The new provision was added at a late stage in the passage of the Children Bill and proved to be one of its most controversial aspects (see Parton 1991, pp 176–190). In order to meet opposition to the measure, the government agreed to provisions that considerably narrow the scope of the new order. As a result, the CAO may prove less attractive than an EPO, especially given that an EPO is available where access to the child has been unreasonably refused

12 CA 1989, s 46(9).
13 CA 1989, s 46(6).
14 CA 1989, s 46(3)(e).
15 CA 1989, s 46(3), (4).
16 CA 1989, s 46(5).
17 CA 1989, s 46(7), (8).
18 CA 1989, s 46(10).
19 CA 1989, s 47(1).

and enables a court to direct precisely the sort of assessment envisaged by a CAO.

However, it seems that the government's intention in introducing the order was to enable social workers to deal with uncooperative rather than dangerous parents (Parton 1991, op cit). Thus, according to official guidance, 'parents should always be told that a CAO may be applied for if they persist in refusing to co-operate . . . [which] . . . may be sufficient to persuade them that the authority are genuinely concerned about the child and that the parents should co-operate with the proposed voluntary arrangements' (DoH 1991, para 4.27).

(i) Grounds

Unlike an EPO, only a local authority or an authorised person (ie, the NSPCC) may apply for a CAO.[20] An applicant must prove:

(i)   that the applicant has reasonable cause to suspect that the child is suffering or is likely to suffer significant harm (the meaning of which is considered below);

(ii) that an assessment of the state of the child's health or development, or of the way he has been treated, is required to enable the applicant to determine whether or not the child is suffering, or is likely to suffer significant harm; and

(iii) that it is unlikely that such an assessment will be made or be satisfactory in the absence of a CAO.[1]

It should be noted that it is sufficient if the applicant has a well-founded suspicion of significant harm. However, if there is firmer evidence available, then an EPO, care or supervision order may be more appropriate; and in any case, condition (ii) may not be satisfied.[2] Paradoxically perhaps, an applicant may be disqualified from seeking a CAO because it has too much information already.[3] Condition (iii) emphasises that an order will only be made where parents are refusing to cooperate with the applicant, for example, by refusing to consent to an assessment of the child.

---

20   CA 1989, s 43(1).

1   CA 1989, s 43(1).The s 1(3) checklist does not apply.

2   Eekelaar (1990) notes that the conditions for a CAO do not cover a case where there is no doubt that the child is suffering harm, but where the cause is unclear.

3   If a local authority considers that the conditions for a CAO exist, then it is also obliged to make such enquiries as it considers necessary to enable it to decide whether to take any action to safeguard or promote the child's welfare: s 47(1)(b) CA 1989.

Although 'reasonable cause to suspect' may appear to set a relatively low threshold for an order, it should be remembered that an EPO is also available to a local authority to whom access to the child has been unreasonably refused (see above).[4] It is possible to envisage circumstances where the applicant may find it easier to pursue an EPO on that ground rather than a CAO. Conversely, as noted above, an applicant may already have too much information to satisfy the conditions of a CAO. It may be, therefore, that only limited use will be made of the CAO.

(ii) Effect

A CAO authorises an assessment of the child in accordance with the terms of the order; and it requires anyone who is in a position to produce the child to do so, and to comply with any directions relating to the assessment as may be specified in the order.[5] An order does not confer parental responsibility on the applicant,[6] although the order may authorise keeping the child away from home for specified periods if it is necessary for the purposes of the assessment.[7] The court may also make such order as it considers fit concerning access to the child during any period that it is away from home.[8]

A CAO lasts for seven days and cannot be extended.[9] This time limit owes more to the notion of 'judicial tariff' (so that a CAO, being an order of lesser significance than an EPO, also had to be shorter in duration) than to a realistic view of the length of time necessary to conduct a full assessment (Parton 1991, p 189). The inadequacy of this time limit may force authorities to seek interim care or supervision orders: 'It is unfortunate that the limitations on the CAO and EPO as aids to investigation could push the case into the context of care proceedings merely for the purpose of completing the assessment' (Eekelaar 1990, p 489).

The court may give directions as to the nature and objective of the assessment, and as to by whom and where it should be conducted.[10]

4   A court may treat an application for a CAO as an application for an EPO and, if there are grounds for making an EPO it must make an EPO: CA 1989, s 43(3), (4).
5   CA 1989, s 43(5)–(7). Thus, a parent could be required to participate in the assessment; but note that the directions relate to the assessment, and not to treatment, so that Eekelaar's assertion (1990, p 488) that parents can be directed to participate in 'family therapy' may be doubted.
6   A CAO will not be necessary where someone with parental responsibility consents to the child being assessed, or where a local authority already has parental responsibility under a care or supervision order.
7   CA 1989, s 43(9).
8   CA 1989, s 43(10).
9   CA 1989, s 43(5).
10   CA 1989, s 43(7).

In doing so, 'the court should take advice from those presenting the case, and if necessary other professionals involved in the case (including the guardian ad litem)' (DoH 1991, para 4.14); but, in general, 'an assessment should always have a multi-disciplinary dimension' (ibid, para 4.25). The outcome of the assessment may indicate the need for further action, which, if voluntary arrangements with the parents cannot be made or will not suffice, may include an application for an EPO or an interim care or supervision order.

(iii) Procedure

An application for a CAO must be heard inter partes, and the normal procedural requirements (discussed below) will apply. The need for an inter partes hearing for an order that only lasts seven days has been questioned (Eekelaar and Dingwall 1990, p 92); but it may be justified in view of the fact that further consequences may flow from the assessment. An applicant for a CAO must take such steps as are reasonably practicable to ensure that notice of the application is given to the child's parents, anyone with parental responsibility, any person caring for the child, anyone with an order for contact with the child and the child.[11]

Compulsory orders: care and supervision orders

So far in this chapter, we have been concerned with the voluntary, investigatory and emergency aspects of a local authority's child care responsibilities. In the course of discharging these responsibilities, an authority may conclude that more extensive compulsory measures are required in order to promote the child's welfare. The 1989 Act provides two forms of such measures: a care order and a supervision order. The former entitles the local authority to remove the child from its family for an indefinite period, the latter to supervise the child in its family setting. The criteria for initiating proceedings for either of these orders are considered below.

If a local authority wishes to obtain a care or supervision order in respect of a child,[12] it may now do so only under s 31 of the Children Act 1989. A local authority cannot apply for residence or contact

---

11 CA 1989, s 43(11).
12 Care and supervision orders cannot be made in respect of children who have reached the age of 17 (or 16 in the case of married children): CA 1989, s 31(3).

orders[13] and the power of a court to make care or supervision orders in wardship proceedings has been removed.[14] A local authority may apply for a care or supervision order in any family proceedings as well as applying for a care or supervision order alone.[15] A court in any family proceedings may, if it considers that a care or supervision order may be appropriate, direct a local authority to investigate a child's circumstances[16] and make an interim care order.[17] In each case, however, the conditions of s 31 will have to be satisfied before a full care order can be made.

Thus, the s 31 conditions assume a central importance which those previously contained in the Children and Young Persons Act 1969 did not possess, since the old CYPA grounds were not the only route into care. However, the grounds themselves have been reformulated to take account of criticisms that were made of the 1969 Act grounds (DHSS 1985, Ch 15).

(i) Initiating proceedings

We have seen that, in certain circumstances, a local authority is obliged to make inquiries to enable them to decide whether to take any action to safeguard or promote the child's welfare.[18] However, there is no obligation on local authorities (as there was under the previous law) to initiate care proceedings if it appears that the conditions for care proceedings are satisfied. Instead, an authority which concludes that action is necessary 'shall take that action (so far as it is within their power and reasonably practicable for them to do so)'.[19]

It has been suggested that this change 'might be taken to signal political coolness towards the use of compulsory measures' (Eekelaar and Dingwall 1990, p 83). This is emphasised in official guidance accompanying the Act, which states that 'no decision to initiate proceedings should be taken without clear evidence that provision of

---

13 CA 1989, s 9(2). Local authorities can apply for specific issue or prohibited steps orders, but a court cannot make such an order with a view to (i) achieving a result which could be achieved by making a residence or contact order or (ii) exercising its power in a way denied to the High Court (by s 100(2)) in the exercise of its inherent jurisdiction: s 9(5) CA 1989.
14 CA 1989, s 100(1), (2).
15 CA 1989, s 31(4).
16 CA 1989, s 37(1).
17 CA 1989, s 38(1). A full care order may only be made if the authority decides to apply for one. If it decides not to apply, the authority must provide the court with reasons for its decision: CA 1989, s 37(3).
18 CA 1989, s 47(1).
19 CA 1989, s 47(8).

services for the child and his family . . . has failed or would be likely to fail to meet the child's needs adequately . . . and that there is no suitable person prepared to apply to take over care of the child under a residence order' (DoH 1991, para 3.10). Compulsory orders, in other words, are a measure of last resort to be used only where the original family cannot be successfully supported in looking after the child and where no suitable substitute carer can be found. Further, '[b]efore proceeding with an application, the local authority . . . should always seek legal advice' (DoH 1991, para 3.12).

Any local authority or 'authorised person' may apply for a care or supervision order.[20] It seems that the applicant authority need not be the one in whose area the child is resident, although the authority designated in the care order must be.[1] The Act specifies the NSPCC as an 'authorised person' and empowers the Secretary of State to add others to the category by order.[2] An authorised person must, if it is reasonably practicable to do so, consult the local authority in whose area the child is resident before making the application.[3] There are provisions relating to the representation of the child and the attendance of the child at hearings, which are considered below. All parties have full rights of appeal to the High Court (see below).

(ii) The conditions

The conditions contained in s 31 originate in (but in some respects differ from) those proposed by the Review of Child Care Law (DHSS 1985, Ch 15). As proposed by the Review, the concept central to the new conditions was to be that of 'harm' to the child. The Review's objectives were:

(i) to clarify the concept of harm, and in particular to include a subjective element for the child concerned;
(ii) to ensure that action could only be taken where the harm was substantial;
(iii) to require evidence that the harm was attributable to a failure of parenting;
(iv) to enable action to be taken where harm was foreseeable but had not yet occurred; and

20 The powers of education authorities and the police to apply for orders have been removed.
1 CA 1989, s 31(8).
2 CA 1989, s 31(9).
3 CA 1989, s 31(6): 'what is reasonably practicable should be considered in the context of *Working Together* and local guidelines on inter-agency relationships, responsibility and accountability for effective case management' (DoH 1991, para 3.13).

(v) to ensure that compulsory orders were only made where the order was the only means available of promoting the child's welfare (ibid, para 15.25).

This, according to the review, would 'provide better protection in every respect for parents and children' (ibid). By including forward-looking conditions, it was thought that the use of wardship as a route into care could be reduced (and, as we have seen, it has now been eliminated).

In its final form, s 31 sets out the following conditions:

-   that the child is suffering, or is likely to suffer, significant harm; and
-   the harm, or likelihood of harm, is attributable to either:
    (a) the care given to the child, or likely to be given to him if the order were not made, not being what it would be reasonable to expect a parent to give him; or
    (b) the child's being beyond parental control.

In addition, a court is obliged to apply the s 1(3) checklist[4] and to observe the principle that no order shall be made unless doing so would be better than making no order at all.[5] It is for this reason that it is more accurate to describe the criteria set out above as 'minimum conditions' for making an order, rather than 'grounds': '. . . it is only if those conditions are satisfied that a court has power to decide whether to make a care or supervision order. That final decision, however, is not governed by the conditions but rather by the welfare principle' (Lord Mackay 1989, p 506).

Each element of these conditions will now be considered in turn.

Harm

The Act defines 'harm' as 'ill-treatment or the impairment of health or development'.[6] These are thus alternative rather than cumulative definitions of harm. Each of these terms is further defined. 'Ill-treatment' is defined as including (and is thus not confined to) sexual abuse (which is not defined[7]) and forms of ill-treatment which are not physical; but it clearly also includes physical ill-treatment and emotional abuse. 'Development' is defined as 'physical, intellectual, emotional, social or behavioural development' and would include, for example, 'a child that is failing to control his anti-social

4   CA 1989, s 1(4).
5   CA 1989, s 1(5).
6   CA 1989, s 31(9).
7   On the difficulties of defining sexual abuse, see Freeman (1990), pp 140–142.

behaviour' (DoH 1991, para 3.20). 'Health' is defined as 'physical or mental health'.

'Significant'

The Act provides little assistance in determining whether harm is 'significant'. However, where the 'harm' relied on is impairment of health or development, the Act states that in order to determine whether the harm is 'significant', the health or development of the child in question shall be compared with that which can be reasonably expected of a 'similar child'.[8] This recognises that in cases of impairment to health or development there is 'a need to use a standard appropriate to the child in question . . . because some children have characteristics or handicaps which mean that they cannot be as healthy or well-developed as others' (DoH 1991, para 3.20). This suggests that the 'similarities' with which a court should be concerned are those specific to the particular child (eg deafness) rather than those to do with the child's class or ethnic background. Thus it has been said that '[o]n this test a child from a deprived background is expected to achieve intellectual growth and emotional maturity comparable to children who come from well-ordered, well-heeled and stimulating environments' (Freeman 1990, p 147).

Where the harm in question is ill-treatment, the meaning of 'significant' is not defined. The intention, however, was to ensure that '[m]inor shortcomings . . . should not give rise to compulsory intervention unless they are having or are likely to have, serious and lasting effects on the child' (DHSS 1985, para 15.15).

'Is suffering or is likely to suffer'

This wording introduces for the first time a generalised forward-looking element into the conditions. Thus it will be possible to seek an order where no harm has occurred, but where it is 'likely to occur'. This presupposes that it is possible to make predictions concerning 'dangerous' parental behaviour. Parton (1991) has argued that the concept of 'dangerousness' forms a key premise of the 1989 Act: namely, that it is possible to identify clearly the dangerous parent from the rest, and to treat different categories of parent accordingly. The concept permits 'a clear division between the voluntary services available to children in need and the care system' (p 198). This is related to the argument, made above and in Chapter 9, that under the 1989 Act 'the role of the state is not so

8   CA 1989, s 31(10).

much reduced but redirected' (ibid, p 203). In the public context, the intervention is targeted more precisely (so it is thought[9]) at dangerous parents; in the private, at those parents who cannot agree (see Ch 9). For the rest, the emphasis is on voluntariness and private agreement.

'Likely' is not defined, but it is probably not as strict as 'imminent' nor as relaxed as 'possible'. The inclusion of this forward-looking element was thought to justify closing off wardship as a route to compulsory orders, since wardship was often used by local authorities to get around their lack of power to take preventive action under the old law. The Act requires in the alternative that the child 'is suffering' harm. Concern has been expressed that this will prevent authorities taking action where harm has occurred in the past, but is not occurring in the present. Indeed, if taken literally, no child that has been removed to care in an emergency from abusing parents will be suffering harm at the date of the hearing. Much will depend on judicial interpretation. Past events may, however, be relevant in two ways. First, they may be evidence of the likelihood of harm occurring again; and second, they may be evidence of a current impairment of development since development is a continuing process.[10]

Attributable to lack of reasonable parental care

As noted above, one of the purposes of the new conditions was to focus attention on failures in parenting and so provide greater protection to parents. This means that harm that occurs to a child for some reason other than a failure in parental care will not be a ground for an order. However, there are a number of ambiguities here.

First, what is meant by 'care'? There may be a number of cases in which a child has not been residing with its parents but has, for example, been accommodated by a local authority or with foster parents, and where an authority wishes to prevent the child's return to its parents. Even assuming that harm or a likelihood of harm can be established, can it be said to be attributable to a failure in parental care? In the example given above, it could be argued that the parents in question have not been able to 'care' for the child in question and so cannot be said to have failed to provide it. However, it seems likely that 'care' will be interpreted broadly so as to encompass more than just physical care. Official Guidance asserts

---

9 On the problems of predicting dangerous parents, see Parton (1985); Dingwall (1990).

10 *F v Suffolk County Council* (1981) 2 FLR 208; *M v Westminster City Council* [1985] FLR 325.

that care 'must mean providing for the child's health and total development . . . and not just having physical charge of him' (DoH 1991, para 3.23).

Thus, in the above example, 'care' may include keeping in regular contact with the child, so that a parent who has failed to do that may be said to have 'failed' to care (White, Carr and Lowe 1990, para 6.13). However, the harm or likelihood of it must be attributable to this failure; but it could be argued that there is here a likelihood of parental failure, since the Act talks of 'the care given to the child, or likely to be given to him if the order were not made'. In the above example, it could be argued that the likelihood of harm is attributable to a likely parental failure. Yet in this way, the Act permits compulsory measures to be taken for harm that has not yet occurred which is attributable to parental failure that has not taken place. Much will depend on how the courts interpret these provisions, but there is at least the possibility of compulsory orders being granted in circumstances where both the harm and the parental failure is predicted rather than actual. This could significantly reduce the protection which the reformulated conditions were originally intended to confer on parents.

Another difficulty concerns the meaning of 'attributable to'. It is arguably wider than 'caused by'. For example, a parent who knows of, but does nothing to prevent, sexual abuse of a child by a third party, may not have 'caused' the harm to the child; but the harm may be said to be 'attributable to' a parental failure to 'care' (ie, 'care' in the broad sense) (see Freeman 1990, p 150).

Finally, the standard of care expected of a parent is that which it would be reasonable for a parent to give the child. It is thus an objective standard. However, this standard is objective only as far as the parents are concerned. For example, some children may have particular needs which a reasonable parent would regard as requiring a higher level of care than required by other children (DoH 1991, para 3.23). By contrast, it is not open to the parents to argue that the relevant standard of care is what it is reasonable to expect *them* to provide. Thus, no allowance may be made for particular problems the parents may have in caring for their children: all are expected to meet the standard of the hypothetical reasonable parent. Again, it may be questioned whether this adequately protects parents.

Beyond parental control

This is an alternative to proving parental failure and 'provides for cases where, whatever the standard of care available to the child, he is not benefiting from it because of lack of parental control' (DoH 1991, para 3.25). It is a survivor from the old law,[11] but, unlike the old law, is linked to the requirement to prove actual or likely harm to the child concerned. The fact that the child causes harm to others will not of itself be sufficient, but we have already seen that a 'failure to control anti-social behaviour' may be taken as evidence that the child is suffering harm. There need be no failure of parenting: 'even the best of parents might lose "control" over a child' (Eekelaar and Dingwall 1990, p 104).

The checklist

In deciding whether to make an order, the court is obliged to apply the s 1(3) checklist. In some respects, the checklist repeats matters which the court will already have taken into account, such as 'any harm which he has suffered or is at risk of suffering' (para (e)) and the capability of his parents to meet his needs (para (f)). Further, the 'range of powers available to the court' (para (g)) will also be a matter for the court to consider in the context of the presumption of no order (see below).

Presumption of no order

The purpose of this provision in the context of child care proceedings is to require 'positive proof that a care or supervision order will result in [the child's] needs being met or at least better catered for, and further that intervention will not do more overall harm than good' (DHSS 1985, para 15.24) The fact that the conditions are made out is thus not a sufficient condition of making a care order, and the court may make another order (such as a residence order, but not in favour of the authority). Alternatively, a court may simply make no order at all, such as where 'the prognosis for change is reasonable and parents show a willingness to co-operate with voluntary arrangements' (DoH 1991, para 3.16). This emphasises that a care or supervision order is a matter of last resort, but that its possible availability may be helpful in persuading parents to cooperate with local authorities.

(iii) The effect of a care order

The Act clarifies the relationship between care orders and other forms of order or proceeding. In particular, it establishes the

11 CYPA 1969, s 1(2)(d).

principle that care orders, s 8 orders and wardship are mutually exclusive. Thus, a care order automatically discharges a s 8 order[12] and brings wardship to an end.[13] Conversely, a child who is subject to a care order may not be made a ward of court[14] and, with the exception of residence orders, a court cannot make a s 8 order with respect to a child subject to a care order.[15] If made, a residence order automatically brings a care order to an end[16] (so that an application for a residence order operates in effect as an application to discharge a care order). Otherwise, a care order lasts until the child reaches the age of 18 unless it is brought to an end earlier (by a residence order or a successful discharge application).[17]

A care order imposes a duty on the authority designated in the order to receive the child into their care and to keep him there during the currency of the order.[18] The designated authority obtains parental responsibility for the child,[19] which is shared with the parents,[20] but cannot cause the child to be brought up in a religious persuasion other than that in which he would have been brought up had the order not been made.[1] Nor may an authority consent to the child's adoption or appoint a guardian for it.[2] During the currency of a care order, a change in the child's surname or the removal of the child from the United Kingdom requires either the consent of every person with parental responsibility or the leave of court.[3]

Although parents retain parental responsibility, an authority has the power to determine the extent to which a parent or guardian may meet his parental responsibility for him, but only if satisfied that it is necessary to do so in order to safeguard or promote the child's welfare.[4] This power does not extend to 'any right, duty, power, responsibility or authority which a parent or guardian of a child has in relation to the child or his property by virtue of any other enactment', which would include the right to consent to the child's marriage, rights under the Education Act 1981 in relation to the child's special educational needs, and financial responsibility for the

---

12 CA 1989, s 91(2).
13 CA 1989, s 91(4). A care order also automatically discharges a supervision order and a school attendance order: CA 1989, s 91(3), (5).
14 CA 1989, s 100(2)(c).
15 CA 1989, s 9(1).
16 CA 1989, s 91(1).
17 CA 1989, s 91(12). On discharge, see CA 1989, s 39.
18 CA 1989, s 33(1).
19 CA 1989, s 33(3)(a).
20 CA 1989, s 2(5), (6).
1 CA 1989, s 33(6)(a).
2 CA 1989, s 33(6)(b).
3 CA 1989, s 33(7).
4 CA 1989, s 33(3)(b), (4).

child.[5] Nor does this power prevent a parent or guardian who has
care of the child from doing what is reasonable in all the
circumstances of the case for the purpose of safeguarding or
promoting the child's welfare.[6] This last provision would apply, for
example, where a child is in the care of a parent or guardian on a
weekend visit.

The effect of these provisions is not entirely clear.[7] Although
parents retain parental responsibility, we have seen that they cannot
apply for s 8 orders while a child is in care (except for a residence
order, which if made has the effect of terminating the care order). It
has been said that 'for what can only be ideological reasons, . . . the
parent retains responsibility, but . . . the means to exercise it [have
been removed]' (Eekelaar and Dingwall 1990, p 137). According to
official guidance, the effect of this provision is to allow 'the local
authority to deal with any conflict that may arise between the
authority and the parents in exercising their respective parental
responsibilities' (DoH 1991, para 3.67). However, it is also stated
that 'where a local authority intend to limit the way in which a
parent meets his responsibility this should be discussed with the
parent and incorporated within the plan of arrangements for the
child while in care so that it may be subject to periodic review' (ibid,
para 3.68).

This flows from the fact that local authorities are required to
consult parents 'so far as practicable' before making any decisions in
relation to a child being looked after by them[8] (which includes a
child in care under a care order: see below); and parents are entitled
to take advantage of the complaints procedure established by the
Act[9] (see below) and to have reasonable contact with the child[10] (see
also below). Nevertheless, the fact that a child in care cannot be
warded, and that only residence orders are available under s 8 where
a child is in care, may lead to parents seeking forms of legal redress
other than those provided for in the Act itself (Eekelaar and
Dingwall 1990, pp 137–138), such as judicial review (see below).

Once in care, a local authority may discharge its duty in relation to
the child by placing the child with its family, a relative or foster
parent or in a recognised children's home.[11] This is discussed further
below.

5   CA 1989, s 33(9).
6   CA 1989, s 33(5).
7   For example, would a local authority have the parental power, identified in *Re R
    (a minor)* [1992] Fam 11 (discussed in Ch 3), to override a '*Gillick* competent'
    child's veto of medical treatment, or would that power remain with the parents?
8   CA 1989, s 22(4).
9   CA 1989, s 29(3).
10 CA 1989, s 34.
11 CA 1989, s 23.

(iv) Contact with children in care

Once a child is in compulsory care, the local authority may take the view that the best permanent plan for the child's future is that it should either be fostered on a long-term basis, or placed for adoption; and that the parents should have no future contact with the child. In this sense, the denial of parental contact to a child in care is a purely operational decision. However, the continuance of parental contact with the child will be crucial in determining the long-term chances of parents regaining care of the child (Gibson and Parsloe 1984), and the decision as to contact is arguably too important to be left to professional discretion. Issues of contact become especially acute where it is proposed that the child should be adopted (see Ch 11). The Review of Child Care Law did not think that 'access could be regarded as simply a matter of management over which local authorities should have sole control' (DHSS 1985, para 21.1).

It is only since 1983 that parents have had the legal right to challenge the termination or refusal of arrangements for access (now 'contact') under CCA 1980, ss 12A–12G; but those provisions suffered from a number of shortcomings, particularly in that they only permitted challenge to a refusal or termination of access rather than establishing a prima facie right to it. The Review proposed to remove the anomaly in the old law that allowed 'a court to specify in detail what access should be allowed once it had been totally denied but [precluded it] from considering cases where it may be severely or unreasonably restricted' (para 21.15) by proposing that there should be a statutory presumption in favour of access.

As a result, s 34(1) contains a presumption that a local authority shall permit a child in care to have reasonable contact with his parents (including an unmarried father), a guardian, any person in whose favour a residence order was in force immediately prior to the care order being made and any person who had care of the child by virtue of an order made by the High Court in the exercise of its inherent jurisdiction. In addition, any of these people (together with anyone who has the leave of the court) may apply for contact, and the court may make such order, and subject to such conditions, as it thinks appropriate.[12] Before making a care order, a court must consider the arrangements proposed by the local authority for contact and invite parties to the proceedings to comment on them.[13] This means that authorities applying for a care order will have to consider their plans for contact at the time of applying for the order.

---

12 CA 1989, s 34(3), (7).
13 CA 1989, s 34(11).

It is envisaged that issues of contact will be resolved primarily by agreement between parents and the local authority, with a court order being used only in cases of disagreement.[14] We will see below that local authorities are in any case required to promote contact between parents and children being looked after by them and are obliged, for example, to keep parents informed of the whereabouts of their child(ren) and have the power to provide financial assistance to parents to enable contact to take place.[15] Thus, according to official guidance, 'the underlying principle is that the authority, child and other persons concerned should as far as possible agree reasonable arrangements before the care order is made, but should be able to seek the court's assistance if agreement cannot be reached or the authority want to deny contact to a person who is entitled to it under the Act' (DoH 1991, para 3.76).

As this implies, it is open to a court to restrict contact with a child in care. Thus, a child or a local authority may apply for an order that only limited contact take place between the child and a named person, or for an order prohibiting contact altogether.[16] A court may make such orders (on application or of its own motion) either when making the original care order, or in any family proceedings relating to a child in care.[17] In addition, a local authority may, without court authority, refuse to allow contact for up to seven days if it is decided as a matter of urgency that it is necessary to do so to safeguard or promote the child's welfare.[18] Before using this power, however, the authority should consider negotiating an agreed reduction in access, applying for an order imposing conditions on contact or authorising refusal of contact altogether,[19] or seeking a discharge or variation of an existing contact order (DoH 1991, para 3.81).[20]

These provisions appear to give with one hand and take with the other in that, while establishing a presumption in favour of contact, they give the courts considerable power to restrict contact or dictate the terms on which it will take place. It has also been questioned whether the courts are the appropriate fori in which decisions of this

---

14 See the guidance contained in DoH 1991b, Ch 6, which replaces the previous Code of Practice on Access to Children in Care (HMSO 1983).

15 CA 1989, Sch 2, paras 15, 16.

16 CA 1989, s 34(2), (4).

17 CA 1989, s 34(5): this would include, for example, an application for a residence order or for adoption.

18 CA 1989, s 34(6). The exercise of this power is subject to the Contact with Children Regulations 1991: CA 1989, s 34(7).

19 CA 1989, s 91(17) requires the leave of court for applications under s 34 where a previous application has been refused in the preceding six months. This applies equally to local authorities, but they are expected 'to carry out good child care practice' and seek leave as necessary (DoH 1991, para 3.83).

20 The court may vary or discharge any contact order on the application of the authority, the child, or the person named in the order: CA 1989, s 34(9).

sort should be made (Eekelaar and Dingwall 1990, p 142). This view is not shared by official Guidance, which sees 'the pro-active role of the court . . . [as reflecting] . . . the importance of the subject' (DoH 1991, para 3.77). It remains to be seen whether the compulsory 'screening' by the courts of local authorities' plans for contact will have any significant impact on the extent of permitted parental contact, or whether the new provisions will simply effect a relocation of formal decision-making from local authorities to the courts with the latter consistently acceding to the views of the former.[1]

(v) The effect of a supervision order

This is an order placing the child under the supervision of a designated supervisor, who may be a local authority or a probation officer. The supervisor must 'advise, assist and befriend the supervised child' and take such steps as are reasonably necessary to give effect to the order.[2] A supervision order permits the supervisor to require the child to comply with directions given by the supervisor to the child to do all or any of a number of specified things.[3] These include requirements to live at specified places, to present himself to a specified person at specified times and to participate in specified activities.[4] A supervision order may also require the child to keep the supervisor informed of any change of his address and to allow the supervisor to visit him at the place where he is living.[5] A supervisor does not have the power to give directions concerning medical or psychiatric examinations or treatment: these may only be directed by the court.[6] An order lasts for a year, but the supervisor may apply for an extension of the order subject to a maximum total duration of three years.[7] The one-year initial limit is new, its purpose being to 'ensure that after a reasonable period the effectiveness of the order and the circumstances of the child are reviewed' (DoH 1991, para 3.96).

1 Recent authority suggests that the courts will be slow to make decisions relating to contact that will interfere with a local authority's long-term plans for the child: see *Re S (a minor)(access application)* [1991] 1 FLR 161.
2 CA 1989, s 35(1). There is also a new power to make an education supervision order which has the effect of putting the child under the supervision of a designated education authority: CA 1989, s 36 and Part III, Sch 3.
3 CA 1989, Sch 3.
4 CA 1989, Sch 3, para 2. The number of days in respect of which a child (or responsible person: see below) may be required to comply with directions shall not exceed a total of 90 days: CA 1989, Sch 3, para 7.
5 CA 1989, Sch 3, para 8.
6 CA 1989, Sch 3, paras 4, 5. A court cannot make such an order if a child who has sufficient understanding to make an informed decision does not consent.
7 CA 1989, Sch 3, para 6.

Following the recommendations of the Review of Child Care Law (DHSS 1985, Ch 18) the 1989 Act imposes certain duties on 'responsible persons', who are defined as a person with parental responsibility for the child and any other person with whom the child is living.[8] The objective is to increase the attractiveness of the supervision order[9] as against a care order, especially where the local authority propose to return the child home to the parents on trial if a care order is made (ibid, para 18.5). Thus, a responsible person must inform the supervisor of his own and the child's address and, if he is living with the child, allow the supervisor reasonable contact with the child.[10] Further requirements may be imposed, but only with the consent of the responsible person concerned. Thus, an order may require a consenting responsible person to take all reasonable steps to ensure that the supervised child complies with any direction given by the supervisor, or by the court in relation to medical or psychiatric examination or treatment. A consenting responsible person may also be required to attend at a specified place to take part in specified activities.[11]

Despite these new provisions, the supervision order has been criticised as being too weak (Eekelaar and Dingwall 1990, pp 134–136). For example, there are no specific sanctions attaching to a breach of a supervision order. If an order is not complied with, the supervisor may only apply to court for its variation or discharge.[12] The power that existed under the old law to 'vary' a supervision order to a care order has been removed, so that a full rehearing will be required if a care order is thought necessary. Further, a supervision order itself confers no power to enter premises where the child is living if entry is refused, in which case the supervisor will need to apply for a warrant authorising a constable to assist the supervisor in exercising the statutory powers, or for an emergency protection order (see above).

It may be, therefore, that the supervision order will not be used more widely, as hoped. For example, it has been suggested that 'if there are reasonable doubts about the prospects of a supervision order being workable, fieldworkers should apply for a care order, even if it is administered initially as if it were supervision' (Eekelaar and Dingwall 1990, p 136). This suggests a different approach from that advocated in official Guidance: 'The local authority should at

---

8 CA 1989, Sch 3, para 1.
9 In 1983 there were about 1,400 supervision orders made in care proceedings, compared with about 3,000 care orders (DHSS 1985, para 18.5).
10 CA 1989, Sch 3, para 8(2).
11 CA 1989, Sch 3, para 3.
12 CA 1989, s 35(1)(c).

all times respond to non co-operation in a positive and constructive way designed to regain that co-operation' (DoH 1991, para 3.95).

(vi) **Discharge and variation of compulsory orders**

Care orders

A care order may be brought to an end either by the making of a residence order or by a successful discharge application. An application to discharge a care order may be made by (i) any person with parental responsibility for the child,[13] (ii) the child, or (iii) the local authority.[14] If an application is refused, a further application may only be made after six months from the preceding application unless the court grants leave to make a further application earlier.[15] The court may substitute a supervision order for a care order on a discharge application, in which case the threshold criterion in s 31 do not have to be satisfied at the time of the application.[16] This permits a supervised return of the child from care. There is no power to vary a care order. The criterion for deciding whether to discharge the order is the child's welfare, and the court is obliged to apply the s 1(3) checklist. There are provisions concerning representation of the child in discharge proceedings, which are similar to those applicable in applications for care orders (see below). All parties have a full right of appeal to the High Court (see below).

Supervision orders

A supervision order may be varied or discharged on the application of (i) any person with parental responsibility for the child, (ii) the child or (iii) the supervisor.[17] As noted above, there is no power to substitute a care order for a supervision order. The rules that apply to applications to discharge care orders concerning repeat applications, representation of the child and appeals apply also in this context.

(vii) **Other outcomes (including interim orders)**

We have seen that, as a result of the presumption of no order, a compulsory order is not an inevitable consequence of the s 31

---

13 This will not include an unmarried father unless he has parental responsibility. An unmarried father without parental responsibility may bring a care order to an end by obtaining a residence order.
14 CA 1989, s 39(1).
15 CA 1989, s 91(15).
16 CA 1989, s 39(4), (5).
17 CA 1989, s 39(2).

conditions being made out. A number of other possibilities theoretically exist. One is to make no order at all; another is to make a residence order. In addition, on an application for a care order, a court may make a supervision order, and vice versa.[18]

If proceedings on an application for a care or supervision order are adjourned, the court may also make an interim care or supervision order,[19] but only if it is satisfied that there are reasonable grounds for believing that the conditions for a care or supervision order exist.[20] Under the old law, the grounds for an interim order were extremely vague, and practice varied between courts (DHSS 1985, para 17.7 and Annex C, p 175). There was also evidence that interim orders were used for a variety of purposes, for example, to allow a guardian ad litem to complete her report, to 'give the child a salutary experience' or to allow for delays arising from full court lists (DHSS 1985, para 17.3 and Annex C, pp 173–174; Morris et al 1980, pp 89–90). The effect of the new criteria will be to create greater uniformity in practice, and to ensure that interim orders are only made where the applicant has gone some way to making out the case.

The rules relating to s 8 orders are also sufficiently flexible to permit a court to make what is, in effect, an interim residence order.[1]

Procedure

The Children Act 1989, and the accompanying rules of court,[2] make significant changes to the procedure to be followed in child care cases. The changes are based on the wide-ranging review of procedure undertaken by the Review of Child Care Law (DHSS 1985, Chs 14 and 16). The Review was particularly concerned with the parents' status in the proceedings, the rules concerning representation of the child, pre-hearing procedure (especially pre-hearing disclosure of oral and documentary evidence) and the rules of evidence applicable to child care proceedings. We will consider each of these in turn.

18 CA 1989, s 31(5).
19 CA 1989, s 38(1). A similar power exists where a court has ordered an investigation of the child's circumstances under CA 1989, s 37(1).
20 CA 1989, s 38(2).
1 CA 1989, s 11(7)(a) permits a court to make a residence order for a specified period, and CA 1989, s 11(3) permits a court to make a residence order at any time in the course of proceedings even though it is not in a position finally to dispose of them.
2 Family Proceedings Courts (Children Act) 1989 Rules 1991; Family Proceedings Rules 1991.

(i) **Party status**

Under the CYPA 1969, only the local authority and the child were parties to care proceedings. The position of parents was complex and obscure. They were not automatically entitled to party status, although they could acquire it under certain circumstances; and they had certain procedural rights to appear in court to represent the child and to answer allegations.[3] The lack of automatic party status for parents had a number of consequences. For example, they were not entitled to legal representation or legal aid, they had no right of appeal except when acting on behalf of the child and had very limited rights to call evidence, cross-examine witnesses or make submissions to court. The Review argued that parents should have automatic full party status since 'care proceedings are usually in substance a dispute between the parents and the local authority in which local authorities are alleging that the parents have failed to care for their child; often they involve allegations not only of neglect but of positive abuse and ill-treatment' (para 14.4). The Review also recommended that the court should have power to join others interested in the proceedings as parties.

These proposals have now been implemented.[4] The basic position is that, in addition to an applicant for an order, the following shall be treated as parties to all applications made under the Children Act 1989:

(i)   every person whom the applicant believes to have parental responsibility for the child;
(ii) if the child is subject to a care order, every person who had parental responsibility immediately prior to the making of the order;[5]
(iii) in the case of an application to extend, vary or discharge an order, the parties to the proceedings leading to the original order; and
(iv) the child.[6]

In addition, the court has a wide power to join any other person as a party.[7] Certain others are entitled to be given notice of an application. In particular, in the case of applications for care or

3 For a discussion of the old law, see Dewar (1989), pp 296–299.
4 FPR 1991, r 4.7 and Appendix 3; FPC(CA 1989)R 1991, r 7 and Sch 2.
5 Category (ii) will include non-parents who had a residence order in their favour prior to the making of the order, but who lost parental responsibility as a result of the care order.
6 A child is automatically made a party in 'specified proceedings', defined in CA 1989, s 41(6), which include all proceedings referred to in this chapter.
7 FPR 1991, r 4.7; FPC(CA 1989)R 1991, r 7.

supervision orders, or for orders concerning parental contact, this category includes every parent of the child who does not have parental responsibility (ie, unmarried fathers who have not acquired parental responsibility). The purpose of requiring notice to be given is presumably to enable the recipient of the notice to seek to be made a party to the proceedings.

(ii) Representation of the child[8]

Background

Although under the old law a child was a party to care proceedings, this did not always guarantee that the child's point of view was separately represented to the court. Certain provisions of the Children Act 1975 permitted the appointment of a 'guardian ad litem' for the child; but it was only in 1984 that these provisions were fully implemented and that local authorities were obliged to establish panels of guardians ad litem to service their area.[9] A 'guardian ad litem' will usually be a qualified social worker independent of the local authority involved in the proceedings in question, selected from a panel established in the local authority's area.[10] The function of a guardian (discussed further below) is 'not to act as an *advocate* for the child in court, but rather to investigate the case by speaking to the relevant social workers, reading the social services' file on the case, interviewing the parents and, where possible, ascertaining the child's views' (Eekelaar and Dingwall 1990, p 116).

The 1989 Act, following the recommendations of the Review of Child Care Law (DHSS 1985, paras 14.10–14.18), seeks to enlarge the number of cases in which the guardian is appointed by introducing the presumption that an appointment of a guardian will be made in all 'specified proceedings'[11] unless it is not necessary to

8   A court may order the child to attend any stage of the proceedings: CA 1989, s 95(1). The court also has wide powers to order that the proceedings take place without the child present: FPR 1991, r 4.16(2); FPC(CA 1989)R 1991, r 16(2).

9   Guardians ad litem and Reporting Officers (Panels) Regulations 1983; see also LAC (83)21. For an account of the work of guardians ad litem under the pre-1989 regulations, see Masson and Shaw (1988).

10   On selection of guardians, see Atherton (1984) and Masson and Shaw (1988) at pp 168–170. Local authorities have devised a number of strategies for ensuring an adequate supply of independent guardians: reciprocal arrangements with other local authorities, the use of freelance social workers and consortium arrangements under which a group of authorities appoint a group of full-time guardians: BASW (1986); Kerr et al (1990), pp 1–5.

11   Defined in CA 1989, s 41(6) as: any proceedings for a care or supervision order (or for their variation or discharge), proceedings in which the court has ordered an investigation under CA 1989, s 37(1), proceedings in which the court is considering whether to make a residence order with respect to a child who is subject to a care

safeguard the child's interests.[12] One consequence of this should be the elimination of regional variations in the appointment of guardians. The rules of court made under the Act also clarify the role of the guardian and the relationship between the guardian and any solicitor appointed for the child (see below).[13] However, the Act does not remedy some of the criticisms that have been levelled at the guardian ad litem system since its inception in 1984. For example, it has been argued that there are some areas where the controls on selection of guardians to the panel are minimal, and there is no guarantee that the elected guardians are genuinely independent of the authority bringing the proceedings.[14] Further, the Act itself creates a need for more guardians to be appointed, yet there was already evidence of a shortage of guardians under the old system (Fortin 1990, p 307).

The problem is well illustrated in *R v Cornwall County Council, ex p Cornwall and Isles of Scilly guardians ad litem and Reporting Officers Panel*,[15] in which a decision by a director of social services to limit the time for which guardians would be paid to 65 hours per case was quashed on an application for judicial review as an abuse of authority. The case illustrates the dilemma in which those responsible for social service budgets will find themselves: the cost of a guardian ad litem comes out of their budget, but they have no control over that head of expenditure. The problem can be expected to become especially acute now that guardians are to be appointed in more cases.

The duties of a guardian

The duties of a guardian once appointed are set out in the rules of court[16] which both reiterate and expand those that were applicable under the old law. The guardian is enjoined to observe the principle of no delay[17] and the s 1(3) checklist,[18] to appoint and instruct a solicitor for the child and to 'give such advice to the child as is

---

order, proceedings concerning contact with a child in care, proceedings for EPOs and CAOs and appeals from these proceedings. Rules of court may add more proceedings to this list: see, for example, FPR 1991, r 4.2(2).

12 CA 1989, s 41(1).
13 FPR 1991, r 4.11; FPC(CA 1989)R 1991, r 11.
14 By CA 1989, s 41(7) the Secretary of State may make regulations concerning the establishment of panels of guardians, so that some further change in selection procedures is possible. See also FPR 1991, r 4.10(7) and FPC(CA 1989)R 1991, r 10(7) which seek to define when a guardian is independent of the relevant authority.
15 (1991) Times, 20 November.
16 FPR 1991, r 4.11; FPC(CA 1989)R 1991, r 11.
17 CA 1989, s 1(2).
18 FPR 1991, r 4.11(1); FPC(CA 1989)R 1991, r 11(1).

appropriate having regard to his understanding'.[19] In addition, there are a number of specific duties, including advising the court on the child's wishes, the appropriate level of court for the proceedings to be heard, and advice on what order should be made.[20] A guardian must make whatever investigations may be necessary for the performance of these duties and has the right to examine relevant local authority records.[1] The guardian must also file a written report 'advising on the interests of the child'.[2] There is also a general duty to provide the court with such other assistance as the court may require.[3]

In the past, reporting to the court has been the focus of the guardian's role (Lyons 1986)[4] but the extension in the use of guardians envisaged by the Children Act 1989, and the wider range of duties imposed on them by the rules of court, seems certain to increase the influence of the guardian (Kerr et al 1990, pp 112–114; Fortin 1990). Local authorities are also increasingly obliged to include a guardian in the decision-making process with respect to the child.[5] In addition, it should be remembered that the 1989 Act increases the significance of court procedures generally, and the guardian's report and general advice will be an increasingly important basis for magisterial and judicial decision-making. This serves to underline the importance of ensuring that sufficient numbers of guardians are appointed and that those appointed are genuinely independent of the relevant authority. It has been pointed out that 'it is the local authority, the prime instigator of care proceedings, who has the responsibility for setting up and administering guardian panels, and it is the local authority of the child under scrutiny who pays the guardian' (Kerr et al 1990, p 111).

Solicitors

A solicitor may be appointed to represent the child, either by the guardian, by the court or by the child. The solicitor will usually be drawn from a panel of local solicitors recognised as specialists in child care law.[6]

19 FPR 1991, r 4.11(2)(b); FPC(CA 1989)R 1991, r 11(2)(b).
20 FPR 1991, r 4.11(4); FP(CA 1989)R 1991, r 11(4).
1 CA 1989, s 42.
2 Detailed guidance as to the contents of the report is contained in Volume 7 of the Department of Health's *Regulation and Guidance* (1990).
3 FPR 1991, r 4.11(10); FPC(CA 1989)R 1991, r 11(10).
4 On the contents of guardians' reports, see Masson and Shaw (1988), pp 177–180.
5 Failure to inform a guardian of a major change in the child's circumstances and to listen to a guardian's views may be grounds for judicial review of a local authority's decision: *R v North Yorkshire County Council, ex p M* [1989] QB 411.
6 The Law Society (1991a) has proposed a new set of criteria for those solicitors wishing to hold themselves out as recognised child care specialists.

As we have seen, it is a responsibility of the guardian to appoint and instruct a solicitor.[7] The solicitor must act in accordance with those instructions, unless the solicitor considers that the child wishes to give instructions that conflict with those of the guardian, in which case, and provided the child has sufficient understanding, the solicitor may act in accordance with the child's instructions.[8] This recognises the fact that guardians and solicitors perform different functions – the guardian must form a view as to the child's best interests, while the solicitor must represent the wishes of the client (Levin 1984; Lyons 1986).

However, a guardian may not always be appointed, in which case the court may also appoint a solicitor, if none has otherwise been appointed, and if certain other conditions are satisfied.[9] The rules also envisage a child instructing a solicitor direct rather than through a guardian or the court.[10]

(iii) Pre-hearing procedure

The criminal antecedence of the CYPA 1969 meant that proceedings under it bore little resemblance to the civil proceedings they in fact were. For example, there were almost no obligations on a local authority to disclose its case before the hearing, save to specify the grounds on which the proceedings would be based. Further, normal civil rules concerning discovery of documents had no application in the magistrates' court; nor was there any provision for a pre-hearing review or appointment for directions. This created a 'real risk that the court's final decision will be based on undisclosed information' (Hayes and Bevan 1986, p 58). The Review of Child Care Law proposed that these shortcomings be rectified with the overall aim of making care proceedings more like ordinary civil proceedings and to create a framework that is 'less accusatorial and more flexibly structured' (DHSS 1985, para 16.1).

These changes have been incorporated in the relevant rules of court. For example, a party to proceedings is obliged to file written

---

7 FPR 1991, r 4.11(2)(a); FPC(CA 1989)R 1991, r 11(2)(a). The rules appear to be couched in mandatory terms, so the guardian has no discretion over whether to make an appointment.
8 FPR 1991, r 4.12(1)(a); FPC(CA 1989)R 1991, r 12(1)(a).
9 CA 1989, s 41(3), (4).
10 FPR 1991, r 4.11(3)(a); FPC(CA 1989)R 1991, r 11(3)(a). In such cases, the guardian will take a more limited role in the proceedings, as directed by the court.

426 *The state as parent*

statements[11] of the substance of any oral evidence which that party intends to adduce at the hearing together with copies of any documents, including experts' reports, on which that party intends to rely.[12] Failure to disclose evidence or documents in this way means that they cannot be relied on without the leave of court. The court also has extensive powers to make directions (either of its own motion or at the request of a party to the proceedings) concerning various aspects of the conduct of proceedings, including the submission of evidence.[13] These rules should ensure that local authorities will be obliged to disclose their case well before the hearing.

A number of other changes flow from the introduction of the principle of 'no delay' (see Ch 3) and the obligation imposed on courts to draw up timetables.[14] Thus, the date for a hearing or directions appointment (which amounts, in effect, to a preliminary hearing) will be automatically fixed by the court,[15] and one of the purposes of the court's extensive direction-making power is to enable the court to ensure that the parties stick to the timetable. It is for this reason that the 1989 Act has been said to have created a more managerial role for the court (Cretney 1990b).

(iv) Evidence

The rules of evidence, especially those concerning hearsay,[16] are of particular importance in care proceedings. The Review of Child Care Law was concerned that the more liberal rules concerning the admissibility of hearsay that apply in the county and High courts were not applicable to care proceedings in magistrates' courts (paras 16.30–16.38). For this reason, the Children Act 1989 contains a number of changes to the law of evidence in cases involving children. Some are specific, such as those concerning the contents and admissibility of a guardian ad litem's report which might otherwise be hearsay;[17] others are more general, such as the provisions

11 Such a statement need not be a sworn affidavit but must be (i) dated, (ii) signed by the person making it and (iii) contain a declaration that its maker believes it to be true and understands that it may be placed before the court: FPR 1991, r 4.17(1)(a); FPC(CA 1989)R 1991, r 17(1)(a).
12 FPR 1991, r 4.17; FPC(CA 1989)R 1991, r 17. This does not amount to full discovery, since a party may not be required to disclose documents adverse to their case (see Spon-Smith 1990).
13 FPR 1991, r 4.14; FPC(CA 1989)R 1991, r 14.
14 CA 1989, s 32.
15 FPR 1991, r 4.4(2); FPC(CA 1989)R 1991, r 4(2).
16 Evidence given by one person as to what another person, not before the court, said or did, when given as evidence of the truth of any issue before the court. Thus, evidence given by A that a child made allegations of abuse to A would be hearsay if produced as evidence of the truth of the allegation.
17 CA 1989, s 41(11), 42(2), (3).

enabling a child to give unsworn evidence and conferring a power on the Lord Chancellor to provide by order for the admissibility of hearsay evidence in a prescribed form (including 'any prescribed method of recording', which would include video evidence).[18]

Jurisdiction and appeals

We saw in Chapter 1 that the Children Act 1989 was accompanied by a reorganisation of jurisdiction in proceedings concerning children, the purpose of which was to create concurrent jurisdiction in matters relating to children between the magistrates', county and High courts.[19] This in turn enables such cases to be heard at the level appropriate to their complexity, and to enable a single court to have jurisdiction over all legal proceedings relating to the child. In the context of 'public' law proceedings, the main significance of this is that while all the proceedings considered in this chapter still have to be commenced in the magistrates' court[20] (which, for these purposes, will be known as the 'family proceedings court'[1]), it is now possible for certain proceedings to be transferred up to a higher court. The factors relevant to transfer are:

(i) whether the proceedings raise exceptionally grave, important or complex issues;

(ii) whether it would be appropriate for those proceedings to be heard together with other family proceedings being heard in another court; or

(iii) whether transfer would accelerate a final determination of the issue.[2]

The procedural rules, discussed above, apply in every court.

All parties to proceedings have full rights of appeal. Appeals from a decision of the magistrates' court either to make or to refuse to make any order under the 1989 Act lie to the High Court.[3]

---

18 CA 1989, s 96.
19 CA 1989, s 92(7).
20 Children (Allocation of Proceedings) Order 1991, r 3.
1 CA 1989, s 92(1).
2 Children (Allocation of Proceedings) Order 1991, r 7. The Lord Chancellor's Department estimates that, applying these criteria, about 25% of all public law cases will be transferred to a higher court (17% to the county court and 8% to the High Court, the latter figure roughly equating with the number of public wardships originated annually under the old law): see *Children Act Progress Report* Number 6, May 1991.
3 CA 1989, s 94(1).

The position of children 'looked after' by local authorities

We have seen that children may come to be looked after by a local authority in two ways: they may be provided with accommodation by an authority, or they may be committed to an authority's care under a care order. In either case, such a child is referred to in the legislation as being 'looked after' by the authority.[4] Although the legal effects of the provision of accommodation and a care order are different, the duties owed by local authorities to both sets of children are in many respects the same.

The theme of partnership with, and involvement of, parents is pursued in both cases (see DoH 1991b, para 2.12), although in practice the degree to which parents will be involved will depend very much on how the child came to be looked after by the authority. It will be remembered that where a child is being voluntarily accommodated, the authority acquires no parental responsibility for the child (except to the extent that parents agree) and parents may remove the child at any time (see above). This will put parents in a stronger position than where there is a care order under which, as we have seen, a local authority has the upper hand (even though parental responsibility is described as being shared between parents and the authority: see above). This is emphasised by the fact an authority is obliged to agree written arrangements for the child's placement where a child is being voluntarily accommodated, but not where the child is in care.[5] However, official guidance asserts that in such cases 'the local authority should still seek to work in partnership and reach agreement with the parents, wherever possible' (DoH 1991b, para 2.19).

As we shall see, the theme of parental involvement with children in care is underlined by certain duties imposed on authorities by the Act itself: but much will depend on the extent to which social services departments embrace the philosophy of the Act, and possibly on the extent to which they can be legally required to do so (see 'Challenging local authorities' decisions', below).

(i) General duties

A local authority has a duty to any child looked after by it to:

4   CA 1989, s 22(1). This will include a child who is in local authority accommodation under an EPO. Note that it is only a child with respect to whom a care order has been made that will be 'in care' for the purposes of the legislation and for this discussion.

5   Arrangements for Placement of Children (General) Regulations 1991, r 3(4).

- safeguard and promote its welfare;[6]
- make such use of services available for children cared for by their own parents (ie, those discussed under 'Family support and prevention', above) as appear to the authority to be reasonable in each case;[7]
- provide accommodation for the child (in one of the ways discussed below) and maintain him in other respects;[8] and
- advise, assist and befriend the child with a view to promoting his welfare when he ceases to be looked after by them.[9]

In addition, an authority must, before making any decision with respect to a child looked after by them, and so far as it is reasonably practicable to do so, ascertain the wishes and feelings of the child, his parents, any other person with parental responsibility and any other person whose wishes and feelings the authority considers relevant.[10] In making any such decision, the authority must give 'due consideration' to the wishes and feelings of the child that they have been able to ascertain (having regard to his age and understanding) and to the wishes of any of those listed above.[11] As we shall see, the written arrangements that authorities must prepare should include provisions concerning consultation with parents and others; but since, as noted above, such arrangements do not have to be agreed with parents where the child is in care, it may be that in some cases parents will only be able to rely on this general provision to establish a right to be involved in decision-making.

In making decisions, the authority must also have regard to the child's religious persuasion, racial origin and cultural and linguistic background.[12] This will be especially relevant to decisions about fostering arrangements.[13]

An authority is permitted to act inconsistently with these duties if necessary to do so in the interests of protecting the public from serious injury; and the Secretary of State may direct them to do so.[14]

---

6   CA 1989, s 22(3)(a).
7   CA 1989, s 22(3)(b).
8   CA 1989, s 23(1).
9   CA 1989, s 24(1).
10 CA 1989, s 22(4).
11 CA 1989, s 22(5)(a)(b).
12 CA 1989, s 22(5)(c).
13 See Foster Placement (Children) Regulations 1991, r 5, which obliges authorities to secure that 'where possible' the foster parent is of the same religious persuasion as the child. No mention is made in the regulations of the other factors in CA 1989, s 22(5)(c).
14 CA 1989, s 22(6)–(8).

(ii) Placement

The Act specifies the ways in which an authority shall discharge its duties to provide accommodation for the child.[15] Before considering these, it should be remembered that the parents of a child who is voluntarily accommodated may remove the child from any organised placement at any time, although the length and termination of the placement should form part of the agreed arrangements for the child. This does not apply to parents whose children are in care under a care order. They are permitted to meet their parental responsibility for a child in care only so far as the authority decides (see above).

Further, whatever placement is made, authorities are under a duty to promote contact between the child and its parents, any other person with parental responsibility and any relative, friend or other person connected with him 'unless it is not reasonably practicable or consistent with his welfare';[16] and the authority should keep such persons informed of where the child is being accommodated.[17] Where the child is the subject of a care order, this duty must be read in the light of the provisions concerning regulation of contact with children in care (see above). In addition, an authority is obliged, so far as is reasonably practicable and consistent with the child's welfare, to secure that a child is accommodated near its home and that siblings are accommodated together.[18]

We will now consider the different forms of placement, all of which are heavily regulated.

Fostering

Fostering is a well established and integral part of local authority child care practice (see Packman 1981, Ch 2; Rowe 1983; Social Services Select Committee 1983–1984, paras 151–190; Hoggett and Pearl 1991, pp 622–629). A substantial minority of children looked after by local authorities are cared for in this way. The Act defines a foster placement as a placement with a family, relative or other suitable person provided that the person with whom the child is placed is neither a parent of the child, a person with parental responsibility for the child or (where the child is in care) a person in whose favour a residence order was in force immediately before the

---

15 CA 1989, s 23(2).
16 CA 1989, Sch 2, para 15.
17 Ibid.
18 CA 1989, s 23(7).

making of the care order.[19] Placements with those falling within this excluded category are separately regulated (see below).

Foster placements are regulated by the Foster Placement (Children) Regulations 1991, which contain detailed provisions relating to approval of foster parents, supervision and termination of foster placements, and record-keeping. In particular, the regulations require a local authority not to foster a child unless it is the most suitable way of discharging their duty to safeguard and promote the child's welfare and that placement with the particular foster parent is the most suitable placement in all the circumstances.[20] In making arrangements, an authority must ensure that 'where possible' the foster parent is of the same religious persuasion as the child, or gives an undertaking that the child will be brought up in that persuasion.[1] The legal position of foster parents themselves is considered in the next chapter. At this stage, it need only be noted that foster parents may in some cases be able to seek a residence order; and they are entitled to invoke the complaints procedure that authorities are obliged to establish (see below).

As noted above, local authorities should seek to ensure that the foster home is near the child's original home and that siblings are fostered together.

Children's homes

Another permitted form of placement is in a community home, voluntary home or registered children's home.[2] Local authorities are given extensive powers to regulate the provision of accommodation in children's homes (Parts VI–VIII), and this is accompanied by extensive guidance and regulation,[3] part of which was drafted in the light of the Staffordshire Child Care Inquiry (the so-called 'pin down' inquiry). This revealed deficiencies in the training and supervision of staff working in residential homes and the use of excessively harsh disciplinary measures. The complaints procedure, discussed below, will (once established) cover complaints concerning the running of children's homes, and it is hoped that this will lead to better practice in residential care, or at least lead to quicker exposure of bad practice (Riches 1991).

---

19 CA 1989, s 23(3)(4).
20 Foster Placement (Children) Regulations 1991, r 5(1).
1   The Foster Placement (Children) Regulations 1991, r 5(2).
2   CA 1989, s 23(2)(b)–(d).
3   See DoH (1991c); Children's Homes Regulations 1991. The use of secure accommodation is also regulated by the Act: CA 1989, s 25.

Return to the family

A child who is being provided with accommodation may, as we have seen, be removed from accommodation by anyone with parental responsibility for the child at any time. This is not the case with a child subject to a care order; but a local authority may take the view that there is a possibility of returning the child to its family. Indeed, local authorities are obliged to make arrangements to enable the child to live with its parents, any other person with parental responsibility, anyone who had a residence order in their favour immediately before the care order was made, or any relative, friend or other person connected with the child.[4] There is thus a presumption in favour of returning the child to its family (although not necessarily to its natural parents). One way of achieving this would be simply to seek a discharge of the care order. However, an authority may take the view that a trial period is necessary before finally relinquishing all responsibility for the child.

A trial period of this sort is closely regulated.[5] Before returning a child, an authority must (among other things) conduct extensive enquiries, reach a written agreement with those with whom the child is to be placed and make arrangements for the supervision of the placement (including visits). According to official guidance, the 'management of the placement should aim to enhance the parents' role and support the family relationship' with the aim of making progress towards the discharge of the care order (DoH 1991b, para 5.3). It is also stressed that 'it is important that the purpose of the placement is clearly identified and discussed with all concerned during consideration of the placement and that the aims and objectives are clearly understood by the child, the proposed carer and others prior to the placement' (ibid, para 5.20).

(iii) Planning and parental involvement

We have seen that a key philosophy underpinning the 1989 Act is that of parental involvement in decision-making about, and in the responsibility for, children who are looked after by local authorities. This is underwritten by the obligation imposed on authorities to

---

4   CA 1989, s 23(6).
5   The Placement of Children with Parents etc Regulations 1991 (replacing the Accommodation of Children (Charge and Control) Regulations 1988). These regulations do not apply to placements of children who are not in care, nor to placements of children with relatives or friends who do not have parental responsibility, which are subject to the Foster Placement (Children) Regulations 1991.

consult parents wherever 'reasonably practicable' before making any decision relating to a child who is being looked after,[6] by the presumption in favour of returning children to their families[7] and by the presumption in favour of parental contact with children in care.[8] In addition, authorities are obliged to draw up a plan in writing for a child whom they are proposing to look after,[9] the purpose of which is 'to prevent drift and help to focus work with the family and the child' (DoH 1991b, para 2.20).

Where the child is being provided with accommodation and is not in care, the authority must 'so far as reasonably practicable' agree the arrangements in writing with either any person with parental responsibility for the child or with anyone who is caring for the child.[10] There is no obligation to agree arrangements where the child is in care.[11] Even in care cases, however, authorities are encouraged to work in cooperation with the parents (DoH 1991b, para 2.19). Parents in such cases who are not satisfied with the extent to which they have been consulted may use the complaints procedure (see below) or seek an order for contact (see above). In more serious cases of parental exclusion, judicial review of a local authority's action may be possible (see below).

The written plan for the child, whether required to be agreed with the parents or not, must be drawn up with regard to certain considerations.[12] These include the child's health and education, the authorities' immediate and long-term arrangements for the child, arrangements for contact and whether the care order should be discharged. Where the child is not in care but is being provided with accommodation, the regulations specify a number of matters to be included in the written arrangements.[13] These include the type of accommodation to be provided, the respective responsibilities of the parents and the authority and the extent to which the parents have delegated any responsibility to the authority, the arrangements for taking decisions and for contact as well as the expected duration of the placement and its termination. There is no prescribed content for

---

6   CA 1989, s 22(4).
7   CA 1989, s 23(6).
8   CA 1989, s 34(1).
9   Arrangements for Placement of Children (General) Regulations 1991, r 3.
10 Arrangements for Placement of Children (General) Regulations 1991, r 3(4).
11 A parent of a child in care is only entitled to notification of the arrangements where either s/he has been consulted by the authority under CA 1989, s 22(4) or has contact with the child under CA 1989, s 34: Arrangements for Placement of Children (General) Regulations 1991, r 5(1). Although good practice requires notification to parents in all cases, authorities may choose to interpret the regulations according to the letter rather than the spirit.
12 Arrangements for Placement of Children (General) Regulations 1991, Schs 1–3.
13 Arrangements for Placement of Children (General) Regulations 1991, Sch 4.

the arrangements made for children in care: but authorities are still obliged in such cases to draw up arrangements in writing and to notify certain third parties of its contents.[14]

There is no doubt that where the child is being accommodated, the position of parents is much stronger than previously under the old regime of voluntary care. Where the child is in care, the position of the parents will depend on a variety of factors: the practice of authorities, the effectiveness of the complaints procedure and court decisions regarding contact. In both cases, however, there is no obligation to agree the arrangements with the child: there is only a general duty to consult and to safeguard and promote the child's welfare (see above). A child being looked after by an authority, or a child in need, may also make use of the complaints procedure (see below), but it remains to be seen how effective this will be. It may thus be said that the emphasis of the Act is on improving the position of the parents rather than the child: on parental responsibility for, rather than to, children (Eekelaar 1991a).

(iv) Reviews

Under the old law, local authorities were obliged to review the cases of children in their care, whether under a care order or in voluntary care, at six-monthly intervals.[15] However, there was no guidance on the conduct or purpose of reviews and there was evidence that not all authorities conducted them (Sinclair 1984; Social Services Select Committee 1983/4, paras 238–246). The Children Act 1989 clarifies the scope and purpose of the obligation to conduct reviews,[16] primarily through the Review of Children's Cases Regulations 1991. The purpose of a review is to 'ensure that the child's welfare is safeguarded and promoted in the most effective way throughout the period he is being looked after or accommodated' (DoH 1991b, para 8.1; and see generally ibid, Ch 8). The regulations provide for the frequency and form of reviews, the considerations to which authorities are to have regard in conducting reviews and for the consultation and involvement of parents, the child and others.

14 Arrangements for Placement of Children (General) Regulations 1991, r 3, 5.
15 CYPA 1969, s 27(4); CCA 1980, s 20(2).
16 See CA 1989, s 26(1).

Wardship and local authorities

(i) Introduction

Under the old law, wardship[17] was available to local authorities as a means of obtaining a care or supervision order with respect to a child.[18] Local authorities made considerable use of the jurisdiction (see Masson and Morton 1989, Table 1). Its chief advantage was that any decision made in wardship proceedings was based entirely on the welfare principle, so that local authorities did not have to prove that the statutory grounds for a care or supervision order existed (see Morgan 1984; Dewar 1989, pp 302–306). However, the opportunities presented by wardship to bypass the statutory grounds were considered unfair to parents (see Law Commission 1987, para 3.38), who in addition were effectively prevented from using wardship against local authorities (see below).

The 1989 Act has removed wardship as a route into care. In order to understand the changes made by the Act, it is necessary to distinguish wardship (the full effects of which are considered in Ch 12) from the 'inherent jurisdiction' of the High Court to protect children. Wardship, which has the effect of requiring the court's approval for any important decision relating to the ward, is merely one way in which the court may exercise its inherent jurisdiction; it may also make other specific orders in the exercise of the inherent jurisdiction which have a less far-reaching effect (Lord Mackay 1989, p 507). Although the 1989 Act does not directly alter the scope of the wardship and the inherent jurisdiction, it significantly restricts its use by local authorities and where a child is in care.

(ii) The effect of the 1989 Act

The statutory power of the High Court to place a ward of court in care or under the supervision of a local authority has been removed.[19] Further, no court may exercise the inherent jurisdiction with respect to children so as to require a child to be placed in the care, or under the supervision, of a local authority; nor may it be exercised so as to require a child to be accommodated by or on behalf of a local authority.[20] Thus, a local authority may only obtain a

17 Discussed in more detail in Ch 12.
18 FLRA 1969, s 7(2). The courts also exercised a non-statutory inherent power to commit a ward of court to care or supervision: *Re CB (a minor)* [1981] 1 All ER 16.
19 CA 1989, s 100(1).
20 CA 1989, s 100(2)(a), (b).

care or supervision order under s 31, and the voluntary nature of provision of accommodation is preserved. The primacy of the statutory code is further underlined by the fact that the inherent jurisdiction cannot be used for the purpose of conferring on a local authority the power to determine any question which has arisen, or which may arise, in connection with any aspect of parental responsibility for the child.[1] Again, the powers of a local authority can only be derived from the statutory code. Finally, wardship and a care order are mutually exclusive: a child who is in care cannot be made a ward of court.[2]

(iii) The continuing relevance of the inherent jurisdiction

Although a child in care cannot be made a ward of court, and although the jurisdiction cannot be used to confer on authorities wider powers than they have under the statutory code, it may still be possible to invoke the inherent jurisdiction in other ways. For example, a local authority may seek approval for certain decisions it may need to take in the course of discharging its parental responsibility for a child in care: indeed, there are some decisions relating to medical treatment, such as abortion, sterilisation or the continuation of life-support treatment, which may require the court's approval.[3] However, a local authority seeking to invoke the inherent jurisdiction in this way will need to obtain the leave of court to do so. The criteria for granting leave are that:

(i) the result which the local authority wish to achieve cannot be achieved through the making of any order (other than an order made in the exercise of the inherent jurisdiction) which the local authority is entitled to apply for;[4] and

(ii) there is reasonable cause to believe that if the inherent jurisdiction is not exercised, the child is likely to suffer significant harm.[5]

It has been suggested that the purpose of these leave criteria is to ensure that 'having acquired control, the authority should exercise parental responsibility to the full. It should not generally seek to pass

1 CA 1989, s 100(2)(d).
2 CA 1989, s 100(2)(c).
3 Per Lord Templeman in *Re B (a minor) (wardship: sterilisation)* [1987] 2 All ER 206, at pp 214–215. See Ch 12.
4 In the case of any application which may only be made with leave (such as an application for a prohibited steps or specific issue order), it is assumed for these purposes that leave is granted: CA 1989, s 100(5)(b).
5 CA 1989, s 100(3)–(5).

this to the High Court and the court should not seek it of its own volition' (Bainham 1991c, p 272).

In the example of medical treatment given above, the fact that a court cannot make specific issue or prohibited steps orders with respect to a child in care[6] means that the inherent jurisdiction will be the only way of seeking the necessary approval, although whether the courts will regard the 'significant harm' criterion as satisfied in such cases remains to be seen.[7] The jurisdiction may be useful in other circumstances, for example, to prevent parents from harassing foster parents with whom a child in care has been placed (Eekelaar and Dingwall 1990, p 39). Where a child is not in their care, the fact that a local authority may seek leave to apply for a prohibited steps or specific issue order[8] will probably mean that the leave criterion for the inherent jurisdiction will not be satisfied, unless the issue relates to something other than the exercise of parental responsibility.[9] An example would be harassment of the child, or other forms of interference, by someone without parental responsibility. In such cases, it would be equally open to the parents to invoke the jurisdiction.

(iv) Are the restrictions justified?

The net effect of these provisions is to assert the primacy of the statutory code as the source of local authorities' powers. Wardship will lose its role as a 'safety net' procedure available to local authorities in cases where their statutory powers are inadequate. The inherent jurisdiction will only be available in restricted circumstances and for limited purposes. This has been justified on three grounds. First, the statutory powers have themselves been reformulated to take account of some of the perceived shortcomings of the old law, and those powers set out clear and exhaustive criteria for intervention: 'To provide otherwise would make it lawful for children to be removed from their families simply on the basis that a court considered that the state could do better for the child than his family' (Lord Mackay 1989, p 508). Second, it was not thought appropriate to place a child in the care of a local authority and then to subject that authority to directions from the court concerning the

---

6   CA 1989, s 9(1).
7   The application of the significant harm test in this context has been criticised: see Eekelaar and Dingwall (1989); Lowe (1989); White, Carr and Lowe (1990), para 10.12.
8   CA 1989, s 10(1)(a)(ii).
9   A prohibited steps order relates only to a 'step which could be taken by a parent in meeting his parental responsibility for a child'; and a specific issue order relates only to a specific issue which has arisen 'in connection with any aspect of parental responsibility': CA 1989, s 8(1). See further Ch 9.

child (ibid). Finally, it is possible under the court structure (see Ch 1) for more serious cases to be heard at a higher level, so that the experience of senior judges may still be called on (ibid).

It has also been argued that 'the High Court in wardship is excessively slow, it is unable to monitor and direct upbringing of wards adequately and it fails to supervise the conduct of proceedings' and that where wardship was invoked by a local authority 'the High Court generally [relied] on the local authority's plan and rarely [exercised] its particular powers' (Masson and Morton 1989, pp 787–788). Concern has been expressed, however, that it is at least premature to prohibit the use of wardship as a route to care or supervision before the practical effects of the new law, especially the conditions contained in s 31, are known (Lowe 1989; but see Eekelaar and Dingwall 1989 and Masson and Morton 1989, pp 787–789).

Challenging local authorities' decisions[10]

In our earlier discussion of local authorities' powers and duties to children in need, and to children being looked after by them, it was noted that the legislation (and regulations) leave authorities a considerable degree of discretion as to how they fulfil their duties or exercise their powers. We saw that the duties laid on authorities are qualified by terms such as 'reasonableness', 'appropriateness', 'practicability' or by reference to the child's welfare. Although, as we have seen, local authorities are encouraged to involve parents and others in decision-making and in caring for the child, there remains the question of the extent to which local authorities may be held accountable for the decisions they make. The question may arise in a number of ways. For example, an authority may decide to close a children's home, or cease to provide a particular service. At a more specific level, an authority may decide to initiate care proceedings in relation to a child rather than provide family support services to the child's family. In this section, we will consider briefly some of the means by which such decisions may be challenged.

(i) Complaints procedure

The 1989 Act for the first time places a statutory duty on local authorities to establish a procedure for considering 'representations', which is defined to include complaints.[11] The procedure must cover any representations or complaints relating to the discharge by the

---

10 See Hadfield and Lavery (1991).
11 CA 1989, s 26(3)–(8). See also the Representations Procedure (Children) Regulations 1991.

authority of its duties and powers to children in need or to children being looked after by it. Thus, the range of matters that may be complained about is wide. It should include 'complaints about day care, services to support children within their family home, accommodation of a child, aftercare and decisions relating to the placement of a child or the handling of a child's case' as well as the 'processes involved in decision-making or the denial of a service' (DoH 1991b, para 5.8). It should not be confined to matters that affect an individual child. Thus, 'inappropriate restrictions on the lives of children in residential care such as preventing children's activities for the convenience of staff, fixing meal times to suit staff rather than to fit in with the normal needs of children or preventing children's normal activities outside the home' (ibid, para 5.9) would be included. It is also suggested that, although not strictly required by the Act, complaints about the inclusion of a child's name on the child protection register should be covered (ibid, para 5.10).

The procedure may be invoked by:

(i) any child who is in need or who is being looked after by the authority;
(ii) any parent of such a child;
(iii) any person who is not a parent but who has parental responsibility for such a child;
(iv) any local authority foster parent; and
(v) any other person that the authority considers has a sufficient interest in the child's welfare to warrant his representations being considered.[12]

This last category could include a guardian ad litem, a doctor or a relative. At least one person involved in hearing the complaint must be independent of the local authority concerned.[13]

There is no obligation on an authority to do anything once a complaint has been made out: they must simply have 'due regard' to the findings of those considering it. If they decide to take any action in the light of the complaint, the action proposed must be notified to the complainant, the child and anyone else likely to be affected.[14] The authority must also notify these people of their decision in writing.[15]

The value and effectiveness of the procedure will greatly depend on local authorities' responses to complaints that have been substantiated. Failure to act on substantiated complaints may lead to greater use of judicial review (see below), either as an alternative to

12 CA 1989, s 26(3).
13 CA 1989, s 26(4).
14 CA 1989, s 26(7).
15 Ibid.

the complaints procedure, or as a means of forcing an authority to take action in the light of a complaint. Alternatively, authorities may find that greater use will be made of other court proceedings (such as applications for discharge of care orders, for residence orders or for contact) as a way of airing grievances (White, Carr and Lowe 1990, p 72).

(ii) Wardship

We have seen that the 1989 Act places restrictions on the use of wardship by local authorities and where a child is in care.[16] Where a child is in care, however, there is nothing in the legislation to prevent a parent or other interested person from seeking to invoke the inherent jurisdiction by means other than wardship so as to challenge a local authority's decision relating to that child. Such applications would not be subject to the requirement to obtain leave of the court. Nevertheless, it is unclear whether the courts will accept jurisdiction in such cases.

Under the old law, the courts had adopted the rule that the wardship jurisdiction would not be exercised where a child was in the care of a local authority.[17] The basis for this was that the wardship jurisdiction should not be used as a means of reviewing the discharge by authorities of their functions under the statutory code of child care law. This rule has now been effectively enacted in the Children Act 1989 (because wardship and care orders are now mutually axclusive): but it is unclear whether the earlier judicial position with respect to wardship would now be treated as extending to the exercise of the inherent jurisdiction as a whole.[18] One view would be that, in view of the new complaints procedure, the 1989 Act now provides a comprehensive statutory framework for hearing complaints and that parents should be confined to this form of redress. A contrary argument would be that parents who are refused access to the inherent jurisdiction would turn instead to judicial review, which is in many respects a less suitable procedure for resolving disputes over children (see below); and that there was in any case some evidence of judicial disagreement over the desirability of a rigid rule requiring the court to decline jurisdiction.[19] It could also be argued

16 CA 1989, s 100(2)(c).
17 *A v Liverpool City Council* [1982] AC 363; *Re W (a minor)* [1985] AC 791.
18 Nor is it clear whether it now extends to children who are being looked after but who are not in care, although parents in such cases have the option either of removing the child, or of seeking a s 8 order to resolve the dispute, and thus may have no need to resort to wardship (see Bainham 1990c).
19 See, eg, *R v London Borough of Newham, ex p McL* [1988] Fam Law 125; *R v North Yorkshire County Council, ex p M (No 3)* [1989] 2 FLR 82.

that wardship implied much greater control over local authorities than does the inherent jurisdiction, so that objections to the use of the former against authorities would not apply to the latter. This is one area that will require judicial clarification.

(iii) Judicial review

Since, under the old law, parents, and others wishing to challenge local authorities, were debarred from using the wardship jurisdiction, greater use came to be made of the powers of the courts to review the actions of local authorities as administrative bodies under the procedure for judicial review.[20] One commentator who foresaw this possibility described it as a 'disastrous development' (Lowe 1982, p 99), and there are many reasons why it is an unsatisfactory procedure in this context. First, judicial review is only available where the local authority has exceeded its legal powers, where it has unreasonably exercised a discretion entrusted to it or where there has been a serious procedural impropriety.[1] The grounds of review are thus 'inappropriate for the review of cases of children in care'.[2] Second, judicial review under Order 53 is heard by judges who may not be as experienced in family and child care matters as the judges who hear wardship cases.[3] Third, the power of a court in proceedings for judicial review is limited to remitting the case to the local authority for reconsideration rather than having the power to make an immediate and specific order.

The improved legal position of parents in child care law, and the establishment of complaints procedures, may reduce the need for judicial review.[4] In addition, the courts may refuse jurisdiction unless the complaints procedure has been invoked, at least in relation to

---

20 See *R v Bedfordshire County Council ex p C, R v Hertfordshire County Council ex p B* [1987] 1 FLR 239; *R v North Yorkshire County Council, ex p M* [1989] 1 FLR 203.
1 *Council of Civil Service Unions v Minister for the Civil Service* [1985] AC 374.
2 Per Latey J in *R v London Borough of Newham, ex p McL* [1988] Fam Law 125.
3 Such applications may increasingly be heard by judges of the Family Division – per Woolf LJ in *Re D (a minor)* [1987] 3 All ER 717 at 732.
4 A decision to place a child on an 'at risk' register and the conduct of case conferences have been held to be judicially reviewable: *R v Bedfordshire County Council, ex p C, R v Hertfordshire County Council, ex p B* (above); *R v Norfolk County Council, ex p M* [1989] 2 All ER 359; *R v Harrow London Borough Council, ex p D* [1990] 1 FLR 79. As we have seen, these matters are not necessarily covered by the statutory complaints procedure, although official guidance has suggested that it would be good practice for them to be included within their scope (see above). A decision made without consulting a guardian ad litem may also be reviewable: see *R v North Yorkshire County Council, ex p M* (above). See also *R v Cornwall County Council, ex p Cornwall and Isles of Scilly guardians ad litem and Reporting Officers Panel* [1992] 1 WLR 427 (discussed above).

those issues within the scope of the procedure.[5] The qualified nature of the duties imposed on local authorities under the 1989 Act will also make it difficult to establish that the grounds for review exist: there will have to be evidence that a particular decision is unreasonable, or that there has been a serious failure to consult or to provide an opportunity to be heard.[6] In this respect, the volumes of official Guidance, which seek to lay down principles of good practice, may be relied on as evidence of unreasonableness in a particular case (DoH 1989, p 2).[7] It remains to be seen how the courts will react to applications for judicial review in the future (see Everall 1991).

5   *R v Chief Constable of Merseyside Police, ex p Calveley* [1986] QB 424; *R v Secretary of State for the Home Department, ex p Swati* [1986] 1 WLR 477.
6   See, for example, *R v East Sussex County Council, ex p R* [1991] 2 FLR 358, in which the parent failed to show that a local authority's decision to place a child on an 'at risk' register was either unfairly reached or unreasonable.
7   See, for example, *R v Cornwall County Council, ex p Cornwall and Isles of Scilly guardians ad litem and Reporting Officers Panel* [1992] 1 WLR 427 (discussed above) in which the court, in quashing the decision, referred to Volume 7 of Department of Health Guidance and Regulations on the 1989 Act.

Chapter 11
Social parenthood

Introduction

In Chapter 3 we identified a number of ways in which the law recognises someone as a parent. We considered there the position of parents identified by means of marriage and the presumption of legitimacy, biology, and by the rules governing the parentage of children born as a result of reproductive technologies. Anyone qualifying by these means will be a 'parent' for the purposes of the Children Act 1989 and hence will be entitled as of right to apply for the full range of s 8 orders.[1] In this chapter, we are concerned with a further type of link, which we have termed 'social parenthood'. The category of social parent includes foster parents, relatives and step-parents.

For present purposes, a 'social parent' is someone who has de facto care of a child but who cannot claim a legal link with it (that is, be accorded recognition for legal purposes as the person with parental responsibility) by any of the other means. Such a person will not count automatically as a 'parent' for Children Act purposes and will thus have to take some positive step to acquire parental responsibility for the child, and may not automatically be entitled to apply for all s 8 orders. Although a parent may arrange for some or all of his or her parental responsibility to be met by one or more persons acting on his or her behalf, this does not of itself confer parental responsibility on the de facto carer: this remains with the parent and cannot be surrendered.[2] However, a person with actual care of a child may do whatever is reasonable to safeguard or promote the child's welfare.[3] It is unclear how much authority this invests in a de facto carer, but it would not of itself entitle the carer to prevent the parent removing the child from their care.

---

1 CA 1989, s 10(4). Not all 'parents' automatically acquire parental responsibility: for example, an unmarried father must either (i) seek an order under CA 1989, s 4, (ii) enter into a parental responsibility agreement with the mother or (iii) obtain a s 8 order (see Ch 3 for further discussion).
2 CA 1989, s 2(9), (11).
3 CA 1989, s 3(5).

There are a number of ways in which a legal link between a social parent and a child may be established. In this chapter, we shall look particularly at the availability and effects of orders under the 1989 Act, and at adoption; but this does not exhaust the possibilities. For example, it would be possible for a social parent to invoke the wardship procedure as a way of obtaining legal recognition,[4] although the Children Act will reduce the need to rely on wardship for these purposes (see below and Ch 12). Another alternative would be guardianship, but the legal concept of guardianship does not require that the guardian act in any way as a social parent, either before or after appointment. For this (and other) reasons, guardianship has been considered separately in Chapter 3.

The degree of legal recognition accorded to a social parent will vary according to the means by which it has been granted. Thus, while adoption amounts to a complete and irrevocable transfer of exclusive parental responsibility to the adoptive parent,[5] other forms of order may transfer lesser rights and responsibilities.[6]

The legal recognition of social parenthood raises a number of important issues. First, how far should legal recognition of social parenthood extend? The answer to this may vary considerably according to the identity of the social parent in question. For example, it may be that we would want to regard the claims of a foster parent in a different light from those of, say, a relative or step-parent. The former may raise issues of the involvement of the state in the family (since, as we shall see, most foster parents will be acting as quasi-employees of local authorities) while the latter may raise issues concerning the 'distortion' of family relations. Second, should the recognition of social parenthood be based on an 'exclusive' model of parenthood, according to which a child would have only one legally recognised set of parents at a time; or should it be based on a more 'inclusive' model according to which other categories of parent might retain a degree of legal recognition?

The legal position of social parents

We will now consider the legal position of the different possible categories of social parent. In each case, the question is how far and

---

4 Eg, *J v C* [1970] AC 668 (private foster parents); *Re P (a minor)* [1990] 1 FLR 96 and *Re JK* [1991] 2 FLR 340 (local authority foster parents); *Re H (a minor)* [1991] 2 FLR 109 (maternal grandmother).
5 Adoption Act 1976, s 12 (as amended by the CA 1989).
6 For example, a residence order will confer parental responsibility on the person in whose favour it is made (CA 1989, s 12(2)), but responsibility will be shared with anyone else who already has it (CA 1989, s 2(5), (6)). Other s 8 orders do not confer parental responsibility on those in whose favour they are made.

in what form should a legal relationship with the child be recognised. The answers may not be the same in each case.

Before the 1989 Act, the means for resolving these issues were considered complex, inconsistent and confusing (Law Commission 1988, paras 4.25–4.49; see Dewar 1989, pp 318–328 for a discussion of the pre-1989 law). The Children Act 1989, which in this respect largely implements the Law Commission's proposals (1988, paras 4.29–4.49), now provides a coherent and unified means by which they may be resolved. In particular, the 1989 Act abolishes custodianship, which was introduced by the Children Act 1975 as a way of enabling certain categories of social parent to obtain 'legal custody' of a child.[7] The focus now is on the rules concerning the availability and effects of s 8 orders, especially residence orders (see further Chs 3 and 9). In defining eligibility for the new range of orders, the Law Commission's objective was 'to devise a unified scheme which is consistent and clear' while retaining sufficient flexibility 'to enable anyone with a genuine interest in the child's welfare to make applications relating to his upbringing' (1988, paras 4.33 and 4.41).

Three features of s 8 orders are especially important in this context. The first is that s 8 orders are available in all 'family proceedings' (which include applications for s 8 orders themselves) and may be made by a court of its own motion in any family proceedings.[8] The second is that the jurisdiction to make s 8 orders extends to *any* child in relation to whose welfare a question has arisen in family proceedings.[9] This gives the court a potentially wide jurisdiction. The third is that a residence order, if made, has the effect of conferring parental responsibility on the person in whose favour it is made for as long as the residence order is in force.[10] The residence order is therefore the primary means by which the legal status of non-parents may be recognised. In this context, the residence order performs a much more significant function than merely settling the practical arrangements for the child: it serves also as a status-conferring mechanism.

This is especially significant in the light of the new rules concerning eligibility to apply for s 8 orders (see Ch 3). At one level, the new

---

7 CA 1975, Part III, which was brought into force in 1985. Despite its short life-span, custodianship attracted criticism and was not much used: see Rowe et al (1984); Adcock and White (1985); Law Commission (1986), paras 5.15–5.28; Dewar (1989), pp 322–330; Hoggett and Pearl (1991), pp 632–635. The use of custodianship is discussed by Bullard (1991), who estimates that about 2,000 custodianship orders were made in total.

8 CA 1989, ss 8(3), (4), 10(1)(b).

9 CA 1989, s 10(1).

10 CA 1989, s 12(2).

rules rationalise and simplify the position and introduce greater flexibility; at another, they serve to provide a legal framework for ensuring as far as possible that children are brought up in private families rather than in state institutions. Primary responsibility is to rest with parents; but in the event of their failing in their responsibility, alternative means of providing for child care within 'the family' are now accorded clearer legal recognition (see Law Commission 1985, para 3.10; 1988, para 2.1).

Parental responsibility acquired under a residence order will be shared with anyone else (such as a parent) who already has it;[11] but in this case, either person may act independently of the other in meeting their parental responsibility provided that they do not act inconsistently with the terms of a court order.[12] In this way, the 1989 Act favours an 'inclusive' model of parenting in that a child may simultaneously have legal links with more than one set of 'parents'; the precise significance of this, however, is likely to turn on how the courts exercise their powers to make orders and to specify conditions attaching to any orders they may make (see Ch 9). Parental responsibility confers further entitlements under the statutory code. For example, anyone with parental responsibility is entitled to apply for all s 8 orders;[13] and a person with parental responsibility acquires a legal standing in relation to local authorities where the child is being accommodated or is in care,[14] and may be entitled to party status in any court proceedings.[15]

(a) Foster parents

Introduction

A foster parent is someone who undertakes to look after a child to which they are not related, either on a long- or short-term basis. Fostering is a well-established and integral part of local authority

---

11 CA 1989, s 2(5), (6). See Ch 9 for a discussion of this in the context of post-divorce arrangements between parents.

12 CA 1989, s 2(7), (8).

13 CA 1989, s 10(4)(b).

14 Eg, to remove a child from local authority accommodation (CA 1989, s 20(8)); to be consulted by a local authority before making any decision in relation to a child being looked after (CA 1989, s 22(4)(c)); to make use of the complaints procedure (CA 1989, s 26(3)(c)); to have contact with children in care where a residence order was in force in their favour immediately before the care order was made (CA 1989, s 34A(10(c)); and to apply for discharge of a care order (CA 1989, s 39(1)(a)).

15 See Ch 10.

child care practice, and a substantial minority (about 40%) of children in the care of local authorities are cared for in this way (DHSS 1982, Diagram One; on the development of fostering, see Packman 1981, Ch 2; Rowe 1983; Social Services Select Committee 1983–1984, paras 151–190; Hoggett and Pearl 1991, pp 622–629).

Foster parenting does not in itself confer any legal status on the foster parent. However, most fostering arrangements will be subject to regulation. Where the fostering placement has been arranged by a local authority in discharge of its duty to provide for children in its care,[16] the arrangement is subject to the Foster Placement (Children) Regulations 1991 (see Ch 10). These regulations are confined to dealing with the selection and duties of foster parents and with the supervision of the foster placement, and are not concerned to confer on the foster parents any legal status akin to parenthood. Apart from the provisions discussed in this chapter, the only entitlement of a foster parent will be to fostering allowances. Despite its close association with local authority child care practice, some fostering may be privately arranged and these arrangements may fall within the scope of Part IX of the Children Act 1989,[17] which requires notification to and supervision by a local authority of the fostering arrangement (see Priest 1986, pp 83–86; White, Carr and Lowe 1990, paras 14.11–14.19).[18]

The case for according foster parents a degree of legal recognition is that it safeguards the child's need for the maintenance of well established relationships, and offers the foster parents a security of expectation concerning the child. The case for legal recognition will thus become stronger the longer the fostering placement. It would also accord with the prevailing child care policy of planning for permanence wherever possible. However, where the fostering has been arranged by a local authority, it could be argued that to give the foster parents legal rights with respect to the child would not only restrict the local authority's discretion to act in what it considered to be the child's best interests, but would also make it more difficult for the child's natural parents to secure the child's return from accommodation. It could also discourage parents from using fostering or local authority accommodation in the first place.

---

16 CA 1989, s 23(1)(a).
17 See also the Children (Private Arrangements for Fostering) Regulations 1991.
18 For the statutory definitions of fostering, see CA 1989, s 23(3), (4) ('local authority foster parent') and s 66(1) CA 1989 ('privately fostered child'). Someone who is a parent of the child or who has parental responsibility for the child will not be a foster parent of it for statutory purposes. For the relevant guidance, see DoH (1991b, Chs 3–4 and 1991d).

Obtaining a legal status

There are a number of means by which a foster parent may acquire a legal status with respect to the child. The first is adoption (considered below), although many foster parents will have no·wish to adopt their foster children (Rowe et al 1984, Table 10). The second is a s 8 order. A foster parent will qualify as someone entitled to seek a residence or contact order (but not a specific issue or prohibited steps order) if they (i) have had the child living with them for at least three years[19] or (ii) have the consent of those with parental responsibility for the child.[20] If they do not qualify under either (i) or (ii), or if they wish to seek a specific issue or prohibited steps order, then they will have to seek leave of court (see Ch 3).[1]

The 1989 Act singles out local authority foster parents[2] for special treatment in this respect, since it prohibits them from applying for leave unless (a) they have the consent of the authority, (b) they are a relative of the child or (c) the child has lived with them for at least three years preceding the application.[3] The effect of this restriction is that anyone who is not entitled to seek a residence or contact order under (i) or (ii) above, or who wishes to obtain a specific issue or prohibited steps order, and who is not a relative of the child and who has had the child living with them for only a short time, will need both the local authority's permission and the leave of court before applying for an order. The purpose of the restriction, which was included against the advice of the Law Commission (1988, para 4.43), is

'. . . to prevent applications by foster parents at a stage when the local authority is still trying to assess what is best for the child in the long

19 CA 1989, s 10(5)(b).
20 Where there is a residence or a care order in force with respect to the child, then consent must be sought from the person in whose favour the residence order has been made or from the local authority with care of the child. If neither of these two orders is in force, then consent must be obtained from each of those with parental responsibility: CA 1989, s 10(5)(c).
1   CA 1989, s 10(2)(b), (9).
2   A 'local authority foster parent' is defined as any person with whom a child has been placed by a local authority in discharge of its duty to provide accommodation for children whom it is looking after under CA 1989, s 23 (2): see CA 1989, s 23(3).
3   CA 1989, s 9(3). The statutory definition of 'relative' is considered below. For the purposes of s 9(3), the child must have lived with the applicant 'for at last three years preceding the application', a period which need not be continuous but which must have begun not more than five years before the application (s 9(4)); the relevant definition for the purposes of s 10(5)(b) (which defines entitlement to apply for residence and contact orders) is similar, except that the three-year period must not have ended more than three months before the application (s 10(10)). A foster parent who satisfies the three-year requirement will not require leave for a residence or contact order, but will require leave for a prohibited steps or specific issue order.
4   CA 1989, s 9(1), 91(1).

term and also so that parents will not be deterred from asking for their child to be accommodated with a local authority foster parent if the need arises.' (DoH 1991, para 2.45)

It should also be remembered that once a child is in care, a court may only make a residence order which, if made, will have the effect of discharging the care order.[4]

Wardship remains a theoretical means by which a foster parent may obtain some security with respect to the child;[5] but given that residence and contact orders are now available to qualifying foster parents in the lower courts, and that specific issue and prohibited steps orders may be obtained if the leave hurdle can be overcome, there may be little to be gained in future from invoking the expensive wardship jurisdiction. Nevertheless, the High Court's power to resolve issues of residence[6] presumably remains, and it is conceivable that foster parents may seek to invoke the inherent powers in order to escape the limitations as to eligibility to apply for s 8 orders imposed by the statutory code. It remains to be seen how the High Court will respond to requests of this sort. It seems unlikely that it would apply more generous criteria than those that apply to granting leave under the 1989 Act: but it is conceivable that there may be cases in which adhering rigorously to the statutory leave criteria could endanger a child's welfare. Wardship may therefore continue to have a limited 'safety net' role.

Where a child is in care, it should be remembered that the courts are specifically prohibited from making a child who is in care a ward of court;[7] but there is nothing to prevent a foster parent from seeking to invoke the wider inherent jurisdiction to challenge a particular decision reached by a local authority. It remains to be seen whether the courts will accept jurisdiction in such cases given that the statutory scheme is against court interference where a child is in care (especially by foster parents)[8] and that foster parents are entitled to make use of the statutory complaints procedure.[9]

The likely effect of the Children Act on the use of the wardship and the inherent jurisdiction is considered further in Chapter 12.

(b) Relatives

Circumstances may arise in which the care of children has been entrusted on a short- or long-term basis to relatives of the child, such

5 See, for example, *J v C* [1970] AC 668; *Re P (a minor)* [1990] 1 FLR 96; *Re JK* [1991] 2 FLR 340.
6 See Ch 12.
7 CA 1989, s 100(2)(c).
8 Eg, CA 1989, s 9(1).
9 CA 1989, s 26(3)(d): see Ch 10.

as grandparents or aunts and uncles. The case for recognising the legal status of relatives rests on the same basis as for foster parents, that is, the protection of well-established relationships. However, there is the additional factor that the de facto care-giver is already related to the child in some way, which may raise the problem that treating the relative as parent may serve to create a distorted parent–child relationship. In such cases, the argument for a more 'inclusive' legal notion of parenthood, in which the natural parents (if they wish to) may retain a role, becomes stronger.

The claims of relatives will most likely be heard by means of s 8 orders. In this respect, relatives are in the same legal position as foster parents except that the requirement of local authority consent, as a precondition of seeking leave to apply for a s 8 order, does not apply.[10] It remains to be seen whether relatives will make use of s 8 orders. Although there were various means under the old law by which relatives could obtain custody of a child, the evidence suggested that relatives rarely made use of them (Douglas and Lowe 1989; Kaganas and Piper 1990). This has been explained by the fact that 'few [relatives] would be anxious to take the speculative and sometimes costly step of litigation without a very good reason, nor would those who required it be granted legal aid unless they could demonstrate that there were reasonable grounds for the action' (Law Commission 1986, para 5.38).

It has also been suggested that solicitors often advise relatives against taking legal action and that those involved in assisting the parties to resolve disputes (especially conciliators) are sceptical of the value of formal legal orders as a way of resolving issues of contact with relatives (Kaganas and Piper 1990, pp 43–48). Similar restraining factors may continue to operate under the new law. A formal order was found to be more likely under the old law where the grandparents had fallen out with the parents, or where the parents were unfit (Priest and Whybrow 1986, paras 7.2–7.5). In addition, relatives, and especially grandparents, seem to be excluded from the process of consultation that precedes the preparation of a Divorce Court Welfare Officer's report (McCarthy and Simpson 1990).

Relatives could continue to make use of the wardship jurisdiction,[11] although the points made above about the likely future role of wardship would also apply in this context. It is presumably still official policy to discourage adoption by relatives, as evidenced by

---

10 Either because the relatives will not be 'local authority foster parents' (see above) or, if they are, because the leave restrictions do not apply to 'local authority foster parents' who are relatives of the child: CA 1989, s 9(3)(b). A 'relative' is defined as a grandparent, brother, sister, uncle or aunt (whether of the full blood or the half blood or by affinity) or step-parent: CA 1989, s 105(1).

11 As, for example, in *Re H (a minor)* [1991] 2 FLR 109.

the introduction of custodianship (Houghton 1972, paras 116ff); but the provisions requiring a court in certain circumstances to treat an adoption application by relatives as an application for custodianship[12] have been repealed along with the concept of custodianship itself. The matter would now fall to be dealt with under the welfare principle alone,[13] bearing in mind that an adoption application is itself a 'family proceeding'[14] so that the full menu of s 8 orders would be available. We will return below to the question of adoption by relatives.

(c) Step-parents

There are a number of reasons why children may come to live in a household in which one of the adults is not his or her 'natural' parent. The most obvious are divorce, separation and death accompanied by either remarriage or cohabitation by the custodial parent with a new partner. Here again there are a number of different interests to be considered, such as the claim of the non-custodial parent to retain some form of legal link with the children and the claims of the children to retain links with the absent parent. It may be that the case for an inclusive concept of social parenthood is at its strongest here, although the custodial parent and new partner may feel that this prevents the new family achieving a degree of 'normality'.[15] Disputes may thus surface indirectly over, for example, the surname by which a child is to be known.[16]

A step-parent may acquire legal status in relation to a child in a variety of ways. The most controversial of these is adoption. As we shall see, it has been official policy to discourage step-parent adoptions, although the Children Act has removed the alternative of custodianship as well as the provisions requiring a court hearing

---

12 CA 1975, s 37(1). For a brief summary of the shortcomings of this provision, see Dewar (1989), pp 328–330.
13 Although there would be competing formulations of it: CA 1989, s 1(1) ('paramount consideration') and s 6 AA 1976 ('first consideration'). This is discussed further below in the context of adoption.
14 CA 1989, s 8(4)(d).
15 Studies of step-families have found a widespread desire to achieve the appearance of normality, although this is not always possible: see Burgoyne and Clarke (1984); Clulow (1991), pp 182–185. For a useful summary of research on 'post-divorce' step-families, see Maidment (1984), pp 224–229; and see the materials assembled in Hoggett and Pearl (1991), at pp 555–566.
16 Where a residence order is in force with respect to a child, no person may cause the child to be known by a new surname without either the written consent of every person with parental responsibility or the leave of court: CA 1989, s 13(1). See *W v A* [1981] Fam 14.

an adoption application to refuse the application if the matter would be better dealt with by means of custody (now residence and parental responsibility).[17] As with adoption applications made by relatives, the choice between an adoption or a residence order would now fall to be dealt with under the welfare principle alone.[18]

The alternative to adoption is a residence order, for which a step-parent may be eligible to apply. The 1989 Act has substantially simplified and, in effect, extended the eligibility requirements for s 8 orders as far as step-parents are concerned (for a discussion of the pre-1989 law, see Dewar 1989, pp 318–320). A step-parent may satisfy the eligibility requirements for residence and contact orders, already discussed in this chapter, if either the child has been living with the applicant for at least three years or if the relevant consents have been obtained.[19] In addition, any party to a marriage, whether or not subsisting, in relation to whom a child is a 'child of the family' may apply as of right for a residence or contact order either as an end in itself or by making an application in existing 'family proceedings' (for example, divorce proceedings).[20]

A 'child of the family' is defined as any child 'treated by both of those parties as a child of their family', which may include a child which is not the natural child of one of the parties.[1] To come within this formula, there must be a recognisable family to which both the child and the adults belong, as well as a marriage between the adult parties. Thus, to link a social parent to a child by means of this formula there must have been matrimonial cohabitation in a household in which the child is a fully accepted member. The test is an objective one and does not depend upon the expressed intention of the parties.[2] This formula applies to any children under 18,[3] but not to a child who has been placed with the parties as foster parents either by a local authority or a voluntary organisation.[4]

Despite the availability of residence orders, there may still be reasons why a step-parent would find adoption preferable. Although a residence order confers parental responsibility on the person in whose favour it is made (see above), it will not give a step-parent the

17 AA 1976, ss 14(3), 15(4) (now repealed).
18 See note 13, p 450, above.
19 A step-parent who does not satisfy these requirements, or who wishes to apply for a specific issue or prohibited steps order, will require leave of court: see Ch 3.
20 CA 1989, s 10(5)(a) CA.
1   CA 1989, s 105(1). The same definition applies to the powers of the court to make financial orders under the MCA 1973, DPMCA 1978 or under CA 1989, Sch 1: see CA 1989, Sch 1, para 16(2), and Sch 12 para 33.
2   *M v M* [1981] 2 FLR 39, CA; *D v D* [1981] 2 FLR 93, CA; *Teeling v Teeling* [1984] FLR 808, CA; *W v W* [1984] FLR 796, CA; *Carron v Carron* [1984] FLR 805, CA.
3   CA 1989, s 105(1) defines a 'child' as a person under the age of 18.
4   CA 1989, s 105(1).

power to appoint a guardian for the child[5] or to withhold consent to the child's adoption (see below); nor may the child succeed on the step-parent's intestacy. Further, a residence order does not remove all the rights of the natural parent, who continues to share parental responsibility.[6] Finally, a residence order imposes requirements of parental or court approval on a change in the child's surname and on the child's removal from the jurisdiction for more than a month.[7] For many step-parents, therefore, a residence order will be seen as less desirable than adoption. The question of step-parent adoptions is considered further below.

Adoption

Adoption is the most permanent and irrevocable means by which the ties of social parenthood may be recognised. An adoption order, which may be made only by a court under a statutory procedure, has the effect of extinguishing the parental responsibility of the child's natural parents,[8] and replacing them with a set of legal relations with the adoptive parents and the adopter's family that are almost entirely equivalent to those that the child had with the natural parents.

Legal adoption first became a possibility with the passage of the Adoption of Children Act 1926. Since then, the law and practice of adoption has changed considerably. The adoption process has become more professionalised and increasingly subject to the supervision of central and local government. Thus, whereas it was initially possible for parents or other private intermediaries to arrange for the child's placement with adopters, it is now the case that most private adoption placements are not allowed, and must be effected either through a government-approved adoption agency or a local authority acting as an adoption agency (see Packman 1981, pp 86–101).

Perceptions as to the possible uses of adoption have also changed from being a means of providing childless couples with children, most of whom would be illegitimate children of unmarried mothers, to being one of a range of possibilities for the substitute care of children in need. The number of illegitimate babies becoming available for adoption has decreased, owing to greater acceptance of

---

5 This power is confined to a *parent* with parental responsibility: CA 1989, s 5(3).
6 CA 1989, s 2(6).
7 CA 1989, s 13(1).
8 AA 1976, s 12(1).

unmarried parenthood and the wider availability of abortion and contraception (Houghton 1972, para 20); and adoption is increasingly seen as a way of providing permanent substitute homes for children with special needs and for older children who, perhaps, have spent a long time in care (DoH 1990, paras 1–6; 1991g, Part 1). This is reflected in statistical evidence, which suggests that while the annual number of adoptions has declined steadily, there has been a gradual shift towards adoption of older children.[9] Adoption is also widely, and more controversially, used within families, for example by step-parents or relatives (see below). The growth in the adoption of older and special needs children, as well as the widespread use of adoption within a family, have been said to be 'indicative of a trend towards adoptions in which the "total transplant" concept of adoption is not necessarily appropriate' (DoH 1990, para 6). This is one of the issues addressed in the Interdepartmental Review of Adoption Law established by the Department of Health, whose proposals for a move towards more 'open' adoption are considered at the end of this chapter.

Adoption has also become increasingly integrated into the child care policies and programmes of local authorities (see Hoggett and Pearl 1987, pp 601–606). This is associated with the two major developments of child care policy noted in the previous chapter; that is, a shift towards a recognition of social parenthood in preference to the 'blood tie' (see Fox 1982), and an emphasis on permanence in the planning of a child's future, with which adoption has become closely associated (Social Services Select Committee 1983/4, paras 191–198; Adcock 1984). This is evidenced by the fact that despite a decline in the annual number of adoptions, the number of children adopted from care grows steadily each year.[10]

Many of these features of modern adoption stem from the Children Act 1975, which introduced several modifications to the previous law, designed to 'give far greater control to local authorities over the lives of children in their care, to allow for an easier severance of parental ties and give greater security to children in their substitute

---

9 Between 1974 and 1989, the total number of adoptions fell from 22,502 to 7,044; over the same period, the proportion of all adoptions involving babies aged under one fell from 23% to 16%, while the equivalent proportions for adoptions involving children aged between 10 and 17 rose from 17% to 26%: Department of Health (1991g), Tables 1 and 2.

10 In 1979, there were 1,488 children adopted from care; in 1989, there were 2,411. Over the same period, the total number of adoptions fell from 10,870 to 7,044: see the *Second Report to Parliament on the Children Act 1975* (1984), Tables A and C; DoH (1991g), Tables 1 and 3. Only a small proportion of children in care are placed for adoption, although the proportion has grown from 1.4% in the year ending in March 1987 to 2.6% in the year ending in March 1990: DoH (1991g), para 9.

homes' (Parton 1985, p 116). In particular, the Act imposed a ban on private adoption placements, imposed a duty on local authorities to provide an adoption service, introduced the 'freeing' procedure under which children could be made more easily available for adoption, extended the grounds for dispensing with parental consent, imposed restrictions on the removal of children from prospective adopters once the adoption application had been made, and introduced adoption allowances.

Although these provisions have been introduced in a piecemeal fashion (and some only very recently), their overall purpose is to encourage the use of adoption as part of a well-supervised and integrated child care service (see Houghton 1973, paras 33–36). However, it may be that a side-effect of these changes, when combined with a growing philosophy of 'permanence', has been to '[encourage] social workers to look for potential adoptive families earlier and so [discourage] whole-hearted and persistent efforts to rehabilitate a child with his natural family' (Social Services Select Committee 1983/4, para 193). This is in turn associated with an increasing tendency to pursue adoption against the wishes of the natural parents, and thus to place greater reliance on the provisions for dispensing with parental consent (Rowe et al 1984, p 23). Although the Children Act 1989 does not deal in any detail with the law of adoption, it may nevertheless be that the emphasis now placed by that Act on cooperation with, and involvement of, parents will lead to a change in the way adoption is viewed by local authorities. The 1989 Act itself makes some changes to adoption law, but most are consequential on changes made by the 1989 Act to child care law. The most important substantive change is that it is now more difficult for a local authority to 'free' a child for adoption where the child is not in the care of the authority (see below).

The adoption legislation (as amended by the 1989 Act) is consolidated in the Adoption Act 1976,[11] and all references are to that statute.

(a) Adoption services

As we have seen, it is one of the purposes of modern adoption law to create the framework for a well-supervised and integrated adoption service. For this reason, the 1976 Act imposes on each local authority a duty to maintain an adoption service, either by acting itself as an adoption agency, or by ensuring that a service is provided by a

---

11 Children Act 1975 and Adoption Act 1976 (Commencement No 2) Order 1987, SI 1987/1242.

voluntary adoption society which has been approved by the Secretary of State in accordance with the provisions of the Act.[12] The service should 'meet the needs in relation to adoption' of children who have been or may be adopted, of parents and guardians of such children, and of persons who have adopted or may adopt.[13] This will include, but is not confined to, making arrangements for the assessment of children and prospective adopters, placing children for adoption and providing counselling for persons (including children) with problems in relation to adoption.[14] The local authority should ensure that the service is provided in conjunction with the authority's other social services, particularly those relating to the care and supervision of children, and with other adoption organisations.[15]

A body providing such a service, whether it is a local authority or an approved voluntary adoption society, is known as an 'adoption agency'.[16] In reaching any decision relating to the adoption of a child, an agency shall have regard to all the circumstances, giving 'first consideration' to the need to safeguard and promote the child's welfare throughout his childhood, and so far as practicable ascertain the wishes and feelings of the child regarding the decision and give due weight to them.[17] It should be noted that the child's welfare is not to be regarded as the 'paramount' consideration (as it is under s 1(1) of the Children Act 1989). The difference is explained by the fact that there are other interests at stake in adoption, such as those of the natural parents, which deserve consideration. The precise duties of adoption agencies are further specified by the Adoption Agencies Regulations 1983. These spell out the duties of adoption agencies to the child, its parents and the adopters, which include the maintenance of case records, provision of information concerning the adoption procedures to those involved, and of counselling services. The regulations also specify the procedures for adoption placements (see below).

---

12 AA 1976, s 1; procedures for the approval of adoption societies are contained in AA 1976, ss 3, 5, 8 and 9.

13 AA 1976, s 1(1).

14 AA 1976, s 1(2). See also Local Authority Circular LAC (87)8 and DoH (1991g), Parts 4 and 5 for discussion.

15 AA 1976, s 1(3), (4) and 2.

16 AA 1976, s 1(4). The CA 1989 has harmonised the law of the United Kingdom and Northern Ireland in this respect so that, for example, approved Scottish and Northern Irish adoption societies may operate in England and Wales: CA 1989, Sch 10, para 2.

17 AA 1976, s 6.

(b) Placement

(i) Private placements

The purpose of the elaborate rules concerning adoption services and their supervision is to ensure that children are given the greatest chance that the placement will be successful. This objective would be undermined if it were possible for private individuals, who may have no experience of adoption, to arrange for the placement of children with prospective adopters (see Houghton 1972, para 88). Accordingly, it is an offence punishable by fine or imprisonment for any person other than an adoption agency to make arrangements for the adoption of a child, unless the proposed adopter is a relative[18] of the child or the person making the arrangement is acting in pursuance of an order of the High Court.[19] The second of these two exceptions is unlikely to be of much significance; and the significance of the first will depend on how far relatives will be persuaded against adoption by the availability of residence orders.

Of greater significance is the fact that there is nothing to prevent a private individual arranging a foster placement and the foster parents later applying to adopt, provided that the arrangement was not initially intended as an adoption placement and that the rules for eligibility (discussed below) are complied with:

'. . . it would not be in the interests of the child to deny him the opportunity of adoption where, with the passage of time and changes in circumstances, carers find themselves fulfilling the role of parent and a child has come to look upon the carer as parent.' (DoH 1991g, para 20)

However, the legislation here imposes a requirement that the applicant give three months' notice to the local authority of an intention to apply for adoption, and, once notified, the authority is obliged to investigate and prepare a report for the court.[20] Notice must be given within the two years preceding the application.[1] Once notice has been given, the child becomes a 'protected child' and the local authority is obliged to visit the child 'from time to time' and satisfy itself of the well-being of the child.[2] If it is not satisfied, it may make use of its emergency powers under the 1989 Act (see Ch 10). A child ceases to be 'protected' if no adoption application is made

---

18 Defined in AA 1976, s 72(1) as a grandparent, sibling, aunt or uncle, whether of the full- or half-blood; an unmarried father; and where the child is born to unmarried parents, anyone who would be a relative within the above definition if the child had been born to parents who were married.
19 AA 1976, s 11.
20 AA 1976, s 22.
1 AA 1976, s 22(1A) (inserted by CA 1989, Sch 10, para 10(1)).
2 AA 1976, s 32, 33.

within two years of notice of an intention to make an application being given.[3]

It may emerge from the local authority's investigation that the child was placed in breach of the criminal prohibition, in which case criminal proceedings may ensue. The court hearing the criminal case may have the power[4] under the 1989 Act to order a local authority investigation into the child's circumstances[5] with a view to the authority seeking a care or supervision order, but a conviction will not prevent an adoption order being made by the court hearing the adoption application. If no investigation is ordered, or the authority does not seek a care or supervision order, it is unclear what steps a court dealing with the adoption application should take in the event of a conviction. It has been argued that 'the legislation fails satisfactorily to resolve the conflict between the assertion of the general principle that private placements are unsatisfactory and the need to accept that a particular private placement may well be very much in the child's interests' (Cretney 1984, p 430).

As we saw in Chapter 3, it is a common element of a surrogacy arrangement that the commissioning parents apply to adopt the child once it has been given to them by the surrogate mother. This amounts to a private placement, although it may fall within the exception accorded to relatives where the husband of the commissioning couple is the genetic father of the child (for discussion, see Wright 1986). Such an arrangement potentially also falls foul of the prohibition on making or giving any payment or reward for or in consideration of the adoption or arrangements for it,[6] since most surrogacy arrangements will involve payment to the surrogate mother. It has been held, however, that payments to surrogate mothers do not amount to 'payment or reward' within the Act, and that even if they did it would be open to the court to authorise such payments retroactively where the adoption was clearly in the child's interests.[7] In any case, the significance of adoption in this context is now diminished following the introduction of the procedure contained in Human Fertilisation and Embryology Act 1990, s 30, discussed in Chapter 3.

3 CA 1989, s 32(4). The same subsection sets out a number of other ways in which 'protection' will cease.
4 It is unclear whether criminal proceedings under the 1976 Act amount to 'family proceedings' for Children Act purposes.
5 CA 1989, s 37. See Ch 10.
6 AA 1976, s 57(1). Contravention of this prohibition prevents a court from making an adoption order: AA 1976, s 24(2).
7 AA 1976, s 57 (3); *Re Adoption Application (adoption: payment)* [1987] 2 All ER 826; see also *Re A (adoption placement)* [1988] Fam Law 293; *Re Adoption Application 113/67* (1988) FCR 723 (adoption arranged abroad for a fee).

Where an application is made to adopt a child placed independently, the local authority to whom notice was given is obliged to prepare a report to assist the court in making a decision on the application.[8] The contents of this report are the same as those required of adoption agencies where the application relates to a child placed by the agency, and are discussed further below.

(ii) Agency placements

Given the prohibition on non-agency placements, most placements will be arranged through an adoption agency. Such placements will either be by a local authority (acting as an adoption agency) of children already in compulsory care, or by an adoption agency (whether a local authority or approved voluntary body) of children whose parents have approached the agency wishing to have their child adopted. Adoptions by foster-parents or relatives, where the child was not placed by an agency, will come within the notification and reporting provisions discussed above.

Before placing a child for adoption, an agency must refer the proposed placement to an 'adoption panel',[9] which is a body composed of agency employees and independent persons,[10] together with a written report on the proposal and any other relevant information. The agency's report will be based largely on the information it is obliged to collect under the Adoption Agencies Regulations 1983 concerning the child, its parents and the prospective adopters. The function of the panel is to make recommendations to the agency as to whether adoption is in the best interests of the child and, if it is, whether a 'freeing' application (see below) should be made in respect of the child; and whether a prospective adopter is suitable to be an adoptive parent either generally or in relation to the child in question.[11]

The agency must wait for the panel's recommendation before making a decision on any of these matters. If it decides that adoption is in the child's best interests, that the child should be freed for adoption, or that a prospective adopter is suitable to be an adoptive parent either generally or in relation to the particular child, it must inform the child's parents or the prospective adopter as soon as possible.[12] If the agency decides to place a child with a particular adopter, it must inform the adopter, the child, the child's parents,

8 Adoption Rules 1984, r 22(2).
9 Adoption Agencies Regulations 1983, reg 9.
10 Ibid, reg 5.
11 Ibid, reg 10(1).
12 Ibid, reg 11.

and the health, education and local authorities. It must also ensure that the child is visited within one week of being placed and as often as considered necessary thereafter, and that written reports of such visits are maintained. If no application to adopt has been made within three months of the placement, the placement must be reviewed.[13]

Where an application is made to adopt a child placed by an agency, the agency is obliged to prepare a report for the court hearing the application.[14] The contents of the report are specified in Schedule 2 of the Adoption Rules 1984. These require particulars relating to the child, the parents or guardians, the prospective adopters, together with opinions concerning the desirability of adoption and conclusions on whether the order sought should be made.

(c) Restrictions on removing the child from prospective adopters[15]

Unless an adoption or freeing application has been made, the prospective adopter has no security with respect to the child, who may be removed by the person with parental responsibility. Further, an adoption agency may, in the case of an agency placement, remove the child from the prospective adopters having given notice of its intention to do so.[16] However, once an application to adopt has been made, to which the parents have consented, the parents cannot remove the child against the wishes of the applicant except by leave of court.[17] Once a freeing application has been made by an agency, a similar restriction arises except that it applies also to parents who have not agreed to the freeing application.[18] Similarly, an adoption agency may not remove a child from prospective adopters with whom the agency has placed the child once an application to adopt has been made without the leave of the court to which the application has been made.[19]

Where the child has had his home with the applicants for five years, and an application to adopt has been made or (in the case of a non-agency placement) the local authority have been notified of an

---

13 Adoptions Agencies Regulations 1983, reg 12.
14 AR 1984, r 22(1).
15 See DoH (1991g), Part 8.
16 AA 1976, s 30(1).
17 AA 1976, s 27(1).
18 AA 1976, s 27(2). In either case, the prospective adopters could agree to the child going back to the parents.
19 AA 1976, s 30(2); see *Re W (a minor)* [1990] 2 FLR 470 (decision of adoption agency to remove a child from prospective adopters not reviewable in wardship).

intention to adopt, the child cannot be removed against the applicant's will either by a parent (whether or not they have consented) or by a local authority with compulsory care of the child, except by the leave of the court.[20] This provision was designed to protect long-term foster parents who wished to adopt. In practice, it seems that it is 'relied on [by foster parents] . . . as a way of exerting pressure on social services to agree to an adoption plan or to speed up proceedings' and it '[gives] courage to them and to social workers in making approaches to natural parents in situations where it was feared they might resist adoption and seek to upset the fostering placement' (Rowe et al 1984, p 18; see also DoH 1991g, paras 153–155). Nevertheless, the provision does not seem to have led to a great increase in applications by foster parents to adopt (Rowe et al 1984, p 16). It has been suggested that the five-year period be reduced to three to mirror the qualifying period of three years for a residence or contact order under the Children Act 1989[1] (DoH 1991g, paras 22 and 152).

(d) Eligibility to adopt

The rules concerning eligibility to adopt 'make some attempt to reproduce a normal family structure' (Hoggett 1987, p 171). However, it should be noted that a person who satisfies these requirements is not entitled to adopt: there are still questions relating to parental consent, and before making an order the court must be satisfied, giving first consideration to the need to safeguard and promote the child's welfare, that adoption is the right course for the child.[2] Further, '[t]here is a distinction between the eligibility criteria laid down by statute and the criteria which agencies apply in assessing the suitability of people who would like to adopt' which can sometimes create 'a sense of unease and unfairness' among prospective adopters (DoH 1991g, paras 35–36; see also Part 3 generally, in which the possibility of specifying eligibility criteria more precisely in legislation or regulations is considered).

To be adopted, a child must be under 18 years of age.[3] Subject to one exception, the applicant(s) must be at least 21 years of age.[4] The

20 AA 1976, s 28. This section introduces an exception to the rule that a person with parental responsibility may remove a child from local authority accommodation at any time, since CA 1989, s 20(8) is expressly disapplied where the conditions in AA 1976, s 28 are met: AA 1976, s 28(2A).
1 CA 1989, s 10(5).
2 AA 1976, s 6.
3 AA 1976, s 72(1).
4 AA 1976, s 14(1A), 15(1).

exception is where the applicants are a married couple and one of the applicants is either the mother or father of the child. In this case, the child's mother or father need only have reached the age of 18 while the parent's spouse must be aged at least 21.[5] At least one of the applicants must be domiciled in the United Kingdom.[6] Joint applications may only be made by married couples.[7]

Sole applications are also possible, provided that the applicant is domiciled in the United Kingdom and has reached the age of 21.[8] If a sole applicant is married, the court must be satisfied that:

(i)   his spouse cannot be found; or
(ii) the spouses have separated and are living apart and the separation is likely to be permanent; or
(iii) that the spouse is incapable of making an application by reason of ill-health.[9]

The purpose here is to ensure that both adults in the adoptive home are in favour of the adoption. Where the sole applicant is the mother or father of the child, the court must be satisfied that either (i) the other natural parent is dead or cannot be found; or (ii) there is some other reason justifying the exclusion of the other natural parent. If an adoption order is made on the sole application of a mother or father, the court's reasons for doing so must be recorded.[10] The circumstances in which a natural parent may seek to adopt are considered below. The prohibition on single parent adoptions probably applies to an unmarried father whether he has parental responsibility or not, since in this context the Act uses the terms 'mother' and 'father' rather than the term 'parent';[11] and the reference in s 15(3)(a) to 'the *other* natural parent' suggests that the prohibition applies to all 'natural' rather than just marital parents.

Where the child has been placed by an adoption agency, the child must be at least 19 weeks old and must have had his home at all times with the applicants for the 13 weeks preceding the adoption order (but, note, not the adoption application[12]). The same period applies to applicants who are parents, step-parents or relatives of the child. In other cases, for example where there has been an

5   AA 1976, s 14(1B) (inserted by CA 1989, Sch 10, para 4).
6   AA 1976, ss 14(2).
7   AA 1976, s 14(1A).
8   AA 1976, ss 14(1), (2), 15(1), (2).
9   AA 1976, s 15(1).
10 AA 1976, s 15(3).
11 For the purposes of the AA 1976, the term 'parent' means a parent with parental responsibility: AA 1976, s 72(1).
12 See DoH (1991g), para 23, where a minimum period before an application is proposed. In the case of applications by step-parents and relatives, the Review suggests a qualifying period of more than 13 weeks: DoH (1991g), paras 26–33.

independent placement or where foster parents wish to adopt, the qualifying period is 12 months and the child must be at least 12 months old.[13] The purpose of this provision is to prevent 'the prohibition on private adoption placements [being] evaded by a placement ostensibly for private fostering' (DoH 1991g, para 20).

Many applications for adoption will be the result of an agency placement, and most placements will be with married couples unrelated to the child. These cases will present no problem of eligibility. However, there are three cases where the rules may give rise to some complexity.

(i) Natural parents

There are a number of circumstances in which a natural parent may wish to adopt their own child, although they may arise only rarely.[14] The first is where a parent wishes to adopt jointly with a new spouse. This would count as a step-parent adoption, and is discussed separately below. The second is where the parties are either separated or divorced (so that the prohibition on married sole applicants does not apply) and a parent makes a sole application. The motive here may be to exclude the other party from the child's life altogether. Unless the other parent cannot be found, the applicant will have to prove that there is a good reason to exclude the other parent by means of adoption; but since the court will also have to dispense with the other parent's consent[15] in order to make the adoption order, the two issues may come to be treated as one. In *Re C (a minor)*,[16] it was held that the burden is on the applicant parent to prove that reasons existed for excluding the other parent, and that it is only in exceptional circumstances that the burden would be discharged. It was not enough that the child had extremely strong and negative views concerning the father, or that the father had lost touch with the child since the divorce.

Finally, it may be that an unmarried mother or father may wish to adopt the child alone, although many of the possible reasons for doing so from the child's point of view have been removed by the improvements to the child's legal position effected by the FLRA 1987, now consolidated in the Children Act 1989 (see Ch 3). If the applicant simply wishes to exclude the other from the child's life,

---

13 AA 1976, s 13.
14 There are comparatively few adoptions granted to sole applicants: *Second Report to Parliament on the Children Act 1975* (1984), Table A.
15 A divorced spouse retains parental responsibility and is thus a 'parent' for the purposes of the 1976 Act (AA 1976, s 72(1)) whose consent must be obtained or dispensed with (see below).
16 [1986] Fam Law 360.

then he or she will have to show that there is a reason justifying the other parent's exclusion.[17] However, as we shall see below, an unmarried father is in a less strong position to oppose an adoption than a married one since his consent to an adoption is not required unless he has obtained parental responsibility under the Children Act 1989 (see Ch 3).

(ii) Relatives

We have seen that it is official policy to discourage adoptions by relatives.[18] This found expression in CA 1975, s 37(1) which required a court in certain circumstances to treat an application by relatives to adopt as an application for custodianship. As noted above, this provision has been repealed by the 1989 Act along with custodianship itself. Given that, owing partly to bad drafting and partly to judicial interpretation,[19] s 37(1) had in any case proved ineffective (Dewar 1989, pp 328–330), its repeal may make little difference, although there is some evidence that relatives were beginning to make greater use of the custodianship (DoH 1990, para 49).

Adoption proceedings are 'family proceedings' for the purposes of the Children Act, so that a court hearing an adoption application may grant a residence order instead of adoption either on application or of its own motion. Thus, residence orders have in effect replaced custodianship as the primary alternative to adoption. There is now, however, no directive to the courts to consider whether a residence order would be better than adoption: it is entirely a matter of applying the welfare principle. The question then arises as to which formulation of the welfare principle is relevant: the Children Act requires the court to treat the child's welfare as 'paramount',[20] whereas the Adoption Act merely requires the court to have regard 'to all the circumstances, first consideration being given to the need to safeguard and promote the welfare of the child throughout his childhood'[1] in considering any question relating to the adoption of a child (which would, presumably, include a decision not to grant an adoption order). Although some writers (eg, Bevan 1989, p 210) have suggested that the difference between the two tests is so fine that it would be simplest to adopt the 'paramount' formula, there may

---

17 AA 1976, s 15(3)(b).
18 Adoptions by relatives account for only a small proportion of all adoptions: DoH (1990), para 47.
19 Eg, *Re S (a minor)* [1987] Fam 98; *Re M* [1987] 2 All ER 88; *Re J (a minor)* [1987] 1 FLR 455; *Re A* [1987] 2 FLR 184; *Re W (a minor)* [1988] Fam Law 92.
20 CA 1989, s 1(1). The Children Act checklist in s 1(3) only applies in certain cases (eg, where a s 8 application is contested).
1 AA 1976, s 6.

nevertheless be some difference in the meanings of the two tests: while 'paramount' means that welfare outweighs all other considerations, 'first' means that it outweighs any other consideration.[2] Assuming that there is a difference in the tests, it has been asked why, '[i]f the rationale for having a different "welfare test" in adoption cases is the severance of family ties involved, is it logical for a court to apply one test when deciding whether to make the adoption order and another if it considers an additional or alternative order under the new s 8?' (DoH 1990, para 86). Official guidance, in explaining the absence of any directive to consider residence orders instead of adoption, appears to prefer the 'paramount' formulation in the Children Act: '[t]hese measures accord with the Children Act's intention of giving the courts a free hand to make whatever orders best serve the interests of the child' (DoH 1991e, para 1.14).

(iii) Step-parents

Applications by step-parents to adopt a child, whether as sole applicants or jointly with one of the parents of the child, may arise where the parents of the child are unmarried; where the parents have divorced; or where one of the parents has died; and, in each case, where one of the natural parents wishes to adopt together with a new partner (see Masson, Norbury and Chatterton 1983). Step-parent adoptions are considered undesirable in that the effect is to cut off all legal links with one of the children's natural parents and with that parent's family (Houghton 1972, paras 116ff; but see Masson et al, pp 49–50 who suggest that this concern may be unfounded).

This concern was manifested under the pre-1989 law by two provisions. The first, already discussed, required the courts to treat certain step-parent adoption applications as applications for custodianship; and the second which required a court to dismiss such an application if it considered that the matter could be better dealt with by an order for custody.[3] The 1989 Act repeals both these provisions. As we have seen, it is now official policy to allow the courts freedom to decide whether, according to the welfare principle (see above), to make an adoption order or a residence order without any statutory directive. The significance of this should not be overestimated, however, since, as we have seen, the custodianship provisions were not widely used; and the courts had restrictively

---

2 Per Lord Simon in *Re D* [1977] AC 602 at 638.
3 AA 1976, ss 14(3), 15(4). See DoH 1991g, paras 32–40 for a discussion of the effect of these provisions.

construed the statutory preference for a custody order.[4] There may nevertheless be room under the new law for differing views as to whether a court should consider a residence order before granting an adoption order.

For many step-families, adoption may be seen as the only way in which the family may be made 'normal' (see Burgoyne and Clark 1984; Masson et al, p 47): its purpose is to 'cement the family unit and put away the past' (DoH 1990, para 127). The alternative of a residence order is unlikely to be attractive since, as we have seen, this will mean that the step-parent will share parental responsibility with the absent natural parent. Thus, despite the policy of discouraging step-parent adoptions, they account (and seem likely to continue to account) for a significant, though declining, proportion of all adoptions. In 1983, just under 32% of all adoptions were by joint adopters one of whom was a parent. This compares with a figure of 43.5% for 1975.[5] The Interdepartmental Review raises again the question whether, in view of the differing circumstances in which applications by step-parents to adopt may arise (especially as to the quality of the child's links with the absent natural parent's family), step-parent adoptions should be prevented altogether; and whether there should be some lesser means of recognising the legal status of a step-parent, such as the automatic acquisition of parental responsibility through marriage to the natural parent (1990, paras 125–134).

(e) Parental consent[6]

An adoption order cannot be made unless the parent(s) or guardian(s) of the child give consent to the order,[7] except where either (i) parental consent has been dispensed with, or (ii) an order 'freeing' the child for adoption has been made (both discussed below). Consent, which must be to a specific application, must be given freely and unconditionally,[8] with full understanding of what is involved.[9] The consent will usually be in writing, evidence of which

4   *Re S* (1978) 9 Fam Law 88, CA; *Re D (minors) (adoption by step-parent)* (1980) 2 FLR 102; *Re P (minors) (adoption by step-parent)* [1988] FCR 401.
5   Table D, *Second Report to Parliament on the Children Act 1975* (1984); DoH (1991g), para 12 and Table 4.
6   See DoH (1991f), Part 1.
7   AA 1976, s 16(1). An unmarried father's consent is only required if he has acquired parental responsibility under the Children Act 1989: see below, and Ch 3.
8   Birth parents thus have no legally enforceable voice in the selection of the adopters: DoH (1991f), paras 4–11.
9   AA 1976, s 16(1)(b)(i).

may be produced;[10] but it may be withdrawn at any time up to the making of the order, subject to the court's power to dispense with consent. A mother cannot give a legally valid consent to adoption within six weeks of the birth of the child,[11] although where the child has been placed from birth with the applicants it may be that the mother will find it hard to change her mind in the light of the power to dispense with the need for consent.[12] When coupled with an application to adopt, parental agreement (even when only oral), will have the effect of bringing the restriction on removal of the child (above) into force.

It is the consent of the child's 'parent' or 'guardian' that is required. For these purposes, 'parent' means any parent with parental responsibility for the child[13] so that an unmarried father's consent will only be required if he has obtained parental responsibility. Thus, where an unmarried father wishes to challenge an adoption application, his best course is to seek parental responsibility.[14] If he does so by means of an application to court for a residence or parental responsibility order, then this application will be heard together with the adoption application,[15] the issue being determined according to the child's welfare (though, again, whether as the 'paramount' or merely 'first' consideration is unclear). The outcome of such proceedings will depend on the circumstances. Thus, where the adoption application is by non-relatives with whom the child has been placed since birth, it is unlikely that a court would refuse adoption and order residence or contact to the father;[16] but where the applicants are the mother and her new partner, the court may be more willing to resolve the issue either in terms of a residence order rather than adoption[17] or to make an adoption order subject to conditions of contact in favour of the father.[18] It may also be possible to make an adoption order coupled with a s 8 order for contact (see below).

10 See AR 1984, Sch 1, Form 7 for a standard form of agreement. Formal written evidence of agreement is not an essential precondition of a mother 'agreeing' for statutory purposes: *Re T (a minor)* [1986] Fam 160.
11 AA 1976, s 16(4).
12 *Re H (infants) (adoption: parental consent)* [1977] 2 All ER 339n, CA.
13 AA 1976, s 72(1). It does *not* mean anyone with parental responsibility.
14 Wardship may be another possibility (see, eg, *Re N*, below), but not if the child is in local authority care: CA 1989, s 100(2)(c).
15 *Re Adoption Application 41/61* [1962] 2 All ER 833.
16 *Re Adoption Application (No 2) 41/61* [1963] 2 All ER 1082; but see *Re C (MA) (an infant)* [1966] 1 All ER 838; and *Re N* [1990] 1 FLR 58, in which a father succeeded in wardship proceedings in preventing the adoption of his daughter and in obtaining reasonable access to her.
17 CA 1975, s 37(1).
18 *Re J (a minor) (adoption order: conditions)* [1973] 2 All ER 410; but see *Re E (P) (an infant)* [1969] 1 All ER 323, where adoption was ordered against the father's wishes in order to remove the 'stigma of bastardy'.

Even if an unmarried father is unsuccessful in obtaining a residence order, a parental responsibility order under s 4 of the 1989 Act in his favour may still have some value, for example where the child has been freed for adoption (on which, see below). Here, the father would retain a parent's residual right to receive progress reports on the child and to apply in certain circumstances to revoke the freeing order[19] in his capacity as a 'parent'.[20] Where the father has not sought parental responsibility (so that he is not a 'parent' for these purposes), he may still be involved in the adoption process in a number of ways. For example, an adoption agency is obliged to obtain various particulars of an unmarried father of a child where his identity is known,[1] and the agency is specifically required to ascertain whether he intends to apply for residence or parental responsibility.[2] In addition, a court must be satisfied before making a freeing order that the father has no intention of seeking a residence or parental responsibility order, or that if he did make such an application it would be refused.[3] This is a potentially powerful weapon in the hands of a father since, as we saw in Chapter 3, the courts seem willing to grant parental responsibility to the unmarried father even though it does not confer any immediately exercisable rights on him and despite the fact that it is likely that his consent to adoption will be dispensed with.[4]

If the father is contributing to the child's maintenance under either a court order or an agreement, he will be made respondent to the application and is entitled to be heard on its merits (but not to withhold his consent).[5] In any other case, he may be made a respondent by virtue of the court's general power to add as respondent anyone with an interest in the proceedings.[6]

(f) Dispensing with consent

The extent and effectiveness of the parental veto of adoption is considerably qualified by the power vested in the court to dispense with parental consent. In recent years, the courts have become

---

19 Under AA 1976, ss 19, 20: see *Re H (minors)(No 2)* [1991] 1 FLR 214. On revocation of freeing orders, see below.
20 Ie, a parent with parental responsibility: AA 1976, s 72(1).
1 There is no absolute requirement that the father be named in the application if he has not obtained parental responsibility: *Re L* [1991] 1 FLR 171.
2 AAR 1983, r 7(3).
3 AA 1976, s 18(7).
4 Eg, *Re H (No 2)* (above).
5 Adoption Rules 1984, r 15(2)(h).
6 AR 1984, r 15(3).

increasingly willing to dispense with consent[7] and this, together with the introduction of the 'freeing' procedure (below) and the growing importance attached to permanence in child care practice, may go some way towards explaining the growing use of adoption in the face of parental opposition. This is evidenced by the gradual but significant increase in the proportion of adoption applications which are contested by parents. Although some of these cases may be parents opposed to step-parent adoption, many will be parents attempting to challenge a local authority's decision to sever the parents' links with the children and to provide the child with a permanent future through adoption,[8] a policy which the authority may have been encouraged to pursue by the court's willingness to dispense with consent. The policy of the courts with respect to dispensation of agreement is thus an important factor influencing the use of adoption as a child care measure. The proportion of cases in which consent was dispensed with grew from 6% in 1979 to 11% in 1983.[9]

Consent may only be dispensed with on the grounds specified in Adoption Act 1976, s 16(2). This means that, in theory, dispensation is not simply a matter of determining where the child's interests lie. However, in relation to the most widely used ground, that the consent is being withheld unreasonably (below), the courts have at times come close to the position that there is no scope for a reasonable withholding of consent where the child's interests require adoption.[10] This substantially diminishes the protection accorded to parents through the insistence on proof of specified grounds; but more recently, the courts have tended to separate the issues of welfare from reasonableness.

The grounds are as follows.

(a) That the parent or guardian cannot be found or is incapable of giving agreement[11]

(b) That the parent or guardian is withholding his agreement unreasonably[12] This is the most widely used ground for dispensing with consent, accounting for about 45% of all cases in which consent

---

7   See the comments of Ormrod LJ in *Re H (infants) (adoption: parental consent)* [1977] 2 All ER 339n, CA and Rowe et al (1984), pp 23–24.
8   Research evidence suggests, however, that it is not always clear why a parent may be withholding consent. There are cases where the parent is reconciled to the child being adopted, but refuses to give formal consent 'because they do not want to be seen to be rejecting the child' (DoH 1991f, para 27: see also paras 28–30).
9   *Second Report to Parliament on the Children Act 1975* (1984), Table B.
10   But see *Re H; Re W (adoption: parental agreement)* (1983) 4 FLR 614 (below).
11   AA 1976, s 16(2)(a).
12   AA 1976, s 16(2)(b).

is dispensed with.[13] The widespread use of this ground has been attributed to the fact that adoption agencies 'may prefer to let both parents and child down lightly by selecting a ground which now rests heavily on the child's welfare rather than on parental misbehaviour' (DoH 1991f, para 36).

The current law under this head stems from the House of Lords' decision in *Re W (an infant)*[14] in which it was held that 'unreasonableness' is neither a question of parental culpability or indifference, nor simply one of the child's welfare.[15] Rather, it is a question of postulating whether the parent in question is acting as a reasonable parent would in all the circumstances. A reasonable parent is entitled to make a band of reasonable decisions, and will not reach a right or wrong answer in every set of circumstances, otherwise the court would simply be substituting its own views for those of the parents; however, in deciding what a reasonable parent would do, the court is entitled to take account of the requirements of the child's welfare, since a reasonable parent would regard this as relevant to the decision to grant or withhold consent. If a reasonable parent would regard it as decisive in a particular case, then it will be so regarded in determining the issue of reasonableness.[16] Reasonableness must be judged at the date of the hearing.[17]

The emphasis is on the totality of the circumstances, including the interests of the applicants, and each case will turn on its facts. Relevant factors might include the future for the child offered by the parents and adopters, the harm associated with removal of the child from an established setting, the risks of impermanence if adoption is not ordered and the past and likely future relationship between the parent and the child.[18] A justifiable sense of grievance about the way the case has been handled (eg where the authority has not attempted to rehabilitate the child with the birth parents) will not of itself make reasonable an otherwise unreasonable refusal of consent.[19] Nevertheless, a parent who has not been given an

13 This has only been the case since 1981, before which ground (a) was the most widely used – *Second Report to Parliament on the Children Act 1975* (1984), Table B.
14 [1971] AC 682, [1971] 2 All ER 49.
15 The welfare principle as formulated in AA 1976, s 6 applies only to decisions taken by agencies and the courts, not to parental decisions and thus has no relevance to dispensing with agreement under this head: *Re P (an infant)* [1977] Fam 25; *Re H; Re W (adoption: parental agreement)* (1983) 4 FLR 614; *Re E (a minor)* [1989] 1 FLR 126; further, the issues of reasonableness and the child's welfare must be decided separately and not treated as equivalent to each other: *Re D (a minor) (adoption: freeing order)* [1991] 1 FLR 48, per Butler-Sloss LJ.
16 *Re B (a minor)(adoption: parental agreement)* [1990] 2 FLR 383.
17 *Re L (a minor)(adoption: statutory criteria)* [1990] 1 FLR 305 at 309.
18 See, eg, *O'Connor v A and B* [1971] 2 All ER 1230; *Re S (an infant) (adoption: parental consent)* [1973] 3 All ER 88; *Re D (an infant) (parent's consent)* [1977] AC 602.
19 *Re B (a minor)(adoption: parental agreement)* [1990] 2 FLR 383.

opportunity to demonstrate the benefits of continued access as a consequence of a local authority's premature freeing application may be justified in withholding consent even though adoption may be in the child's best interests.[20] In this respect, the courts seem willing to police local authorities' use of their powers through their interpretation of reasonableness.

Despite the diversity of factors that may be relevant, it is possible to identify two types of case where the courts have adopted differing approaches. The first type of case, of which *Re W* was an example, is where the child has been placed with the applicants at birth following a decision by the mother to consent to an adoption which she later wishes to withdraw. Here, the courts have taken the view that once the child is placed with adopters and formal consent has been given, the more time that elapses before the mother seeks to withdraw consent, the greater the likelihood of her withdrawal of consent being regarded as unreasonable.[1]

A problem here is how far the court should take account of the individual circumstances of the mother. In *Re R (a minor) (adoption: parental consent)*,[2] the mother was 16 years old at the time of birth and gave her consent under what she later claimed to be duress from her parents. The county court judge had regarded this as relevant to the question of reasonableness, but on appeal the Court of Appeal regarded the matter from the objective point of view of the reasonable parent, and held that the welfare of the child and the interests of the adopters justified dispensing with her consent.[3] Given the restrictions on removal of a child from prospective adopters that apply once an adoption application has been made (see above), and given also the frequent delays in adoption applications being heard, it has been said that once a child has been placed with adopters 'the birth mother's chances of securing the child's return are slight' and that 'once agreement has been given for the child to be placed for adoption, assumptions of good practice undermine for all practical purposes the birth parents' legal rights' even where consent is subsequently withdrawn (DoH 1991f, paras 62–63).

The second type of case is where the parents have never consented to the adoption, for example, where the child is being adopted from care following a decision that rehabilitation with the natural parents is unlikely or undesirable. Here, the issue is not whether the child

20 *Re E (minors)(adoption: parental agreement)* [1990] 2 FLR 397: 'an injustice has been done to the mother . . . I would be unhappy if this court felt compelled, for whatever reason, to perpetuate an acknowledged injustice' (per Balcombe LJ at p 410).

1 *Re H (infants)(adoption: parental agreement)* [1977] 2 All ER 339n; *Re W (adoption: parental agreement)* (1981) 3 FLR 75, CA.

2 [1987] 1 FLR 391.

3 See also *Re V (a minor)(adoption: parental agreement)* [1987] 2 FLR 89.

should return to the parents, but the terms on which the child will remain in the substitute home. The courts' approach to such cases appears to have changed somewhat recently. Thus, while in cases like *Re F*[4] and *Re EL-G*[5] the issue of the child's welfare had become a dominant consideration so that adoption was ordered where the parent had had no contact with the child for some time and where the child had developed a strong bond with the foster parents, the emphasis in more recent cases has been on refusing adoption where there is or has been contact between the child and the parent and, more significantly, where there is the possibility that contact might successfully take place in the future.[6] Although it may be that these cases can all be explained as turning on their own facts, and particularly on the question of past, present or future contact, the Court of Appeal in *Re H; Re W*[7] made it clear that there is room for a reasonable withholding of consent even where the evidence suggests that adoption is in the child's interests.[8] However, it may be that such cases will in future be dealt with by an adoption order subject to a condition permitting contact with the birth family, or an adoption order coupled with a contact order under s 8 of the Children Act 1989, rather than a refusal of the adoption order altogether.[9]

Where the child is in local authority care, there is likely to be a close interrelation in the second type of case between the issue of dispensing with consent and that of parental contact with the child (discussed in Ch 10). One issue that arose under the pre-1989 law was the order in which the issues of parental access (now contact) and adoption should be dealt with: some courts had favoured adjourning the access proceedings until the outcome of the adoption application was known, while others had taken the opposite view.[10]

4　*Re F (a minor)(adoption: parental consent)* [1982] 1 All ER 321.
5　*Re EL-G (minors)(wardship and adoption)* (1983) 4 FLR 589, CA.
6　*Re H; Re W (adoption: parental agreement)* (1983) 4 FLR 614; *Re M (a minor) (adoption order: access)* [1986] 1 FLR 51; *Hampshire County Council v C* [1988] FCR 133, CA; *Re E (a minor)* [1989] 1 FLR 126 (contact with sibling). If the adopters are willing to permit post-adoption contact, this may add force to the arguments for an adoption order: see, eg, *Re B (a minor)(adoption: parental agreement)* [1990] 2 FLR 383, in which 'quite wonderful and selfless' adopters were prepared to permit contact with the natural parents and the court considered that contact would be more secure with an adoption order than without it.
7　Above.
8　See also *Re J (a minor)(wardship: adoption: custodianship)* [1987] 1 FLR 455; *Re B (a minor)(adoption)* [1988] Fam Law 172.
9　Eg, *Re C (a minor)(adoption order: conditions)* [1988] 1 All ER 705. See below, for a discussion of the courts' powers to make conditional orders and s 8 orders.
10　Compare *Re M (a minor)* [1985] Fam 60; *Southwark London Borough Council v H* [1985] 2 All ER 657 and *Re E (minors)* [1990] 2 FLR 397 with *R v Tower Hamlets Juvenile Court, ex p London Borough of Tower Hamlets* [1984] FLR 907, *Re PB (a minor)* [1985] FLR 394 and *C v Berkshire County Council* [1987] 2 FLR 210.

The new provisions concerning contact with children in care introduced by the Children Act 1989[11] will ensure that the issue of contact is dealt with at the time that the care order is made, rather than at the time that contact is terminated (as was the case under the pre-1989 law). If the parents do maintain contact with their child, this will make it more difficult to dispense with their consent; but, as we saw in Chapter 10, it is still possible under the new law for a local authority to apply for contact to be terminated. It remains to be seen how the courts will deal with such applications where the authority's plan for the child is to place it for adoption. In a recent decision, for example, the Court of Appeal has held that a court should be slow to make orders permitting parental contact where doing so would frustrate the authority's long-term plan for the child to be adopted.[12]

It has been said that the new general framework introduced by the 1989 Act will go some way to rectifying the problem that, except in wardship proceedings, 'there is no way that all disputed issues [such as contact, alternatives to adoption and conditional orders] can be resolved before it is too late'; but that, '[n]evertheless, the basic problem will remain, that birth parents' theoretical right to withhold agreement may be rendered worthless by the way in which the professionals have decided to handle the case' (DoH 1991f, para 78).

(c)   That the parent or guardian has persistently failed without reasonable cause to discharge the parental duties in relation to the child[13]   For these purposes, parental duties include those of showing affection towards and interest in the child, as well as the legal duties of maintenance and restraint from injury.[14] The failure must be culpable to a high degree and so grave that the child could gain no benefit through continued contact.[15] 'Persistent' means permanent, and would be evidenced by a parental failure over a long period of time.[16] Since the failure must be without 'reasonable cause', it is reasonable to assume that the circumstances giving rise to the adoption application would be relevant. Thus, a case where a child is placed for adoption out of care, having come into care as a result of parental neglect or abandonment, would more clearly come within this section than a case where the child was given to an agency by the mother, who then ceases to visit the child.

---

11 See Ch 10 at pp 415–417.
12 *Re S (a minor)(access application)* [1991] 1 FLR 161. Although decided under the old law, the reasoning in the case is equally applicable to the 1989 Act's provisions.
13 AA 1976, s 16(2)(c).
14 *Re P (infants)* [1962] 3 All ER 789.
15 *Re D (minors)(adoption by parent)* [1973] 3 All ER 1001.
16 Ibid.

(d) That the parent or guardian has abandoned or neglected the child[17]   This refers exclusively to criminal abandonment under s 27 of the Offences Against the Person Act 1861 or abandonment or neglect under CYPA 1933, s 1.[18]

(e) That the parent or guardian has persistently ill-treated the child[19]

(f) That the parent or guardian has seriously ill-treated the child[20]   Like the previous two grounds, this would appear to require evidence of criminal conduct. Under this head, the ill-treatment has to be serious, but not persistent, so that a single act would suffice; under the previous ground, it need only be persistent rather than serious. Grounds (d)–(f) will be particularly relevant to cases where the child is being adopted out of care, having come into care through parental abuse. Ground (f) will only apply if the rehabilitation of the child within the household of the parent or guardian is unlikely, whether because of the ill-treatment or for some other reason.[1]

(g) The 'freeing' procedure

(i) Introduction

Under the procedure described above, parental consent is given to a specific adoption application and, subject to the power to dispense with consent, must be operative at the time of the order and may be withdrawn at any time before then. The 'freeing procedure', which was introduced as part of the Children Act 1975 and implemented in 1984, enables the issue of parental consent to be dealt with prior to the hearing of an adoption application, and permits parents to give a general consent to adoption (or to have consent dispensed with) rather than in relation to a specific application.

The purpose of this procedure is two-fold. First, it avoids the period of uncertainty between the application and the order that is inevitable under the conventional procedure, and which is undesirable from the point of view of the parents, adopters and the child. Second, it enables a local authority to plan more positively for the child's future safe in the knowledge that the parents are out of the picture (Houghton 1972, paras 168–169, 221). These two objectives each rest on slightly differing views of the nature and purpose of adoption in that while the former assumes uncontested adoptions,

---

17 AA 1976, s 16(2)(d).
18 *Watson v Nickolaisen* [1955] 2 QB 286.
19 AA 1976, s 16(2)(e).
20 AA 1976, s 16(2)(f).
1   AA 1976, s 16(5).

the latter assumes that adoption will be used more as part of a child care strategy in which the agreement of the parents is not taken for granted. While at the time of the 1975 Children Act's passage the former purpose may have been uppermost, the latter may now be regarded as the most significant purpose of the new procedure (Adcock and White 1984).

(ii) The freeing application

A freeing application is made by an adoption agency, and may only be made with the consent of at least one of the child's parents or guardians.[2] If neither parent consents to the application, an application may only be made if the child is in the care of the agency making the application and if the agency is applying also to dispense with parental consent.[3] For these purposes, a child is not 'in care' if it is being accommodated by a local authority: there must be a care order.[4] This marks a change from the previous law under which a freeing application could be made in respect of a child in voluntary care. This change is attributable to the Children Act 1989[5] and is designed 'to enable parents to have confidence in the voluntary nature of "accommodation"' (DoH 1991e, para 1.18). It means that if a local authority (which is also an adoption agency) wishes to free for adoption a child it is accommodating, and the parents do not consent, it will first of all have to seek a care order or will have to apply to have the parents' consent dispensed with in the context of a specific adoption application. This has been criticised on the ground that '[n]either of these is entirely satisfactory: the former will result in increased delay and involvement in court procedure, the latter may result in a decreased pool of potential adopters, a placement breaking down because the application is not granted, or a reluctance in the local authority to pursue the course which it thinks would be in the child's best interests' (DoH 1991f, para 122).

Since the purpose of a freeing application is to deal with the issue of consent, the court must ensure that the consent requirements outlined above have been complied with. A court may only dispense with parental consent on the grounds set out above if the child is already placed for adoption or if the court is satisfied that it is likely that the child will be placed for adoption.[6] If the court makes the

---

2   AA 1976, s 18(2)(a).
3   AA 1976, s 18(2)(b).
4   AA 1976, s 18(2A). Research conducted under the old law showed that 33% of children who were the subject of freeing applications were in voluntary care: DoH (1991f), para 124.
5   CA 1989, Sch 10, para 6(1).
6   AA 1976, s 18(1)–(3).

order freeing the child, the effect is to vest all parental responsibility with respect to the child in the adoption agency, until either the child is adopted or the freeing order is revoked.[7]

(iii) Revocation

An application to revoke may be made by a parent or guardian at any time after 12 months since the making of the order, provided that the child has not been adopted or placed for adoption.[8] A parent is entitled to be informed of the child's position after 12 months, unless the parent has declared that s/he no longer wishes to be involved with the child.[9] Once an application for revocation has been made, the agency cannot place the child for adoption without the leave of the court.[10] In deciding whether to revoke the order, the court must have regard to the child's welfare as the first consideration.[11] The effect of revocation of a freeing order is to extinguish the adoption agency's parental responsibility and to give it to the child's mother and, if the father was married to the mother at the time of the child's birth, to the father.[12] In the case of unmarried fathers, revocation 'revives' any parental responsibility agreement or order under s 4 of the 1989 Act granting the father parental responsibility.[13] It will also revive the appointment of a guardian.[14] The revocation of a freeing order does not affect any person's parental responsibility so far as it relates to the period between the making and revocation of the freeing order.[15]

(iv) Freeing in practice

A number of problems with this procedure have emerged. The freeing procedure does not appear to be as speedy a means of resolving the consent issue as had been hoped (Bell 1988). One reason for this is that a decision to place a child for adoption may be coupled with additional proceedings regarding parental contact with children in care under the relevant sections of the Children Act 1989 (see above and Ch 10, pp 415–417), which may have the effect of slowing the freeing procedure down. Although it has been assumed

---

7   AA 1976, s 18(5).
8   AA 1976, s 20(1).
9   AA 1976, ss 18(6), 19.
10 AA 1976, s 19(2).
11 AA 1976, s 6.
12 AA 1976, s 20(3)(a), (b) (inserted by CA 1989, Sch 10, para 8(2)).
13 AA 1976, s 20(3)(c)(i), (ii).
14 AA 1976, s 20(3)(c)(iii).
15 AA 1976, s 20(3A).

that freeing applications will usually be made before the child is placed, this may make it difficult to make out a case for dispensing with parental consent where necessary since there will be no evidence of a successful placement as an alternative to parental care; further, a child that has been freed but whose placement has broken down will be in limbo (Adcock and White 1984). However, if an application is not made until after a placement, the uncertainty still remains for all parties until the freeing order is made.

More recent evidence[16] (summarised in DoH 1991f, paras 145–175) suggests that the procedure has met with mixed success. There are wide regional variations in its use, accounting on average for about a quarter of all adoption applications (ibid, paras 146–147). A high proportion are contested (para 138). One explanation for this is that where the parents do not intend to contest the application, and where prospective adopters have already been found, there is little point in going through two procedures (ie freeing followed by adoption) rather than one. The majority concern children adopted from care rather than young children (ie the second of the two objectives for the procedure identified by Houghton) (para 139) and freeing applications seem to be used in cases involving children with more complicated histories (paras 152–156). The advantages of the procedure were found to be that it enabled the local authority to settle its 'battle' with the parents, and so begin making a long-term plan, at an earlier stage than might be the case with an adoption application; and that it enables those parents who agree to adoption to withdraw at an early stage in the process. It is also popular with adopters, because the agency takes on the fight with the parents (paras 162–167). However, there is evidence of lengthy delays in the procedure, attributable to, amongst other things, the need to prepare and obtain reports, a shortage of Reporting Officers and guardians ad litem, and delays in court listings (paras 168–175).

The Interdepartmental Review of Adoption Law suggests that '[j]udged on the Houghton Committee's criteria, freeing has failed' (1991f, para 179): the procedure is rarely used for young babies voluntarily relinquished by their mothers for adoption, and the delays that seem to be endemic in the procedure prevent the realisation of many of the goals that Houghton wished to achieve. Its use in relation to children in care has arguably led to more contested applications. The Review thus leaves open the question of whether the procedure should be retained, while considering a number of changes that could be made to the procedure if it is to be retained (see paras 180–194).

16 See Lowe (1990); Lambert, Buist, Triseliotis and Hill (1989, 1990).

(h) **Procedure**[17]

(i) *The application*

An application to adopt is made by the prospective adopters. Application may be made to a High, county or magistrates' court,[18] although in practice most are made to the county court. Unless the child has been freed for adoption, the parents or guardian of the child must be made a respondent to the application, together with the adoption agency which placed the child or the local authority to whom notice of a private placement was given, any person liable to contribute to the maintenance of the child and anyone else the court chooses to add.[19] Where the applicant intends to request the court to dispense with the parent's consent, the application must be accompanied by a statement of the facts on which the applicant intends to rely in arguing for dispensation, copies of which must be sent to the parent or guardian.[20]

(ii) *Reporting Officer and guardian ad litem*

If it appears that the parents or guardian of the child are willing to agree to the adoption of the child, the court must as soon as possible after the application[1] has been made appoint a Reporting Officer in respect of the parent or guardian of the child.[2] The Reporting Officer's task is to verify that the requirements concerning parental consent, for example that it has been given freely, unconditionally and with full understanding, are satisfied. The officer must also make a report to the court drawing the court's attention to any matters which may be of assistance in considering the application.[3]

If, on the other hand, it appears that the parent or guardian is unwilling to give consent, the court must as soon as possible appoint a guardian ad litem. The guardian's task is to safeguard the interests of the child before the court by investigating and reporting on any relevant matters, particularly the matters covered in the agency or local authority report (see above) or the statement of facts to be relied upon for dispensing with consent. The guardian should also

---

17 See DoH (1991g), Parts 12–14.
18 AA 1976, s 62. Procedure in the High and county courts is governed by the Adoption Rules 1984; that in the magistrates' by the Magistrates' Courts (Adoption) Rules 1984. Since the two are substantially the same, reference here is to the Adoption Rules 1984 only.
19 AR 1984, r 4, 15.
20 AR 1984, r 19; the same rule applies to freeing applications, except that the particulars must be supplied by the applying agency – r 7 A.R 1984.
1   This includes an application for a freeing order.
2   AR 1984, r 17(1).
3   AR 1984, r 17(4).

advise on whether the child should attend the hearing and should perform any other duty considered necessary by the court.[4] The court also has the power to appoint a guardian ad litem wherever there are special circumstances and it appears to the court that the welfare of the child requires it, and the guardian's function will be to investigate any matter that the court directs.[5]

Reporting Officers and guardians must be independent of any agency or local authority which is respondent to the application, and must be appointed from a panel established for the purpose.[6] In the High Court, the role of guardian may be taken by the Official Solicitor.[7] Where parents or guardians do not agree between themselves on whether to give consent, or where they change their mind, so that both a Reporting Officer and guardian are required, the same person may perform both tasks.[8]

(iii) The hearing

The hearing is held in private. The child and the applicants must usually attend, and any person who is respondent to the application may attend. The court may require the attendance of any person if that is considered necessary.[9]

(iv) Making the order

Before making an adoption order, the court must first be satisfied that all the requirements for making an order have been complied with, for example, that the applicants are qualified and that the requisite consent has been given. The court must also be satisfied that an adoption order is appropriate in view of its duty to regard the child's welfare as the first consideration.[10] Where the court is requested to dispense with parental consent, it now appears to have been established (after some doubt on the matter) that the court should deal with the issue of dispensation at the same time as the issue of whether or not to make an order, rather than dealing with the two matters separately.[11]

In deciding whether to make the order (and, presumably, whether to dispense with consent) the court will have available the reports

---

4   AR 1984, r 18(6).
5   AR 1984, r 18(2).
6   Under the Guardian ad Litem and Reporting Officers (Panels) Regulations 1983.
7   AR 1984, r 18(4). The Official Solicitor will not usually act in uncontested cases: *Practice Direction* [1986] 1 WLR 933.
8   AR 1984, r 18(3).
9   AR 1984, r 23.
10 AA 1975, s 6.
11 *Re K (a minor) (adoption: procedure)* [1986] 1 FLR 295; *Re R (a minor) (adoption)* [1987] 1 FLR 391.

from the agency who placed the child or the local authority to whom notification of a private placement was given, and those of the Reporting Officer and/or the guardian ad litem. The factors relevant to the court's decision will include 'material and financial prospects, education, general surroundings, happiness, stability of home and the like'.[12] Specific factors will vary from case to case, but in every case the court is directed to give due consideration to the wishes and feelings of the child having regard to his age and understanding.[13]

(v) Powers of the court

If satisfied that adoption is the best course in the circumstances, the court may make the order. If it is not satisfied, then it may either:

(i)   make an interim order vesting parental responsibility for the child in the applicants for a probationary period of two years;[14]
(ii) refuse an order, in which case a child placed with the applicants by an agency must be returned to the agency within seven days;[15] or
(iii) make a residence or other s 8 order (see above).

Applicants who are refused an order are debarred from making a further adoption application unless the court making the refusal directs otherwise or there has been a change of circumstances making it reasonable to proceed.[16] The power that existed under the old law to make supervision or care orders in respect of the child on refusal of an adoption application[17] have been removed by the Children Act 1989[18] in line with the philosophy that there should be only one route into care or supervision, namely s 31 of the 1989 Act. A court may, however, direct a local authority investigation of the child's circumstances.[19]

The court also has the power to impose conditions on the adoption order relating, for example, to contact with the natural parent or relative.[20] However, the courts are generally reluctant to make such

---

12 Per Davies LJ in *Re B (an infant)* [1970] 3 All ER 1008 at 1012.
13 AA 1976, s 6.
14 AA 1976, s 25.
15 AA 1976, s 30(3).
16 AA 1976, s 24(1).
17 AA 1976, s 26.
18 CA 1989, s 108(7) and Sch 15.
19 CA 1989, s 37.
20 AA 1976, s 12(6). The power does not enable the court to add to the parental responsibilities of the adopters, for example, by granting an injunction restraining the birth family from contacting the child: *Re D (a minor)* [1991] 3 ALL ER 461 (disapproving *Re F (a minor) (adoption order: injunction)* [1990] 3 All ER 580). An injunction of this sort can only be obtained in wardship proceedings or, after the 1989 Act, under the inherent jurisdiction of the High Court.

conditions since they detract from the rights and duties of the adoptive parents in a way that is inconsistent with the nature of adoption.[1] In particular, contact and adoption would appear to be incompatible, since if the case is appropriate for a contact condition, it is probably an unsuitable case for adoption.[2] Nevertheless, there may be exceptional cases where, provided all the parties are agreed, a contact condition will be imposed. In *Re W (a minor)*[3] an access (as it then was) condition was granted in favour of the parents on an adoption application by the child's grandparents; and in *Re C (a minor)*,[4] the House of Lords approved an access condition in favour of the adopted child's brother. However, in view of the availability of the alternative of a residence order, it may be asked whether adoption was the appropriate course in either of these cases.

The same end may be achieved by making a contact order under the Children Act 1989, since adoption proceedings are (family proceedings). Although the effect of an adoption order is to extinguish any order made under the 1989 Act,[5] this arguably does not prevent a court from making a s 8 order at the same time as, or at any time after, an adoption order. Nevertheless, the considerations outlined above would apply equally in this context.[6]

(i) Effects of an order

An adoption order vests parental responsibility in the adopters prospectively from the date of the order, and extinguishes the parental responsibility which any person has for the child immediately before the making of the order.[7] An adopted child is treated as if it were the legitimate child of the adoptive parents and not the child of anyone other than the adopters;[8] but for certain purposes, such as entitlement to citizenship, for the rules concerning prohibited degrees of marriage and the law of incest, the child is regarded as a

---

1 *Re GR (adoption: access)* [1985] FLR 643; *Re C (a minor) (adoption order: condition)* [1986] 1 FLR 315, CA.
2 *Re V (a minor) (adoption: consent)* [1986] 1 All ER 752, [1987] 2 FLR 89.
3 [1988] Fam Law 92.
4 [1988] 1 All ER 705.
5 CA 1989, s 12(3)(aa).
6 See, for example, *Re R (a minor)* [1991] 2 FLR 78, in which it was held that, under the pre-1989 law, there was no power to hear an unmarried father's application for access once an unconditional adoption order had been made: 'To make an adoption order, and to leave over indefinitely a question as to access by the natural father, would be to invite unknown problems, and could not be considered consistent with a proper approach to the making of an adoption order' (per Sir Stephen Brown P), at p 84.
7 AA 1976, s 12.
8 AA 1976, s 39.

member of its natural family.[9] An adoption does not affect succession to peerages or other titles.[10] An adoption order is irrevocable, except where the child has been adopted by a single parent who subsequently marries the other parent so that the child is legitimated by operation of law.[11]

(j) Information about origins

An adoption is registered in the Adopted Children Register[12] and, on reaching the age of 18, the adopted person has the right to a copy of his or her original birth certificate.[13] Where the adoption order was made before 12 November 1975, the certificate will only be released after the adopted person has received counselling from either the General Register Office, the local authority in whose area the application is made or in whose area the original order was made, or from the adoption society who arranged the adoption. In every other case, the applicant is informed that such counselling is available.[14] It seems that only a minority of adopted persons make use of this provision (Triseliotis 1984; DoH 1990b, pp 18–19).

The Children Act 1989 establishes a new Adoption Contact Register, the purpose of which is to enable an adopted person to make contact with their birth parents or other relatives.[15] This potentially provides an adopted person with more information about their origins than merely their birth certificate. The Register is open only to adopted persons who are aged 18 or over. On an application by an adopted person, the Registrar General must pass on to the applicant any details that have been placed on the register by a relative. For these purposes, a relative is any person (other than an adoptive relation) who is related to the adopted person by blood or marriage.[16] The Registrar General may pass information contained in the register only to the adopted person. A relative, for example, cannot seek information about the adopted person. Thus, the decision to make contact is entirely for the adopted person and presupposes that he or she knows that s/he is adopted. It also depends on the relative concerned being willing to register his or her details.

9 AA 1976, ss 47–49. See Department of Health (1990), Part A, for discussion.
10 AA 1976, s 44(1).
11 AA 1976, s 52.
12 AA 1976, s 50.
13 AA 1976, s 51. This right is subject to public policy considerations. Thus, an inmate of Broadmoor who had murdered a fellow prisoner in the mistaken belief that the victim was his adoptive mother could be refused access to birth records on the grounds that there were reasons to fear for the safety of the applicant's natural mother: *R v Registrar General, ex p Smith* [1991] 1 FLR 255.
14 AA 1976, s 51(3), (4), (6).
15 AA 1976, s 51A (inserted by CA 1989, Sch 10, para 21).
16 AA 1976, s 51A(13)(a).

It has been suggested that these provisions could be extended so that, for example, a natural parent should be given the right to trace a child of theirs who has been adopted, or the right to refuse contact altogether; and, from the adopted person's point of view, that a procedure for tracing the addresses of birth parents should be introduced (see DoH 1990, para 81; 1991g, paras 93–97 and Part 10; for discussion, see Haimes 1988; O'Donovan 1989; Walby and Symons 1990). It has been said that 'this is altogether an area of great difficulty and sensitivity in which it barely seems possible that the needs and wishes of all the parties can be satisfactorily reconciled' (DoH 1991g, para 97).

(k) A new model for adoption?

In the light of evidence that adoption is increasingly used for older children who have some knowledge of their birth family, it has been suggested that the 'legal transplant' model of adoption is no longer appropriate and that there should be a move towards greater flexibility in adoption to take account of the wide range of circumstances in which it is now used. Amongst other things, this could mean that the child would retain some continuing and formal link with the birth family.

The Department of Health's Review of Adoption Law has recently canvassed three more flexible models for adoption (1990, Part E[17]).

Option A: the retention of the existing 'legal transplant' model, but with greater flexibility and emphasis on 'openness'. This could be achieved through greater emphasis on pre- and post-adoption contact between the child and its birth parents, for example by allowing the parents a greater say in the choice of adopters, by granting the parents a contact order under the 1989 Act and by giving birth parents a right to information about their child after the adoption. The retention of the 'legal transplant' model may also require a reintroduction of a duty on the courts to consider the alternatives to adoption, especially residence orders, before making an adoption order. The Review recognises that alternatives to adoption would need to be 'sold' to carers, since they could be considered unfamiliar and lacking the desired degree of security. The experience of custodianship suggests that, in part, it was the perception by applicants for adoption that custodianship was

---

17 See Graham Hall and Martin (1991), who suggest an intermediate form of order falling between full adoption on the one hand and a residence order on the other, which they term a 'dual family order'. This would amount, in effect, to a form of irrevocable residence order.

unfamiliar and an unknown quantity that may have accounted for its lack of popularity (Bullard 1991).

Option B: the introduction of two different types of irrevocable order, one of which would correspond to the current 'legal transplant' model of adoption, the other amounting to 'a simpler form which could be used whenever a less extreme result is desired' (para 115). This could be achieved, for example, by an irrevocable residence order, which would guarantee permanence to the carers while leaving the child's legal relationships with its birth family intact, possibly (though not necessarily) including the retention of parental responsibility by the birth parents. If this model were to be adopted, a number of questions would arise: when would the different types of order be appropriate and should this be enshrined in rules? To what extent should a limited form of order assimilate the child into the new family from a legal point of view (eg, in relation to emigration and changes of surname)? Would parental consent be required?

Option C: the replacement of adoption as currently understood with a basic form of adoption with a number of additional features that could be added on to suit individual circumstances. In this model, 'adoption' could mean anything from the equivalent of an irrevocable residence order with the birth parents retaining parental responsibility, to a full 'legal transplant' form of adoption, together with all possible variations in between. The additional features that could be added would include the severance of existing familial relationships and their transfer to the adopters and conditions as to contact with the birth family.

As we have seen in this chapter, there are a wide range of circumstances in which social parents may seek some legal status with respect to children, often through adoption, and a variety of circumstances in which adoption is used. It may be that it is no longer possible to embrace all these instances in one unitary concept of adoption. Two points arise, however: first, how far can adoption be made more flexible while still retaining the essential features of permanence and irrevocability that it is popularly thought to possess, and which seem to make it attractive? Second, assuming that 'adoption' retains broadly its current meaning, how vigorously should alternatives to adoption be pursued? As we have seen, the 1989 Act leaves residence orders as the main alternative and leaves the choice to be judged entirely according to the child's welfare; but we have also seen that, technically, the 1989 Act also permits a move towards greater 'openness' in adoption through the making of contact orders in conjunction with adoption orders. It may be wise to wait and see how these powers are used by the courts before making any further changes to the law.

Chapter 12
Wardship and the inherent jurisdiction

Introduction

(a) Historical development

Wardship is a means by which disputes involving the welfare of children may be referred speedily to a court for resolution. It is an inherent non-statutory jurisdiction that has its origins in the sovereign's prerogative as *parens patriae* to care for those who cannot care for themselves. This prerogative was originally an incident of the feudal system of tenure, and was thus closely associated with the management of property and so provided the Crown with a valuable source of revenue (Bevan 1989, para 8.01). The prerogative was delegated to the Court of Wards, then to the Court of Chancery and finally to the Family Division of the High Court.[1] Even though the emphasis of wardship had by the nineteenth century altered from the management of a ward's property to the care and protection of the ward's person,[2] it remained the case that, for procedural reasons, the jurisdiction could only be invoked in respect of wealthy children. These restrictions were removed in 1949,[3] with the effect that wardship became a jurisdiction potentially available with respect to any child.

The use of wardship has grown considerably since 1949 (see Parry 1990). In 1951 there were 74 applications to ward a child; in 1985, there were 2,815 (Lowe and White 1986, p 10). A number of explanations may be advanced for this (ibid, pp 9–12). Some of these are technical, such as the removal of the procedural limits on the jurisdiction in 1949, the availability of legal aid for wardship proceedings also in 1949, and the transfer of the jurisdiction to the

---

1 Administration of Justice Act 1970, s 1(2), Sch 1.
2 *R v Gyngall* [1893] 2 QB 232.
3 Law Reform (Miscellaneous Provisions) Act 1949, s 9; Supreme Court Act 1981, s 41, Sch 1, para 3(ii).

Family Division in 1971.[4] Some relate to changing perceptions of the usefulness of the jurisdiction, such as the growing use of wardship by local authorities to supplement or circumvent their statutory powers and by non-parents, who may otherwise have no means of acquiring legal security with respect to the child; and the growing mobility of the population with has led to a growth in 'kidnapping' cases for which wardship has proved useful. Wardship has also been increasingly used to resolve questions relating to the medical treatment of children (see below).

(b) The effect of the Children Act 1989

The Children Act 1989 will have a major impact on the use of wardship. Although the Act does not abolish the jurisdiction, it will affect it in three ways.

(a) As we saw in Chapter 10, the 1989 Act specifically prohibits the use of wardship as a means of placing a child in the care, or under the supervision, of a local authority.[5] Before the implementation of the 1989 Act, local authorities made significant use of the jurisdiction for this purpose (Masson and Morton 1989). The implications of the 1989 Act for local authorities has already been discussed in Chapter 10.

(b) By providing a more comprehensive statutory code for resolving issues relating to children, for example through more flexible eligibility rules and more flexible court orders, the 1989 Act will greatly reduce the need to invoke the jurisdiction at all. Those for whom wardship was previously the only means of acquiring a legal status in relation to the child, such as relatives, may now be able to apply as of right for residence or contact orders, and at the very least will be able to seek leave to apply for a s 8 order (see Ch 11). Those who wish to obtain a court order resolving a specific point of disagreement, or to prevent a parent taking a particular step in relation to a child, may now do so by using the appropriate s 8 order, provided that the matter in question relates to the exercise of parental reponsibility. The 1989 Act does not expressly prohibit the use of wardship for these purposes: it merely reduces the need to do so;

(c) The 1989 Act introduces, or clarifies, the distinction between wardship on the one hand and the inherent jursidiction of the High Court to act for the protection of children on the other. Wardship is

4 Certain matters in wardship may now be heard in the county court – Matrimonial and Family Proceedings Act 1984, s 37; *Practice Direction* (6 April 1988, unreported).
5 CA 1989, s 100(1), (2)(a), (b).

now seen as merely one means by which the broader inherent jurisdiction may be exercised (Mackay 1989, p 507). Although this inherent jurisdiction is not new, 'it has so far been little developed' (White, Carr and Lowe 1990, para 10.5). Its significance is that it confers jurisdiction on the High Court to hear and resolve questions about the upbringing of children without the full effects of wardship coming into operation. As we shall see, once wardship is invoked, it operates to vest parental responsibility for the warded child in the court itself and stipulates that no important step may be taken in relation to the child without the court's prior consent. The fact that this does not apply to the inherent jurisdiction removes what in the past may have been seen as a disadvantage of the wardship jurisdiction.

In this chapter, we will consider the legal characteristics of wardship and consider some examples of its uses. It will be assumed that, subject to the important differences just outlined, the inherent jurisdiction will operate in a similar way to wardship.

Legal aspects of wardship

(a) The effects of wardship

Wardship has been described as 'a system whereby any person may, by issuing proceedings for the purpose, make the High Court guardian of any child within its jurisdiction, with the result that (a) no important steps in the child's life can be taken without the court's leave, and (b) the court may make and enforce any order or direction consistent with the principle that the first and paramount consideration is the welfare of the child' (Law Commission 1987, para 2.2). Only the second of these would apply to the inherent jurisdiction; it is the first that is the distinctive feature of wardship. It should be noted that the court in wardship assumes control over the child immediately from the issue of the originating summons. Although the court is described as 'guardian', this is merely a way of describing a situation in which the court has control and supervision of the child, and may also be described as 'custody in the wide sense'.[6] Following the Children Act 1989, this would now be described as 'parental responsibility'. Actual care and control of the child (now residence) will be delegated, since the court cannot itself

---

6   *Re W (an infant)* [1963] 3 All ER 459; *Re E(SA) (a minor)(wardship)* [1984] 1 All ER 289.

literally care for the child. The court's control continues until the child is dewarded, the wardship lapses or the ward attains majority.

Although there is no precise definition of what counts as an 'important step' requiring the leave of the court, it would seem to include those matters that are comprised in parental responsibility. On this basis, it would include the following: marriage,[7] adoption,[8] removal from the jurisdiction,[9] change of education,[10] blood tests,[11] certain forms of non-therapeutic medical treatment, such as sterilisation or abortion,[12] and psychiatric or psychological examinations.[13] Failure to obtain leave before taking such steps will be a contempt of court. There remains, however, considerable uncertainty over what counts as an 'important step' and thus how far the automatic supervision of the court extends (Lowe and White 1986, pp 93–94).

(b) Which children may be warded?

The jurisdiction is available in respect of all[14] children under the age of 18 who are British subjects,[15] irrespective of place of birth, domicile or place of residence. It may thus be invoked in respect of children who are physically abroad, subject to the limitations imposed on such proceedings by the Child Abduction and Custody Act 1985 where an application has been made under that Act for the return of a child from abroad.[16] It is also available with respect to any alien child who is physically present within the jurisdiction at the time of the wardship application, and may extend to one, who though not physically present, is 'ordinarily resident' within the jurisdiction.[17] Following the Children Act 1989, an important limitation is that a child who is subject to a care order cannot be

7 This is explicitly stated in the Notice of Wardship (see Barnard 1983, p 132).
8 *Re F (wardship: adoption)* [1984] FLR 60.
9 *Practice Direction* [1986] 1 All ER 983.
10 See Notice of Wardship.
11 See Lowe and White (1986), pp 89–90.
12 *Re B (a minor)(sterilisation)* [1987] 2 All ER 206 (on which see de Cruz (1988)); *Re G-U (a minor)(wardship)* [1984] FLR 811. See further below.
13 *Re A-W (minors)* (1974) 5 Fam Law 95.
14 It is not available with respect to unborn children – *Re F (in utero)* (1988) 2 All ER 193, CA.
15 It is unclear whether the jurisdiction turns on the common law concept of nationality or the statutory concept of citizenship – see Lowe and White (1986), pp 19–21.
16 Child Abduction and Custody Act 1985, ss 9, 20, 27 and Sch 3.
17 *Re P (GE)(an infant)* [1965] Ch 568.

made a ward of court,[18] although a local authority may still invoke the inherent jurisdiction in such cases (see Ch 10 for discussion).

There are statutory limits on the court's powers to make orders in wardship proceedings for the care of a child or orders providing for contact with, or the education of, a child where either (i) the child is not habitually resident in England or Wales or is neither physically present in England and Wales nor habitually resident in Scotland or Northern Ireland or (ii) where there are divorce proceedings between the child's parents in either Scotland or Northern Ireland.[19] The purpose of these restrictions is to prevent conflicts arising between different jurisdictions within the United Kingdom, but the effect is to impose the restrictions even in cases where the child is not habitually resident or physically present in any of the United Kingdom jurisdictions and in which no possibility of conflict arises. These restrictions do not apply to other kinds of order, to which the ordinary jurisdictional rules apply; nor do they apply where the court considers that it should exercise its powers for the child's protection, in which case it is sufficient if the child is physically present in England and Wales[20] (see further Lowe and White (1986) Ch 2).

(c) Who may apply?

Although there are no formal rules concerning those who may invoke the jurisdiction, it will in practice be invoked by those who have some interest in the child, such as a parent, step-parent, foster parent, relative or local authority. However, this is not an exhaustive list, and the procedure may in theory be invoked by anyone, subject to the requirement that the applicant must state his or her relationship to the ward on production of the application so that either the district judge or court may refuse the application if it is considered to be an abuse of process.[1] The child, acting by a next friend,[2] may invoke the jurisdiction with respect to itself.

The defendant to the proceedings will be the person or body against whom an order is sought. There are powers to add others as parties to the proceedings, including the child who, if added, will be represented by a guardian ad litem (usually the Official Solicitor[3]); however, owing to the greater time and expense involved, a child will

18 CA 1989, s 100(2)(c).
19 Family Law Act 1986, ss 1(1)(d), 2, 3.
20 FLA 1986, s 2(2), 3.
1   *Practice Direction* [1967] 1 All ER 828.
2   Family Proceedings Rules 1991, r 9.2.
3   *Re JD (wardship: guardian ad litem)* [1984] FLR 359.

only be joined as a party in exceptional circumstances.[4] Finally, any person with an interest in the proceedings may apply to be joined as a party at the discretion of the district judge.

(d) Procedure

A child becomes a ward of court by virtue of a court order to that effect, application for which is made by originating summons issued in the Family Division of the High Court.[5] However, the child is effectively subject to the guardianship of the court from the time of the issue of the originating summons, subject to the rule that the child will cease to be a ward if an appointment for a hearing of the summons is not made within 21 days of its issue.[6] In urgent cases, for example where it is anticipated that the child is about to be removed from the jurisdiction, it is possible to obtain a preliminary injunction ex parte before the issue of an originating summons.[7] Once issued, the summons is served on the defendant and on any other interested party, together with the Notice of Wardship which states that the court's leave is required for certain matters, such as a change in the arrangements for the ward's welfare, care and control and education (Barnard 1983, p 132).

The first hearing of the summons will be by a district judge, who will make directions on a number of matters. These will include: directions as to the filing and giving of evidence, the addition of parties, the appointment of the Official Solicitor as guardian ad litem for the child, requests for a welfare report, and appointments for conciliation if appropriate.[8] The district judge may make any orders that are agreed between the parties;[9] but must otherwise either adjourn the proceedings for further directions from himself, or certify that the case may be heard by a judge, who will make any contested orders and decide all points of law. It may also be directed that certain matters in the proceedings be heard in the county court.[10]

A welfare report may be requested either at this initial stage, or at any time in the proceedings. The report will be prepared by the court welfare service, and will concern itself with the child's circumstances and background. It is official policy that this report

---

4   *Practice Note* [1961] 1 All ER 319; *Re A, B, C and D (minors)* [1988] 2 FLR 500.
5   Family Proceedings Rules 1991, r 5.
6   CA 1989, s 41(2)(2A); Family Proceedings Rules 1991, r 5.
7   RSC Ord 29, r 1.
8   *Practice Direction* [1966] 3 All ER 84; *Practice Direction (child: custody: conciliation: guardianship and wardship)* [1984] 3 All ER 800.
9   *Practice Direction* [1980] 1 All ER 813.
10 *Practice Direction* [1985] FLR 536.

will usually be sufficient to protect the child's welfare, so that the Official Solicitor will only be appointed as guardian ad litem in exceptional cases.[11] Such cases will be:

(i)   cases where the ward is of sufficient age to express an independent view on the substance of the proceedings which should be communicated to the court;
(ii) 'teenage wardship' cases where the ward is associating with an undesirable person;
(iii) where the court requires a specific task or independent inquiry to be carried out, such as a psychiatric examination; and
(iv) where there is a difficult point of law or international element (Lowe and White 1986, pp 201–203).

If appointed, the Official Solicitor's role is to conduct the proceedings on behalf of the child and to give the child a voice in the proceedings. This latter function will usually be performed by means of a report which is compiled after an investigation of all the circumstances of the case. The report will also make submissions to the court on the child's behalf, and may contain specific recommendations (Lowe and White 1986, pp 208–212).

Once all the evidence and reports are available, the matter will be heard by a judge. Evidence at the hearing will be by affidavit evidence, supplemented by oral evidence and cross-examination of witnesses and deponents of affidavits. Owing to the supervisory nature of the jurisdiction, the court's procedure will be less rigid than in adversarial cases so that, for example, it will be possible to treat reports (such as that of the Official Solicitor) as confidential, and to admit otherwise inadmissible hearsay evidence.[12]

(e) Powers of the court

We have already seen that one of the effects of wardship is to require the leave of the court before taking certain steps in relation to a ward of court. Wardship proceedings, and proceedings invoking the inherent jurisdiction, are also 'family proceedings' for the purposes of the Children Act 1989, so that the court has the power to make the full range of s 8, and other, orders.[13] In addition, the court has power to make a variety of other orders concerning the child which are enforceable through the law of contempt (see Lowe and White,

---

11 *Practice Direction* [1982] 1 All ER 319; *Re A, B, C and D (minors)* [1988] 2 FLR 500.
12 *Official Solicitor v K* [1965] AC 201, [1963] 3 All ER 191, HL.
13 CA 1989, s 8(3)(a).

Ch 8). Where the child's residence or upbringing is directly in issue, the court will have regard to the child's welfare as the first and paramount consideration. This will not always be the case; for example, where a child has been warded to prevent publication of certain material, the child's welfare will be balanced against other interests, such as the right to freedom of publication.[14]

The most important orders (other than s 8 orders) are as follows.

(i) Care and control

Since in wardship the court itself retains custody of the ward 'in the wide sense' (or, now, parental responsibility), a court may only make orders concerning the care and control (or residence) of the ward. The person with residence is subject to the 'important steps' restriction outlined above as well as to any specific directions that the court may make relating, for example, to the exercise of contact by third parties, or to the education of the ward (Lowe and White 1986, pp 98–99 and 114–120).

(ii) Maintenance

The court has the same powers to make orders for the financial provision of children as are available to other courts[15] (see Ch 4).

(iii) Other orders

The court may make a variety of other orders. These include: orders restraining named individuals or groups from associating or communicating with the ward, orders restraining the marriage of the ward, non-molestation orders and orders either restraining or sanctioning certain forms of medical treatment (Lowe and White 1986, pp 126–134).

(f) Jurisdictional limitations

Although wardship is in principle generally available (unless a child is in care), there are some cases in which the courts have refused to accept jurisdiction. The court may refuse jurisdiction if it would not

---

14 *Re X (a minor) (wardship: jurisdiction)* [1975] 1 All ER 697; *Re C (a minor) (wardship: medical treatment) (No 2)* [1989] 2 All ER 791; *Re M and N (minors) (wardship: freedom of publication)* [1990] 1 All ER 205.
15 CA 1989, s 15 and Sch 1.

be in the child's interests for the court to hear the application, for example, where the dispute over the child was before another court in other proceedings,[16] or where the child is out of the jurisdiction and there is little chance of the court's order being obeyed.[17] The court may also refuse to make orders or may stay the proceedings for the same reasons.

The uses of wardship

There are three main potential groups of litigant in wardship proceedings. They are:

(i)   local authorities;
(ii) parents, most of whom will be seeking to prevent removal (or 'kidnapping') of a child by the other parent, or to recover a child already removed; and
(iii) non-parents, such as foster parents, relatives or interested third parties (Law Commission 1987, para 3.3).

We shall consider the use of the jurisdiction by these groups in turn.

Before doing so, it should be remembered that the Children Act 1989 will reduce the use of wardship and the inherent jurisdiction by drastically curtailing its use by local authorities and by filling in the gaps in the statutory code of child law which in the past wardship has been used to fill. Although s 8 orders under the 1989 Act will be sufficient for most purposes, so that there may be no need to invoke the wardship or inherent jurisdiction at all, there may still be some cases in which the statutory orders will be inadequate. For example, prohibited steps and specific issue orders may only relate to some aspect of the exercise of parental responsibility.[18] This would not include an order prohibiting a third party, who does not have parental responsibility, from doing something in relation to the child. One example would be an order relating to newspaper or other publicity concerning a ward. Another would be an injunction preventing a child's natural parents from contacting a child following its adoption.[19]

---

16 FLA 1986, s 5.
17 *Re S (M)(an infant)* [1971] 1 All ER 459.
18 CA 1989, s 8(1).
19 *Re D (a minor) (adoption order: injunction)* [1991] 3 All ER 461: by definition, a child's natural parents following an adoption do not have parental responsibility and so cannot be caught by s 8 orders; and, according to the decision in *Re D*, the court has no power to impose such an injunction as part of the adoption order itself. The only alternative, therefore, is to seek an order under the inherent jurisdiction or wardship.

In addition, there may still be reasons for invoking wardship even where the statutory orders would be available. For example, it may be desirable to obtain immediate court protection (although s 8 orders may be obtained ex parte) and to preserve the status quo pending the court hearing, or to have continuing supervision by the High Court of a particularly complex case (eg, one involving an international dimension). There may thus still be cases where there is either no alternative to invoking the wardship or inherent jurisdiction, or where wardship and the inherent jurisdiction offer significant advantages over the other available procedures. Nevertheless, it has been suggested that the future of wardship after the 1989 Act 'will depend on whether it is perceived to have something distinctive to offer to children which is different in kind from that available under the statutory code' (Bainham 1990c, p 273).

(a) Local authorities

The impact of the Children Act 1989 on the use of wardship both by and against local authorities has already been considered in Chapter 10. It will be remembered that the 1989 Act permits local authorities limited access to the inherent jurisdiction, conditional on obtaining the leave of court.[20]

(b) Parents

Disputes between parents concerning residence, contact or the upbringing of children will in future be resolved mainly under the 1989 Act. Nevertheless, wardship will still be available to resolve inter-parental disputes of this kind,[1] but not where the purpose is to effect an appeal from or review of a decision of a court made under the statutory procedures.[2] In practice, however, it is unlikely that wardship would be used by parents to resolve disputes of this sort since the cost of wardship proceedings is extremely high, and legal aid may not be available where the dispute may be resolved through resort to another court acting under the statutory powers. However, the fact that wardship has immediate effect and invokes the continuing supervision of the court, together with the fact that the court may make a wide range of orders for the protection of the

---

20 CA 1989, s 100(3), (4).
1   *Re P (infants)* [1967] 2 All ER 229, [1967] 1 WLR 818.
2   *Re A-H (infants)* [1963] Ch 232.

child, may make wardship attractive to those who can afford it (Law Commission 1987, paras 3.5–3.11).

The most likely use of wardship between parents will be in cases of 'kidnapping'. Owing to the wide jurisdictional rules and the broad range of orders that may be made, wardship may be useful in preventing the removal of the child from the jurisdiction, in recovering a child from a foreign jurisdiction, or in assisting in the return of a child 'kidnapped' to this country. However, as a result of recent changes in legislation and practice, wardship may have lost its pre-eminence as a means of preventing or remedying kidnapping. Kidnapping is already a criminal offence,[3] and may thus involve the police without any need for wardship; further, since 1986 it has been possible for the police to operate the 'all ports warning' system, by which ports and airports are notified of the imminent unlawful removal of a child from the jurisdiction, without any need for a court order.[4] However, wardship will be useful where the child's removal may not have been in contravention of any criminal prohibition, in which case an order in wardship restraining the child's removal will itself be sufficient to invoke the assistance of the police and the 'all ports warning' procedure. Further, the issuing of wardship proceedings will have the effect of preventing the child being issued with a passport.[5]

Once the child has been removed, there may be few advantages in invoking wardship. Where the child is still within England and Wales, the child may be recovered through *habeus corpus* or by an order for the return of a child taken in breach of a custody order.[6] However, it may be that the parents are in dispute over the child's residence and no court order has yet been made, in which case wardship may be appropriate both as a means of resolving the residence issue and of securing the child's return to the parent with whom it is to live. Where the child is within the United Kingdom (ie including Scotland and Northern Ireland), the Family Law Act 1986 provides for the reciprocal enforcement of residence orders between jurisdictions.[7]

Finally, where the child has been taken outside the United Kingdom, the Child Abduction and Custody Act 1985 provides for

---

3   (i) At common law (see *R v D* [1984] AC 778, [1984] 2 All ER 449); (ii) Child Abduction Act 1984, ss 1, 2; (iii) Sexual Offences Act 1956, s 20. See further, Lowe and White (1986), pp 325–327.

4   *Practice Direction* [1986] 1 All ER 983, [1986] 1 WLR 475; see Lowe and White (1986), pp 328–333.

5   *Practice Direction (minor: preventing removal abroad)* [1986] 1 All ER 983, [1986] 1 WLR 475; see Lowe and White (1986), pp 323–324.

6   FLA 1986, s 34.

7   FLA 1986, ss 25–32.

the reciprocal enforcement of custody orders between those states who are signatories to certain international conventions concerning child abduction.[8] A court in whose jurisdiction the child is must usually order the return of the child to the country where the original order was made. Where the child has been removed to a country to which the 1985 Act does not apply, an order for residence, whether made in wardship proceedings or not, would not be enforceable. Residence orders in wardship are otherwise no more enforceable than those made in other family proceedings; thus, while kidnapping would be a contempt of court, this would only be enforceable against the kidnapper if s/he returned to this country. For these reasons, the Law Commission concluded that, in this context, 'wardship has no obvious advantage over the other jurisdictions' (1987, para 3.23.; see also paras 3.17–3.22)

(c) Non-parents

We have seen in Chapter 11 that non-parents, such as relatives or foster parents, may acquire a legal status with respect to a child without the need to resort to wardship proceedings. In addition, we saw in Chapter 3 that anyone may apply for leave to seek a s 8 order. It is conceivable that someone who is unsuccessful in obtaining leave under the 1989 Act may achieve their desired result in wardship or under the inherent jurisdiction, but it seems unlikely that the courts will allow the jurisdiction to be used in this way. However, as noted above, there may still be some advantages in using wardship or the inherent jursidiction rather than relying on the statutory code; and more complex cases involving non-parents, such as *Re D*[9] (in which an educational psychologist successfully prevented the mother of a handicapped girl from having the girl sterilised), may still appropriately be dealt with in wardship even though the statutory code could theoretically apply.

(d) Other uses

There are a number of other cases in which wardship may be appropriate. Wardship may be a means of controlling the behaviour

---

8   (i) The Hague Convention on the Civil Aspects of International Child Abduction (1980); and (ii) The Council of Europe Convention on the Recognition and Enforcement of Decisions Concerning Custody of Children and on Restoration of Custody of Children (1981).

9   [1976] Fam 185.

of the child, for example by restraining the ward from entering into or continuing certain undesirable relations or associations,[10] although the enforcement of any order that the court might make through committal for contempt may have adverse consequences for the ward (Law Commission 1987, para 3.49). Wardship is appropriate for hearing novel or complex cases, such as those involving surrogacy arrangements (although the creation of a statutory framework for resolving some of these issues will reduce the need for wardship: see Ch 3).

Wardship may also be a means of resolving questions relating to consent to the medical treatment of children. It is well established that a court in wardship may override the refusal of consent by parents to medical treatment,[11] just as it may override the giving of consent.[12] It has also been suggested (albeit obiter) that the same applies to a '*Gillick* competent' child, so that a court in wardship may override the refusal of consent by such a child (and, presumably, may override the giving of consent by such a child).[13] In so far as the issue of parental consent or veto is concerned, the matter may now be dealt with under the statutory code, since it is a matter that relates squarely to the exercise of parental responsibility.[14] This is not true of the child's consent, so that wardship (or, possibly, the inherent jurisdiction) will be one way of challenging a *Gillick* competent child's veto of medical treatment. It is not the only way, however, since (as we saw in Chapter 3) it has also been suggested[15] that a parent may override a *Gillick* competent child's decision to say 'no' (but not, as *Gillick* itself decided, such a child's decision to say 'yes'). It is unclear whether this parental power (ie the power to override a *Gillick* competent child's veto) is part of 'parental responsibility', and therefore within the scope of the statutory code (see further, Ch 3).

---

10 See, eg, *Re SW (a minor)* [1986] 1 FLR 24.
11 See, eg, *Re P (a minor)* [1986] 1 FLR 272 (abortion authorised against parents' wishes); *Re B (a minor)(wardship: medical treatment)* [1990] 3 All ER 927 (life-saving treatment for a Downs syndrome child authorised by the court against the wishes of the parents).
12 *Re D (a minor)(wardship: sterilisation)* [1976] 1 All ER 326 (sterilisation of child prevented).
13 Per Lord Donaldson MR in *Re R (a minor)(wardship: consent to treatment)* [1991] 4 All ER 177.
14 There may be limits, however, to the effectiveness of parental consent. There may, for example, be a distinction between treatment carried out for therapeutic reasons on the one hand, and treatment (such as sterilisation) which is not therapeutically necessary, on the other: decisions of the latter sort should be referred to court, although this is probably a matter of good practice rather than a legal requirement. See *Re F (mental patient: sterilisation)* [1990] 2 AC 1 (per Lord Bridge) and *Re E (a minor)(medical treatment)* [1991] 2 FLR 585.
15 *Re R (a minor)(wardship: consent to treatment)* (above).

Even where consent is not in issue, there are nevertheless some serious forms of medical treatment in respect of which court approval[16] may be sought.[17] This would include sterilisation,[18] abortion or life-saving treatment.[19] As far as local authorities are concerned, this may be one of the few contexts in which they might now invoke the inherent jurisdiction, always assuming that the relevant leave criteria can be satisfied.[20]

16 The court may give consent to treatment, but cannot dictate to doctors that the treatment take place: per Lord Donaldson MR in *Re J (a minor)(wardship: medical treatment)* [1990] 3 All ER 930, CA.
17 It may be that court approval *must* be sought: per Lord Templeman in *Re B (a minor)(wardship: sterilisation)* [1987] 2 All ER 206 at 214–215, although the House of Lords' decision in *Re F (mental patient: sterilisation)* [1990] 2 AC 1 suggests that although the consent of the court should be sought as a matter of good practice, it is not required as a matter of law. Wardship may be be used by doctors (or their insurers) as a means of clarifying their legal position: see, for example, *Re E (a minor)(medical treatment)* [1991] 2 FLR 585.
18 *Re B (A minor)(wardship: medical treatment)* [1988] AC 199 (authorisation of the sterilisation of a mentally retarded child in care).
19 Eg, *Re B (a minor)(wardship: medical treatment)* (above); *Re J (a minor)(wardship: medical treatment)* [1990] 3 All ER 930, CA (in which it was decided that a court could decline to authorise life-saving treatment in certain cases, even where the child was not terminally ill: see Wells, Alldridge and Morgan 1990).
20 CA 1989, s 100(4). See Ch 10 for discussion.

References and bibliography

Adcock, M & White, R (1984) 'Freeing for Adoption and the Access Provisions', 8 (2) Adoption and Fostering 11–17

Alston, P, Parker, S & Seymour, J (eds) (1991) *Children, rights and the law* Oxford, OUP

Anderson, S (1984) 'Legislative Divorce – Law for the Aristocracy' in G Rubin & D Sugarman (eds) *Law, Society and Economy: Essays in Legal History* Abingdon, Professional Books

Armstrong, C and Walton, T (1990) 'Transsexuals and the law' 140 New Law Journal 1384

Atherton, C (1984) 'Appointing and Monitoring Guardians' 8 (3) Adoption and Fostering 24–6

Austin, J (1863) *Lectures on Jurisprudence, Volume II* London, John Murray

Bainham, A (1988) *Children, parents and the state* London, Sweet & Maxwell

Bainham, A (1990) 'The privatisation of the public interest in children' 53 Modern Law Review 206–220

Bainham, A (1990a) 'The Children Act 1989: Welfare and Non-interventionism' Family Law 143-145

Bainham, A (1990b) 'The Children Act 1989: The state and the family' Family Law 231-234

Bainham, A (1990c) 'The Children Act 1989: The future of wardship' Family Law 270–273

Ball, M (1983) *Housing Policy and Economic Power: The Political Economy of Owner Occupation* London, Methuen

Barnard, D (1983) *The Family Court in Action* London, Butterworths

Barrington Baker, W, Eekelaar, J, Gibson, C & Raikes, S (1977) *The Matrimonial Jurisdiction of Registrars: The Exercise of the Matrimonial Jurisdiction by Registrars of England and Wales* Oxford, SSRC

Barron, J (1990) *Not worth the paper . . . ?: The effectiveness of legal protection for women and children experiencing domestic violence* Bristol, Women's Aid Federation England

Barton, C (1985) *Cohabitation contracts* Aldershot, Gower

Barton, C (1990) 'Pre-"marriage" contracts – work for practitioners?'
140 New Law Journal 626–627

Barton, C (1991) 'Rape within marriage' Family Law 73–75

Beck, C, Glavis, G, Glover, S, Jenkins, M & Nardi, R (1978) 'The
Rights of Children: A Trust Model', 46 Fordham Law Review
669–780

Bell, M (1988) 'Freeing Orders', 12 Adoption and Fostering 10–17

Bennett, M (1990) 'The mechanics of the offer: The art of settlement'
Family Law 249–252

Bevan, H (1989) *Child Law* London, Butterworths

Binney, V, Harkell, G & Nixon, J (1981) *Leaving Violent Men: A Study
of Refuges and Housing for Battered Women* Women's Aid Federation of
England/Department of Environment

Bird, R (1991) 'The Child Support Act 1991: An outline' Family
Law 478–480

Black, J & Bridge, J (1989) *A Practical Approach to Family Law* 2nd
edn, Blackstone Press, London

Block, J, Block, J & Gierde, P (1986) 'The personality of children
prior to divorce: a prospective study' 57 Child Development
827–840

Booth, Hon Mrs Justice (1985) *Report of the Matrimonial Causes
Procedure Committee* London, HMSO

Borkowski, M, Murch, M & Walker, V (1983) *Marital Violence – The
Community Response* London, Tavistock Publications

Bottomley, A (1984) 'Resolving Family Disputes: A Critical View' in
M D A Freeman (ed) *State, Law and the Family: Critical Perspectives*
London, Tavistock, 292–303

Bottomley, A (1985) 'What is Happening to Family Law?: A
Feminist Critique of Conciliation' in J Brophy & C Smart (eds)
Women in Law: Explorations in Law, Family and Sexuality London,
Routledge and Kegan Paul, 162–187

Bradney, A (1986) 'Blood Tests, Paternity and the Double Helix'
Family Law 378–380

British Association of Social Workers (1984) *Family Courts: A
Discussion Document* London, BASW

Bromley, P & Lowe, NV (1987) *Bromley's Family Law* 7th edn,
London, Butterworths

Brophy, J & Smart, C (1981) 'From Disregard to Disrepute: The
Position of Women in Family Law' 9 Feminist Review 3–15

Brown, B (1986) 'Book Review', 13 Journal of Law and Society
433–439

Bryan, M (1984) 'Domestic Violence: A Question of Housing?'
Journal of Social Welfare Law 195–207

Burgoyne, J, Ormrod, R & Richards, M (1987) *Divorce Matters*
Harmondsworth, Penguin

Bowlby, J (1965) *Child care and the growth of love* 2nd edn, Harmondsworth, Penguin

Bowler, J, Jackson, J & Loughridge, K (1989) *Living together precedents* London, Waterlow

Bowler, J, Jackson, J & Loughridge, K (1991) *Living together* London, Century Hutchinson

British Association of Social Workers (1986) *Guardians ad litem and reporting officers* London, BASW

Buck, T (1990) 'Distribution on intestacy: The Law Commission Report No 187' Family Law 267–269

Bullard, E (1991) 'Custodianship and the review of adoption law' Family Law 188–191

Burgoyne, J & Clark, D (1984) *Making a go of it – A study of stepfamilies in Sheffield* London, Routledge

Campbell, B (1988) *Unofficial secrets* London, Virago

Campbell, T (1991) 'The Rights of the Minor: As Person, As Child, As Juvenile, As Future Adult' in Alston, P, Parker, S & Seymour, J (eds) *Children, Rights and the Law* Oxford, Oxford University Press

Central Statistical Office (1987) *Social Trends 17* London, HMSO

Central Statistical Office (1991) *Social Trends 21* London, HMSO

Clark, D (ed) (1991) *Marriage, domestic life and social change: Writings for Jacqueline Burgoyne* London, Routledge

Clive, EM (1980) 'Marriage: An Unnecessary Legal Concept?' in J Eekelaar & S Katz (eds) *Marriage & Cohabitation in Contemporary Societies: Areas of Legal, Social & Economic Change* Ch 8

Clulow, C & Vincent, C (1987) *In the Child's Best Interests? Divorce Court Welfare and the Search for a Settlement* London, Tavistock Publications

Clulow, C (1991) 'Making, breaking and remaking marriage' in Clark, D (ed) *Marriage, domestic life and social change: Writings for Jacqueline Burgoyne* London, Routledge, Ch 7

Commaille, J (1982) *Famille San Justice? Le Droit et la Justice Face aux Transformations de la Famille* Paris, Editions du Centurion

Coward, J (1987) 'Conceptions outside marriage: Regional differences' 49 Population Trends, OPCS, London, HMSO, 24–30

Cretney, S (1984) *Principles of Family Law* 4th edn, London, Sweet & Maxwell

Cretney, S (1986) 'Money After Divorce: The Mistakes We Have Made?' in M Freeman (ed) *Essays in Family Law 1985* London, Stevens, 34–54

Cretney, S (1987) *Elements of Family Law* London, Sweet & Maxwell

Cretney, S (1990) 'Money and divorce, A quarterly retrospect: Needs and principles' Family Law 89–91

Cretney, S (1990a) 'Divorce and the low income family' Family Law 377–379

Cretney, S (1990b) 'Defining the limits of state intervention: The child and the courts' in Freestone, D (ed) *Children and the law* Hull, HUP, Ch 3

Cretney, S (1991) 'Divorce and the high income family' Family Law 171–173

Cretney, S & Masson, J *Principles of Family Law* 5th edn (1990) London, Sweet & Maxwell

Criminal Law Revision Committee (1984) *Fifteenth Report, Sexual Offences* Cmnd 9213, London, HMSO

Curtis, M (1946) *Report of the Care of Children Committee* Cmnd 6922, London, HMSO

Cusine, D (1990) *New reproductive technologies: A legal perspective* Aldershot, Dartmouth

David, M (1983) 'The New Right and Sex Education Policy: Towards a New Moral Economy in Britain and the USA' in J Lewis (ed) *Women's Welfare/Women's Rights* London, Croom Helm

Davis, G (1982) 'Conciliation: A Dilemma for the Divorce Court Welfare Service' 29 (4) Probation Journal 123–128

Davis, G (1983) 'Conciliation and the Professions' Family Law 6–13

Davis, G (1983a) 'Mediation in Divorce: A Theoretical Perspective' Journal of Social Welfare Law 131–140

Davis, G (1987) 'Public Issues and Private Troubles: The Case of Divorce', Family Law 299–308

Davis, G (1988) 'The halls of justice and justice in the halls' in Dingwall, R & Eekelaar, J (eds) *Divorce mediation and the legal process* Oxford, OUP, Ch 6

Davis, G (1988a) *Partisans and Mediators* Oxford, Clarendon

Davis, G (1991) 'Mediation appointments on money and property in the Bristol County Court' Family Law 130–135

Davis, G (1991a) 'Mediation – an addition to the judicial repertoire' New Law Journal 396–397

Davis, G & Bader, K (1985) 'In-Court Mediation: The Consumer View' Family Law 42–49 and 82–86

Davis, G, Macleod, A & Murch, M (1982) 'Special Procedure in Divorce and the Solicitor's Role' Family Law 39–44

Davis, G, Macleod, A & Murch, M (1983) 'Divorce: Who supports the Family?' Family Law 217–224

Davis, G, Macleod, A & Murch, M (1983a) 'Undefended Divorce: Should secton 41 of the Matrimonial Causes Act be repealed?' 46 Modern Law Review 121–146

Davis, G & Murch, M (1988) *Grounds for divorce* Oxford, OUP

de Cruz, SP (1987) 'Parents, Doctors and Children: The Gillick Case and Beyond' Journal of Social Welfare Law 93–108

de Cruz, SP (1987a) 'Abortion, *C v S* and the Law' Family Law 319–323 de Cruz, SP (1987b) 'Protecting the Unborn Child: *Re D*' Family Law 207–211

de Cruz, SP (1988) 'Sterilization, Wardship & Human Rights' Family Law 6–12

Deech, R (1977) 'The Principles of Maintenance' 7 Family Law 229

Deech, R (1980) 'The Reform of Illegitimacy Law' Family Law 101–104

Deech, R (1980a) '*Williams and Glyn's* and Family Law' New Law Journal 896

Deech, R (1980b) 'The Case Against Legal Recognition of Cohabitation' in J Eekelaar & S Katz (eds) *Marriage and Cohabitation in Contemporary Societies* Toronto, Butterworths, Ch 30

Deech, R (1982) 'Financial Relief: The Retreat from Precedent and Principle' 98 Law Quarterly Review 621–652

Deech, R (1984) 'Matrimonial Property and Divorce: A Century of Progress?' in M Freeman (ed) *The State, The Law and The Family: Critical Perspectives* London, Tavistock, 245–261

Deech, R (1990) 'Divorce law and empirical studies' 106 Law Quarterly Review 229–245

Department of Health (1989) *An introduction to the Children Act 1989* London, HMSO

Department of Health (1989a) *The Care of Children: Principles and Practice in Regulation and Guidance* London, HMSO

Department of Health (1990) *Interdepartmental Review of Adoption Law, Discussion Paper No 1: The nature and effect of adoption* London, Department of Health

Department of Health (1990a) *Interdepartmental Review of Adoption Law, Background Paper No 1: International perspectives* London, Department of Health

Department of Health (1990b) *Interdepartmental Review of Adoption Law, Background Paper No 2: Review of research relating to adoption* London, Department of Health

Department of Health (1991) *The Children Act 1989 Guidance and Regulations: Volume 1, Court Orders* London, HMSO

Department of Health (1991a) *The Children Act 1989 Guidance and Regulations: Volume 2, Family support, day care and educational provision for young children* London, HMSO

Department of Health (1991b) *The Children Act 1989 Guidance and Regulations: Volume 3, Family placements* London, HMSO

Department of Health (1991c) *The Children Act 1989 Guidance and Regulations: Volume 4, Residential care* London, HMSO

Department of Health (1991d) *The Children Act 1989 Guidance and Regulations: Volume 8, Private fostering and miscellaneous* London, HMSO

Department of Health (1991e) *The Children Act 1989 Guidance and Regulations: Volume 9, Adoption issues* London, HMSO

Department of Health (1991f) *Interdepartmental Review of Adoption Law, Discussion Paper No 2: Agreement and freeing* London, Department of Health

Department of Health (1991g) *Interdepartmental Review of Adoption Law, Discussion Paper No 3: The adoption process* London, Department of Health

Devereux, J (1991) 'The capacity of a child to consent to medical treatment in Australia – Gillick revisited?' 11 Oxford Journal of Legal Studies 283–302

Dewar, J (1982) 'Cohabitees: Contributions and Consideration' 12 Family Law 158–160

Dewar, J (1984) 'Promises, Promises' 47 Modern Law Review 735–740

Dewar, J (1984a) 'Reforming Financial Provision: The Alternatives' Journal of Social Welfare Law 1–13

Dewar, J (1985) 'Transsexualism and Marriage' 15 Kingston Law Review 58–76

Dewar, J (1986) 'Financial Provision Reformed: An Abdication of responsibility?' Conveyancer and Property Lawyer 96–106

Dewar, J (1989) 'Fathers in Law?: The Case of A.I.D.' in R Lee and D Morgan (eds) *Birthrights: Law and Ethics at the Beginnings of Life* London, Croom Helm, Ch 7

Dewar, J (1989) *Law and the family* London, Butterworths

Dewar, J (1991) 'The Children Act 1989: Rolling back the state?' Student Law Review, Summer 1991, 36–37

DHSS (1974) *Report of the Committee of Inquiry into the Care and Supervision Provided in Relation to Maria Colwell* London, HMSO

DHSS (1974a) *Non Accidental Injury to Children*, Local Authority Social Services Letter (LASSL) (74) 13

DHSS (1976) *Non Accidental Injury to Children: Area Review Committee*, Local Authority Social Services Letter (LASSL) (76) 2

DHSS (1982) *Memorandum by the Department of Health and Social Security and the Home Office to the Social Services Select Committee on Children in Care 1983/4* London, HMSO

DHSS (1982a) *Child Abuse: A Study of Inquiry Reports 1973–1981* London, HMSO

DHSS (1985) *Review of Child Care Law* London, HMSO

DHSS (1985a) *Social Work Decisions in Child Care: Recent Research Findings and their Implications* London, HMSO

DHSS (1986) *Legislation on Human Infertility Services and Embryo Research: A Consultation Paper* Cmnd 46, London, HMSO

DHSS (1986a) *Low Income Families – 1983* London, DHSS

DHSS (1987) *Human Fertilization and Embryology: A Framework for Legislation*, Cmnd 259, London, HMSO

Dickens, BM (1981) 'The Modern Function and Limits of Parental Rights', 97 Law Quarterly Review 462–485

Dickens, B (1990) 'Reproductive technology and the "new" family' in Sutherland, E & McCall-Smith, A (eds) *Family rights: Family law and medical advance* Edinburgh, Edinburgh University Press

Dingwall, R, Eekelaar, J & Murray, T (1983) *The Protection of Children: State Intervention and Family Life* Oxford, Basil Blackwell

Dingwall, R (1988) 'Empowerment or enforcement? Some questions about power and control in divorce mediation' in Dingwall, R and Eekelaar, J (eds) *Divorce mediation and the legal process* Oxford, OUP, Ch 10

Dingwall, R & Eekelaar, J (eds) (1988) *Divorce mediation and the legal process* Oxford, OUP

Dobash, R & Dobash, R (1980) *Violence Against Wives: A Case Against Patriarchy* London, Open Books

Dodd, B (1980) 'When Blood is their Argument', 20 Medicine, Science and Law 231–238

Dodd, B (1986) 'DNA Fingerprinting in Matters of Family Law and Crime', 25 Medicine, Science & Law 25–32

Dodds, M (1983) 'Children and Divorce', Journal of Social Welfare Law 228–237

Dominian, J (1982) 'Families in Divorce' in RN Rapoport, MP Fogarty & R Rapoport (eds) *Families in Britain*, London, Routledge and Kegan Paul, Ch 13

Donzelot, J (1979) *The Policing of Families: Welfare versus the State* London, Hutchinson

Douglas, G (1981) 'The Clean Break on Divorce', 11 Family Law 42–48

Douglas, G (1990) 'Family Law under the Thatcher government' 17 Journal of Law and Society 411–426

Douglas, G (1991) 'The Human Fertilisation and Embryology Act 1990' Family Law 110–116

Douglas, G (1991a) *Law, fertility and reproduction* London, Sweet & Maxwell

Douglas, G & Lowe, N (1989) 'The grandparent-grandchildren relationship in English law' in Eekelaar, J & Pearl, D (eds) *An aging world: Dilemmas and challenges for law and social policy* Oxford, OUP

Dow, M (1976) 'Police Involvement' in M Borland (ed) *Violence in the Family* Manchester, Manchester UP, 132–133

Edgell, S *Middle Class Couples* (1980) London, George Allen & Unwin

Edwards, S (1989) *Policing 'domestic' violence* London, Sage

Edwards, S & Halpern, A (1987) 'Financial Provision, Case-Law and Statistical Trends since 1984' Family Law 354–357

Edwards, S & Halpern, A (1988) 'Maintenance in 1987: Fact or Fantasy?' Family Law 117–121

Edwards, S & Halpern, A (1988a) 'Conflicting interests: Protecting children or protecting title to property' Journal of Social Welfare Law 110–124

Edwards, S & Halpern, A (1990) 'Regional "injustice": Financial provisions on divorce' Journal of Social Welfare Law 71–88

Edwards, S & Halpern, A (1990a) 'The stark reality?: The meal ticket for life' 140 New Law Journal 821–822

Edwards, S & Halpern, A (1990b) 'Making fathers pay' 140 New Law Journal 1687–1691

Edwards, S & Halpern, A (1991) 'Protection for the victim of domestic violence: Time for radical revision?' Journal of Social Welfare and Family Law 94–109

Edwards, S & Halpern, A (1991a) 'The cost of truth' 141 New Law Journal 1340–1342

Edwards, S, Gould, C & Halpern, A (1990) 'The continuing saga of maintaining the children after divorce' Family Law 31–35

Eekelaar, J (1978) *Family Law and Social Policy* London, Weidenfeld & Nicholson

Eekelaar, J (1982) 'Children in Divorce: Some Further Data', 2 Oxford Journal of Legal Studies 63–85

Eekelaar, J (1984) *Family Law and Social Policy* 2nd edn, London, Weidenfeld & Nicholson

Eekelaar, J (1986) 'The Emergence of Children's Rights' 6 Oxford Journal of Legal Studies 161–182

Eekelaar, J (1986a) 'Gillick in the Divorce Court', 136 New Law Journal 184

Eekelaar, J (1987) 'Family law and social control' in Eekelaar, J & Bell, J (eds) *Oxford essays in jurisprudence*, Third series, Oxford, OUP, Ch 6

Eekelaar, J (1989) 'What is "critical" family law?' 105 Law Quarterly Review 244–261

Eekelaar, J (1990) 'Investigation under the Children Act 1989' Family Law 486–489

Eekelaar, J *Regulating divorce* (1991) Oxford, OUP

Eekelaar, J (1991a) 'Parental responsibility: State of nature or nature of the state?' Journal of Social Welfare and Family Law 37–50

Eekelaar, J (1991b) 'Are parents morally obliged to care for their children?' Oxford Journal of Legal Studies 340–353

Eekelaar, J (1991c) 'The Importance of Thinking that Children Have Rights' in Alston, P, Parker, S & Seymour, J (eds) *Children, Rights and the Law* Oxford, OUP

Eekelaar, J (1991d) 'A child support scheme for the United Kingdom: An analysis of the White Paper' Family Law 15–21

Eekelaar, J (1991e) 'Child support – an evaluation' Family Law 511–517

Eekelaar, J & Clive, E (with K Clarke & S Raikes) (1977) *Custody After Divorce: The Disposition of Custody in Divorce Cases in Great Britain* Oxford, SSRC, Family Law Studies No 1

Eekelaar, J & Maclean, M (1986) *Maintenance After Divorce* Oxford, Oxford University Press

Eekelaar, J & Dingwall, R (eds) (1988) *Divorce mediation and the legal process* Oxford, OUP

Eekelaar, J & Dingwall, R (1988a) 'The development of conciliation in England' in Dingwall, R & Eekelaar, J (eds) *Divorce mediation and the legal process* Oxford, OUP, Ch 1

Eekelaar, J & Dingwall, R (1989) 'The role of the courts under the Children Bill' 139 New Law Journal 217–218

Eekelaar, J & Dingwall, R (1990) *The reform of child care law: A practical guide to the Children Act 1989* London, Routledge

Eekelaar, J & Maclean, M (1988) 'The evolution of private law maintenance obligations: The common law' in Meulders-Klein, M-T & Eekelaar, J (eds) *Family, State and individual economic security*, Vols 1 and 2, Brussels, Story Scientia, Ch 6

Eekelaar, J & Maclean, M (1990) 'Divorce law and empirical studies – a reply' 106 Law Quarterly Review 621–631

Elliott, J (1991) 'Demographic trends in domestic life, 1945–87' in Clark, D (ed) *Marriage, domestic life and social change: Writings for Jacqueline Burgoyne* London, Routledge, Ch 4

Elliott, J, Ochiltree, G, Richards, M, Sinclair, C & Tasker, F (1990) 'Divorce and children: A British challenge to the Wallerstein view' Family Law 309–310

Elliott, B & Richards, M (1991) 'Children and divorce: Educational performance and behaviour before and after parental separation' 5 International Journal of Law and the Family, 258–276

Elliott, J & Richards, M (1991a) 'Parental divorce and the life chances of children' Family Law 481–484

Elston, E, Fuller, J & Murch, M (1975) 'Judicial Hearings of Undefended Divorce Petitions' 38 Modern Law Review 609–640

Everall, M (1991) 'Judicial review of Local Authorities after the Children Act 1989' Family Law 212–216

Family Policy Studies Centre (1991) *Supporting Our Children* London, FPSC

Faragher, T (1985) 'The Police Response to Violence Against Women in the Home' in J Pahl (ed) *Private Violence and Public Policy* London, Routledge & Kegan Paul, Ch 8

Finer, M (1974) *Report of the Committee on One-Parent Families* (Chairman: The Hon Sir Morris Finer) Cmnd 5629, London, HMSO

Finer, M & McGregor OR (1974) 'The History of the Obligation to Maintain', Appendix 5 to the *Report of the Committee on One Parent Families*, Cmnd 5629–I, London, HMSO

Finlay, H & Bailey-Harris, R (1989) *Family law in Australia* Sydney, Butterworths

Fitzgerald, T (1983) 'The New Right and the Family' in M Loney, D Boswell & J Clarke (eds) *Social Policy and Social Welfare* Milton Keynes, Open University Press, Ch 4

Foden, A & Wells, T (1990) 'Unresolved attachment: Role and organisational ambiguities for the Divorce Court Welfare Officer' Family Law 189–191

Fortin, J (1990) 'The guardian ad litem in care proceedings: The developing role' Family Law 303–308

Foster, K, Wilmot, A & Dobbs, J (1990) *General Household Survey 1988* London, HMSO

Foucault, M (1977) *Discipline and Punish: The Birth of the Prison* Harmondsworth, Penguin

Foucault, M (1979) 'Governmentality' 6 Ideology and Consciousness 5–21

Foucault, M (1981) *The History of Sexuality, Volume I: An Introducton* (R Hurley trans) Harmondsworth, Penguin

Fox, R (1967) *Kinship & Marriage, An Anthropological Perspective* Harmondsworth, Penguin

Fox Harding, L (1991) 'The Children Act 1989 in context: Four perspectives in child care law and policy' Journal of Social Welfare and Family Law 179–193 and 285–302

Fraser, R (1990) 'Running an independent service' in T Fisher (ed) *Family Conciliation within the UK: Policy and practice* Bristol, Jordan & Sons, Ch 18

Freedman, J, Hammond, E, Masson, J & Morris, N (1988) *Property and marriage: An integrated approach* London, Institute for Fiscal Studies

Freeman, MDA (1976) 'Divorce Without Legal Aid' 6 Family Law 255–259

Freeman, MDA (1980) 'Violence Against Women: Does the Legal System Provide Solutions or Itself Constitute the Problem?' 7 British Journal of Law and Society 215

Freeman, MDA (1983) *The Rights and Wrongs of Children* London, Frances Pinter

Freeman, MDA (1985) 'Doing His Best to Maintain the Sanctity of Marriage' in J Johnson (ed) *Marital Violence* London, RKP

Freeman, MDA (1985a) 'Towards a Critical Theory of Family Law' 38 Current Legal Problems 153–185

Freeman, MDA (1986) *Essays in Family Law 1985* London, Sweet & Maxwell

Freeman, MDA (1986a) *Dealing with Domestic Violence* London, CCH

Freeman, MDA (1986b) 'After Warnock: Whither the Law?' 39 Current Legal Problems 33–55

Freeman, MDA & Lyon, CM (1983) *Cohabitation Without Marriage* Aldershot, Gower

Freeman, M D A (1991) 'Taking Children's Rights More Seriously' in Alston, P, Parker, S and Seymour, J (eds) *Children, Rights and the Law* Oxford, OUP

Freestone, D (ed) (1990) *Children and the law: Essays in honour of Professor HK Bevan* Hull, HUP

Gardner, S (1991) 'A woman's work . . .' 54 Modern Law Review 126–129

Garlick, P (1983) 'Judicial Separation: A Research Study' 46 Modern Law Review 719–737

Garrison, M (1990) 'The economics of divorce: Changing rules, changing results' in Sugarman, S and Kay, H (eds) *Divorce reform at the crossroads* New Haven, Yale University Press, Ch 3

General Synod of the Church of England (1988) *An Honourable Estate* London, Church House Publishing

Gibson, C (1980) 'Divorce and the Recourse to Legal Aid' 43 Modern Law Review 609–625

Gibson, C (1982) 'Maintenance and the Magistrates' Courts in the 1980s' Family Law 138–141

Gibson, P & Parsloe, P (1984) 'What stops parental access to children in care?' 8 (2) Adoption and Fostering 18–24

Gibson, S (1991) 'Bellum Pax Rursum' 12 The Journal of Legal History 148–154

Giddens, A (1984) *The Constitution of Society* Cambridge, Polity Press

Glendon, MA (1977) *Family Law in Transition in the United States and Western Europe* Amsterdam, North Holland

Glendon, MA (1981) *The New Family and the New Property* Toronto, Butterworths

Glendon, MA (1989) *The transformation of Family Law: State, Law and Family in the United States and Western Europe* Chicago, University of Chicago Press

Goldstein, J, Freud, A & Solnit, AJ (1973) *Beyond the Best Interests of the Child* NY, The Free Press

Goodhart, W (1988) 'Occupational pension schemes and divorce – a new proposal' Trusts Law and Practice 120–124

Gordon, D (1987) 'Arranged Marriages: For Entry or for Love?' Family Law 224–227

Government Green Paper (1989) *Registration: A modern service*, Cm 531, London, HMSO

Government White Paper (1990) *Registration: Proposals for change* Cm 939, London, HMSO

Graham Hall, J (1977) 'Outline of a Proposal for a Family Court' Family Law 6–8

Graham Hall, J & Martin, N (1991) 'A new approach to adoption' 12 Law Society's Gazette 27–28

Gray, K (1977) *Reallocation of Property on Divorce* Abingdon, Professional Books

Gray, K (1987) *Elements of Land Law* London, Butterworths

Green, D (1987) *Maintenance and capital provision on divorce: A need for precision?* London, Law Society

Greenslade, R (1988) *Matrimonial Advocacy and Litigation* London, Butterworths

Gregory, J & Foster, K (1990) *The consequences of divorce* London, HMSO

Guymer, A & Bywaters, P (1984) 'Conciliation and Reconciliation in Magistrates' Domestic Courts' in T Marshall (ed) *Magistrates' Domestic Courts* Home Office Research and Planning Paper 28, London, Home Office

Hadfield, B & Lavery, R (1991) 'Public and private law controls on decision-making for children' Journal of Social Welfare and Family Law 454–468

Haimes, E (1988) '"Secrecy": What can artificial reproduction learn from adoption?' 2 International Journal of Law and the Family 46–61

Hall, J (1990) 'Children and Divorce' in Freestone, D (ed) *Children and the law* Hull, HUP, Ch 8

Harding, L (1987) 'The Debate on Surrogate Motherhood: The Current Situation, Some Arguments and Issues; Questions Facing Law and Policy' Journal of Social Welfare Law 37–63

Harris, P & Scanlon, D (1991) *The Children Act 1989: A procedural handbook* London, Butterworths

Harris, R & Webb, D (1987) *Welfare, Power and Juvenile Justice: The Social Control of Delinquent Youth* Tavistock, London

Harris, R (1990) 'A matter of balance: Power and resistance in child protection policy' Journal of Social Welfare Law 332–340

Haskey, J (1984) 'Social Class and Socio-Economic Differentials in Divorce in England and Wales' 38 Population Studies

Haskey, J (1986) 'One Parent Families in Britain' 45 Population Trends, London, OPCS

Haskey, J (1989) 'Current prospects for the proportion of marriages ending in divorce' Population Trends 55, London, HMSO, 34–37

Haskey, J (1989a) 'Cohabitation in Great Britain – Characteristics and estimated numbers of cohabiting partners' Population Trends 58, London, HMSO

Haskey, J & Kiernan, K (1990) 'Cohabitation: Some demographic statistics' Family Law 442–444

Hayes, M (1978/9) 'Supplementary Benefit and Financial Provision Orders' Journal of Social Welfare Law 216–225

Hayes, M (1980) 'Law Commission Working Paper No 74: Illegitimacy' 43 Modern Law Review 299–306

Hayes, M (1990) 'The Law Commission and the Family Home' 53 Modern Law Review 222–229

Hayes, M (1991) 'Making and enforcing child maintenance obligations' Family Law 105–109

Hayes, M & Battersby, G (1985) 'Property Adjustments: Further Thoughts on Charge Orders' Family Law 142

Hayton, D (1990) 'The equitable rights of cohabitees' The Conveyancer 370–387

Hodson, D (1990) 'The new partner after divorce' Family Law 27–30, 68–71

Hogg, J (1991) 'Surrogacy – Nobody's child' Family Law 276–278

Hoggett, B (1980) 'Ends and Means: The Utility of Marriage as a Legal Institution' in Eekelaar, J & Katz, S *Marriage & Cohabitation in Contemporary Societies* Toronto, Butterworths, Ch 10

Hoggett, B (1986) 'Family Courts or Family Law Reform: Which Should Come First?' 6 Legal Studies 1–17

Hoggett, B & Pearl, D (1991) *The family, law and society: Cases and materials* London, Butterworths

Holcombe, L (1983) *Wives and Property* Oxford, Martin Robertson

Holmes, R (1991) 'Name any man . . . or else' 141 New Law Journal 244–245

Home Office (1989) *Magistrates' Courts: Report of a scrutiny 1989* Vols 1 and 2 London, HMSO

Home Office (1991) *Working together under the Children Act 1989: A guide to arrangements for inter-agency co-operation for the protection of children from abuse* London, HMSO

House of Commons (1986) 32nd Report of the Committee of Public Accounts, 1985/6 *Provision of Legal Aid in England & Wales* London, HMSO

Houghton Committee (1972) *Report of the Departmental Committee on the Adoption of Children* Cmnd 5107, London, HMSO

Ingleby, R (1988) 'Buy Now, Pay Later: The Hidden Costs of Negotiated Settlements to Matrimonial Disputes' Journal of Social Welfare Law 50–55

Ingleby, R (1988a) 'The Solicitor as Intermediary' in Dingwall, R & Eekelaar, J (eds) *Divorce Mediation and the Legal Process* Oxford, Clarendon

Inland Revenue (1980) *The Taxation of Husband and Wife* Cmnd 8093, London, HMSO

Inland Revenue (1986) *The Reform of Personal Taxation* Cmnd 9756, London, HMSO

Jackson, H & Maclean, M (1990) *The resolution of financial disputes on divorce: A cross national review of current models of policy and practice* Edinburgh, Scottish Office

Jackson, J (1990) 'People who live together should put their affairs in order' Family Law 439–441

James, A (1988) '"Civil work" in the probation service' in Dingwall, R and Eekelaar, J (eds) *Divorce mediation and the legal process* Oxford, OUP, Ch 4

James, AL & Wilson, K (1984) 'Reports for the Court: The Work of the Divorce Court Welfare Officer' Journal of Social Welfare Law 89–103

James, TE (1957) 'The Illegitimate and Deprived Child: Legitimation and Adoption' in Graveson, RH and Crane, FR (eds) *A Century of Family Law* London, Sweet & Maxwell, 39–55

Joshi, H and Davies, H (1991) *The pension consequences of divorce* Centre for Economic Policy Research Discussion Paper No 550, London, CEPR

Kaganas, F & Piper, C (1990) 'Grandparents and the limits of law' 4 International Journal of Law and the Family 27–51

Kerr, A, Gregory, E, Howard, S & Hudson, F (1990) *On behalf of the child: The work of the guardian ad litem* Birmingham, Venture Press

Kerridge, R (1990) 'Distribution on intestacy: The Law Commission's Report (1989)' The Conveyancer 358–369

King, M (1981) 'Welfare and Justice' in King, M (ed) *Childhood Welfare and Justice* London, Batsford, Ch 5

King, M (1987) 'Playing the Symbols: Custody and the Law Commission' Family Law 186–191

King, M (1991) 'Child welfare within law: The emergence of a hybrid discourse' 18 Journal of Law and Society 303–321

Kingdom, E (1988) 'Cohabitation contracts: A socialist–feminist issue' 15 Journal of Law and Society 77–89

Kingsley, J (1990) 'The Court Welfare Officer: Aims, procedures and practice – A research project' Family Law 183–188

Kleanthous, V & Kane, M (1987) 'The Development of In-Court Conciliation' Family Law 175–178

Lacey, N, Wells, C, Meure, D (1990) *Reconstructing Criminal Law* London, Weidenfeld and Nicholson

Lambert, L, Buist, M, Triseliotis, J and Hill, M (1989) *Freeing children for adoption – Final Report to the Social Work Services Group* Edinburgh, Scottish Office

Lambert, L, Buist, M, Triseliotis, J and Hill, M (1990) *Freeing children for adoption* London, BAAF

Land, H (1976) 'Women: Supporters or Supported?' in Barker, DL & Allen, S (eds) *Sexual Divisions in Society: Progress and Change* London, Tavistock 109–132

Land, H (1983) 'Who Still Cares for the Family? Recent Development in Income Maintenance, Taxation & Family Law' in Lewis, J (ed) *Women's Welfare/Women's Rights* London, Croom Helm, 64–85

Latham, CT (1986) 'Welfare Reports and Conciliation' Family Law 195–197

Law Commission (1966) *Reform of the Grounds of Divorce: The Field of Choice* Cmnd 3123, London, HMSO

Law Commission (1969) *Financial Provision in Matrimonial Proceedings*, Law Com No 25, London, HMSO

Law Commission (1970) *Report on Nullity of Marriage*, Law Com No 33, London, HMSO

Law Commission (1971) *Family Property Law* Working Paper No 42, London, HMSO

Law Commission (1973) *First Report on Family Property: A New Approach* Law Com No 52, London, HMSO

Law Commission (1973a) *Report on Solemnisation of Marriage in England and Wales* Law Com No 53, London, HMSO

Law Commission (1973b) *Matrimonial Proceedings in Magistrates' Courts* Working Paper No 63, London, HMSO

Law Commission (1974) *Second Report on Family Property: Family Provision on Death* Law Com No 61, London, HMSO

Law Commission (1978) *Third Report on Family Property: The Matrimonial Home* Law Com No 86, London, HMSO

Law Commission (1979) *Illegitimacy* Working Paper No 74, London, HMSO

Law Commission (1980) *The Financial Consequences of Divorce: The Basic Policy* Law Com No 103, London, HMSO

Law Commission (1981) *The Financial Consequences of Divorce* Law Com No 112, London, HMSO

Law Commission (1982) *Report on Illegitimacy* Law Com No 118, London, HMSO

Law Commission (1982a) *Property Law: The Implications of Williams and Glyn's Bank Ltd v Boland* Law Com No 155, London, HMSO

Law Commission (1982b) *Time Restrictions on Presentation of Divorce and Nullity Petitions* Law Com No 116, London, HMSO

Law Commission (1984) *Report on Declarations in Family Matters* Law Com No 132, London, HMSO

Law Commission (1985) *Transfer of Money Between Spouses: The Married Women's Property Act 1964* Working Paper No 90, London, HMSO

Law Commission (1985a) *Review of Child Law: Guardianship* Working Paper No 91, London, HMSO

Law Commission (1985b) *Capacity to Contract a Polygamous Marriage and Related Issues* Law Com No 146, London, HMSO

Law Commission (1986) *Review of Child Law: Custody* Working Paper No 96, London, HMSO

Law Commission (1986a) *Illegitimacy, Second Report* Law Com No 157, London, HMSO

Law Commission (1987) *Review of Child Law: Care, Supervision and Interim Orders in Custody Proceedings* Working Paper No 97, London, HMSO

Law Commission (1987a) *Review of Child Law: Wards of Court* Working Paper No 101, London, HMSO

Law Commission (1988) *Review of Child Law: Guardianship and Custody* Law Com No 172, London, HMSO

Law Commission (1988a) *Facing the Future: A Discussion Paper on the Grounds for Divorce* Law Com No 170, London, HMSO

Law Commission (1988b) *Distribution on Intestacy* Working Paper No 108, London, HMSO

Law Commission (1988c) *Matrimonial Property* Law Com No 175, London, HMSO

Law Commission (1989) *Trusts of Land* Law Com No 181, London, HMSO

Law Commission (1989a) *Trusts of Land: Overreaching* Law Com No 188, London, HMSO

Law Commission (1989b) *Distribution on Intestacy* Law Com No 187, London, HMSO

Law Commission (1989c) *A Criminal Code for England and Wales* Law Com No 177, London, HMSO

Law Commission (1989d) *Domestic violence and occupation of the family home* Working Paper No 113, London, HMSO

Law Commission (1990) *Rape within marriage* Working Paper No 116, London, HMSO

Law Commission (1990a) *The ground for divorce* Law Com No 192, London, HMSO

Law Society (1985) *A Family Court: Consultation Paper* London, Law Society

Law Society (1988) *Legal Aid: 37th Annual Report of the Law Society 1986–87* London, HMSO

Law Society (1990) *The Guide to the Professional Conduct of Solicitors* London, The Law Society

Law Society (1991) *Maintenance and capital provision on divorce* London, Law Society Legal Practice Directorate

Law Society (1991a) *The Child Care Panel after the Children Act 1989* London, Law Society Legal Practice Directorate

Law Society (1991b) *Professional Standards Bulletin No 5* London, The Law Society

Lawrence, T (1990) 'Duxbury, disclosure and other matters: An accountant's view' Family Law 12–16

Levin, J (1984) 'Guardians ad Litem in the Juvenile Court' Family Law 269–299

Lewis, J & Cannell, F (1986) 'The Politics of Motherhood in the 1980s: Warnock, Gillick and Feminists' 13 Journal of Law & Society 321–342

Lord Chancellor's Department (1985) *Occupational Pension Rights on Divorce* Consultation Paper, London, Lord Chancellor's Department

Lord Chancellor's Department (1986) *Interdepartmental Review of Family and Domestic Jurisdiction: A Consultation Paper* London, Lord Chancellor's Department

Lord Chancellor's Department (1986a) *Legal Aid: Efficiency Scrutiny* London, Lord Chancellor's Department

Lord Chancellor's Department (1987) *Legal Aid in England and Wales: A New Framework* Cm 118, London, HMSO

Lord Chancellor's Department (1988) *Judicial Statistics, England and Wales for the Year 1987* London, HMSO

Lord Chancellor's Department (1990) *Judicial Statistics, Annual Report 1989* London, HMSO

Lord Chancellor's Department (1990a) *Children Come First*, 2 vols, London, HMSO

Lowe, NV (1982) 'To Review or Not to Review?' 45 Modern Law Review 96–100

Lowe, N (1989) 'Caring for children' 139 New Law Journal 87–89

Lowe, N (1990) 'Freeing for adoption – the experience of the 1980s' Journal of Social Welfare Law 220–233

Lowe, N & White, R (1986) *Wards of Court* 2nd edn, London, Kluwer Law Publications

Luckhouse, L (1984) 'Social Security: The Equal Treatment Reforms' Journal of Social Welfare Law 325–334

Luhmann, N (1982) *The Differentiation of Society* trans by S Holmes & C Larmore, New York, Columbia University Press

Luhmann, N (1985) *A Sociological Theory of Law* trans by E King & M Albrow, London, Routledge & Kegan Paul

Luhmann, N (1986) *Love As Passion: The Codification of Intimacy* (trans by J Gaines & D Jones) Cambridge, Polity Press

Lygo, J (1991) 'Sharpening the focus' 141 New Law Journal 448–451

Lyon, CN (1986) 'Safeguarding Children's Interests? – Some Problematic Issues Surrounding Separate Representation in Care and Associated Proceedings' in MDA Freeman (ed) *Essays in Family Law 1985* London, Sweet & Maxwell, 1–19

McCann, K (1985) 'Battered Women and the Law: The Limits of the Legislation' in Brophy, J & Smart, C (eds) *Women in Law* London, Routledge & Kegan Paul, Ch 4

McCarthy, P & Simpson, B (1990) 'Grandparents and family conflict: Another view' Family Law 480–482

McDonald, P (1985) *The Economic Consequences of Marriage Breakdown in Australia* Melbourne, Institute of Family Studies

MacFarlane, A (1986) *Marriage and Love in England: Modes of Reproduction, 1300–1840* Oxford, Basil Blackwell

McGregor, Lord, of Durris (1987) 'Family Courts?' 6 Civil Justice Quarterly 44–55

Mackay, Lord (1989) 'Perceptions of the Children Bill and beyond (Joseph Jackson Memorial Lecture)' 139 New Law Journal 505–508

Maclean, M (1991) *Surviving divorce: Women's resources after separation* London, Macmillan

Maclean, M & Eekelaar, J (1986) 'Divorce and Self-Sufficiency' Family Law 310–312

Maclean, M & Johnston, J (1990) 'Alimony or compensation: What can we learn from the language of economists?' Fam Law 148–149

Maclean, M & Wadsworth, M (1988) 'The interests of children after parental divorce: A long-term perspective' 2 International Journal of Law and the Family 155–166

MacPherson, CB (1978) *Property: Critical and Mainstream Positions* Toronto, University of Toronto Press

Maidment, S (1977) 'The Law's Response to Marital Violence in England and the USA' 26 International and Comparative Law Quarterly 403

Maidment, S (1980) 'The Relevance of the Criminal Law to Domestic Violence' Journal of Social Welfare Law 26–32

Maidment, S (1982) *Judicial Separation: A Research Study* Centre for Socio-Legal Studies, Oxford, SSRC

Maidment, S (1984) *Child custody and divorce* London, Croom Helm

Maidment, S (1984a) 'MCA 1973, s 41 and the Children of Divorce: Theoretical and Empirical Considerations' in M Freeman (ed) *State Law and the Family* London, Tavistock

Maine, H (1861) *Ancient Law* London, John Murray

Maitland, FW (1936) *Lectures on Equity* Cambridge, CUP

Manners, A & Rauta, I (1981) *Family Property in Scotland* London, HMSO

Martin, JP (ed) (1978) *Violence & the Family* Chichester, Wiley

Masson (1986) 'Pensions, Dependency and Divorce' Journal of Social Welfare Law 343–361

Masson, J (1988) 'A New Approach to Matrimonial Property' Family Law 327–330

Masson, J (1988) 'Pensions, the family and dependency' in Meulders-Klein, M-T & Eekelaar, J (eds) *Family, State and individual economic security*, Vols 1 and 2, Brussels, Story Scientia, Ch 39

Masson, J (1991) 'Adolescent crisis and parental power' Family Law 528–531

Masson, J & Morton, S (1989) 'The use of wardship by local authorities' 52 Modern Law Review 762–789

Masson, J, Norbury, D & Chatterton, S (1983) *Mine, yours or ours? A study of step-parent adoption* London, HMSO

Masson, P (1980) 'Parental Choice in State Education' Journal of Social Welfare Law 193–208

Mears, M (1991) 'Consent orders and the clean break principle' 135 Solicitors' Journal 546–548

Mendes da Costa, D (1957) 'Criminal Law' in RH Graveson & FR Crane (eds) *A Century of Family Law* London, Sweet & Maxwell, Ch 8

Meulders-Klein, M-T & Eekelaar, J (eds) (1988) *Family, State and individual economic security*, Vols 1 and 2, Brussels, Story Scientia

Meyer, P (1977) *L'Enfant et la Raison d'Etat* Paris, Editions du Seuil

Millam, S, Bullock, R, Hosie, J & Haak, M (1985) *Children Lost in Care: The Family Contact of Children in Care* Aldershot, Gower

Miller, J (1986) 'Occupation of the family home and the Insolvency Act 1985' The Conveyancer 393–405

Minor, I (1979) 'Working-Class Women and Matrimonial Law Reform, 1890–1914' in Martin, D & Rubinstein, D (eds) *Ideology and the Labour Movement* London, Croom Helm

Minson, J (1985) *Genealogies of Morals: Nietzsche, Foucault, Donzelot and the Eccentricity of Ethics* London, Macmillan

Mnookin, RH (1975) 'Child-Custody Adjudication: Judicial Functions in the Face of Indeterminacy' 39 Law and Contemporary Problems 226–293

Moffat, G & Chesterman (1988) *Trusts Law: Text and Materials* London, Weidenfeld & Nicholson

Monckton, W (1945) *Report by Sir W Monckton on the circumstances which led to the boarding-out of Denis and Terence O'Neill at Bank Farm, Minsterly, and the steps taken to supervise their welfare* Cmd 6636, London, HMSO

Montgomery, J (1988) 'Children as property?' 51 Modern Law Review 323–342

Montgomery, J (1989) 'Rhetoric and welfare' 9 Oxford Journal of Legal Studies 395–402

Montgomery, J (1991) 'Rights, restraints and pragmatism: The Human Fertilisation and Embryology Act 1990' 54 Modern Law Review 524–534

Moran, L (1987) 'Dr Lushington's Sexual Fix' (unpublished, author's draft)

Morgan, D (1985) 'Making Motherhood Male: Surrogacy and the Moral Economy of Women' 12 Journal of Law & Society 219–256

Morgan, D (1986) 'Who to be or not to be: The Surrogacy Story' 49 Modern Law Review 358–368

Morgan, D and Lee, R (1991) *The Human Fertilisation and Embryology Act 1990: Abortion and embryo research, The new law* London, Blackstone Press

Morgan, DM (1975) *Social Theory and the Family* London, Routledge & Kegan Paul

Morrison, CA (1957) 'Contract' in Graveson, RH & Crane, FR (eds) *A Century of Family Law* (1957) London, Sweet & Maxwell, Ch 6

Morrison, CA (1957a) 'Tort' in Graveson, RH & Crane, FR (eds) *A Century of Family Law* London, Sweet & Maxwell, Ch 5

Morton Report (1956) *Royal Commission on Marriage and Divorce 1951–55* Cmnd 9678 (Chairman, Lord Morton of Henryton)

Murch, M (1980) *Justice and Welfare in Divorce* London, Sweet & Maxwell

Murphy, WT (1979) 'Monied Might and Social Justice' 42 Modern Law Review 567

Murphy, WT (1983) 'After *Boland*: Law Com No 115' 46 Modern Law Review 330–337

Murphy, WT & Clark, H (1987) *The Family Home* London, Sweet & Maxwell

Murphy, WT & Rawlings, R (1980) 'The Matrimonial Homes (Co-Ownership) Bill: The Right Way Forward?' Family Law 136–140

Murphy, WT & Roberts, S (1987) *Understanding Property Law* London, Fontana

New South Wales Law Reform Commission (1983) *Report on De Facto Relationships* LRC 36, Sydney, NSWLRC

Norris, T & Parton, N (1987) 'The Administration of Place of Safety Orders' Journal of Social Welfare Law 1–14

Newcastle Conciliation Project Unit (1989) *Report to the Lord Chancellor on the costs and effectiveness of conciliation in England and Wales* University of Newcastle

O'Donovan, K (1978) 'The Principles of Maintenance: An Alternative View' 8 Family Law 18–24

O'Donovan, K (1982) 'Should All Maintenance of Spouses Be Abolished?' 45 Modern Law Review 424–433

O'Donovan, K (1984) 'Legal Marriage – Who Needs It?' 47 Modern Law Review 112–118

O'Donovan, K (1985) *Sexual Divisions in Law* London, Weidenfeld & Nicholson

Office of Population Census & Surveys (OPCS) (1987) *General Household Survey 1985* London, HMSO

Olsen, F (1983) 'The Family and the Market: A Study of Ideology & Legal Reform' 96 Harvard Law Review 1497–1578

Olsen, F (1991) 'Children's Rights: Some Feminist Approaches with Special Reference to the Convention on the Rights of the Child' in Alston, P, Parker, S & Seymour, J (eds) *Children, Rights and the Law* Oxford, OUP

O'Donovan, K (1989) 'What shall we tell the children?' in Lee, R & Morgan, D (eds) *Birthrights: Law and ethics at the beginnings of life* London, Routledge, Ch 5

Offe, C (1984) '"Ungovernability": The renaissance of conservative theories of crisis' in *Contradictions of the Welfare State* London, Hutchinson, Ch 2

Office of Population Census and Surveys (1991) *Marriage and Divorce Statistics 1989* London, HMSO

One Parent Families (1980) *An Accident of Birth: A Response to the Law Commission's Working Paper on Illegitimacy* London, OPF

One Parent Families (1981) *Lone Parents and Family Taxation* London, OPF

One Parent Families (1982) *Against Natural Justice: A Study of the Procedures used by Local Authorities in Taking Parental Rights Resolutions Over Children in Voluntary Care* London, OPF

Packman, J (1981) *The Child's Generation: Child Care Policy in Britain* (2nd edn) Oxford, Basil Blackwell/Martin Robertson

Packman, J (with Randall, J & Jaques, N) (1986) *Who Needs Care? Social Work Decisions About Children* Oxford, Basil Blackwell

Pahl, J (1980) 'Patterns of Money Management Within Marriage' 9 Journal of Social Policy 313

Pahl, J (1982) 'Police Response to Battered Women' Journal of Social Welfare Law 337–343

Pahl, J (1984) 'The Allocation of Money Within the Household' in Freeman, M (ed) *The State, The Law and the Family: Critical Perspectives* London, Tavistock, pp 36–50

Pahl, J (ed) (1985) *Private Violence and Public Policy: The Needs of Battered Women and the Response of the Public Services* London, Routledge & Kegan Paul

Pahl, J (1989) *Money and marriage* London, Macmillan

Parker, S (1985) 'The Legal Background' in Pahl, J (ed) *Private Violence and Public Policy* London, Routledge & Kegan Paul, Ch 7

Parker, S (1987) 'The Marriage Act 1753: A Case Study of Family Law-Making' (1) International Journal of Law and the Family 133–154

Parker, S (1990) *Informal marriage, cohabitation and the law, 1750–1989* London, Macmillan

Parker, S (1991) 'Rights and utility in Anglo–Australian family law' (forthcoming, author's draft)

Parker, S (1991a) 'Child Support in Australia: Children's Rights or Public Interest?' 5 International Journal of Law and the Family 24

Parker, S (1991b) *Cohabitees* 3rd edn, London, Longman

Parkinson, L (1986) *Conciliation and Separation in Divorce: Finding Common Ground* London, Croom Helm

Parkinson, L (1987) 'Independent Divorce Mediation Services in Britain' in *The Role of Mediation in Divorce Proceedings: A Comparative Perspective* Vermont Law School Dispute Resolution Project, Vermont, Vermont Law School, 111–122

Parkinson, PN (1986) 'The Gillick Case: Just What Has It Decided?' Family Law 11–14

Parmiter, G (1981) 'Bristol In-Court Conciliation Procedure' Law Society's Gazette, February 1981, 196

Parnas, R (1978) 'The Relevance of the Criminal Law to Interspousal Violence' in Eekelaar, J & Katz, SA (eds) *Family Violence: An International & Interdisciplinary Study* Toronto, Butterworths, 188–191

Parry, M (1990) 'The changing face of wardship' in Freestone, D (ed) *Children and the Law* Ch 10

Parton, N (1985) *The Politics of Child Abuse* London, Macmillan

Parton, N (1990) 'Taking child abuse seriously' in *Taking child abuse seriously, by the Violence Against Children Study Group* London, Unwin, Ch 1

Parton, N (1991) *Governing the family: Child care, child protection and the state* Basingstoke, Macmillan

Parton, N and Martin, M (1989) 'Public inquiries, legalism and child care in England and Wales' 3 International Journal of Law and the Family 21–39

Parton, N & Thomas, T (1983) 'Child Abuse & Citizenship' in Jordan, B & Parton, N (eds) *The Political Dimensions of Social Work* Oxford, Basil Blackwell, 55–73

Passingham, B & Harmer, C (1985) *Law and Practice in Matrimonial Causes* (4th edn) London, Butterworths

Pearce, B (1990) 'An overview of the National Family Conciliation Council' in Fisher, T (ed) *Family Conciliation within the UK: Policy and practice* Bristol, Jordan & Sons

Pearl, D (1986) 'Public Housing Allocation and Domestic Disputes' in Freeman, M (ed) *Essays in Family Law 1985* London, Stevens 20–33

Pearl, D (1986a) *Family Law and the Immigrant Communities* Bristol, Jordan & Sons

Pettitt, PH (1957) 'Parental Control and Guardianship' in Graveson, FR & Crane, RH (eds) *A Century of Family Law* London, Sweet & Maxwell, 56–87

Poulter, S (1986) *English Law and Ethnic Minority Customs* London, Butterworths

Powell, JV (1984) 'Pension Considerations on Marriage Breakdown' Family Law 187–189

Priest, J (1985) 'The Report of the Warnock Committee on Human Fertilisation & Embryology' 48 Modern Law Review 73–85

Priest, J & Whybrow, J (1986) *Custody Law in Practice in the Divorce and Domestic Courts* Supplement to Law Commission Working Paper No 96, London, HMSO

Pugsley, J & Wilkinson, M (1984) 'The Court Welfare Officer's Role: Taking it Seriously?' 31 (3) Probation Journal 89–92

Report of the Inter-Departmental Committee on Conciliation (1983) London, HMSO

Report of the Inquiry into Child Abuse in Cleveland Cm 412 (1988) London, HMSO

Report of the Select Committee on Violence in Marriage (1975) HC 553-II (1974–5) London, HMSO

Rheinstein, M & Glendon, MA (1980) 'Interspousal Relations' 4 International Encyclopedia of International Law, Ch 4

Richards, M (1982) 'Post-divorce arrangements for children: A psychological perspective' Journal of Social Welfare Law 133–151

Richards, M (1982a) 'Post-Divorce Arrangements for Children: A Psychological Perspective' Journal of Social Welfare Law 133–151

Richards, M (1986) 'Behind the Best Interests of the Child: An Examination of the Arguments of Goldstein, Freud and Solnit Concerning Custody and Access at Divorce' Journal of Social Welfare Law 77–95

Richards, M (1991) 'Divorce research today' Family Law 70–72

Riches, P (1991) 'Pindown – Would the Children Act 1989 have made a difference?' Family Law 292–294

Rights of Women Family Law Sub-Group (1985) 'Campaigning Around Family Law: Politics & Practice' in Brophy, J & Smart, C (eds) *Women in Law* London, Routledge & Kegan Paul, Ch 9

Rights of Women Lesbian Custody Group (1986) *Lesbian Mothers' Legal Handbook* London, The Women's Press

Roberts, S (1983) 'Mediation in family law disputes' 46 Modern Law Review 537–557

Roberts, S (1988) 'Three models of family mediation' in Dingwall, R & Eekelaar, J (eds) *Divorce mediation and the legal process* Oxford, OUP, Ch 9

Roberts, S (1990) 'A blueprint for family conciliation?' 53 Modern Law Review 88–90

Robinson, P (1983) see *Report of the Inter-Departmental Committee on Conciliation*

Roche, J (1991) 'The Children Act 1989: Once a parent always a parent?' Journal of Social Welfare and Family Law 345–361

Rose, G & Gerlis, S (1991) 'Conciliation for family finance' Family Law 92–93

Rose, N (1987) 'Beyond the Public/Private Divide: Law, Power & the Family' 14 Journal of Law & Society 61–76

Rose, N (1989) *Governing the soul: The shaping of the private self* London, Routledge

Rowe, J (1983) *Fostering in the Eighties* London, BAAF

Rowe, J, Cain, H, Hundleby, M & Keane, A (1984) *Long-Term fostering and the Children Act* London, BAAF

Rowe, J & Lambert, L (1973) *Children Who Wait: A Study of Children Needing Substitute Families* London, ABAA

Sanders, A (1988) 'Personal Violence and Public Order: The Prosecution of "Domestic" Violence in England and Wales' 16 International Journal of the Sociology of Law 359–382

Sarat, A & Felstiner, W (1986) 'Law and strategy in the divorce lawyer's office' 20 Law and Society Review 93

Sax, R, Crowther, F & Haws, J (1987) 'Child Maintenance: A Fresh Look' Family Law 275–276

Schaffer, H (1990) *Making decisions about children: Psychological questions and answers* Oxford, Basil Blackwell

Scott, T & White, F (1990) 'Setting aside for non-disclosure: Practice and procedure' Family Law 326–328

Scottish Law Commission (1981) *Report on Aliment and Financial Provision* Scot Law Com No 67, Edinburgh, HMSO

Scottish Law Commission (1983) *Consultative Memorandum No 57: Matrimonial Property* Edinburgh, HMSO

Scottish Law Commission (1984) *Family Law Report on Matrimonial Property* Scot Law Com No 86, Edinburgh, HMSO

Scottish Law Commission (1984a) *Report on Illegitimacy* SLC No 82, Edinburgh, HMSO

Scottish Law Commission (1988) *The Ground for Divorce: Should the Law be Changed?* Discussion Paper No 76, Edinburgh, Scottish Law Commission

Scottish Law Commission (1990) *The effects of cohabitation in private law* Discussion Paper No 86, Edinburgh, Scottish Law Commission

Second Report to Parliament on the Children Act 1975 (1984) London, HMSO

Secretary of State for Social Services (1988) *Report of the Inquiry into Child Abuse in Cleveland 1987* London, HMSO

Seebohm, Lord (1968) *Report of the Committee on Local Authority and Allied Personal Social Services* Cmnd 3703, London, HMSO

Segalen, M (1986) *Historical Anthropology of the Family* (JC Whitehouse & S Matthews, trans) Cambridge, Cambridge University Press

Sevenhuijsen, S (1986) 'Fatherhood and the Political Theory of Rights: Theoretical Perspectives of Feminism' 14 International Journal of the Sociology of Law 329–340

Shultz, M (1982) 'Contractual Ordering of Marriage: A New Model for State Policy' 70 California LR 207–334

Sinclair, R (1984) *Decision Making in Statutory Reviews on Children in Care* Aldershot, Gower

Smart, C (1984) *The Ties that Bind: Law, Marriage and the Reproduction of Patriarchal Relations* London, Routledge & Kegan Paul

Smart, C (1984a) 'Marriage, Divorce and Women's Economic Dependency: A Discussion of the Politics of Private Maintenance' in Freeman, M (ed) *State, Law and the Family* London, Tavistock, Ch 1

Smart, C (1986) 'Feminism and Law: Some Problems of Analysis and Strategy' 14 International Journal of the Sociology of Law 109–123

Smart, C (1987) '"There is of course the distinction dictated by nature": Law and the Problem of Paternity' in Stanworth, M (ed) *Reproductive Technologies: Gender, Motherhood and Medicine* Oxford, Polity Press, 98–117

Smart, C (1989) 'Power and the politics of child custody' in Smart, C and Sevenhuijsen, S (eds) *Child custody and the politics of gender* London, Routledge, Ch 1

Smart, C & Brophy, J (1985) 'Locating Law: A Discussion of the Place of Law in Feminist Politics' in Brophy, J & Smart, C (eds) *Women-in-Law: Explorations in Law, Family & Sexuality* London, Routledge & Kegan Paul

Smart, C and Sevenhuijsen, S (eds) (1989) *Child custody and the politics of gender* London, Routledge

Smith, R (1991) 'Who benefits?' 141 New Law Journal 644

Smith, L (1989) *Domestic violence: Home Office Research Study 107* London, HMSO

Snowden, R & Mitchell, G (1981) *The Artificial Family* London, George Allen & Unwin

Social Services Select Committee (1983–4) *Children in Care* Second Report, London, HMSO

Sparkes, P (1989) 'Purchasers and rights of occupation under the Matrimonial Homes Act 1983' 52 Modern Law Review 110

Sparkes, P (1991) 'The quantification of beneficial interests: Problems arising from contributions to deposits, mortgage advances and mortgage instalments' 11 Oxford Journal of Legal Studies 39–62

SPCK (1966) *Putting Assunder – A Divorce Law for Contemporary Society* Report of a group appointed by the Archbishop of Canterbury, London, SPCK

Spon-Smith, R (1990) 'Duty of disclosure in children cases' Family Law 289–292

Steinman, E (1981) 'The Experience of Children in a Joint Custody Arrangement: A Report of a Study' 51/3 American Journal of Orthopsychiatry 403–412

Stone, L (1979) *The Family, Sex and Marriage in England 1500–1800* Harmondsworth, Penguin

Stone, L & Stone, JCF (1984) *An Open Elite? England, 1540–1880* Harmondsworth, Penguin

Sufrin, B (1987) 'Intention and Detriment' 50 Modern Law Review 94–100

Sugarman, S (1990) 'Dividing financial interests on divorce' in Sugarman, S & Kay, H (eds) *Divorce reform at the crossroads* New Haven, Yale University Press, Ch 5

Sugarman, S & Kay, H (eds) (1990) *Divorce reform at the crossroads* New Haven, Yale University Press

Symes, P (1985) 'Indissolubility and the Clean Break' 48 Modern Law Review 44–60

Szwed, E (1984) 'The Family Court' in Freeman, M (ed) *State, Law and the Family* London, Tavistock, Ch 16

Taitz, J (1988) 'A transsexual's nightmare: The determination of sexual identity in English law' 2 International Journal of Law and the Family 139–154

Tasker, F and Golombok, S (1991) 'Children raised by lesbian mothers: The empirical evidence' Family Law 184–187

Temkin, J (1987) *Rape and the Legal Process* London, Sweet & Maxwell

Thery, I (1986) '"The Interests of the Child" and the Post-Divorce Family' 14 International Journal of the Sociology of Law 341–358

Thery, I (1989) 'The "interests of the child" and the regulation of the post-divorce family' in Smart, C and Sevenhuijsen, S (eds) *Child custody and the politics of gender* Ch 4

Theweleit, K (1986) *Male Fantasies, Volume I: Women, Floods, Bodies, History* Cambridge, Polity

Thornton, R (1989) 'Homelessness through relationship breakdown: The Local Authorities' response' Journal of Social Welfare Law 67–84

Timms, J (1986) 'The Guardian ad Litem: A Practitioner's Perspective' Family Law 339–344

Todd, J & Jones, L (1972) *Matrimonial Property* London, HMSO

Triseliotis, J (1984) 'Obtaining Birth Certificates' in Bean, P (ed) *Adoption: Essays in Social Policy, Law and Sociology* London, Tavistock

Walby, S and Symons, B (1990) *Who am I? Identity, adoption and human fertilisation* London, BAAF

Wallerstein, J and Blakeslee, S (1989) *Second chances: Men, women and children a decade after divorce* London, Bantam

Wallerstein, J & Kelly, J (1980) *Surviving the Breakup: How Children and Parents Cope with Divorce* London, Grant McIntyre

WAR (1990) 'The rapist who pays the rent' 140 New Law Journal 1599

Warburton, J (1991) 'Trusts, common intention, detriment and proprietary estoppel' Trusts Law International 9–12

Warnock, M (1985) *A Question of Life* Oxford, Basil Blackwell

Wasoff, F, Dobash, R & Harcus, D (1990) *The impact of the Family Law (Scotland) Act 1985 on solicitors' divorce practice* Edinburgh, Scottish Office

Webb, A & Wistow, G (1987) *Social Work, Social Care and Social Planning: The Personal Social Services Since Seebohm* Social Policy in Modern Britain Series (J Campling, ed) London, Longman

Webb, D (1986) 'The Use of Blood Groupings and DNA "Finger Printing" Tests in Immigration Proceedings' 1 Immigration and Nationality Law & Practice 53–55

Webb, J (1988) 'Maintenance Payments, Social Security and the Liable Relative' Family Law 267–270 and 307–311

Weitzman, L (1981) *The Marriage Contract* New York, Free Press

Weitzman, L (1985) *The Divorce Revolution: The Unexpected Social and Economic Consequences for Women and Children in America* New York, Free Press

Weitzman, L (1988) 'The divorce revolution in the United States: The unexpected consequences for women and children' in Meulders-Klein, M-T and Eekelaar, J (eds) *Family, State and individual economic security*, Vols 1 and 2, Brussels, Story Scientia, Ch 28

Wells, C, Alldridge, P and Morgan, D (1990) 'An unsuitable case for treatment' 140 New Law Journal 1544–1545

Westcott, J (1987) 'Enforcement of Matrimonial Orders' Family Law 106–108

Weyrauch, W (1980) 'Metamorphosis of Marriage' 13 Family Law Quarterly 415–440

Wheeler, S (1989) 'Protection for the matrimonial home' Journal of Social Welfare Law 101–107

White, R (1991) *The administration of justice* 2nd edn, Oxford, Basil Blackwell

White, R, Carr, P and Lowe, N (1990) *A guide to the Children Act 1989* London, Butterworths

White Paper (1987) *The Law Relating to Child Care and Family Services* Cm 62, London, HMSO

Wikeley, N (1991) 'The Maintenance Enforcement Act 1991' Family Law 353–355

Wilkinson, M (1981) *Children and divorce* Oxford, Basil Blackwell

Wilson, E (1977) *Women and the Welfare State* London, Tavistock

Williams, G (1991) 'The problem of domestic rape' 141 New Law Journal 205–206, 246–247

Wishik, HR (1986) 'Economics of Divorce: An Exploratory Study' 20 Family Law Quarterly 70–103

Wood, J (1991) 'The Social Security Act 1990: The clean break rejoined' Family Law 31–33

Wright, M (1986) 'Surrogacy and Adoption: Problems and Possibilities' Family Law 109–113

Wright, M (1991) 'Financial provision, the clean break and the search for consistency' Family Law 76–79

Zander, M (1988) *A matter of justice: The legal system in ferment* Oxford, OUP

Zipper, J & Sevenhuijsen, S (1987) 'Rethinking Feminist Notions on Motherhood' in M Stanworth (ed) *Reproductive Technologies: Gender, Motherhood and Medicines* Oxford, Polity

Zuckerman, AAS (1978) 'Ownership of the Matrimonial Home: Common Sense and Reformist Nonsense' 94 Law Quarterly Review 26

Index

546   *Index*

Wardship – *contd*
local authorities 435-438
relationship to care orders 413
relatives 450
section 8 orders 492
uses 493-499
Wardship applications
children in care 440-441
kidnapping by parents 495
litigants 493-499
local authorities 495
social parenthood 444
Wardship procedure 491-492
Wardship proceedings 491-492
county courts 12
evidence 491-492
foster parents 497
freedom of publication 493
jurisdiction 486, 489-490, 493-494
parties 490-491, 494-499
relatives 497
unborn children 54
welfare reports 491-492
Warrants of execution 307
Wealthy families *See* HIGH INCOME
FAMILIES
Welfare
agencies 16
children
divorce 266, 345-347
local authorities 428-429
maintenance, children 312-314
reports
Divorce Court Welfare Service
372-374
wardship proceedings 491-492
support services 16
Welfare benefits 163-173

Welfare benefits – *contd*
cohabitation 65
Welfare of children paramount 381
Welfare officers 27-29, 285-286
Welfare reports, children 74
Wife's property, legal history
176-178
Wills
family provision 209-214
orders 213-214
freedom of disposition 205, 209
Wishes of the child
care proceedings 424
looked after by LA 429
Witnesses
formalities of marriage 37
See also EVIDENCE
Wives, bargaining power 291, 293
Women
compensation for criminal injuries 227
conciliation, subordinated to child
welfare 288
divorce, finance and custody 354
economic consequences of divorce
299-301
income 126
from employment 301
oppression 8
rights over their own bodies 55-58
social class, economic consequences of
divorce 302
status 8
violence against *See* DOMESTIC
VIOLENCE
welfare benefits, cohabitation 65
**Written agreements, parental
responsibilities, local
authorities** 393-394